AMERICAN DIPLOMACY

BY

CARL RUSSELL FISH

PROFESSOR OF HISTORY IN THE UNIVERSITY
OF WISCONSIN

WITH SIXTEEN MAPS

NEW YORK
HENRY HOLT AND COMPANY
1915

TO MY MOTHER AND SISTER

PREFACE

THIS book is intended as a comprehensive and balanced, though brief, review of the history of American diplomacy. It is hoped that it will prove useful both to the student in the classroom and to the general reader, and will help to diffuse a knowledge of our diplomacy at a time when it is becoming increasingly important that public opinion should be internationally minded. While it is for the most part based upon an independent study of the sources, it is not presented as a contribution to knowledge but rather as a condensation of ascertained conclusions. The footnotes, therefore, contain few specific references to support the text, but rather suggest to the reader material for further study; either the more important sources, which in the case of diplomatic history are exceptionally readable, or those accounts and monographs which are most useful.

CONTENTS

Chapter		Page
I.	Phases and Problems of American Diplomacy	1
II.	Pre-Revolutionary Boundaries	10
III.	Recognition	21
IV.	Spain and Holland	31
V.	Peace	40
VI.	Religion and Commerce	51
VII.	The West	63
VIII.	Old Problems in New Hands	79
IX.	The Establishment of Neutrality	94
X.	The Jay Treaty	108
XI.	War and Peace with France	126
XII.	The Louisiana Purchase	140
XIII.	The Embargo	152
XIV.	War with England	163
XV.	Peace	176
XVI.	Commerce and Boundaries	188
XVII.	The Monroe Doctrine	203
XVIII.	Reciprocity, Claims, Boundaries, and the Slave Trade	220
XIX.	Expansion	243
XX.	Annexation	260
XXI.	Diplomacy and Politics	280
XXII.	The Civil War	304
XXIII.	The Civil War and the Monroe Doctrine	324
XXIV.	The Aftermath of the Civil War	336
XXV.	Routine, 1861 to 1877	349
XXVI.	Baiting the Lion, 1877–1897	370
XXVII.	Blaine, Olney and the Monroe Doctrine	384
XXVIII.	Growth of American Influence in the Pacific	396

x CONTENTS

Chapter		Page
XXIX.	The Spanish War	408
XXX.	Imperialism and Great Britain	423
XXXI.	Spanish America	439
XXXII.	The Pacific	454
XXXIII.	Routine and Arbitration	464
XXXIV.	Mexico	480
XXXV.	The Great War	491
XXXVI.	Success and its Causes	497

MAPS

IN COLOR

PAGE

Establishment of Diplomatic Posts by the United States, 1776–1914
Inside front cover

West Indies, 1776 to 1898 20

United States, 1783 to 1790 70

Changes on Southeast, 1760 to final establishment of United States ownership 218

Possessions and Dependencies of the United States and other great Powers in the Pacific 460

Development of United States Consular Service, 1876–1891 *Inside back cover*

IN TEXT

Boundary Discussions, 1763 to 1783 47

Northeastern Boundary Controversies 229

Northwesternmost Head of Connecticut River 231

Rouse's Point Controversy 232

Oregon Boundary Controversies 268

Texan Boundary 272

Central America, 1850 to 1860 294

Alaska Boundary Controversy 433

West Indies, 1898 to 1915 445

Territorial Expansion of the United States 488

AMERICAN DIPLOMACY

CHAPTER I

PHASES AND PROBLEMS OF AMERICAN DIPLOMACY

BEFORE the Spanish war most Americans regarded diplomacy as a foreign luxury. Some thought that we should import a little of it; others regarded it as a deleterious appendage of effete civilizations which we, in our young strength, had forever cast aside. Not that this had always been our attitude. During the Revolution and the Confederation diplomacy was recognized by the intelligent to be as essential to the establishment of our national existence as arms, diplomats were as carefully chosen as generals; the news of the negotiations of Franklin, Adams, and Jay was as anxiously awaited as that from the army, and their successes brought almost as great a reward of popular acclaim as did those of commanders in the field.

Birth of American diplomacy, 1774 to 1789

By 1789 the joint efforts of our soldiers, diplomats, and constitution-builders had assured our national existence, but the broader question as to whether we could gain real freedom to pursue our national development in our own way remained. European statesmen regarded us but as a weight to be used in fixing or unfixing the balance of power. The strong wind of the French Revolution swept across the Atlantic and divided our own citizens. Foreign affairs absorbed attention that was needed for domestic problems, the fate of administrations came to hang upon their foreign

Development of the Monroe Doctrine, 1789 to 1829

1

policy. Dissertations on diplomatic problems created political reputations. Of the five presidents who succeeded Washington all had had diplomatic experience and four had served as secretaries of state. Practically devoid of a permanent army or navy, we relied for defence upon our diplomats and the ocean. The Treaty of Ghent in 1814, followed by the peace of Europe in 1815, gave us real freedom, and our struggle left as its by-products an intelligent public opinion, and a staff so well trained that the period from 1815 to 1829 may in many ways be regarded as the golden age of American diplomacy. As Marshall was during those years codifying the constitutional practices of the past in form to serve as a guide for a considerable future, so John Quincy Adams was codifying our diplomatic opinions. By 1829 we had not only shaken ourselves loose from the entanglements of European international politics, but we had formulated rules of conduct designed to make that separation permanent.

Our isolation achieved, diplomacy ceased to attract our ablest men or to interest the public. Of seventeen presidents

Subordination of diplomacy to politics, 1829 to 1844

between 1829 and the Spanish war, two only, Van Buren and Buchanan, had served in diplomatic posts. Between 1829 and 1844 a few episodes gained a momentary attention; but not many persons took the trouble to connect them with one another and with the past, or to free their vision from the blurring mist of internal politics. Between 1844 and

Expansion, 1844 to 1860

1860 a consciousness of our growing strength and "manifest destiny" began to arouse a new interest in diplomacy not as a protective art but as a weapon of acquisition. Fearless, often shameless, and with little deference for the feelings or conventions of others, our diplomats helped to extend the boundaries of the republic; but they were unable to win for their labors much applause from a people absorbed in its home concerns and the coming storm of civil war.

By the war the work of diplomacy was once more rendered vital. If our diplomatic policy had failed then, the country would inevitably have been divided, and the system of equipoise which causes all Europe to vibrate to the slightest international happening, that balance of power to which we had by such earnest effort avoided becoming a party, would have been established in America. Again we were successful; but the clang of battle for the most part deafened the public ear to the diplomatic struggle, while the political, social, and economic reconstruction of the next few years gave the public time for only an occasional glance at the diplomatic reconstruction, which was satisfactorily completed in 1872.

War and Reconstruction, 1860 to 1872

The period from Reconstruction to the Spanish war marked the lowest point in the quality of our diplomacy and in the amount of public attention devoted to it. With no fear of foreign powers and with no definite international aspirations, most of our leading men ignored foreign affairs. Some to be sure, used them to add ginger to their public speeches, but only a handful devoted any gray matter to their management. The situation, however, was gradually changing, the world was growing closer together; nations were actually becoming more intimate than English counties were a century ago; isolation was no longer possible, at least to the degree in which it had existed when the Monroe Doctrine was announced. During the nineties there was a growing appreciation that our national life must become less secluded, and in 1898 the Spanish war brought us suddenly and dramatically upon the world stage. Our policies, no longer those of the anxious pigmy of a hundred years before, but of a great power seeking influence and opportunity, became of moment to the world and to ourselves. In an atmosphere of growing intelligence, statesmen with a broader grasp of international relations than had been held for three-quarters of a century emerged to

The nadir of diplomacy, 1872 to 1898

The United States a world power, 1898

undertake the readjustment, with the result that the United States has become a world power and an international influence, though without losing its tradition of living mainly to itself and letting others do the same. Never again in the future, however, can we ignore our international relations as we did from 1829 to 1898.

The popular interest aroused by the questions of policy of the last fifteen years has furnished incentive for a wide-spread study of our diplomatic activity in the past. Monographs, essays, and books on diplomatic history and international law have been rapidly multiplying, and it is upon these studies that this book is in large part based. It is hoped that its brief outline will be supplemented by the intensive works to which reference is made, and that it may thus serve to broaden the basis of public opinion upon which the usefulness and ultimate safety of the United States must depend.

It is, of course, apparent that popular interest alone has not been the measure of our diplomatic activity. At no time have we lived wholly to ourselves. Whenever an American citizen or an American product crosses a neighbor's border, or whenever foreigners and their goods cross ours, there is material for diplomacy. Problems, some perennial, some transient, have at all times confronted our administrations, however ill-manned, however feebly supported.

When in 1783 we won recognition of our independence, we possessed scarcely one undisputed boundary line, and, even had every contention been decided in our favor, the territory enclosed would not have sufficed for a well-rounded and self-sufficient national growth. Our boundaries have only just been adjusted, and whether the limits of our national expansion have been reached must still be regarded as an open question. At no time in our history have these problems been absent, and at no time have they failed to influence other nations in their attitude toward us; in some periods they have been the very pivots upon which our national policy has turned.

American citizens have never been content with the resources of their own land; to protect them, therefore, in the pursuit of the cod and mackerel of the north- Extra terri-
torial re- east coast, of the seal of Behring sea, of the sources and oceanic whale, and of the guano deposits of the international
pathways islands of the sea, has been an unending task. Of greater difficulty, however, has been the effort to free the paths of intercourse. For many years the products of our lower Middle West were bottled up by Spain's hold on the Mississippi, till the nation itself was in peril of disruption on that account. Then, too, many of our northern water outlets east of the Rockies run through Canada, while west of the mountains the Canadian outlets run through our territories; and, further, the most tempting road between our Atlantic and Pacific coast lies far south of our own boundaries. From problems such as these we have never been free, and with regard to no others have we changed our mind so often. Generally favoring liberality, we have done much to free the lanes of commerce in which our interest is only general, such as the international rivers of South America, the Danish straits, the Scheldt, and many other paths.

More important and more varied have been the problems of our trafficking. The direct exchange of our own products for those of other countries has in itself occasioned Commerce little controversy with other nations, and has been steady and increasing; but whether these exchanges should be carried in our own vessels or in those of other countries has always been a matter of concern and difficulty. Mainly a question of diplomacy in the beginning, it has become more and more one of economic conditions and internal policy. In the matter of opening up the colonies of other nations to our ships and exports, however, diplomacy has found no respite; the situation in the foreign spheres of influence in China to-day is as knotty as was that of West

Indian trade in the early years of the last century. Our merchants, moreover, have not always been satisfied with handling our own business. They have acted as carriers for others, sometimes in open competition, sometimes by seeking to make a profit from our neutrality.

For no other nation has neutrality assumed such protean shapes as for the United States. For more than half of our national existence we have been either a neutral or else a belligerent interested in the neutrality of others. After independence had been established the vital question was whether we could remain neutral in the struggle that divided Europe. From our effort to remain so grew our positive policy of isolation, which, designed to guard our weakness, still governs the use of our strength. Coincident with this problem was that of the protection of our rights as a neutral, in behalf of which we were in 1812 stirred to war. As soon as the general peace in Europe in 1815 assured us that our earthen jar had floated safely through the contest of the iron pots, we became concerned in the problem of our duty as a neutral in the strife of weaker neighbors, and from that time to this the question has presented itself in every conceivable form,—in the struggle of Spain with her colonies, in which the latter so much engaged our sympathies; in the later struggle between Spain and the Cubans, where desire was added to sympathy; in revolutions and petty wars in which our only interest as a people was in peace but into which many of our citizens entered on one or the other or on both sides. The protection of lives and property during these conflicts, the securing of damages for the loss of the one or the other after peace was reëstablished, has been the unending task of our diplomats and foreign office. Then in the Civil War we were violently confronted with the reverse side of the proposition,—with questions as to the duties which neutral nations owed to us as belligerents. The experiences of the United States in handling neutrality have been uniquely varied, its record on the whole is honorable, and the experience of the past has been a growing force to guide the future.

More unique still has been our experience in affording protection to our citizens. A nation made up of emigrants, we have not always found other countries as willing to give up their claims to allegiance as we are to welcome the newcomers. Since we achieved independence the whole question of naturalization and change of nationality has been completely reviewed, and, largely by our insistence, the conclusions of international and municipal law have been almost directly reversed. New phases have lately arisen, however, from our wish to discriminate in our welcome between the various races; hence, while the problems of emigration—that is, the relationship of the individual to the country he is leaving—are fairly well settled, those of the immigrant with the country to which he desires to shift, remain uncertain. Naturalization

Besides establishing our national identity and making elbow room for the activities of our citizens, we have been obliged to assume a social position in the world. Since the rise of the Spanish-American nations our policy of individualism has been modified by a feeling of special interest in their welfare. While avoiding entangling alliances with them, as with others, we have always desired a close association from which the nations of other continents should be excluded; and over the states that lie between us and the equator we have increasingly exhibited a tendency to assume a modified guardianship. Moreover, we have never been able to avoid connections with the nations outside the American continents. Deeply concerned in the formulation of international law, we have been forced to recognize the weight of international opinion, and have contributed not a little to give it its present form. At first a matter of separate treaties and of diplomatic and judicial precedents, it has in the last thirty years exhibited a striking tendency to codify results by general agreements reached by International association international congresses. From these developments we have not stood aloof, and we have shared fully in the still more recent establishment of an international judiciary. Whether international law as interpreted by the Hague court will ultimately be provided with a police to carry out its decisions, and whether we will coöperate in this extension, are questions that will inevitably concern us in the future.

The diplomatic problems of the United States have always had more than an intrinsic interest for the rest of the world. **Democracy** The method of their handling has been more unique than their quality. To those who, whether with approval or with apprehension, believe that civilization is tending more and more toward democracy, the experience of this country, which has been more democratic than any other in the control of its diplomacy, has the value of an experiment.

To the casual observer, as to the close student, it is obvious that our democracy has not abolished personality. More **Personality** than in any other branch of our activity has the personal element counted in determining our diplomatic controversies. Great figures like Franklin, John Quincy Adams, and Hay stand out by their achievements more conspicuously than do any of our legislators and than all but a few of our administrators; and the encounters of Madison and Napoleon, Adams and Canning, Charles Francis Adams and Russell, Blaine, Olney, and Lord Salisbury have all the fascination of the days of the tournament and the duel.

Personality has perhaps shone all the more conspicuously because our democracy has not chosen permanently to equip **Diplomatic staff** itself with a trained staff. In selecting our champions we have been governed at best by opportunism. When great crises have arisen we have usually sent great men, who have in most cases outclassed their opponents; when the stake has been or has seemed to be of minor importance, we have allowed the exigencies of internal politics to dictate the choice. The result has been representative perhaps, but representative of the worst as well as of the best that was in us. Quite as disturbing a factor as the motley composition of our foreign corps has been the unfortunate circumstance that our foreign minister, the secretary of state, is expected, under the President, to be the political head of the administration. Insuring, as this fact does, the handling of foreign affairs by a man of ability and power, it does not always involve special fitness for the task. Although some selections have been ideal, others have been seriously bad,—seriously, but not impossibly so, for the permanent force of the state department has been able to guide the willing but untutored secretary and to modify the eccentricities of the obdurate.

More fundamental than differences in the choice of the protagonists has been the difference in the location of the power that has determined the policies upon   Control by the which they have acted. Has the broadening   people of the basis upon which the expression of the national will rests meant loss or increase of power, fluctuation or steadiness of purpose? On this point all sorts of opinions have been held. It has been said that the people, without ability to acquire the information necessary to form intelligent opinions on questions so remote from their daily life, would be at the mercy of every whiff of opinion which a designing or a shifting press might express; that, swept away by sudden passions, they would rush into wars from which the sage reticence of experienced men of affairs had previously saved them; or, on the other hand, that if those who suffered the pains of war could control it, there would come an era of peace on earth from which universal good will might ultimately flow. At all events, the controlling element in our diplomacy has been the people at large; and if our policy has on the whole secured us what we wanted, and done so without unnecessary friction, it is a justification of our democracy and an argument in favor of democracy in general.

CHAPTER II

PRE–REVOLUTIONARY BOUNDARIES

The return of Columbus in 1493 at once brought his discoveries before the forum of the world's diplomacy, Rome; The papal bulls for the first thought of his "Most Catholic" sovereigns, Ferdinand and Isabella, was to secure a title to these new lands from the pope. Alexander VI was a Spaniard by birth and feeling, and at the instance of the royal ambassadors he promptly issued two bulls giving to Spain "all and singular the aforesaid countries and islands thus unknown and hitherto discovered by your envoys and to be discovered hereafter, providing however they at no time have been in the actual temporal possession of any Christian owner." These bulls were issued almost as a matter of course, as the confirmation of a miner's claim would be granted by the United States government to-day; but they were unsatisfactory to Spain in that they did not prohibit discoveries and the establishment of claims by others. To meet these wishes a third bull was accordingly issued, May 4, 1493, which fixed a meridian one hundred leagues westward of "any" of the Azores or Cape Verde islands beyond which all other nations were prohibited from voyaging for the purposes of fishing and discovery.[1]

The general bearing of these bulls upon American diplomacy seems to have been greatly exaggerated. They did not prevent that good Catholic, Henry VII of England, from Their general significance sending out John Cabot to emulate Columbus in 1496, nor his "Most Christian" Majesty, Francis I of France, from attempting to found a French colonial empire thirty years later. The most peremptory

[1] E. H. Blair and J. A. Robertson, *The Philippine Islands* (55 vols., Cleveland, 1903–09), i. 97–129.

challenge to Spain's claim, moreover, was to come from Protestants, to whom the pope's grant was rather an incitement than a restraint. As a matter of fact the bulls were not much relied upon by Spanish diplomats in their general negotiations, although they may have contributed to the feeling on their part, remarked in 1565 by one of the Venetian ambassadors, that like Israel of old, the Spaniards were a people chosen of God to occupy a promised land.[1]

In determining the relations between the two great oceanic powers of that day, Spain and Portugal, however, the third bull proved to have a great and lasting influ- **Demarcation** ence. Accepting its principle, the two countries **line and Brazil** agreed in the treaty of Tordesillas in 1494 to make the meridian fixed by the pope, or rather one somewhat to the west of it, the dividing line between their "spheres of influence," each respecting the rights of the other to the exclusive enjoyment of everything discovered within its sphere, Spain taking what lay to the west, Portugal to the east. As the drawing of the line was beyond the scientific abilities of the day, its exact location was never determined. Nevertheless, to the surprise of both nations it soon became evident that, even allowing the most easterly position possible for the boundary, a portion of South America projected beyond it into the Portuguese sphere. To this line of demarcation laid down by Alexander VI in 1493 and modified by the treaty of Tordesillas in 1494 the existence of the Portuguese language and civilization in Brazil to-day is distinctly traceable, and the first event in American diplomacy is thus still a factor in our daily life.[2]

When Magellan circumnavigated the world and made "east" and "west" relative terms, it was at once realized that if the demarcation line were to remain useful it must

[1] C. R. Fish, *Guide to the Materials for American History in Roman and other Italian Archives* (Washington, 1911), 239.

[2] Henry Harrisse, *The Diplomatic History of America, its first Chapter, 1452-1494*, London, 1897.

girdle the globe. The matter was one of great scientific difficulty, and national interests did not leave science to work unfettered, but by the treaties of Victoria in 1524 and Zaragoza in 1529 the boundary was reduced to terms. In point of fact the line was incorrectly drawn, but, as is often the case when an accident occurs in times of flux and uncertainty, the error has become embedded in history. The Philippines, properly Portuguese, became Spanish, and, being Spanish, ultimately became American. This second permanent result of Pope Alexander's demarcation line can, of course, hardly be attributed to its influence alone; for Spain by discovery and occupation, and by her actual power, helped produce the error in location. In spite of inaccuracies, however, the existence of the principle of a dividing line, aided in the early and peaceful settlement of the question.[1]

Demarcation line and the Philippines

In America the effect of the treaty of Tordesillas was to leave Spain a free hand west of Brazil. By voyages of discovery, followed up by conquests and settlements, she speedily established a firm hold on all the territory as far north as Mexico and Florida, and presently came to regard the entire continent and adjacent seas as hers by all rights divine and human. In 1555 Charles V on relinquishing his authority to his son Philip II drew up a set of instructions to guide him in his government, in which, among the problems relating to the various portions of his vast territories, he discussed the situation in the Indies. In 1558 he issued another instruction, dealing for the first time with the subject of the defence of the Indies.[2]

Spanish empire

We may, therefore, believe that during this interval the Spanish government first became seriously alarmed for the safety of its American possessions. Although the attacks

[1] Blair and Robertson, *Philippine Islands*, i. 159–164, 222–239; Justin Winsor, *Narrative and Critical History of America* (8 vols., Boston, 1884–89), ii. 441.

[2] Fish, *Guide*, 113.

upon them which excited the apprehension of the dying statesman were not at that time such as to test the strength of
his son's empire, yet the enormous extent of Rise of the
Spanish dominions rendered defence difficult, pirates
and its riches attracted the hardy adventurer. The assail-
ants, moreover,—Mohammedans from Barbary, French
Huguenots, and, a little later, Dutch and English Protestants,—were in a position to give to their plundering expeditions the sanction of religion. But although they rendered
property unsafe, they were not powerful enough to cope
with the organized forces of Spain, their only serious attempt
upon the integrity of the empire being thwarted in the awe-
inspiring massacre of the French Huguenots on the river
St. John in 1563.

With the defeat of the Spanish Armada by England in
1588 the situation changed. Fear of Spain was almost for-
gotten, and information spread as to the pos- English,
sibilities of the vast areas to the north of French, and
Spanish settlement. To these regions Eng- Dutch settle-
land, France, and Holland set up rival claims, ments
based on the discoveries of the Cabots, Verrazzano and
Cartier, and Hendrik Hudson respectively; and each country
began permanent settlements. By 1625 the English were established in Virginia and New England, the French in Canada
and Acadia, or Nova Scotia, and the Dutch on the Hudson;
but there was as yet no mutual recognition of each other's
rights, and no recognition of any alien rights by Spain.

The first treaty after Tordesillas which referred to
America was that of St. Germain in 1632, according to the
terms of which England restored to France International
the post of Quebec and other American forts recognition of
taken in the preceding war, and which may colonies
therefore be taken as a recognition by each country that the
other had American possessions.[1] By royal patent of 1645

[1] Thomas Rymer, *Foedera*, etc. (3d ed., 10 vols., The Hague, 1739–45),
viii. pt. iii. 228–229.

Spain tacitly acknowledged the presence of the English in America by permitting them to import into Spain certain products peculiar to America;[1] in the famous treaty of Munster, in 1648, she recognized the American possessions of the Dutch;[2] and by the treaty of Madrid in 1670 she formally acknowledged the existence of the English colonies.[3] By 1670, therefore, the colonial empires of these four rival countries had acquired international standing, but no definite boundary line in North America had international recognition.

Of these rivals the Dutch were the first to disappear. Already by the treaty of Breda in 1667 Holland had ceded to Elimination of England not only her own settlements about Dutch from the Hudson but also those of the Swedes on North America the Delaware which she had seized in 1655.[4] Recaptured by the Dutch a few years later, these were finally ceded by the treaty of Westminster, in 1674, to remain united forever with their English neighbors.[5]   Almost more important was the fusion of Dutch and English interests in 1688 on the accession of the stadtholder of Holland to the throne of England as William III.   United by strict treaties, by which the Dutch practically conceded naval supremacy to England in return for the profits to be derived from a liberal grant of rights to their neutral vessels when England was at war,[6] the latter rose to world power, while Holland sank into a desuetude which was innocuous to all except her own citizens.

[1] George Chalmers, *A Collection of Treaties between Great Britain and other Powers* (2 vols., London, 1790), ii. 27.

[2] P. J. Blok, *Geschiedenis van het Nederlandsche Volk* (8 vols., Groningen, etc., 1892–1908), iv. 444; translated by O. A. Bierstadt, *History of the People of the Netherlands* (5 vols., New York, etc., 1898–1912), iv. 148.

[3] *Cambridge Modern History* (1908), v. 105.

[4] Comte de Garden, *Histoire générale des traités de paix* (15 vols., Paris, 1848–87), ii. 52.

[5] *Cambridge Modern History*, v. 161.

[6] Garden, *Traités de paix*, ii. 129, iii. 9–10; Charles Jenkinson, *Collection of . . . Treaties* (3 vols., London, 1785), i. 190, 279, 364.

Of the rivals that remained Spain was on the defensive. To the effort to fortify and defend that which she had already occupied she devoted great energy, and, with Spanish de-the assistance of Rome, was in the main suc- fence cessful for over a hundred years. It was not so easy to monopolize the commerce of her possessions in the face of the persistent intrusions of Dutch and English merchants; but by concentrating it in certain ports and confining ocean traffic to the regular passage of great protected fleets, she went far toward accomplishing her purpose.

France and England confronted the situation in a different spirit. The conspicuously great powers of the day both aimed at world empire, and regarded France and America as a field for contest and a prize England for the victor. Between 1688 and 1815 they seven times engaged in war, and for sixty-three years out of the one hundred and twenty-seven they were in open conflict. All these wars involved America, and out of them emerged American boundaries, American foreign policies, and to a considerable extent the spirit of American nationality.

The first two of these wars grew out of European causes, and the third from Spanish-American trade; but in each case the French and English colonists of North America Colonial wars were drawn into the conflict. Although the two groups were still separated by hundreds of miles of wilderness, the Indians constituted a medium by which the shock of hostility was communicated: the burning of Schenectady in 1690 by the French and Indians caused a first thrill of mutual dependence and helpfulness to run through the northern group of English colonies. The point of closest contact, however, was in the northeast, where ever since 1613 the absence of a boundary between the French and English spheres of influence had given rise to occasional encounters. In particular the depredations of the French privateers, first from Port Royal, later from Louisburg, made the possession of those ports a practical question to the New England merchants, who in each war, and mainly by their own efforts, captured the offensive seaport but were foiled in their designs on the seat of French power, Quebec.

Peace treaties, or more properly truce agreements, however, were made in Europe and in accordance with European conditions. The first, that of Ryswick in 1697, restored Port Royal to France.[1] The second, that of Utrecht in 1713, marked a defeat for France as well as the first attempt to define by treaty North American boundaries.[2] France gave up all claim to Newfoundland and to the Hudson Bay country, and a commission was appointed to draw a boundary for the latter region. Of more immediate interest was the cession to England of Acadia or Nova Scotia, including Port Royal; but in this case a boundary controversy resulted instead of a boundary, for the country was granted "with its ancient boundaries," which can scarcely be said to have existed. In 1745 the colonists captured Louisburg, the French substitute for Port Royal, but by the treaty of Aix-la-Chapelle, in 1748, they had to return it to France.[3] The disadvantages of their European connection were beginning to unfold themselves to the British settlers.

With this peace a new condition began to develop, which resulted in the first American war fought for American causes. The centre of interest was now shifted to the Ohio valley. This region the French claimed on three grounds,—because by their settlement at New Orleans they held the mouth of the Mississippi which drained it, because in 1749 they officially explored it and left formal evidences of their claims, and because they had at Vincennes the only actual white settlement in the main valley. For three reasons, too, they were

European treaties

The contest for the Ohio valley

[1] William MacDonald, *Select Charters* (New York, 1899), 223.
[2] *Ibid.*, 229–232.
[3] R. G. Thwaites, "France in America" (*American Nation*, vol. vii.), 122.

willing to fight to maintain their claims,—because of the value of the fur trade of the region, because the valley was necessary if they were to weld Canada and Louisiana into one imperial colony, and because by holding it they would restrict the English to the seacoast. They prepared, therefore, to establish a chain of forts from the lakes to the gulf. The English colonists, on the other hand, desired the valley in order to thwart the plans of the French, and because the far-sighted were already anticipating that the westward push of American settlement would at no distant period turn its rich lands into pioneer farms. Their claims they based partly upon the right of a nation occupying a coast to possession of the back country,—a view of international law early incorporated into the colonial charters,—partly upon what would to-day be called a protectorate over the Iroquois Indians, whose visionary claims extended over nearly all the Northwest, and partly upon their trade relations with the valley Indians.

Not by such arguments but by arms alone could so great a controversy be decided. In 1754 the French secured the strategic point, the junction at which the **An American** Monongahela and the Allegheny unite to **war** form the Ohio. A body of Virginia militia advanced against them. The French awaited them in ambush without the fort. Warned by an Indian, the Virginians surprised the French, and the first battle of the war took place. As Voltaire said: "A torch lighted in the forests of America set all Europe in conflagration." How essentially this was an American war is illustrated by the fact that, although hostilities began here in 1754, it was not till 1756 that France and England officially broke off diplomatic relations. It is not without significance that the command for the first shot was given by Major George Washington.

In William Pitt, the great English war minister, the colonists found a leader who brought out their comparatively great resources. By 1760 Canada was conquered. In this emergency France called upon Spain for assistance. These two monarchies had since 1702 been united dynastically by **The "Family Alliance"** the succession of a French prince to the Spanish throne, and in 1761 they became by treaty diplomatically bound together in what is known as the Family Alliance.[1] In accordance with this agreement either country might, if engaged in a defensive war, call for the assistance of the other, but in such case it must make good any losses which the succoring party should sustain. This union, though unable to check the progress of English arms, yet brought Spain and her possessions into the peace negotiations and caused readjustments of fundamental importance.

The war resulted in four documents which together constituted the basis of American territorial diplomacy till well **The cession of Canada** into the nineteenth century. First came the treaty between England and France, made at Paris in 1763.[2] For a long time the English government hung in uncertainty as to whether it should take as part of the spoils of war the rich sugar island of Guadaloupe in the West Indies, or Canada. Fortunately for the colonies, however, they were at this crisis represented in London by an agent of exceptional force and adroitness, Benjamin Franklin of Pennsylvania, who made it clear that they would be greatly dissatisfied if they should again be deprived of their conquests. The English government therefore concluded to hold Canada, but not without some misgiving that it might have been safer to face discontented colonists than to free them from the continual menace of French hostility, a point of view which gave some consolation to the French statesmen, who confidently predicted that England could not long hold colonies to whose safety she was not necessary.

[1] Comte de Flassan, *Histoire générale et raisonnée de la diplomatie française* (2d ed., 7 vols., Paris, 1811), vi. 314–320.

[2] From this point all treaties mentioned to which the United States was not a party may be found in G. F. de Martens's *Recueil de traités des puissances et états de l'Europe*, which begins with 1761 and is continued by supplements and new editions to 1913.

In addition to Canada, France ceded all her claims to the Ohio valley and all of the province of Louisiana east of the Mississippi and north of the little river Iberville, which ran from the Mississippi to the gulf, retaining to the east of the Mississippi only the Ile d'Orléans, which contained the city now called New Orleans. The eastern limit of this French cession was not defined by treaty, but by custom had been established at the river Perdido, halfway between the French Mobile and the Spanish Pensacola. This boundary was for the present, however, obliterated by the second document in the series, the treaty between Spain and England, by which the former ceded to England all of Florida, thus absorbing also the boundary disputes between that province and its northern neighbor, Georgia.

French Louisiana and Spanish Florida

By a third document France gave to Spain what remained of Louisiana, the Ile d'Orléans and an undefined territory west of the Mississippi, to indemnify her for the loss of Florida.[1] Thus the whole mainland of North America came to be divided between Spain and England by the waters of the Mississippi and the Iberville. The far-sighted, however, realized that, with the French navy in existence, with a French population in Canada and Louisiana, and with so wide a difference in the relative strength of Spain and France, the latter was not yet eliminated as a factor in American development.

Spanish Louisiana

The fourth document was an English royal proclamation, issued October 7, 1763, dividing the new conquests into administrative provinces.[2] Florida was extended to include the portion of French Louisiana ceded to England, and was divided into east and west provinces by the Appalachicola river, Pensacola thus falling to

The English Floridas

[1] B. A. Hinsdale, *The Establishment of the First Southern Boundary of the United States*, Amer. Hist. Assoc., *Report*, 1893, pp. 329–366.

[2] William MacDonald, *Documentary Source Book of American History* (New York, 1908), 113–116, see also C. E. Carter, "Some Aspects of British Administration in West Florida," *Mississippi Valley Hist. Review*, 1914, i. 364–375.

the western province. The boundary between East Florida and Georgia was fixed as it stands to-day; the northern boundary of West Florida was set at the thirty-first parallel. In 1764 this boundary was shifted to a line running from the mouth of the Yazoo, or 32′ 28″.

To the north the province of Quebec was created, with a southern boundary extending from the "South end of lake

Quebec Nipissing." Thence the said line, crossing the river St. Lawrence and the lake Champlain in 45 degrees of north latitude, passed along the "High Lands, which divide the rivers which empty themselves into the river St. Lawrence, from those which fall into the sea, and also along the North coast of the Bayes des Chaleurs." In 1774, by the Quebec Act, the province was enlarged by the inclusion of the region north of the Ohio river. The area between Quebec and Florida, bounded on the east by a line connecting the head waters of the rivers flowing into the Atlantic, was left unorganized, a preserve for Indians and fur-bearing animals.[1]

With this settlement the ground plan of American diplomacy was laid. Indians, English, French, and Spanish colo-

Factors and problems nists, as well as the mother countries with their rivalry of interests and traditions, were all alert to their positions. Nor may one overlook the situation in the West Indies, so much more important at that day than at this, and so much more closely connected with the continent by ties of business and of government. There all the rival nations had footholds, and there the fate of European and American wars was sometimes determined. Under these circumstances were to be settled such great questions as the direction of English and Spanish-American commerce, the governmental relationship of Europe and America, and the racial ownership of the Mississippi valley and the region of the great lakes.

[1] C. E. Carter, *Great Britain and the Illinois Country* (Washington, 1910), 13–26.

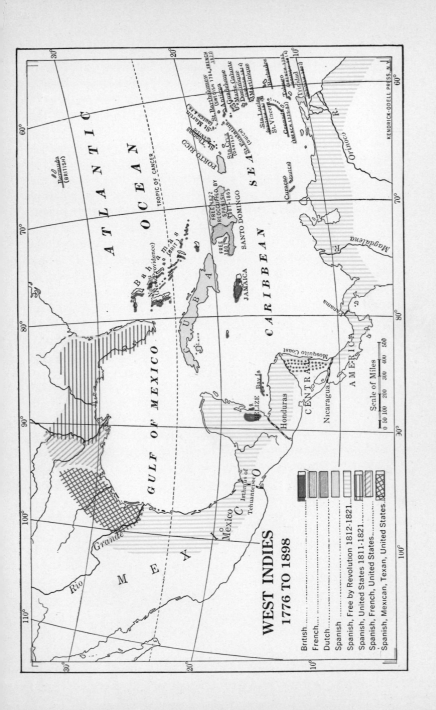

WEST INDIES
1776 TO 1898

British..............
French..............
Dutch..............
Spanish..............
Spanish, Free by Revolution 1812-1821..
Spanish, United States 1811-1821......
Spanish, French, United States........
Spanish, Mexican, Texan, United States..

Scale of Miles
0 50 100   200   300   400   500

KENDRICK-ODELL PRESS, N.Y.

ATLANTIC   OCEAN

Bermuda
(BRITISH)

TROPIC OF CANCER

Bahamas

New Providence
(BRITISH)

CUBA

PORTO RICO
(SPANISH)

St. Thomas (DANISH)
St. John (DANISH)
Sta. Cruz (DANISH)
St. Martin (DUTCH & FRENCH)
St. Bartholomew (SWEDISH 1784, FRENCH 1877)
Anguilla
Barbuda
Guadaloupe (FRENCH)
Marie Galante
Dominica
Martinique

FREE 1822
RECONQUERED BY
SPANISH
1861-1865

FREE
1801

SANTO DOMINGO

JAMAICA

Sta. Lucia
St. Vincent
Grenada (FRENCH 1779)
Barbadoes
Tobago
Trinidad

Curaçao (DUTCH)

CARIBBEAN   SEAS

Mosquito Coast

CENTRAL   AMERICA

Honduras

Nicaragua

BELIZE Bay's

Isthmus of
Tehuantepec

Mexico

M   E   X   I   C   O

Rio Grande

Orinoco R.

Magdalena R.

Atrato R.

Panama

CHAPTER III

RECOGNITION [1]

THE early diplomatic successes of the Americans are often enhanced by the commentary that the first representatives of the new country faced, as untrained novices, Diplomacy and international law. Europeans who were masters of their art. This lack of preparation, however, extended only to lack of practice in the formal art of diplomatic intercourse and to lack of acquaintance with international law. Of these apparent defects the first was a distinct advantage, for the diplomatic code of the eighteenth century had become rigid and formal to the point of breaking, and the directness of the Americans was like a fresh breeze under which it began to totter to a fall. International law, on the other hand, was then so far from being the formal and inclusive system which it is to-day that it was not beyond the comprehension of amateurs.

Of men trained in the more essential elements of diplomacy, the colonies had a greater proportion than any other country of the time. They had been engaged in continual negotiations, almost independently of Colonial experience. Great Britain, with the Indian tribes, and frequently with the French and Spaniards. Every colony had had semi-diplomatic disputes with its neighbors, and all had supported agents in England whose functions included virtually all the elements of a diplomatic mission. Almost continuously from 1758 to 1774 Benjamin Franklin, as general agent, had occupied a post in England essentially equivalent to minister

[1] For a general bibliography of American diplomacy to 1901, see A. B. Hart, *Foundations of American Foreign Policy* (New York, 1905), 241–293; also Channing, Hart, and Turner, *Guide to the Study of American History* (Boston, etc., 1912), which has special sections on diplomacy to 1912.

to that government. Moreover, the whole movement toward union between the colonies was diplomatic in its character, and constantly involved the most delicate questions of management.

The colonists had therefore had experience with alliances, with treaties of peace, of boundary, and of cession, with the

Arbitration conduct of joint military expeditions, and with dealing with men of differing habits and customs. They were thoroughly at home with the great American questions of boundary, fisheries, Indians, and foreign trade. They were accustomed to discuss difficult problems with able men, and to recognize the necessity of compromise. In one respect their peculiar experience as colonists prepared them even to take the lead in a new departure in international law,—the science of international arbitration. Accustomed as they were to see intercolonial disputes ultimately settled by judicial process in England, they thought of arbitration as a natural expedient. Further, having no trained diplomatic staff, they sent over their ablest men of affairs, who usually overmatched in ability the men with whom they had to deal.

This diplomatic readiness was indeed an essential resource, for without foreign aid the cause of the colonists would have

Necessity for been well-nigh hopeless. In the final event foreign aid the French army was a decisive factor at Yorktown; but the French army was less significant than the French navy, which rendered the situation at Yorktown possible.[1] Still more important, however, was the fact that the colonies were not self-sufficing industrially, and so could not have withstood the first shock of war without the supplies of arms and other manufactured goods which from the beginning of the conflict found their way into the country through the lax neutrality of Holland, Spain, and France.[2]

[1] A. T. Mahan, *The Influence of Sea Power upon History, 1660–1783* (Boston, 1890), 382–400.

[2] J. F. Jameson, "Saint Eustatius in the American Revolution," *Amer. Hist. Review*, 1903, viii. 683–708.

From the meeting of the Continental Congress, September 5, 1774, until the Declaration of Independence, July 4, 1776, the position of the colonists was extremely Groping for delicate. Professing loyalty to George III, aid they realized more and more the necessity of foreign assistance, for which, however, it would have been treason to apply. Groping for support, Congress on October 21, 1774, sent an address to the other continental British colonies, on June 3, 1775, it addressed the people of Ireland, and on June 16 it appointed a committee to secure the friendship of the Indian nations. On November 29, 1775, though veiling its design in ambiguity of language, it took a more decisive step by appointing a committee of five to correspond with friends of the colonies in Great Britain, Ireland, "and other parts of the world"; and finally, in the spring of 1776 it sent Silas Deane as agent to France, his mission, however, disguised under a pretence of private business.[1]

Before following Deane in his delicate task it is desirable to have some understanding of the general conditions under which diplomatic intercourse was con- Diplomatic or-ducted during the Revolution. In general the ganization development of diplomatic organization resembled that of other departments. The committee of correspondence lasted till April, 1777. It was succeeded by a committee on foreign affairs, which gave way in October, 1781 to a secretary of foreign affairs, Robert Livingston. Under all these successive régimes, however, the main questions were debated in Congress itself, which received foreign ministers, and whose president sometimes acted as the national representative before the world. Communication Communica-between the directing body and its agents tion abroad was slow and uncertain. Even in summer two months was considered good time between Philadelphia and

---

[1] *The Revolutionary Diplomatic Correspondence of the United States*, ed. Francis Wharton, 6 vols., Washington, 1889; also *Secret Journals of Congress, 1775–1788*, 4 vols., Boston, 1821.

Paris, and in winter there were few opportunities to send letters; moreover, if they escaped the constant peril of capture by the English, they were liable to be read by the foreign postal authorities. Months often passed without the successful exchange of a letter, and some of the most important papers fell into the hands of the enemy. Under such circumstances the American representatives abroad were to a remarkable degree thrown upon their own responsibility, and might well feel that the fate of a nation depended upon their wisdom.[1]

More important than such facts was the attitude in which Deane would find Europe waiting. Primarily that attitude was one of intense interest. From the first moment that the Revolution took form the chancelleries of Europe watched with minute attention. The press of Amsterdam teemed with translations of American pamphlets and original discussions of the American situation. From 1774 half the bulk of the Paris and London correspondence of every court of Europe consisted of American news; the ministry of Naples knew in detail of every happening in Philadelphia; at Rome Mgr. Lazzari began a diary of the American Revolution. Never since then, unless possibly in 1900, has this country absorbed so much of the attention of continental Europe.[2]

European interest

The vogue of America rested largely on the belief that in that far-off non-contagious land the vision of Rousseau was being materialized. The American leaders, such as Patrick Henry and Samuel Adams, were picturesque and appealing in their sentiments and eloquence; in one section of French society liberalism was fashionable; if one may judge from the conduct of the nobility early in the French Revolution it was more than fashionable. Even to those to whom it did not appeal, the liberal experiment was compelling in its possibilities. Sympathy

Sentimental sympathy

[1] See page 23, note 1.
[2] Fish, *Guide*, 74, 75, 118, 233–235, 240–241, 246, 250.

hung in the balance, but the audience was on tiptoe following the action.[1]

If America seemed less picturesque to the men of affairs, it seemed also less remote. For a hundred years every war had tended to become a general war. Since 1763 England had been regarded as the bully of Europe, and the strength of England was believed to lie in her commerce and her colonies. The possible disintegration of the British empire was a subject that nearly touched that holy of holies of the European statesman, the balance of power. To France the situation came not entirely as a surprise. Choiseul had predicted it in 1763, France had maintained secret agents in the colonies from that time, and the king himself had attended to their reports. Toward France, therefore, the eyes of the nations were directed as closely as toward London and America.

Hatred of England

In France Louis XVI, "the Good," had succeeded to the throne in 1774. Neither he nor the prime minister, Maurepas, was the driving force; the energy of the government lay with Turgot, the minister of finance, and Vergennes, the minister of foreign affairs. Both intent upon revenge on England, Turgot wished for a longer period of recuperation, whereas Vergennes was eager to take advantage of this unique opportunity. In two papers entitled "Réflexions" and "Considérations," the latter urged his views. The colonists, he said, must be supported. If they were conquered, England would turn her armies in America upon the French and Spanish West Indies. It was more likely, however, that the war would cause the overthrow of the existing British ministry and the recall of William Pitt, now earl of Chatham. That sinister genius, the idol of the colonies, would probably effect a reconciliation, and, with

Vergennes and Turgot

[1] For a running account, see J. B. Perkins, *France in the American Revolution*, Boston, etc., 1911; for the documents, Henri Doniol, *Histoire de la participation de la France à l'établissement des États Unis d'Amérique*, 5 vols., Paris, 1886–92.

the combined forces of England and America, "une epée nue dans les mains d'un furieux," would devastate the world.[1]

France, however, could not well act openly without Spain. Their fleets together might hope to meet that of England, but that of France alone could not. Spain, under Charles III and his minister Florida Blanca, was somewhat more energetic than usual. She was still united with France in the Family Alliance, and she desired to regain Florida and Gibraltar. On the other hand, it seemed rash for the greatest colonial power to encourage revolting colonies; besides, she was not fully ready for war, and again the habitual Spanish procrastination stood in the way of prompt action. While goading Spain into activity, Vergennes advised Louis XVI to await her decision before going to war, but meantime by secret succor to prevent the colonies from falling before British arms or promises.

Spain delays French action

It was possibly the opening of this middle way, rendering unnecessary a definite decision, from which Louis XVI shrank almost as nervously as did Charles III, that secured for Vergennes his victory over Turgot and the direction of French policy. On May 2, 1776, he was authorized to use a million francs for the colonies, to which Spain soon added another million. To employ these sums for the colonists, without the knowledge, or at any rate without the proved knowledge, of England, Vergennes had recourse to Pierre de Beaumarchais, a playwright and litterateur, who escaped being a charlatan by being something of a genius, and who had served as a special agent for Vergennes in England.[2]

Tentative assistance

Beaumarchais organized a commercial company, under the name of Rodriguez Hortalie and Company, to deal in American products. Through Dumas, a Dutch friend of

---

[1] Charlemagne Tower, *The Marquis de La Fayette* (2 vols., Philadelphia, 1895), i. 74, 92–97, 108–113.

[2] C. J. Stillé, *Beaumarchais and " The Lost Million,"* (Philadelphia, 1886).

Franklin, he was put in touch with Arthur Lee, an American just then in Paris. When, therefore, Deane arrived in France he found everything prepared for him. The initiative came from neither side alone, but each putting forth its antennæ encountered the other. Nor was the preparation confined to that of the government. In that military age war anywhere attracted the adventurous. Soldiers of fortune looked to America as a field for possible glory and emolument, while some men, like the young Marquis de Lafayette, burned to baptize their swords in the cause of liberty. Deane was overwhelmed with offers of assistance, as well as with requests for commissions in the American army; and he sent home not only a number of officers, good and bad, but, what was still more necessary, arms from French arsenals, paid for by the French and Spanish millions or to be paid for by cargoes of tobacco. Beaumarchais wrote to Congress, "Your deputies, gentlemen, will find in me a sure friend, an asylum in my house, money in my coffers, and every means of prosecuting their operations whether of a public or a secret nature."

Meantime the Declaration of Independence had been issued and the new United States could reveal its policy. Its representatives need no longer be inconspicuous; accordingly, in September it sent to France its most illustrious citizen, Benjamin Franklin. From his arrival in 1776 till his departure in 1785, sometimes as one of several commissioners, sometimes as sole minister to France, Franklin was universally thought of as the representative of the American cause in Europe. Arriving in Paris at the age of seventy, and preceded by his reputation as a statesman, but still better known as the author of *Poor Richard's Almanac* and by his discoveries in electricity, he presented to the curious gaze of those who thought to see for the first time in the flesh one of those Arcadians who were becoming the support of conversation, a benignant countenance with gray locks "appearing under a martin fur cap." His lack of acquaintance with French court etiquette he concealed under a cloak of agreeable eccentricity, which he knew how to render interesting and not too strange, just as he kept his costume simple but not too simple. Honesty had so long been his policy that it shone from his face, and he captured at once, and contrived to deserve, the complete confidence of the entire diplomatic corps. Perhaps only those who had business with him realized that his disarming ingenuousness of appearance was not unaccompanied by a subtlety based upon a knowledge of human nature more comprehensive than that of Lincoln, though not so profound. All, however, came to realize that the intellect under the fur cap was unique, and that of all great minds produced by America his was the most nearly akin to the Gallic. His pregnant wit passed rapidly from mouth to mouth. His satiric skits were expressed with an artistic delicacy as pleasing to the Parisian as unusual among Americans. Moreover, his artistic sense for language seems but to have reflected his mastery of the art of living. His tact and sympathetic consideration won those who associated intimately with him, while he did not disdain to employ a nicely calculated breadth of acting which gained the remote spectators of the gallery.[1]

Franklin took Paris by storm. His piquant sayings and writings caught the public attention, his shoe buckles be-

Franklin captures Paris
came the fashion, his pictures were everywhere for sale. The best Latin verse since the Augustan age was forged in his honor: "Eripuit cælo fulmen, sceptrumque tyrannis," "He snatched from Heaven the thunderbolt, the scepter also from tyrants." Hesitant society swung to the American side, and society was at that period the public in France. That Franklin enjoyed himself is clear, and that he liked the French, who liked him, was only natural. It is true that he became very close to those

---

[1] E. E. Hale and E. E. Hale, Jr., *Franklin in France*, 2 vols., Boston, 1887–88; and, more particularly, Franklin's Works (ed. John Bigelow, 10 vols., New York, 1887–88), vols. vi.–ix.

in authority, but that the glamor blinded in any way his clear view of American interests may well be doubted. In December, 1776, it was said of him, "That popular man became more powerful than power itself;" and Jefferson wrote later, "He possessed the confidence of that government in the highest degree, insomuch that it may truly be said that they were more under his influence than he under theirs."

Franklin's success rendered the triumph of Vergennes's policy comparatively easy. American merchant ships, privateers, and war vessels found harborage in **Friendship and** French ports; and finally, when the news of the **alliance** surrender of Burgoyne reached France, early in 1778, the king consented to act without waiting upon Spain. On February 6 of that year two treaties were signed between France and the United States,—one of amity and commerce, and, in case England should resent that, one of alliance. The treaty of amity was framed upon principles of free mutual intercourse which were somewhat in advance of the time, and incorporated certain rules of international law, as that free ships make free goods, long laid down by the Dutch and French writers but denied by the English. The treaty of alliance guaranteed, on the part of France, the independence of the United States; on the part of the latter the existing possessions of France in America. To the United States it gave a free hand in the conquest of British continental possessions and of the Bermudas; to France it granted similar rights in the West Indies. "Neither of the two parties," it ran, "shall conclude either truce or peace with Great Britain without the formal consent of the other first obtained; and they mutually engage not to lay down their arms until the independence of the United States shall have been formally or tacitly assured by the treaty or treaties that shall terminate the war." [1]

[1] For these and all subsequent treaties to which the United States was a party, see *Treaties, Conventions,* etc., ed., W. M. Malloy and Charles Garfield, 2 vols. to 1909, and supplement to 1913 (Senate Doc., 61 Con. 2 sess., No. 357).

England, on hearing of the recognition of American independence by France, did not accept the view of Louis XVI,
France enters who wrote to George III that he was assured
the war that the latter would regard it as one more manifestation of his friendly disposition; and in April war between France and England began. Thanks largely to the tact of Franklin, the alliance worked smoothly. The French government loaned money and guaranteed other loans; it sent ships and troops to America. As the chief American authority in Europe, Franklin was financial and purchasing agent for the states; he directed the employment of the American navy under Commodore John Paul Jones; and, through his friends, the Foxes of Falmouth, he looked after the welfare of the American prisoners in England. American trade was legitimatized, and the final independence of the United States became a reasonable certainty.

CHAPTER IV

SPAIN AND HOLLAND

Two parties arose in Congress. One, which came to be known as the Gallican, or French, party, favored the entrusting of American interests in Europe to France, advised by Franklin. The other, sometimes known as the party of the Lees and Adamses, distrusted French sincerity and Franklin's ability and wished to preserve an independent course. The friends of Franklin, who in domestic affairs were also in general the supporters of Washington, succeeded in maintaining him at Paris, but their rivals obtained the appointment of a swarm of agents commissioned to other countries. Silas Deane was recalled in 1778, and in 1779 Franklin was appointed sole minister to France; but from time to time Ralph Izard was sent to Tuscany, Arthur Lee was for a time co-commissioner to France and was appointed to undertake missions to Spain and Prussia, William Lee was sent to Berlin and Vienna, Francis Dana to Russia, Henry Laurens to the Netherlands. None of these were received at their posts, but at Paris and in their wanderings about Europe they now and again touched wires in a manner disturbing to the controlling authorities. It was, however, at Paris, and by Franklin and Vergennes, that the international status of the alliance had to be determined.[1]

The first essential was the Spanish fleet, and the Spanish negotiation at once became the central point of diplomatic interest. Charles III was annoyed at the independent action of France; the Spanish government was irritated at the persistent attempts of Arthur Lee to gain admission to the Spanish court, and vacillated with the success or the failure of American arms. Spain

[1] Wharton, *Diplomatic Correspondence*, introduction.

31

was still unready; she asserted that France was the offending party and that the Family Alliance did not compel her to assist France in an offensive war. Instead she offered mediation, in return for which she was to receive the cession of the Floridas and a considerable proportion of the territory between the Floridas and the Ohio, a proposal which was virtually an offer to accept a bribe from England for her inactivity. The offer was refused, but European opinion still believed that she would remain at peace, when rather unexpectedly, in 1779, she declared war on Great Britain.

Thus united, the French and Spanish fleets for some years neutralized British naval supremacy. Since Spain, however, though allied with France, had not as yet even recognized the United States, in the autumn of 1779 Congress sent John Jay to treat with her. Jay was thirty-four years old, a man of decided talent and great energy. Although a gentleman in the conventional sense and descended from French Huguenots, he was provincial in experience and point of view and retained no spark of appreciation for French civilization. Given to self-confidence, he was alert to American interests up to the point of being suspicious of all who opposed his view of them. He was instructed to offer Spain permission to take the Floridas from Great Britain and to hold them; but in return he was to insist on the right of the Americans to navigate the Mississippi to the sea,—a right in respect to which he declared in 1780, "The Americans, almost to a man, believed that God Almighty had made that river a highway for the people of the upper country to go to the sea by,"—and he was to request permission to use similarly the rivers flowing into the Gulf of Mexico to the eastward. In 1781 under the pressure of accumulated woes, Congress released him from that part of his instructions relating to the Mississippi; but he disregarded the modification.[1]

John Jay

---

[1] John Jay, *Correspondence and Public Papers* (ed. H. P. Johnston, 4 vols., New York, 1890–93), i. 248–461, ii. 1–296.

Jay was not officially received in Spain, but he was put in touch with Don Diego de Gardoqui, a Spanish merchant versed in American affairs, who represented Spanish the Spanish government. It soon appeared policies that Spain was as insistent on closing the Mississippi as Jay was on opening it. One great boon which she expected to obtain from the war was the banishment of all foreign commerce from the Gulf of Mexico. Ever timid as to her American possessions, she wished to hold all neighbors at arm's length. Indeed, she was not satisfied with the narrow fringe of coast afforded by the Floridas; but in the project of a treaty presented in her behalf to Congress by Luzerne, the French minister at Philadelphia, she renewed the suggestion contained in her mediating offer to England, that she receive a portion of the region between the Floridas and the Ohio.[1] Money she was willing to offer; vital concession she would not make.

Fully cognizant of Spanish views, and with his suspicions excited by an outside view of a negotiation with England which took place at Madrid during his stay, Spanish nego-Jay, having obtained nothing but some slight tiation in pecuniary aid, returned to Paris, where in Paris 1782 he renewed negotiations with the Spanish minister at that capital, Count d'Aranda. To assist in these negotiations Vergennes delegated his secretary Rayneval, who seemed to Jay to support the Spanish contentions.

Meantime the question was not left to diplomatic controversy alone. In 1778 and 1779, the American, George Rogers Clark had captured Kaskaskia on the War in the Mississippi and Vincennes on the Wabash, West within the territory added to Quebec by the act of 1774. Between 1779 and 1781 Spain captured the British forts in West Florida. At Natchez on the Mississippi between the parallels of 31' and 32' 28'', in or out of West Florida as one might view it, the Spaniards and Americans almost

[1] *Secret Journals of Congress*, ii. 310, etc.

came to blows. In the winter of 1781 a Spanish expedition from St. Louis penetrated to the British fort of St. Joseph in Michigan and burned it.[1] Jay wrote to Livingston, "When you consider the ostensible object of this expedition, the distance of it, the formalities with which the place, the country, and the rivers were taken possession of in the name of His Catholic Majesty, I am persuaded it will not be necessary for me to swell this letter with remarks that would occur to a reader of far less penetration than yourself."

By 1782 Jay was, therefore, thoroughly convinced that Spain wished no good to the United States, but rather that she would curtail it within the narrowest limits. He believed also that France was co-operating with Spain and was moved by similar desires. John Adams writing in November of that year confided to his diary: "Mr. Jay likes Frenchmen as little as Mr. Lee and Mr. Izard did. He says they are not a moral people; they know not what it is; he don't like any Frenchman; the Marquis de Lafayette is clever, but he is a Frenchman. Our allies don't play fair, he told me." Adams's reference to allies is a little ambiguous; but he must have referred to the French alone, for by the close of 1782 there was still no agreement between Spain and the United States. France was the ally of each, but they were not allies of each other.

While Jay was negotiating with Spain, the centre of interest had shifted to the Netherlands. With the only comparatively free press on the continent, that country, and particularly Amsterdam, was a centre for the publication of polemical literature; and as the chief money-lender of Europe, the Dutch bourse reflected all shades of all the diplomatic changes of the world. The interest of the Dutch in America, and of the Americans in the Dutch, however, was far from being wholly platonic. Until our treaty

Jay's conclusions

Holland

---

[1] Justin Winsor, *The Westward Movement* (Boston, etc., 1897), 116–202; Doniol, *La participation de la France*, iv. 101.

with France, Dutch neutrality was the chief foreign asset of the colonies.

Dutch smugglers had always been the bane of honest English officials in the colonies; the smuggling question had, indeed, been one of the causes of irritation that produced the Revolution. In the event of independence, the Dutch seemed most likely to inherit the American trade. When communication between England and America was cut off and British war vessels began to patrol the American coast, the safest expedient was to drop with the generally favoring winds into the maze of West Indian islands to seek a market for sale and purchase; and the Dutch merchants took care that the Americans should find what they came for. European goods could be safely shipped from Holland to some Dutch island, and in particular the little island of St. Eustatius became from 1776 to 1779 the entrepôt of American trade. Lying in close juxtaposition to St. Christopher, which was British, St. Bartholomew, which was French, St. Croix, which was Danish, and Spanish Porto Rico, and enjoying the privileges of a free port, it was a natural depot of exchange. Through St. Eustatius, Amsterdam took the place of London as the market for American tobacco and indigo; she exported to London instead of receiving from her. Through St. Eustatius, also, cloth and iron and war material from Europe, and even from England herself, reached the colonies. In thirteen months of the years 1778–79, 3182 vessels sailed from the island, and through its ports was carried on most of the American correspondence with Europe.[1]

St. Eustatius

England was naturally exasperated at this situation, which was enriching her most important rival in merchant tonnage and at the same time rendering her task in America the more difficult. Particularly irritating was the fact that the

[1] Jameson, "Saint Eustatius," *Amer. Hist. Review*, 1903, viii. 683–708; also Hansard, *Parliamentary Debates*, xxii. 218–262, May 14, 1781 (discussion by Burke).

treaties made in the time of William III when the relative position of the two powers was quite different, gave the England and Dutch ships special advantages by allowing the Dutch the principle of free ships, free goods, and by confining contraband within narrow bounds. In terms Holland and England were practically allies, but the Dutch refused to carry out the agreement by lending England troops, which the latter had the treaty right to require. The Dutch government did indeed send out instructions calling for the strict enforcement of neutrality on the part of its colonial officers; yet one governor of St. Eustatius ordered a salute to an American vessel, and of his successor the American agent, Van Bibber, wrote in 1776, "We are as well fixed with him now as we were with the former." During 1777 the British naval vessels off St. Eustatius were ordered to search for contraband all vessels entering and leaving the island, and to send those found with it to an admiralty court for adjudication. In 1779, a further cause for complaint was given by the refuge afforded to John Paul Jones in the *Texel* after his raid in English waters. In 1780, therefore, England, after due notice, announced the suspension of the Dutch treaties and began to seize and confiscate Dutch vessels carrying American goods or any kind of war material.

Meantime the Netherlands drifted, anxious to secure the last dollar from the neutral trade, and unable to determine Dutch parties which side to take up when neutrality ceased to be possible. The stadholder was pro-English, but was without energy or power. Of the people, a very strong party, sedulously encouraged by the skilful diplomacy of Vergennes, had for many years been coming to favor France; and this faction was now supported by an emotional body of "patriots" who felt a sentimental sympathy with American republicanism. In 1778, during this deadlock, the city of Amsterdam, on the responsibility of its burgomaster, Van Berkel, had the draft of a treaty with the United States drawn up by a M. de Neufville, who secretly at Frankfort met William Lee, who acted on his own responsibility. This draft, utterly without standing in diplomacy, was sent to repose in the archives of Amsterdam and the United States; but it did not sleep.[1]

While affairs were in this state, Catharine of Russia suddenly entered the lists. England had at first counted upon Russian support, and had sent her ablest dip- Catharine of
lomat, Sir James Harris, afterwards earl of Russia
Malmesbury, to cajole the capricious empress. When, however, George III in an autograph note asked for Russian mercenaries, Catharine, who posed as a ruler of advanced ideas, replied that she was not in that business. Moreover, since France was also ably represented at the court, Harris was not able to efface the ill effect created by the English treatment of the vessels of the northern neutral powers, Denmark, Sweden, and Russia, a subject especially aggravating to Catharine because among her many aspirations was that of making Russia a great mercantile power. This difficulty, however, arose chiefly after the entrance of France and Spain into the war, as ships of these northern countries seldom reached America.

Under these circumstances Catharine resolved upon a dramatic stroke which should at once enhance both her power and her prestige as a leader of liberal thought. The Armed
On March 10, 1780, she announced to the world Neutrality
the following principles of international law: that neutral vessels may engage in the coast trade of a belligerent country so long as the ports are unblockaded; that enemies' goods in neutral vessels are free from seizure; that contraband is limited to goods directly used in war; and that a blockade must be maintained off the port blockaded. To enforce the observance of these views by the belligerent powers she prepared a strong fleet, and united with Denmark and Sweden in what is known as the Armed Neutrality.[2]

[1] H. W. van Loon, *The Fall of the Dutch Republic*, London, 1913.
[2] Francis Wharton, *Digest of the International Law of the United States* (3

France and Spain joyfully accepted this declaration which would open their ports to neutral vessels, and Frederick the Great approved. England, though protesting, could observe the rules with little hurt so far as the signatory powers were concerned; but, should the Dutch come under them, trade with the United States would become a pastime for the trafficker, and the policy of attrition which she had been attempting since 1779 would be nothing but a dead letter. War with Holland without offence to the northern powers was the necessity of English diplomacy, and, while the slow wheels of Dutch governmental machinery were rolling toward incorporation in the alliance, luck threw in England's hands an instrument which secured her first diplomatic victory since hostilities began.

In 1779 Henry Laurens had been elected minister to the Netherlands. With his papers he naturally carried the draft **War between England and Holland** of the treaty which William Lee had made. Captured on the ocean, he threw his papers overboard, but they were rescued by the British, the draft among them. This was sent to Holland, November 11, 1780, with a demand for an explanation. The Dutch were not able to satisfy the British minister, York, who was accordingly withdrawn on December 16. On the 19th, Holland acceded to the alliance, but it was too late. St. Eustatius received the first news of war from the British admiral, Rodney, who demanded its surrender; and the Dutch, in ceasing to be neutrals, ceased forever to carry American trade.

The task of establishing relations between the United States and England's new enemy fell to John Adams. A substantial **John Adams** lawyer of forty-five, he had been in France for a brief period in 1778 as co-commissioner, and had now returned as commissioner to secure the peace with England which as yet was only a hope. On April 6, 1781,

vols., Washington, 1886), iii. 262–264; Paul Fauchille, *La diplomatie française et la ligue des neutres de 1780*, Paris, 1893.

he received a further commission to treat with Holland. Of Puritan breeding and ideas, he was American to the backbone. With a fund of solid information and a penetration and sound judgment which marked him out among his contemporaries, he was also conceited, obstinate, and disagreeable. His disapproval of the frivolities of Philadelphia when he attended Congress there foreshadowed his opinion of Paris, and indeed of Franklin. Referring to the latter, he wrote, "Congress will not be put to any expense for my family, for my coaches and retinues of servants." July 13, 1780, he wrote to Vergennes, "The United States are a great and powerful people, whatever European statesmen may think." On August 9, 1780, Franklin wrote to the president of Congress, "M. de Vergennes, who appears much offended, told me yesterday that he would enter into no further discussions with Mr. Adams."

Happy in the thought that an understanding with Holland might render the United States "less dependent on France," Adams was also happy in the quieter atmos- **Treaty with** phere of the Dutch capital and the substantial **Holland** methods of her statesmen, who on their part appreciated his qualities. On October 8, 1782, therefore, an admirable treaty of amity and commerce was signed, and an American loan was floated on the Dutch market. In his diary he records the remark made to him, "Sir, you have struck the greatest blow in the American cause, and the most decisive." [1]

[1] John Adams, *Works* (ed. C. F. Adams, 10 vols., Boston, 1850–56), iii. 94–304.

CHAPTER V

PEACE

DURING the spring of 1779 Congress devoted much of its time to a consideration of the terms upon which it would American de- consent to make peace. It decided that the sires recognition of independence must precede negotiation and not form part of the treaty. On the subject of boundaries it determined to make the cession of the unorganized Indian country between the Floridas, the mountains, the Ohio, and the Mississippi an ultimatum. To the north it wanted the 1763 boundary of Quebec, that is, Lake Nipissing to the point where the forty-fifth parallel crosses the St. Lawrence, then along that parallel to the highlands, and then along the highlands, giving us the country from Lake Nipissing westward to the source of the Mississippi; but the whole portion of the line west of the St. Lawrence it was willing to leave subject to negotiation. To the northeast, the line was to descend from the highlands along the river St. John, but some more western river might be chosen if thereby the war could be shortened. Congress expressed its readiness to take Nova Scotia and the Bermudas, and made other interesting suggestions which were, however, not to be insisted upon.[1]

In the discussions two points of dispute arose. New England could not conceive of happiness without the Newfound-Fisheries and land fisheries. Her representatives demanded the Mississippi the right to fish on the "Banks," and in addition the privilege of landing on unoccupied coasts to dry fish and for other purposes. The southern states, on the con-

[1] *Secret Journals of Congress*, ii. 132–261; *Diplomatic Correspondence of the United States, from 1783 to 1789*, 3 vols., Washington, 1837.

trary, were unwilling to prolong the war for such ends, but
demanded on their part that the free navigation of the
Mississippi be an ultimatum, a grant for which the New
Englanders were not prepared to fight. When Congress
voted to include in the ultimatum merely the common right
of fishing on the "Banks" without the in-shore privileges,
Samuel Adams was heard to say that one saw more and more
that the separation of the East and the South was inevitable.[1]

The French minister, Gerard, not unnaturally urged that
the fixed points in the instructions be as few as possible, and
the final draft, August 14, 1779, left out both   Final instruc-
fisheries and Mississippi. Two years more of   tions
war, with the disasters in the South, still further broke the
spirit of Congress, and June 15, 1781, the commissioners
were informed that, although the desires of Congress remained the same they were not to be insisted upon. "We
think it unsafe at this distance," ran the instructions, "to
tie you up by absolute and peremptory directions upon any
other subject than the two essential articles [independence
and the observance of the French treaties]. . . . You are
therefore at liberty to secure the interest of the United States
in such manner as circumstances may direct, and as the state
of the belligerent and disposition of the mediating powers
[Russia and Austria were offering their mediation] may
require. For this purpose, you are to make the most candid
and confidential communications, upon all subjects, to the
ministers of our generous ally the king of France; to undertake nothing in the negotiations for peace or truce, without
their knowledge and concurrence; and ultimately to govern
yourself by their advice and opinion." [2]   John Adams was in
1779 appointed to carry out the negotiations, and in 1781 four
other commissioners were added,—Franklin, Jay, Laurens,
and Thomas Jefferson. Of these Jefferson did not cross the

[1] Doniol, *La participation de la France*, iv. 105–107.
[2] *Secret Journals of Congress*, ii. 424–439.

ocean, and Laurens was in the Tower of London until just before the signing of the preliminary articles.

From the beginning of the war till the end of 1778 Great Britain was continually and increasingly anxious to negotiate **Great Britain opens negotiations** with the colonies on some basis less than that of independence.[1] These attempts were a constant source of anxiety to France, and were in fact given by Louis XVI to Charles III as his excuse for recognizing our independence without waiting for action by Spain. The attempt of 1778 was earnestly undertaken but was unsuccessful, and after that date such negotiations were not seriously renewed. The surrender of Cornwallis at Yorktown, October 14, 1781, brought England to the point of acknowledging independence. On March 20, 1782, Lord North resigned, and was succeeded by the marquis of Rockingham, whose program was peace. The new ministry, however, was divided as to method. Lord Shelburne, secretary of state for the colonies, held that the Americans were still colonists, that independence should be granted as a valuable concession, and that the negotiations should be conducted by his department. Charles James Fox, secretary of foreign affairs, the friend of the colonists and the avowed enemy of Shelburne, wished to recognize independence at once, to make the terms so generous as to reconcile America to England and alienate her from France, and desired to conduct the negotiation himself. In this deadlock, in the spring of 1782, Thomas Grenville appeared in France from the English foreign office being known as Mr. Fox's minister, and Richard Oswald from the colonial office being known as Lord Shelburne's minister.[2]

[1] For negotiations in the field, see Washington's *Works* (ed. W. C. Ford, 14 vols., New York, etc., 1889–93), iii. 77, 79, 90, 248, 282. For peace negotiations with Howe, see *ibid.*, iv. 249, 263, 309; Wharton's *Diplomatic Correspondence*, ii. 98, 103; Franklin's *Works* (ed. Bigelow), vi. 28; *Secret Journals of Congress*. For negotiations of 1778, see *Secret Journals*, vol. ii. 13; Franklin's *Works*, vi. 124–238.

[2] Winsor, *America*, vii. 89–184; Lord Fitzmaurice, *Life of William Earl of Shelburne* (2d ed., 2 vols., London, 1912), ii. 111–223.

The central figure in the diplomatic situation was the
Count de Vergennes. The pivot of European affairs from
1776 to 1783, leader of France in her only suc-   The objects of
cessful war with England during the long   Vergennes
struggle between 1688 and 1815, master of a distinctly noble
style of correspondence, active, and successful in the choice of
agents, he has failed to impress history as has Necker, who
was less able, or Turgot, who was less powerful. Possibly
his failure in half of his main conception has blurred his impress on our memory: in separating the American colonies
from England he succeeded, in binding them to France he
failed. To accomplish the latter purpose he counted on a
gratitude that was not forthcoming, on a trade that did not
develop, on a dependent weakness that was avoided.[1]

Certainly his position in 1782 must command our sympathy. The ally of Spain and of the United States, who were
not on terms with each other and who had dif-   Vergennes's
ferent and conflicting purposes, he felt also   program
responsibility for the Netherlands, whom he had incited
to enter the war. On the side of the United States he was
bound to conclude no treaty without her consent, to obtain
independence "formally or tacitly," and also to secure her
possessions and conquests; moreover, the United States
would not be content with the territory actually occupied
nor without further stipulations, such as those concerning
the Mississippi and the fisheries. On the side of Spain he
was bound to conclude a simultaneous treaty, and Spain
would not be satisfied without Gibraltar, which the allies
had been for years besieging, and the Floridas. His policy
was to compel England to offer terms. To Oswald he wrote:
"There are four nations engaged in the war against you, who
cannot, till they have consulted and know each other's minds,
be ready to make propositions. Your court being without
allies and alone, knowing its own mind, can express it immediately; it is, therefore, more natural to expect the first

[1] For Franklin's opinion of Vergennes, see his *Works*, viii. 305–307.

proposition from you." To Franklin he wrote, May 28: "You will treat for yourselves and every one of the powers at war with England will make its own treaty. All that is necessary for our common security is that the treaties go hand in hand, and be signed all on the same day." As to the necessity of standing together Franklin agreed with him. He wrote Congress, "The firm united resolution of France, Spain and Holland, joined with ours, not to treat of a particular, but a general peace, notwithstanding the separate tempting offers to each, will in the end give us command of peace." The first commission to Grenville having been to France alone, Vergennes refused to treat with him; whereupon, June 15, Grenville was invested with additional power to treat with any other prince of state that might be concerned. This seemed sufficient to Vergennes, and the final negotiations appeared about to begin.[1]

Kaleidoscopically the situation changed. On June 23 Jay arrived from Spain, and at about the same time Franklin

Jay's suspicions

became to a considerable degree incapacitated by an attack of gout. Jay's suspicions of France, already aroused, were rapidly augmented. He insisted that Grenville's new commission was still unsatisfactory, that it must acknowledge the independence of the United States, but Vergennes argued that this was not necessary. Early in September the same Rayneval who was defending the views of Spain in the negotiation between Jay and d'Aranda was despatched on a secret mission to England. Actually sent over to test the English views about Gibraltar, he refused to discuss the affairs of the United States;[2] but Jay not unnaturally suspected that he was sent to bargain for a peace on the terms of dividing the West between England and Spain. At about the same time Jay received from British sources the translation of a *mémoire*

---

[1] For the opening negotiations, see particularly Franklin's *Works*, viii. 1–119.

[2] Doniol, *La participation de la France*, v. 132–133, 255–256, 603–626.

of Barbé Marbois, French secretary of legation at Philadelphia, which, like the Dutch treaty, had been rescued from the waves into which it had been thrown from a captured ship, and which presented an argument against the American claim to share in the Newfoundland fisheries. Jay concluded that France was planning to buy a peace from England favorable to Spain and at the expense of the United States. He believed that his country must depend upon itself alone, and that, in the illness and pro-French weakness of Franklin, the responsibility rested on him. Accordingly, on September 11, without consulting Franklin, he sent Vaughan, one of the English agents in Paris, on a secret mission to the English government. The coöperation between France and the United States was no longer complete.[1]

In England, also, the situation had changed. The death of the Marquis of Rockingham in June left no Whig leader who could manage Fox and Shelburne together. Fox retired, and the control of the ministry fell to Shelburne on July 2. Grenville was recalled from France and Alleyne Fitzherbert was sent in his place. A master of finesse, Shelburne, who had been seeking an opportunity to separate England's enemies, welcomed the news brought by Vaughan, and accepted the suggestion of Jay. Independence was recognized in a new commission to Oswald, and instructions were given as to terms which seemed to insure success. The negotiation was to be secret from France. Shelburne told Oswald, September 23, "We have put the greatest confidence, I believe, ever placed in man in the American commissioners. It is now to be seen how far they or America are to be depended upon. . . . I hope the public will be the gainer, else our heads must answer for it, and deservedly."

On September 27 Vaughan returned to Paris, and the American commissioners had to decide whether to accept the offer. To do so involved the breaking of their instructions

Shelburne treats with Jay

---

[1] Jay, *Papers*, ii. 366–452.

from Congress, which authorized them to treat only with the full knowledge of the French ministers and to govern themselves by their advice. The very form of these instructions seemed to Jay to confirm his suspicions of a malign and pervasive French influence in Congress itself, and he hesitated not a moment. On October 26 John Adams arrived from his successful mission in Holland, and proved to be, as Jay wrote, "a very able and agreeable coadjutor." He sided with Jay, and together they outvoted Franklin. The negotiations therefore began, their progress being kept secret from Vergennes.[1]

Americans negotiate separately from France

In the conduct of the negotiations the American had the advantage over the British representatives both in ability and in local knowledge. They might have obtained even better terms than they did, had not the British government from time to time braced the backbone of its commissioners. The boundaries agreed upon were almost identical with those described by Congress. On the northeast the St. Croix was substituted for the St. John, a change that somewhat curtailed the limits of Massachusetts. West of the St. Lawrence it was agreed to compromise between the 1763 and 1774 boundaries of Quebec. The American commissioners offered to accept either the extension of the forty-fifth parallel to the Mississippi, or a line through lakes Ontario, Erie, Huron, Superior, and the Lake of the Woods, to the northwestern point of the latter, and thence due westward to the Mississippi. Fortunately the British chose the latter, a selection which ultimately proved even more advantageous to the United States than the line from Lake Nipissing would have been. The western boundary was the Mississippi, the southern was the northern boundaries of the Floridas, that of West Florida being considered as the thirty-first parallel. By a secret article, however, it was agreed that, should Great Britain retain West Florida, the northern

Boundaries

[1] John Adams, *Works*, iii. 300–387.

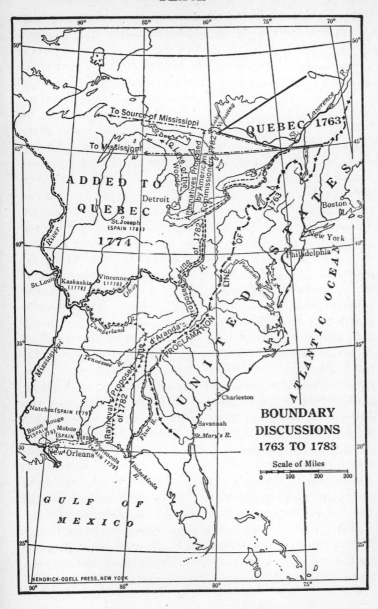

BOUNDARY
DISCUSSIONS
1763 TO 1783

Scale of Miles

0   100   200   300

KENDRICK-ODELL PRESS, NEW YORK

boundary of that province should run eastward from the mouth of the Yazoo, or in other words along the parallel of 32' 28''.

The question of the fisheries fell to the lot of John Adams, who had special instructions on that subject from the legislature of Massachusetts. Master of the facts, he
Fisheries,
debts, and succeeded in incorporating into the treaty a
loyalists recognition of American rights to fish on the
"Banks," and sufficient in-shore privileges to make fishing profitable. The navigation of the Mississippi was also obtained. The American commissioners readily agreed to an article that creditors on either side should "meet with no lawful impediment to the recovery of the full value in sterling money of all bona fide debts heretofore contracted," a provision which had special reference to debts due by Americans to British merchants when hostilities began. The most troublesome question was that concerning the loyalists, whose property had been confiscated and who had been subjected to various persecutions. Naturally, the British government felt a proper regard for their interests; but, since the laws against them had been made by the states, Congress could not promise restitution. A compromise was finally reached by the agreement that Congress would "earnestly recommend" restitution and the repeal of all laws not in harmony with "that spirit of conciliation which, on the return of the blessings of peace, should universally prevail." With a provision for the mutual restoration of property the preliminary articles were concluded and signed, November 30, 1782.

Triumphant in their negotiations with England, the commissioners had now to face France. Although they had
Effect of the broken their instructions from Congress, they
treaty on had not violated the letter of the French com-
France pact, for they had not signed a definitive
treaty. In spirit and in effect, however, they had done so. When the news of the articles reached London, the British

cabinet was on the point of exchanging Gibraltar for Guadaloupe, a transfer ardently desired by Spain, and by France
in behalf of Spain.[1] From this proposal it immediately
withdrew and gave orders for an amnesty with the United
States in order that the British troops there might be employed in the West Indies.

Upon Franklin, who disagreed with his colleagues as to the
sinister designs of the French, and who believed that by
coöperation with Vergennes he could have **Franklin and**
obtained terms equally good, fell the burden **Vergennes**
of reconciliation. When the question of forwarding the
articles to America came up, the commissioners again acted
with secrecy, hastening to send the good news although
Vergennes wished delay. The latter wrote to Franklin in
terms of surprise and of dignified reproach. The letter of
Franklin in reply, December 17, was a masterpiece of diplomatic art, even to the adoption of a certain touch of pathos
in its slightly rambling quality, natural to his age but not
characteristic of his writing even later. "But," he explained,
"as this was not from want of respect for the king, whom we
all love and honor, we hope it will be excused, and that the
great work, which has hitherto been so happily conducted,
is so nearly brought to perfection, and is so glorious to his
reign, will not be ruined by a single indiscretion of ours. And
certainly the whole edifice sinks to the ground immediately
if you refuse on that account to give us any further assistance." He lays down his pen, but taking it up again, adds:
"The English, I just now learn, flatter themselves they
have already divided us. I hope this little misunderstanding
will therefore be kept a secret, and that they will find themselves totally mistaken." [2]

It was indeed true that if Vergennes stood in the way of
this generous treaty, his whole work would turn to ashes in
his hands: England and America would again unite against

---

[1] Fitzmaurice, *Shelburne,* ii. 214.
[2] Franklin, *Works,* viii. 228–230.

France. Accordingly, on December 21 he wrote to his representative in Philadelphia, Luzanne, not to complain **Vergennes's conclusions** to Congress of the action of the American commissioners, and he arranged a new loan of six million francs to the United States.

Meantime the French and Spanish treaties gradually progressed, till on September 3, 1783, definitive treaties of **The end of the war** peace were signed between Great Britain and France, Spain and the United States. The latter was identical with the provisional articles, except for the secret article, which was left out as no longer necessary, since the status of the Floridas was determined by their cession to Spain. France gained Tobago. The Netherlands, after a long negotiation, made their peace in 1784, accepting the loss of their mercantile privileges and of several colonies.

The peace meant that our national existence, announced to the world by the Declaration of Independence July 4, **What had been accomplished** 1776, had been established. Further, the treaty gave us a territory, not indeed logical and satisfactory, but ample for present needs. We had not won our independence and our field for growth by the force of arms alone, but by our success in manipulating the divisions of Europe to our advantage, a success largely due to our diplomats. Elate though they were, their task was by no means finished; for the boundaries of our territories were nearly all vague or questionable, and we were still a weak nation among the strong. Until we could develop our own strength it would continue to be necessary to take wise advantage of the divisions of Europe in order to insure our safety and our winnings.

CHAPTER VI

RELIGION AND COMMERCE

INDEPENDENT and at peace, the United States faced the diplomatic problems of national existence. One of these, which still continues to vex some nations, was at once and definitively settled. The connection of a portion of their subjects with a non-resident religious authority had always been a matter of national concern. Expecting that such would be the policy of the new government, and that it would wish to free its Catholic citizens from English control, the papal nuncio at Paris addressed Franklin, July 28, 1783, with the proposal that Congress consent to the establishment in some city of the United States of "one of its Catholic subjects" with ecclesiastical authority as bishop or apostolic prefect. Franklin properly informed the nuncio that neither Congress nor any state could take action on such a matter, but that a dignitary thus appointed by Rome would nevertheless be cordially welcomed, a position in which he was upheld by Congress. Less wisely he recommended that Roman control be exercised through the medium of some French ecclesiastic, who would thus replace the vicar-general at London. This latter plan was heartily embraced by the French government, which hoped by French education and connection to render the Catholic element a weapon of French influence, and possibly had in mind the prestige accruing to France from the French protectorate of Catholics in the Orient. The Roman Propaganda investigated the question, however, and, after testing the sentiment of the American Catholics, decided to appoint an American bishop, John

The United States and the Papacy

Carroll, and thus deal with its members without the mediation of any foreign nation.[1]

These two wise decisions were paralleled in what was perhaps the more trying case of the American adherents of the Church of England. They at once assumed the position that national independence should be reflected in a national church organization; but to secure a continuation of the apostolic succession it was necessary to have recourse to the mother country, since there were no bishops in America. In order to obtain consecration, moreover, a bishop must swear allegiance to the English crown, and the colonial opposition to the appointment of a bishop before the Revolution caused England to doubt the reception of one now. Samuel Seabury, the first applicant, was forced to accept his consecration from a small independent branch of the church in Scotland. The attitude of Congress, however, and a declaration to the same effect by Connecticut soon removed apprehension as to American opposition; and John Adams while minister in England exerted himself unofficially, as Franklin had done in Paris, to make matters smooth. The result was the consecration, in 1787, and by English bishops, of two additional American bishops without the hampering oath.[2]

With religion thus freed from foreign governmental control and not interfered with by the home government, religious questions were practically removed from diplomacy until, with the beginning of the missionary movement, they reappeared in the form of demands for the protection of American religious workers and property in foreign countries.

Meanwhile popular interest in diplomacy was chiefly directed toward commercial affairs. One reason why the

[1] C. R. Fish, "Documents relative to the Adjustment of the Roman Catholic Organization in the United States to the Conditions of National Independence, 1783–1789," *Amer. Hist. Review*, 1910, xv. 800–829.

[2] Richard Hildreth, *History of the United States of America* (6 vols., New York, 1880–82), iii. 479–481.

colonies had chafed against dependence on England was the fact that their trade had for the most part been curtailed by the limits of the British empire, and, worse still, had been regulated within those limits by an authority in which they did not share. One of the chief advantages of independence was to be the opening of new channels of trade. International trade, however, is as dependent upon legalized relationships as is domestic trade upon the preservation of law and order; and in the eighteenth century such legal basis must depend, even more than in the twentieth, upon special treaty agreements; for general international law was at that time less uniform and less pervasive than it is to-day, besides including many rules and regulations discriminating against foreigners which lingered on from the middle ages.

Commercial necessity for treaties

At the commencement of peace such treaties existed only with France and the Netherlands. It did not, however, seem difficult to extend the series, for every nation of Europe was intent on diverting to itself the golden current of American trade to which so much of England's prosperity was attributed.

European desire for treaties of commerce

No sooner was American independence assured than Franklin was besieged with requests to enter into negotiation. On December 24, 1782, he wrote to Livingston, "The Swedish ambassador has exchanged full powers with me." In February, 1783, the Danish minister was instructed to arrange a treaty similar to that between the United States and Holland. In July Franklin wrote that the electors of Saxony and Bavaria, the king of Prussia, and the emperor were thinking of treaties, and in September that Russia wanted trade. April 15 of the same year he wrote to Livingston that he had received offers to serve as consul for America from merchants in every port of France and from most of those of Europe.[1]

Not all these projects materialized into treaties; but in

[1] Franklin, *Works*, viii. 172–313.

1783 Franklin concluded one with Sweden, and in 1785 Adams, Franklin, and Jefferson made one with Prussia.

Character of our early treaties

These compacts, like those with France and Holland, were exceeding liberal in their provisions. They granted freedom of religion to the citizens of one country who were occupied in the other, and abolished the *droit d'aubaine*, or tax on the estates of deceased foreigners. With regard to trade during time of war, these treaties aligned the United States with the Dutch, or continental, views rather than with those of the English. The interests of most European nations were similar to those of the United States in opposition to those of Great Britain, they were the interests of nations weak at sea against the strong. In the end the continental views for the most part triumphed, but they can scarcely be regarded as accepted international law in the eighteenth century. They expressed desires rather than accomplished facts. Among the provisions bearing on the subject were those by which the belligerent right of search was strictly limited, contraband was narrowly interpreted, neutral ships were allowed to carry enemies' goods, and in the case of Prussia privateering was prohibited between the two powers. The French treaty, however, allowed the capture of neutral goods on enemies' ships. In 1788 Jefferson, then serving as minister to France, concluded an elaborate treaty with that country regulating the rights of consuls.

Meanwhile, not waiting for treaties, adventurous American merchants were striking out for trade beyond the limits

Trade in Asia and Africa

of Europe in the Far East, which had beckoned Columbus, and whose most cherished product, tea, had caused one of the dramatic preludes of the Revolution. Previously debarred from this trade by the monopoly granted to the East India Company, the colonists were nevertheless somewhat familiar with it, and had long used Asiatic commodities. Once free, they hastened to make use of their opportunities. In 1784 the first American vessel

reached Canton, in 1786 an American commercial agent
was in residence there, and soon American vessels were frequenting the northwest coast of America in search of the
furs and ginseng which the Chinese wished in exchange for
their tea and silk. Moreover, on the coming of peace, Americans had resumed their traffic on the slave coast of Africa,
where there were no governments with which they must
come to terms.[1]

In the Mediterranean, however, no progress was made.
This was not due to a neglect on the part of the Italian
powers to cultivate the United States. The   Mediterranean
papal nuncio, while writing of religion in be-   trade
half of the church, had also mentioned trade in behalf of
the states of the church; and Naples, Venice, and Malta
all made similar advances. Nor was it because the United
States was unfamiliar with trade conditions in that inland
sea; for as colonists the Puritan New Englanders had constantly supplied the Mediterranean countries with salted
cod for fast-day fare, and wheat and rice, and had smuggled
away ribbons, silks, Leghorn hats, and other commodities.
The difficulty lay in the fact that here was encountered one
of the disadvantages of separation from England. The
English navy no longer protected American ships from the
Barbary pirates.[2]

The North African states, Morocco, Algiers, Tunis, and
Tripoli, constituted an anachronism that was a blot upon the
civilization of Europe. Their official navies   The Barbary
consisted of pirate craft, which swept down   states
upon peaceful trading-vessels and sold, with ship and goods,
the sailors and passengers into captivity. So well recognized
was their activity that there existed an active "Society of the
Holy Trinity for the Redemption of Captives," whose work

---

[1] Katharine Coman, *The Industrial History of the United States* (New
York, 1910), 135–137; Hildreth, *United States*, iii. 510.

[2] Eugene Schuyler, *American Diplomacy* (New York, 1886), 193–208;
E. Dupuy, *Américains et Barbaresques*, Paris, 1910.

went on from century to century. At the time of the Revolution these pirates respected the flags of certain countries, as England, France, and Spain, in return for heavy payments. That these nations, whose fleets could have cleared the sea as Pompey's did in 67 B. C., failed to do so, was for reasons similar to those which cause the police of some large cities to tolerate "gunmen" and vice. Franklin wrote, July 22, 1783, that it was a maxim among English merchants that, "if there were no Algiers, it would be worth England's while to build one." By preventing the smaller nations from competing in trade, the pirates increased the employment of the protected merchant marines.

In July, 1785, an American schooner, *Maria*, and the ship *Dauphin* were captured, and American trade in the Mediterranean ceased. The United States had hoped to substitute the French navy as protector in place of the English, but France would promise nothing except assistance in making a treaty. In May, 1784, Adams, Franklin, and Jefferson were empowered to negotiate with them; but negotiation was expensive and the agents themselves were not agreed as to method. Adams favored the European practice of buying peace, whereas Jefferson was opposed to such a policy, and broached the impractical scheme of forming a general confederation to put the pirates down. In July, 1787, Thomas Barclay, being specially delegated by Adams and Jefferson, had the astonishing good luck to conclude a treaty with Morocco without tribute. Success, however, failed to attend the negotiations with the other powers, and at the close of the Confederation trade in the Mediterranean was still closed to American vessels and a number of Americans still remained as slaves in Algerian households.

Spain and Portugal, however, were accessible. To these countries had always gone the best of the colonial fish, and when fishing was resumed after the war it was again sent there for sale. Meal, lumber products, rice, and some other goods also sought these markets. With independence it was hoped that this trade might be made more profitable by the securing of return cargoes, which had for the most part previously been prohibited by the English navigation acts. Both countries

Trade with Spain and Portugal

permitted trade, but American merchants and sea-captains found themselves under disadvantages due to the absence of the treaty protection which they had enjoyed as English subjects. Rates and regulations were now arbitrarily changed, and religious difficulties kept arising. It was hoped to settle these discords by negotiation, and also to induce Spain to open up, in some degree, a direct trade with her colonies, for much of what Americans sold in Spain was reëxported to the Spanish settlements.

In 1784 Jay succeeded Livingston as secretary of foreign affairs, and Spain sent over Gardoqui to continue the negotiations which had been begun in 1779. They found agreement on commercial matters easy; but the old difficulty of the Mississippi persisted, and Spain's ambitions with regard to

Failure of negotiations with Spain and Portugal

the West assumed a new phase, so that no treaty was consummated. As none was made with Portugal either, the Confederation government thus failed to satisfy the demand of the commercial community that trade with these two nations be put upon a solid basis.

However great might be the future development of the new channels of trade opened up by independence, the greatest present change felt by the people of the United States was that concerning their relations with the British empire. Heretofore they

Trade with the British empire

had been free of the empire, but debarred from the rest of the world; now they had the world before them, but were strangers within the empire. Unless diplomacy could secure them some of their old advantages, the new might not suffice to make good their losses. Trade with Great Britain itself was still allowed, and afforded a market for tobacco, tar and turpentine, and some other products; but our exports to that country had never paid for our imports, and did not bid fair to do so in the future. The balance had been paid by the excess in our favor resulting from the trade with the British West India islands.[1]

This trade had been the most important of all branches of colonial commerce. Those islands were devoted to raising British West staple products, such as sugar, and they relied Indies in large measure on the continental colonies for food, including wheat, cheese, and salt pork; for lumber, including barrel staves and framed houses ready to set up; for horses, and for many of their slaves; and particularly they bought for their slaves the poorer qualities of cod and mackerel which, indiscriminately with the good, were caught by the fisherman but which could not be sold in Europe. This trade had not only afforded a market for our farms and industries, but had also given employment to our ships, and thereby fostered ship-building and all the gamut of subsidiary occupations. It had been the corner stone of American commerce, and its preservation was a primary object of American diplomacy.

As soon as the preliminary articles of peace were signed in November, 1782, work upon a treaty of commerce was Shelburne's begun. The Duke of Manchester and David plans and de- Hartly were commissioned by the English feat government for "opening, promoting, and rendering perpetual the mutual intercourse of trade and commerce between our kingdom and the dominions of the United States." Lord Shelburne was deeply influenced by the views of Adam Smith. He was inclined to continue the policy which he had adopted in response to Jay's offer, and by liberal arrangements with America to prevent the per-

[1] Edward Channing, *History of the United States* (vols. i.–iii. New York, 1905–12), iii. 412–424; Phineas Bond, *Letters*, Amer. Hist. Assoc., *Report*, 1896, i. 513–659; Stephen Higginson, *Letters, ibid.*, 711–841; Marquis of Buckingham, *Letters to Sir John Temple*, Mass. Hist. Soc., *Proceedings*, 1866, pp. 69–80.

manent alignment of the United States with France. His power, however, was limited. To some degree, it may be said, his ministry was tolerated by Parliament for the sole purpose of performing the disagreeable task of sanctioning the partition of the empire. On February 24, 1783, he was forced to resign, and was succeeded by an incongruous combination headed jointly by the inveterate contestants, Fox and North. Vaughan wrote to Franklin the next day, "But the overthrow of parties is nothing to the overthrow of systems relative to English commerce, which was intended to be placed on a footing that would have been an example to all mankind, and probably have restored England to her pinnacle again." [1]

The new government was to a considerable extent influenced by Lord Sheffield, whose "Observations on the Commerce of the United States," published in 1783, set forth the long-established view of England's policy with regard to trade and navigation. On July 2, 1783, a royal proclamation confined the West Indian trade to British ships; July 27, the commissioners found "it best to drop all commercial articles in our definitive treaty." The subject, however, was one which the United States could not afford to drop, and John Adams was sent as minister to England to renew negotiations. Arriving in February, 1785, as first representative from America to the British crown, himself a leading figure in the struggle for independence, he was in a position of some delicacy, but nevertheless he found his new post eminently congenial. The ponderous seriousness of English public life sufficiently resembled respectability to win his lively approbation. On examining the library of George III., he felt that it contained every book which a king should have and no other. His sturdy Americanism, however, asserted itself. When the king somewhat jocularly remarked upon Adams's well known dislike of the French, the latter replied, "I must avow to your ma-

[1] Franklin, *Works*, viii. 261.

jesty, I have no attachment but to my own country." The king responded, "quick as lightning," "An honest man will never have any other." [1]

In spite of this auspicious opening Adams's mission failed of its main object. In fact, in 1788 an act of Parliament

Adams's mission

made permanent the policy of the proclamation of 1783, and this in spite of the succession to the premiership of William Pitt, who in 1783 had shared Lord Shelburne's liberal convictions. Not only were American ships prohibited from engaging in the West Indian trade, but the policy of encouraging Canada to supply the islands with the goods they needed was adopted, with the result that British ships were allowed to carry United States goods to the islands only at such times and to such a degree as was absolutely necessary.

One reason for this policy was explained in the following words by the Duke of Dorset, with whom Adams was treat-

Great Britain distrusts the Confederation

ing: "The apparent determination of the respective states to regulate their own separate interests, renders it absolutely necessary, towards forming a permanent system of commerce, that my court should be informed how far the commissioners can be duly authorized to enter into any engagement with Great Britain, which it may not be in the power of any one of the states to render totally useless and inefficient." This point was well taken to the extent that the sole power over commerce given to Congress by the Articles of Confederation was that of preventing the states from levying discriminating duties against nations with which the country was in treaty relations. Moreover, England had practical demonstration of the inefficiency of Congress in the fact that, in spite of the treaty of peace, various states still put obstacles in the way of the collection of British debts and refused to heed the recommendation of Congress for a greater leniency toward loyalists. This impotence of Congress not only

[1] J. Q. and C. F. Adams, *John Adams*, vol. ii.

caused the British government to doubt the efficacy of a treaty on commercial subjects with the United States, but relieved it from any apprehension of effective retaliation. Congress could not pass retaliatory laws; and although some of the states, as Virginia and Georgia, did so, the English statesmen correctly judged that any universal agreement to such an end was not within the realm of practical politics.[1]

Still more conclusive to the English mind was the fact that Great Britain, without a treaty, was nevertheless enjoying the most essential advantages of American trade. The Americans were familiar with English goods, liked them, and found them on the whole the cheapest in the world. The British merchants more easily resumed American connections than other nations established them; and particularly they were willing to grant the long credits which the Americans desired. London, moreover, was actually the most convenient distributing centre of the world, and its merchants continued to handle many articles, such as German linens, which the Americans desired from the continent. In 1789 probably three quarters of our imports came from Great Britain, who in turn received perhaps half of our exports. France, although coaxing our trade by liberal concessions to our whale oil, fish, grains, and such products in 1787, and seeking earnestly to develop in the United States a taste for French brandy, secured but a small and not increasing portion of the American traffic. Naturally, therefore, England saw no necessity for granting favors, when without them she continued to enjoy that market for her factories and employment for her vessels of which Vergennes had thought to deprive her.

Thus the government under the Confederation was not able to reopen the British West Indies to trade. Although the trade of the French islands was open to small Amer-

Great Britain holds American trade

---

[1] *Secret Journals of Congress*, iv. 185–286; W. C. Fisher, *American Trade Regulations before 1789*, Amer. Hist. Assoc., *Papers*, 1889, iii. 467–493.

ican vessels trading directly there and back, yet it was subject to such disadvantages that it by no means took the Failures of the place of what we had lost. In fact this was not Confederation entirely a gain after all, for the colonies had to some degree engaged in it before the Revolution, albeit illegally. With the loss of the Mediterranean traffic and the uncertainties in Spain and Portugal, the total effect of the Revolution on commerce could in 1789 hardly be said to have been satisfactory, and the failure of negotiations was rightly felt to have been due in large measure to the lack of a strong national government capable of making itself respected abroad.

CHAPTER VII

THE WEST

THE failure of the negotiations with Great Britain and Spain on the question of commerce was not by any means due entirely to the intrinsic difficulties of the subject. Both nations were our neighbors, and the problems of territorial propinquity were in both cases more complicated and disturbing than those of oceanic traffic. The cession to the United States of the region bounded by the Appalachian mountains, the Great Lakes, the Mississippi, and the Floridas was not regarded by European statesmen as finally determining the future. As it stood, moreover, this area did not constitute a satisfactory territorial unit; for, as conditions of transportation then were, its commercial outlets fell to the control, not of the United States, but, as to the southern half, to Spain, who held the mouth of the Mississippi, and as to the northern half to Great Britain, who held the St. Lawrence. Its population was during the period of the Confederation about equally divided between Indians, who held themselves to be independent, and frontiersmen, whose loyalty to the central government of the United States was yet to be created and would depend upon the ability of that government to solve their problems. Thus, as Washington said, the western settlers "stood upon a pivot, the touch of a feather would turn them any way."

At the close of hostilities Great Britain still held important posts in the ceded area, at such strategic positions as Detroit, Michilimackinac, Niagara, and Oswego. In July, 1783, Washington sent Baron Steuben to General Haldiman, the governor-general of Canada, to accept the surrender of these forts. The latter said that he had received no instructions on the point and refused to discuss the question. In June, 1784, instructions did indeed reach him, but they were to the effect that the posts should be held, a position that was later justified by the British minister, Hammond, on the ground that the United States had failed to live up to the terms of the treaty as to the payment of British debts and the treatment of the loyalists. The balance of evidence would seem to indicate that the refusal to give up the posts preceded any definite information as to the disregard by the states of the injunctions of the treaty and the requests of Congress. If this excuse had not been afforded, however, it is possible that the British might later have yielded the point; in fact, the British foreign office carefully framed its own dispatches on this view of the matter. But the first refusal was based on other grounds.[1]

One of these was the complaint of the British fur-traders, who protested as soon as the terms of the provisional articles were announced. Their trade made London the most important fur-market of the world; the carrying out of the treaty, they claimed, would practically destroy their occupation; for half their furs came from the forests and streams allotted to the Americans, and the best trails, portages, and river channels were on the American side of the boundary.

The fur-trade

More important than the fur-traders were the Indians, who, though in many tribes, comprised only two main groups. One of these was the Iroquois, who had so long maintained themselves in the fair valleys of central New York, exercising by their valor and their shrewdness in diplomacy a potent influence on the struggles between the French, Dutch, English, and Americans. Although the real power of the Iroquois confederacy had been broken by the expedition of the American army under General Sullivan in 1779, they still retained the title to their lands and a great

The Iroquois

[1] A. C. McLaughlin, "The Western Posts and the British Debts," Amer. Hist. Assoc., *Report*, 1894, pp. 413–444.

name. During the period of the Confederation they divided
into two groups, one of which made friends with the Americans and retained their homes, while the other and larger
band preferred their traditional friendship with the British
and removed to a grant given to them by the British
government west of the Niagara river. The leader of this
portion was the famous Joseph Brant, a man of ability
and distinction who stood high in the councils of the
English.[1]

The other main group, consisting of the Delaware, Wyandot, Shawanee, Miami, and other tribes, and comprising
about five thousand warriors, was known col- The North-
lectively, although there was but slight co- western In-
hesion among the several tribes, as the North- dians
western Indians. They occupied, geographically, the region
which is to-day Ohio and Indiana, and politically held the
same strategic relation to boundaries and settlements which
the Iroquois had formerly held. By the British they were
regarded as still under the influence of the Iroquois, but as a
matter of fact, being less civilized and more independent,
they were no longer inclined to accept the leadership of that
confederation or of Brant.

When the tribes heard of the treaty of peace their anger
against the British was intense, because they were not included in its terms. They had for the most The Indian
part been engaged in the war as allies of the peril
British, the treaty left them at the mercy of the Americans.
So violent was their tone that the British feared some such
general and concerted movement among them as had taken
place under Pontiac in 1764, when the Indians had been
similarly deserted by the French. Against such an attack the
feeble British garrisons along the lakes would be but a frail
defence; but, should these be withdrawn, the little settlements of French about the trading centres, and of American

---

[1] I. J. Cox, "The Indian as a Diplomatic Factor in the History of the
Old Northwest," *Ohio Archæol. and Hist. Quarterly*, 1909, xviii. 542–565.

loyalists who were beginning to occupy what is now Ontario, would fall like brush before the fire. To prevent such a catastrophe, the British commissioners in Paris had suggested that Great Britain retain the forts for three years, or until American garrisons arrived; but this proposition had been rejected.[1]

Angry as the tribes were with the British, they felt a more fundamental hostility to the "Long Knives" or Americans, Indians and whose advancing settlements drove wild life Americans before them. They were loath to make peace with them particularly because to the Americans a treaty with Indians meant acquisition of territory. The Indians continued to trade with the British agents, to frequent the British forts, to speak of George III, the great chief with the red coat, as father; but if they were to be obedient children they wished protection from their enemies. The Indians were, therefore, a weapon for the British, but one which required careful handling.

The policy of the British government was one of peace and pacification, but it could not command the Indians to The British accept American terms without the danger of Indian policy a great uprising. Nor could it entirely control its own agents so far away on the frontier and necessarily invested with large personal responsibility. Many of these were American loyalists, as bitter against their former countrymen as were the Indians. Guns and ammunition were sold, indiscreet utterances were made, ardent young Englishmen and Canadians occasionally joined the Indian forays; and the Americans interpreted British policy as a careful nursing of the tribes to be used as a lash to castigate the United States frontier when occasion should arise.[1]

The most important European settlement in the drainage basin of the St. Lawrence, except for the French Canadian

[1] Papers drawn from the Canadian archives, the Simcoe papers, and the British Public Record Office, by Miss Orpha Leavitt, for use in a Wisconsin doctor's thesis as yet unpublished.

farmers along the main river, was that of the "Green Mountain Boys" in the valley of Lake Champlain. Their position was a peculiar one. Although they were organized as a separate state, their lands were claimed by both New Hampshire and New York and their government was not recognized by Congress. During the Revolution they had fought on the American side, but they had negotiated with Great Britain independently. With peace, their great desire was incorporation into the American Union, within whose boundaries they were living; and yet they realized that Great Britain held their welfare in her hands, for the only outlet for their lumber and grain was down the Richelieu, or Sorrel, river to Montreal.[1]

Vermont

To obtain the privilege of this route they determined to negotiate on their own account, and in 1786 sent three commissioners to frame a treaty of commerce with Lord Dorchester, then governor-general of Canada. In 1787 and 1788, the British government granted them certain privileges by proclamation and ordinance; but the Vermonters, wishing a formal treaty, continued negotiations through 1790. On April 17, 1790, Cattrell, in behalf of the Canadian government, wrote to W. W. Grenville of the British foreign office: "It belongs not to the Committee to decide how far any article in the late Treaty of Peace, by which the Independence of the United States was acknowledged and the extent of their Territories defined, may make it improper for the government of this Country to form a separate Treaty with the State of Vermont, or whether it may be politically prudent all circumstances considered, to risk giving offence to the Congress of the United States, by such a measure." He thought, however, that it would certainly be of commercial benefit to Great Britain "to prevent Vermont and Kentuck and all the other settlements now forming in the Interior parts of

Influence of the St. Lawrence

[1] F. J. Turner, "English policy toward America in 1790–1791," *Amer. Hist. Review*, 1902, viii. 78–86.

the great Continent of North America, from becoming dependent on the Government of the United States or on that of any Foreign Country, and to preserve them on the contrary in a state of Independence, and to induce them to form Treaties of Commerce and Friendship with Great Britain."

Great Britain had less to offer Kentucky than she could give to Vermont; moreover, her relations with the Indians caused the settlers there to be, some of them suspicious, and an increasing number violently hostile. Yet the portages between the northern branches of the Ohio and the Great Lakes might be used as an outlet for Kentucky products, and in 1788, according to the report of John Connolly, a British agent in that region, the people were thinking of bargaining for this outlet down the St. Lawrence.[1]

It is not necessary to suppose that the Vermonters and Kentuckians were actually planning local independence, in order to realize that the continued failure of the United States to open a channel for their commerce, combined with the possibility of accomplishing such a result by their own endeavors, was calculated speedily to develop a desire and a purpose for independence. Furthermore, while the British government had no direct policy for bringing about a dissolution of the Union, it is evident that it was closely observing conditions in the West and was not inclined to relinquish anything that it held. With its control of the Indians and of the St. Lawrence, it remained a factor in the development of the whole Northwest, irrespective of boundaries. The future of the valley of the Great Lakes and of the northern part of the Ohio valley might yet prove to lie with Great Britain rather than with the United States.

Of more immediate interest was the problem of the Southwest, where the situation was similar to that in the north,

Kentucky and the St. Lawrence

Possibilities of British control

[1] Theodore Roosevelt, *Winning of the West* (4 vols., New York, etc., 1889–96), vol. iii. chs. iv.–v.

although the various factors differed in their relative weight
and the need for a solution was more urgent. The future
of the Mississippi valley probably lay in the   **Kentucky and**
hands of the American pioneers who were pour-   **Cumberland**
ing into that region. Their settlements constituted two oases
in the wilderness. The more important, consisting of Scotch-
Irish mountaineers and Revolutionary veterans largely from
Virginia, was in the blue-grass district of Kentucky. Increasing with great rapidity throughout the Confederation,
it had in 1790 about 70,000 inhabitants. The other settlement, one hundred and fifty miles to the southwest, was in
the Tennessee blue grass, about Nashville, and was known
as the Cumberland district. Settled more exclusively by the
mountaineer type, it had in 1790 less than half as large a population as Kentucky, and was also more exposed, being surrounded by the powerful tribes of the southwestern Indians.

Like the Vermonters, these invaders of the wilderness had
shown their patriotism during the Revolution by fighting
against the British; they had assisted George   **Spirit of in-**
Rogers Clark in the capture of Kaskaskia and   **dependence**
Vincennes, and had themselves delivered the great blow at
King's Mountain of which the story in ballad and fireside
tale enlivened many a forest cabin for years to come. Like
the Vermonters, however, it was independence that fired
them, and not particularly loyalty to the American Union
or even to their states. Tennessee had a government, headed
by John Sevier, which claimed separation from the parent
state of North Carolina; and Kentucky was anxious to organize separately from Virginia.

Their virgin farms produced abundant crops, and nearly all
were on the banks of rivers hurrying to meet the Mississippi
and the sea. The forests furnished ready material for rafts and rude boats, and all nature   **Traffic**
invited to this easy path of export. It was only necessary to
obtain the permission of the Spaniards to drift down to some
point near the gulf, there tranship their goods at some place

of deposit, and to return with the proceeds, either by sea to Philadelphia and thence home across the mountains, or buying a horse at New Orleans or Natchez ride home through the forests. During the Revolution, when we were to some extent coöperating with Spain, they had tested the advantages of this traffic; but in 1786 Spain closed the route. To reopen it was the work of Congress.[1]

Jay, treating with Gardoqui at Philadelphia, pointed to the treaty of peace with England, which specifically declared

The "right" of navigation that the navigation of the Mississippi should be free from its source to the ocean, and to the treaty of 1763 between Great Britain and Spain, which had given England this right. Gardoqui claimed that the concession to England was a specific grant, which she had no power to transfer to another country. He refused to accept Jay's argument that the United States had a natural right to follow to the ocean all rivers on which any of its territory bordered; as a matter of fact, moreover, free navigation was of comparatively little use unless accompanied by the privilege of a place of deposit where rafts could be broken up and transhipment to ocean-going vessels made.[2]

Spain was the more tenacious of her position because of a misunderstanding regarding the Florida boundary. The

The Florida boundary treaty of 1783 between England and Spain read, "His Britannic Majesty likewise cedes and guarantees, in full right, to His Catholic Majesty East Florida, as also West Florida." In the treaty of even date between England and the United States the northern boundary of West Florida was fixed at the thirty-first parallel. As between these two documents, the one indefinite, the other definite, the latter would naturally govern. Spain, however, claimed that "West Florida" was a definite term, that England had in 1764 extended the province to a line running through the mouth of the Yazoo. Moreover, her

[1] Winsor, *Westward Movement,* 247–256.
[2] *Secret Journals of Congress,* iv. 42–132.

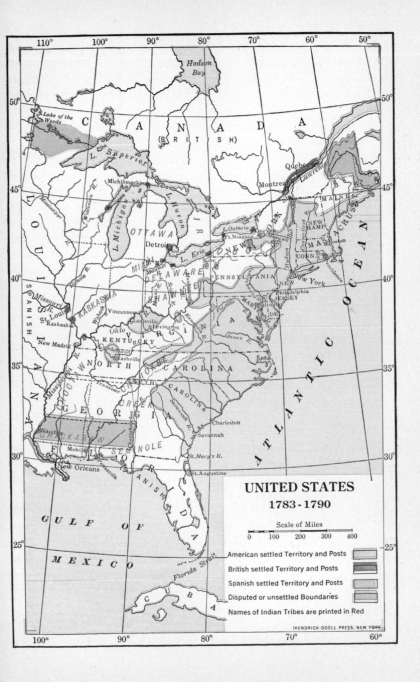

UNITED STATES
1783 - 1790

Scale of Miles
0   100   200   300   400

American settled Territory and Posts
British settled Territory and Posts
Spanish settled Territory and Posts
Disputed or unsettled Boundaries
Names of Indian Tribes are printed in Red

[KENDRICK-ODELL PRESS, NEW YORK]

claim in equity is improved by a study of the preliminary articles of both treaties; for those of the American treaty agreed to the Yazoo boundary in case England remained in possession of West Florida, whereas the agreement with Spain was that she should "continue" to hold West Florida. Now, she actually did hold Natchez, the only important post in the disputed region. Technically the arguments balanced, but Spain "continued" to hold Natchez, which not only was a Spanish garrison town, but was peopled for the most part with American loyalists, who were averse to a transfer of authority. Congress was, therefore as unable to clear the national territory of foreign control to the southwest as to the northwest.

Meantime the commercial interests of the coast were impatient at having an agreement held up because of these western questions, which they felt to be of little concern. Not all, moreover, favored the open- **"East" and "West"** ing of the Mississippi. In addition to a feeling that western emigration weakened the older parts of the country, there was a distinct fear, voiced by such men as Rufus King, that, should the West learn to face down the Mississippi, the country would be divided into two spheres so distinct that union would cease to be possible. He believed that the development of the West had best wait on the slow process of creating transportation routes across the mountains.

The position of Congress had been vacillating. In 1779 it had made the navigation of the Mississippi an ultimatum in any treaty with Spain; in 1781 it had withdrawn this condition; in 1784 it had returned to it. **Jay's proposal** In 1786 Jay, who had ignored the instructions of 1781, concluded that he could not carry out those of 1784, and arranged a treaty with Gardoqui on the basis that the United States should forego the navigation for twenty-five years, without prejudicing her rights. This plan he recommended to Congress, with whom the question assumed a sectional aspect. The commercial regions, New England and the middle states, were in favor of it, the southern states, less interested in general commerce and more closely in touch with the West, were opposed. On one vote seven states out of the thirteen favored the proposal, but the decision was ultimately left over to the new government under the constitution.

It was not till 1788, in the discussion of the Virginia convention over the ratification of the constitution, that the Western discontent West learned of this proposed betrayal of its birthright. For several years, however, its inhabitants had been growing restless at the protracted failure of Congress to meet their wishes, a restiveness that was aggravated by the similar failure of Congress to deal effectually with their Indian enemies.

The Southwestern Indians were more numerous than the Northwestern, and better organized; the five great tribes, Cherokee, Creeks, Choctaw, Chickasaw, and Chicamauga, could together furnish perhaps twenty thousand warriors. The close of the war found these tribes at enmity with the Americans. In 1785 commissioners arranged a treaty with the Cherokee, but the boundary provided was not satisfactory to the frontiersmen, and North Carolina stood by her citizens. The articles of Confederation gave Congress control of Indian affairs only in the case of tribes not living within the limits of a single state. North Carolina, therefore, claiming to comprehend the Cherokee, denied the validity of the treaty. To the failure of Congress to open the Mississippi was thus added the failure to quiet the Indians upon satisfactory terms, and the people of the West came to believe that their happiness must depend on their own exertions.

Under these circumstances the West became fertile ground for the development of plans and plots and conspiracies. Western projects They grew up, withered, and revived again; they adjusted themselves to times and conditions; they flourished now successively, and now simultaneously even in the same mind. They stretched their threads to Congress and the coast, and across the ocean to Madrid, Paris, and London; they connected themselves with the general history of the age. At times secret and unobserved, at times the central objects of attention, they together form one of the two leading themes of our diplomatic history until after 1803. During the Confederation they were practically all directed to the solution of western problems by some one of the following four methods,—by the self-reliant seizure of New Orleans, a task somewhat beyond existing resources; by submission to the control of Spain; by independence and alliance with Spain; or by independence and alliance with Great Britain. It is probable that the majority of the inhabitants were at most times disposed to follow a fifth course,—the obvious and legal one of urging their grievances upon the government of the United States in the hope that it would acquire the power to redress them. The supporters of this view, however, were often discouraged, for they were not sustained by any such deep-seated loyalty as developed when the nation had proved itself deserving of their devotion.

Fully aware of the situation, Spain was disposed to pull every string of intrigue in order to manipulate it to her own advantage. Her Indian policy was well con- *The Spanish* ceived and well executed. The government *Indian policy* encouraged the great Scotch firm of Panton, Leslie and Company, whose American headquarters were at Pensacola. It saw to it that traders frequented the Indian villages, and that their rates for goods were moderate. It allowed a secret trade in firearms. It distributed generous presents. To the great chief of the Creeks, the most powerful man among the Indians, Alexander McGillivray, it paid a yearly pension. Of this man, Navarro, intendant or civil officer of Louisiana, wrote, April 15, 1786: "So long as we shall have this chief on our side, we may rely on having established, between the Floridas and Georgia, a barrier which it will not be easy to break through. The Indians are now fully convinced of the ambition of the Americans; the recollection of past injuries still dwells on their minds, and, with it, the fear that these greedy neighbors may one day seize upon their lands, and strip them of a property to which they consider themselves as having a right derived from nature herself. It ought to be one of the chief points in the policy of this Government to keep this sentiment alive in their breasts." Upon these Indians, with the creole population, the Spanish government placed its greatest dependence for the defence of Louisiana, and through Louisiana of the mines of Mexico.[1]

It hoped, however, by intrigue with the western settlers to create a still more advanced barrier, namely, to acquire

The coloniza-   or to control the region which it had endeavored
tion plan   to obtain in the negotiation of 1779 with England and of 1782 with Jay. Alert and eager as it was, however, the Spanish government lacked unity of purpose. One of the plans considered was that of Navarro, who wrote, December 19, 1787: "It is necessary to keep in mind that, between this province and the territories of New Spain, there is nothing but the feeble barrier of the Mississippi, which it is as easy to pass as it is impossible to protect, and that, if it be good policy to fortify this province by drawing a large population within its limits, there are no other means than that of granting certain franchises to commerce, leaving aside, as much as possible, all restrictions and shackles, or at least postponing them to a future time, if they must exist. In addition, the government must distinguish itself by the equity of its administration, the suavity of its relations with the people, and the disinterestedness of its officers in their dealings with the foreigners who may resort to the colony. This is the only way to form, in a short time, a solid rampart for the protection of the kingdom of Mexico." [2]

[1] Charles Gayarré, *History of Louisiana* (3d ed., 4 vols., New Orleans, 1885), iii. 175 and *passim;* Roosevelt, *Winning of the West,* vol. iii.; Winsor, *Westward Movement.*

[2] Gayarré, *Louisiana,* iii. 189.

This plan was fostered by Gardoqui, who at Philadelphia entered into relations with Colonel George Morgan and arranged a deal with him. Morgan received a grant of land and undertook to establish a colony, New Madrid, at the strategic point in what is now Missouri, opposite the mouth of the Ohio. George Rogers Clark was interested in a scheme to organize a similar colony on the Yazoo, and joined with him were James Wilkinson, John Brown, a delegate in Congress, Harry Inness, the attorney-general of the Kentucky district, and other men of influence and ambition. To make settlement in these new grants desirable it was proposed to allow emigrants to bring in their property free of duty and to enjoy religious tolerance; but of course the main inducement would be freedom to use the Mississippi. The essential point was to keep the river tight closed to those living in the American districts.[1]

With regard to the wisdom of this plan it may be remarked that, as immigrants of this kind would change their flag only for their personal advantage, the durability of their loyalty to the Spanish crown might well be suspected. James Wilkinson It was like asking the fox to guard the chickens. Something like this was felt by Miro, the governor of Louisiana, to whom the tempter came in the form of James Wilkinson. During the winter of 1775 a few hundred Americans, suffering sickness, icy cold, and want, had besieged Quebec. That little group must have possessed distinguished courage and a spirit of high adventure, but it contained also the three well-known traitors of our history, Benedict Arnold, Aaron Burr, and James Wilkinson. One can hardly refrain from supposing that over their camp-fires conversation often ran to the fascinating possibilities of Spanish America, to the mines of Mexico and Peru. Of the three, Wilkinson was the least, but the most enduring.

Settling in Kentucky, this man no sooner won confidence

[1] C. H. Haskins, *The Yazoo Land Companies*, Amer. Hist. Assoc., *Papers,* 1891, v. 395–437.

by a successful raid against the Indians than he began to tread the shady paths of forest diplomacy. In 1786 he visited Natchez and established relations with Gayoso, the Spanish commandant. The next year he descended the river with a cargo of tobacco, flour, butter, and bacon. He secured an interview with Miro, to whom he presented a plan for allowing a few prominent men of the American settlements the privileges of commerce, in return for which they would devote themselves to persuading the whole region to declare its independence and form an alliance with Spain. Miro wrote, January 8, 1788: "The delivery of Kentucky into his Majesty's hands, which is the main object to which Wilkinson has promised to devote himself entirely, would forever constitute this province a rampart for the protection of New Spain." Wilkinson was allowed to complete his transactions, and with such of his profits as he did not hand over to Miro he went home by way of Philadelphia.[1]

Independence and alliance

It is obvious that this project was somewhat at variance with the colonization scheme, for it would furnish relief to some at least of the inhabitants of Kentucky. Instead of deciding definitively upon one plan or the other, however, the Spanish authorities tried to ride both. They somewhat distrusted Wilkinson, as they did the proposed colonizers, and by limiting trading privileges to a few they hoped still to attract immigration. Wilkinson, meantime, whatever his ultimate intentions may have been, pushed his plans. He hoped to secure the consent of Virginia to the organization of Kentucky as a separate state, and then to apply the process later known as secession. In July, 1788, he made his proposals to the Kentucky constitutional convention, and, although he did not win their adoption, he secured a postponement of the final decision. In June, Miro had written home that he heard from Kentucky that in various conversations "among the most distinguished

Kentucky undecided

[1] T. M. Green, *Spanish Conspiracy*, Cincinnati, 1891.

citizens of that State," it had been said "that the direction of the current of the rivers which run in front of their dwellings points clearly to the power to which they ought to ally themselves."

Miro did not neglect Tennessee. Of the settlers in the Nashville region the most prominent was James Robertson. Restless under the restraint of trade, but even more under the Indian attacks, he at any rate coquetted with the Spaniards. McGillivray wrote, April 25, 1788, that the Cumberland settlers had asked for terms, "and added that they would throw themselves into the arms of his Majesty as subjects, and that Cumberland and Kentucky are determined to free themselves from their dependence on Congress, because that body cannot protect either their persons or their property, or favor their commerce. They therefore, believe that they owe no obedience to a power which is incapable of benefiting them." Even in the valleys of East Tennessee, John Sevier, foremost man of the district, in 1788 offered his services to Miro and Gardoqui, although he subsequently withdrew from the connection.[1]

Miro and Tennessee

The government under the Confederation, therefore, not only failed to open up commerce with the Mediterranean and the West Indies, and to put that with Spain upon a desirable basis, but it was unable to occupy the territory granted to the United States by the treaty of 1783, either in the northwest or on the Florida border. It was unable to quiet the Indians of north or south, or to provide commercial outlets for the trans-Appalachian settlers. Its failure was causing not only discontent but disloyalty, and to such a degree that, although the racial control of the great valley was probably determined by the character of the aggressive population already on the spot, its governmental future was still uncertain.

Diplomatic failure

[1] Roosevelt, *Winning of the West*, iii. chs. iii.–v.; Winsor, *Westward Movement*, 334.

While the western situation was not widely appreciated in the older portion of the country, the financial plight was

The danger of the debt

fully realized. Owing to the lack of national resources, the interest on our foreign debt was met only by occasional sales of such portions of the Dutch loan arranged by Adams as had not been immediately taken up.[1] The loans from France were still unprovided for, and it was the gossip of diplomatic circles that France might take the island of Rhode Island as her payment.[2] To the public mind of Europe in 1789, the acquisition of a French naval base on the United States coast seemed no more improbable than the acquisition of a United States naval base in Cuba seems to-day. It was by no means an accepted opinion that the United States would prove to be more than what we call to-day a protectorate, under French or English influence. The public debt was one of the weapons of France, as it has since so often been the key to European interference in the weaker countries of the world. Even though we were not actually in danger of being forced into political dependency, Europe had yet to be convinced that we were not. The future independence as well as the future limits of the country were in 1789 felt to be undetermined.

[1] John Adams, *Works*, see index under *loans*.

[2] For the French position, see "Correspondence of the Comte de Moustier [French Minister in the United States] with the Comte de Montmorin," *Amer. Hist. Review*, 1903, viii. 709–733; for rumors, see Buckingham's letter to Temple, Mass. Hist. Soc., *Proceedings*, 1866, p. 75.

CHAPTER VIII

OLD PROBLEMS IN NEW HANDS [1]

UNDER the Articles of Confederation the administration had proved too weak to perform the duties of a national government in maintaining the rights and interests of its citizens among the nations of the world. This failure in diplomacy was one of the causes for the formation of a stronger central authority. Naturally, therefore, the constitution gave the new government a freer hand in dealing with international affairs. The states conceded to the nation almost complete control of war, peace, treaty-making, army and navy, commerce, naturalization, and Indian affairs; and treaties were made the law of the land, enforceable by the national supreme court. The only limitations were that the importation of slaves was not to be prohibited for twenty years, that no taxes should be levied on exports, and no preference given to the ports of one state over those of another. In actual practice, these limitations proved to give rise to little controversy and to hamper the national government

Diplomatic powers of the national government

[1] J. D. Richardson, *Messages and Papers of the Presidents*, 10 vols., to 1899, with continuations by other editors (contains valuable summaries and discussions); *Journal of the Executive Proceedings of the Senate, 1789–1901*, 32 vols. in 34, Washington, 1828–1911 (contains votes on treaties and appointments); *Compilation of Reports of [Senate] Committee on Foreign Relations, 1789–1901*, 8 vols., Washington, 1901 (Senate Doc., 56 Cong., 2 sess., No. 231); *American State Papers, Foreign Relations*, 6 vols., Washington, 1832–59 (gives such correspondence as was submitted to Congress from 1789 to 1828; that between 1828 and 1860 is not collected [see Hart, *Foundations of American Foreign Policy*, 281–283]; since 1860 selected material has been published each year, although further papers are still presented to Congress on call from time to time); J. B. Moore, *Digest of International Law as embodied . . . especially in Documents . . . of the United States*, 8 vols., Washington, 1906 (House Doc., 56 Cong., 2 sess., No. 551; an invaluable aid, discussing all points involving questions of law).

very little in its negotiations; but the failure to give the government full control of aliens within the limits of the states, coupled with the fact that foreign nations have held it to be responsible for them, has occasionally caused trouble.

Within the government, the direction of foreign affairs was given to the President, but the appointment of "ambas- The executive and Congress sadors, other public ministers, and consuls" requires the confirmation of the Senate, and treaties must be ratified by a two-thirds vote of the same body. The relation of the House of Representatives to diplomacy has proved one of the most baffling ambiguities of the constitution. A minister appointed by the President and confirmed by the Senate is an official of the United States. He can, however, draw no salary unless one is provided for by Congress as a whole. In the same way a treaty confirmed by the Senate is the law of the land and enforceable by the supreme court; but if it provides for the expenditure of money it cannot be executed unless the House consents. A treaty, moreover, often fixes rates to be paid on imported articles and on the vessels carrying them; but of no power are the representatives more jealous than that of regulating customs duties, a function clearly granted by the constitution to Congress as a whole. Although these questions have never been authoritatively adjudicated upon, and perhaps never can be, it may be said that Congress as a body has directed the expansion of the diplomatic service, that the House, although it has sometimes delayed discharging financial obligations laid upon the nation by treaties, has never failed to do so eventually, and that, on the other hand, it has never yielded its direction of commercial policy.

When Washington took office in April, 1789, he found no organization by means of which he could execute his diplo- The determin- ation of policy matic powers. Congress, however, speedily provided for a department of state, charged chiefly with that function, its secretary becoming in effect foreign minister. The natural selection for this office was

John Jay, but he preferred the position of chief justice. Washington therefore appointed Thomas Jefferson, who had served on the committee of correspondence of the Continental Congress and since 1784 had been minister to France. Foreign affairs were, however, of such critical moment throughout the Federalist period that all questions of policy were discussed by the whole cabinet, together with Jay and the vice-president John Adams. As a matter of fact, Jefferson's opinion was seldom followed; his influence was modifying rather than directing. The responsibility and the credit belong primarily to the presidents, Washington and, later, Adams.[1]

Although conditions of intercourse were better than during the Revolution, they were still poor, and a close-knit policy was impossible. It was very difficult, moreover, to induce fit men to accept appointments in the regular diplomatic service. Salaries, while perhaps more adequate than they are to-day, were smaller than during the Revolution. The social allure which now renders so many patriots willing to spend abroad for their country was not strong enough to cross the Atlantic in the cheerless barks of that day. Old men feared the voyage; young men like John Quincy Adams disliked to abandon their professions for positions of "nominal respectability and real insignificance." Consequently it was found impossible to keep first-class ministers except at London and Paris. Spain was ill-supplied, and the missions to Holland, Portugal, Russia, and Prussia were only occasionally filled. In this situation the government resorted to the expedient of sending special missions in important crises, and at such times it was well served.

Federalist diplomatic service

The consular service was still less satisfactory. The only positions that carried salaries were those to the Barbary states, which were semi-diplomatic in character. In all

[1] On organization, see Schuyler, *American Diplomacy*, chs. i–iii; J. W. Foster, *The Practice of Diplomacy*, Boston, 1910; Gaillard Hunt, *Department of State*, New Haven, 1914.

other cases compensation came from fees alone. The result was that consuls usually had to be chosen from merchants The consular trading at the ports, who in many cases were service not Americans. The whole idea of using consuls as a means of advancing national commercial interests was of later growth in the United States. At that time their services were purely those of trade regulation and registration.

The strength of the new government was first apparent at home, and next appeared in the handling of those diplomatic Financial problems which were also in part domestic. strength The financial resources developed by Hamilton's management at once settled the question of credit, and never since that time has the United States offered an excuse for foreign interference by failing to meet its financial obligations, or even by being in danger of such failure. The repudiation of portions of their debts by some of the individual states, however, has at times caused trouble, though never danger.

While settling its finances, the new government took a first step toward developing the loyalty of the frontier by Representa- admitting Vermont, Kentucky, and Tennessee tion of the to statehood, the first two in 1791 and 1792 West respectively, the last in 1796. Thus recognized, the new states were inclined to await somewhat more loyally, if not more patiently, the solution of their special problems.

The Indian question was taken up vigorously, though not with entire success. Various laws were passed to diminish the Indian policy friction between the savages and the pioneers and traders; and finally Washington, in his fifth annual message, recommended the establishment of government trading-houses among them "to conciliate their attachment." In 1796 this system was adopted, in the hope thereby to detach them from the Spaniards and English. Tackle wrote to Lord Bathurst, November 24, 1812: "Of all the

projects of Genl. Washington, after effecting the separation
of those Colonies from the mother country; I apprehend
this of the Trading houses, best calculated to undermine the
influence of Great Britain, with the Indians." [1]

While this general policy was being worked out, negotiations were carried on with the various tribes. McGillivray
and other chiefs were brought to New York, fêted, and
bribed. In spite of obstacles which the Spaniards were supposed to, and probably did, interpose, a treaty was arranged
with the Creeks in 1790; [2] and in the same year orders were
given that the treaty of Hopewell, made in 1785 with the
Cherokee, be observed by the white settlers. Peace was thus
established in the southwest, although the situation was not
conducive to slumber.

In the northwest, negotiation proved futile, and Washington advised that economy would "point to prompt and decisive effort rather than to defensive and linger-   Indian wars
ing operations." The means at his disposal
were, however, insufficient. In 1790 General Harmer was sent
against the Indians and disastrously defeated, and the following year a more formidable expedition under St. Clair,
governor of Northwest Territory, went down in utter rout.
General Wayne, whose nickname "Mad Anthony" is appropriate only if it is considered as implying the presence of
dash and not the absence of judgment, was then appointed
to the command of the western department. It was the
spring of 1794 before he moved against the Indians. In
February they had been encouraged by an injudicious speech
of Lord Dorchester, and they now took their stand near a
newly-established British fort at the rapids of the Maumee,
twenty miles within American territory. General Knox,
secretary of war, wrote to Wayne: "If, therefore, in the

---

[1] Wisconsin Hist. Soc., *Collections*, 1911, xx. 4–5; Washington, *Works*
(ed. Ford), xi. 465.

[2] John Marshall, *Life of Washington* (5 vols., Philadelphia, 1804–07),
v. 274.

course of your operations against the Indian enemy, it should become necessary to dislodge the party at the rapids of the Miami, [sic] you are hereby authorized, in the name of the President of the United States, to do it." Wayne, however, succeeded in inflicting a decisive defeat upon the Indians in the battle of Fallen Timbers, without becoming officially involved with the British, though he notified General Knox, "It is with infinite pleasure that I announce to you the brilliant success of the Federal army under my command, in a general action with the combined force of the hostile Indians, and a considerable number of the volunteers and militia of Detroit." Peace with the Indians, however, did not come until the next year, 1795, after the Jay treaty had been framed and continued peace between Great Britain and America seemed assured. Defeated and deserted, the Indians agreed to the treaty of Greenville, which granted the Americans a large portion of what is now Ohio and a part of Indiana. By 1795, therefore, the new government had accomplished one of its tasks in restoring peace to the frontier and making itself respected by the Indians. It could not, however, put an end to the inevitable conflict between the onward-pushing forces of American civilization and the inhabitants of the forest, who continued to lean for support upon the less aggressive Spaniards and English. This peace constituted merely a truce, but a truce which allowed tens of thousands of American pioneers to establish themselves in the wilderness and to tip the balance substantially in favor of the United States before the hostile forces closed in final struggle.[1]

One problem did not wait upon another, and during these same years the questions of commerce were being discussed. With regard to the Barbary states the administration adopted the European practice of purchasing peace. Yet, even with

[1] B. A. Hinsdale, *Old Northwest* (New York, 1888), 184ff.; also unpublished theses by Shong and Groves in the library of the University of Wisconsin.

money and a willingness to use it, the difficulties remained serious. It was not till 1795 that a treaty was arranged with Algiers, to be followed in 1796 by a Mediterranean similar one with Tripoli, and finally, in 1799, trade by one with Tunis. Then the coast seemed clear. In spite of these treaties and the expenditure of nearly two million dollars, however, there continued to be such constant trouble that the Federalist administration can hardly be said to have made the Mediterranean a safe route for American commerce.[1]

But far more important was the question of general commercial policy, the source which was expected not merely to provide the government with most of its reve- The merchant nue, but also to advance the interests of Amer- marine ican merchants and ship-owners. It was a question which lay with Congress rather than with the administration. The first point, after the imposition of a customs tariff, was whether there should be discrimination in favor of American as opposed to foreign vessels, a policy that was opposed by the agricultural interests on the ground that it would inevitably mean higher freight rates. By the commercial interests it was of course strongly urged, and with them sided what we may call the nationalists. Jefferson, although from an agricultural state, argued: "In times of general peace, it multiplies competition for employment in transportation, and so keeps it at its proper level, and in times of war, that is to say, when those nations who may be our principal carriers, shall be at war with each other, if we have not within ourselves the means of transportation, our products must be exported in belligerent vessels, at the increased expense of war freights and insurance, and the articles which will not bear it, must perish on our hands." It was finally voted that American vessels should pay six cents duty per ton on entering a port, and foreign vessels fifty cents. To encourage American ship-building, American-built, foreign-owned ves-

[1] J. B. Moore, *American Diplomacy* (New York, etc., 1905), 63–72.

sels were to pay a middle rate, thirty cents. In addition, American vessels were to receive ten per cent rebate from the duties imposed on their cargoes.

Keener discussion raged on a second point,—whether there should be discrimination between the vessels of various Discrimina- foreign countries according to their treatment tion of our vessels. The strongest advocate of this policy was Jefferson, who in December, 1793, submitted to Congress a remarkably able report setting forth his views. "Our commerce," he declared, "is certainly of a character to entitle it to favor in most countries. The commodities we offer are either necessaries of life, or materials for manufacture, or convenient subjects of revenue; and we take in exchange, either manufactures, when they have received the last finish of art and industry, or mere luxuries." He thought that by discrimination we could force the nations of the world, and Great Britain in particular, to throw open their ports on our own terms.[1]

By the commercial classes this plan was opposed as impracticable. They realized that trade is seldom much more profit-Retaliation able to one nation than to another, that actually the greater bulk of our commerce was with Great Britain, and that she might retaliate. Fisher Ames wrote, July 2, 1789: "But are we Yankees invulnerable, if a war of regulations should be waged with Britain? Are they not able to retaliate? Are they not rich enough to bear some loss and inconvenience? Would not their pride spurn at the idea of being forced into a treaty?" [2] Jefferson's plan, therefore, although supported warmly by Madison in the House of Representatives, was defeated, and he was forced to pigeon-hole it among those policies which were awaiting the day, which he believed certain to come, when the people would confide their welfare to his willing hands.

[1] *Amer. State Papers, Foreign*, i. 300–304.
[2] Fisher Ames, *Works* (ed. Seth Ames, 2 vols., Boston, 1854), i. 57–60.

These measures for fostering the American merchant marine actually worked, and, in combination with circumstance, worked marvellously. American ships rapidly Diplomatic failures secured not only our whole coasting trade but about eighty per cent of our foreign trade, and held it for many years. The commercial classes became enthusiastic for a government that could do so much by its own regulations. In matters which required the mutual consent of other governments, however, success was not so immediate. Spain could not be persuaded to open the Mississippi, and Great Britain allowed the use of the St. Lawrence only by highly exceptionable special agreements with Vermont. The British West Indies remained closed.

While these essential matters were still unsettled, we did force from Great Britain an important courtesy. That country had steadily refused to commission a First minister from England minister to the United States, her commercial interests being well attended to by a consul-general, Sir John Temple, and the active Phineas Bond, consul at Philadelphia. With the return of Adams in 1788 we were equally unrepresented in England, nor could we, consistently with our self-respect, again appoint a minister until Great Britain was willing to reciprocate. To meet the situation, which was not only inconvenient but, considering all conditions, dangerous as well, Washington sent Gouverneur Morris unofficially to England. He succeeded in impressing the English ministry with the friendliness of the American administration, and the probability of hostile commercial legislation by Congress if England remained obdurate, with the result that in 1791 George Hammond was appointed minister just in time, as Lord Grenville was informed, to prevent the passage of an act discriminating against English commerce. The next year Thomas Pinckney was sent as American minister to Great Britain. Although neither Pinckney nor Hammond accomplished definite results, the exchange of ministers somewhat enhanced the prestige of the United States.[1]

While formulating these general policies, the government found itself confronted by an episode which for a moment **Nootka Sound** pulled taut all the strings of American diplomacy. The situation quickly relaxed, it is true, but in that moment were brought to view motives and forces which were to play a vital part in the history of the United States for many years to come. In the same month in which Washington was inaugurated, two Spanish war vessels, unauthorized by their government, seized some goods left by an English company which intended upon its own responsibility to form a permanent commercial settlement at Nootka Sound, on what is now called the island of Vancouver, at that time one of the most remote spots on the sea-washed earth. As fast as the wind could carry the ships of the day, the news was brought to the courts of England and Spain.[2]

The affair was accidental, but it involved the fundamental interests and the long-established views of both countries. **The verge of war** England could not let the seizure go unnoticed without recognizing the Spanish claim to the unoccupied coast of North America, a claim resting entirely upon a questioned discovery. A virile growing power, she had for two hundred years denied such prescriptive rights. Spain, on the other hand, could not make amends without either giving up her claims to ownership or acknowledging the breakdown of her policy of commercial exclusion. Both nations prepared for war. Spain called on France, who, although the Revolution had begun, was still bound to her by the Family Alliance. Pitt made ready to regain the

---

[1] E. D. Adams, *The Influence of Grenville on Pitt's Foreign Policy*, 1787–1798, Washington, 1904; *Dropmore Papers* (British Hist. Mss. Commission, *Report*, 1894, xiv. pt. v.), ii. 228, 250, 263, 444.

[2] W. R. Manning, *The Nootka Sound Controversy*, Amer. Hist. Assoc., *Report*, 1904, pp. 279–478; W. E. H. Lecky, *England in the Eighteenth Century* (8 vols., London, 1878–90), v. 206–209; H. H. Bancroft, *Northwest Coast* (2 vols., San Francisco, 1884), i. 180–225.

golden colonies of Spain won by his father but lost through the policy of George III.

To Pitt's hand lay many strange instruments. Among them was William A. Bowles, a fantastic American loyalist, a portrait-painter, an actor, a soldier, who was at this time adventuring for a fortune in trade with the southwestern Indians. A rival of the Spanish-sympathizing McGillivray, he offered to organize among the Indians a force to capture the mines of Mexico. "I should inform your Lordship," he wrote to Lord Grenville, January 13, 1791, "that these Speculations would meet with other support than the force of the Creek and Cherokee Nation. There are now settled in the Cumberland Country [a] set of men, who are the Relicts of the American Army; These people are weary of their Situation. . . . I have had a request from . . . [them] to lead them on an expedition to the Spanish settlements, that being the object of adventure now most thought of, in that part of the world. . . . These people are desirous on any terms, of coming to settle amongst us, as well for the objects of peace as those of War. For, at present, they are shut out from the sea. They feel no attachment to the Americans and would be glad to abandon everything for a situation near the Sea in our Country [the Indian lands]." [1]

More formidable than Bowles was the mysterious Francisco de Miranda. A native of that hive of revolution, Caracas of Venezuela, he left a Spanish post in 1782 and devoted his life to the cause of freeing Spanish America. Had he directed his efforts toward internal preparation rather than to securing foreign assistance, he might perhaps have anticipated Bolivar as the successful leader of that movement; but, again, he might have been shot sooner than he was. From 1790 till 1810 he is always to be found hovering about the courts of whatever powers seemed most

[1] F. J. Turner, "English Policy toward America in 1790–1791," *Amer. Hist. Review*, 1902, vii. 706–735.

likely to welcome a project against Spain. A man of ability and with an unusual capacity for winning confidence, he was successively in close contact with England, France, England again, and at times with Russia and the United States. His plan at this time was the formation of a great independent Spanish-American constitutional monarchy in commercial alliance with Great Britain.[1]

It is obvious that such proposals touched the United States very nearly, and would have much disturbed its government had it known of them. Still more important, however, and more apparent was the prevalent feeling that, should a general war break out, the United States would necessarily become involved in it. Spain sought American favor by failing to seize two American ships that were at Nootka Sound. She also began to speak soft on the Mississippi question. Pitt, however, brought the subject up in more concrete form. Influenced by Miranda or by his own designs, he made arrangements for a descent upon New Spain. He had agents at Charleston and New York; he considered the advisability of sending troops from India against the west coast of Mexico; and particularly he thought it possible to use the troops at Detroit against New Orleans. As this project involved crossing American territory, he sent an agent to sound the American government as to its attitude. This agent, Major Beckwith, met Hamilton in July, 1790, and requested permission thus to use American territory should it prove desirable. He spoke of the cause of the expected rupture, observing that "it was one in which all commercial nations must be supposed to favor the views of Great Britain, that it was therefore presumed, should war take place, that the United States

Spain, England, and the United States

[1] F. J. Turner, "English Policy toward America in 1790–1791," *Amer. Hist. Review*, 1902, vii. 706–735; also W. S. Robertson, *Francisco de Miranda and the Revolutionizing of Spanish America*, Amer. Hist. Assoc., *Report*, 1907, i. 189–539; Hubert Hall, "Pitt and General Miranda," *Athenæum*, April 19, 1902, pp. 498–499.

would find it to their interest to take part with Great Britain rather than with Spain."

This was the first question of high diplomacy presented to the new government. Our two neighbors were apparently about to go to war. Should we side with Spain, United States or with Great Britain, or remain neutral? policy What would be the obligations of neutrality? what its rights? On August 27 Washington asked his advisers for their opinions on the crisis. They discussed it broadly. Jefferson feared an English conquest of Florida and Louisiana. "Embraced from the St. Croix to the St. Mary on Jefferson's the one side by their possessions," he wrote, views "on the other by their fleet, we need not hesitate to say that they would soon find means to unite to them all the territory covered by the ramifications of the Mississippi." Under such circumstances he looked forward to "bloody and eternal war or indissoluble confederacy" with her. "In my opinion," he said, "we ought to make ourselves parties in the general war expected to take place, should this be the only means of preventing the calamity." He hoped that by way of compromise England might allow us Florida and New Orleans; and on the immediate question of permission to cross our territory he advised delay.[1]

Hamilton inclined toward England. "It is not to be doubted," he wrote, September 15, 1790, "that the part which the courts of France and Spain took in Hamilton's our quarrel with Great Britain, is to be attrib- views uted, not to an attachment to our independence or liberty, but to a desire of diminishing the power of Great Britain by severing the British empire," a view in which Jay naturally agreed with him. Although Hamilton recognized the danger of permitting Great Britain to take Florida and Louisiana, he felt that our refusal to allow the expedition would not prevent it, but would involve us in the war on the

[1] Thomas Jefferson, *Writings* (ed. P. L. Ford, 10 vols., New York, etc., 1892-99), v. 228, 238, August 28, 1790.

side of Spain, who was sure to lose. He too would delay, but would grant the permission if the issue were forced.[1]

John Adams alone struck the note of absolute neutrality which was to characterize American diplomacy. Already **Adams and neutrality** in 1782 he had written Livingston: "America has been long enough involved in the wars of Europe. She has been a football between contending nations from the beginning, and it is easy to foresee, that France and England both will endeavor to involve us in their future wars. It is our interest and duty to avoid them as much as possible, and to be completely independent, and to have nothing to do with either of them, but in commerce." He therefore advised refusal. Should the troops be sent without permission, we could remonstrate.[2]

Fortunately the real issue had already been decided by the defeat of Mirabeau in the debate of May 20-22 in the **War averted** National Assembly of France. Louis XVI and his advisers had hoped by war to turn the rising tide of revolution into patriotism. In that case the King needed to retain the right of making peace and war, and to this end Mirabeau exerted himself. When, however, the Assembly voted that it alone possessed the right, the chance that France might join Spain passed, and Spain was forced to seek terms of England.[3]

The treaty between them, signed October 28, 1790, was of importance to the United States both immediately and **Nootka Sound treaty** subsequently. The third and sixth articles allowed freedom of trade and settlement on the coasts of the Pacific, "in places not already occupied," north of "the parts occupied by Spain," that is, practically above San Francisco bay. Although this relaxation of

---

[1] Alexander Hamilton, *Works* (ed. J. C. Hamilton, 7 vols., New York, 1850-51), iv. 48-69, September 15, 1790.

[2] John Adams, *Works*, viii. 9, 497-500, August 29, 1790.

[3] F. M. Fling, *Mirabeau and the French Revolution*, N. Y., 1908. Albert Sorel, *L'Europe et la révolution française* (8 vols., Paris, 1885-1904) ii. 61, 84-95.

Spanish control applied specifically to England, the Americans profited by it. Already frequenting the coast for its furs and gingseng, they would in the long run at least have been annoyed by Spanish interference, had it not been for this treaty. As it was, in the next year Captain Gray sailed, the first white man, into the great river of the region and named it after his ship, the Columbia, thus establishing the first link in the chain of claims which was to bring Oregon to the United States.

It is plain that, when the end of Washington's first term approached in 1793, the diplomatic situation did not warrant his withdrawal with the sense of leaving a task **Uncompleted** accomplished. Nearly everything was still **tasks** unsettled, and he consented to serve again in hope of carrying the various problems to solution. Nevertheless, the government was feeling the good influence of improved stability, the administration had determined its policy on some important questions, and on most others its individual members had begun to find themselves.

CHAPTER IX

THE ESTABLISHMENT OF NEUTRALITY

THUS prepared, the United States was in the spring of 1793 overtaken by a hurricane of diplomatic disturbance which was to blow with increasing violence for twenty-two years. The revolution which began to take form in 1789 was, in the minds of its leaders, only accidentally French. Its ideals were equally applicable to all nations in which the people were oppressed by their rulers. This international character of its professions, which it retained to the end, was at the beginning in some degree actually true. It was welcomed by liberals in all countries. It crossed the channel into England. As Wordsworth wrote,

> "Bliss was it in that dawn to be alive,
> But to be young was very heaven."

When the Bastile fell Lafayette sent its keys to Washington, a recognition of the indebtedness which the cause of revolution owed to America. French fashions for the first time invaded our country; and civic feasts, liberty caps, and the salutation of "citizen" and "citizeness" became common in our streets.

As one wave of radicalism succeeded another in France, each raising the tide of revolution higher toward the final fury of the Terror, the enthusiasm of the more moderate cooled, died, and turned to opposition. By 1793 England had become in effect a unit in resisting the spread of Revolution, and for the majority of Englishmen Revolution had come to be embodied in France. The inoculation of humanity was not able to cope with the traditional antipathies of French and English.

France continued to fight for the ideal of "Liberty," but England had come to personify for her the forces of oppression. In February, 1793, she anticipated a declaration of war on the part of England by declaring war with that country herself.

In America sentiment divided. Jefferson liked the French, as had Franklin. He had played a part in the beginning of their revolution and knew many of their leaders. He had a French cook, and he intro- *American sympathies* duced from France the revival of classic forms of architecture. Himself as peaceful as a Quaker, he was not troubled over a little blood-letting. He had said at the time of the Shays Rebellion that the tree of liberty must from time to time be watered by the blood of patriots and tyrants; " it is its natural manure." Serene in his belief in the ultimate triumph of right and reason, he looked without flinching upon the excesses of the Terror, and maintained his sympathy with the fundamental purpose of the movement. Hamilton, on the other hand, to whom civilization seemed based upon the slow and precarious triumph of informed intelligence over brutish ignorance, saw the whole structure tottering in France with the successes of the *sans culottes*, and imperilled in the world at large. Between the two was every shade of opinion, and in fact many were more radical than either. To the danger that would inevitably come to the United States of being drawn into the vortex of any war between France and Great Britain was added the peril of being divided within itself over the issue. It was probably fortunate that at this crisis both opinions were represented in the cabinet, and it was incalculably advantageous that the government was presided over by Washington's force, prestige, and balance.[1]

France, taking arms against the "impious hand of tyrants," —the governments of England, Prussia, Austria, Holland,

[1] C. D. Hazen, *Contemporary American Opinion of the French Revolution*, Baltimore, 1897.

and Spain,—did not lose sight of America. Even in the kaleidoscopic whirl of Paris Americans were conspicuous.

French hopes of the United States Thomas Paine sought to become the essayist of the new revolution, as he had been of the American; John Paul Jones was ready to repeat his naval triumphs in its behalf; the poet, Joel Barlow, dabbled now in land speculation, now in politics. Brissot de Warville, "who ruled the council," had in 1788 completed a voyage through America. When, therefore, the French republic was proclaimed, September 22, 1792, there was a reasonable hope on the part of its leaders that it would find sympathy and support from the sister republic across the ocean. The two countries were bound together by the intimate treaties of 1778 and 1788; the United States owed France money, the hastened payment of which would ease her finances; the American merchant marine could be useful to France in many ways and would find such occupation profitable. To announce the new republic, to realize these advantages, to replace the existing treaties by a still closer one, by "a true family compact" on a "liberal and fraternal basis," Edmund C. Genêt, an enthusiastic patriot, only twenty-eight years of age and yet trained for many years in the foreign office under Vergennes, was sent as minister to the United States.[1]

But Genêt was not to be a mere diplomatic representative, as that term is now understood. French ministers during the **Genêt's task** Revolution felt themselves commissioned, not from government to government, but from people to people. They embodied revolution; their functions were unlimited; and in this case Genêt's instructions definitely launched him into colossal enterprises. All America was his province. Miranda was now high in the counsels of the French; Dumouriez wrote to Lebrun, November 30, 1792, of the "superb project of General Miranda" for revolu-

[1] McMaster, *History of the People of the United States* (8 vols., New York, 1883–1913), ii. 89–141.

tionizing Spanish America. The foreign office, however, was somewhat more conservative and more French: "To embrace all at once the immense country which stretches from New Mexico to Chili to make revolutions, is to be willing to lose realities, to occupy oneself with Chimeras. Without doubt these immense possessions will not remain always under the yoke of Spain, but it does not depend upon us to-day to deliver them."

Permanent national interests, however, survive all changes in the form of government. The recovery of Louisiana had been constantly in the mind of the French France and ever since its loss in 1763. No longer ago than Louisiana 1787, indeed, a project for the accomplishment of this end had been presented to the French government. With the new vigor of the Revolution throbbing in her veins France was not likely to forget that she had once had a vast American empire, that tens of thousands of French were living in Louisiana, to say nothing of Canada. On the contrary, the old end was sought with new energy. The recovery of Louisiana was among the duties assigned to Genêt.

His means were to be found in the United States: first, money, which Hamilton was to give in repayment of the French loans; second, an army, which was to Genêt's in- consist of the American frontiersmen, spurred structions by promise of abundant loot and by that persistent motive, the navigation of the Mississippi. The foremost of the frontiersmen, George Rogers Clark, anticipated the desires of France by offering his services. His letter probably reached France before Genêt sailed; at any rate, the latter counted upon him.

Even to the French enthusiasts of 1792 it occurred that this plan of organizing within the United States, and by the resources of the United States, forces to attack Genêt and the Spain, with whom the nation was at peace, United States involved delicate questions. Nor were they unaware that a reaction had taken place in this country, for the foreign office took care to inform Genêt, "The enjoyment of liberty has rendered them [the Americans] more calm, they no longer treat it as lovers but as husbands." He was to be cautious, therefore, in revealing his plans, and the more so in view of the possibilities of the future. Was Louisiana to become free, French, or part of the United States?

France was concerned with the future, not of Louisiana alone, but of all the rest of the West as well. "Nature," France and Genêt was instructed, "has traced the future the West revolutions of North America." It is divided into two parts by the Appalachian Mountains. "The East part is peopled, that of the West is almost not. The climates of the two countries offer as many differences as are found in the interests of the inhabitants. The one direct their speculations toward New Orleans, which will be their only outlet, the other toward the cities established on the borders of the Atlantic sea. . . . This liberty of navigation and the independence of Louisiana will draw into this country an immense population at the expense of the United States. By the progressive growth of this population the schism between the Atlantic states and those of the West will be inevitable. The Americans know it and do their best to delay the epoch." The question might, therefore, he was told, be safely left to time. Louisiana would need French aid, and the West would ultimately join her; but naturally such plans were not for the ears of the American cabinet.

On April 8, 1793, Genêt arrived at Charleston. Welcomed with official sympathy by Governor Moultrie and by popular Genêt's ar- demonstration, he devoted himself, perhaps rival more openly than was intended, to the organization of operations against the enemies of France. Against English commerce he issued a number of privateering commissions (of which he was said to have brought three hundred) to American vessels manned by Americans; and in accordance with a decree of the National Convention, he authorized the French consuls in American ports to act as courts of admiralty for the trial, condemnation, and sale of prizes. The business of these courts was not long in beginning, for unwarned British vessels promptly fell into the hands of the French-commissioned American privateers. Against Spain, he arranged an expedition of southeastern American frontiersmen to attack St. Augustine. To promote the cause of Revolution, he also organized a Jacobin club. Leaving these affairs at Charleston in the hands of the consul, Mangourit, he then started north. In an atmosphere warm with popular sympathy, to which he knew how to respond in a manner piquant and provocative, he rode to Philadelphia, which he reached May 16, prepared to repeat the part which Franklin had sustained in Paris.[1]

On April 8, the day on which Genêt made Charleston, the American cabinet, chilled by the news of the proscription of Lafayette and the beheading of Louis XVI, heard of the war between France and England. They had five weeks for consultation before Genêt would reach the capital. The questions which Washington presented to the members included the following: Whether Genêt should be received; whether the republican authorities should be recognized as the government of France; whether the treaties were still binding, and, if they were, whether the guarantee of the French West Indies was still obligatory; and exactly what the favors granted to the French consuls, war vessels, and privateers involved. The primary question, however, was whether a proclamation of neutrality should be issued, and, if so, what form should be given to it. The answers to these questions brought out clearly the opposing views of Jefferson and Hamilton. Over the validity of the French treaties they were particularly at odds. Jay had already,

Cabinet discussions

Jefferson versus Hamilton

[1] F. J. Turner, "The Origin of Genêt's Projected Attack on Louisiana and the Floridas," *Amer. Hist. Review*, 1898, iii. 650–671; *Correspondence of Clark and Genêt*, Amer. Hist. Assoc., *Report*, 1896, i. 930–1107; *Mangourit Correspondence*, ibid., 1897, pp. 569–679.

in 1788, maintained that the treaty of alliance terminated with the war, that is in 1783, and Hamilton had supported him. The latter now held that the treaty had been made with the government of Louis XVI, and could not be regarded as binding with the new government of France. Jefferson more correctly maintained that a treaty was the action of a nation, not of a government, and therefore survived all changes of form. Madison expressed the same idea in the words, "A nation, by exercising the right of changing the organ of its will, can neither disengage itself from the obligations, nor forfeit the benefit of its treaties." A more promising lever, however, for releasing us from the uncomfortable obligations resulting from the warmth of our relations with France during our own Revolution lay in the disregard, by the new French government, of some of its corresponding obligations; but the facts were not yet sufficiently well ascertained to justify more than a protest. On neutrality all were agreed; nor did its preservation seem to them so difficult as it had at the time of the Nootka Sound affair, for they were as yet in ignorance of the territorial ambitions of France.[1] In this case it seemed to be a problem of the sea alone.

The final decision lay with Washington, and his first step was to issue, on April 19, a proclamation of neutrality. In Proclamation deference to Jefferson's wish, however, the of neutrality word neutrality was omitted, as it was thought that some uncertainty in regard to our position might be of advantage. This document, announcing "a conduct friendly and impartial towards the belligerent powers," and warning all citizens of the United States to avoid hostilities and not to trade with the powers at war in any of "those articles which are deemed contraband by the modern usage of nations," has assumed unique position in the development of American diplomacy. It really represented not merely an

[1] Hamilton, *Works* (ed. H. C. Lodge, 9 vols., New York, etc., 1885–86), iv. 20–135; Jefferson, *Writings* (ed. Ford), vi. 219–231.

intention to keep out of the war then in progress, but also the national determination to resist the centripetal forces of European politics and to be left free to work out our national development. As the first public announcement of this determination, it forms the basis of our most characteristic diplomatic policy.[1]

It was further resolved to receive Genêt, a step which ultimately meant recognition of the French republic. This instance became a precedent, which the United Recognition of States has nearly always followed, for promptly the republic recognizing accomplished changes of government in foreign countries. It is a policy equally consistent with our professed belief in the right of revolution and with the practical common sense which has usually been found in American diplomacy. The other questions at issue were left for future decision. That of the West India guarantee, which Hamilton claimed could not hold in case of an offensive war such as France was then waging against Great Britain even if the treaties were still in force, was soon happily settled by the decision of France not to insist upon it. The validity of the treaties, and their exact bearing upon the neutral rights and duties of the United States, remained topics of controversy until Napoleon cut the knot in 1801.

Genêt was probably more incensed than disappointed by the proclamation, and he was still further angered by his official greeting at Philadelphia, where he was Reception of received by Washington in a room decorated Genêt with medallions of Louis Capet and Marie Antoinette, and with a rather frigid bow in place of the fraternal embrace and kiss symbolic of the Revolution. Hamilton, moreover, courteously explained the impossibility of anticipating in any large way the payment of the French loans, and Genêt was thus left without the financial resources upon which he had relied. Nevertheless, he proceeded with his plans. He

[1] Washington, *Writings* (ed. Ford), xii. 281–282; Moore, *American Diplomacy*, 33–62.

forwarded a commission of commander-in-chief to George
Rogers Clark, and stirred the Kentucky settlements on the
Ohio and those of Tennessee on the Cumberland with the
preparation of flat boats and provisions. On June 19, he
wrote to Lebrun that he was provisioning the West Indies,
inciting the Canadians, arming Kentucky, and preparing
an expedition by sea to assist in the attack on New Orleans.

On July 5 Genêt discreetly unfolded his Louisiana project
to Jefferson. The latter, understanding that the rendezvous
Jefferson and   was to be outside of the United States and
Genêt   that Louisiana was to be independent, expressed indifference, but warned him that the halter would
be the fate of the participants in such an expedition. Nevertheless, he gave a letter to Michaux, who under the guise of
an explorer was to act as French agent in the West, com-
mending him to Governor Shelby of Kentucky.

Meantime Genêt was involved with Jefferson in constant
discussion on questions of neutrality. The treaty with France
Neutrality   declared that in time of war it should not be
                lawful for citizens of other countries "to fit their
ships in the ports of either the one or the other of the aforesaid parties." This certainly forbade the fitting out of
British war vessels in American ports, but Genêt claimed
that by implication it allowed that privilege to the French.
This Jefferson denied; indeed, to have held otherwise would
have meant immediate war with England. Again, the seventeenth article of the treaty of commerce provided that prizes
should not "be arrested or seized when they come to or enter
the ports of either party." Genêt claimed that this conceded
complete jurisdiction over prizes to the French consular
courts, Jefferson, that the United States retained in full the
rights necessary to enforce her own neutrality regulations
in case of captures in violation thereof. Jefferson held that
Americans enlisting in French privateers, were violating our
declared neutrality and should be punished. On this charge
Henfield and Singleterry, Americans enlisted on one of

Genêt's Charleston privateers, were arrested. Genêt protested, "The crime laid to their charge, the crime which my pen almost refuses to state, is the serving of France, and the defending, with her children, the common and glorious cause of liberty."

The inevitable crisis came in July, when *l'Ambuscade*, the French frigate which had brought Genêt, captured within the capes of the Delaware, and hence clearly illegally because within American waters, the British vessel *Little Sarah*, and brought her to Philadelphia. The government ordered her surrender, but instead of complying, Genêt renamed her the *Little Democrat* and fitted her out for a privateer. Brought to task for this by Jefferson, he promised that she should not sail until the matter was adjusted. Nevertheless, she secretly dropped down the river and put to sea, whereupon the government, in a letter of August 23, demanded of France the recall of Genêt.

The Little Democrat

Pending an answer, Genêt remained in the country. A large portion of the press sympathized with France, and attacked the government for its lack of sympathy. Particularly Freneau's *National Gazette* lashed Washington with scorpions, until he doubted whether free government and free speech could coexist. Thus spurred, Genêt resolved to turn from the government to the people, and straightway addressed the President in a letter of bombastic insult which found its way into the newspapers. When Congress came together in December the whole correspondence was submitted to it, and then Genêt found that the Americans had indeed cooled to the passions of liberty. He received some applause but no effective support; even the Democratic societies formed upon the model of the Jacobin club were unwilling to push to extremes.

Genêt's appeal to the people

In February his mission ended. His friends, the Girondists had fallen; and their successors the Jacobins, Danton and Robespierre, were anxious for his head and did not hesitate to recall him. He failed to respond, however, remaining to become a citizen of the United States; but he ceased to be minister and to figure in the national life. As a balm to the Recall of Genêt pride of the republic, France asked the corresponding recall of Gouverneur Morris, since 1792 our minister there. An aristocrat to the finger-tips, Morris had on the whole maintained a commendable impartiality during those two dreadful years in Paris; but his Recall of Morris sympathies with the king and the nobility were well known, and he was not *persona grata* to the French government. The United States, therefore, properly acceded to the request and withdrew him.

On December 31, 1793, Jefferson resigned from the cabinet. The strain of acting as a spokesman of a policy which Retirement of Jefferson came steadily to be directed more and more by Washington in accordance with Hamilton's advice was too great for him, and he was also torn within himself between his sympathy for France and his belief in neutrality. Genêt complained, perhaps not unjustly, that he had an official and a confidential language which widely differed. His service in remaining throughout the Genêt affair, however, cannot be overestimated. The majority still sympathized with France, and the fact that the position of the government had been expounded by a known French sympathizer did much to maintain confidence at home and to present to foreign nations an appearance of national solidarity.

Jefferson was succeeded by Edmund Randolph of Virginia, who as attorney-general had, on the whole, supported him, Randolph and Monroe although he was somewhat aptly described by John Quincy Adams as "a body devoid of weight dragged along by the current of events." To succeed Morris, Washington appointed James Monroe, another friend of Jefferson and an avowed sympathizer with France. He had desired to send Jefferson's leading supporter, Madison, who declined; the pro-French senators had urged Aaron Burr; yet Monroe's appointment was regarded as conciliatory both at home and abroad, and it was hoped that he would inaugurate an era of friendly understanding with France on the basis of absolute neutrality.

Meantime the government was developing the details of its system. News of the still active western preparations reached it, and in March Washington issued a *Enforcement* supplementary proclamation dealing with this *of neutrality* phase of the situation. Governor Shelby expressed his unwillingness to act under a proclamation against "men whom he considered as friends and brethren," in behalf of the king of Spain, whom he viewed as "an enemy and a tyrrant"; but General Wayne, by occupying a strategic position at the junction of the Cumberland and the Ohio, succeeded in separating Clark's Kentucky and Tennessee forces. Whether the government could have held its own had the issue been forced, is a question; but at least it showed vigor and purpose. In regard to the ocean still greater energy was exhibited. The only advantage allowed to the French over the English, as a result of the treaties, was that the former were allowed to sell prizes in American ports and the latter were not. Thus far the enforcement of neutrality had been wholly by executive discretion; but there was some criticism that this had been stretched too far, and the courts had in some instances refused to enforce executive orders. The government's position was therefore strengthened when, June 5, 1794, Congress passed our first neutrality act.

This law made all persons entering the service of any foreign state, or enlisting others in such service, liable to a fine of $1,000 and three years' imprisonment; *Neutrality law* it likewise made punishable the fitting out, *of 1794* or increasing the armament, of any foreign ship or cruiser. The government's good faith was further indicated by the appropriation of eighty thousand dollars for the purposes of enforcement. This act, taken in connection with the president's proclamations and the rules adopted by the cabinet on August 3, 1793, "as to the equipment of vessels in the ports of the United States by belligerent powers," was important not only in establishing the American policy, but also in developing the general principles of international law. The American position represented the most advanced views of the day in regard to the obligations of neutrals, and its practice far exceeded that of any other nation up to that time.

Fortunately, the attitude of France was for the moment complaisant. Genêt was succeeded by a commission of which Fauchet's mission J. A. J. Fauchet was chief with the title of minister, its instructions being dated November 25, 1793, at the very abyss of French fortunes. Hostile armies, insurrections, and famine were pressing in upon the new republic. Genêt's actions were disavowed, the western plans were given up, and American neutrality was recognized. France was, in short, coming to an appreciation of the fact that American neutrality was one of her strongest assets. The chief need was food, and the carrying of provisions in neutral American vessels was the chief concern of the commissioners. Desirable as such provisions were for the famine-stricken capital, they were a matter of absolute necessity for the West Indian colonies of France. Fauchet wrote, February 4, 1795: "You recall, Citizen, that when the legation was sent, the Republic was in danger. We saw in the United States a point useful for our provisioning which caused us not a little alarm, and other political interests were entirely subordinated to this powerful consideration." In the same letter he wrote: "'The force of things,' said Mr. Jefferson, 'delivers the French colonies to us; France enjoys the sovereignty, we the profit.' Mr. Jefferson thought justly," he went on. "Colonies which America can cast into famine in time of war . . . must form close bonds with a people which can from fortnight to fortnight satisfy their needs. . . . France has to fear for her colonies." To assist in this emergency Hamilton did advance some money not yet due. Monroe was welcomed in France with lively satisfaction, and for the moment cordiality reigned.[1]

The Genêt episode, therefore, passed. It had threatened to drag the United States into the general war of Europe either directly through sympathetic attraction for France, or indirectly by the use of her soil, *Close of the episode* citizens, and waters for the military purposes of that country. It had threatened to divide the United States into two warring factions. Instead, it left her resolute in the possession of a well-developed policy, and still presenting a united front to a divided Europe.

[1] F. J. Turner, *Correspondence of the French Ministers to the United States, 1791–1797*, Amer. Hist. Assoc., *Report*, 1903, vol. ii.

CHAPTER X

THE JAY TREATY

WHILE relations with France were thus assuming a quiet tone, a new episode was taking shape. In 1793 it seemed that Changed con- we might be stampeded into war with England ditions by our French sympathies; in 1794 it looked as if England might force us into war by her aggressions. In 1793 it was a question of our obligations as neutrals, in 1794 of our rights as neutrals.

The trade between France and her West India colonies constituted perhaps two-thirds of her sea-borne commerce. The French It provided France with her breakfast,—coffee, West Indies sugar, and chocolate. In return, France supplied not only manufactured goods, but also, until the demoralization of agriculture in 1793, grain. The French fishermen of Brittany, moreover, caught on the banks of Newfoundland the short cod and mackerel which fed the slaves of San Domingo, Guadaloupe, and Martinique, while the best were taken across the ocean to serve the lenten fare of the French at home. Should these branches of trade be cut off, it would cause financial loss and inconvenience in France, it would cause starvation in the colonies. In fact, the Revolution increased the needs of trade, since for a time France ceased to be able to feed herself and so became an importer of foodstuffs.

The protection of this trade was the underlying function of the French navy. While, however, the French fleet was strong and efficient, it was less powerful than that of Neutral trade England. Except in the war of the American Revolution, when it joined forces with Spain, it proved unequal to the task, and direct trade in French vessels was generally in time of war so insecure as to be impracticable. To meet this situation, it had been the custom of France in such emergencies to open the colonial trade to neutral nations, and the Dutch, protected by their English treaties, had enjoyed the lion's share. The natural convenience of the American granaries, however, the hunger of San Domingo, and the seamanship and commercial spirit of the American colonists often overcame the obstacles of legality and enmity. During the Seven Years' war colonial vessels laden with grain often dropped down to the vicinity of the French islands, and, by collusion with the authorities, allowed themselves to be captured, their cargoes being ostensibly seized but actually paid for.[1]

For these precarious advantages the new war promised to substitute a legal and extensive trade. Almost simultaneously with the declaration of hostilities France opened her colonial ports. The Dutch no longer had their treaties with England; in fact, they may scarcely be said to have had a merchant marine. To the Americans, therefore, possessing as they did the world's most important neutral marine, was offered the opportunity not only of provisioning the islands, but of serving as intermediaries between the colonies and the mother country, in addition to supplying the latter with provisions. Our merchants were quick to take advantage of the situation. They carried our products to the islands, exchanged them for island products, and carried the latter to France, or brought them back to the United States and then took or sent them to France. In 1791 we exported 2,000,000 pounds of coffee and 1,200,000 pounds of sugar; in 1793, 34,000,000 pounds of coffee and 18,000,000 pounds of sugar. Merchants throve, ship-owners turned their capital with unprecedented rapidity, shipyards were pressed to complete

The United States and the French West Indies

---

[1] T. L. Stoddard, *The French Revolution in San Domingo* (Boston, 1914); A. T. Mahan, *Influence of Sea Power upon the French Revolution and Empire, 1793-1812* (10th ed., 2 vols., Boston, 1898), vol. i. ch. iv., vol. ii. chs. vii.-viii.

new vessels, sailmakers and ropemakers were busy; farmers opened new fields to supply the demand for grain, salt pork, hemp, butter, and other staple articles; fishermen enlarged their ventures and their catches to supply what the Bretons could no longer furnish. In part, but not mainly, the sympathy for France was due to the general prosperity which resulted from the outbreak of hostilities.

To England the situation was doubly distasteful, first because it was of advantage to France, and second because **English attitude** it served to build up the American merchant marine, the only one, since the fall of the Dutch, which endangered the supremacy of her commercial fleet, upon which rested her naval power, her colonies, and her wealth. Her navy was of little use to her if American vessels, in an impenetrable armor of neutrality, could serve all the customary routes of French commerce. It was not thus that the first Pitt had made commerce flourish by means of war. England had never shown a disposition to stand passive before an international opinion, which had been formulated by Dutch publicists, was without the backing of effective force, and could hardly be dignified by the name of international law. She had rather, as a result of her experience, devised a variety of practices which furnished her navy with weapons as effective against neutrals as against enemies, and she was prepared to use them.

The first of these was the principle that enemies' goods at sea might be seized and confiscated even when carried in **"Free ships, free goods"** neutral ships. There was a growing sentiment that "free ships" should make "free goods." This had been one of the declarations of the Armed Neutrality, and was embodied in all the commercial treaties of the United States. England's practice, however, was the older, and she refused to recognize the new idea as having the force of law. Neutrals could escape the consequences of her rule by becoming the actual owners of the cargo, but to do so involved a large capital. Such a purchase, moreover, was looked upon as collusive; hence, being subject to examination in the English admiralty courts, the practice involved no little risk.

A second difference in England's policy had reference to contraband. It was universally admitted that for a neutral to carry war material to a belligerent was law- Contraband less, and justified the seizure of the material in question, the freight, and possibly the ship itself. There was, however, disagreement as to what constituted war material. The weaker maritime powers thought that the term should be narrowly interpreted; England, on the contrary, except when bound by treaty, as in the case of Russia, held for a broad interpretation. On June 8, 1793, she issued an order in council authorizing the seizure of "all ships laden with corn, flour, or meal." This measure she defended as being not only within her rights but in retaliation for a similar French decree of May. The French claimed that their decree had been of a special rather than a general character and had already been withdrawn when the British order had been issued. Failing to secure the withdrawal of the latter, the French in July renewed their decree, and provisions became seizable by both parties. In September, however, the British ordered that provisions so seized be paid for and the vessels released. The provision trade continued to grow, but its fortunes were checkered and its success a gamble. It should be observed that while Great Britain and France were ostensibly pursuing the same policy, it was, of course, the British navy which made the most seizures and won the most hatred.

Another point upon which England maintained a position at variance with that of most nations was regarding blockade. All nations recognized that a vessel endeavor- Blockade ing to enter a port publicly blockaded incurred the risk of capture and confiscation. The continental school of international law held that in such cases the blockade must be properly announced, and that it must be effectively maintained off the actual port. England upheld what her enemies derisively called the "Paper Blockade," to the effect that a considerable area of coast might be blockaded by a single fleet cruising along it, and that the rule might be enforced upon any vessel, anywhere, whose papers indicated that it was destined for one of the blockaded harbors. In accordance with this policy, England in 1793 blockaded numerous West Indian ports.

In addition to these interpretations of general principles, England had another rule adapted to meet the special case "Rule of 1756" of the French West India islands. Announced by an order in council of 1756, it is known as the "Rule of 1756." Briefly, it meant that, when a nation closed its colonies to other nations in time of peace, it had no right to open them in time of war, and that, if it did, all such commerce was liable to seizure. English instructions of November 6, 1793, ordered naval officers to "stay and detain all ships laden with goods the produce of any colony belonging to France, or carrying provisions or other supplies for the use of any such colony, and" to "bring the same, with their cargoes, to legal adjudication in our courts of admiralty." This instruction was modified January 8, 1794, in such a way as to leave open the trade between the United States and unblockaded ports in the West Indies, in articles not contraband and not of French ownership. The goods thus introduced into the United States might then be shipped to unblockaded ports in France. The West Indian trade was thus not destroyed, but it was hampered. Moreover, one hundred and fifty American vessels had been seized under the first instruction, and in the spring of 1794 were condemned by the admiralty courts of various British West India Islands.

It is obvious that a British war vessel cruising in the open sea had many questions to ask of any merchantman it met. The display of a flag was not sufficient answer; in fact, the standard of morality concerning the use of national emblems at sea has never been high. In such cases international law permits the war vessel to "visit" the merchantman to examine her papers. It was unquestionably true **" Visit " and** that these papers often failed to tell the whole **" search "** story: the port of destination was frequently given falsely, and the captain often took on questionable cargo after the clearance papers had been made out. The British, therefore, claimed the right to "search" the cargo. This privilege the United States and most other powers strenuously denied. On this point America was perhaps in worse case than other countries, for their merchant vessels often sailed in fleets under convoy of a war vessel, which assumed responsibility, whereas we had no navy, and our commerce was too scattered to allow such concentration.[1]

Such searches, moreover, brought up another vexed point of dispute which was peculiarly our own, and which waxed constantly in importance until it overshadowed all **Impressments** the rest. It is only by an appreciation of the rock-bottomed belief of Englishmen that everything which they held sacred rested upon their fleet, that we can comprehend the spectacle of a people, on the verge of the nineteenth century, submitting to the "press." Every British-born subject was bound to serve the nation, if the fleet needed men. British war vessels, if short-handed, might stop any British vessel and take off such sailors as it needed, leaving only the absolute minimum number required for navigation. In their searches of American vessels, British officers often saw British subjects aiding to build up a merchant marine which, if not indeed belligerent, was, they believed, sapping the strength of Great Britain. In such cases they took them off. Misled by similarities of language and appearance, they sometimes took native Americans. Such instances were more annoying than serious, for the Americans were returned when nationality was proved,—a matter, to

[1] Mahan, *Sea Power in its Relations to the War of 1812* (2 vols., Boston, 1905), i. 42–99.

be sure, of delay and sometimes of difficulty, owing to our lax methods of registration. More often they took British-born subjects who had been naturalized in the United States. In such instances the chasm of misunderstanding was unbridgable. England claimed that a man British-born could never expatriate himself; whereas the United States held that all her citizens, native and naturalized, stood upon the same basis and were equally entitled to protection.

When one remembers that the British naval officers were spurred in the performance of their duties by the distribution among them of the major portion of the proceeds of the prizes they captured, and that nearly every little British West India island had its own prize court, often incompetent and sometimes venal, at least to the extent of preferring a condemnation with fees to an acquittal without them, one sees that the opportunities for friction were countless. Added to all these considerations was a maladroit action of the British government, as a result of which the Portuguese fleet, which customarily guarded the straits of Gibraltar, was in the summer of 1793 withdrawn from that duty. Algerian corsairs now dashed out into the Atlantic, and by the end of the year ten American vessels had fallen into their hands. The final pitch of excitement was reached when, in March, 1794, came the reports of the speech of Lord Dorchester, the governor general of Canada and just back from London, to the Canadian Indians, predicting war with the United States and bidding them prepare.

As news of one unfriendly act after another reached America, excitement increased day by day. Congress was in session, and in the spring of 1794 came to be divided between those who hoped for and those who dreaded a war with Great Britain. Fisher Ames, an ardent sympathizer with England, wrote, March 26: "The English are absolutely madmen. Order in this country is endangered by their hostility, no less than by the French friendship. They act, on almost every point, against their interests and their real wishes." The House voted to suspend commercial intercourse with Great Britain until restitution should be made, but by the assistance of the Senate, the administration was enabled to carry out its own less belligerent policy. A general embargo was passed, on the ground that the seas were unsafe for American shipping; the first steps were taken in the construction of a navy; and, most important of all, a final solemn embassy was sent to Great Britain to present the case of the United States and demand satisfaction.[1]

For this task the chief justice, John Jay, was chosen. It seems to have been felt that, since in Monroe a friendly minister had been sent to France, so an English sympathizer should be sent to England. **Jay's mission** Hamilton was distrusted by the Republicans. Jay had more experience than any other American except Adams, who was disliked by many Federalists; but even Jay was attacked because of his Mississippi proposal of 1786. He was now instructed to adjust all the multifarious difficulties growing out of the treaty of 1783, particularly the continued occupation of the posts by the British. He was to arrange a treaty of commerce. He was to secure compensation for seizures of American vessels, and agreements concerning impressments, blockades, and other points of international law. On these latter points he was to accept no settlement except along the line of his instructions, which in each case laid down the American view of the matter. With this heavy burden, and weighted down with the sense of his responsibility to prevent a war which he felt to be almost inevitable, Jay set sail for England.

The "madness" of England was twofold. In so far as it related to her principles of maritime conduct, it was basic, four-square with her conceptions of national safety. From

[1] Trescot, W. H., *The Diplomatic History of the Administrations of Washington and Adams* (Boston, 1857), chs. ii.–iv.

these she would not move while a war-ship was afloat. Her vexatious conduct in other matters, however, was very England's largely connected with her belief that war with "madness" the United States was sure to come. Equally unable with France to understand the American desire for isolation, she felt that France would ultimately win our alliance.

Her greatest anxiety was in regard to the West. The Northwestern Indians still called upon her for support against English appre- the Americans, and threatened to turn on hensions Great Britain if aid was refused. The fur-traders were more distressed than before, because of the discovery that the source of the Mississippi probably lay south of the Lake of the Woods, a circumstance that rendered the British right to navigate that river worthless. To meet both difficulties, Hammond had in 1792 urged the formation of an Indian buffer state to stretch everywhere between the United States and Canada, or at least to include the country northwest of the Ohio. This means of settlement was then rejected by the Americans, even in spite of the sting of St. Clair's recent defeat; and now, in 1794, the situation was in their favor. Wayne's army, which seemed to the Americans a valiant David going into the wilderness to meet the Goliath of Indians and British, was known by the latter to be larger than the combined British forces in all the posts, and seemed to loom menacingly over all British America. England's real efforts to bring about peace between the Indians and the Americans had caused both to be suspicious; and the mistake of a subordinate had furnished the United States with a new grievance by the establishment of the fort on the Maumee. Finally, Lord Dorchester's speech to the Canadian Indians, which had been made public, had roused the hope of the Indians on American soil, while hardening the American distrust into conviction. In the early summer of 1794, therefore, Pitt and his foreign minister, Lord Gren-ville, feared that there could be no escape from a clash on the frontier which would bring the United States into the war.[1] Nor did England want war. From the abyss of November, 1793, France was emerging triumphant; her armies and Revolution were everywhere advancing. The first coalition against her was falling to pieces.

Jay, therefore, was warmly welcomed when he reached England. In estimating his chances of success, one feels that he was under some psychological dis- Jay and Gren-advantage. His mere arrival reassured Lord ville Grenville, who was at once convinced that a treaty could be made, and who even anticipated that the United States, recoiling from France, might actually join England. Jay, on the other hand, was to the end fearful lest no treaty could be arranged and that war would result. Throughout the negotiations the fortunes of France rose higher, and in the midst of them came news of Wayne's victory over the Indians. Of this international situation Jay, trembling for his treaty, seems to have taken no advantage.

The treaty which was signed on November 19, 1794, was most comprehensive. It embodied for the first time two principles since then common in American Settlement of diplomacy.[2] The settlement of many vexed the treaty of points it left to commissions authorized to 1783 determine results by judicial or semi-judicial process, and it provided for the mutual extradition of persons "charged with murder and forgery." The difficulties arising out of the treaty of 1783 were compromised, but to the advantage of the United States. Great Britain agreed to evacuate the posts on or before June 1, 1796. A commission provided to determine what river was intended to be described as the "St. Croix" on the northeast boundary ultimately accepted

[1] Unpublished thesis on the Jay treaty, by Orpha Leavitt; also *Dropmore Papers*, ii.

[2] For this and all subsequent instances of arbitration, to 1897, see J. B. Moore, *History and Digest of International Arbitrations*, 6 vols., Washington, 1898 (House Misc. Doc., 53 Cong. 2 sess., No. 212). In every case this work gives an admirable sketch of the origin and settlement of the dispute.

the river now known by that name, although an additional convention of 1798 was required to determine its source. A commission was to ascertain the source of the Mississippi, which, however, failed in its object. Another commission was to adjudicate on the question of the pre-revolutionary debts due to British merchants, of which the United States was to assume the obligation. Difficulties arising on this subject, a new convention became necessary in 1802, and ultimately we had to pay something over two million and a half dollars. The question of compensation by the United States to loyalists was dropped, and also that of indemnity by Great Britain for slaves carried away in 1783, a demand which we based on the general provision for the mutual restoration of property. It is probable that Jay might have obtained the latter point, had he forced the issue.[1]

A commission was also charged with the settlement of claims by British merchants because of the failure of the United States to perform properly her neutral Settlement for violations of neutrality duties during 1793, and of those by American merchants because of "irregular or illegal captures or condemnations" by the British in violation of our neutral rights. After many delays, this commission awarded American claimants nearly six million dollars and British claimants about one hundred and fifty thousand.

A permanent commercial provision in the treaty allowed trade from Vermont to Montreal and Quebec, and freedom Commercial clauses of trade with the Indian tribes across the border, except in the Hudson Bay region,— reciprocal advantages. For a limited time the British East Indian trade was opened to Americans. That of the West Indies, so long and earnestly desired, was made free to American vessels of seventy tons' burden,—that is, those that were too small to cross the ocean and so were confined to direct voyages. This provision, however, was bound up with a

[1] F. A. Ogg, *Jay's Treaty and the Slavery Interests of the United States,* Amer. Hist. Assoc., *Report,* 1901, i. 273–298.

promise on the part of the United States to refrain from "carrying any molasses, sugar, coffee, cocoa, or cotton in American vessels, either from His Majesty's islands or from the United States" to any country except the United States, a promise that was an utterly inexcusable error on the part of Jay, for in the case of cotton it forbade us to export our own products in our own vessels. The Senate cut this article from the treaty, and trade with the British West Indies remained subject to temporary regulations. Between England herself and the United States commerce and navigation were to be for twelve years on the basis of the most favored nation.

Jay was soon and properly convinced that he could not obtain a recognition of the American position on any points of international law. In the event of such an International emergency he had been instructed to conclude practices nothing on the subject. He felt, however, that minor modifications of the English position and definite understandings would be advantageous; and he had always been accustomed to break instructions. He therefore concluded articles, to last twelve years, admitting that provisions might in some cases be contraband although they should be paid for, and that enemies' goods on neutral vessels might be seized. Article xvii. provided that due notice of blockade should be given, but said nothing of "paper" blockades; article xxiv. forbade "foreign" privateers to sell prizes in the ports of either party; article xxv. admitted British prizes to American harbors; but these articles were not to be construed in such a way as to violate any previous treaty, the fact being that they apparently clashed with our treaties with France.

Once signed, the Jay treaty began a series of adventures that remind one of a Baron Munchausen tale. Not till June, 1795, did it reach America. The Senate, Acceptance by promptly called in special session, ratified it the Senate June 24, with the exception of the West Indian article. For a time it was doubtful what the effect of such partial ratification would be; but in the end England accepted the change, and a precedent was established which has many times been followed. Meanwhile the treaty itself had been kept secret, but a copy was presently furnished to the press by Senator Mason of Virginia. Instantly there followed an outburst of popular indignation which swept from one end of the country to the other, and for a moment united all classes of the population. Jay, according to the cheerful custom of the day, was burned in effigy, and Hamilton, who attempted to defend him, was stoned.

While the popular tumult was raging, Washington was at Mount Vernon, deferring his signature. He chafed at Jay's disregard for his instructions, and was disturbed over a new British order for the seizure of provisions, which, the United States claimed, was not warranted by circumstances. Randolph, the secretary of state, was urging that he withhold his signature altogether. At this juncture the sea once more gave up its prey, this time dispatches of Fauchet thrown overboard to avoid capture by the British but secured by their sailors. One of these, No. 10, which Hammond handed to Hamilton, referred to the "precious confessions" of Randolph disclosed in a previous letter, No. 6. Despite the subsequent publication of the latter, with a letter of explanation by Fauchet and a *Vindication* by Randolph, the exact nature of these precious confessions remains unproved. Randolph and Fauchet claimed that they had to do with internal affairs, the Whiskey Rebellion in particular. From the internal evidence, however, John Quincy Adams concluded, and not without some force, that they had reference to the enforcement of neutrality. At all events, that there was revealed an amazing condition of confidential intercourse between the secretary of state and a foreign minister, is undoubted. This circumstance, to be sure, appears less remarkable in view of later revelations of the astonishing intimacy of Hamilton, secretary of the treasury, and other Federalists, with the British minister; but there is this difference, that Randolph en-

deavored to obtain money from Fauchet, a fact which turns
his indiscretion into moral obliquity.[1]

At any rate, Washington considered that the new situation demanded immediate action, and decided to sign the
treaty in spite of his dissatisfaction with it.   Washington
With a grimness closely allied with humor, he signs the
ordered Randolph to complete a protest to   treaty
Great Britain at the seizure of provisions, and, when it was
completed, showed him the dispatch.   Randolph at once resigned, and, after a succession of attempts to bring in some
notable personage, was replaced by Timothy Pickering, a decided partisan of England, a man able and honest, but without poise.

Not even yet was the treaty safe. It called for the appointment of commissioners and the appropriation of money, and
the latter must come by vote of the House of   The House ac-
Representatives.   Should the appropriation   cepts the
fail, the treaty could not be executed. All the   treaty
forces hostile to England, favorable to France, and opposed
to the administration and the treaty, rallied for a final struggle. The year before Fisher Ames had said of certain resolutions that they had French stamped on their face, and Parker
of Virginia had replied that he wished everybody had a stamp
on his forehead to show whether he was for France or Great
Britain. Now the feeling was even more intense. The House,
led by Edward Livingston, demanded that it be furnished
with copies of the papers in the case. This request Washington refused. It could not force him, nor could he force it.
He could refuse the papers, but it was more important that
the House could refuse the money. The debate became the
leading question of the session. On the whole the treaty
gained support as the commercial classes came to accept
Washington's view, that, although the treaty was not a

[1] Edmund Randolph, *Vindication of Mr. Randolph's Resignation*, Philadelphia, 1795; M. D. Conway, *Omitted Chapters of History, disclosed in the
Life and Papers of Edmund Randolph*, New York, etc., 1888.

good one, the existing choice lay not between it and a better one, but between it and war. This view was most forcibly expressed by Fisher Ames in the greatest speech till then made in Congress; and at length, on April 30, 1796, the appropriation was passed and the treaty became an established fact.[1]

The Jay treaty worked more satisfactorily than was expected. Grenville had promised Jay some concessions not formally mentioned, and these were fulfilled. The admiralty courts in the West Indies were reorganized and made respectable. Hammond was replaced by Liston, who proved to be somewhat more pleasing personally. From 1796, moreover, in spite of the excision of the West Indian article from the treaty, that trade was thrown open to American vessels under certain limitations. Best of all was the quieting effect on the northern frontier. Vermont was relieved by the opening of trade to Montreal, the national power was vindicated by the occupation of the whole national territory, and with the Jay treaty added to Wayne's treaty of 1795 came sixteen years of comparative peace with the Indians. On September 8, 1796, the British consul, Bond, wrote to Lord Grenville that the treaty had a "tendency to retain this infant country in a state of peace with the most powerful empire in the universe."

Working of the treaty

The effect of the Jay treaty was not confined to the relations between the United States and Great Britain. The document was observed by all the cabinets of Europe with varying emotions, but everywhere from the point of view of the obsession that the United States must be upon one side or the other. If she had rejected the overtures of France and made a treaty with England, it must mean that she was to be counted on the side of England. Nowhere was the effect so immediate and pronounced as in Spain.[2]

European opinion

---

[1] S. B. Crandall, *Treaties, their Making and Enforcement*, New York, 1904.
[2] C. C. Pinckney, *Thomas Pinckney*, Boston, etc., 1895; Schuyler, *American Diplomacy*, 271–281.

Important as were the questions at issue with that country, no progress had been made in solving them. In part this was due to the inadequacy, nearly always Relations with Spain characteristic, of our representation at that court. Carmichael exhibited a nonchalance that excites suspicions as to his good intent. His industrious successor, Short, was *persona non grata*. At length, in August, 1794, Spain distinctly declared that "at least His Majesty expected that the ministers appointed by the United States should bo poroono of such character, distinction, and temper as would become a residence near his royal person."

Meantime Spain had continued her various policies, keeping on good terms with the Indians and bribing Wilkinson. In 1794 Gayoso had hopes of Kentucky, but Spanish policies feared that, if the settlers there knew of the Spanish relations with the Indians, they would, instead of continuing their negotiations, "become our most cruel enemies." Washington wrote in September, 1794: "Spain by a similar conduct to that of Great Britain has imposed the necessity of sending an envoy extraordinary to her. They coöperate; cordial in their hatred, they have agreed to employ the Indians against us."

The envoy selected was Thomas Pinckney, the resident minister at London, whose position was perhaps rendered slightly invidious in consequence of Jay's mis- Pinckney's mission sion. The attitude of Spain always varied with the changes in European conditions. By her defeats of 1794 she had been forced to turn from England to France; the treaty of Basle, July 22, 1795, revived the old "family" alliance, although the dynastic situation had so tragically changed. It was in this new condition that news of the Jay treaty found Spain. Her court, believing that it meant the alliance of the United States and Great Britain, saw in imagination irresistible forces descending upon her frail defences in Louisiana and attacking the mines of Mexico. Although convinced of the necessity of coming to terms, her ministers could not shake off their constitutional habits of delay, until on October 24, 1795, Pinckney announced his immediate departure for London. His bluff was successful, and on October 27 the treaty of San Lorenzo was signed.

As the first treaty between United States and Spain, it laid down the general rules of intercourse upon liberal terms. Treaty of San Lorenzo In regard to neutral rights it provided that provisions should not be contraband of war, and that free ships make free goods. Until 1794 the Spanish fleet had coöperated with that of Great Britain, and had acted upon somewhat the same principles. To settle questions arising from this conduct, a commission was arranged for, which came to an end in 1800 after having awarded over three hundred thousand dollars to American claimants. But these questions were of less interest than those relating to boundaries and the use of the Mississippi. As to the former, Spain accepted the American contention, the thirty-first parallel, and agreed to evacuate her posts in the disputed region. She opened the navigation of the Mississippi to the Americans, and engaged that for three years New Orleans was to serve them as a "place of deposit" with the right to export their goods therefrom free of duty. "And His Majesty promises either to continue this permission, if he finds during that time that it is not prejudicial to the interests of Spain, or if he should not agree to continue it there, he will assign to them on another part of the banks of the Mississippi an equivalent establishment."

With the prompt ratification of this favorable treaty, Washington could indeed feel that the new government had Success of the national government justified itself to the people as their representative before the world. The diplomatic problems that had helped cause the fall of the Confederation had all been solved. Commercial treaties had been made with Spain and Great Britain. If the latter had not permanently opened her West India islands, at any rate they were open now. The Indians north and south had been quieted. Outlets had been obtained down the St. Lawrence to Montreal and Quebec, and down the Mississippi to the Gulf of Mexico. The occupation of the entire national territory had been provided for. In addition, the policy of national independence from European disputes had been effectively laid down, the worst irregularities of belligerent interference with our commerce had been done away with, and compensation for our losses provided for. If these settlements were not all to prove permanent, at least they established precedents which we were steadily gaining added strength to enforce. For many of these suc- *Washington's* cesses Washington could take personal credit, *influence* over and above that of choosing the men who accomplished them. The Indian policy was peculiarly his own. His selection from the various alternatives proposed by Hamilton and Jefferson for handling the Genêt affair made the policy adopted essentially his. In view of the conflicting forces within him and without, his decision to sign the Jay treaty was a great act which proved to be a wise one. Finally in his farewell address he gave the policy of neutrality a consecration in the minds of the people which still persists. The points on which he might have done better were comparatively minor. He was able to retire in March, 1797, not, to be sure, leaving all problems solved, but having settled all those, except the opening of the Mediterranean, that he was chosen to deal with, and more.

CHAPTER XI

WAR AND PEACE WITH FRANCE

THE Jay treaty, which settled so many of our difficulties,
served to intensify those with France. That country, in
Permanent   addition to a continued insistence on the execu-
French policies tion of the treaties of 1778 and 1788, was pressing two lines of policy which animated her diplomacy throughout the period of her final struggle with England. One
was the claim, which gradually took clearer and clearer form,
that the rights of the neutral were the possession of the belligerent. She held that it was the duty of the United States
to maintain in full her neutral rights against England, that
the failure to do so constituted practical alliance with England and justified retaliatory disregard of neutral rights by
France. Her second policy was the attempt to destroy English trade by attacking her commerce, "to force the English
to a shameful bankruptcy." John Quincy Adams wrote,
August 21, 1796: "But the French Government are evi-
dently making their preparations to put in execution their
singular plan of war against Britain, the season ensuing.
That they will succeed in cutting off the communication
between that island and all the rest of Europe, is not at all
impossible." [1]

The mission of Monroe had been accepted as an indica-
tion of regard for France. He had been publicly and en-
Monroe in   thusiastically received by the convention in
France   August, 1794, and had pleased it by his response. "America and France," he said in effect, "have
the same interests and principles, the recollection of common

[1] Volume ii. of his *Writings* (ed. W. C. Ford, New York, 1913, etc.) throws
much light on this period.

dangers and difficulties will cement the union. The United States is sincerely attached to the liberty, prosperity, and happiness of the French Republic. I know that in perpetuating the harmony between the two republics, I shall promote the interests of both." Nor had the mission of Jay as explained by Monroe caused any alarm, for he was sent to assert American neutral rights.[1] The French believed that he would be unsuccessful and that his mission would result in war with England.

Under these circumstances Monroe had been successful in obtaining some useful concessions. In July, 1795, the retaliatory decree of France making English French friend- goods in American vessels seizable was re- liness pealed. "It is amidst her triumphs that the Republic loves to give this striking mark of its fidelity. Victorious France knows no other concern than that of justice; no other diplomatic language than that of truth." P. A. Adet, who arrived in America in June, 1795, to replace Fauchet, had received most amicable instructions. Monroe had even encouraged France to hope for a loan from the United States, and had urged it on our government alleging that France was fighting our battles.

The news of the signature of the Jay treaty alarmed France, and the Committee of Public Safety turned to Monroe for information as to its details; but The Jay treaty since, as the result of a policy rather difficult in France to account for, he had been left uninformed by Jay and by the United States government, he could give only vague assurances that the compact was not inconsistent with our obligations to France. Confident rumor, however, speedily detailed its terms, and a copy of the treaty itself, sent by Adet, reached France in the summer of 1795. Monroe and the French leaders equally were stunned. Instead of vindicating the status of neutrality laid down in our treaties with

[1] James Monroe, *A View of the Conduct of the Executive in the Foreign Affairs of the United States*, Philadelphia, 1797.

France, it accepted a totally different status, permitting to
England practices against which we had protested in the
case of France. The English had just touched France to the
quick by their second order for the seizure of provisions as
contraband, and it was seen that they were justified by the
new treaty. Monroe was unable to meet the situation. In
February, 1796, France declared her alliance with the United
States at an end. On July 2, 1796, a decree of the French
executive Directory announced that France would treat
neutrals as England did, and actually went further by declaring all goods destined for England contraband. In November, Adet announced to the American government that
he had been ordered to terminate his mission.

On August 22, 1796, the American government had recalled Monroe and appointed in his place Charles Cotes-
worth Pinckney. Monroe's recall was due
partly to his failure to press American claims
in all cases to the satisfaction of the government; particularly
the claim for compensation for captures under the decrees
ordering the seizure of English goods in American vessels and
making provisions contraband, both of them in violation of
the treaty of 1778, but defended by France on the basis of
retaliation. Still more was his recall due to the general tone
of his correspondence, which constituted a protest against the
policy of his own country and a defence of France. It may
be said, however, that he did secure more concessions from
France than Jay could obtain from England, and that he
had been instructed to cultivate French friendship. He was
undoubtedly indiscreet, but part of the blame must be laid
to the policy of sending in such a delicate crisis a minister
known to be out of touch with his superiors. The most
serious fault of Monroe was his conduct after he became ac-
quainted with the details of Jay's treaty, and still more after
his own recall. In close touch with the French leaders,
he impressed upon them the difference, which they were
only too prone to believe, between the government of the

United States and the people. He acknowledged that the
government was hostile to France, but he urged them to wait
for justice until after the next presidential election, which
he was sure would bring Jefferson into the presidency. He
assisted in destroying that impression of national solidarity
for which Washington had labored so hard, and which Jefferson
himself had confirmed by his correspondence with Genêt.

France and Monroe were not without some justification
for believing that the existing American government was
not only anti-French but to some degree pro-English. Washington, indeed, remained impartially American, but he had been forced to
give up his vision of an administration comprehending all
parties. His assistants were Federalists, and they sympathized with England. In 1796 Thomas Pinckney was replaced at London by an ardent English partisan, Rufus King.
In 1797 John Quincy Adams was commissioned to reframe
our treaties with Prussia and Sweden, of which the first had
expired and the other was about to expire. He was instructed
by Pickering to leave out the former provisions regarding
free ships, free goods. "It is a principle," wrote Pickering,
"that the United States have adopted in all their treaties
(except that with Great Britain), and which they sincerely
desire might become universal: but treaties formed for this
object they find to be of little or no avail, because the principle
is not universally admitted among the maritime nations." He was also to enlarge the definition of contraband.
Against these changes in the American policy, showing so
marked a leaning to the English practice, Adams vigorously
protested, but his instructions remained unchanged. Although such details were not generally known, the atmosphere of the administration became increasingly hostile to
France.

Under these circumstances the French government took
occasion to show its friendliness for Monroe upon his withdrawal as minister. It refused to receive his successor,

Pro-English policy in the United States

Pinckney, and on February 3, 1797, ordered him to leave the country. Although it withdrew Adet from his mission, it allowed him to remain in the United States in the hope that he might influence the presidential election of 1796. Adet announced his withdrawal in a letter which he published in the press, explaining it not as "a rupture between France and the United States, but as a mark of just discontent, which was to last until the government of the United States returned to sentiments and to measures more conformable to the interests of the alliance; and to the sworn friendship between the two nations." His interference was perhaps not without some weight, but it did not secure the election of Jefferson. John Adams was chosen to the presidency, and the officials as well as the policy of the old administration bade fair to be continued for at least four years more.[1]

France and the election of 1796

Hopeless of American friendship, France turned with more energy toward other plans. In February, 1795, Fauchet had in a long letter advised that the only way of offsetting the effects of the Jay treaty, of which he did not then know the details, was by the acquisition of Louisiana. That colony could feed the islands and so wrench them free from their dependence on the United States. This familiar policy France determined to pursue. With Spain as an ally, cession and not capture must be the method. Accordingly, the French commissioners for the treaty of Basle were instructed, "The restitution of Louisiana is of all the conditions we have proposed the one to which we attach the greatest importance." Failing at that time, France instructed General Perignon, her ambassador at Madrid, March 16, 1796, to urge the point: "Our possession of Louisiana would give us the means to offset the marked predilection of the Federal government for our enemy and keep it within the line of duty by the fear of a dismemberment, we might cause."

France and Louisiana

[1] McMaster, *People of the United States*, ii. 209–416, 429–476.

This dismemberment of the United States, so clearly fore-shadowed in the instructions to Genêt, continued to haunt the minds of the French ministers. Adet, New French while striving to excite the French Canadians intrigues against England,[1] sent his ablest agent, General Collot, into the American West. He was to nourish sentiments of dissension among the leaders "by observing that the interests of the eastern and western parts of the United States were in collision, that the period was not distant when a separation must take place, and the range of mountains on this side of the Ohio was the natural boundary of the new government, and that in the event of separation the western people ought to look to France as their natural ally and protector." On July 15, 1797, Talleyrand became French minister of foreign affairs. Just returned from banishment in the United States, he had recently read before the Institute papers on "The Commercial Relations of the United States" and "The Colonial Interests of France." Although primarily concerned at the moment with Bonaparte's plan to divert attention to Africa, he maintained that the eastern part of the United States was irrevocably bound to England by language, habits, and trade, but that the country beyond the mountains would in time separate and need France.[2]

The American government only suspected these western designs; but the official insult involved in the treatment of Pinckney was patent, and the constant seiz- Adams's com-ure and condemnation of American vessels un- mission to der successive decrees, unjustifiable and often France contradictory, demanded attention. As experiments with Monroe, a Republican, and Pinckney, a Federalist, had proved unsatisfactory, Adams, with general approval, decided to send a joint commission of three,—to Pinckney,

[1] *Canadian Archives*, 1891, pp. 63–79; 1894, p. 527.
[2] A. Cans, "Les idées de Talleyrand sur la politique coloniale de la France au lendemain de la Révolution," *Revue d'Histoire Moderne*, 1900, ii. 58–63; F. J. Turner, "The Policy of France toward the Mississippi Valley," *Amer. Hist. Review*, 1905, x. 249–279.

were added John Marshall, a Federalist, and Elbridge Gerry, a Republican. On the day on which Talleyrand took office they received their instructions.

Arriving in Paris at the very crest of the Revolution, they found themselves confronting a situation unparalleled since the last century of the Roman republic. Triumphant France was surrounded by nations buying peace; the dazzling private expenditure which betokened the coming empire tempted public officials to demand private douceurs for the favor of their nod. The world seemed melting into new shapes at the whim of those who from moment to moment dominated Paris. America was a minor consideration; she was treated as were other powers. Even the astute Talleyrand, master of finesse, could see the need of no more subtle weapon than the threat, to be parried by the bribe.

French revolutionary diplomacy

He refused to receive the commissioners until redress of grievances was made and the President's message of May 16, 1797, dealing with the French situation, atoned for. Privately, however, he met them, and introduced them to certain individuals as possessing his confidence. These persons explained that as a preliminary to negotiation France expected the United States to buy from her, at par, certain Dutch bonds worth about fifty cents on the dollar,—two satellite republics were to combine to feed the great one. To set the whole in motion, a million francs, it was hinted, would be expected by the proper officials. This proposal was not so likely to surprise a trained diplomat at that time as now, if indeed anything in the Paris of 1798 could have surprised a trained diplomat. It was in effect a renewal in a different form of the loan proposition of 1794 so warmly endorsed by Monroe. We had not hesitated to buy peace from the Barbary pirates, and there was really no need of being more scrupulous about corrupting Talleyrand's morals than theirs. Pitt himself was at this very time seriously considering the purchase of

Secret negotiations

peace on similar, but dearer, terms.[1] I believe, however, that Americans remain glad that their commissioners were shocked, and that Pinckney replied, "No! no! no! not a sixpence!" Pinckney and Marshall at once broke off negotiations. Gerry lingered for three months more, but without being trapped into any concessions by Talleyrand; then he too left France, in August, 1798.

Meanwhile the commissioners' dispatches had been received in America. On March 19 Adams announced that they rendered peace no longer possible. In April they were published, the letters X, Y and Z being used to designate the intermediaries; and their contents convinced a large majority of Americans that Adams was right. Congress authorized an increase in army and navy, and on June 21 Adams was widely applauded for his announcement that he would "never send another minister to France without assurances that he will [would] be received, respected, and honored as the representative of a great, free, powerful, and independent nation."

The X, Y, Z correspondence

Although peace was at an end, war was not begun. It was hoped that we might hang between the two. On July 7 Adams declared our treaties with France suspended. An act of June 12 had already suspended all commercial intercourse with her, and on June 15 merchant vessels were authorized to arm and to defend themselves against search, seizure, or interference by French vessels. On July 8 authority was given to naval vessels to capture any armed French vessels, and the president was empowered to commission privateers to do the same. As practically all French merchantmen sailed armed, this licence offered a wide field. Three hundred and sixty-five privateers were commissioned, France lost ninety ships, and several naval duels were fought.[2]

American reprisals

[1] Adams, *Influence of Grenville on Pitt's Foreign Policy,* 67.
[2] G. W. Allen, *Our Naval War with France,* Boston, etc., 1909; G. N. ricoche, "Une page peu connue de l'histoire de France, la guerre franco-néricaine (1798–1801)," *Revue Historique,* 1904, lxxxv. 288–299.

In order to avoid the losses to American merchants which would come from a closing of the trade with the West Indies, West Indian Adams, June 26, 1799, declared suspended the trade suspension of French commerce in the case of certain ports of San Domingo. That colony was then under the control of Toussaint L'Ouverture, and its political connection with France was but slight. It is probable, also, that American merchants even continued to supply the more loyal islands of Guadaloupe and Martinique by means of collusive captures. Hostilities therefore brought little inconvenience to the United States, and, as for danger, Adams said that he no more expected to see a French army in America, than in heaven.[1]

Although we did not consider ourselves at war with France, we were fighting her. The policy of isolation had been in The Blount part deviated from. Were we going to give it conspiracy up wholly by becoming the ally of England, and so be enmeshed in the general European conflict? There were many circumstances that rendered such an event probable and many men who desired it. The new British minister, Liston, proved pleasing. He won confidence at once, in 1797, by helping to disclose a project of William Blount, senator from Tennessee, for a joint expedition of frontiersmen and the British fleet to seize Louisiana and put it under the control of Great Britain. Impeached by the House of Representatives, Blount resigned to escape conviction, and was promptly elected governor of his state; his plan serves to show how minds in the West were turning. Since Spain was loath to live up to the treaty of 1795, it was becoming doubtful whether that settlement would prove permanent; Great Britain, therefore, in becoming the enemy of Spain, became the natural friend of the frontiersman.

For similar reasons Miranda left France, now the ally of Spain, and sought England, where in 1797 he was once more deep in the confidence of Pitt. His plans resembled those

[1] Hildreth, *United States*, v. 267-270.

of 1790, except that the United States had swum into his ken. He would now give the Floridas and New Orleans to that country, "the Mississippi being in every re- Miranda's spect the best and most solid barrier that one plan can establish between the two great nations which occupy the American continent." England was to have Porto Rico and other islands. To all these nations—England, the United States, and Spanish America—the use of the isthmuses of Panama and Nicaragua was to be guaranteed. The instruments to secure all this were to be the United States army, the English navy, and Spanish-American discontent.[1]

These plans were accepted with enthusiasm by Rufus King, who communicated them to Pickering, our secretary of state, and to Hamilton, who under Washing- Federalists' ton commanded the new army. The plan plans for war pleased Hamilton. He wrote to Senator Gunn of Georgia, December 22, 1798: "This, you perceive, looks to offensive operations. If we are to engage in war, our game will be to attack where we can. France is not to be considered as separated from her ally. Tempting objects will be within our grasp." King wrote, October 20, 1798, "Things are here, as we could desire: there will be precisely such a co-operation as we wish the moment we are ready;" and again, on January 21, 1799: "For God's sake, attend to the very interesting subject treated of in my ciphered dispatches to the Secretary of State of the 10th, 18th, & 19th instant. Connect it, as it should be, with the main object, the time to accomplish which has arrived. Without superstition, Providence seems to have prepared the way, and to have pointed out the instruments of its will. Our children will reproach us if we neglect our duty, and humanity will escape many scourges if we act with wisdom and decision." On March 22 he wrote less hopefully to the secretary of state, "one is tired with beholding, and with endeavoring in vain to account for the blindness that even yet prevents an honest

[1] Robertson, *Miranda*, Amer. Hist. Assoc., *Report*, 1907, i. 189–539.

and general confederacy against the overbearing Power of France." On March 12, 1799, Dr. Edward Stevens was appointed consul-general to San Domingo, to enter into relations with Toussaint L'Ouverture, and to coöperate with the English consul in encouraging the independence of the island. It is significant that Hamilton was at this time in touch with Wilkinson.[1]

Whatever advantages this plan might have secured to the United States, it certainly involved the abandonment of the policy of neutrality. It involved

Dr. Logan's mission for peace

also the risk of internal disunion. How widely apart the opposing factions in the nation were already leaning is indicated by the mission of Dr. Logan, a Philadelphia Quaker, who went to France in 1798 to treat for peace upon his own account. Instead of passports he carried letters from Jefferson and from Thomas McKean, chief justice of Pennsylvania. In 1799 such private missions were prohibited by law, but his action is symptomatic of the way in which a war with France would have divided the nation.

Talleyrand had intended by his bullying to produce, not war, but money. American hostility was inconvenient to

Talleyrand offers to negotiate

France; actual war and alliance with England on the part of the United States might be dangerous to her. Moreover, the French expedition to Egypt had proved disappointing, and in his brain were revolving American projects which required, for the time, peace with the United States. On September 28, 1798, therefore, he informed William Vans Murray, our minister at The Hague, that any minister whom the United States might send would

[1] George Gibbs, *Memoirs of the Administrations of Washington and John Adams*, 2 vols., New York, 1846; J. Q. and C. F. Adams, *John Adams*, i. 516 ff.; John Adams, *Works*, vols. iii., viii., app.; C. R. King, *Life and Correspondence of Rufus King* (6 vols., New York, 1894–1900), vol. ii.; Hamilton, *Works* (ed. Lodge), vol. viii. (ed. Hamilton), vol. v.; "Letters of Toussaint Louverture and of Edward Stevens, 1798–1800," *Amer. Hist. Review*, 1910, xvi. 64–101.

be received with the respect due to the "representative of a free, independent, and powerful nation." This letter was at once seized upon by Adams as complying with the conditions that he had laid down in his message of June 21. His sturdy and persistent Americanism had accepted hostility, not from preference, but as necessary to the national honor and prestige. He was anxious to return to neutrality and diplomatic isolation, and on February 18, 1799, he nominated Murray to the Senate, as minister to France.

Of all personal decisions in American diplomacy, this was the most important, unless it be that Jay was justified in his suspicions of Vergennes in 1782 and so deflected the course of history at that point. Of the wisdom and justice of Adams's course there can be no doubt. He could, however, be counted upon to be as disagreeable as he was right. He sent in the nomination without consulting even his secretary of state. For this unusual discourtesy it is, however, possible that there was some excuse. Had the proposition been submitted to his cabinet, dominated as it was by Hamilton, it would undoubtedly have been rejected and further action would have been difficult. Once Talleyrand's offer became public, however, an overwhelming public opinion, all Republicans and the moderate Federalists, demanded its acceptance. Pickering, Hamilton, and their associates were aghast, but did not dare oppose the mission. Yet they succeeded in substituting for a minister a commission, comprising, in addition to Murray, the chief justice Oliver Ellsworth, and Patrick Henry, upon whose refusal Governor Davie of North Carolina was substituted. Concerning the instructions to this commission, Pinckney wrote to King, March 12, 1799: "These terms are what we have a clear right to, and our interest and honor oblige us to insist on. Yet I very much doubt whether France will yield them. I am morally sure she will not; and this has put us all much at our ease."

In spite of this confidence, however, Adams had personally to intervene to secure the departure of the envoys. Pickering Cabinet dis-sensions did not choose to take the course of resignation, which his difference of purpose and his personal relations with Adams made obvious. He clung to his position until May 12, 1800, when Adams removed him. With him went also Hamilton's influence over diplomacy, which since 1789 had largely controlled details. Yet none of the great decisions or policies of the period had been Hamilton's, although in some such cases his view had coincided with that followed and had often helped to shape it. In this final clash, however brilliant and fascinating were his ideas and however great his capacity to realize them, it cannot be doubted that Adams, bred of the soil, stood for the desires John Marshall secretary and best interests of his country. Pickering was replaced by John Marshall, whose term was too short and quiet to test his diplomatic abilities.

In Paris the negotiations, having the good will of Talleyrand and of the rising Bonaparte, progressed rapidly. On Convention of 1800 September 30, 1800, a convention was concluded. This agreement was generally satisfactory on points relating to navigation. It laid down the French view, which was also the American, with regard to free ships making free goods, and also with regard to contraband. In one point, however, we were obliged to accept the French view, as Jay had accepted the English,—namely, the provision that neutral goods on enemies' vessels might be seized. The chief difficulty lay in the American demand that indemnity be paid for illegal condemnations by the French, on which were based nearly twenty-three hundred sound claims, and the French demand for the execution of the treaties of 1778 and 1788. The commissioners finally decided to leave these questions for future negotiation "at a convenient time," the treaties meanwhile to be inoperative. This proposal the United States Senate amended by the provision that the convention should remain in force for eight years. Bonaparte, by this time Napoleon and consul, with his usual clear headedness accepted this amendment, "provided that by this retrenchment the two States renounce the respective pretensions which are the object of the said article."

Thus were disposed of forever the treaties which constituted our first "entangling alliance." The advantage that accrued to the nation is obvious. The justice of thus exchanging private claims for national gain has since then many times engaged the attention of Congress, but these particular "French Spoliation Claims" became henceforth a domestic problem.

End of " French treaties "

The end thus arrived at is to be attributed not only to Adams's decision to make peace, but to his willingness, previously shown, to make war. The brief brush with France had, moreover, brought other results. Fearing some such scheme as Miranda was elaborating, Spain at length, and reluctantly, in March, 1798, evacuated her posts between the Yazoo and the thirty-first parallel, and the United States for the first time actually possessed in full the boundaries awarded her by the peace of 1783.

Origin of " French spoliations "

To the achievements noted at the close of Washington's administration, therefore, the Adams administration added that of meeting the most acute crisis that had yet confronted the nation, and of emerging from it with the fundamental policy of neutrality still intact, and relieved from treaty complications. It left the affairs of the nation in a condition superficially satisfactory and actually strong.

Close of Federalist period

CHAPTER XII

THE LOUISIANA PURCHASE

THE succession of Jefferson to the presidency made less immediate change in the current of American diplomacy than

A change of régime

was expected, much less than in domestic affairs. The formal etiquette with which Washington had surrounded himself was modified and its neglect caused some friction with the foreign ministers at Washington; but the essential practice of having all governmental intercourse with them pass through the hands of the secretary of state was retained. Jefferson, moreover, was a gentleman and of cosmopolitan experience; and on the whole the administration was well-mannered. Jefferson had long held that ministers should not be retained abroad more than six or eight years, for fear that they would cease to be true representatives of Americanism, a principle for which there was much to be said in those days, when foreign politics tended so to engage American sympathies and antipathies and communication was so scant. Charles Pinckney was therefore nominated minister at Madrid, "vice David Humphreys, recalled on account of long absence from the United States," and Robert Livingston was substituted for Short, in France, for the same reason; but comparatively little more was heard of the practice.[1] In the interests of economy the missions to Prussia, Holland, and Portugal were discontinued, a step which John Quincy Adams considered a mistake, as it left us at the mercy of the two great belligerent powers by putting us out of touch with our natural friends, the neutral maritime nations; but the neutral nations were so weak that the loss cannot be considered great. Most of the men appointed by

[1] C. R. Fish, *The Civil Service and the Patronage* (New York, etc., 1905), 38.

Jefferson were of ability and training, though his leading agent, Monroe, seems to have been framed for other tasks than diplomacy. Jefferson's most important advisers were James Madison, secretary of state, and Albert Gallatin, secretary of the treasury; but his own power, ability, and experience served to give him control.[1]

The first question which confronted the administration resulted from a tangle in that particular thread of diplomacy which the Federalists had failed to unravel. Mediterranean trade Our treaties with the Barbary states were not highly regarded by those powers. The Dey of Algiers had objected to making one. "If I were to make peace with every body," said he, "what should I do with my corsairs? What should I do with my soldiers? They would take off my head for the want of other prizes, not being able to live upon their miserable allowance." Nor did the treaty once made lie very heavily upon him; it seemed in fact to offer him some amusement. In 1800 Captain Bainbridge, arriving at Algiers with the usual tribute, was ordered to carry dispatches to Constantinople. "You pay me tribute," explained the Dey, "by which you become my slaves, and therefore I have a right to order you as I think proper." Jefferson had long been familiar with the situation, and had always opposed the policy of tribute. Now he proposed to use force to exact respect. Inconsistent as this policy seems to be with his general belief in the supremacy of reason, it was probably based upon a still more fundamental sense of honor, and a somewhat emotional reaction from so barbaric an anachronism as the Barbary coast. At any rate, he sent a squadron to the Mediterranean, where for several years American ships and men, captains and consuls, performed their parts in romantic adventures which smack of the

[1] Jefferson, *Writings*, ed. Ford, 10 vols.; James Madison, *Writings*, ed. Gaillard Hunt, 9 vols., New York, 1900–1910; Albert Gallatin, *Writings*, ed. Henry Adams, 3 vols., Philadelphia, 1879; James Monroe, *Writings*, ed. S. M. Hamilton, 9 vols., New York, etc., 1898–1903.

Arabian Nights rather than of the nineteenth century. Independent of home support, as only sailing-vessels can be, they so successfully impressed the rulers of the several states that by 1805 the sea was comparatively safe for American traders.[1]

Even at Jefferson's inauguration the great event of his administration was taking shape behind carefully closed doors.

Plan of Talleyrand and Napoleon
There was no novelty in what was being planned; except what lay in the ability of the actors and the strength of the forces at their command. Talleyrand and Napoleon had definitely taken up the plans for dominating the Mississippi valley, and through it the western world, with which so many men had been playing now for fifty years. At their back they had the virility and enthusiasm of revolutionary France, now disciplined into military effectiveness; they had the defeated and demoralized, but still powerful, French navy.[2]

The first step was to get Louisiana, to get it quickly and undamaged. Talleyrand wrote to his representative at

Cession of Louisiana to France
Madrid in the summer of 1798: "The Court of Madrid, ever blind to its own interests, and never docile to the lessons of experience, has again recently adopted a measure which cannot fail to produce the worst effects upon its political existence and on the preservation of its colonies. The United States has been put in possession of the forts situated along the Mississippi, which the Spaniards had occupied as posts essential to arrest the progress of the Americans in those countries." The Americans, he said, must be shut up within "the limits which nature seems to have traced for them,"—the same limits, of course, which Rayneval had traced for d'Aranda and Jay in 1782. Spain, continued Talleyrand, should "yield a small part of her immense domain to preserve the

---

[1] G. W. Allen, *Our Navy and the Barbary Corsairs*, Boston, etc., 1905.

[2] Gustav Roloff, *Die Kolonialpolitik Napoleons I*, Munich, etc., 1899; Henry Adams, "Napoléon Ier et Saint Domingue," *Revue Historique*, 1884, xxiv. 92–130.

rest." Let Spain cede the Floridas and Louisiana to France, "and from that moment the power of the United States is bounded by the limits which it may suit the interests and tranquillity of France and Spain to assign her." Spain still resisted the inevitable, but at length on October 1, 1800, the treaty of San Ildefonso was signed, "retroceding" Louisiana to France in exchange for some Italian provinces. With a persistence worthy of a more hopeful cause Spain still clung to the Floridas.[1]

Twenty-four hours before, the convention bringing about the necessary truce with the United States had been signed. There remained necessary, peace with Great Britain to free the ocean for French operations. *Reduction of San Domingo* On October 1, 1801, preliminary articles were signed with that country, and on March 27, 1802, the peace of Amiens was concluded. One detail was still incomplete, but it seemed to offer small difficulty. The key to the new colonial empire of France must be the island of San Domingo, still dominated by the negro Toussaint L'Ouverture, whose loyalty to France was insufficient for the purposes in view. In January, 1802, Napoleon's brother-in-law, Leclerc, with ten thousand men and a large fleet, arrived off the island to restore it to its dependence. His military successes paved the way for the reëstablishment of slavery, and Toussaint L'Ouverture was sent prisoner to France. Napoleon then prepared his expedition to Louisiana, and drew up instructions to General Victor, who was to command it.

The central feature of this plan, the cession of Louisiana, was still a secret; Talleyrand even denied it, yet rumor spread. In April, 1801, John Quincy Adams had heard of it at Berlin. In 1802 Godoy, "Prince of the Peace" and the leading figure in *The news reaches America* Spain, being pressed by France for the Floridas, seems to have allowed a copy of the treaty to fall into our hands. In

[1] See F. L. Riley, *Spanish Policy in Mississippi after the Treaty of San Lorenzo,* Amer. Hist. Assoc., *Report,* 1897, 175–192.

November, 1802, a premonition was given of what might happen should the transfer take place. The Spanish intendant at New Orleans, at French instigation, as it was believed, forbade the Americans the use of that city as a place of deposit, and refused to designate another. The first action was in accordance with our treaty with Spain, more than the three years specified having elapsed; but the refusal to assign a new port was a violation of that treaty. It again clogged the Mississippi and stirred all the forces of the restless West.[1]

Fortunately, Jefferson was familiar with every factor of this new combination of long-existing conditions. He flour-

Jefferson threatens ished before France the danger of an alliance between the United States and England. In a letter intended to be read by the French leaders he wrote: "The day that France takes possession of New Orleans fixes the sentence which is to restrain her forever within her low water mark. It seals the union of two nations, which in conjunction can maintain exclusive possession of the ocean. From that moment we must marry ourselves to the British fleet and nation." He showed marked favoritism to the British representative, Thornton, and scared the French minister, Pinchon, into a promise to endeavor to secure the opening of the Mississippi from France. Yrujo, the Spanish minister, did obtain a temporary restoration of the right of deposit at New Orleans.

For the serious handling of the question Jefferson reverted to the method thrice employed by the Federalists, a special

Jefferson's policy mission; and he chose Monroe for the office. The latter was instructed to purchase New Orleans and the Floridas, being allowed to bid anything up to ten million dollars. Congress had just appropriated two million for the purpose. If the purchase could not be made,

[1] Henry Adams, *History of the United States during the Administrations of Jefferson and Madison*, 9 vols., New York, 1889–91 (gives an incomparable account of the diplomacy of the period). See also F. A. Ogg, *The Opening of the Mississippi*, New York, 1904.

he was to secure an acknowledgment of the right of deposit. If this could not be obtained, he was to await new instructions. The cabinet decided that in such case negotiations should be protracted until the next inevitable war between England and France broke out, and then coöperation should be arranged with England. In accordance with this policy of delay the departure of Monroe was not hurried, and he did not leave till March 8, 1803.

Jefferson's policy was exactly adapted to the situation. The only criticism is, that he ought to have overcome his scruples against a navy and have strengthened our position in order that we might be in readiness for the war which was so definite a possibility. The event, however, was in no wise dependent upon him, and had practically been consummated before Monroe reached Paris. In January, 1803, news reached France of the death, from disease, of Leclerc and a large part of the French army in San Domingo and of the revival of revolt. Napoleon, while steadfast in the pursuit of fundamental purposes, never shot a second arrow to recover one lost in a side issue. He was already interesting himself in the prospect of a new European war. On March 12, 1803, he practically broke with England. Under such circumstances he was not so foolish as to squander another army on America. The colonial empire was dropped.

Napoleon's change of plans

Napoleon was too able an economist to keep intact machinery for which he now had no use: he would scrap it for what it would bring. On April 10 he spoke of Louisiana to Barbé Marbois, who, familiar with American affairs from our own Revolution, was negotiating with Livingston. England, he said, would seize it at the first moment of war, and added: "I think of ceding it to the United States. I can hardly say that I cede it to them, for it is not yet in our possession. If, however, I leave the least time to our enemies, I shall only transmit an empty title to those republicans whose

Napoleon scraps Louisiana

friendship I seek. . . . Irresolution and deliberation are no longer in reason; I renounce Louisiana. It is not only New Orleans that I cede, it is the whole colony, without reserve. I know the price of what I abandon." Marbois was to get at least fifty million francs for the cession.

On April 11 this proposal was broached to Livingston, and the next day Monroe arrived. Negotiations proceeded with the rapidity customary when Napoleon was in command, and on April 30 the treaty was signed. In return for the cession we agreed to pay sixty million francs, and we assumed the payment to our own citizens of claims against France to the extent of not over twenty million francs.

That Napoleon made a good bargain must be conceded. He received more money than the minimum he had set; he won, too, some of that feeling of friendship which he had mentioned; and he kept Louisiana out of the hands of England. Moreover, there seems to be no reason to believe that he had any idea that he was renouncing Louisiana. Perhaps his mind saw things too simply: his struggle was with England; once England was downed, the world was his to command. The very difficulty in disposing of Louisiana which even he had with his advisers and with public opinion illustrates the hold which the vision of America had on the French mind. Actually with the delivery of New Orleans to the United States, December 20, 1803, and the independence of Hayti, or western San Domingo, proclaimed November 29 of the same year, France was eliminated as a territorial factor in our history; but although the crisis had passed, her policies and ambitions continued to be of moment.

In America the news of the treaty was confounding. It was more than had been hoped for; it was not exactly what was desired. It raised a score of opportunities for dispute and distraction. In the first place, there was no specific power to annex territory granted in the constitution, although it was easily inferred from the power to make treaties. More seriously discussed was the clause of the treaty providing that the inhabitants of the ceded territory should be "incorporated in the Union." The Federalists were willing to annex territories to govern, but not to give them a share in the government. By the acceptance of the treaty, however, this question was at least quieted. The treaty also provided that France and Spain be exempted from discriminating duties in the ports of Louisiana for twelve years, and that France remain forever after that on the basis of the most favored nation. The first of these provisions was of doubtful constitutionality, while the second was long a source of dispute with France.

These were problems that could be settled at leisure, and they were but pin-pricks compared with those which the purchase solved. The navigation of the Mississippi was now completely freed, and its *Results of the treaty* future was not dependent upon the continued favor of any foreign nation. All the interests which had drawn the frontiersmen toward Spain or Great Britain, dividing their allegiance, now were added ties to strengthen their natural bonds of race and sympathy with the American government. The completeness of the change was shown by the utter collapse of Burr's conspiracy in 1806.

What his plans were is not entirely clear; probably he himself changed them so often that they lost their definiteness. At any rate, he played on all the customary strings of western adventure. His *Burr's conspiracy* objective was Spanish America. England's coöperation he sought, offering through the British minister, Merry, in 1804 "to effect a separation of the western part of the United States from that which lies between the Atlantic and the mountains, in its whole extent." While still vice-president he journeyed through the West and collected material for an expedition; he was also in touch with Wilkinson, now in command of the western department. The latter, however, was more weatherwise than Burr, and, bribed by Spain, he betrayed Burr, and the whole bubble burst. In fact, it never had any semblance of real strength, for there was no motive for disloyalty, or even lack of loyalty, in the West. The government of the United States had obtained for it its most conspicuous desire.[1]

So much the purchase of Louisiana had accomplished, while it was not yet clear just what Louisiana was. To the westward it had never had a boundary; even such boundary agreements as had once existed had been absorbed by the Spanish annexation of 1763, and were lost to memory. Napoleon had ordered Victor to occupy to the Rio Grande, but this fact was unknown to the American government. Jefferson's imagination, however, stretched to the uttermost limits of the opportunity. Even before he had acquired Louisiana he had planned its exploration, and in 1804 started the Lewis and Clark expedition westward, up the Missouri, across the mountains, and beyond any conceivable limits of the purchase, to the Pacific. In 1805 the expedition descended the Columbia and thus added a link to the chain of our claims to the Oregon country, the first of which had been forged when Captain Gray in 1791 had entered the mouth of that river. The record of the expedition, put in popular form by Nicholas Biddle on its return, engaged the imagination of the far-seeing in dreams which made the purchase of Louisiana seem but a step in our progress. In 1805 and 1807 Captain Zebulon Pike was sent into the region south of the Missouri, where he felt the Spaniards, and gained an idea of the actual limits of what we had acquired.[2]

To the eastward the situation was more definite, in fact it was definite. Our treaty of cession recited as its definition of Louisiana the description given in the treaty of San

Western limits of Louisiana

---

[1] W. F. McCaleb, *The Aaron Burr Conspiracy*, New York, 1903.

[2] Henry Gannett, *Boundaries of the United States and of the several States and Territories*, 2d edition, 1900 (U. S. Geological Survey, *Bulletin*, No. 171); H. E. Chambers, *West Florida*, Baltimore, 1898.

Ildefonso between France and Spain: "The Colony or Province of Louisiana with the same extent that it now has in the hands of Spain, and that it had when France possessed it, and such as it should be after the treaties subsequently entered into between Spain and other states." This definition was obviously self-contradictory. Louisiana, when France possessed it, stretched eastward to the Perdido river and included Mobile; the province as it was in the hands of Spain extended only to the Iberville. The meaning, however, was clear enough. The treaty was entitled one of "retrocession." Spain could retrocede to France only what she had received from France; that is the region from the Iberville westward given her in 1763. Although in 1800 she held that between the Iberville and the Perdido, it was by cession from England in 1783, and was separately organized as part of the province of West Florida. This was well understood by the French. Berthier wrote, "After the general peace, the King might decide to cede a part of the Floridas between the Mississippi and the Mobile, on the special demand which the First Consul might make of it." Talleyrand wrote to Napoleon, November 18, 1802, "West Florida suffices for the desired enlargement of Louisiana, it completes the retrocession of the French Colony, such as it was given to Spain." The instructions to General Victor ordered him to take possession only to the Iberville.

Eastern boundary of Louisiana

Madison, Livingston, and Monroe, however, seized upon the ambiguity. In a small way each of the rivers flowing into the gulf presented the same problem as the Mississippi. Population was occupying their upper banks, and desired to use them as outlets for their products. So far as immediate utility was concerned, the securing of the territory beyond the Mississippi, which no one had thought of buying, was not a compensation for the gulf fringe of West Florida, which Livingston and Monroe had been instructed to purchase. Our relations with Spain,

United States claims

moreover, were sure to be unpleasant whether we pressed this additional claim or not, for Napoleon had promised Spain never to give Louisiana to a foreign power. This promise, to be sure, was not incorporated in the treaty of San Ildefonso and did not impair our title, but it afforded a starting-point of disagreement. Under these circumstances the government decided that we had actually purchased the territory to the Perdido, the wish having a very close relation to the thought.

The dispute, of course, was with Spain, but as a matter of fact Napoleon controlled Spain. Except for a brief and un-**Napoleon's game** successful mission of Monroe to Madrid, the American government recognized the logic of the situation, and directed its efforts to the fountain head at Paris. Though claiming title, it was nevertheless willing to pay for the recognition of it, and to purchase other portions of the derelict Spanish empire. Napoleon might have settled the question as to the boundary by opening his records. He preferred, however, mystery and confusion. Talleyrand said to Livingston, "You have made a noble bargain and I suppose you will make the most of it." From 1804 to 1812, indeed, the Florida question became a barometer of European conditions. When pressure was heavy, Napoleon was ready to treat for a money consideration: December 24, 1804, Armstrong wrote to Madison, "This country has determined to convert the negotiation into a job, and to draw from it advantages merely pecuniary to herself." When pressure was light, Napoleon was shocked at the assumption that he might sell property belonging to his ally. When by the accession of his brother Joseph to the throne of Spain the possessions of that crown became part of the estate of the house of Bonaparte, he warned the United States against interference.

On the whole, it may be said that Napoleon used the Florida question as a bait to keep the United States in the vicinity of his hook, and that he was not without some success.   In the end, however, fate and Madison got the better of him.   That portion of the disputed region on the east bank of the Mississippi between the thirty-first parallel and the Iberville was being occupied by American settlers, regardless of its international status.   In September, 1810, these people proclaimed their independence and asked for annexation to the United States.   October 27, 1810, Madison, acting on the supposition that it was already United States territory, ordered its occupation, whereupon Claiborne, governor of Orleans territory, took possession to the Pearl river, the present boundary between the states of Louisiana and Mississippi.   In 1813 General Wilkinson occupied Mobile and the region eastward to the Perdido.   From that time the United States remained in possession of its utmost claims as to the eastern boundary of Louisiana, but its title to that part of it between the Iberville and the Perdido had yet to be determined.

Occupation of disputed territory

CHAPTER XIII

THE EMBARGO

THE war renewed between France and England in 1803, the shadow of which brought us Louisiana, had many other things in store for us, both pleasant and unpleasant. The course of the struggle from 1803 to 1815 parallels in many ways that between 1793 and 1802. Some of the factors, however, had changed. Our own West had become strong enough to master its own destiny; it was now so firmly attached to the government that it ceased for the present to enter into the plans of European states. The policy of our government continued to be that of neutrality, but its sympathies were now French instead of English. Its methods of preserving neutrality, moreover, were so decidedly different as to change the whole character of our diplomacy. In the case of both France and England, the preceding war had witnessed experiments; the new one found determined policies. The defeat of Napoleon's navies at Trafalgar in 1805 gave England a more complete control of the sea than she had ever had before, while his victories by land isolated her from the continent in a manner new and menacing.

With the diplomatic elimination of the West, American commerce with the belligerents became the focus of attention. Its steady-going element consisted in the exchange of our raw products for England's manufactures. Carried on largely in our own vessels, it was safe, fairly unvarying in quantity, and brought in reasonable profits to respectable established firms. Less important was that carried on with the British colonies under temporary suspensions of the navigation laws and by special licences.

Change of conditions

American commerce

Part of this trade, it is true, was practically regular and suited to the conservative temperament. As however, the permissions were based on the needs of the moment, there was a fluctuating margin, which gave opportunity to those with a keen scent for special venture and quick turnovers. News of crops and markets was eagerly read, and the British government was besieged with special applications. In 1809 it refused a licence to export ice and snow from the United States to the West Indies; those were commodities sufficiently abundant in the loyal colony of Canada.

More adventurous, and after 1805 partaking somewhat of the nature of speculation, was the continued attempt to supply France with her breakfast of West Indian coffee, sugar, and cocoa. Hayti was *American carrying-trade* now practically free, but its market continued to be France; and the other islands furnished their quota. In return the islands wanted provisions, which we ourselves could furnish, and manufactured goods, which should have come from France but which we often secured for them from England. This trade demanded high freight rates and protected itself by insurance. It produced both fortunes and bankruptcies. By 1805 it overshadowed the safer trade with England. Between 1803 and 1806 our exports of domestic goods sank from $42,206,000 to $41,253,000; those of foreign goods rose from $13,594,000 to $60,283,000.[1]

Still choicer titbits invited those who frankly disregarded business principles and resorted to speculation pure and simple. To add to their lading of French colonial *Speculative ventures* products some of the manufactures of England so eagerly desired and so highly priced on the continent, and, protected by licences from England and France, to carry on trade between the enemies, or to carry it on unprotected, induced many to risk ships and liberty. To disregard the

[1] Mathew Carey, *The Olive Branch*, Philadelphia, 1815 (contains many original documents and statistics); *British and Foreign State Papers* (an annual series).

restrictive laws framed with such rapidity by the United States government, to gamble on a change of regulation before reaching port or on the possibility of bribing officials, to coast from one French port to another, to rove at will over the ocean using whatever flag and papers were convenient at the moment, involved serious risks, but not sufficient danger to exclude such practices. Everywhere the Americans found and made business. Gallatin estimated that our merchant marine grew seventy thousand tons a year and called for over four thousand additional men; and Phineas Bond had already in 1796 referred to the enterprising spirit of so many of our traders in "forcing the prescribed channels of commerce." To shepherd such a reckless crew was no easy task for an administration so firmly based on the idea of self-government, but at heart so paternalistic, as was that of Jefferson.

The attitude of Great Britain toward this trade was not a simple one. Underlying all her actions was a sensitive Great Britain's national jealousy at the growth of a rival merpolicy chant marine, and a constant purpose to give every possible advantage to her own. She did not wish to cut off all trade with the enemy; she was especially anxious to sell all the manufactured goods possible. She tried, therefore, to confine trade to channels favorable to herself, and to cause it to pass under her watchful eye. Agricultural conditions had so readjusted themselves on the continent that there was less chance of starving France into submission; hence the question of regarding provisions as contraband of war was not so important as in the previous war. In the execution of her policy she showed an arrogance and a carelessness of others that often caused her to persist in practices not essential to her general policy and yet provocative of retaliation. England's policy cannot be considered apart from her bad manners.

The policy of Napoleon toward neutral trade was based on the ideas of the Directory. It was subsidiary to his central idea of destroying England by destroying her commerce. He would close all the ports of the world to British trade, he would cause her ships to be idle and her Napoleon's factories to be glutted with unsalable goods; policy then bankruptcy and submission would be inevitable. This was the fundamental purpose which underlay his entire foreign policy from 1805, and which resulted in the climatic tragedy of the Russian invasion. While he undoubtedly miscalculated the tenacity of the British will, and thought that less pressure would be necessary to bring a nation of shopkeepers to terms than proved to be the case, his plan was not fantastic and he may have come within sight of success. He himself, when at Elba, reviewing and magnifying, like so many lesser of the fallen, the turns of fortune against him, said that he should have succeeded had not the Spanish revolt opened up to England, after 1808, the trade of Spanish America which she had so long desired and which gave a new market for her surplus products.[1] It should not be held against him as an inconsistency, or as an evidence of the impossibility of his plan, that his armies were often clothed in British goods. He realized the temporary necessity, but under the protection of his system he expected to develop self-sufficing industry on the continent. Indeed, one of the most permanent results of his rule has been found to be precisely this development. With such a policy Napoleon knew no neutrals: trade with his enemy was vital assistance to his enemy. This policy, however, was diplomatically veiled so as to enable him to employ neutral vessels for his own purposes. The details of his regulations therefore change from time to time. Without a navy, he was driven to such measures as could be enforced in his own ports.

In the United States the policy formulated to defend our trade was emphatically Jefferson's, although it so closely resembled Napoleon's that it was attributed to French in-

[1] T. B. Richards, "An Unpublished Talk with Napoleon," *Harper's Magazine*, January 1911, pp. 165–175.

fluence. If there was any connection, however, it was Jefferson who originated the plan. Even as a youth he had
Jefferson's policy   been much impressed with the rapidity with which the colonial non-importation agreements had brought England to terms, and he believed that similar pressure would be as effective between nations as it had proved between colony and mother country. He may well have discussed the matter with the French revolutionary leaders during his residence in France. Certainly on his return he urged it upon Congress in his report of 1793. Now as president he intended to use it as the bulwark of defence for our commerce and our merchant marine.

The first serious difficulty arose with England over the trade of the French West Indies. As a result of decisions
England and the French West Indies   of Sir William Scott in the cases of the *Emanuel* in 1799 and the *Polly* in 1800, that trade had been allowed to the Americans if carried on from the colonies to the United States and from the United States to France. July 23, 1805, in the case of the *Essex,* Scott practically reversed himself, declaring that on an innocent voyage between the United States and Europe the neutral owner of such colonial goods must be able to prove by something more than evidence of a custom-house entry that his original intention had been to terminate his venture in an American port. Upon this theory several American vessels were condemned, and the trade, while not prohibited, was rendered uncertain and difficult; for it was, of course, almost never the intention of the American owner to terminate his venture in the United States, and he was actually in most cases owner merely in form and not in substance, a situation that might be revealed by the British courts which it was framed to deceive. This trade, as well as other branches of traffic, was soon additionally hampered by a British order in council of May 16, 1806, blockading the coast from Havre to Ostend and prohibiting the coast trade to neutrals from Havre to the Elbe.

Another source of difficulty arose from the discovery by the British that this blockade could be more effectively and conveniently enforced off the American than the French coast. For years, it became customary for every American vessel leaving New York, the Chesapeake, and other harbors to heave to, and submit to a vigorous search. If the result created suspicion, the vessel was put in charge of a British officer and sent to Halifax for adjudication by the admiralty court there. In 1806, in the execution of this police duty, the British accidentally shot and killed an American sea-captain. *Blockade of American coast*

Usually the vessel was allowed to proceed, but in a large number of cases with the loss of members of its crew. The impressment problem gave increasing trouble. Of the four thousand new seamen demanded each year by the merchant marine twenty-five hundred, it was reckoned, were British born, most of them sailors who preferred the better wages, food, and treatment to be found on American vessels. Such transfer of allegiance in the heat of the national life-and-death struggle was regarded by British public opinion as no less than desertion; hence the navy vigorously resorted to impressment to redress the balance. It is estimated that there were a thousand cases annually. *Impressments*

It was in this state of affairs that the clauses of the Jay treaty relating to neutral rights expired. Jefferson prepared to substitute for them a new and better treaty. To bring pressure to bear upon England, he had Congress pass a non-importation act, prohibiting the entry of certain British goods which he esteemed not necessary to our happiness. Its operation was not to be immediate, but it was to hang like a sword of Damocles over the negotiations. Many doubted its efficiency. John Randolph derided it as "a milk and water bill, a dose of chicken broth to be taken nine months hence." To bring it to the attention of England, Jefferson appointed *Monroe and Pinkney in England* a commission consisting of Monroe, who had succeeded King as minister, and William Pinkney. Their instructions, drawn up by Madison, insisted upon three ultimata,—namely, an agreement regarding impressments, indemnity for American vessels and cargoes condemned, as we held, unjustly, and a satisfactory provision regarding the trade of the French West Indies. "We begin to broach the idea that we consider the whole Gulf stream as our waters," said Madison, a remark which reminds one of Fauchet's comment in 1795, that America "puffs itself up with its position and the future power to which it can pretend."

Happy in beginning their negotiations under the auspices of Charles James Fox, always the friend of America and now foreign minister, they found their hopes soon dashed by his death. It is probable, however, that this made little difference, for on the subjects upon which they desired acquiescence no British minister would have dared offer even compromise. Unable to obtain a single important concession they nevertheless signed a treaty on December 31, 1806, which was as unsatisfactory as that of Jay on matters of international law, besides affording none of the compensations which that treaty offered, for there were no outstanding matters at issue of a character not thought to be necessary to England's national existence. The treaty was not consummated; Jefferson never presented it to the Senate.

With the failure of the treaty, the lightning began to play in dead earnest. In November, 1806, Napoleon had Napoleon's de- issued his Berlin decree declaring the British cree isles blockaded, with the result, as concerned neutrals, that no vessel coming from England or her colonies should after a nine months' notice be admitted into any French port. This was followed by the Milan decree of December 17, 1807, which declared that any vessel submitting to search by a British ship, paying duty to the British government, or coming from or destined for a British port should be good prize.

Meantime an English order in council of January 7, 1807, known as Lord Howick's order, forbade neutral vessels to engage in the French coasting trade, even British orders between unblockaded ports. The British at- in council titude is indicated in a dispatch from Lord Howick to Erskine, the British minister to the United States: "His Majesty, with that forbearance and moderation which has at all times distinguished his conduct, has determined for the present to confine himself to the exercise of the powers given him by his decided naval superiority in such manner only as is authorized by the acknowledged principles of the law of nations." On November 11, 1807, an order known as Spencer Perceval's established a "paper" blockade of the whole European coast from Trieste to Copenhagen. No neutral vessel could enter any port from which British vessels were excluded, unless clearing from a British port and under British regulations, including the payment of duties, a condition which *ipso facto* rendered it liable to seizure by France.

While this clash of decrees and orders sounded but dimly in the ears of most Americans, uncertain as yet as to what they portended, an episode on the coast of The Leopard-America roused the nation, so observers said, Chesapeake more than anything had done since Lexington. affair The *Chesapeake*, an American frigate fitting for the Mediterranean, enrolled a number of men whom the British admiral off the coast claimed as deserters. Commodore Barron satisfied himself that such was not the case, and on June 22, 1807, set sail. The *Chesapeake* was followed by the *Leopard*, one of the vessels enforcing the blockade of Europe off Chesapeake Bay, and was ordered to heave to. After a formal resistance, she lowered her flag, officers from the *Leopard* took off the men in question, and left the *Chesapeake*, which promptly returned to Norfolk.

This extension of the practice of impressment to national naval vessels found no support even in the elastic international law of the day. The British government did not attempt to defend it, but it handled the matter with so un-

Popular indignation pardonable a stupidity that the episode remained an open sore for four years. Jefferson expressed his indignation in a proclamation of July 2, which forbade the use of American harbors to British war vessels, and on July 30 he called a special session of Congress.

The measure that he recommended was not war, but it no less reflected the seriousness of his view of the situation. War

The embargo he believed a barbarism; for it he would substitute the appeal to interest. As he believed that under normal conditions commercial discrimination was an effective instrument, so he believed that under abnormal conditions a total cessation of trade would exert all the compulsive efforts of war without its horrors. In other words, he would have us withdraw from the commerce of the world, in the belief that it would not be long before the nations would be clamoring for us to reopen our ports on our own terms. As a result of his recommendation, on December 21, 1807, a general and indefinite embargo was established. No vessel was to leave port, except (1) foreign vessels in ballast, or with such cargo as they had laded before the passage of the act, and (2) vessels engaged in the coasting trade. This embargo seemed to resemble that established at the time of Jay's mission to England; but it is to be differentiated from that because it was regarded by those who adopted it, not as a temporary expedient providing for the safety of our shipping, but as a weapon to conquer favorable terms from our adversaries.

So it happened that, before our merchants could be sure what effect the rival orders and decrees might have upon

Effect of the embargo on commerce their business,—although they felt certain that there would be loopholes in both the French and English systems,—their own government laid a restraining hand on all their ventures. It was the steady-going merchants who suffered most, those who were

engaged in the regular trade with England and her colonies, and so were comparatively untouched by the regulations either of that country or of France. The more adventurous could always find opportunities for traffic by evading or disregarding the law. Until stopped by a supplementary act, many vessels cleared for an American port but found themselves driven by stress of weather to the West Indies. Once there, they sold their goods. Even when this practice was stopped, some preserved freedom by remaining away from home. April 11, 1808, an English order in council forbade the seizure of American vessels in the West Indies and South America, even if without papers. In March, April, and May sixteen American vessels were allowed to enter English ports. Although numbers of American vessels thus found employment it was, however, in carrying on the business of others, not in supplying the United States with what she desired and taking from her ports what she had for sale. Our commerce was dead.

Whether or not Jefferson was right in claiming that American commerce was more essential to other nations than to ourselves, at any rate we had a governmental **Failure of the** organization more sensitive to public distress **embargo** than other nations. The embargo did cause suffering in the British empire: Newfoundland was on the point of starvation, and English mills shut down, with all the attendant woes. England, however, remained firm.

In the United States opposition swept down the coast. In New England the criticism of the commercial classes, unappreciative of this attempt to clear the **Repeal of the** seas by forbidding the use of them, rose to **embargo** fury. New England statesmen talked of disunion. In the middle states the farmer, for whose crops the home market was inadequate, added his voice to that of the merchant of New York, Philadelphia, and Baltimore. Washington Irving, in his Knickerbocker history of New York, ridiculed the embargo: "Never was a more comprehensive, a more ex-

peditious, or, what is still better, a more economical measure
devised, than this of defeating the Yankees by proclamation—an expedient, likewise, so gentle and humane, there
were ten chances to one in favor of its succeeding,—but
then there was one chance to ten that it would not succeed,—
as the ill-natured fates would have it, that single chance carried the day." Even the Virginia planters, groaning under
the burden of supporting their slaves, whose products remained unsold on the plantation, protested. On February 28,
1809, the embargo was repealed, having brought about no
amelioration of our international position.

CHAPTER XIV

WAR WITH ENGLAND

THE succession of Madison to the presidency on March 4, 1809, meant no change of ideas. In fact, it hardly involved a change of personnel; for Jefferson was still consulted, and the new secretary of state, Robert Smith, was scarcely more than a figure-head, Madison himself often writing his dispatches. The embargo had failed, but a substitute had been provided. This took the form of a non-intercourse act, which opened up commerce to the rest of the world but prohibited it with France, England, and their colonies. To them America remained tight closed. The law set forth, however, that should England withdraw her orders, or France her decrees, the President could resume intercourse with the complaisant power.

In spite of the importance of the restrictions that remained, the merchant marine soon found unparalleled opportunities for employment. That of Massachusetts increased from 310,000 tons in 1807 to 352,000 tons in 1810. The British armies in Spain and Portugal needed provisions, and those countries were open to our trade. To the north, Russia was free to neutrals after December 31, 1810, and we were practically the only neutrals. This opportunity was not too far afield for our enterprize. By way of the Baltic and the port of Riga, and even by the Arctic port of Archangel, the route to which had the advantage of lying far from the haunts of the British navy, we sent to Russia, in 1810, $3,975,000 worth of goods, in 1811, $6,137,000 worth. To guard this new trade, we exchanged ministers with that country in 1809, sending thither John Quincy Adams, who had now affiliated with the dominant party. Holland and Naples, moreover, and other stretches of European coast, though actually under Napoleonic control, were not legally French and did not fall within our prohibition. To them we could send such things as Napoleon wished and England did not object to. Fish and oil were permitted, but cotton England banned as tending to build up French manufactures. Nor did prohibition by law actually prevent American vessels from dropping into the harbors of France herself, when the way was open. In addition, our ships were licensed by the belligerents to carry on some of that exchange between them which was so beneficial that it defied the dictates of policy. Increasingly, however, this trade was given to their own vessels, and it never was so large as the unlicensed smuggling carried on by the boatmen of the Channel in the teeth of the authorities of both countries. If by this description the ocean may seem to have been a smooth road to the Americans, it must be borne in mind that there were always the perils of search and impressment, and the chances of sudden changes in regulations, involving delay, seizure, and confiscation. Worse still, the standard trade of bringing English manufactures into the United States, and of exporting tobacco and other goods to England and provisions to her colonies, was practically ended.[1]

It was under these circumstances that George Canning, now British minister of foreign affairs, resolved to take advantage of the offer contained in the non-intercourse act in order to reopen the American market to British manufactures. This negotiation was to take place in America, and he instructed his minister at Washington to announce that the orders would be recalled on condition that we withdraw non-intercourse with Eng-

Erskine arrangement

[1] For the study of the actual course of commerce during these years the *Guide to the Material in London Archives for the History of the United States since 1783*, by C. O. Paullin and F. L. Paxson, is useful. It describes the papers to the period of the Civil War. The records of the Board of Trade are found to contain the most novel material.

land, that we forego trade with the French West Indies, and that we allow England to enforce our non-intercourse act with France. The British minister at this time was David Montague Erskine, a young Whig appointed by Fox in 1806, very friendly toward America and married to an American wife. With him an agreement was made which dealt with the *Chesapeake* affair and the recall of the orders, and looked to the formation of a general treaty of commerce between the United States and Great Britain, but which left out Canning's last two conditions. In accordance with this arrangement, Madison, on June 10, 1809, declared intercourse with Great Britain restored.

Canning at once rejected the agreement, recalled Erskine, and sent in his place Francis James Jackson, who was not expected to repeat Erskine's mistake of over- **Canning disavows Erskine** friendliness to America, and who lived up to his reputation. After five weeks' exchange of notes, which grew increasingly unpleasant, the American government refused to deal further with him. Canning, however, had promised him a year in America, and he was not recalled until the end of it. Until the autumn of 1810, therefore, the United States and Great Britain were provided with a burr under the saddle which the tact of Pinkney, our minister at London, could scarcely be expected to make comfortable.

Meanwhile Napoleon had not been unconscious of the United States, though he had not needed to give her much of his attention, since her policy conformed **Napoleon and the embargo** to his own, and he seemed to be reaping the reward for the sale of Louisiana. As if in accordance with his desires,—but in reality because of the southern objection to recognizing a republic founded on a slave insurrection,—intercourse had in 1806 been prohibited with his revolted colony of Hayti, in which he took a fleeting interest. The embargo again, though a measure based on Jefferson's philosophy, exactly fitted into Napoleon's continental system. Although he objected to it as regarded

France, he could not have devised a plan better suited to his purposes had he been dictator of America. "The Emperor applauds the embargo," said Turreau, French minister at Washington. On April 5, 1808, Napoleon issued from Bayonne a decree ordering the sequestration of all American vessels arriving in France, as presumably British property sailing under false papers, no American vessels being legally afloat.

The repeal of the embargo was therefore a rebuff, and its form, by grouping England and France together and differ-

Napoleon and non-inter-course

entiating between France and her dependent states, was still more so. Moreover, the prohibition of Haytian trade, which had never been effective, lapsed about the same time. Napoleon therefore ordered his minister to withdraw from Washington. On August 4, 1809, after Canning's disavowal of the Erskine agreement had assured a return to non-intercourse and a period of aggravation between England and the United States, while the battle of Wagram gave him command of Europe, he issued the decree of Vienna, ordering the seizure and confiscation of "every American ship which shall enter the ports of France, Spain, or Italy." This step he justified by the arguments that those entering French ports were violating the law of the United States, and that the other countries under French control should not be allowed to enjoy trade forbidden to France. The decree was kept secret apparently in order to induce American vessels to enter. Thiers says: "To admit false neutrals in order to confiscate them afterwards, greatly pleased his astute mind, little scrupulous in the choice of means, especially in regard to shameless smugglers who violated at once the laws of their own country and those of the country that consented to admit them." [1] Napoleon himself wrote to Danzig: "Let the American ships enter your ports! Seize them afterwards

[1] M. J. L. A. Thiers, *Histoire du consulat et de l'empire* (21 vols., Paris etc., 1845–69), vol. xii.

You shall deliver the cargoes to me, and I will take them in part payment of the Prussian war debt." On March 25, 1810, he published the Rambouillet decree, which was practically a public announcement of that of Vienna, but with this difference, that it merely sequestered the American vessels instead of confiscating them. He thus held in his hands over eight million dollars' worth of American property as hostage for our behavior. The number of vessels seized in the various countries indicated the state of trade: 51 in France, 44 in Spain, 28 in Naples, and 11 in Holland. To carry out this vigorous policy he was forced to depose his brother Louis, king of Holland, and annex that country to France, as well as to drive from the cabinet his valuable assistant, Fouché. He still continued, however, to license American vessels to import specified goods, and they continued to pay high for such licences.

In spite of the attention that he devoted to it, American trade can hardly be said to have been a leading consideration with Napoleon at this time; his main desire, the closing of the American market to British goods, was still fulfilled. Very different, however, was the situation created by the next change in the American system. Restive under our own regulations, public sentiment, after a hard struggle, at length, May 1, 1810, obtained a practical abandonment of the restrictive system by means of an act popularly known as "Macon Bill No. 2," which allowed trade with all the world. The only continuance of the policy of using commercial regulation as a weapon of diplomacy is found in the provision authorizing the President, in case either Great Britain or France should, before the third day of March following, "so revoke or modify her edicts" as to "cease to violate the neutral commerce of the United States," and the other country should not do so, to renew the non-intercourse act against the obdurate power.

This was indeed a blow to Napoleon's continental system, for it reopened to England her most valuable single market.

It is said that he devoted three days to a consideration of the situation. The result was a letter from his foreign minister, Cadore, of August 5, 1810: "In this new state of things, I am authorized to declare to you, sir, that the decrees of Berlin and Milan are revoked, and that after the 1st of November they will cease to have effect; it being understood that, in consequence of this declaration, the English shall revoke their orders in council, and renounce the new principles of blockade which they have wished to establish; or that the United States, conformably to the act you have just communicated, shall cause their rights to be respected by the English. It is with the most particular satisfaction, sir, that I make known to you this determination of the Emperor. His majesty loves the Americans. Their prosperity and their commerce are within the scope of his policy."

But Napoleon's purpose was not the abandonment of his system. "It is evident," said he, "that we commit ourselves to nothing." He explained to his council that, should the English withdraw their orders, he could achieve his results by customs regulation. What he hoped was that by the ambiguity of his letter he might once more embroil England and the United States. Meantime, to clean the slate of the past, he ordered the American vessels sequestered by the Rambouillet decree to be confiscated. This order was not published; but, when its effects became evident, Cadore explained that it did not affect the future, that it was in reprisal for our non-intercourse act, and that the law of reprisal was final.

Madison seized upon this letter with avidity. He at once demanded that Great Britain withdraw her orders, including **Napoleon and Madison** the blockade of 1806, and threatened nonintercourse should she fail to do so. The Marquis of Wellesley, who had succeeded Canning, was more favorably disposed toward the United States; but as he read the Cadore letter it contained a conditional offer, not a statement of fact. He thought it meant that, if Great Britain should withdraw her orders, Napoleon would withdraw his decrees; that if she should not do so the decrees would also remain in force unless the United States made her neutrality respected, that is, unless she forced England to recall her orders. In this *impasse* the United States would not, he believed, be justified in differentiating between the belligerents until she received evidence of the withdrawal of the decrees. He also found in the letter an additional condition, —namely, that Great Britain must renounce her principle of blockade. Madison, however, understanding that the decrees were actually withdrawn,—for Napoleon failed to answer the riddle which he had set,—declared non-intercourse with England reëstablished after February 2, 1811. He was sustained by an act of Congress of March 2, 1811, and in April, as an expression of his discontent, he withdrew Pinkney from London. Once more, therefore, Napoleon closed the American market to England.

His wall, however, was crumbling at its opposite extremity. It has been noted that on December 31, 1810, Russia opened her ports to neutral vessels. American ship- **Napoleon and** ping straightway crowded her ports, and much **Russia** that they brought was British. Of our exports to Russia in 1811, amounting to over $6,000,000, only $1,630,499 were of our own products. Nor did the total amount given in our figures include cargoes taken in England and admitted by Russia because of the American flag borne by the ship carrying them, a flag which in many cases it had no right to fly. Napoleon called upon the czar to close this breach. The Russian court was divided, torn by factions. Curiously, Romanzoff, who was sympathetic with France, wished to encourage the American merchant marine in order to release Russia from her former dependence on England; Nesselrode, whose inclinations were English, objected to extending privileges to the United States not granted to Great Britain. He wished alliance with the latter power. American trade, long torn by the dogs of war, thus became the bone of contention to set them fighting among themselves. John Quincy Adams found himself at St. Petersburg,—familiar to him as a boyhood memory from his stay there while secretary to Francis Dana, our first minister,—more vitally involved in European entanglements than had been any American minister since Franklin. Napoleon would assent to no compromise, the czar would not close his ports, and events marched rapidly toward war and Napoleon's invasion.[1]

In behalf of our commerce, Russia was preparing for war with France and alliance with England; Napoleon was preparing to force Russia to close her ports to neutral trade. Could we still preserve our neutrality in this supreme moment of struggle? To which side did our interests ally us? To Russia, fighting to defend our rights but allied with England, our great commercial rival? or to Napoleon, endeavoring to shut us out of Europe, but professing himself, if he won and brought England to terms, willing to establish peace on earth and freedom on the seas? Even if these professions were not to be accepted at their face value, at any rate it was probable that a victorious Napoleon would not be lenient, should one have stirred his wrath.

During the spring of 1811 Madison and Monroe, the latter of whom had just replaced Smith at the state department, Napoleonic triumph debated over the question. The immediate issue was whether we should send a minister to France to take the place of Armstrong, who had returned to America. Evidence accumulated that Napoleon's decrees still operated and that the sequestered American vessels were actually confiscated. The balance turned against France. At this critical moment, however, Napoleon once more proved himself equal to the emergency. His foreign minister, the Duke of Bassano, informed Jonathan Russell, our secretary of legation, that the emperor had authorized "the admission of the American cargoes which had been

[1] J. Q. Adams, *Memoirs* (12 vols., Philadelphia, 1874–77), ii. 491–662, iii. 1–144.

provisionally placed on deposit." This turned the scale; Joel Barlow was appointed minister, and relations were continued.

The administration still hoped for peace, although leaning toward France; but its plans were set at naught by the entrance into national politics of two new factors. The first was a general fighting spirit brought to Congress, when it met in the autumn of 1811, by a number of young men who soon began to act together and to be known as the "War Hawks." The aroma of war had for twenty years floated across the Atlantic, but it had brought only its glories and not its sorrows. To the younger generation war seemed to be almost the normal condition, and to offer opportunities of distinction and advancement which peace denied. If, however, the wars of Europe had an effect on American youth, the effect was general. No longer, as in 1793, did the particular issues of European politics divide the majority of Americans into partisans of France and of England. The new war leaders were nationalists; they wished to fight to vindicate the honor of their country, smirched, they believed, by her long supine submission to the whacks and blows of the belligerents. Isolation they accepted, but they did not believe that it must necessarily be passive. Many of the leaders were indifferent as to whom they fought; Calhoun, the logical, with the enthusiasm of youth, would fight both.[1]

Direction was given to this warlike spirit by the second factor. Once more western problems became vital: they were to determine the issue. This time it was primarily a question of the northwest, though its views were voiced in Congress by Henry Clay of Kentucky, speaker of the new House of Representatives.[2] The most obvious

---

[1] J. C. Calhoun, *Works* (ed. R. K. Crallé, 6 vols., New York, 1853–55), vol. ii.

[2] Henry Clay, *Works* (ed. C. Colton, 7 vols., New York, 1897), vol. i. ch. ix.

motive for discontent resulted from the Indian situation. Steadily since 1796 the pioneer had pressed into the wilderness, steadily the government had made broad his way by contriving one purchase of Indian land after another. The Indians, grumbling, had yielded to necessity; but dissatisfaction grew among them, and recently had resulted in combination to resist encroachment. Under the leadership of two brothers, Tecumseh, the war chief, and Olliwochica,

The Indians the prophet, the beginnings of a confederacy were formed, the leaders conceiving of a union not only of the northern tribes but also between the northern and southern groups. In 1811 war began in the battle of Tippecanoe, near the Wabash.

That the Indian hostility was encouraged by the British, and that the latter would aid the savages in the coming war,

British and Indians was firmly believed by the sanest heads on the frontier. William Henry Harrison, governor of Indiana territory and in command at Tippecanoe, said that he could always tell the state of relations between United States and Great Britain by the behavior of the Indians. Great Britain's policy was actually not different from that pursued during Washington's administration. There was on the part of the government no incitement to hostility; rather, the effort was to keep the peace. On the other hand, it maintained, though not entirely of its own choice, relations with the Indians which, considering the fact that these tribes were within the limits of the United States, were not compatible with any principle of international comity. Moreover, as was natural on so wild a frontier, its control over its own agents and subjects was so lax that it was sometimes involved by their acts in complications for which it was not directly responsible but which it was by its international duty required to prevent.

The British subjects concerned in these relations were nearly all fur-traders. Scotch, French-Canadians, English, and half-breeds, they led lives of the most unfettered freedom, with the exception of an almost complete economic dependence upon the two great British companies, the Hudson Bay, and the Northwestern. Together these companies dominated the whole region west- *Fur-trade rivalries* ward from Lake Michigan, including what is now Wisconsin and the upper reaches of the Mississippi and the Missouri. Wide as was the area, its paths, the rivers and trails, were none too numerous, and the traders of the two companies were continually encountering each other, as well as the rivals of both, the Americans. The latter had hitherto not been so well organized as the British subjects; but of late the American Fur Company, of which John Jacob Astor was the leading spirit, had been bringing order out of chaos. Astor's imperial plans were now taking the form of establishing a permanent settlement on the Pacific coast. He engaged experts from the Northwestern Company, and in 1811 founded the post of Astoria on the Columbia. This distant enterprise did not, however, diminish the rivalry nearer home. From St. Louis and Michilimackinac went forth better and better equipped bands of American traders, who competed with those sent out by the British companies. The emulation in the forests and plains was transmitted, with the skins, to Montreal and to New York, which supplied the capital for the expeditions and for the establishment of the posts, and which competed in the disposal of the furs. Relatively the British were losing ground; they asked for government support; they bemoaned the influence of the United States government factories which had been established at Washington's behest. To the American frontiersmen, their own government seemed inert and spineless as compared with that of Great Britain, and particularly they protested at the free use of American soil which the British companies enjoyed under the Jay treaty. This growing rivalry was temporarily embittered by the fall in the price of furs as a result of the European wars. The pressure for assistance was equally strong upon both governments, but it was most effective at this time in strengthening the call for war from the American frontier.[1]

It is not to be supposed that the purpose of the virile West was purely self-defence. To north, to west, to south, Conquest of it felt nothing stronger than itself, except the Canada bonds of the United States government which held it in. It strained at the leash. It felt competent, if left alone, to settle all its difficulties in the completest manner by wiping out opposition. It wished merely permission to use its strength. February 22, 1810, Henry Clay said to the Senate: "The conquest of Canada is in your power, I trust I shall not be deemed presumptuous when I state that I verily believe that the militia of Kentucky are alone competent to place Montreal and Upper Canada at your feet."

The new national spirit, thus directed by the West, swept the administration fluttering before it. The breeze was fanned, War declared to be sure, by some new episodes, such as the encounter in 1811 of the *President* and the *Little Belt*, in which the former avenged our navy for the maltreatment of the *Chesapeake* by the *Leopard*, and the publication by Congress in 1812 of the papers of John Henry, a British secret agent; but these things counted little. On April 1, 1812, in a secret message, Madison recommended an embargo preparatory to war. On June 1 he recommended war, and on July 18 Congress accepted the recommendation.

England at the eleventh hour sought to preserve peace. She sent over the comparatively agreeable Augustus John England's ef- Foster. Apology and reparation for the fort for peace *Leopard-Chesapeake* affair were at length arranged. On June 16 the recall of the orders was voted by Parliament. Madison, however, deemed this insufficient. He demanded assurance that blockades should not be made

[1] Washington Irving, *Astoria*, 2 vols., Philadelphia, 1836; H. M. Chittenden, *The American Fur Trade of the Far West*, 3 vols., New York, 1902; *The Fur-trade in Wisconsin*, Wisconsin Hist. Soc., *Collections*, 1911, vol. xx.

to do the duty of the orders, that the enforcement of English blockades off the American coast should cease, and that the impressment of seamen should be suspended, pending a treaty which should settle the matter definitively. In the election of 1812 the country supported Madison by reëlecting him. It is noticeable that the commercial states voted against him, protesting at this final attempt of **Causes of war** an administration of agriculturists to protect our commercial interests. The West solidly supported him. The causes of the war were not Great Britain's failure to agree with us as to the position of neutrals, nor did they spring from the jockeying of Napoleon; they lay rather in the national anger roused by twenty years' disregard of our neutral rights. It was not detailed arguments, but accumulated woes, that moved the "War Hawks" of the East, while those of the West felt the added impulse to obtain a free hand for the settlement of their own problems.

CHAPTER XV

PEACE

UNTIL the spring of 1814 Great Britain did not blockade the coast north of Cape Cod. In part this forbearance may
Great Britain and New England
have been due to a hope, based upon the reports of secret agents like John Henry and John Howe, her consuls, and Jackson her minister, that the discontent of that region might find expression in separation from the United States.[1] It was true that its leading men doubted whether they could forever endure a government so distasteful in its policies; and their anger mounted higher when, in this supreme moment of the contest between Napoleon representing the forces of revolution, and England the supporter of order, the administration threw its weight into what they believed was the wrong scale. Their view was expressed by Pickering's toast to Jackson in 1810, "The world's last hope,—Britain's fast-anchored isle." This feeling extended to heckling the government, and later to action looking toward a break-up of the Union; but it did not reach the point of treating with the national enemy, nor did it prevent New England from doing its fair share in the war.[2]

Great Britain did not lose by her leniency, however, and probably her motive was less political than commercial. The
War trade
West Indies and the armies in Canada needed supplies, and New England could furnish them, and did. As, in the wars between England and France when we were colonies, our ship-captains helped supply the French

[1] "Secret Reports of John Howe, 1808," *Amer. Hist. Review*, 1911–12, xvii. 70–102, 332–354; see also Paullin and Paxson, *Guide*, "Lady Jackson Papers."
[2] Edmund Quincy, *Life of Josiah Quincy* (Boston, 1867), 242–306.

West India islands,[1] so now, under one disguise or another, the New England ships brought to Halifax and other ports the needed provisions, and from one point or another gathered cargoes to import into Boston and other open ports. In fact, war proved to have less effect on New England commerce than the embargo had had. South of Cape Cod the blockade was so far from being of the "paper" variety that practically no trade could go on without the assent of Great Britain. Her armies in Spain, however, must be fed, and they continued to draw their supplies from the ample granaries about the Chesapeake, brought to them in American vessels equipped with special licences. Privateering, moreover, was not much more hazardous than were many other branches of the trade which Americans had been pursuing. Many merchants strengthened their craft, enlarged their crews, and scoured the seas for British merchantmen. The national balance of captures and losses was not very unequal, about seventeen hundred captures of merchant vessels being credited to the Americans as against about fourteen hundred losses; but wealth changed hands rapidly. Fortunes running over a million were won. The losses made less impression because, owing to various kinds of insurance, they actually did not fall with corresponding heaviness upon individuals.

Most avenues of trade, however, were closed, and particularly the ordinary unromantic routes. The severest blow was the cutting-off of the coast trade, Changed conditions in 1814 which had been steadily growing since the end of the Revolution, and which alone had escaped the dead hand of the embargo. The Newfoundland fisheries also were closed. With the fall of Napoleon in the spring of 1814, England, on the day after her final peace with France, shut up the United States so completely that during that summer her commerce was represented on the ocean by nothing but some forty or fifty privateers.

[1] G. S. Kimball, *Correspondence of William Pitt . . . with Colonial Governors*, 2 vols., New York, etc., 1906.

To the West, which had wanted the war, it brought both satisfaction and disappointment. The Indians were thor-

Western campaigns oughly and, as it proved, finally overwhelmed, both to the south in the battle of Horseshoe Bend, and to the north in the battle of Thames. This latter result, however, was not due to the unassisted efforts of the frontiersmen themselves, as Clay had boasted that it would be. The navy, which after a brilliant and important struggle had been driven from the ocean, sent of its personnel to the lakes, where, in the battles of Lake Erie and Lake Champlain, it established a control, which it continued to maintain, over all the border lakes except Ontario, where neither side obtained supremacy. Even with this assistance Upper Canada remained unconquered. The western leaders had overlooked one element in the situation,—the people of the region which is now Ontario. The nucleus of this sturdy population consisted of American loyalists and their descendants. Hearty in their hatred of the United States, they were situated nearer the strategic points than were the Americans, and they afforded a substantial support to the British troops, which until 1814 were none too numerous. After the release of Wellington's veterans by the closing of the European wars, conquest by the Americans was of course out of question. In fact, in that year the British held points on American soil all along the northern boundary.[1]

While these events were taking place negotiations for peace were in progress.[2] It was displeasing to the czar that,

Russia offers mediation just when Napoleon was invading Russia to close her ports to American trade, the United States should go to war with Great Britain, his friend and leading ally. He, therefore, September 21, 1812, offered

[1] C. P. Lucas, *The Canadian War of 1812*, Oxford, 1906.

[2] For the peace negotiations, the *Memoirs* of J. Q. Adams, and the *Writings* of Gallatin are the most valuable and interesting sources, taken, of course, in connection with the official dispatches in the *American State Papers, Foreign Relations*. The best historical account is that in the last chapter of Mahan's *Sea Power in its Relations to the War of 1812*.

mediation, and Adams at once sent word of the offer to Washington. It reached there with the news of Napoleon's reverses. We had bet on the wrong horse. We had carefully refrained from allying ourselves with Napoleon, but the fact that he too was fighting England had undoubtedly lent us courage. Madison did not relish the idea of carrying on the war alone. Indeed, there was no reason why he should not negotiate, or why he should not accept the mediation of Russia, whose useful friendship our commerce had experienced. The offer was therefore accepted, March 11, 1813, and a mission was appointed consisting of Albert Gallatin and Adams of the administration party, and James A. Bayard, a Federalist.

When Gallatin and Bayard reached Europe they found the offer of mediation rejected by England. Although Great Britain and Russia were united in fighting Napoleon, their ideas did not harmonize on *Russia versus Great Britain* many other subjects. Particularly on those involved in the dispute between Great Britain and the United States were they poles apart, Russia clinging to the pronouncements of Catharine's Armed Neutrality, England to the principles that had so long controlled her conduct. "Maritime law!" said Lord Walpole at one time to Adams. "Why, Russia may fight us till she sinks, and she will get no maritime law from us; that is no change in the maritime law. Maritime law submitted to the Congress! What can there be upon earth more absurd?" Alexander, moreover, became less intent upon pressing the matter as the allies became more successful and it was seen that the weight of America was not sufficient to prevent the balance tipping against Napoleon. Mediation failed.

On July 13, 1813, Castlereagh offered to negotiate directly. This offer, made while victory in Europe was still undetermined, was eagerly accepted by Madison after the defeat of Napoleon in the campaigns of that year had become patent. He added to the American commission Henry Clay to represent the West, and Jonathan Russell, who had served in France. After some troublesome preliminaries it was ar-

Opening of ne- ranged that the negotiations take place at Ghent.
gotiations The two commissions were well chosen and rep-
resentative. On the British side Lord Gambier was an admiral, Henry Goulburn was member of Parliament and undersecretary for the colonies, and William Adams was a doctor of law. Expert and skilful as they were, however, they were no match for the American commissioners. Three of these, Gallatin, Bayard, and Clay, were without diplomatic experience, but Gallatin and Clay, with Adams, were among the ablest half-dozen men of our country. They were thoroughly at home in handling American questions; they were used to dealing with men; and they had an intellectual power and a driving force which utterly overshadowed that of their opponents. England was at the disadvantage of having her best talent diverted to the more important Congress of Vienna, but even her delegation there could not have overmatched the Americans at Ghent. Though Adams was the head of the American commission, Gallatin was its most influential member. A French Swiss by birth and education, and of noble family, he was regarded by Europeans as one of themselves, familiar with their standards and mode of life, a solace in their intercourse with the, if not untutored at least differently tutored, Americans. At the most critical moment of the negotiation the duke of Wellington did not hesitate to write to him privately of his wish for peace. Gallatin acted as mediator between the members of the commission and between the commission as a whole and European public men.[1]

Our best efforts were indeed needed. England was at her pinnacle. The *Times*, in June, 1814, when Gallatin and Bayard were in London, said: "Having disposed of all our enemies in Europe, let us have no cant of moderation. There

[1] *A Great Peace Maker, the Diary of James Gallatin*, New York, 1914, 34–35.

is no public feeling in the country stronger than that of indignation against the Americans. As we urged the principle of no peace with Bonaparte, so we English opinmust maintain the doctrine of no peace with ion James Madison." The same paper, announcing the American victory at Plattsburg, said, October 14, 1814: "This is a lamentable event to the civilized world. The subversion of the whole system of the Jeffersonian school . . . was an event to which we should have bent and yet must bend all our energies. The present American government must be displaced, or it will sooner or later plant its poisoned dagger in the heart of the parent state." Again it declared, "Mr. Madison's dirty swindling manœuvers in respect to Louisiana and the Floridas remain to be punished." The British were at this time in Spanish Florida; they threatened Mobile; and throughout the negotiations news was awaited of the fleet and the army under Pakenham which was advancing upon New Orleans. Louisiana had as yet but a small American population, it was isolated from the settled West, and the loyalty of its creoles was in doubt. It seemed possible, therefore, that the mouth of the Mississippi might be lost and all the attendant problems once more arise.

More definite was the danger to the northward. The *Canadian Gazette* insisted that the United States surrender the northern part of New York State, so as The "buffer to give Canada both banks of the St. Lawrence state" and of the Niagara. It insisted also on a guaranteed buffer Indian country, bounded toward the United States by a line from Sandusky to Kaskaskia. This old idea, which Hammond had been instructed to act upon in 1792, was now being continually urged upon the British ministry. Tackle wrote to Lord Bathurst, November 24, 1812, suggesting that the Indian territory extend to the Maumee and the Wabash. "It would be, in my feeble judgment," he urged, "if occupied exclusively by Indians, an all important barrier to the designs of the United States against the influence, and intercourse of the British, with the immense regions extending Westerly even to the Pacific Ocean." The fur-traders and the Indians had fought well during the war, the latter especially had suffered; now both demanded that protection which they had persistently been claiming from the British government since 1783.

Under these circumstances, Castlereagh issued his instructions, July 28, 1814. Maritime law was not to be touched. The boundary should be "rectified" so to give the British a road from Halifax to Quebec, with Sackett's harbor to command the St. Lawrence, Fort Niagara to command the river of the same name, and Moose island and Eastport to command the mouth of the St. Croix. The Indians should be included in the treaty, and should be assured of a mutually guaranteed boundary,— that fixed by Wayne's treaty of 1795. The United States must give up its privileges in the fisheries, and the navigation of the lakes; England, having access to the Mississippi through the Indian country, must continue to enjoy its navigation. The American instructions, prepared by Monroe, January 14, 1814, were to obtain first of all an acknowledgment of the American position on points of maritime law, though a compromise was suggested on the subject of impressment whereby Great Britain was to yield the right and the United States was to forbid British born sailors to serve in American vessels. Indemnity was to be secured for illegal captures. The commissioners were to urge "the advantages to both countries which are promised by a transfer of the upper parts and even the whole of Canada to the United States," and were to point out that experience had shown that Great Britain could not "participate in the dominion and navigation of the lakes without incurring the danger of an early renewal of the war."

These differences seemed to preclude the possibility of agreement, especially since the British terms were presented in the form of an ultimatum. On August 24, the American

commissioners returned a "unanimous and decided negative,"
in a very able vote setting forth that the English claims were
"founded neither on reciprocity, nor any of the
usual bases of negotiation, neither that of *uti* Check
possedetis nor of *status quo ante bellum*." Openly, but not
hastily, they prepared to leave Ghent. While thus delaying
they talked much with the British commissioners, particularly in regard to the buffer state. Gallatin asked what
would become of the hundred thousand Americans already
living within the boundary proposed. Goulburn, perhaps
hearing of them for the first time, thought that the line
might be slightly changed, but that on the whole the Americans could shift for themselves: the Indians would treat them
well; he knew an Indian who was very intelligent. Adams
said that such a treaty provision was opposing a feather
to a torrent. Population, he declared, was increasing: "As
it continued to increase in such proportions, was it in human
experience, or in human power, to check its progress by a
bond of paper purporting to exclude posterity from the
natural means of subsistence?" Bayard, the Federalist, told
Goulburn that, when it became known that the negotiation
had broken off on such terms, the Federalist party in the
United States would be overwhelmed.

In the end the Americans succeeded in making an impression on the British commissioners, and through them on
the ministry. Since England had been put
in the position of continuing the war for conquest, the ministry became satisfied that if
the negotiations ended at this point the war would become
"quite popular" in America. "It is very material," they
said, "to throw the rupture of the negotiations, if it take
place, upon the Americans." It was, indeed, feared that the
war might become unpopular in England: the *Times* did
not represent the whole nation. The same elements of
distress which, anxious for the American market, had all
too late forced the recall of the orders in council, would be

little inclined to forego their trade much longer for remote accessions of territory in the wilds of America. The ministry, moreover, was full of anxiety over the wrangles of the late allies at the Congress of Vienna, where events were rapidly shaping themselves for a new European alignment,— England, France, and Austria against Russia and Prussia— and a new war. Moved by these considerations, it sent new instructions to Ghent, September 1. Far from satisfactory in themselves, these new terms put the British in the awkward position of having retreated from an ultimatum. The American commissioners were quick to take advantage of this weakness. They refused to treat on the proposed new basis of *uti possedetis*, that is to say the situation then existing. Under these circumstances the duke of Wellington was asked if he would go to America. He expressed his willingness, but declared that nothing could be accomplished while the Americans held the lakes, and said that England was not justified by the military situation in demanding any territory. The ministry once more receded, and offered to negotiate on the basis of *status quo ante bellum*, or the condition before the war. Indeed, it is difficult to see how they could do anything else. If they doubted the support of public opinion in demanding important posts and a buffer state, they could scarcely expect it in fighting for the apparently trivial bits of American territory which they were holding in 1814.

On the other hand, the American commissioners found that in insisting on an adjustment of maritime law they ran into the stone-wall of British determination. Fortunately, however, they were instructed from America, where Madison was oppressed by the impending British attack on New Orleans, the harrying of the coast and burning of Washington, and the prospect of the Hartford convention, to omit such clauses from the treaty if necessary.

Maritime law

With these points out of the way, negotiations progressed

rapidly. On the question of fisheries, it is true, the American commission divided. Adams and Russell wished to restate the terms of 1783, which meant that the British right to navigate the Mississippi must be conceded also. Clay, mindful of the usefulness of that river to the British fur-traders, and afraid that such a right would be used by Great Britain to back a claim for territorial access to the Mississippi by pushing south the northern boundary of the Louisiana Purchase, was unwilling to admit the privilege. Finally, at Gallatin's suggestion, both points were omitted, and on December 24, 1814, the treaty was signed.

Fisheries versus the Mississippi

Great triumph of American diplomacy as the treaty was in the light of the British instructions, yet, considered from the point of view that the Americans began the war to obtain satisfaction for what they considered infractions of maritime law, it registered a defeat. It is more important, however, to note that from 1815 until the present year (1914), Great Britain was at war with European powers for only three years (1853 to 1856), and so the treaty marked the end of our suffering as neutrals from her exactions for a hundred years. The West more nearly obtained what it wanted. The treaty provided: "The United States engage to put an end, immediately after the ratification of the present treaty, to hostilities with all the tribes or nations of Indians," on the basis of 1812, if they should agree. No provision guaranteed these boundaries, however, and though the United States continued to press them westward, Great Britain never after meddled in the matter. The Indian power east of the Mississippi was broken, and never again within the United States did any Indians play a part as a factor in American diplomacy. The general restoration of property, moreover, included the raising of the United States flag over the post of Astoria, although the property title to it had passed into the hands of the British Northwestern Company, to be absorbed later

Gains and losses

into the Great, or Hudson Bay, Company. By this recognition was added a third link to our claim to Oregon.

The treaty provided also for the settlement of the numerous points of dispute that had arisen regarding the exact **Boundary** location of the boundary between Canada and **commissions** the United States. Once more, as in the case of the Jay treaty, these questions were to be determined by semi-judicial process,—that is, by commissions of two members each, or, if the commissions failed to agree, by arbitration. Four such commissions were arranged for. The first one was to divide the islands in Passamaquoddy Bay, in submitting one of which, Moose island, to question, the Americans suffered the only defeat, so far as details were concerned, in the framing of the treaty. This commission worked satisfactorily on the whole, although the final water boundary was not determined until an arbitration of 1908. Another commission ultimately fixed the boundary from the crossing of the forty-fifth parallel and the St. Lawrence through Lake Huron. The problems of the boundary from the St. Croix to the St. Lawrence and from Lake Huron to the Lake of the Woods proved too complicated; the commissions charged with them failed to agree, and subsequent arbitration was unsuccessful. Nevertheless, another long step had been taken in clearing up the ambiguities and vagueness of the treaty of 1783.

From the peace of Ghent the United States emerged, not a "great power" in the conventional sense, but a nation of **Our position in** assured position. Thereafter our strength was **1815** sufficient for our defence, and our safety ceased to depend on the oscillations of the European balance of power. The way was open for us to enter into the European **National exist-** system as a participating member, or to pursue **ence and terri-** our own path without serious molestation. **tory** There were just as many unsettled stretches of our boundary as in 1783, but their vagueness was now an advantage to our growing power rather than a danger. The area of dispute, moreover, had been pushed back and our territory was much more self-sufficing than it had been. We had secured the outlet of our greatest river, and we actually possessed the mouths of nearly all those flowing from our territory into the Gulf of Mexico. The great western expanse of the Louisiana Purchase assured us that the Mississippi was destined to become what a river should be, a magnet to unite and not a boundary to divide. Had we rested where we were in 1815 our destiny as a great nation would have been certain; but we were already pushing our claims across the mountains to the Pacific, and it required no great prophetic power to foresee that our forty-five degrees of longitude would irresistibly grasp the almost uninhabited ten degrees of the Pacific slope.

Our commerce for years had been abnormal, and was for the moment almost swept from the seas; international law had been so strained and broken by twenty years of ceaseless strife that one might have feared that two centuries of development in the regulation of international relationships would be lost and anarchy return. A world-wide readjustment must follow the overthrow of Napoleon, and we must share in it. Fortunately, we were increasingly producing things that other nations needed, besides affording a growing market for their products. Fortunately, too, we entered into the new era of negotiation free from entangling agreements, and with a remarkably consistent record of action in the past from which we could develop policies for the future.

Commerce and international law

CHAPTER XVI

COMMERCE AND BOUNDARIES

THE period from the treaty of Ghent to the inauguration of Jackson is notable for the continuity and the brilliancy of our diplomatic service. In 1817 Monroe, having been secretary of state, became President. Unsuccessful in all his early diplomatic undertakings except the purchase of Louisiana, which was in no wise due to him, he had nevertheless an experience dating back to 1793, and he showed improvement.[1]

The diplomatic service

But, although the responsibility was Monroe's, the burden fortunately fell on John Quincy Adams. As a boy Adams had known the diplomatic circles of Paris and St. Petersburg. From 1795 to 1801 he had conducted negotiations with England, Holland, Prussia, and Sweden. At the close of his work at Ghent, he became minister to Great Britain, to return home in 1817 as secretary of state, an office which he retained until his elevation to the presidency in 1825. Although perhaps not intended by nature for a career in diplomacy, by intellect and industry he forced himself ahead of all his contemporaries and made fundamental contributions to American diplomacy on a par with those of Franklin, Washington, his father John Adams, and Hay. Unprofitably obstinate and exacting, and without personal charm, he had a more comprehensive view of our national future than any of his associates, a view somewhat obscured in later life, it is true, when his emotions were stirred by his opposition to slavery and his imagination by his fear of the slavocracy. His chief opponent

Characteristics of Adams

[1] Monroe, *Writings*, 7 vols, N. Y., 1898–1903.

was George Canning, after 1822 foreign minister of Great
Britain.   Both players of consummate ability, Adams
showed perhaps more genius, Canning more   Canning
adaptability.   If neither definitely triumphed
over the other, at least neither lost tricks; each won when
he held the cards.[1]

Of subordinates, Gallatin gained golden opinions during
his mission to France from 1816 to 1823, and served as
minister to England in 1826 and 1827.[2]   Clay,   Gallatin
as Adams remarks, had been much influenced
by his residence abroad on the peace commission.   With his
ready adaptability he had added a polish of manner to his
natural magnetism, and had acquired interest   Clay
in foreign affairs and a broad, if somewhat
superficial, knowledge of them.   Disappointed at not receiving the state department in 1817, he was for years
a thorn in the side of the administration; but during
his service as secretary of state, from 1825 to 1829,
he was a sympathetic coadjutor of Adams.   Richard
Rush and Rufus King, ministers to England   Rush and King
from 1817 to 1825, were highly competent
representatives of the country.[3]   In general, indeed, the
service had begun to attract men of a high class, and the
administration was willing to employ them.

This condition was both a cause and a result of the higher
standing which the United States had taken in the world's
estimation.   Perhaps no one thing had con-   Enhanced
tributed more to this added prestige than the   prestige
glorious, though apparently futile, record of our navy in the
war.   Not since the French Revolution beheaded the naval
officers of the old régime had the British found rivals able to
stand before them on any basis approaching equality.   The

[1] J. Q. Adams, *Memoirs*, 12 vols., Phila., 1874–77. H. W. V. Temperley,
Life of Canning, London, 1905.

[2] Gallatin, *Writings*, 3 vols., Phila., 1879.

[3] Richard Rush, *Memoranda of a Residence at the Court of London*, Philadelphia, 1833; C. R. King, *Life and Correspondence of Rufus King*, 6 vols.

successful naval duels fought by the *Constitution*, the *Wasp*, and the *United States*, to say nothing of the battles on the lakes, amazed Europe. England sought to minimize this impression by pointing to inequalities in the strength of the vessels, and by claiming the crews as renegade Englishmen; but she failed to shake their effect. The potential strength of the American navy, and the actual strength of the merchant marine on which it rested, gained us a hearing at every court.[1]

The problems that engaged the attention of the government during this period were less vital than those which **Decline of Commerce** occupied our diplomacy before 1815, and consequently attracted less public interest. To a large degree our long-sought isolation had been attained. The European situation was also less absorbing, and our growth had rendered us less malleable to European intrigues. Moreover, Jefferson's restrictive policy had hastened the same natural process here which Napoleon's continental system had brought about in Europe. Manufacturing had developed. We were less dependent upon foreign imports, and our own markets consumed a greater proportion of our agricultural products. We were approaching more nearly to an economic equilibrium, and commerce was not so important to us as it had been. Our diplomacy was less interesting and less vital, and it was conducted under less pressure.

The treaty of Ghent had so rigidly excluded contentious matters that many subjects were left to the future. This **Continuation of negotiation with Great Britain** was on the whole to the advantage of the United States. In fact, the statesmen of the rising generation, conscious of our steadily growing power and not confronted by the pressing necessity of the Confederation and early constitutional periods, were usually ready to let issues drag, confidently believing that

[1] C. F. Adams, "Wednesday, August 19, 1812, 6:30 P. M. the Birth of a World Power," *Amer. Hist. Review*, 1913, xviii. 513–521.

time was working with them. The settlement of many of these problems, however, was not long delayed; for the treaty proved to be not the end of agreement, but merely the first step toward it.

In 1817 Bagot, the British minister at Washington, and Richard Rush, the acting secretary of state, exchanged notes dealing with the navigation of the Great   Use of the Lakes. This simple arrangement provided for   lakes the maintenance of small and equal armed forces by the two powers. Although revocable at six months' notice, it has, adjusted to meet the changing conditions of ship-construction and revenue patrol, lasted to the present time.[1]

A disagreement arose over the interpretation of the treaty of Ghent. The Americans claimed that its provision for the return of property of all kinds included slaves,   Indemnity for many of whom had been taken on board by   slaves British war vessels in the Chesapeake and elsewhere; Great Britain, on the contrary, maintained that they ceased to be slaves on entering a British war vessel and so could not be returned. By a convention of 1818 this question was submitted to a true arbitration by the emperor of Russia, who decided that we could claim indemnification but not restitution. In accordance with this decision, a new claims convention was framed in 1822, by which we ultimately received nearly a million and a quarter dollars in compensation. The demand for the restitution of slaves taken at the close of the Revolution was not pressed.

A more disturbing question was that of the status of previous agreements between the two nations. The effect of a war upon earlier treaties is a subject which   Effect of war had not then, and indeed has not yet, been   on treaties reduced to rule. The courts of this country and of others have continued to enforce provisions respecting individual rights established under earlier treaties, though this does not

[1] J. M. Callahan, *Agreement of 1817; Reduction of Naval Forces upon the American Lakes*, Amer. Hist. Assoc., *Report*, 1895, pp. 369–392.

include a recognition of the power to create fresh rights from the provisions of an earlier treaty after a war has intervened. Again, many treaties contain provisions relating to conduct during hostilities which would be meaningless were they supposed to lapse with a declaration of war. Special privileges and arrangements, on the other hand, are commonly understood so to lapse. In discussing this problem, Adams was particularly anxious to obtain recognition of the rights and privileges accorded to American fishermen on the coast of British America by the treaty of 1783. The British held that these clauses had ceased to operate; consequently fifteen hundred New England vessels previously employed in this occupation were now barred from it. Adams could not press his point as he might have wished; for we on our part treated as void the permanent clause of the Jay treaty giving mutual privileges in the fur trade, by passing, April 29, 1816, an act forbidding licences for trade with the Indians to any except United States citizens, unless by special permission of the President. Adams attempted to draw a distinction between the two treaties, on the ground that the first "was not, in the general provisions, one of those which, by the common understanding and usage of civilized nations, is or can be considered as annulled by a subsequent war." This Lord Bathurst denied; but he admitted that this treaty, "like many others, contained provisions of different character—some in their own nature irrevocable, and others of a temporary character."

Upon this basis the convention of 1818 dealt with the question. The "right" of Americans to fish off the Banks of Newfoundland, "acknowledged" by the treaty of 1783, remained acknowledged; the "liberties," however, were treated as void, and a substitute arrangement was entered into. This contract gave us the right to take fish within the three-mile limit on the coast of Labrador and certain specified coasts of Newfoundland, and to use for drying fish the same shores so long

Convention of 1818 and the fisheries

as they remained unsettled. Our fishermen might also use the settled harbors "for the purpose of shelter and of repairing damages therein, of purchasing wood, and of obtaining water, and for no other purpose whatever." But, runs the treaty, "they shall be under such restrictions as may be necessary to prevent their taking, drying or curing fish therein, or in any other manner whatever abusing the privileges hereby reserved to them."

Under this convention, which is still in force, the American fishermen at once resumed their occupation. In spite of its apparently liberal provisions, however, the document proved to be a Pandora's box of discords, and its ambiguities have been sources *Later problems of the fisheries* of dispute almost to the present day. There were stretches of coast where we wished to fish which were not included in the treaty definition. Here we certainly could not encroach within the three-mile limit, but it was not certain what the three-mile limit meant. Great Britain insisted that a number of bays, even though their mouths exceeded six miles across, were closed waters; and we desired to use the Gut of Canso, separating Nova Scotia from the island of Cape Breton, although it was less than six miles broad. The important, almost necessary, privilege of purchasing bait was not mentioned in the treaty and was often denied, as was that also of using the harbors for transshipment of fish from one vessel to another.

The local port regulations admitted of being made very burdensome, and the spirit to make them so developed, for the rivalry between American and Canadian fishermen became constantly keener. Hereto- *Fishermen's rivalries* fore the Canadians had had the best of it, for the most important common market for both countries, the British West Indies, had been regulated to their advantage. Now the United States was developing into the most important market, and here the Americans had the aid of tariff protection. They also received bounties from the national government, as an offset to the duty on the salt they used and in recognition of the fisheries as a "nursery of seamen." The less fortunate Canadians were eager to embarrass the Americans by disagreeable regulations, but they were not unwilling to sell them fish, upon which many Americans unblushingly collected bounties and which they sold at prices enhanced by the tariff.[1]

A somewhat similar question, which can hardly be said ever to have risen to the surface of diplomacy, related to the annuities granted by the United States, in payment for Indian lands, to certain tribes which subsequently removed to Canada. Although paid before the war, the annuities were discontinued afterwards, and are now (1914) the subject of arbitration.

Indian claims

The most important unsettled question, however, though not of so immediate concern as the fisheries, was that of boundary. At the "most northwestern point of the Lake of the Woods" the dividing line between the two nations vanished into thin air. The direction of the treaty of 1783 to continue a line westward until it struck the Mississippi could not be carried out, as such a line would not strike the Mississippi. Perhaps the most logical thing would have been to draw the shortest line to that point, but there was no entirely obvious course. Moreover, the matter had been further complicated by our purchase of Louisiana, which had no northern boundary. Finally, however, the two questions were combined and settled in the convention of 1818, by the dropping of a line due south from the termination of the boundary to the forty-ninth parallel, along which it continued westward to the "Stony," or, as we say, Rocky Mountains. This adjustment was eminently satisfactory, as it gave us almost exactly the natural drainage basin of the Mississippi, which practically constituted our claim by the Louisiana purchase. Although some commun-

Northwestern boundary

[1] Raymond McFarland, *A History of the New England Fisheries*, New York, 1911.

ities along the northern border might to-day be somewhat better accommodated had the natural line been followed, the national area would not be noticeably different, and the national temper would have been many times tried, and might have been lost, in the attempt to locate it. Astronomical boundaries have the advantage of being ascertained by mechanical rather than by human instruments, although, as we shall discover, astronomers may themselves go wrong.

The obscuration of the Mississippi by this line, which left it entirely within United States territory, gave a curious and final twist to the problem of its navigation, until then a perennial question. Had the Mississippi taken its rise in British territory, the clause of the treaty of 1783 giving Great Britain its free use must probably have been interpreted as on a par with that giving us the "right" to fish on the Banks. As the river lay wholly in our territory, however, we successfully asserted that the clause in question lapsed with the one that gave us fishing "liberties." Subsequent discovery, it is true, has shown that the Milk river and a few other branches of the Missouri do rise in Canada; but their navigation will scarcely serve to revive the question, although their use for irrigation is perhaps not without diplomatic significance.

The navigation of the Mississippi

In the same convention a fourth link was added to our claim to the Oregon country by Great Britain's recognition of our pretensions to it. Neither side acknowledged more than the fact that the other had a claim, and it was agreed that the subjects of both might for ten years jointly use the whole region.

Joint occupation of Oregon

With the convention of 1818 practically all the immediate and special questions between the United States and Great Britain had been put in process of settlement. The issues that remained were for the most part in the nature of permanent conflicts of interest and opinion, which do not admit of final determination.

Permanent issues

Of these, commercial intercourse was the most important. The commercial problem of diplomacy was now less than Commercial previously one of opening up markets for our conditions goods. Our fish, that bone of contention, we were coming to eat ourselves; most of the rest were raw materials eminently desired by other countries. England had a small duty on our cotton, but it was soon removed because of internal policy. The foreign products that we handled, as tea from Asia, occasioned more difficulty. The main problem, however, was to protect and encourage the employment of our vessels. For years Great Britain and the United States, the former under the protection of her navy, the latter as the sole important neutral, had almost monopolized the world's shipping. Both suffered from the peace. The neutral trade had been a constant source of embarrassment, but now there was no neutral trade. Our feelings were relieved, but we suffered in pocket. The vessels of other countries came out of their seclusion, and their governments sought to encourage and favor them. One result of this general revival of interest in navigation was that at length, and with difficulty, international coöperation was brought to bear on the Barbary states, till by degrees that pest was wiped out and the Mediterranean was opened to all nations. We did not join in the coöperation, which was under the direction of the quadruple alliance; but we sent a squadron there, and we shared the advantages.[8]

Our method of favoring the merchant marine rested on Jefferson's idea of commercial discrimination. It was em-Commercial bodied in what was called a policy of reciprocity policy which was based on an act of March 3, 1815, providing for the abolition of all discriminations against foreign vessels in our ports in the case of those nations who would reciprocally abolish their discriminating duties. The execution of this policy was to be by means of diplomacy. On this basis, a convention was in the same year arranged with

[1] Moore, *American Diplomacy*, 63–130.

Great Britain which included her European possessions and enumerated ports in the East Indies, but which applied only to goods that were the produce of the respective countries or colonies involved.   In 1822 a somewhat similar convention was arranged with France.   In 1826 a treaty with Denmark, in 1827 treaties with the Hanse towns, Hamburg, Lübeck, and Bremen, and with the kingdoms of Sweden and Norway, and in 1828 a treaty with Prussia opened up complete reciprocity in all kinds of goods.   By an act of 1828 the President was authorized to abolish such discriminating dues by proclamation alone in the case of any country where he should become convinced that a similar freedom was offered to American vessels.   Under this law successive proclamations gradually admitted one country after another to reciprocity.   The discriminations of 1789 disappeared, but with them disappeared also the countervailing discriminations of other countries.

One demand was for an agreement concerning British North America.   With the extinction of the permanent clauses of the Jay treaty vanished the right *The St. Law-* which it gave to Vermont and northern New *rence* York to take their goods to Montreal and Quebec.[1]   The loss of this privilege did not destroy the trade, which continued to be allowed under British regulations till 1822; but no permanent agreement could be reached.   Great Britain wished to blend the matter with the general question of colonial trade; the United States insisted on our natural right to navigate to the sea a river on which we bordered. We were as unable to obtain a recognition of this principle from Great Britain as we had been to secure the assent of Spain in the case of the Mississippi, and a deadlock ensued. Fortunately, the completion of canals from Lake Champlain to the Hudson and from Lake Erie to the Erie canal unbottled those districts, and so diminished the importance of the question.

[1] Schuyler, *American Diplomacy*, 282-291.

The old question of trade with the West Indies continued
to be the most vexing issue between the two governments.

The British Here again it was our shipping and not our
West Indies exports that caused trouble. Under the reciprocity convention of 1815 British vessels brought British
goods to the United States, took aboard United States products needed in the West Indies, and there exchanged them
for island products which they took to England. The American ships, on the contrary, were in general barred from the
islands, and even in the direct trade with England they felt
the competition of the British vessels, which in the greater
flexibility of their opportunity enjoyed a substantial advantage.

Though loath to do so, the United States submitted to
the exclusion from the trade between the colonies and Great

Policy of the Britain, but she insisted on the privilege of
United States carrying on trade between the colonies and
countries mutually foreign. Believing that her products
were so essential to the existence of the West Indian colonies
that she could force her own terms by prohibiting trade there
entirely, she passed acts to that effect in 1818 and 1820, with
the qualification that the President was to suspend them
when he was convinced that their object had been attained.
In 1822 they were in part suspended pending further negotiations under a new British act.

Meanwhile, under the leadership of Huskisson, who in
1823 became president of the Board of Trade, Great Britain

Change in Brit- was undergoing a change of heart, or at least
ish policy of mind, on the subject of the navigation laws.
The old system was breaking down, but, like all other British
institutions, it did not break down suddenly. The ultimate
result, ultimate that is for this period, of the change in British
policy was reached in the acts of June 27 and July 5, 1825,
which opened the colonies to the direct trade of all nations,
that is, to trade in the products of the colony and of the nation to which the vessel employed belonged. The traffic

between the colonies and Great Britain was retained as "coasting trade" for British vessels, as was all indirect trade, as for instance, that in China tea by way of New York. Enjoyment of the benefits of the acts was to depend upon reciprocal advantages granted to Great Britain within the year.

These terms seemed to offer an opportunity for a final settlement, but the United States would not take them as they stood, insisting on the right to take British West Indian goods to all countries ex- **Stale-mate** cept Great Britain. Accordingly, the year having expired before an agreement was reached, Great Britain withdrew her offer. Adams thereupon let the acts of 1818 and 1820 go once more into operation. The West Indian trade was therefore again absolutely closed, as to both products and shipping. Moreover, with the greater efficiency of governmental action, the laws were now so vigorously enforced that there was less commercial intercourse between the United States and the islands than ever before, whether in peace or in war.

More important than these negotiations with Great Britain concerning commerce were those with Spain in regard to boundaries. When in 1815 the Spanish **Disputes with** monarchy reëmerged from the blanket of **Spain** French and English control, it found itself confronted by issues with the United States which would have excused a war had it been in a position to undertake one. Although Spain held title to West Florida, we occupied most of the province; furthermore, though Spain now accepted the validity of the Louisiana Purchase, its western limits were still undetermined. We, on our part, insisted upon the execution of a claims convention framed in 1802, we were fully of a mind to keep West Florida, and were equally determined to obtain East Florida.

Our claim to the latter territory was inherently grounded in that "Manifest Destiny" which was to play so important a part in our history. More concretely, it was based on the argument that Spain was not able to take care of the country,—on the self-constituted right of the stronger nations United States of the world to demand and enforce the claims elimination of international nuisances, an idea which succeeded "Manifest Destiny" as the chief diplomatic slogan of "imperial" statesmen. This argument found its justification in the use of East Florida by the British during the war of 1812, the use of Amelia island just south of Georgia by Spanish American privateers until a later period, and the incursions of Florida Indians into the United States after cattle and slaves.

The negotiations were conducted at Washington by Adams with Don Luis de Onis, whose titles fill nine lines Negotiations of the treaty. They were assisted by the French minister, Baron Hyde de Neuville to whose tact success was in part due. The United States emphasized its views in 1817 by ordering the temporary occupation, for the suppression of piratical privateering, of Amelia island on the one side and Galveston on the other. More important were the orders given to General Andrew Jackson, commanding the southern department, to follow across the border, and chastise in their homes, any Indians marauding United States territory. Jackson, misconceiving the scope of his orders, invaded Florida in the winter of 1818, and not only dealt with the Indians but seized the Spanish forts of St. Marks and Pensacola, and hanged, after a court-martial, two Englishmen, Arbuthnot and Ambrister, who were accused of assisting the Indians.[1]

This episode, which under other circumstances might have embroiled us with both Spain and England, Adams used to quicken the negotiation. Knowing that the latter country did not care to trouble itself over two cosmopolitan adven-

[1] H. B. Fuller, *The Purchase of Florida, its History and Diplomacy*, Cleveland, 1906; James Schouler, *Historical Briefs* (New York, 1896), "Monroe and the Rhea Letter"; R. C. H. Catterall, *A French Diplomat and the Treaty with Spain, 1819*, Amer. Hist. Assoc., *Report*, 1905, i. 21; Frances Jackson, *Memoir of Baron Hyde de Neuville*, St. Louis, 1913.

turers, he set up the claim that they had expatriated themselves by their activities. To De Onis he wrote: "If, as the
commanders both at Pensacola and St. Marks **Adams de-**
have alleged, this has been the result of their **fends Jackson**
weakness rather than their will; if they have assisted the
Indians against the United States to avert their hostilities
from the province which they have not sufficient force to
defend against them, it may serve in some measure to ex-
culpate, individually, those officers; but it must carry demonstration irresistible to the Spanish government, that the right
of the United States can as little compound with impotence
as with perfidy, and that Spain must immediately make
her election, either to place a force in Florida adequate at
once to the protection of her territory, and to the fulfillment
of her engagements, or cede to the United States a province,
of which she retains nothing but the nominal possession, but
which is, in fact, a derelict, open to the occupancy of every
enemy, civilized or savage, of the United States, and serving
no other earthly purpose than as a post of annoyance to them."

Meantime the settlement of the western boundary was
under discussion. We claimed to the Rio Grande, on the
basis of French exploration under La Salle. **The Texas**
Since, however, La Salle went there by mis- **question**
take, and was intent upon leaving as rapidly as possible
when he was murdered, the claim was lacking in convincing
force. A slightly stronger basis for our claim is found in
Napoleon's instructions to Victor in 1802 to occupy to that
river, but of this instruction Adams did not know. Spain,
on her part, claimed to the watershed of the Mississippi, a
limit which would have brought her close to its mouth and
made her an inconvenience if not a menace to its navigation.
De Neuville suggested that Spain give up Florida and that
Adams compromise to the westward. This the latter was
unwilling to do, but he yielded to the pressure of Monroe
and others, and, after discussing nearly every river of the
coast, accepted the Sabine. Curiously, this boundary gave

us more nearly what we had purchased than any other would have done; for although there had never been a western boundary to Louisiana, the most western French fort had been at Natchitoches, about forty miles east of the Sabine, and the most eastern Spanish post had been Nacogdoches, about the same distance to the west.[1] The Sabine, moreover had been agreed upon as a temporary military boundary in 1806.

In return for the cession of the Floridas we released Spain from all claims under the convention of 1802, which had just Terms of the been renewed, and agreed to assume the pay-treaty ment of them to the amount of five million dollars. The treaty resembled that relating to the purchase of Louisiana, in providing that "The inhabitants of the territories which His Catholic Majesty cedes to the United States, by this treaty, shall be incorporated in the Union of the United States, as soon as may be consistent with the principles of the Federal Constitution, and admitted to the enjoyment of all the privileges, rights, and immunities of the citizens of the United States."

To Adams's mind, the most important provision of the treaty was that which described the boundary between the Boundary to United States and the possessions of Spain the Pacific north of the Sabine. This line zigzagged by rivers and parallels of latitude, until it followed the forty-second parallel to the Pacific. Instead, therefore, of completing the bounding of Louisiana, it departed from that purchase and, running westward, created the first international boundary-line that touched the western ocean. It thus added a fifth link to our claim to Oregon.

The treaty was signed February 22, 1819, but its ratification was delayed both in the United States, because of opposition to the so-called surrender of Texas, Ratification and in Spain; so that ratifications were not finally exchanged until February 22, 1821.

[1] R. C. Clark, *The Beginnings of Texas*, Texas Hist. Assoc., *Quarterly*, 1902, v. 171–205.

CHAPTER XVII

THE MONROE DOCTRINE [1]

THE elevation of Joseph Bonaparte to the throne of Spain in 1808 snapped the worn bands that held her American colonies. Miranda was correct in his diagnosis of sentiment in Spanish America. Innumerable causes, local and general, preventable and inevitable, had long nourished a discontent that but awaited an opportunity to manifest itself. In 1810 Miranda, who had of late been making his headquarters in the United States, lost his life in a tragic effort to start the blaze in his home province of Venezuela. In the same year a more successful beginning was made at Buenos Ayres by leaders who still professed loyalty to the Spanish nation, which also, with the fostering aid of England, was resisting the Bonapartist dynasty. When, however, in 1815 Ferdinand VII was restored, this loyalty disappeared; Buenos Ayres never permitted the exercise of his power, and soon the flames of revolt were sweeping over the continent. In 1822 the conflagration raging northward from Buenos Ayres met, in Peru, that which Bolivar had kindled in Venezuela from the ashes of Miranda's movement. In 1821 Mexico had thrown off the yoke; and there was left of the Spanish empire almost nothing except an army in the heights of the Andes which was to succumb in 1824, and the islands of Cuba and Porto Rico. Brazil separated from Portugal in 1822.

To the European mind this outbreak seemed a continuation of the revolution that had begun in the United States and had swept through Europe under the leadership of the French.

[1] D. C. Gilman, *James Monroe*, revised ed., Boston, etc., [1900]. The appendix contains a bibliography of the Monroe Doctrine to 1897.

Brazil, indeed, established an empire; but Spain's former possessions broke up into federal republics based on the model of the United States. In 1820 the movement seemed to rebound to Europe, and insurrections and revolts broke out in Spain herself, in Naples, in Sardinia, and in Greece.

European revolutions

This time, however, revolution found monarchy organized to resist it. September 26, 1815, there had been signed at Paris, at the earnest solicitation of Czar Alexander, the so-called Holy Alliance, by which Russia, Austria, and Prussia united to defend religion and morality, and, what they believed to be the only sure foundation for them, government by divine right. While the Holy Alliance of itself did little, it inspired with its principles the quadruple alliance, of which France was a member and with which England sometimes coöperated, as in the joint demonstration against the Barbary pirates. In 1821 the meeting of the allies at Troppau authorized Austria to quench the revolts in Italy, and it was done. In 1822 the meeting at Verona commissioned France to restore the Spanish monarchy, and that task was accomplished in 1823.

The Holy Alliance

The Congress of Verona resolved "that the system of representative government is equally incompatible with the monarchical principles as the maxim of the sovereignty of the people is with the divine right "; and the members engaged, "mutually and in the most solemn manner, to use all their efforts to put an end to the system of representative governments in whatsoever country it may exist in Europe, and to prevent its being introduced in those countries where it is not yet known." It is to be observed that the qualifying clause "in Europe" applies to the suppression of representative government where it then existed. It does not apply to the countries into which its future introduction should not be allowed. This precise reading of a phrase which was probably carefully framed leaves the United States unthreatened, but it seems to

European intervention

imply a purpose to interfere in Spanish America. Nor was there any reason why European statesmen should recognize the Atlantic as a dividing line. Ideas crossed it all too readily for their taste, and they had always looked upon the whole world of European culture as one. It was the rumor, also, that France expected reward for her services to Spain in the shape of a Mexican kingdom for one of her princes, or in the cession of Cuba.[1] Besides, Russia was certainly advancing along the northwest coast, and might find cause and power to demand California from a grateful Spain.

Great Britain, although she had opposed Revolution as exemplified in France, was as little in sympathy with Divine Right. She was alarmed at the disturbance **Great Britain** in that delicate adjustment, the balance of **and Spain** power in Europe, which the alliance of all the great powers brought about. Her special interests, too, differed from those of continental Europe. If the Spanish-American revolutions of 1810 had not saved her from bankruptcy, as Napoleon believed, they had at any rate opened a rich and long-sought opportunity for wealth. If the dreams of Hawkins, of the speculators in the South Sea Bubble, of the colonists to Darien, were perhaps not fully realized, they at least became substantial. Ferdinand VII, after his restoration, though profuse in his rewards to his protector Wellington, was less obviously grateful to the nation that had sent Wellington to help him. He restored the old colonial system.[2]

No longer bound by any ties of consideration for Spain, Great Britain was unwilling to let Spanish-American trade slip through her fingers. She had no territorial ambitions; in a free competition she would gain the trade which was her principal object. Consequently she looked with pleasure on

[1] Marquis de Chateaubriand, *Oeuvres complètes* (12 vols., Paris, 1865–73), x. 359, etc.

[2] J. R. Seeley, *The Expansion of England*, Boston, 1883, and later editions; Montagu Burrows, *History of the Foreign Policy of Great Britain*, New York, 1895; Viscount Castlereagh, *Memoirs and Correspondence*, etc. (12 vols., London, 1850–53), vii. 257–456, etc.

the progress of the revolution, one of the impulses of which was the desire to do business with her. England's interests and her moral convictions generally coincide,

Great Britain and Spanish America and she has never spared her blood to advance them both. English volunteers, therefore, flocked to the banners of the revolutionary leaders. Admiral Cockrane commanded the fleet, practically a British one, which turned the tide on the Pacific coast, and a British legion was one of Bolivar's strongest weapons.[1] In 1819 the government passed a neutrality act, ordering its subjects to stand aloof, it did not recognize the independence of the new states; but its sympathy was well known, and when Canning became foreign minister, in 1822, he made the question his leading interest. England would object to any action which might close the ports of Spanish America to her, she would object to the acquisition of Cuba by France, and to the extension of Russian territory. How she would object was not known.

For the United States the situation was a difficult one. Our republican sympathies were aroused by the vision of a people shaking off the yoke of a European

Sympathy in the United States country. Our pride was touched by an apparent effort to imitate our methods. In 1811 both houses of Congress resolved "that they beheld with friendly interest the establishment of independent sovereignties by the Spanish provinces of America." In 1810 Joel Poinsett was sent to Buenos Ayres "to ascertain the real condition of the South American peoples, as well as their prospects of success." His report of 1818 was unfavorable; but we continued to maintain an agent at that city, and Clay made his sympathy for the movement his chief political instrument in attacking the administration. In 1818 trade with Spanish America was authorized.[2] Adventurers threw themselves

[1] Winsor, *America*, vol. viii.

[2] F. L. Paxson, *The Independence of the South American Republics*, Philadelphia, 1903; C. J. Stillé, *The Life and Services of Joel R. Poinsett*, Philadelphia, 1888.

into the cause of the revolutionists. In fact our concern in the cause did not stop with the Atlantic. Dr. Samuel Howe joined the forces of the Greeks; and in 1824 Webster delivered an oration in their behalf. Sympathy with revolution was not unassociated with dread of the forces of oppression. Particularly was Roman Catholicism coming, in the popular mind, to be connected with Divine Right, and the European support of the American missions of that church was for many years regarded as an insidious attack on our institutions.

To this popular interest in Spanish-American affairs the administration obviously could not give free rein without sacrificing the Spanish treaty, which was at **Sympathy versus neutrality** this time being negotiated. Yet we could not ignore a situation which filled the Caribbean with Spanish and Spanish-American warships and privateers, and with pirates who were taking advantage of the new flags. These vessels did not respect the rule of free ships, free goods, and some of them did not respect any rule at all. As a maritime nation we were bound to recognize the divergence from the normal, but to induce Spain to make her cessions we must at the same time preserve the fairest appearance of neutrality. We were, in fact, confronted by a new aspect of neutrality which has troubled us often enough since, namely, our duty in a neighboring contest of forces less strong than our own. In 1815 the President issued a neutrality proclamation, and in 1817 Congress passed a new neutrality act, which, amended in 1818, set a new and higher standard of national obligations.

Fearful of having his hand forced by Congress under the leadership of Clay, Adams, in December, 1817, wrote to his friend Alexander Everett furnishing him with **Neutrality versus recognition** the gist of a scathing indictment of the new republics which he hoped he would put in form for the newspapers.[1] He was not, as he explained later to the cabinet,

[1] Letters to Everett, 1811–1837, *Amer. Hist. Review*, 1905, xi. 88–116.

willing to see the new governments fall, but they were not going to fall, and our record must be clear; the European powers were attempting peaceful mediation, which we must allow. In March, 1818, however, he told the cabinet that, since the Holy Alliance had had a free opportunity to attempt a peaceful adjustment and had failed, as he had believed it would, we must not commit ourselves against recognition of the new republics, for we should ultimately recognize them. At the same time, feeling confident that England sympathized with our position, he assured her minister that we would coöperate with her in preserving the independence of the states, though not in alliance. He had divined the separation of Great Britain from the allies, and he sought to widen the breach. From that date our recognition of the new republics hung on the Florida treaty, and it was not till March 8, 1822 after the final ratifications had been exchanged, that the President recommended it to Congress. Recognition did not, of course, mean a departure from neutrality, which we still professed. It was in this situation, with our Florida chestnuts out of the fire, without having by our acts given the allies any handle for interference, and with a comfortable assurance as to the position of England, that we awaited whatever action might be taken when the pacification of Europe was complete.

The enthusiasm of many of our statesmen for the revolutionary movement had been dampened by other considera-
Our reversion- tions than those of our relations with Spain.
ary interests Ever since our beginnings as a nation certain portions of Spanish America had been earmarked as ultimately ours: the Floridas, Texas, and certainly Cuba—it was unnecessary to define exactly. As early as 1790 we considered the question of asserting our reversionary interest in the Floridas, and from 1808 we were prepared to assert it in Cuba. Afraid that that island might fall either to France or to England, Jefferson wrote to Gallatin, May 17, 1808: "I shall sincerely lament Cuba's falling into any hands

but those of its present owners. Spanish America is at present in the best hands for us, and '*Chi sta bene, non si muove* should be our motto.'" In April, 1809, he wrote to Madison that Napoleon might let us have Cuba "to prevent our aid to Mexico and the other provinces. That would be a price," he added, "and I would immediately erect a column on the southernmost limit of Cuba, and inscribe on it a *ne plus ultra* as to us in that direction. . . . Cuba can be defended by us without a navy, and this develops the principle which ought to limit our views." We were clear that we could not with equanimity see Cuba taken by either France or England; but how inconvenient also would it be should that island, or indeed Texas and possibly California, fall from the hands of Spain, out of which we could so honorably rescue them, only to assume an independence which it would be sacrilege for us to violate! These views were embodied by Adams in a dispatch to Nelson, our minister to Spain, April 28, 1823. They have constituted the rift in the lute of our Spanish-American relations which has until to-day prevented those republics from dancing to our piping.

To the situation, already complex, another element was added by Russia's independent action. Her traders, coming south from Alaska, had in 1816 established a *The Russian* fort in what is now California. In 1821 the *advance* czar issued a *ukase*, or proclamation, giving to a Russian company exclusive right to territory as far south as the fifty-first parallel, and excluding foreigners from the sea for a distance of one hundred Italian miles from the coast. The Russian minister, Baron de Tuhl, also informed Adams that his sovereign would not recognize the independence of Spanish America, and on November 16, 1823, communicated to him a manifesto of the czar, as mouthpiece of the Holy Alliance, setting forth the advantages of Divine Right and the inadequacy of republics. The *ukase* was as distasteful to Great Britain as to us, and the ministers of the two countries were ordered to coöperate in remonstrance. The manifesto was our own affair.[1]

It was at this juncture that Adams received from Rush, our minister at London, a proposal from Canning. The latter conceived that it was hopeless for Spain to try to recover her colonies, but he was not opposed to an amicable arrangement between them and the mother country; the question of the recognition of their independence, he said, was one of time and circumstance. Great Britain, he declared, did not aim at the possession of any portion of Spain's territory herself, but she could not with indifference see the transfer of any portion of it to another power. He informed Rush that he had received unofficial notice that a proposal would be made "for a Congress [of the allied nations], or some less formal concert and consultation, especially upon the affairs of Spanish America." If the United States acceded to his views, a declaration to that effect, concurrently with England, would, he thought, be "the most effectual and the least offensive" mode of making known their joint disapprobation of the suggested interference of Europe in the affairs of America.

Canning's offer

This proposal reached Washington October 9, 1823, and at once precipitated one of the most critical cabinet discussions in our history. There can now remain no doubt that the policy adopted was that continually and aggressively urged by Adams. Monroe was at first in favor of accepting the advance. Adams argued that England and the United States did not stand on an equal basis, because we had recognized the Spanish-American republics and she had not, because we did want portions of Spanish America, and, most significantly, because we were the most interested party. His attempt to put the question "to a test of right and wrong" reads curiously in view of his dispatch to Nelson regarding Cuba; and his objection to co-

Cabinet discussion

[1] Georg Heinz, *Die Beziehungen zwischen Russland, England und Nordamerika im Jahre 1823*, Berlin, 1911.

operation on the ground that it was contrary to our policy of abstaining from entangling alliances seems hardly consistent with the union of American and British interests at St. Petersburg. Yet this latter point really constituted the chief ground of opposition to Canning's proposal; it restruck the note of isolation sounded by John Adams, Washington, and Jefferson. The negotiation with Russia might be defended on the basis that the territory threatened by Russia was legally in the joint occupation of the two countries; but to coöperate in a matter of this importance and publicity, where not special interest but general American policy was at stake, was to throw isolation overboard, to admit that Great Britain was a partner in American affairs. Moreover, coöperation was not essential. Since Great Britain was moved by permanent interests, these would not change because we refused to join her. The British fleet would still stand between Spanish America and united Europe.[1]

The exclusion of coöperation with Great Britain carried with it the use of Canning's idea of a self-denying ordinance as the basis of objection to the proposed inter-

Basis of the Monroe Doctrine

ference. It was necessary to find a different one, and that employed was none other than an extension of the very policy of isolation because of which we refused to coöperate with Great Britain. This policy was extended beyond the primary idea that we as a nation should not be involved in European wars; it was extended beyond Madison's instruction to Monroe that we ought to begin to broach the idea that the whole Gulf Stream is our waters; it was extended to include the whole of both the American continents. As a basis for this extension, and at the same time as an answer to the czar's defence of Divine Right, there was inserted in the President's message a declaration that the political systems of Europe and America were different and incompatible. "Our policy in regard to Europe,

[1] W. C. Ford, "John Quincy Adams and the Monroe Doctrine," *Amer. Hist. Review*, 1902, vii. 676–696, viii. 28–52.

which was adopted at an early stage of the wars which have so long agitated that quarter of the globe, nevertheless remains the same, which is, not to interfere in the internal concerns of any of its powers; to consider the government *de facto* as the legitimate government for us. . . . But in regard to those [the American] continents circumstances are eminently and conspicuously different. It is impossible that the allied powers should extend their political system to any portion of either continent without endangering our peace and happiness; nor can anyone believe that our southern brethren, if left to themselves would adopt it. . . ." This policy forced Monroe to leave out of his message a recommendation for the recognition of revolutionary Greece, as that would have been an interference in European affairs; yet the stand taken was so obviously but a stretching of our oldest policy, of the movement begun by our own Revolution, that it was heartily approved.

So far the policy outlined dealt with the right of the settled portions of the American continents to choose their own

End of coloniz-   governments; it remained to deal with the
ing era   Russian advance on the unsettled northwest

coast. On this point Monroe announced that "the occasion has been judged proper for asserting, as a principle in which the rights and interests of the United States are involved, that the American continents, by the free and independent condition which they have assumed and maintain, are henceforth not to be considered as subjects for future colonization by any European powers." The era of claim-making was past; in the future boundaries were to be found, not made.

The confidence with which these bold declarations were made in Monroe's message of December 2, 1823, rested more

European in-   on the efficiency of the British navy than on
tervention   our own strength. At the same time, it is

evident that in theory they bore as heavily on England as on the powers of the Quadruple Alliance, in actual fact even more heavily, for Great Britain was more interested in America than they were, was in fact as great an American power as we ourselves. Thus to use for one's own purposes the resources of a rival power, while yielding nothing to her rivalry, is daring; but, if justified, it is the highest manifestation of the diplomatic art. In this case Adams proved to be as safe as he believed himself to be. Even before Monroe's announcement, on October 9, France informed England that she would not endeavor to obtain territory in America and did not consider that Spain had any opportunity to regain hers.[1]

While the message did not, therefore, contribute to the defeat of united Europe, it did enable us to gain a *succès d'estime* in the Russian negotiation. The czar was not sufficiently interested in the north- *Check to Russia's expansion* west coast to inconvenience himself over it. He refused the bribe of California which Mexico offered for a recognition of her independence. Willing to yield to the combined protest of England and the United States, he was actually more favorable to the latter in spite of her form of government, because of the traditional Russian desire to build up anywhere a rival to England's merchant marine. When, therefore, Canning withdrew from coöperation with us because "the principle laid down with respect to colonization in the speech of the President of the United States (to which Great Britain does not assent) must be so particularly displeasing to Russia," the czar took the opportunity to conclude a treaty with us before he did with Great Britain. This treaty, signed in 1824, was entirely satisfactory to us. By fixing the parallel of 54° 40′ as the southern limit of Rus-

[1] A. C. Coolidge, *The United States as a World Power* (New York, 1908), 95–120; J. A. Kasson, *Evolution of the Constitution . . . and History of the Monroe Doctrine*, Boston, etc., 1904; T. B. Edington, *The Monroe Doctrine*, Boston, 1904; W. S. Robertson, *The Beginnings of Spanish-American Diplomacy*, in *Turner Essays* (New York, 1910), 231–267; J. H. Kraus, *Monroedoctrin, in ihren Beziehungen zur amerikanischen Diplomatie und zum Völkerecht*.

sian America, it checked her expansion and thus added a sixth link to our claim to Oregon.[1]

Canning's withdrawal from coöperation in the Russian negotiation was the result of a thorough discontent with Canning's opposition the whole doctrine of Monroe's message, which asserted the primacy of the United States in American affairs. It was not for this that he was bringing "a new world into existence"; and, rightly claiming that Monroe's message was but the prelude to an active anti-English, or at least Pan-American, policy on our part, he at once entered into a contest with Adams for the leadership of Spanish America. In 1823 his instructions to his commissioners to the various states direct their attention to danger from France, those of 1824 to danger from the United States. On January 16, 1824, his Mexican commission reported, "Hence the Mexicans are looking anxiously around them in quest of an alliance with one of the great maritime powers of Europe, and if they should be disappointed in their hopes, they will ultimately be forced to throw themselves into the arms of the United States." [2]

The fears of Canning and the hopes of Adams were equally aroused when, in 1825, after Adams had been elected to the Adams's ambitions presidency and Clay had become his secretary of state, the Spanish American powers extended to us an invitation to meet them in the congress to be held at Panama. Adams at once accepted the invitation, and announced to our Congress that he would commission ministers to attend. Canning wrote: "The other and perhaps still more powerful motive of my apprehension is the ambition and ascendency of the United States of America. It is obviously the policy of that government to connect itself with all the powers of America in a general Transatlantic League, of which it would have the sole direction. I need

---

[1] "Correspondence of the Russian Ministers in Washington, 1818-1825," Amer. Hist. Review, 1913, xviii. 309-345, 537-562.

[2] Temperley, Canning, chs. viii.-x.

only say how inconvenient such an ascendency may be in time of peace, and how formidable in case of war." Again he wrote that Great Britain would not object to a Spanish-American league; "but any project of putting the United States of North America at the head of an American Confederacy, as against Europe, would be highly displeasing to your government . . . and it would too probably at no very distant period endanger the peace both of America and of Europe." [1]

At this point Canning had the best cards, and he played them with a shade more skill than Adams did his. The latter had made a point by granting the first recog- Adams versus nition to Spanish America; Canning, however, Canning rightly judged his own later recognition the more potent. December 17, 1824, he wrote of this act, "The deed is done, the nail is driven, Spanish America is free, and if we do not mismanage our affairs badly, she is English." Of the two countries, England was able to exert the greater influence with Spain to secure her recognition of the independence of her former colonies, and she also had more capital for the loans needed by both government and people. Canning referred to such investments in Buenos Ayres as not "mere commercial speculations." Mr. Hervey, the commissioner in Mexico, wrote home, March 30, 1824, "Without the temporary aid afforded by Mr. Staples, the government would have labored under the greatest embarrassment, and must indeed have stopped payment altogether." For an attempt to guarantee this loan Mr. Hervey was recalled, but he himself believed that his recall was due to "the peculiar circum-

[1] British Public Record Office, *Foreign Office Records, Mss., Mexico,* iii., iv., vi.; also *Colombia* and *Buenos Ayres.* In regard to mediation, in 1826 and 1827, between Buenos Ayres and Brazil regarding Montevideo, Canning instructs his minister: "As to taking part with either side in the contest your Lordship cannot too peremptorily repress any expectation of that nature. . . . There is much of the Spanish character in the inhabitants of the colonial establishments of Spain; and there is nothing in the Spanish character more striking than its impatience of foreign advice, and its suspicion of gratuitous service."

stances which have given publicity to correspondence marked with the Stamp of Secrecy." How great was the financial opportunity is indicated by the plan of the Mexican Congress to open bids for a canal across the isthmus of Tehuantepec.

Still more important than the need of money, which England alone could supply, was the fact that Great Britain and Spanish America were commercially supplementary to each other, the one a manufacturing country, the other a producer of raw materials. While the United States could use some South American tropical products, there was nothing which she could supply in return more cheaply than could Great Britain. Adams's obstinacy, too, was somewhat apparent in his commercial negotiations with the new powers; he was extremely loath to admit any deviation from our usual policies. The Spanish-American republics wished to retain the right to discriminate in their commercial relations between Spain and other countries, in hope of thus buying recognition of their independence. Adams would make no treaties except on the basis of most favored nation, while Canning was, within limits, complaisant. The latter, however, had his troubles also, because of his insistence on the suppression of the slave trade. As a result, the year 1829 found us enjoying commercial treaties only with Central America, Brazil, and Colombia, while England had them with Buenos Ayres, Colombia, Brazil, and Mexico.

Meanwhile Congress had been debating the proposition to send ministers to Panama. The administration finally won, and the delegates were sent; but the delay caused them to be too late, and the opportunity did not come again. The instructions growing out of the debate, however, make it doubtful if their presence would have been profitable, for the United States was not prepared to assume the lead in the direction toward which the ambitions of the new republics tended.

Their great purpose was to free Cuba and Porto Rico from Spain; but as this plan was directly opposed to our wishes, our ministers were instructed not to discuss it. Canning, quick to see his advantage, wrote, March 18, 1826, that, while Great Britain also preferred the existing state of things, "So far from denying the right of the new states of America to make a hostile attack upon Cuba . . . we have uniformly refused to join the United States in remonstrating with Mexico against the supposed intention. . . . We should indeed regret it, but we arrogate to ourselves no right to control the operations of one belligerent against another. The government of the United States, however, professes itself of a different opinion, . . ." He adds: " Neither England nor France, could see with indifference the United States in occupation of Cuba." On October 15, 1826, he wrote: "The general influence of the United States is not, in my opinion, to be feared. It certainly exists in Colombia, but it has been very much weakened even there by their protests against the attack on Cuba."

It was still farther weakened among the racially mixed population of Spanish America, which was marching under the banner of universal emancipation, by the widespread publication which the debate over Influence of slavery the Panama congress gave to our racial prejudices, notably the opposition of a strong element among us to negro emancipation, particularly in Cuba, and our unwillingness to sit in the congress with delegates from the negro states of Hayti and the Dominican Republic.

The plan for a United States hegemony of the American continent, therefore, fell before the greater resources of England, and because of our divided policies. England continued until the present generation to enjoy commercial predominance and a Idealization of the Monroe Doctrine certain political leadership. Those policies, however, to which Monroe's message was confined—the separation of the American and European spheres of influence, and the closing of the era of colonization—were grounded on facts, permanent interests, and the waxing strength of the United States. Although not incorporated in law, either national or international, they have stood. Europe has actually respected the territorial integrity and political independence of the Americas, and our people have until to-day embraced as one of their most cherished ideals the statement of Monroe's policy, founded as it was on their fundamental desire to pursue untrammelled the course of their own development and to hold Europe at ocean's length. Possibly its association with the venerable and non-contentious figure of Monroe gave it quicker and more general hold on the public mind than if it had taken its name from its real author, the belligerent Adams. From time to time the mantle of the Monroe Doctrine has been spread over additions and interpretations, till the name now stands for much that was not imagined at its announcement. It is possible that, by tending to crystallize our ideas, it has in the long run hampered our adjustment to conditions; for national interests are only relatively permanent, and their relationship with one another changes constantly. There can be no doubt, however, of the advantage that it was to us, in the period of untutored democracy upon which we were just entering, to have out a sheet anchor of fixed and respected policy.

In the fifteen years between 1815 and 1830 our territory had been further consolidated by the acquisition of Florida, great reaches of our boundary had been defined, and our claims to a Pacific coast line had been vastly strengthened. We had opened the world so far as it interested us to our exports and, with the exception of the British West Indies, to our shipping. We had passed the crisis of the Spanish-American revolution in such a way that the probability of European interference in our affairs was diminished rather than increased, as it had at one time seemed likely to be. Russia was eliminated

Accomplishments, 1815 to 1829

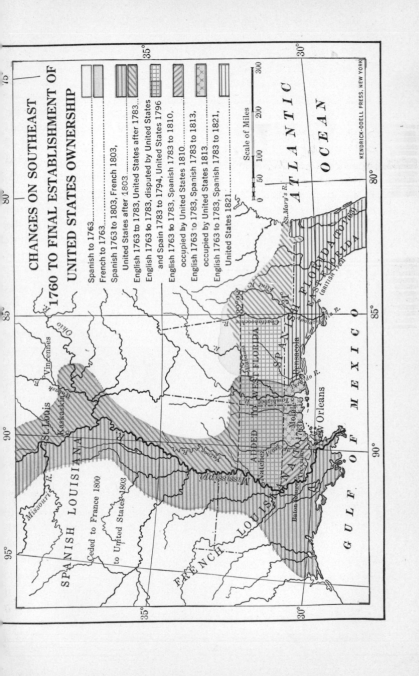

CHANGES ON SOUTHEAST
1760 TO FINAL ESTABLISHMENT OF
UNITED STATES OWNERSHIP

Spanish to 1763................................

French to 1763................................

Spanish 1763 to 1803, French 1803,
United States after 1803................

English 1763 to 1783, United States after 1783...

English 1763 to 1783, disputed by United States
and Spain 1783 to 1794, United States 1796

English 1763 to 1783, Spanish 1783 to 1810,
occupied by United States 1810................

English 1763 to 1783, Spanish 1783 to 1813,
occupied by United States 1813................

English 1763 to 1783, Spanish 1783 to 1821,
United States 1821................

Scale of Miles

0   50   100   200   300

KENDRICK-ODELL PRESS, NEW YORK.

ATLANTIC

OCEAN

GULF OF MEXICO

SPANISH FLORIDA (BRITISH 1763)

EAST FLORIDA (BRITISH 1763)

SPANISH WEST FLORIDA

CEDED TO WEST FLORIDA

FRENCH LOUISIANA

SPANISH LOUISIANA

Ceded to France 1800

to United States 1803

St. Louis

Kaskaskia

Vincennes

Ohio

Wabash

Missouri R.

Mississippi

Yazoo

Natchez

Baton Rouge

New Orleans

Mobile

Pensacola

St. Mary's R.

Chattahoochee

35°

30°

95°   90°   85°   80°

as a potential American power. Threads had been tied together, disagreements healed or bandaged, and our national experience had been crystallized into a policy to guide future manifestations of the national will.

CHAPTER XVIII

RECIPROCITY, CLAIMS, BOUNDARIES, AND THE
SLAVE TRADE

By 1815 diplomacy had ceased to shape politics; after 1830 politics began to shape diplomacy. With Jackson, "shirt-
Change of personnel sleeve" diplomacy began, but it did not reach its zenith till after the Civil War. The most important change in personnel took place in the state department itself: in 1833 only two old officials remained; it was the most nearly complete break ever made in the continuity of that staff. This weakening of the central administration was accompanied by a remanning of the diplomatic corps that was quite as sweeping. Appointments were now eagerly sought, and there were few more satisfactory methods of paying political debts. Many choices were not without merit, but for the most part they reflected the general tendency of politics to rely on mediocrity. Still more apparent was the lack of familiarity with European conditions, which was the product of our realized isolation. Less than the men of 1775, with their colonial interest in "home" affairs, many of them, like the Pinckneys, with an English education, did the new ministers understand world politics.

Of the secretaries of state for the next fifteen years, Van Buren was tactful and suave, but in diplomacy colorless.
Van Buren, McLane, Livingston, Forsyth Louis McLane was without distinction. Edward Livingston was every inch a diplomat, but his service was cut all too short by his death.[1]
Forsyth, who served Jackson and Van Buren for seven years, was skilful and had had experience, but he left no impress.

[1] C. H. Hunt, *Life of Edward Livingston*, New York, 1864.

Legaré and Upshur together were in office only about a year. Webster and Calhoun are the only really great names, and they, properly, are remembered for other things. They serve in fact to illustrate two of the more general weaknesses of the whole service. Webster handled cases; the adaptation of a general policy to the whole field of diplomacy he did not attempt. He was **Webster** primarily a lawyer, only incidentally a diplomat. Hardly any one was primarily a diplomat, or primarily **Literary appointments** interested in diplomacy. When a President wished to gain applause, he appointed an author, like James Fenimore Cooper or Washington Irving, who was expected to repay the nation by writing a book. Of all the statesmen of the time, Calhoun was prob- **Calhoun** ably the best endowed for diplomatic work, but he sacrificed diplomacy to politics. The only really great American who was greatly interested in diplomacy was Henry Wheaton, who spent this period in various **Wheaton** German posts. Performing perfectly the difficult, but not very important, tasks allotted him, he devoted his leisure to the cognate study of international law.[1] He was recalled in 1845, and the fruit of his preparation was never gathered by the nation.

The rank and file of the service possessed characteristics similar to those of the chiefs, except that some of Jackson's appointments, as that of John Randolph to **Diplomatic** Russia and of Butler to Mexico, were con- **and consular** spicuously bad, and Tyler's on the whole con- **service** spicuously good. During this period both the diplomatic and the consular service grew rapidly in numbers. An attempt to improve the consular system was made in 1833; but it failed, and the staff continued to decline in quality.

In spite of these defects, it remains true that American

[1] See his *History of the Law of Nations,* New York, 1845; and his *Elements of International Law,* Philadelphia, 1836, which has been many times edited and brought up to date.

diplomacy, although its wheels creaked and rumbled, accomplished its main ends.   This attainment was, however,
due more to situation than to merit.   We had
only one strong general rival, Great Britain,
and with her, after years of controversy,
Webster finally dealt.   The other countries with whom we
had intimate relationships were too weak to make our errors
painful to us.   American commerce was simpler than it
had been, consisting more and more of the exchange of our
non-competitive agricultural products for manufactures
which other nations were anxious to sell us.   Such direct
commerce needs much less governmental protection than the
carrying trade, which had previously been of so much greater
relative importance, or than the disposal of competitive
goods such as we now produce.

Simplicity of the American position

Jackson, like Jefferson, found the diplomatic board for
the moment almost swept clean of complications.   Yet, as
Jefferson had been able to reap some glory
from a new handling of the Barbary question,
so Jackson scored an early triumph by restoring trade with
the British West Indies.   Van Buren, as senator, had opposed
Adams on that point, claiming that he was too stiff in maintaining non-essentials, a fault which was certainly Adams's
characteristic weakness.   He promptly instructed McLane,
our new minister to Great Britain, to assure the British
government that with the change of administration in the
United States had come a change of policy, and to offer to
renew trade on the basis of the British acts of 1825.   Great
Britain was complaisant, and by proclamation this long-vexed question was finally settled on terms that gave the
United States complete freedom of direct trade, but not of
trade between the islands and other countries.   Van Buren
failed to win the plaudits for which he had hoped, owing to
his unusual and improper reference to domestic politics in a
dispatch intended to be read to a foreign minister.[1]

British West Indies

[1] E. M. Shepard, *Martin Van Buren* (Boston, etc., 1900), chs. vi.–vii.

Partly as a result of the same greater flexibility, the formation of commercial treaties with Spanish America now proceeded more rapidly; in 1831 one was made with Mexico, in 1832 one with Chili, compacts with Peru, Bolivia, and Venezuela followed in 1836, and one with Ecuador in 1839. Probably the policy of the administration had less to do with the framing of our first treaties with Mediterranean powers than had the general amelioration of commercial conditions, especially the final quelling of the Barbary pirates after the capture of Algiers by the French in 1830. At all events, treaties were made with the Ottoman empire in 1830, with Greece in 1837, Sardinia in 1838, and the Two Sicilies, or Naples, in 1845. In 1840 a first treaty was made with Portugal. In 1833 a roving commission to Edmund Roberts resulted in our first Asiatic treaties,—one with Muscat and one with Siam. In 1843 we officially expressed an interest in Hawaii, and in 1844 our first treaty with China was concluded. This latter was relatively satisfactory from a commercial point of view, for it opened the five ports of Kwang-Chow, Amoy, Fuchow, Ningpo, and Shanghai to commerce and residence and elaborately regulated trade. It did not open the way to missionary enterprise.

The Mediterranean

The East

Throughout the period the policy of reciprocity was actively pursued. In so far as the employment of vessels was concerned it was embodied in most of the treaties already mentioned, and it was in some cases extended to reciprocity of customs dues. By a convention of 1831: "The wines of France, from and after the exchange of the ratifications of the present convention, shall be admitted to consumption in the States of the Union at duties which shall not exceed the following rates," and "the proportion existing between the duties on French wines thus reduced, and the general rates of the tariff which went into operation the first of January, 1829, shall be maintained, in case the Government of the United States should think proper

Reciprocity

to diminish those general rates." France in return agreed to establish the same duties on long staple cotton as on the short staple, if carried in French or American vessels, and in "consideration of this stipulation, which shall be binding on the United States for ten years, the French government abandons the reclamations which it had formed in relation to the eighth article of the treaty of cession of Louisiana."

This last clause was in settlement of a dispute regarding the significance of the "most favored nation" provision, "Most fa- which affected our whole reciprocity campaign. vored nation" Nearly all our treaties were on this basis. If thereby every nation on such terms with us were to enjoy every favor granted to any nation, our bargaining power would be much reduced. John Quincy Adams had argued with France that it applied only to favors freely granted, not to special concessions given in exchange for other special favors. This interpretation was incorporated into our treaty with Mexico in 1832, which qualified the "most favored nation" clause by providing that the nations mutually, "shall enjoy the same [favors] freely, if the concession was freely made, or upon the same conditions, if the concession was conditional." [1]

The most important commercial negotiations were those conducted in Germany by Henry Wheaton. At the very German trea- end of the period he secured the abolition, by ties numbers of the sovereign German states, of the *droit d'aubaine*, or tax on estates of foreigners, and of the *droit de détraction*, or tax on emigration. Meantime he was working for commercial reciprocity on the basis of Adams's interpretation of the "most favored nation," which he may be said to have incorporated into international law. In 1840 he arranged a treaty with Hanover. Most of the other North German states were united in the Zollverein, or customs union, of which Prussia was the head. This group of states

[1] Max Farrand, "The Commercial Privileges of the Treaty of 1803," *Amer. Hist. Review*, 1902, vii. 494–499.

consumed half of our tobacco crop and much of our rice. In 1838 Wheaton secured a reduction in the duty on rice. Our tariff of 1842, however, incited retaliation, and in 1844 he made a new arrangement on a reciprocal basis. By this agreement the United States was to impose only rates fixed in the treaty on certain products of the Zollverein, which in return was to reduce to a stipulated rate its duties on tobacco and lard, to forego its contemplated increase in the tax on rice, and to impose no duty at all on raw cotton. These provisions were to apply only to direct trade in German or American vessels.

This treaty, commercially very favorable, was in 1844 recommended by President Tyler to the Senate. Rufus Choate reported for its committee on foreign affairs: "The Committee . . . are not pre- Rejection of pared to sanction so large an innovation Zollverein treaty upon ancient and uniform practice in respect of the department of government by which duties on imports shall be imposed. . . . The . . . committee believe that the general rule of our system is indisputably that the control of trade and the function of taxation belong, without abridgment or participation, to Congress." Calhoun, who was secretary of state, maintained on the other hand that such rate-making, whether by treaty or by international agreement, was a well-established practice: "The only question it is believed that was ever made was, whether an act of Congress was not necessary to sanction and carry the stipulations making the change into effect." Many considerations intervened, such as the unpopularity of Tyler and the Whig objections to any lowering of the customs rates; and the treaty was rejected. Constitutionally the episode is of importance, because the Senate, moved by outside considerations and for once forgetting its *esprit de corps*, put itself on record as supporting the contention of the House as to the limitations on the treaty-making power.[1]

[1] Senate Committee on Foreign Relations, *Reports* (Senate Doc., 56 Cong.

A more exciting occupation than that of commercial negotiation was that of gunning for claims. These claims were of two classes. One kind had arisen, and continued to grow, from the disturbed condition of Spanish America. Revolution had already become chronic and American citizens and their property were often in the way, often in fact were actively involved on one side or the other. Recognition of the resulting claims for damages was obtained, and indemnity provided for, in treaties with Texas in 1838, Mexico in 1839, and Peru in 1841. The other class of claims was grounded on the maltreatment of American shipping during the Napoleonic wars. Such claims made the basis of a treaty with Denmark in 1830, with France in 1831, with the two Sicilies in 1832, and with Spain in 1834. With the addition of Portugal in 1851 the list was complete and the slate clean. Our claims against Great Britain had been wiped out by the war.

Claims treaties

The signing of the treaty with France did not, however, secure immediate payment of claims. On the contrary, its execution involved us in the only strictly diplomatic embroglio which aroused public interest between 1829 and 1840. Although rising at one time to a point at which even sane men expected war, the affair must in reality be considered as opera bouffe rather than drama. The king and peers of France constitutionally agreed that the nation would pay us, for the release from all our claims for seizure and destruction of property, five million dollars in six annual instalments; but the Chamber of Deputies, as our House of Representatives has so often done, refused to grant the money. Jackson mentioned the matter to Congress in 1833, and sent Livingston as minister to France, especially charged with obtaining payment. It is said that an intimation came from France that Jackson

Claims treaty with France

2 sess., No. 231, pt. 8), viii. 36–37, June 14, 1844. Cf. S. M. Cullom, *Fifty Years of Public Service* (Chicago, 1911), 368–374; and E. S. Corwin, *National Supremacy*, New York, 1913.

had better assume a stronger tone in his next message, of 1834; at any rate, he did so. In seven pages he discussed the question with all his peculiar frankness. "Our institutions," said he, "are essentially pacific. Peace and friendly intercourse with all nations are as much the desire of our government as they are the interest of our people. But these objects are not to be permanently secured by surrendering the rights of our citizens or permitting solemn treaties for their indemnity, in cases of flagrant wrong, to be abrogated or set aside." [1]

Interpreting this as a threat of war, French public opinion went up in the air. The government of Louis Philippe, conciliatory but dependent on public opinion, was forced to prepare for war. French fleets sailed for our coasts. The French Chamber, with a characteristic Gallic touch, voted the money, but would not pay it until an apology for Jackson's message was tendered. The French minister at Washington was recalled, and Livingston was given his passports. Our government maintained that a presidential message was a domestic document and hence neither justified official umbrage nor allowed official explanation. John Quincy Adams, now a member of the House of Representatives and chairman of its committee on foreign affairs, supported Jackson and reported in favor of retaliatory legislation, thereby losing an election to the Senate from Whig Massachusetts. In the Senate, the placating Clay delayed war preparation and caused conciliatory resolutions to be adopted.

War clouds again

In his next annual message, December 7, 1835, Jackson explained that of the year before. "The conception," said he, "that it was my intention to menace or insult the Government of France is as unfounded as the attempt to extort from the fears of that nation what her sense of justice may deny would be vain and

Reconciliation with France

---

[1] Richardson, *Messages of the Presidents*, iii. 126–223; A. Danzat, *Du rôle des chambres en matière de traités internationaux.*

ridiculous." After some demur and an informal mediation by Great Britain, this explanation was accepted by France as satisfactory, relations were resumed, and payment was made. For this result the credit was claimed by the friends of Adams, of Clay, and of Jackson. It certainly belonged to whoever made the happy suggestion of explaining one domestic document by another. If presidential messages are not to be considered as international declarations, we neither insulted France nor apologized; our honor was secure. If they are to be so considered, whatever insult the first contained was atoned for in the second, and French honor was satisfied.

Meanwhile our always existing difficulties with Great Britain were again approaching a head: they seem to require lancing about every quarter of a century. **Northeastern boundary** The most important of these concerned the boundary between the crossing of the St. Lawrence by the forty-fifth parallel, and a line drawn due north from the source of the St. Croix. The treaty of 1783 provided that this line run "to the Highlands; along the said Highlands which divide those rivers that empty themselves into the river St. Lawrence, from those which fall into the Atlantic Ocean." The question arose as to whether the St. John, emptying into the Bay of Fundy, flowed into the Atlantic ocean in the sense of the treaty. If it did, then the highlands referred to were those dividing its waters from the tributaries of the St. Lawrence, and quite near the latter; if not, the highlands would be those separating its valley from those of the rivers of Maine. About twelve thousand square miles were involved. The British contended for the second interpretation, holding that the intention had been to divide the river basins, and that this line would give them the whole of the St. John valley. The Americans claimed that the treaty had attempted to define a line already existing,—the southern boundary of Quebec as defined by the proclamation of 1763, in which the highlands were expressly men-

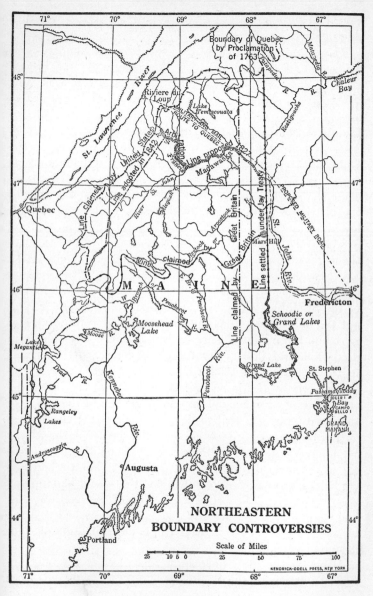

NORTHEASTERN
BOUNDARY CONTROVERSIES

Scale of Miles

tioned as running to the Bay of Chaleurs, and so were undoubtedly the northern chain.

The dispute was somewhat clouded by the hundred-and-fifty-year-old dispute between Massachusetts and French

Border difficulties

Acadia, which British New Brunswick now claimed to represent, and by the presence of an old French fief, Madawaska, situated in the middle of the district and granted by the governor of Canada in 1683. This settlement had unfortunately been overlooked by the United States census of 1810. Obviously it had never *de facto* been a part of Massachusetts, as the United States claimed the whole region had been *de jure*. In the thirties the district was no longer overlooked. In 1831 a riot followed an attempt on the part of Maine to hold an election in Madawaska, and later the British planned a road through the region, connecting Halifax and Quebec. Lumberjacks of the two nations began to clash. In 1838 and 1839 occurred the "Restook war," in the valley of the Aroostook, a branch of the St. John. Congress authorized the President to call out the militia and to accept fifty thousand volunteers, and gave him ten million dollars credit. Maine voted eight hundred thousand dollars for forts. General Scott was sent to the frontier. In 1839 a *modus vivendi* was arranged by the governors of Maine and New Brunswick: "That the civil posse of Maine should retain possession of the valley of the Aroostook, the British denying their right; the British authorities retaining possession of the valley of the Upper St. John, Maine denying their right." The difficulty seemed the more serious because, although in 1827 Gallatin had succeeded in arranging an arbitration, the result had proved unsatisfactory. The arbiter, the king of the Netherlands, had suggested a compromise and both parties had rejected his suggestion. Subsequent attempts at arbitration or compromise had equally failed.

Although the most important, this was not the only unsettled portion of the boundary line. The highlands once agreed upon, the line was to descend to the "North-western most head of Connecticut river." What was the "North-western most head"? There were several Minor boundary disputes that might with no great stretch of the conscience be so described. About one hundred thousand acres were in dispute. More annoying, because a preventable error, was the fact, discovered by one of the commissions

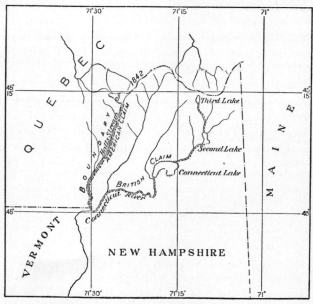

NORTHWESTERNMOST HEAD OF CONNECTICUT RIVER

under the treaty of Ghent, that the forty-fifth parallel had been incorrectly surveyed in 1774 and the report ever since had been accepted. The error was not great, but the tipping of the parallel northward as it went west had given us Rouses Point, which commanded the outlet of Lake Champlain, and upon which we had built a costly fortress. This was.now found to be in territory properly British.[7]

[7] J. F. Sprague, *The North Eastern Boundary Controversy and the Aroostook War*, Dover, Me., [1910]; W. F. Ganong, *Evolution of the Boundaries of the*

These disputes were rendered the more serious by the situation in Canada and the attitude of the United States toward

The Canadian insurrection

it. The years from 1837 to 1840 mark a period of unrest in that colony. There were French Canadian movements and Republican movements to throw off British rule. Until the report of Lord Durham, in 1839, Great Britain was not decided in her attitude. In the United

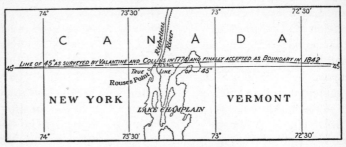

ROUSES POINT CONTROVERSY

States there was sympathy for the revolution and hope of annexation. Once more confronted by the question of neutrality, the government on the whole did its best, and did well. In 1838 Congress strengthened the neutrality law by giving the collectors of customs power to prevent the departure of military expeditions when there was "probable cause to believe" they intended to violate neutrality.[1]

Before the government could bring its force to bear on the frontier, however, the Niagara river had been the scene of

The Caroline

actual hostilities. In 1837 forces equipped in New York gathered on Navy island, in American waters, and were supplied from the United States by the little steamer *Caroline*. On December 26 a party of Canadian militia crossed the river, boarded the *Caroline*, and sent her

Province of New Brunswick, Royal Soc. of Canada, *Trans.*, 1901, vii. sec. ii. 139–449.

[1] William Kingsford, *History of Canada* (10 vols., London, 1888–98), x. 430–457; Shepard, *Van Buren*, 350–356; *House Exec. Docs.*, 25 Cong., 2 sess., No. 74.

drifting and afire over the falls. In the scrimmage one American was killed. The excitement which this violation of our territory caused among the border population, already afire with sympathy for the Canadian movement, was intensified by a new episode which grew out of it. In 1840 Alexander McLeod, a Canadian, boasted in a New York saloon that he had been of the boarding party and had killed the American. He was at once arrested and put on trial for murder. The British government demanded that he be released on the ground that whatever he had done had been done under orders. The United States replied that he was being tried in a state court and that the national government could not interfere. Webster, who became secretary of state in March, 1841, wrote to President Tyler in July, that "Hunters' Lodges" were organized along the border from Maine to Wisconsin, that they were said to number ten thousand members and to desire war with Great Britain, that they were likely to attempt violence against McLeod, and that, if a "mob should kill him, war would be inevitable in ten days." [1]

McLeod

The coming in of Webster at this juncture was fortunate, and it happily coincided with the new British ministry of Sir Robert Peel, favorably inclined to a settlement with the United States. Webster was well known to the ministry, which sent Lord Ashburton over to treat with him. The latter was a member of the firm of Baring Brothers, his wife was an American, and he personally knew Webster, to whom he wrote truly, January 2, 1842, "The principal aim and object of that part of my life devoted to public objects during the thirty-five years that I have had a seat in one or the other House of Parliament, has been to impress on others the necessity of, and to promote myself, peace and harmony between our countries." Under such pleasing auspices the settlement was undertaken, but the mutual friendliness and good fellowship did not prevent either

Webster

[1] Daniel Webster, *Letters* (ed. C. H. Van Tyne, New York, 1902), 233.

party from sturdily maintaining his case, or from withholding from the other evidence which he believed to be damaging to his own position.[1]

The McLeod affair was for Webster to arrange. Great Britain was right about it, but our national government Settlement of was without authority to interfere. Webster McLeod case followed the trial with great interest, used his and Caroline affair influence with the state government, and was not uninfluential in obtaining the final discharge of McLeod, although he was dissatisfied with the form which it took— the acceptance of an *alibi*. He also saw to it that precisely such cases should not arise in the future, by securing an act of Congress providing that a subject of a foreign power on trial in a state court might be brought into a United States court on a writ of *habeas corpus*, and dismissed if the latter court judged proper.[2] The *Caroline* affair was settled by an exchange of notes. Webster admitted that such a violation of our territory was permissible if necessary for self-defence,— we could not well take the opposite view considering our several invasions of Spanish Florida,—but he denied the necessity in this case. Lord Ashburton maintained that the necessity had existed, but nevertheless apologized.

The boundary controversies were settled by a treaty of August 9, 1842. Webster and Ashburton abandoned the Webster-Ash- attempt to discover the boundary intended in burton treaty 1783, and agreed to follow the suggestion of the king of the Netherlands and compromise. To compromise, however, meant the giving up of territory without first ascertaining whether we had title to it or not. It is conceivable that, when the territory in question is part of a state, this exceeds the constitutional power of the national government. It was at any rate necessary to recognize Maine,

[1] E. D. Adams, "Lord Ashburton and the Treaty of Washington," *Amer. Hist. Review*, 1912, xvii. 764–782; J. W. Foster, *A Century of American Diplomacy* (Boston, etc., 1901), 282–286.

[2] Daniel Webster, *Writings and Speeches* (National edition, 18 vols., Boston, 1903), xi. 247–269; *United States Statutes*, 27 Cong., 2 sess., ch. 257.

which was officially represented at the conference and officially compensated by a provision of the treaty. Although Maine assented to the terms, it is possible that her dislike for the settlement cost Webster his last chance for the presidency in 1852. Massachusetts was also involved, having retained, when she permitted the erection of Maine into a separate state, the ownership of certain lands. She too was represented and recognized.[1] The compromise divided the region disputed between Maine and New Brunswick in such a way as to give the former the valley of the Aroostook and the southern part of the valley of the upper St. John. Both nations were admitted to equal use of the St. John for the purpose of logging. This arrangement gave the United States 7,015 miles and Great Britain 5,012, a settlement a little less favorable to us than that suggested by the king of the Netherlands. Our contention as to the head of the Connecticut river was allowed, and the old incorrect location of the parallel of 45° was allowed to stand, as so many vested rights would be disturbed by moving it. The line of the boundary from Lake Huron to the Lake of the Woods, which the Ghent commission had not completed, was also drawn. Thus at length, in 1842, the northern boundary provided by the treaty of 1783 was reduced to intelligible terms, except where it was frankly departed from. The few disputes that have since arisen have been of a minor character and seem now all to be settled.

The treaty also revived and expanded the extradition article of the Jay treaty, which had expired with the war of 1812. As it did not yet, however, cover em- **Extradition** bezzlement, "gone to Canada" was for many years the epitaph of the dishonest American who had been found out.

On one subject with which it dealt the treaty proved unsatisfactory. This was the slave trade, which had been

[1] *Report and Resolves in relation to the North-eastern Boundary* (Massachusetts General Court; Senate Doc., No. 67), Boston, [1838].

the subject of a dispute that for a quarter of a century had been growing more acute. In 1807 Great Britain, as the result of a long philanthropic agitation, abolished the trade as respected her own subjects. Once having repudiated it herself, she was moved by every motive, philanthropic and philistine, to secure its abolition elsewhere. While it continued anywhere, not only were her citizens deprived of its profits, but her colonies were hampered by the competition of other regions where the slave supply was plentiful and cheap. Thus the wily Castlereagh and the beneficent Clarkson together urged abolition before European congresses.

Slave trade

Civilized public sentiment was ready for the movement, at least when unaffected by special considerations. Denmark had preceded Great Britain in 1802, the United States followed in 1808, Sweden in 1813, France in 1815; Spain and Portugal yielded to financial and other inducements in 1817. The trade soon became illegal among all so-called Christian powers. *Sub rosa*, however, it continued to exist. It was necessary for a nation to possess a navy and the will to achieve, if she were to prevent adventurers, either of her own or of other nationalities, from misusing her flag. So long as slavery existed in Brazil, Cuba, and Porto Rico, and the southern states of our country, the rewards of the trade were sufficient to induce men to engage in it despite the law and even in the face of considerable risk.

Difficulty of suppression

During the last years of the Napoleonic wars England had almost stopped the trade by using her belligerent right of search. With peace, however, this right vanished, and her navy saw the flags of other nations fraudulently used to protect a fraudulent traffic and were impotent to interfere. Her great admiralty judge, Sir William Scott, declared in the case of *Le Louis*, 1817, that the slave trade was not piracy, and that no right of search existed. Great Britain, therefore, sought to obtain a

Great Britain's policy

general agreement to a mutual right of search or visit in times of peace; but although she succeeded in making such arrangements with Spain and Portugal, she failed to obtain them from the Holy Alliance in 1818 and again in 1822. As the greatest naval power, she would obviously profit much by a regulation that would give her navy in time of peace almost as effective a police power over the ocean as it exercised in time of war, including a rich harvest of prize money. Interest combined with the highest ideals of patriotism and altruism to press her to the attainment of her goal.

In the United States these ideals stood in a rivalry which grew year by year more bitter. We had agreed in the treaty of Ghent that both the contracting parties should use "their best endeavors to accomplish" the abolition of the slave trade. An act of Congress of May 15, 1820, declared the slave trade piracy, and a growing element among the people of the North urged a continuation of this policy of exterminating a trade which had already been branded by all the European world. The nationalist spirit, however, was not prepared to permit Great Britain to police our flag, to renew in time of peace those practices which had in time of war driven us to fight. In the case of the *Antelope*, in 1825, John Marshall denied that our law of 1820 made the trade piracy in the international sense, or gave other nations any rights over our vessels, however employed. Between 1823 and 1825 Congress discussed the subject of coöperating with Great Britain on the subject. Adams, though forced by a resolution of Congress to negotiate on the basis of a mutual right of search, was personally opposed. He wrote to Gallatin: "The admission of a right for the officers of foreign ships of war to enter and search the vessels of the United States in time of peace, under any circumstances whatever, would meet with universal repugnance in the public opinion of the country." The convention drawn up by Rush and Canning in 1824 was rejected as unsatisfactory, and when Webster and Ashburton met

Attitude of the United States

we had not yet come to an understanding with Great Britain. The United States was so lax in the enforcement of her own law that much of the trade was carried on under the protection of her flag, and some of it in American vessels.

This main difficulty was augmented by questions arising from our domestic maritime slave trade. Vessels carrying

Domestic slave trade

slaves from one of our Atlantic ports to the gulf states were often forced by stress of weather or other circumstances into British West Indian ports. In 1831 and 1833 slaves from the *Comet* and *Encomium* were released and freed by the British authorities there. During the Van Buren administration indemnity was paid in these cases, on the ground that, as slavery was permitted in the islands the principle of British law that slaves on reaching British territory or war vessels became free did not apply there. When, however, in August, 1834, the British West Indian slaves were freed, the application of the principle was extended to those islands. New cases occurred, as those of the *Enterprise* and *Hermosa*, and satisfaction was refused. The most important was that of the big *Creole*, in 1841, whose cargo of slaves arose, killed a passenger, took possession of the ship, and made the port of Nassau. Those guilty of the murder were executed and the remainder freed.

These cases aroused great excitement in the United States. In 1840 Calhoun secured the passage by the Senate of resolu-

Calhoun's propositions

tions declaring that a vessel "in time of peace, engaged in a lawful voyage, is, according to the laws of nations, under the exclusive jurisdiction of the state to which her flag belongs," and that, if forced "by stress of weather, or other unavoidable cause" into the port of another friendly power, "she could, under the same laws, lose none of the rights appertaining to her on the high seas." In his speech defending these resolutions he laid down the doctrine that the constitution made it the duty of the national government, solely charged with the foreign relations of every state, to defend before the world the institutions of every state;

that the protection of the domestic slave trade was a matter of national obligation, and not of choice.

These positions would seem so reasonable and clear as hardly to need statement, but public opinion was blurred by an apparent similarity with another case which during 1840 was being argued by John Quincy Adams in the supreme court. L'Amistad case This case concerned the Spanish vessel, *l'Amistad*, engaged in the Spanish domestic slave trade, whose cargo revolted and which was brought into a United States port. As it developed that these negroes had been recently and illegally captured, it was held that they were not properly slaves, but free persons kidnapped, and they were restored to Africa. It is possible that in strictness we should have turned the whole case over to the Spanish authorities; but the distinction between these facts and those involved in the *Creole* case, in which the negroes were without doubt legal slaves by the laws of Virginia and of the United States, was sufficient to bar its use as a precedent.[1]

Webster entered upon the discussion of these problems with little apparent enthusiasm. In a letter to Lord Ashburton enclosing his statement of the *Creole* case, he said " Using the words of Walter Scott when he sent one of his works to his publisher—I send you my *Creole*—D—n her." No agreement was reached as to this and the other vessels, until after Settlement of the Creole case his return to office under Fillmore; then, in 1853, a claims convention submitted the matter to arbitration, and Great Britain paid indemnity. More important was the question of making arrangements for the more effectual suppression of the slave trade. Great Britain was as insistent as ever on some such provision. The United States was as loath as it had been under Adams to permit the British navy to search our vessels. Finally, at the suggestion of President Tyler there was incorporated into the treaty a plan for the main-

[1] W. E. B. DuBois, *Suppression of the African Slave-trade* (New York, etc., 1896), 131–146, 162–167; Schuyler, *American Diplomacy*, ch. v.

tenance by the two powers of a joint squadron off the coast of Africa.

This agreement was promptly attacked by Lewis Cass, our minister to France, on the ground that Great Britain had not definitely admitted that she did not possess the right of search, and hence that she would in all probability actually exercise it. His fears had been excited by the attempt of that power in 1842 to effect a quintuple agreement by joining with her Austria, Prussia, France, and Russia for such a mutual right. On the basis of this powerful support he believed that Great Britain would assert the right as established international law. Cass therefore wrote a pamphlet attacking the proposal, and, acting without instructions, protested to the French prime minister, Guizot, and secured the defeat of the British plan, France finally adopting the American scheme of a joint squadron. In this action he was endorsed by Webster, and was supported by an article written by Henry Wheaton, entitled "An Inquiry into the Validity of the British Claim to a Right of Visitation and Search." [1]

Cass defeats the quintuple treaty

Nevertheless, by 1849 Great Britain had secured treaties with twenty-four nations, all, except those with the United States and France, permitting a mutual right of search. With this great weight of international support behind her, she justified Cass's fears by acting upon a claim, not indeed to search, but to visit any vessel suspected of the traffic in order to ascertain its nationality, a course to which she was provoked by the facts that otherwise any vessel flying the American flag was immune, and that most vessels used that flag in places where American war-ships were not to be found. If the vessel visited was not American, we did not suffer; but when, as often happened, it was ours, we, with our special sensitiveness to such liberties taken with our flag, resented the visit and

Great Britain yields visitation

---

[1] Daniel Webster, *Works* (ed. Edward Everett, 6 vols., Boston, 1851), v. 78–150; A. C. McLaughlin, *Life of Lewis Cass* (Boston, 1891), 174–192.

became increasingly angry. Finally in 1858, Cass himself having become secretary of state, the issue was forced, and the British government, with the advice of its law officers, admitted that no right of visitation existed.[1]

The American government thus successfully met the attempt of Great Britain to continue in time of peace a practice which we had unsuccessfully resisted *The conflict of* in time of war. It is uncontestably true that *ideals* in accomplishing this object we delayed the abolition of the slave trade to which we stood committed. It was a question of conflict between the national ideal of the freedom of our flag, strengthened later by the rising pro-slavery movement, and the ideal of humanitarianism. With the outburst of the Civil War the latter element got the upper hand in the national government, and in 1862 Seward ar- *Triumph of hu-* ranged a treaty providing for a limited mutual *manitarian* right of search, but protecting American *ideals* interests by a provision for mixed courts to try the cases. Seward said that, had such a treaty been made in 1808, there would have been no Civil War; but Seward was apt to be hyperbolic in expression.

The achievements of the period from 1829 to 1844 were the final settlement of the difficulties growing out of the Napoleonic wars, and the passing of another mile- *The period* stone in the adjustment of our relationships *1829 to 1844* with Great Britain. The latter transaction was a conventional agreement, in which it is doubtful if Webster did as well as John Quincy Adams would have done. The former was the work of Jackson, whose fearless, mannerless method of procedure marks the dominance of the frontier element in political life; it was not in accordance with rule, but it was characteristic and it was effective. More was done for the furtherance of commerce than one would have expected from the ruling elements in the United States at that time. To no small extent this progress must be considered as due to the

[1] McLaughlin, *Lewis Cass*, 323–330.

presence on our staff of a man of Henry Wheaton's preeminent ability; but a factor still more important lay in the character of the commerce itself, now almost wholly noncompetitive and universally desired. The period as a whole, however, would be barren were it considered in relation to actual achievements alone. Its chief interest lies in the rise of new problems which it left for the future to solve.

CHAPTER XIX

EXPANSION

IN a report to the Mexican Congress in 1830, the secretary of foreign affairs, Lucas Alaman, analyzed the process of American expansion: [1]

Alaman's analysis of American expansion

"The United States of the North have been going on successfully acquiring, without awakening public attention, all the territories adjoining theirs. Thus we find that, in less than fifty years, they have succeeded in making themselves masters of extensive colonies belonging to various European Powers, and of districts, still more extensive, formerly in the possession of Indian tribes, which have disappeared from the face of the earth; proceeding in these transactions, not with the noisy pomp of conquest, but with such silence, such constancy, and such uniformity, that they have always succeeded in accomplishing their views. Instead of armies, battles, and invasions, which raise such uproar, and generally prove abortive, they use means which, considered separately, seem slow, ineffectual, and sometimes palpably absurd, but which united, and in the course of time, are certain and irresistible.

"They commence by introducing themselves into the territory which they covet, upon pretence of commercial negotiations, or of the establishment of colonies, with or without the assent of the Government to which it belongs. These colonies grow, multiply, become the predominant party in the population, and as soon as a support is found in this manner, they begin to set up rights which it is impossible to sustain in a serious discussion, and to bring forward ridiculous pretensions, founded upon historical facts which

[1] *House Exec. Docs.*, 25 Cong., 2 sess., No. 351, pp. 312–322.

are admitted by nobody. . . . These extravagant opinions are, for the first time, presented to the world by unknown writers; and the labor which is employed by others, in offering proofs and reasonings, is spent by them in repetitions and multiplied allegations, for the purpose of drawing the attention of their fellow-citizens, not upon the justice of the proposition, but upon the advantages and interests to be obtained or subserved by their admission.

"Their machinations in the country they wish to acquire are then brought to light by the appearance of explorers, some of whom settle on the soil, alleging that their presence does not affect the question of the right of sovereignty or possession to the land. These pioneers excite, by degrees, movements which disturb the political state of the country in dispute. . . . When things have come to this pass, which is precisely the present state of things in Texas, the diplomatic management commences: the inquietude they have excited in the territory in dispute, the interests of the colonists therein established, the insurrections of adventurers and savages instigated by them, and the pertinacity with which the opinion is set up as to their right of possession, become the subjects of notes, full of expressions of justice and moderation, until, with the aid of other incidents, which are never wanting in the course of diplomatic relations, the desired end is attained of concluding an arrangement as onerous for one party as it is advantageous to the other."

In the *History Teachers' Magazine* for February, 1914, Dr. Jameson of the Carnegie Institution analyzed the natural history of American expansion. He omitted the stage of diplomatic claim-making by the United States and added the final step,—that of popularizing annexation by arousing our fears that some other power would annex if we did not. Otherwise these two analyses harmonize completely, except that Alaman finds the motive force in the malevolent scheming of the government, Dr. Jameson in the working of natural forces. Al-

Process of expansion

though the process described is not entirely realized in every case, and has not always been crowned with success, it may well be used as a basis for the study of the development of our interests in the territory of the Indian tribes, in the Natchez district, West Florida and East Florida, Texas, Oregon, California, Nicaragua, Cuba, Hawaii, Samoa, the Philippines, Panama, and even Mexico.

From the time of the Florida treaty, in 1819, germination began which was to result in the addition of several of these branches to the mother trunk. The imagination of the pioneer had already passed the Frontier characteristics limits of the Louisiana Purchase, and, unrestrained by its western bounds, had begun to busy itself with the lands beyond. The Americans engaged in these movements were similar to those who took the field in the long struggle for the Ohio valley, except that unlike them they were characterized by a loyalty to the United States that at times overrode their immediate material interest. At this period the diplomatic problem never took the form of defending our own undisputed territory, as it had from 1783 to 1815; rather, it was a matter of struggling for disputed regions, as in the case of Oregon, or for those undeniably belonging to other nations, as in the case of Texas and California. The issue was never so vital to our existence as was the struggle for the mouth of the Mississippi, and it only intermittently held the attention of the public or of most political leaders.

The signing of the Florida treaty was immediately followed by the rush of far-sighted speculators into Texas. Linking the old order with the new, General Texan colonists Wilkinson joined the number. These men were attracted by the fact that now for the first time could secure land titles be obtained in that region of which the ownership had previously been so uncertain. They were attracted, too, by the Spanish land system, which was based on the principle of granting favors to managers, or empresarios, who on their part guaranteed to introduce a specified number of colonists.

Nothing, except possibly bribes, had to be paid down, and the terms were such that land could be offered to the individual settler at twelve and a half cents an acre, as against the United States price of a dollar and a quarter.[1]

Mexico, succeeding Spain, continued the same liberal policy. No less anxious than Spain had been during the Con-

Mexico's liberality federation to people her frontiers, she encouraged the incoming settler by an absence of curiosity concerning his religion, by allowing the importation of slaves from the United States, and by an almost entire governmental neglect. In return for his land the settler had only to accept Mexican citizenship.

This halcyon period did not last long, for Great Britain was pressing upon Mexico an anti-slavery policy. In 1823

Omens gradual emancipation was adopted, in 1824 importation of slaves was prohibited. In 1825 and 1827 Adams, who as secretary of state had resented the failure to insist on our claim to Texas, now as President attempted to cover the error by purchasing the country. He urged Mexico to sell all or part of the region between the Sabine and the Rio Grande, using the same line of argument he had employed with Goulburn in 1815 concerning the Indian buffer state, and with de Onis in 1819 concerning Florida. He pointed out that the American settlers would never submit to Mexican authority, that the natural progress of American settlement could not be stopped by paper bonds. "These immigrants," said he, "will carry with them our principles of law, liberty, and religion, and, however much it may be hoped they might be disposed to amalgamate with the ancient inhabitants of Mexico, so far as political freedom is concerned, it would be almost too much to expect that all collisions would be avoided on other subjects. . . . These collisions may insensibly enlist the sympathies and feelings of the two Republics and lead to misunderstandings." Mexico had better now, he urged, accept compensation for territory

[1] G. P. Garrison, *Texas; a Contest of Civilizations*, Boston, etc., 1903.

which she would soon lose without it. Adams's arguments were emphasized by the proclamation of the "Fredonian republic" in 1826. Although this proved to be a premature movement, since the Americans were not yet "the predominant party in the population," it nevertheless foreshadowed what their grumblings at the anti-slavery policy of the government, which was as yet unenforced in Texas, would lead to when the settlers became strong.[1]

Impelled by these facts, by the warnings of Ward, the British minister, and by its Cassandra, Alaman, the Mexican government changed its policy. In 1826 it forbade the importation of colonists from coterminous nations; after 1828 it encouraged the formation of colonies on the border composed of persons not from the United States; in 1827 it joined the territory of Texas to the state of Coahuila to keep the former under better control; in 1829 it declared the immediate emancipation of slaves; and finally, in 1830, it prohibited immigration from the United States. The first actual manifestation of this policy in Texas itself was the establishment of Mexican military posts in 1831. Immediate revolt followed, and separation would probably have resulted, had not the revolting Texans combined with Santa Anna, who was conducting a simultaneous revolution in another part of Mexico to defend the constitution against President Bustamante. The two movements triumphed in 1832, and for a moment the Texans posed as Mexican patriots, defenders of the Mexican constitution.

Meantime the colonists began to be succeeded by the "explorers" mentioned by Alaman, men drawn to Texas not only by the cheapness and richness of the soil, but by the prospect of military glory and political advancement in the

Alarms and excursions

[1] Sir H. G. Ward, *Mexico in 1825-7;* L. G. Bugbee, "Slavery in Early Texas," *Political Science Quarterly*, 1898, xiii. 389–413, 648–668; John and Henry Sayles, *A Treatise on the Laws of Texas relating to Real Estate*, 2 vols., St. Louis, 1890–92.

conflict which it did not require great acumen to foresee. Foremost among them was Samuel Houston, the picturesque

Houston and Jackson

governor of Tennessee, who in 1829 had picturesquely vanished from that position, to be discovered later living among the Indians on the Texan border. A friend and protégé of Jackson, he occasionally visited Washington. Undoubtedly the two talked of the future of Texas, which both expected to become part of the United States. There is no evidence or probability that there was collusion between them to hasten that movement, or indeed that Houston himself did hasten it. Nevertheless, his appointment by Jackson, in 1833, to negotiate with certain Indian tribes in the region introduced him commandingly to the Texans when, in 1835, they felt the imperative need of a leader.

Santa Anna tired of the constitution that he had revived, and overthrew it. In the civil war which followed, the Tex-

Texas declares independence

ans took the losing side, and soon found themselves the sole armed supporters of the Mexican constitution. Thrown thus upon their own responsibility, they could draw upon the experience of scores of groups of Americans similarly situated. Their first step was to organize a committee of safety, then they called a convention, and finally, in 1835, after halting for a moment with a declaration of independence from the state of Coahuila, they declared their entire separation from Mexico, established a republic, and chose Houston as commander-in-chief.

Ever since 1830 "unknown" writers had been exciting the interest of the people of the United States in the affairs

Sympathy in the United States

of Texas, and now the first and ablest of the empresarios, Stephen Austin, came as ambassador to the people to solicit aid. The tragic and heroic stories of the Alamo and Goliad, with the death of David Crockett, the ideal frontier hero of the time, roused sympathy for the Texans and hatred for the Mexicans. During this period there were always thousands of Americans spoiling for a fight, and in this instance, as in most other cases, sympathy was not the only fuel relied on to kindle the flames. Those who came to the rescue were promised not glory and gratitude alone, but land as well,—three hundred and twenty acres for three months' service, twice that amount for six months, four times as much for a year. The war fever spread over the southern states, and with decreasing violence as far north as New York. Thousands volunteered to assist their late fellow-countrymen, whom, after an interval of Mexican citizenship and one of independence, they expected to welcome into what was now the "Old" Union.[1]

As individuals, companies, regiments, and even fleets left the country, either crossing the frontier on the road from Natchatoches to Nacogdoches or sailing from New Orleans, their departure was triumphantly heralded by the press. Yet, when the collectors of customs were asked to enforce the neutrality act, they explained that they could discover no organized expeditions, but only ships with individual passengers and cargoes of arms. It was not, indeed, till 1838 that the law authorizing them to detain vessels on "probable cause" was enacted. Still, a nation is responsible if its laws are not sufficient, and Mexico had good reason to complain. The record of the administration, however, was clear, its orders were correct, and probably no administration could have repressed the determination of the people to aid Texas.

Popular violation of neutrality

If the responsibility for this volunteer assistance rested fundamentally upon the people, the executive was more directly responsible for the action of its agents. In the spring of 1836, when Santa Anna was sweeping northward over Texas and Houston was retreating before him, the frontier of the United States was disturbed by rumors of impending Indian outrages to the southeast

Gaines and the Indians

[1] G. L. Rives, *The United States and Mexico, 1821–1848*, 2 vols., New York, 1913.

among the Seminole, and to the west along the Mexican or Texan border. General Gaines was authorized to call out militia to aid the regular army, and to take proper measures to defend our citizens on both frontiers, even to occupying Nacogdoches, a Mexican town, but within territory to which the United States maintained a rather fantastic claim. This town occupied an important strategic position, for it was at the junction of the coast and inland roads through Texas. Gaines so far deviated from his instructions as to concentrate on the Texan border, paying little attention to Florida, and in July he occupied Nacogdoches.[1]

This occupation had no actual effect on the Texan movement, for the crucial and final battle of independence had been won by Houston at San Jacinta on April 20. Nevertheless, the Mexican minister withdrew from Washington by way of protest. Here again the administration was able to show a clear record. It reprimanded Gaines for calling more militia than was needed to the western frontier; and, although it justified the occupation of Nacogdoches as necessary for self-defence, it ordered the town to be evacuated now that danger from the Indians had passed. When we remember, however, that Gaines knew he was acting under a President who had been elected, if not because of, at any rate in spite of, a similar over-interpretation of orders to defend the frontier by entering foreign territory, and that Jackson knew that Gaines had that knowledge, it is hard to escape the belief that an excess of zeal was expected of him. Gaines's misfortune was that his action came too late to be significant.

Jackson and Gaines

As the Nacogdoches episode reminds one of the invasions of Florida before annexation, so the whole conduct of the Texan affair seems like a less able imitation of Adams's handling of that question. Jackson's administration had for years

[1] H. von Holst, *Constitutional and Political History of the United States* (8 vols., Chicago, 1879–92), ii. 548–714; T. M. Marshall, *A History of the Western Boundary of the Louisiana Purchase, 1819–1841*, Berkeley, 1914.

been carrying hand in hand negotiations for the purchase of Texas and for the settlement of American private claims against Mexico. Adams had secured acknowl- Jackson and edgment of the claims in the first place, and Adams had paid for the territory by assuming them; during the negotiations he had preserved neutrality between Spain and her revolting colonies. On December 21, 1836, Jackson, having received the report of a special agent sent to investigate the condition of Texas, left the question of the recognition of the new republic to Congress with the words, "Prudence, therefore, seems to dictate that we should still stand aloof . . . at least until the lapse of time or the course of events shall have proved beyond cavil or dispute the ability of the people of that country to maintain their separate sovereignty." On February 6, 1837, he sought to bring the question of claims to an issue by a message one stage more advanced than that which led to trouble with France—that is, by recommending reprisals. At the same time he was discussing unofficially with Santa Anna, who was at Washington, and with the Texan representatives, a renewed proposal of purchase.

The plan was too delicate for its originators to carry out and broke down altogether. Mexico, with a persistent determination to reconquer Texas, refused to sell. Congress decided that one more solemn demand for jus- Policy of Congress tice be made upon Mexico for our claims before gress reprisals should be authorized, but voted recognition of the Texan republic. With the strings thus tangled, the proposal to secure Texas from Mexico became impracticable.

Promptly upon recognition the new republic made formal a request for annexation which had already been informally presented. This request at once Annexation refused revealed those fundamental differences which refused were threatening the United States with disunion. Monroe had in 1819 refused to press our claims to the region because of the effect which such action might have upon our national existence at a time when passions were inflamed by the struggle of pro- and anti-slavery forces over the Missouri question. Those forces were in 1837 and 1838 more bitter than ever before. Webster wrote, May 7, 1836: "We are in a peck of troubles here, and I hardly see our way through. My greatest fear at present, is of a war about Texas. . . . This whole subject appears to me to be likely to bring into our politics new causes of embarrassment, and new tendencies to dismemberment." John Quincy Adams, who in 1819 had been unwilling to give up our chance to Texas, now, in a speech running from June 15 to July 8, 1838, put all his powers into opposition to the acceptance of annexation. He believed as firmly as Alaman did that our whole movement into the region was a conspiracy; the only difference was that Alaman believed it a conspiracy of the government and included Adams among the conspirators, whereas Adams believed it a conspiracy of the "Slavocracy" supported by Jackson. Van Buren, to whom the decision came upon his succession to the presidency in 1837, was not inclined, in the face of a divided opinion at home, to press the question of annexing territory still claimed by Mexico; and the party managers were unwilling to take up an issue that was sure to divide their organizations. The question of annexation was dropped.[1]

Texas was therefore left to shift for herself, a juvenile republic with American frontier energy and a dash of Spanish braggadocio. She quickly accumulated a navy

Texas as an independent nation

and a debt. Always at war with Mexico, hostilities were intermittent. Her soldiers when unfortunate, as when captured in an expedition against Santa Fé, remembered their United States origin and sought protection as citizens. At other times they threatened to plant their banners in the halls of the Montezumas, to annex

[1] G. P. Garrison, *Diplomatic Correspondence of the Republic of Texas*, Amer. Hist. Assoc., *Reports*, 1907, vol. ii., 1908, vol. ii.; also his "First Stage of the Movement for the Annexation of Texas," *Amer. Hist. Review*, 1904, x. 72–96.

California, and become a transcontinental nation. Though ever prepared for and expecting annexation to the United States, they nevertheless grew contented with independence. Indeed, the actual disadvantages were not great; when the history of Texas is compared with that of one of our states at the same stage, as Arkansas, the difference is not appreciable.[1]

Internationally there were even advantages in her position. In 1837 France recognized her independence and Great Britain accorded trading privileges to her. Texas and The latter country delayed recognition until Great Britain 1842, but negotiation was constant. Texas and Great Britain were commercially complementary: the one produced cotton, the other manufactured it. Great Britain, while anxious for political reasons to prevent the United States from acquiring the long Texan coast line which would give command of the gulf of Mexico, was equally unwilling to see Texas fall under the United States tariff system, again after 1842 dominated by the manufacturing interests of the North. She also wanted to secure an independent source of cotton supply. The Texans, on their part, realized that Great Britain's influence in Mexico was potent, and that she might exert it to secure Mexican recognition of the new republic. It was, indeed, largely by her good offices that an amnesty was in 1843 arranged between the two countries.

The element of discord was slavery. Texas assented to a treaty on the maritime slave trade which granted a mutual right of search, but she maintained slavery and Slavery in the overland slave trade with the United Texas States. A strong English public opinion resented the creation of a new slave-holding republic out of the free territory of Mexico. Lord Aberdeen, the British minister of foreign affairs, July 31, 1843, instructed his representative in Mexico to urge the Mexican government to make the "absolute

[1] E. D. Adams, *British Interests and Activities in Texas, 1838–1846*, Baltimore, 1910; J. H. Smith, *The Annexation of Texas*, New York, 1911.

abolition of the principle of slavery" a condition of her final recognition of Texan independence. In August, 1843, in reply to a question by Lord Brougham as to the attitude of the government toward slavery in Texas, he said that his unwillingness to tell what was being done "did not arise from indifference, but from quite a contrary reason." This reply naturally aroused interest in the United States. The retention of slavery might prevent a harmonious understanding between Great Britain and Texas; but, should slavery be abolished, their interests would be cemented together, as against the United States, by the strongest ties. The fear of British influence was spurring the United States to renewed interest in annexation.

Texas was not the only fruit that hung ripe, unpicked, and threatened by alien hands in 1843. In 1795 Fauchet had written of the explorations of Alexander McKenzie in the Oregon country. "If this discovery is followed up," said he, "the English will hasten without doubt to forestall the Americans by establishments to put them in a position to secure possession of this important point." Neither government, however, seemed disposed to press the matter. In 1818 the United States and Great Britain had agreed to a joint occupancy for ten years, and by 1828 this agreement had been continued indefinitely, but made terminable by a year's notice. Spain and Russia had been eliminated from the question by their treaties with the United States and Great Britain, and by the same treaties the bounds of the territory we jointly occupied had been fixed by the parallels of 42° on the south and 54° 40' on the north.[1]

Joint occupancy of Oregon

Although American vessels frequented the coast, and Astoria had been founded in 1811, the use of the territory

[1] H. H. Bancroft, *Oregon*, 2 vols., San Francisco, 1886–88; Robert Greenhow, *Memoir, Historical and Political, on the North-west Coast of North America*, Washington, 1840; Sir Travers Twiss, *The Oregon Territory*, New York, etc., 1846.

under the joint occupancy fell at first chiefly to Great Britain, represented by the Hudson Bay Company. The only posts for many years were its fur-trading establish- **Early interest** ments, and the only settlements those of its **in Oregon** retired French-Canadian trappers; the only government was that of its factor, Dr. McLaughlin. During the twenties our government concerned itself somewhat with the subject. A Virginian representative, John Floyd, sought to have Congress secure our rights by the formation of military establishments, and Monroe recommended such action in his message of 1824. With the retirement of Floyd in 1829, however, the matter dropped out of public notice.

That basis of actual occupancy which always seems to be necessary in order to arouse a genuine interest in such questions in the United States was furnished **The mission-** by a new type of pioneer. The wave of mis- **ary movement** sionary impulse whose beginning was marked in 1819 by Bishop Heber's hymn "From Greenland's Icy Mountains" touched all Christian organizations; it started anew the attempt to Christianize the world. In such movements, as in other things, there are fashions, and among the most popular subjects for conversion in the thirties was the American Indian. A series of events attracted the missionary interest to Oregon. Various American denominations sent missionaries to the region, till by 1840 not only were there some seventy or eighty Americans in the country, but the raising of the money which sent and kept them there had aroused a widespread popular interest. Oregon had become a household word.[1]

This renewed interest was naturally reflected in the gov ernment. In 1835 Lewis F. Linn appeared as senator from Missouri, the state which, by means of the river of the same name, was most closely, or rather least distantly, connected with Oregon. He at once made himself champion of the new

[1] R. E. Speer, *Missions and Modern History*, 2 vols., New York, etc., [1904].

country by bringing in a bill to organize the Columbia river region as Oregon territory. The bill itself was reported adversely; but, as ten thousand copies of the report were distributed, it proved to be a new organ for arousing popular attention. In 1840 a squadron under Captain Wilkes was sent to visit the coast; in 1842 Tyler called attention to the problem and in the same year, Adams, as chairman of the house committee on foreign affairs, urged the sending of a special mission to Great Britain to negotiate. Linn continued to press his bill in various forms. Of one of them his colleague Benton said, "I now go for vindicating our rights on the Columbia, and as the first step toward it, passing this bill and making these grants of land, which will soon place thirty or forty thousand rifles beyond the Rocky Mountains."

Renewed interest in Oregon

While the material reason for immediate legislation was the desire for land titles, which could not be secured until the question of sovereignty was determined, there developed a further motive to hasten action. The same impulse which moved Protestant American denominations to enter the Oregon field stirred the church of Rome also. French Canadian priests, under the protection of the Hudson Bay Company, were active there and in their work with the Indians were more successful than the Protestants. Their American rivals, therefore scented a great conspiracy of the priests, the Hudson Bay Company, and the British government to drive the Americans out of Oregon and secure it for Great Britain, and endeavored from 1839 onward to impress their views on the government at Washington.[1]

British and American rivalries in Oregon

The degree to which popular interest had been stimulated was shown in 1842, when an Indian agent, sent out to treat

[1] W. I. Marshall, *Acquisition of Oregon and the long suppressed Evidence about Marcus Whitman*, 2 vols., Seattle, 1911; E. G. Bourne, *The Legend of Marcus Whitman*, in his *Essays in Historical Criticism* (New York, 1901) 3–109; Joseph Schafer, *Oregon Pioneers and American Diplomacy*, in *Turner Essays*, 35–55.

ith the tribes of the region, was joined as he went west
om Washington by nearly one hundred and fifty prospec-
ve settlers. In the spring of 1843, other Settlement of
roups of emigrants from Missouri, Arkansas, Oregon
linois, and neighboring states began promptly, without pre-
oncert, to direct themselves toward Independence, the
arting-point for the long journey to the Pacific. With
agons labelled "For Oregon," and with all their possessions,
out a thousand came together and pushed on to their
oal. In Oregon they found a self-formed provisional gov-
nment of the American settlers, begun in 1841 and per-
cted in the spring of 1843. When, in 1844, the French
anadians and British took a hand in this government,
regon, like Texas, was ready for picking. The difficulty
y in the rival British claims, and in the inability of Great
ritain and the United States to agree upon a division of
rritory.

More desirable in the minds of many than either Texas
Oregon was the California country. Although it was an
ndisputed portion of the Mexican republic, California
ic same elements were nevertheless present
re as in other regions, but in different proportions. Settlers
om the United States were few. There were some mer-
ants on the coast, merchant vessels touched its ports, and
ter 1843 some pioneers came down from Oregon. Few as
ey were, however, they were not without importance, for
e Mexican population itself was so inconsiderable that it
ould take but a small influx of Americans to make the latter
e "predominant party." In 1844 the British consuls at
pic and Monterey wrote of the rapid American emigration
the coast.[1]

The interest of Great Britain in California was keen.
ritish subjects as well as Americans were resident there,
1842 a consul had been sent to Monterey, and a British
val officer had been commissioned to investigate condi-

[1] Paullin and Paxon, *Guide*, 178-187.

tions. In 1844 the British consuls reported that a speedy separation from Mexico was inevitable. Already Great Britain had been asked if she would aid a revolution, and the foreign office had considered the possibility of California's putting herself, when free, "under the protection of any other power whose supremacy might prove injurious to British interests." In 1845 the foreign office tendered its advice to Mexico with regard to the safety of California. Great Britain, it was said, desired that California remain Mexican, she feared that France might secure it, and still more that it might fall to the United States.

Great Britain and California

The latter country was awake to the situation, or at least to a situation. Here again she believed that Great Britain not only barred her way but sought the prize. In 1842 an American squadron was sent to the coast, and, on a false rumor of war between the United States and Mexico, seized Monterey; an act for which, of course, apologies were tendered. From 1842 Captain Frémont was in and about the region at the head of a formidable exploring expedition of United States troops.

The United States and California

The government, moreover, was considering the question. In 1842 Waddy Thompson, our minister to Mexico, wrote to Webster expatiating on the desirability of annexing California. "Our Atlantic border," he urged, "secures us a commercial ascendency there. With the acquisition of Upper California, we should have the same ascendency on the Pacific. . . . I believe that this [the Mexican] government would cede to us Texas and California, and I am thoroughly satisfied that this is all we shall ever get for the claims of our merchants in this country." Webster authorized a negotiation: "You will be particularly careful," he wrote to Thompson, "not to suffer the Mexican Government to suppose that it is an object upon which we have set our hearts, or for the sake of which we should be willing to make large remuneration. The cession must be spoken of rather as a convenience to Mexico, or a mode of discharging her debts."

Possibly our willingness to use our pecuniary claims to secure
the cession of California made us the more ready to accept
the rumored statements that Great Britain was endeavoring
to do the same.[1] On April 4, 1844, B. E. Green wrote to
Calhoun that California was organized for independence.

The year 1844, therefore, found three great diplomatic
problems pressing for solution. Different as they were in
their details, they all concerned the acquisition Diplomacy and
of new territory, and they were all urged not politics
only as desirable in themselves but as necessary to check the
advance of British interests. Of the three, that relating to
Texas was in itself the least difficult; for after eight years of
independence, and an independence that was recognized
by the leading nations of Europe, Mexico's claim to her territory had nothing to rest upon. The reason why Texas
was still out of the United States was not diplomatic, but
political; it lay in the institution of slavery. Her problem
could not be solved without a linking of diplomacy and
politics such as there had not been since 1815.

[1] J. S. Reeves, *American Diplomacy under Tyler and Polk* (Baltimore,
1907), 100–102.

CHAPTER XX

ANNEXATION

When Tyler succeeded to the presidency he privately announced his determination to annex Texas. His secretary of state, Webster, however, was unenthusiastic and no action was taken till 1843. Then Webster resigned. Tyler was at this time unconnected with either political party; he had nothing to lose by a disturbance of political conditions, and he decided to press the matter. He was still delayed, however, by the death of Webster's successor, Hugh S. Legaré, after six weeks' service; but the next secretary, Abel P. Upshur, took the negotiation seriously in hand. It was conducted in secrecy, with the ostensible purpose of preventing speculation in Texan securities. The Texan administration, with Houston at the head, was slow to take the bait. It feared that the treaty might be rejected by our Senate, and Texas thus be left in an embarrassing position, an objection that Upshur met by arguments which appear to have been more satisfying to Texas than they could have been to his own conscience. The treaty drawn up, there remained the question as to the status of Texas between the signing of the treaty and its acceptance by the Senate. This would be Mexico's last chance, her amnesty with Texas would be at an end, Great Britain would no longer stand in the way of hostile action, and the probability was that she would at least reek her anger on the frontier, if not her vengeance on the nation. At this point Upshur was killed.[1]

In seeking to replace him, Tyler's primary object was to obtain political strength, for the diplomatic task was almost

[1] Reeves, *American Diplomacy under Tyler and Polk.*

finished. Unfortunately for him, however, he was brought by the intervention of friends to offer the position to John C. Calhoun, probably of all his genera- Calhoun be-
tion the man most capable of diplomatic great- comes secre-
ness, but one whose name alone was sufficient tary of state
to defeat the treaty, and who did not leave his name to work alone. Calhoun, having obtained by inquiry the opinion that both the Texas and the Oregon question could be settled, accepted the office.

On April 11, 1844, he answered the question as to the protection of Texas during the discussion of the treaty, by the following note: "During the pendency of the Treaty of an-
treaty of annexation, the president would deem nexation con-
it his duty to use all the means placed within cluded
his power by the constitution to protect Texas from all foreign invasion." An enumeration of these powers might have been less impressive than the general statement of them; but the latter proved sufficient for its purpose, and on April 12 the treaty was signed.

Calhoun came into office with a firm conviction of a purposeful policy of aggrandizement on the part of Great Britain. He wrote to Francis Wharton, May 28, 1844: Calhoun's
'As to myself, I am of the impression, if we views of Great
shall have the folly or wickedness to permit Britain
Great Britain to plant the lever of her power between the U. States and Mexico, on the Northern shore of the Gulph of Mexico, we give her a place to stand on, from which she can [brave?] at pleasure the American Continent and control its destiny. There is not a vacant spot left on the Globe, not excepting Cuba, to be seized by her, so well calculated to further the boundless schemes of her ambition and cupidity. If we should permit her to seize on it, we shall deserve the execration of posterity. Reject the treaty, and refuse to annex Texas, and she will certainly seize on it. A treaty of alliance commercial and political will be forthwith proposed by Texas to her, and I doubt not accepted. This

for yourself." On April 29, 1844, he had received a letter from a Texan friend announcing: "We are all prepared if we are spurned again from the Union to enter into a commercial free trade treaty with G. B. and France on a guaranty of our Independence which we can now have and the advantages it promises us in the cotton trade renders it very desirable." With free trade the United States would lose its market for manufactured goods in Texas. The Texan planters, supplied with low-priced British goods, could produce more cheaply than those of the United States. Texas would therefore draw away from us population and wealth, and, backed by the British navy, become our political as well as economic rival.[1]

Although having to his hand such nationalistic arguments, based on a sincere conviction, which would have been absorbed by most of our population or suspicion, Calhoun chose to rest his case or totally different grounds. He found among Upshur's papers a letter of Pakenham, the British minister at Washington enclosing a note from Aberdeen written in answer to a request from Edward Everett, our minister at London, by direction of Upshur, for an explanation of Aberdeen's statement in the House of Lords concerning his interest in the question of Texan slavery. Aberdeen, admitting an interest in Texas, denied that Great Britain had any "occult design . . . even with reference to slavery in Texas." He said, however, that it was well known that Great Britain wished to see slavery abolished "throughout the world But," he added, "the means which she has adopted and will continue to adopt, for this human and virtuous purpose, are open and undisguised. . . . The Governments of the slaveholding states may be assured that, although we shall not desist from those open and honest efforts which we have constantly made for procuring the abolition of slavery . . .

Lord Aberdeen's note

[1] Calhoun, *Correspondence*, ed. J. F. Jameson, Amer. Hist. Assoc., *Rep.* 1899, vol. ii.

we shall neither openly nor secretly resort to any measures which can tend to disturb their internal tranquillity, or thereby to affect the prosperity of the American Union."

This note, though cleverly guarded in its language at essential points, was substantially untrue, for it was intended to appear to deny the rumor that Great Britain was urging Mexico to insist upon abolition in Texas as a condition of recognizing her independence. It was also discourteous in its reference to our established domestic institutions. The disclaimer of any intention to disturb our "internal tranquillity" could certainly not be accepted by our government on its face value: we could scarcely allow Great Britain to be a judge of what would create such a disturbance. When a nation deliberately asserts a policy of meddling with the rest of the world, other nations have a right to demand, not general assurances as to her methods, but explicit itemization.

Lord Aberdeen's note came to Calhoun both as a confirmation of suspicion and as an instrument of action. He at once engaged Pakenham in a correspondence growing out of it, which afterwards formed his case before the Senate for the support of the treaty. *Calhoun-Pakenham correspondence*
He stated that upon hearing of the avowed determination of Great Britain to attempt the abolition of slavery throughout the world, the United States had to consider her own safety; since, therefore, the abolition of slavery in Texas would imperil the internal tranquillity of the nation, a treaty of annexation had been arranged as the only means of preventing such a misfortune. To Aberdeen's expressed hope for abolition in the United States he replied by an argument designed to show that emancipation would prove a national calamity. He did not even refrain from making use of the hackneyed comparison between the American slaves and the British laboring classes.[1]

Calhoun's statement that Aberdeen's note had caused the making of the treaty was, of course, untrue. Essentially,

[1] Calhoun, *Works*, vols. iv.–v.

however, it represented the truth, for the note put into definite public form rumors that had been coming to his ears,
Critique of Calhoun's case
particularly from the London letters of his confidant, Duff Green, who quoted the assertion of the Texan representative, Ashabel Smith, that England would guarantee a loan to Texas to pay the expenses of emancipation. To Calhoun, though not to the President, the main motive for action lay in the danger to slavery. His defence of slavery as an institution has been criticised, and perhaps in form is open to criticism; but Aberdeen's remarks on the subject demanded some answer. There is no doubt that Calhoun believed in the case as he presented it. He wrote to James H. Hammond, May 17, 1844: "There is not a doubt in my mind, that if Texas should not now be annexed, she is lost to our Union. The Senate has been furnished with evidence to that effect, perfectly conclusive."

The defect in Calhoun's argument was that his reasoning was logical rather than political, and that his logic did not
Failure of Calhoun's case
reach to his conclusion. His basis was that of his slave-trade resolutions,—the obligation of the national government to protect any institutions of any state. His second step, that it was the duty of the national government to protect the internal tranquillity of the state, was just as sound; it had been used by Dana in 1809 in reference to the South when he was discussing trade with the negro state of Hayti. His slip came in asserting that the one method of performing these duties was the annexation of Texas. The national government has discretion as to methods, and annexation was not the only one possible. The fact is, Calhoun was so anxious to fix the doctrine of national protection upon the country that his eagerness blinded him to this weakness in his logic. He sacrificed Texas to political theory.

The unpopularity of Tyler and the fear of the slavery issue brought to the front by Calhoun combined to defeat the treaty. Annexation, however, could no longer be held off.

Wiser politicians took it up and changed the basis of argument. In a strong letter Jackson roused the public apprehension of England's political ambitions, and the Democratic convention had the good sense to unite northern with southern interests by joining Oregon with Texas. Referring to our lost settlement at Astoria and our claim to Texas abandoned in 1819, the convention resolved, "That our title to the whole of the territory of Oregon is clear and unquestionable; that no portion of the same ought to be ceded to England or any other power; and that the reoccupation of Oregon and the reannexation of Texas at the earliest practicable period are great American questions."

Defeat of the treaty

The election of the Democratic candidate, James K. Polk, was accepted as a national mandate in favor of annexation. But, if annexation was to come, many believed that it must come quickly. Texas was now the scene of a dramatic contest between the American representative, Duff Green, specially sent to hold the republic in line, and Elliot and Saligny, the British and French representatives respectively, who, backed by their governments, had dropped the slavery question and were promising recognition by Mexico on condition of a promise by Texas to maintain her independence. In order to hasten action by the United States, it was proposed that, since a two-thirds majority for a treaty could not be secured in the Senate, annexation be brought about by a joint resolution of the two houses. The constitutionality of such a method was at least obscure, for previously the power to annex had been implied from that to make treaties. The constitutional argument, however, played little part in the discussion of the main question, which absorbed most of the session from December, 1844, to March, 1845. At length, on March 1, the resolution was passed, but added to it was a curious amendment allowing the President either to proceed with annexation by the authority thereby given or to negotiate a treaty.

Annexation by joint resolution

This double-headed proposition was accepted by a balancing number of senators with the understanding that the Tyler annexes whole matter would be left to Polk for settle-Texas ment, and with the purpose that he should find himself fully empowered to act quickly. Tyler, however, anticipated action by Polk by dispatching a messenger to Texas announcing that she might enter the union on the terms of the joint resolution. Polk acquiesced in the accomplished fact, and the centre of interest shifted from Washington to Texas.[1]

The proposal to Texas was that she be admitted as a state, with such government as should be adopted by the people Struggle for and assented to by the United States. This Texas plan, in contrast with Calhoun's treaty, which resembled previous annexation treaties in merely providing for admission to statehood at some future time, virtually constituted an enabling act, pushing statehood one step further forward. It provided that Texas should hold her public lands for the payment of her debt; whereas Calhoun had agreed that the United States would receive the lands and pay the debt. The question of boundary it left open to settlement by the United States. It further provided that Texas was not to be divided into more than four states, of which those north of the parallel of 36° 30′ should not permit slavery,—points for which there were no equivalents in the Calhoun treaty. The president of Texas, Anson Jones, received the proposal with dignity. He encouraged Elliot to press Mexico for recognition, and when the Texan convention met, July 4, 1845, he offered it the alternatives of independence, recognized by Mexico on condition that it be maintained and with the special friendship of Great Britain and France, or annexation. Without hesitation the convention chose the latter, and in December Texas became a state of the Union. Although chagrined at the result, Great Britain and France were nevertheless, as they had indeed repeatedly

[1] T. H. Benton, *Thirty Years' View*, 2 vols., New York, 1854–56.

declared, not prepared to resist forcibly; hence nothing now remained necessary for a complete settlement of the question but acceptance by Mexico.[1]

Polk came into office with the intention of securing Texas, Oregon, and California. To the accomplishment of this formidable task he brought, not great intellectual ability, but an iron will, a directness of **Polk** purpose, and a conviction of the morality of his intentions inherited from his Scotch-Presbyterian ancestry,—just the equipment for the man of action after discussion has cleared and defined the issue.[2] He found the first part of his three-fold undertaking practically finished, and he accepted the results. Of the two remaining tasks, the Oregon controversy, of which the details had been worked out by Gallatin in 1827, had just been still more closely defined in a correspondence between Calhoun and Pakenham.[3]

In these letters the British practically acknowledged our title from the forty-second parallel to the south bank of the Columbia, and we practically acknowledged **The Oregon** their rights north of the forty-ninth parallel. **question** Within the undistributed middle lay Puget Sound and the tip of Vancouver island. Both countries claimed Spanish recognition of their claims, the British by the Nootka Sound convention of 1790, we by our treaty of 1819. By discovery and exploration we had the stronger claim to the Columbia valley, the British to that of the Fraser. In actual settlements Great Britain had held the advantage; but the United States was gaining, though most of her settlers sought the valley of the Willamette, a southern branch of the Columbia. In 1844 Aberdeen offered to arbitrate, but the United States refused.

---

[1] Anson Jones, *Memoranda and Official Correspondence relating to the Republic of Texas*, New York, 1859.

[2] J. K. Polk, *Diary*, ed. M. M. Quaife, 4 vols., Chicago, 1910.

[3] Calhoun, *Works*, vol. v.

Calhoun expected that Polk would request his continuance in the position of secretary of state, but Polk failed to do so, **Polk's Oregon policy** for his views differed fundamentally from those of Calhoun. Calhoun feared both the intentions and the power of Great Britain, he believed that she could and would maintain her views by force. He was of

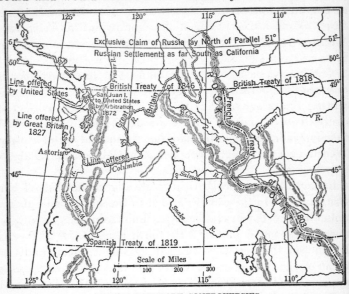

OREGON BOUNDARY CONTROVERSIES

that generation of American statesmen who, confident in our growing strength, preferred to leave such disputes open, trusting to the future. Polk intended to settle the question at once, and chose as his secretary James Buchanan, a man of like mind.

The latter offered Great Britain the line of 49°, which had **Polk revives the Monroe Doctrine** been satisfactory to Calhoun. Upon its rejection, which had been anticipated, Polk took up the question in his message of December, 1845. Referring to the Monroe Doctrine, which he was the first President to revive, he said: "It should be distinctly announced to the world as our settled policy that no future European colony or dominion shall with our consent be planted or established on any part of the North American continent." He rejected the idea of any balance of power as applied to America. Finally he asked Congress to authorize the termination of the joint occupancy with a year's notice, as provided in the convention of 1828. He declared that our title "to the whole Oregon Territory" had already been "asserted, and, as is believed, maintained by irrefragable facts and arguments."

Congress debated the proposal with unusual seriousness and ability. Polk's views found an echo in a style of expansionist oratory new to the country and not confined to Congress. The phrase "Fifty-four-forty or fight" rang through the land. Calhoun and Webster, on the other hand, pleaded for moderation, expressing their belief that the President's policy would result in war, and that war would end in the loss of Oregon to the British fleet. In the end the President was authorized to give notice of the termination of the joint occupancy; but this notice was to be joined with the declaration that it was hoped that the step would lead to a speedy amicable adjustment of the differences between the two governments,—an apparent invitation for a proposal of compromise.[1] *Oregon policy of Congress*

The British government was still under the leadership of Sir Robert Peel, whose friendliness to the United States had resulted in the Webster-Ashburton treaty. It was, indeed, the same government whose machinations, real and exaggerated, in Texas and California had been so effectively used in furthering Texan annexation. The desire of Great Britain to prevent that annexation, however, had been no more inimical than the desire of a merchant to secure a new cus- *British policy*

---

[1] See speeches by Calhoun and Webster in their *Works;* also Joseph Schafer, "The British Attitude toward the Oregon Question, 1815–1846," *Amer. Hist. Review,* 1911, xvi. 273–294.

tomer rather than let him go to a rival. Her methods in the use of her influence with Mexico had perhaps been "unfair"; but if these did indicate a slight moral obliquity, and if Aberdeen's letter on slavery was lacking in tactfulness, such lapses did not come from any hostility or from a failure to realize that the friendship of the United States was more important to Great Britain than that of any other country on the American continent. Great Britain was looking after her own interests to be sure, but her ministers, Aberdeen and Peel, were friendly to the United States. Their friendship, moreover, was greatly stimulated in 1846 by the fact that both nations were just taking the first steps in the new policy of free trade, which, if persisted in, would cement their destinies by an ever-increasing bond of trade.

The British government, therefore, having previously ascertained that its proposal would not be contumaciously Oregon agree- rejected, offered to compromise on the forty-ment ninth parallel to the strait of Georgia, and thence to the ocean, with the right of free navigation on the Columbia. This was more than Great Britain had ever before offered, though less than the United States had expressed its willingness to accept. It gave us Puget Sound, it gave Great Britain the tip of Vancouver island, thus distributing the best harbors on the northwest coast. Polk accepted this proposal as a basis, and a treaty was drawn up. Before concluding it, however, Polk endeavored to relieve himself of responsibility for compromising in a case in which he had asserted our title to the whole to be "clear and unquestionable," by resorting, as has so seldom been done, to the "advice" of the Senate. That body advised signing, and thereby practically committed itself to ratify the treaty, which was promptly done in June, 1846.

Thus was settled the last stretch of our northern boundary, although the division of the smaller islands caused more trouble, which was adjusted by arbitration in 1871. Polk's bluster and the wild speeches in Congress probably made some difference in the result. Whenever we have encountered Great Britain we have been obliged to compromise, but bluff on our part has often hastened agreement. The line decided upon was a reasonable one, and, after the following of the forty-ninth parallel to the Rockies in 1818, was probably inevitable, regardless of claims or of diplomacy. The protrusion of Vancouver island south of forty-nine was disagreeable, but on general principles the island was best considered as a whole. In rousing popular agitation Polk was playing with fire; it was a typical example of "shirt-sleeve" diplomacy. On the other hand, a continuance of the joint occupancy in the face of the actual settlement of the region might well have given rise to frontier squabbles more dangerous than the whiff of spread-eagle oratory.

What was at issue in Oregon?

On April 28, 1846, Polk accepted the British offer as to Oregon, subject to the consent of the Senate; on May 11 he advised war with Mexico. The conjunction of the events was fortunate, but probably not vital, for Great Britain had already signified her intention not to support Mexico. At Polk's inauguration the war had not been expected by those best informed. Webster wrote to his son, March 11, 1845, that Mexico would doubtless "be very angry" over the annexation of Texas, but, he added, "that she will plunge at once into a war, though it is possible, is as yet not thought probable, by the best informed here. . . . Mr. Polk and his cabinet will desire to keep the peace."

Mexico and Texan annexation

Although Mexico withdrew her minister, as she had done in 1837, she did not rush into war. There existed, however, at the outset a question that required careful handling on the part of the United States. As usual, we had annexed not territory alone, but a boundary controversy. The Mexican territory of Texas had been bounded to the south by the Nueces river; the republic of Texas had actually occupied the south bank of this river; the

The Texas boundary

constitution of Texas described the national boundary as the
Rio Grande to its source, and thence northward to the forty-
second parallel. This constitutional boundary, which
swept in Mexican settlements on the north bank of the Rio
Grande near its mouth, together with the important post of
Santa Fé in New Mexico, had been fixed in order to provide a
basis for compromise. Calhoun had recognized its lack of
actuality, and the joint resolutions, seeking to avoid any such
difficulty as had arisen with Maine two years before, had

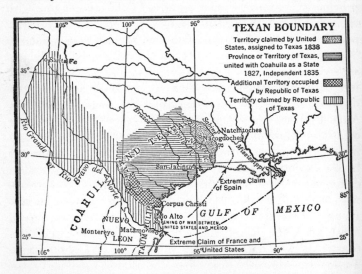

given the United States power to settle the boundary. Meantime, the question as to the protection of Texas until her
formal admission, which could not be consummated till
December, 1845, came up. Calhoun, after the rejection of
his treaty, had promised such defence as the President could
give while negotiations were in process; but this did not mean
much. Polk was in an easier position; for the United States
had assented to the annexation, but until July 4, 1845, Texas
had not. During the interval he wished to send troops, but
President Jones said they were not necessary. When Texas

accepted our offer this difficulty was removed,[1] and Polk could do as he wished.

On June 15, 1845, Polk ordered General Taylor to "select and occupy, on or near the Rio Grande del Norte, such site as will consist with the health of the troops, and will be best adapted to repel invasion, and to Taylor in Texas protect what, in event of annexation, will be our western frontier." Against this order our representative in Texas, A. J. Danelson, protested on the ground that, since Texas had previously accepted a truce leaving Mexico in possession of the north bank of the Rio Grande, and had evinced a disposition to settle the question by negotiation, things might, "to say the least . . . be left by the United States in the same condition." On July 8 Taylor was ordered not to interfere with existing Mexican military establishments in the disputed region, "unless a state of war should exist." On August 30 he was instructed as follows: "The assembling of a large Mexican army on the border of Texas, and crossing the Rio Grande with a considerable force, will be regarded by the executive as an invasion of the United States, and the commencement of hostilities. An attempt to cross the river with such a force will also be considered in the same light." It was obviously the intention of the administration to insist upon the Rio Grande boundary, at least near the coast. It was not, however, till January 17, 1846, that Taylor was explicitly ordered to the Rio Grande.

During the same period Polk was endeavoring to open an approach to negotiation with Mexico. An agent, Parrott, accompanied the withdrawing Mexican minis- Slidell's instructions ter, and in June reported that Mexico would not go to war over Texas. Polk thereupon appointed John Slidell minister to Mexico. He was, first of all, to warn Mexico of the insidious designs of foreign nations and of our

---

[1] Rives, *The United States and Mexico;* William Jay, *Review of the Causes and Consequences of the Mexican War,* Boston, etc., 1849; C. H. Owen, *The Justice of the Mexican War,* New York, etc., 1908.

determination to prevent them. Then he was to insist upon the payment of the claims of American citizens, which had been recognized by a convention of 1839 but which remained unpaid. Realizing the financial inability of Mexico, the government instructed Slidell, "Fortunately the joint resolution of Congress for annexing Texas to the United States presents a means of satisfying these claims, in perfect consistency with the interests as well as the power of both republics." The indisputable character of the Texan claim to the Rio Grande near its mouth, was to be asserted; but a question concerning the right to New Mexico was admitted, and Slidell was authorized to offer to assume claims for five million dollars in return for the title to that territory.

The most important portion of the instructions, however, referred to the reopening, but in a new spirit, of the question Polk and California in regard to California which Thompson and Webster had broached in 1843. Under the pressure of events the situation there was rapidly ripening. Rumors of revolt were multiplying, and Polk did not seek to blast the growth. In October, 1845, Larkin, our consul at Monterey, was instructed: "Whilst the president will make no effort and use no influence to induce the Californians to become one of the free and independent states of this Union, yet if the people should desire to unite their destiny with ours, they would be received as brethren, whenever this can be done without affording Mexico any just cause of complaint." Lieutenant Gillespie was sent to confer with Larkin, Commodore Stockton was ordered to report with his squadron at Monterey, and Frémont was exploring California.

In the midst of these happenings, Slidell was instructed to call the attention of Mexico to the fact that she had small Mexico and California chance of maintaining her hold upon California, and that Great Britain and France were both ambitious to obtain it. He was to say that the United States would never permit its cession to either of these powers, but would herself pay Mexico liberally for possession,—from twenty to twenty-five million dollars according to the inclusion or the exclusion of the peninsula of Lower California. Polk was himself determined to secure at least the bay of San Francisco.

With such instructions Slidell arrived in Mexico. The government of that country was expecting the United States to explain the annexation of Texas; that, to its mind, was the primary question. Accordingly, *Slidell in Mexico* it refused to treat except with a commissioner sent for that express and sole purpose. As a fresh revolution was in progress, Slidell awaited the result, hoping for reception by the new government. Paredes, the successful contestant, was, however, more hostile than Herrera, whom he had turned out. He at length did what had been so often surmised without foundation,—offer California to Great Britain to hold as a security for a loan. When the offer reached her, however, she declined; the security was no longer Mexico's to offer. Toward Slidell he pursued the policy of his predecessor by persistently refusing to receive him, till by the middle of March Slidell gave up hope of accomplishing anything on the existing basis of facts and returned to the United States.

Polk and Buchanan had long before reached this decision, and determined to change the facts. The change was to be not in the instructions themselves but the method of pressing them. War was to be recommended. *Timing war* Such drastic action, however, must, to receive popular support, have been preceded by a patient negotiation such as to their minds Slidell had just carried out. It should also come after a settlement of the Oregon question, not because Polk expected war with Great Britain, but because the possibility of such a war would serve to enhearten Mexico and diminish the moral effect which he hoped would follow his threat. Both these conditions being fulfilled, on Saturday, May 9, the decision was taken, although there was still reason to fear the reception of the message by Congress.

On Sunday news arrived at Washington from Taylor on the frontier. Since January he had been in camp on the Rio Grande, "right in the enemy's country, and actually occupying their corn and cotton fields," as one of his officers wrote. Mexico took the attitude that this occupation constituted war. On April 24 Paredes declared, "Hostilities then have been commenced by the United States"; but he disclaimed the right to declare war until the Mexican Congress assembled. The tinder was ready, however: on April 26 Mexican and United States troops met and fought. It was of this encounter, that Polk heard. It afforded a more appealing if not more solid cause for war than the failure of negotiation. Contrary to his usage, therefore, he prepared his message on Sunday, and sent it to Congress the next day, May 11, 1846. "The cup of forbearance had been exhausted even before the recent information from the frontier of the Del Norte. But now, after reiterated menaces, Mexico has passed the boundary of the United States, has invaded our territory and shed American blood upon the American soil . . . war exists, and, notwithstanding all our efforts to avoid it, exists by the act of Mexico herself."

"War exists"

Polk regarded war not as an object, but as a means: he believed that his ends could be obtained without fighting. Having deprived Mexico of the hope of British assistance, he entered into negotiations with Santa Anna, the exiled Mexican hero, who was in Havana. On June 7 Commander Alexander Slidell MacKenzie, who had been sent to confer with him, reported that he had explained to Santa Anna the President's intentions as to boundaries and other questions, and that Santa Anna had expressed his friendship for the United States as well as his enlightened views for the government of Mexico, and had given certain advice with regard to General Taylor's movements. Accordingly the United States allowed Santa Anna to pass the blockade, and watched with pleasure his rapid success in

Polk and Santa Anna

establishing himself in control of Mexico. She anticipated a speedy ending of hostilities, and a prompt and happy negotiation with the new Mexican government. Santa Anna, however, on gaining power, sought to establish it upon the only basis on which it could continue to exist: he put himself at the head of the national forces to resist the United States. Thus we not only were at war but were also obliged to fight.

On May 13, 1846, Buchanan proposed in the cabinet that our announcement to foreign nations of the fact that we were at war with Mexico be accompanied by a declaration that we would acquire nothing but the Rio Grande boundary. Polk, however, refused to sanction such a promise. "I will not tie up my hands by any such pledge," he declared. "In making peace with our adversary, we shall acquire California, New Mexico, and other further territory, as an indemnity for this war, if we can." In accordance with these ideas, Nicholas P. Trist, chief clerk of the state department, was in April, 1847, commissioned to accompany the army and to make peace whenever he got the chance. Santa Anna twisted him about his fingers throughout the summer, and in the autumn Polk recalled him. The successes of the army, however, rendered Santa Anna's intrigues useless, except as a means of securing money for himself, When, September 14, 1847, the city of Mexico fell, the whole of Mexico became demoralized and its government became anxious to negotiate. Trist, although having now no official position, nevertheless negotiated a treaty at Guadaloupe Hidalgo on February 2, 1848.

By the time this document reached the United States that country was a hustings for the discussion of war. Those who opposed it and its conduct and its purposes were of the better-educated class; they possessed the greater literary ability; they produced careful briefs, studied histories, and imperishable satires, and their voices have outlasted those of their opponents. The loudest voices at the time, however, and the most popular pens, were those that became more and more imbued with the war spirit. A clamor for the whole of Mexico arose.

The "Hard" faction of the New York Democracy said of the war: "It is no more than the restoration of moral

Expansionist feeling

rights by legal means"; the field for work is "opened to us by the conduct of Mexico, and such moral and legal means are offered for our use. Shall we occupy it? Shall we now run with manly vigor the race that is set before us? Or shall we yield to the suggestions of a sickly fanaticism, or sink into an enervating slumber? . . . We feel no emotion but pity for those whose philanthropy, or patriotism, or religion, have led them to believe that they can prescribe a better course of duty than that of the God who made us all." Nor was the feeling sectional. The *National Era*, an antislavery organ, favored the absorption of Mexico, state by state. From England, George Bancroft, our minister, wrote to Buchanan: "People are beginning to say that it would be a blessing to the world if the United States would assume the tutelage of Mexico,"—the first appeal of the British investor for United States protection. Buchanan himself in cabinet discussion said, "We must fulfill that destiny which Providence may have in store for both countries."

With this rising wave of enthusiasm Polk had no sympathy. From the beginning his purpose had been to annex

Peace

Texas, Oregon, and California, and so his purpose remained. He would not imperil what he had won, by waiting for the doubtful result of the next election. Distasteful and irregular as Trist's conduct had been, and his negotiations feeble and even improper, Polk seized upon his treaty as the only means of bringing a prompt end to the war and of checking projects of further conquest. He sent it to the Senate on February 21, 1848, recommending the striking out of one article; on March 10 it was accepted, against the vote of Webster, who wished to acquire no territory at all, and of Hannegan of Indiana, who wanted all Mexico.

The treaty gave us Texas to the Rio Grande, New Mexico including Arizona, and California, with the free navigation of the Colorado and other rivers. Mexicans remaining in the ceded territory were to become incorporated into the United States. We agreed to pay Mexico fifteen million dollars, to exonerate her from all claims of American citizens up to the date of the treaty, and ourselves to satisfy such claims to the extent of three and a quarter million dollars. Two articles were of special interest, the seventeenth, which specifically provided for the revival of the treaty of commerce of 1831, and the twenty-first, which in a lame and hesitating manner introduced into our diplomacy the idea of permanent arbitration.

Terms of peace

With the acceptance of this treaty the third great accession of territory within three years had been consummated. In each case movements long germinating had reached fruition. Texas was over-ripe, Oregon at practical maturity, California was hastened by the hothouse influence of the other two. Polk, the "dark horse," whom "no one knew" at the time he was nominated, had pushed through with relentless energy and indifferent skill the most ambitious diplomatic program with which any President had ever entered office. It is evident that his task had consisted, not in the delicate manipulation of conflicting interests, but in the constant reiteration of the will of a dominant power.

Polk's accomplishment

CHAPTER XXI

DIPLOMACY AND POLITICS, 1848-1861

EXHILARATED by our annexations, we no longer, in the period between the Mexican and Civil wars, feared Europe.

Expansion The star of empire had crossed the Atlantic. "European monarchies" had become "effete." They were still malevolent, but it was no longer necessary for us to defer crises. Our hour had struck; destiny indicated our line of march. Expansion had become a national conviction; the American continents would become united, not under our influence, but under our flag.

This belief in expansion, however, was not imperialism. Our faith in the universal applicability of our political system was as strong as ever. The Spanish-

Republicanism Americans were to be incorporated into the Union, not to be subject to it. For a time, indeed, our ardent republicanism, no longer forced to be on the defensive, seemed likely to involve us in a policy of interference in Europe. The revolutions of 1848 stirred us almost as much as had the first French revolution or that of Spanish America. The Democratic Convention of that year resolved "that, with the recent development of this grand political truth of the sovereignty of the people and their capacity and power for self-government" which was "prostrating thrones and erecting republics on the ruins of despotism in the Old World," it felt a renewed duty to defend liberty at home. This was extremely discreet, and our action was confined to a prompt recognition of the new government of France, and the sending of our first diplomatic representative to the Papal States in appreciation of the liberal sentiments with which Pius IX. came into the pontificate. When, however, in 1851, Louis Kossuth came to this country with the avowed object of securing aid for a new struggle in Hungary designed to established republicanism and independence, sympathy seemed about to plunge us into European politics. It may have been fortunate for us that Polk had recently revived our interest in the Monroe Doctrine; but it was probably the fundamental popular conception on which the doctrine rested that held us in check and caused the enthusiasm which Kossuth aroused to exhaust itself in champagne and oratory.

Our expansionist spirit, self-limited by the ocean and based on republicanism, was also non-military. Seward, most genial of expansionists, said in 1861 at St. Paul that he saw Russia and Great Britain building on the Arctic Ocean and in Canada the outposts of his own country, and that he expected that the future capital of our expanded native land would be in the valley of Mexico; but he continued to assert what he had said in 1846, "I would not give one human life for all the continent that remains to be annexed." The action of Congress, moreover, continued to be based on the principle that the army should be just sufficient to maintain order on the frontier and the navy to protect our merchant marine. President Pierce's first message does show a tendency to stretch the principle to cover a substantial increase in the navy, but the most ardent of the expansionists, Buchanan, showed no appreciation of a connection between a policy of expansion and prepared military strength. Destiny was to furnish her own instruments, of which the peaceful infiltration of armed American immigrants was the chief.

Individualism versus Imperialism

That this popular conviction did not materialize during this period into actual acquisition is in part due to external obstacles, and in part to the fact that diplomacy was not only subordinated to politics but was even actively employed for political ends. Politicians and statesmen alike endeavored to relieve the pressure of the conflict over slavery by pointing to ques-

Influence of politics on diplomacy

tions which would rouse a national interest; they feared those subjects that would embitter sectionalism. Webster wrote in regard to a grandiloquent dispatch which he had sent to Hülseman, the Austrian representative, that his purpose was to "touch the national pride and make a man feel sheepish and look silly who should speak of disunion." The habit of making stump speeches in diplomatic documents became common; Everett made his in a declaration against European interference in Cuba, Marcy his on the case of Martin Koszta. Diplomatic policies, therefore, stood always attendant upon those of politics and fared as secondary interests always do.

Of the men who directed affairs, Buchanan was the most conspicuous. Secretary of state under Polk, minister to

Buchanan

Great Britain from 1853 to 1856, and President from 1857 to 1861, he had experience and considerable dialectic skill. He had also purpose; oblivious of the necessity of domestic policies, he made expansion his program, and himself the leader of the movement. He lacked

Pierce

force, however, to push his policies to conclusion or even to an issue.[1] President Pierce was a lesser light of the same group. Of the secretaries of state,

Clayton

Clayton is remembered chiefly for his treaty with Bulwer, which has proved to be our most entangling agreement with a foreign power since

**Webster,
Everett**

our first treaties with France. Webster and Everett were both worthy of the reputation of the office, though neither particularly enhanced his own.

Cass

Cass, under Buchanan, had already made his career and now added to it merely his extinction of Great Britain's claim to the right of visitation.[2]

William L. Marcy, serving under Pierce, caused a ripple of amusement and annoyance by his famous circular order

[1] James Buchanan, *Works*, ed. J. B. Moore, 12 vols., Philadelphia, etc., 1908–11.

[2] McLaughlin, *Lewis Cass*.

of June 1, 1853, that all our representatives were to confine their sartorial ambitions to "the simple costume of an American citizen." The diplomatic uniforms which had been developed by the practice of our ministers were accordingly discarded for trousers and frock or evening coats; we became *sans culottes.* The long-lived joke about the American minister who was mistaken for a waiter was soon born. With this exception, Marcy was not trivial; he became more fully secretary of state, more conversant with the whole field of our diplomacy, and more universally active in dealing with it than had any secretary since John Quincy Adams.

Marcy

During the fifties there were rumblings of administrative reform along many lines, but there was neither the will to perform nor the evolution of any practicable scheme. In 1856 a general act was passed systematizing the whole diplomatic service. The positions were graded, salaries were fixed, fees were regulated, and a method of control was outlined. Nevertheless, appointments grew to be more and more at the mercy of politics and more and more unsuitable. Most notorious was that of Pierre Soulé to the court of Spain, in the face of the fact that his personal history, to say nothing of his personal characteristics, was sure to produce trouble. The expansion of our commerce began to arouse a special interest in our consular service, with the result that in 1856 an act was passed providing for the appointment of twenty-five "consular-pupils," who were, on showing themselves competent, to be promoted. This act was repealed in 1857, but it indicated a desire to release that service from the perils of rotation in office.[1]

Diplomatic and consular service

Commerce, though but lamely supported by our consuls, was flourishing without interfering with our isolation. Our exports still consisted of non-competitive products, but in bulk these had increased beyond expectation. The growth

[1] Fish, *The Civil Service and the Patronage,* 139–140, 183.

of cotton production and of its consumption in Europe had made that commodity one of the leading features of inter-
Character of national trade. Europe had passed the point
our commerce of self-sufficiency in food supply, and drew more and more from our farms. The development of our manufactures rendered a corresponding increase in our imports unnecessary, and for the first time the balance of direct trade was in our favor. The indirect trade was of steadily diminishing significance; our exports of foreign goods in 1836 amounted to about fifteen per cent of our total exports, in 1856 to about five per cent only. This did not mean that we imported fewer of such articles of trade as Chinese silks and teas; it meant that we kept them.

This commercial prosperity was shared by the merchant marine. Seventy-five per cent of our imports and exports
Merchant were carried in American vessels, and owing
marine to the bulky character of the exports, this meant an immense tonnage. By 1860 we had surpassed Great Britain. Maintained since 1828 on a basis of equal treatment as to port and customs regulations in the case of nearly all countries, our merchant marine was also fostered by the government, which not only continued the bounties on fishing but inaugurated in 1846 a short-lived policy of subsidies to assist in our competition for the fast-mail traffic. The subsidies were, however, discontinued before the end of this period.[1]

Chiefly, however, the energy of the government was displayed in preparing the way for commerce by means of di-
Commercial plomacy. Between 1845 and 1861 the United
treaties States continued her policy of making American commerce respected by enforcing the claims of her citizens, mainly for injuries to person and property received in Spanish-American countries. The integrity of commerce she better assured by the formation of extradition treaties with most of the German states, Austria, France with whom

[1] Coman, *Industrial History*, 264–266.

a first treaty on the subject had been made in 1843, Sweden and Norway, Colombia, and the Two Sicilies. First treaties of commerce were made in Europe with Belgium, Mecklenburg-Schwerin, Oldenburg, and Switzerland; in Spanish America with the Argentine Republic and Paraguay, as well as with Bolivia and Peru, which had now separated, and with Costa Rica, Guatamala, and Salvador, which had formerly been included in our general treaty with Central America. In the near East we made a first treaty with Persia.

The most important commercial treaty was that negotiated by Marcy, in 1854, with Great Britain in behalf of Canada. Arranged on the basis of reciprocity, Reciprocity it harmonized the growing difficulties of the with Canada Newfoundland fisheries, by submitting some points to arbitration, and by securing to us certain desired privileges, in return for which the Canadians were given the right to import their fish into the United States free of duty. It also reciprocally exchanged, subject to a reservation of rights, the navigation of Lake Michigan by the British for that of the St. Lawrence and the canals between the Great Lakes and the ocean by the Americans. The arrangement was for twelve years.[1]

The most interesting field for diplomatic effort, however, was the Pacific. That ocean was filled with our shipping. The whale fishery was at its height, whale oil Trade in the was the most prized illuminant, and we were the Pacific foremost nation in the pursuit. The whalers, often three years away from home, were forced to frequent the islands and coasts of the whole ocean, and the American flag became everywhere familiar. Amid these sturdy little craft shifting nervously about, following their quarry, passed the superb clippers, whose voyages, never deviating, from New York to

[1] Chalfant Robinson, *A History of Two Reciprocity Treaties* [New Haven, 1904]; C. D. Allin and G. M. Jones, *Annexation, Preferential Trade, and Reciprocity*, Toronto, [1912].

Canton could be measured almost to the day, to whom disaster was a word almost unknown. Sailing with the others to the Horn, but then hugging the west coast of South America, had lately come the nondescript fleet bearing adventurers to the newly discovered gold mines of California. From the Isthmus up, the number increased, and the Caribbean was livelier than ever with vessels carrying from the Isthmus to the United States the goods brought down to its Pacific ports, and to the Isthmus those from the United States destined for California. The occasional wrecking of American vessels on the ocean coasts, as in Japan, the employment of islanders (Kanakas) on our vessels, and the use of Kanakas and Chinese labor on the Pacific slope added material for diplomacy.

It is not surprising, therefore, to find these growing interests fructifying into treaty relations. In 1849 a first Treaties with treaty of friendship and commerce was made Pacific powers with the kingdom of Hawaii, in 1850, one with the sultan of Bruni in Borneo. In 1856 a new treaty was made with Siam. In 1858 a treaty with China very much increased the opportunities in that empire which had been offered to us by the treaty of 1844. In particular it granted religious freedom in China, and provided that "any person, whether citizen of the United States or Chinese convert, who, according to these tenets, peaceably teach and practice the principles of Christianity, shall in no case be interfered with or molested." In 1854 a treaty opened up the tightly closed islands of Lew Chew; but most important of all was that made in the same year by Commodore Matthew Perry with the empire of Japan, which, till then closed for generations to the outside world, dates its new life from that event. This treaty was followed by others in 1857 and 1858, the ratification of these last being exchanged with a pomp and circumstance at Washington, by a special embassy from Japan, which did much to arouse popular interest.

A more special endeavor of American diplomacy during

this period was to establish the principle, to which we were now fully committed, of the free use of international rivers and narrow waterways. One of the most im- **Free use of** portant of such straits was the sound between **waterways** Denmark and Sweden, for the passage of which Denmark charged dues. About one hundred of our vessels passed through every year, paying on an average about **Danish sound** a thousand dollars apiece. Against this we had long protested, and finally in 1855 we abrogated our treaty with Denmark. Our action was widely approved, and Denmark herself suggested a convention to discuss the matter. She finally agreed to give up her right or claim upon the payment of a lump sum, of which our share was about a million dollars. We declined thus to recognize the existence of her right by paying for its surrender, and in 1857 established our point in a new treaty by which we agreed to pay about four hundred thousand dollars in consideration of Denmark's service in lighting and buoying the channel. Meantime we were urging the countries of South America to open to the world the navigation of La Plata and its branches **South Amer-** and of the Amazon, broad streams flowing **ican rivers** past several countries, and the former indeed the only outlet for Paraguay and for most of Bolivia. These two countries were naturally willing to accede to our principle, and in 1853 the Argentine Republic opened the Parana and Uruguay, the essential feeders of La Plata. Brazil, however, remained obdurate, and was the centre of an active diplomatic pressure throughout the period.[1]

Analogous to this subject was our controversy with Great Britain as to the limits of marine territorial jurisdiction within bays more than six miles across. The ques- **Maritime ter-** tion was brought up by the seizure of our fish- **ritorial juris-** ing vessels within such bays, and in 1853 was **diction** submitted to arbitration. The decision was on the whole

[1] Schuyler, *American Diplomacy*, 265–366; T. J. Page, *La Plata, the Argentine Confederation, and Paraguay*, New York, 1859.

in our favor, thus marking another step toward the freeing of the world's waters for general use.

Prevalence and expectation of peace on our part did not cause us to lose our interest in the international law of war. International coöperation In 1854, indeed, we again became a neutral owing to the Crimean war between Russia and Great Britain, France, Sardinia, and Turkey. As usual, our shipping was involved; J. M. Forbes of Boston made a fortune by helping provision Sevastopol. The enlistment of British subjects resident in America violated our position as a neutral, and led to a long controversy between Marcy and the British minister, Crampton, whom we ultimately dismissed. Whenever possible, we endeavored to advance our views as to the rights and duties of neutrality in our general treaties, and we made two specially on the subject, one with Russia in 1854 and one with the Two Sicilies in 1855. We took a new step in our diplomatic relationships, moreover, when in 1854 we joined in an international act concerning the treatment of those wounded in war. In the Declaration of Paris of 1856, by which the principal nations of the world agreed to our long-maintained doctrine that free ships make free goods, that neutral goods in enemies' ships are free, and that blockades to be legal must be effective, we refused to join. Marcy gave as his reason our desire to exempt from capture all private property at sea, except when used in violating the laws of blockade and of contraband. We also objected to the first article of the Declaration, which abolished privateering. With our large merchant marine and small navy, it would have been a disadvantage to us to surrender the right of commissioning our private vessels, unless we were compensated by the freedom of movement in time of war which the principle of immunity of enemies' goods in enemies' vessels would give. Nevertheless, the Declaration marked an important step toward that view of neutral rights upon which we had always, except perhaps while Pickering was secretary of state, insisted.

A question that began to take on such importance during this period as to seem new was that of the position of our naturalized citizens. The impressment con- **Status of nat-** troversy with Great Britain had illustrated **uralized citi-** its difficulty. The rising tide of immigration **zens** which the lessening of the European food supply and revolutions, industrial and political, were impelling, and our redoubled prosperity was attracting, to our shores, now that the improvement of ocean transportation had made the carriage of immense numbers possible, brought up the question with almost every country in Europe. The fact that these naturalized citizens had votes made the question political. The seizure of Martin Koszta, a Hungarian revolutionist who had declared his intention of becoming an American citizen, in Turkish waters by an Austrian war ship, gave Marcy, in 1854, an occasion to make a public and forcible expression of our views. Koszta was returned by Austria because of the exceptional circumstances of his arrest; but, although the assertion that it is "the duty of the United States to afford ample and complete protection to all its citizens, whether at home or abroad, and whether native or foreign," began to be made in some form in all party platforms, no definite understanding with other countries resulted during the period. In fact, they all asserted the principle of indefeasible allegiance, while we asserted the right of individual choice of nationality.[1]

While these problems of the past and the future were not neglected, the special task of this period received due attention. With the extension of our population **Problem of** to the Pacific coast, the question of transpor- **transcontinen-** tation between the East and the new West **tal traffic** assumed an importance almost as great as that of an outlet for the Mississippi valley had possessed until the purchase of Louisiana. Our territory was continuous, but the titanic bulk of the Rockies, the aridity of the western plains, and

[1] Moore, *American Diplomacy*, 168-199.

the vastness of the distances rendered, not indeed communication, but traffic by our own roads impossible. All the easier routes lay in foreign countries, and to secure the use of them was the duty of diplomacy.

The favorite idea of the later fifties was that of a railroad. Experts decided that the best line was to the south, involving **Gadsden** the use of Mexican territory; but to trust **treaty** such an enterprise, which must be launched with government aid, to the protection of that still distracted nation seemed impossible. Finally, by the manipulation of a boundary dispute and a liberal use of money, a treaty was arranged in 1853 by James Gadsden which granted us the territory needed in northern Mexico, in return for a payment of ten million dollars. By the same treaty we secured the equal use, even for the passage of troops, of the isthmus of Tehuantepec, over which, the earlier plan for a canal having been given up, it was hoped to run a railroad.

A real transcontinental railroad, however, was during this period merely a rather wild hope. The more practical **Importance of** improvement of the situation lay in a canal **Central-** across one of the narrower isthmuses, as that **American** **isthmuses** of Panama or of Nicaragua, entirely outside of our own territory. Even as things were, the greater bulk of our commerce and travel from coast to coast passed over these isthmuses, and its protection was a national obligation.

The importance of these points at which the two great oceans approached each other so closely had been appreciated **Formulation of** from the time of their discovery; it had been **our policy** more and more appreciated as it became clear that except here the two continents stretched continuous and immense from the Arctic ice almost to that of the Antarctic. Charles V had considered the possibility of a canal. Miranda had envisaged their international status, and, liberal with his paper kingdom, had offered them to the free use of commerce. Clay, in his instructions to the delegates to the Panama Congress, had said of the isthmus there, "The benefits of it ought not to be exclusively appropriated to any one nation, but should be extended to all parts of the globe." We did not quite venture to claim this as a right analogous to that of navigating narrow waterways; but the principle was similar, and formed the basis of our policy.

To turn this policy into action, desire for immediate use was necessary. Our first step, therefore, was a treaty with New Granada or Colombia in 1844, after the Oregon migration had begun. This arrangement was unsatisfactory, and another treaty was drawn up in 1846. It provided absolute equality of use for the commerce and the citizens of both countries; "and," it went on, "in order to secure to themselves the tranquil and constant enjoyment of these advantages, and as an especial compensation for the said advantages—the United States guarantee, positively and efficaciously, to New Granada—the perfect neutrality of the before-mentioned isthmus, with the view that the free transit from the one to the other sea may not be interrupted—and, in consequence, the United States also guarantee, in the same manner, the rights of sovereignty and property which New Granada has and possesses over the said territory." Polk defended this guarantee on the ground that the interests of the United States were highly involved, that capital would not be invested without such security, and that New Granada would not grant us the needed rights on other terms.[1]

Guarantee of the neutrality of Panama

With the discovery of gold in California and the influx of population that followed, the situation became more pressing, and a canal seemed an immediate probability. The advantages of the route through Nicaragua over that at Panama were, however, coming to be

The Nicaraguan route

[1] W. F. Johnson, *Four Centuries of the Panama Canal*, New York, 1906; J. H. Latané, *The Diplomatic Relations of the United States and Spanish America* (Baltimore, 1900), 176–220; L. M. Keasbey, *The Nicaragua Canal and the Monroe Doctrine*, New York, etc., 1896.

strongly urged.[1] By the organizing ability of Commodore
Vanderbilt, that route came to be the more frequented, and
arrangements for its protection became necessary. At this
point we once more encountered our constant rival, Great
Influence of   Britain. She must supply a portion at least
Great Britain   of the capital required, and she was in the possession of certain special interests that seemed to many in
1849 to give her control of the situation. Of these the first
was the settlement of Belize, now British Honduras, an ancient logwood-cutting establishment with elastic boundaries.
Englishmen also were living on the islands of the Bay of Honduras. Moreover, Great Britain had a protectorate, vague
but of long standing, over the, considering the trouble they
gave for forty years, appropriately named Mosquito Indians.
Since these Indians were claimed as subjects by Nicaragua,
the situation was similar to that which would have existed
in the United States when Great Britain was intriguing with
our Indians, had the United States been as weak as Nicaragua was. The Indians professed to own the mouth of the
St. Juan river, the first step in the overland journey; in 1848
the British seized its port, Greytown, as Mosquito territory.[2]

Under these circumstances, Clayton began negotiations
with Sir Henry Lytton Bulwer. Fearing a British protest,
Clayton-   he failed to press treaties made without gov-
Bulwer treaty   ernment authorization by our representatives
in Nicaragua and Honduras which promised us exclusive
rights there, and considered himself fortunate to have the
matter taken up on a basis of equality. On April 14, 1850,
Clayton and Bulwer agreed to a treaty which provided that
neither the United States nor Great Britain was to exercise
any exclusive control over any canal that might be constructed, that no fortifications should be erected to command

[1] D. K. Pangborn, "A Journey from New York to San Francisco in 1850,"
Amer. Hist. Review, 1903, ix. 104–115.

[2] I. D. Travis, *History of the Clayton-Bulwer Treaty*, Michigan Political
Science Assoc., *Publications*, 1900, iii. No. 8.

it, and that neither party should colonize or assume or exercise dominion over any part of Central America. The prospective canal was to be absolutely neutral, even in case of war between the two countries; and this neutrality was mutually guaranteed, other nations being invited to join in maintaining it. These general principles were also extended to all the other isthmuses of the region.

The Clayton-Bulwer treaty was at once attacked as a violation of the Monroe Doctrine. Buchanan declared that it established the doctrine against ourselves rather than against European governments. The Democratic platform of 1856 said, "We can, under no circumstances, surrender our preponderance in the adjustment of all questions arising out of [interoceanic communication]." Though it may well be doubted whether John Quincy Adams would thus have admitted Great Britain to equal partnership, it may be observed that the invidiousness of this partnership might have been somewhat ameliorated had other nations accepted the invitation to join in the guarantee. Adams's second and more practical objection to coöperating with Canning in 1823 had been that his own country wished to acquire territory and Canning's did not. In Clayton's case, the long-expressed intention of the United States was to acquire nothing which all the nations of the globe could not share with us, the free use of the isthmus and its improvement. Subsequently we changed our minds on this latter point, and the treaty became an obstacle.

The fundamental question was, however, lost sight of through the irritating failure of Great Britain to live up to the spirit of the treaty. Clayton acknowledged, before ratification, that Belize should not be regarded as part of Central America,—a sensible decision, as this was one of Great Britain's oldest American settlements. This, however, did not content England, who continued to uphold and extend her interests in the region that was undoubtedly covered by the term Central

America. She continued to exercise her protectorate over the Mosquitoes and began to organize a government in the Bay Islands. In so doing she was not even justified by any deep-laid scheme of villainy, it was mere needless trouble-making. Her excuse, that the self-denying section of the treaty was prospective and not mandatory, could not bear examination in light of the text of the treaty, "assume or

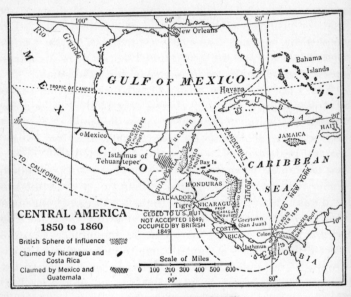

ISTHMIAN CONTROVERSIES

exercise dominion over." Webster and Everett handled the case over delicately, and Great Britain continued in possession of what she claimed were her rights. Pierce sent Buchanan to England charged with the matter, but in the opinion of the latter the decision to treat Canadian questions separately at Washington rendered a settlement impossible. The incoming of Lord Palmerston as Prime Minister in 1855, brought an English administration prone to indulge in the art of bluff into opposition with an American administration with similar characteristics. The nervous feared war, though neither side intended to fight. The American bluff won, as has usually been the case in games of that character with the mother country. In 1856 Buchanan's successor, Dallas, arranged with Lord Clarendon that Great Britain should withdraw her protectorate of the Mosquitoes and surrender her control of the Bay islands which were to become a practically independent state, though nominally under Honduras, and that the boundary of Belize should be definitely fixed. This convention was not formally accepted; but in 1860 Great Britain acted upon its terms, and Buchanan, in his annual message of the same year, announced his satisfaction.[1]

The Clayton-Bulwer treaty, lying between the United States and Great Britain, referred only to their joint policy toward any isthmian canal that might be constructed. Arrangements for construction, and for the protection of traffic before the canal was built, must be made with the several countries concerned.

The extent of our accomplishments

Under the protection of the Colombian treaty of 1846 a railroad was built over the Panama route in 1856, an arrangement that proved reasonably satisfactory and drew the trade from Nicaragua. Since, upon investigation, the project of a canal seemed too immense an undertaking to be practicable, it was dropped, and diplomacy went little farther. A treaty was made with Nicaragua in 1856, but was not ratified. With Honduras, whose isthmus presented another possible thoroughfare, none was made. Up to the Civil war, therefore, the achievements of diplomacy toward the solution of the problem of transcontinental transit consisted of the formulation of a policy, with the securing of the free use of Panama for our commerce and travel, of Tehuantepec for commerce, travel, and troops, and of a route for a railroad through the Gadsden Purchase.

[1] The best account of this episode is that in *Anglo-American Isthmian Diplomacy*, 1815-1914, by M. W. Williams, to be published by the Am. Hist. Assoc. as Winsor Prize Essay for 1914.

It was not, however, upon these routine problems and these solid accomplishments that public attention centred, **Interest in ex- pansion** but upon what proved at the time to be the will-o'-the-wisp of expansion. The first instance arose from the chaos of the Mexican war. On April 29, 1848, Polk informed Congress that the government **Yucatan** of Yucatan, which claimed to be independent of Mexico, was in deadly peril from Indians and requested protection and annexation, that similar appeals had been sent to Great Britain and Spain. He declared that action by those powers would be inconsistent with the Monroe Doctrine, and that to prevent it we must ourselves assume the burden. Although nothing came of this proposition, for Mexico and Yucatan became reconciled, it is nevertheless of interest because Polk made use of it to add the first corollary to the Monroe Doctrine,—namely, our duty to occupy territory if necessary to prevent the introduction of the European political system,—and to enunciate the principle of the white man's burden.[1]

Equally futile were the not entirely haphazard attempts of William Walker, between 1855 and 1858, to secure control of **Nicaragua** Nicaragua and bring it into the United States. Again it is the comment of the President which renders the matter interesting. January 7, 1858, Buchanan announced to Congress: "It is beyond question the destiny of our race to spread themselves over the continent of North America, and this at no distant day should events be permitted to take their natural course. The tide of emigrants will flow to the south, and nothing can eventually arrest its progress. If permitted to go there peacefully, Central America will soon contain an American population which will confer blessings and benefits as well upon the natives as their respective Governments . . . whilst the different transit routes across the Isthmus . . . will have assured protec-

[1] Calhoun, *Works*, iv. 478–479; Eligio Anacona, *Historia de Yucatan desde la época mas remota*, iv. 15–170.

tion. . . . Had one-half the number of American citizens who have miserably perished in the first disastrous expedition of General Walker settled in Nicaragua as peaceful emigrants, the object which we all desire would ere this have been in a great degree accomplished." [1]

Buchanan was not unaware that Mexico lay between the United States and Central America. In 1848 he had come to sympathize with the popular desire for all   Mexico. As President, he looked with distress   **Mexico** upon her growing disorder, and despaired of her ability to govern herself. In 1859 he said, "She is now a wreck upon the ocean, drifting about as she is impelled by different factions." Foreign vultures were awake. Our claims had again accumulated. He recommended that he be granted authority to take possession of "a sufficient portion of the remote and unsettled territory of Mexico, to be held in pledge." Congress, however, failed him.

Marcy's treaty of annexation with Hawaii, in 1854, raised still another point, by tacitly including those islands within the sphere of influence of the American con-   **Hawaii** tinents. Although the treaty did not succeed, we continued to maintain the principle of a dominant influence over the group.

The chief treasure that we sought, however, was the pearl of the Antilles, Cuba. In 1848 it seemed to many that the period had arrived, predicted in Adams's instructions   **Cuba** to Nelson in 1823, when the annexation of Cuba to our Federal republic had become "indispensable to the continuance and integrity of the union itself," when we could cease our constant ward of Spain's sovereignty and grasp the prize ourselves. The position of the island, though perhaps not, as was often asserted, essential to the navigation of the Mississippi, nevertheless strategically commanded

---

[1] J. F. Rhodes, *History of the United States* (7 vols., New York, 1893–1906), ii. 242, 288–290. A good account, as are his descriptions of other diplomatic episodes from 1850 to 1877.

much of our commerce. The existence of slavery was an inducement to annexation sentiment in the South, and the fear of emancipation in Cuba by English influence affected thousands now as it had Calhoun in the case of Texas. This sectional interest, however, did more to weaken the influence of the nationalistic argument in the North than to strengthen the cause in the South. From 1848 the press teemed with articles on Cuba, till that island became more familiar to Americans than any other portion of Spanish-America ever has been, except itself again forty years later, and Mexico since the recent outbreak of revolution there. This newspaper interest rested on the diplomatic situation, and not on actual bonds between us and Cuba. Of tangible relationships the most important were trade and the fact that many Cubans sent their sons to be educated in the United States. The real reason for our change from a passive to an aggressive policy was within ourselves: we felt able to handle the question.[1]

During the next twelve years three methods of securing Cuba were conceived,—by purchase from Spain, by conquest from Spain, or by annexation after a real or a forced revolution. The effort to apply the last of these means was naturally the work of individuals. Filibustering became the fashion of the day, and engaged men of social and political standing. The Cuban leader was General Narcisco Lopez; among the Americans the foremost was General Quitman, a dashing hero of the Mexican war. "Cuba once free," said the latter, "the regeneration of Mexico and of the distracted governments to the south of it would follow, and a new empire, the centre of the world's production and commerce, governed by the great principle of unrestricted free trade, would soon be established." Such

Filibustering

[1] A bibliography of Cuba has been published (1898) by the Library of Congress, as is customary when such questions assume general importance. There are similar bibliographies on the Interoceanic Canal, Hawaii, Neutrality (1914), etc. The most nearly complete account of this period is J. M. Callahan, *Cuba and International Relations*, Baltimore, 1899.

movements were widely heralded by the press, and in New Orleans and New York expeditions were openly fitted out. Spain was naturally alarmed. We assured her that our neutrality laws would be enforced, but to at least one of the invasions, that of 1849, our state department was privy. This attempt failed, as did that of 1850, in which many Americans were captured, whose fate held the country in suspense. They were eventually pardoned; but those captured during the unsuccessful attempt of 1851 were shot in cold blood. Nevertheless in 1854 Lopez led a final band to their doom, and lost his own life. With him died for the time the attempt to revolutionize Cuba.

Alarmed by these efforts, in 1851 England and France ordered their navies to prevent the landing of unauthorized vessels in Cuba, and requested us to join in a   Everett's dispatch tripartite agreement to secure the island to Spain. It was this request which gave Edward Everett his opportunity for a dispatch ringing with patriotism, in which he asserted the primacy of our interests, our determination that no foreign power should succeed Spain in possession of the island, and our intention to regulate our own conduct toward it as we thought fit.

The failure of irregular attempts to secure it, coupled with the assertion of our interest in the island by a man who could certainly not be regarded as a pro-slavery advocate, turned attention, if it needed turning, to acquisition by more regular means. In 1848 Buchanan had offered to buy it from Spain. In 1852 it was proposed to link its annexation with that of Canada as a Democratic campaign issue; but the second half of this proposition was too risky, and without some sop to the North Cuba was not suited to appeal to a nation sectionalized as we were at that time. The proposal was therefore dropped and expansion was left out of the platform.

This fact, however, did not prevent the new administration from taking it up. Buchanan advised Pierce to make Cuban annexation the distinctive measure of his administration, and wished, as secretary of state, to have the handling of it.

Pierce's policy Pierce, preferring to gain the glory himself, sent Buchanan to England, and, unfortunately for his purposes, chose Marcy as secretary. In his inaugural he announced his purpose. "The policy of my administration," he declared, "will not be controlled by any timid forebodings of evil from expansion. Indeed, it is not to be disguised that our attitude as a nation and our position on the globe render the acquisition of certain possessions not within our jurisdiction eminently important for our protection."

In the spring of 1854 Pierce seemed likely to win Cuba by conquest. The *Black Warrior*, a United States merchant Black Warrior steamer engaged in the Cuban trade, was affair seized by the Spanish customs officials for a trifling violation of some new port regulation. Marcy instructed Soulé, our minister in Spain, to demand three hundred thousand dollars damages. Meantime the island authorities withdrew from their position, restored the vessel, and returned to their former rules. Before this news, unassisted by cable, reached Spain, however, Soulé had acted. Intent on bringing about war, he presented his demand as an ultimatum to be answered in forty-eight hours. His note, nicely calculated to arouse all the Spanish pride and obstinacy, produced its result, for the answer met the tone of the demand with an eloquent refusal. Straightway public opinion in the United States, just quieted from the episode itself, again took fire. General Quitman, now in the House of Representatives, moved that the neutrality laws be suspended and our fighting spirit let loose. Marcy, however, realizing that the situation did not warrant war, instructed Soulé to take no further steps in the matter.[1]

It was decided to undertake the formulation of a complete program. Distrustful of Soulé, Marcy wrote to him that

[1] H. L. Janes, "The Black Warrior Affair," *Amer. Hist. Review*, 1907, xii. 280–298.

the President thought that "weight and perhaps efficiency" would be gained if "two other of our most distinguished citizens" should be associated with him. Renewed ne-These two were James Buchanan, minister to gotiations Great Britain, and John Y. Mason, minister to France. A revolution in Spain seemed to offer an occasion, and in the Fall after the *Black Warrior* affair the three met at Ostend to formulate a policy.

This took the form of the "Ostend Manifesto," a declaration setting forth that the position of Cuba made its acquisition necessary to the United States. We Ostend Mani-should offer Spain one hundred and twenty festo millions for it. If she refused the offer, "it will then be time to consider the question, does Cuba in the possession of Spain seriously endanger our internal peace and the existence of our cherished union." This, it was urged, was actually the case, because emancipation was threatened by the overwhelming influence of Great Britain on Spain. The situation was similar to that which existed when emancipation was threatened in Texas, but it was more serious because of the number of the Cuban negroes; emancipation meant "Africanization," which would be a constant incentive to negro revolt in the United States. "Then, by every law, human and divine," concluded the manifesto, "we shall be justified in wresting it from Spain if we possess the power; and this upon the very same principle that would justify an individual in tearing down the burning house of his neighbor if there were no other means of preventing the flames from destroying his own home." It was another combination of the arguments of "manifest destiny" and international nuisance which were becoming so familiar to us.

The force of these arguments was, however, counteracted in the United States by the development of the slavery struggle. Politicians and statesmen alike were divided between the possibility of distracting public attention from internal conflict by pointing the way to national glory, and the

fear that the sections would divide all the more quickly in fighting for the spoils. Spain refused to sell, the foreign min-
Cuba and slavery   ister declaring that "to part with Cuba would be to part with national honor." Yet Marcy would not follow the policy of the manifesto, and Congress during the next administration steadily refused to endorse Buchanan's earnest plans for action.

An attempt was made to inject the subject into the campaign of 1860. Both branches of the Democracy declared
Expansion and the failure of compromise   in favor of annexation, upon terms "honorable to us and just to Spain." Although forced out of the campaign discussions by other issues, it reappeared conspicuously between December, 1860, and March, 1861, in the deliberations over the question of compromise. In fact, it was the universal belief that we were destined to absorb the country to the south of us, or at least that the question of such absorption would continue to be pressed, that created the final obstacle to compromise. The sections were able to agree upon the status of slavery in all our then existing territory, but not upon that in future annexations to the south.

One dominant fact characterizes the period from 1844 to 1860,—the national territory had expanded about fifty
Territorial expansion   per cent. The result was our possession of a region consolidated and self-contained, so situated that we could never have a neighbor, unless with European connections, strong enough to cause us anxiety, and giving us outlet on both oceans. To this diplomacy had contributed but little. The people had expanded, diplomacy was expected merely to justify and confirm their action. This it had done with decided success. Never before had our boundary been so unquestioned; only at the extreme northwestern corner was controversy still serious. In its attempt to extend our territory beyond the limits of actual expansion, however, diplomacy had signally failed.

Commercially our efforts had been mainly devoted to securing equality of rights for the shipping of all nations on such pathways of commerce as were indis- **Commercial gains** pensable to world trade but yet fell territorially under the jurisdiction of some one power. In this field decided progress had been made, and even the question of isthmian transit seemed solved. The opening of Japan and the increased use of the Pacific had presented less difficulty, and our success had been even more marked and momentous.

We had definitely refrained from using our strength to play a part in world politics. The question of our diplomatic quietude seemed to rest almost wholly with **Prospect of peace** ourselves. Unless we decided to press forward our territorial expansion beyond the limits which our citizens actually occupied, the only important question that remained was that of establishing the status of our naturalized citizens when abroad. When Lincoln came into office he found, as had Jefferson and Jackson, a sky which seemed to be almost clear of foreign complications.

CHAPTER XXII

THE CIVIL WAR [1]

NOVEMBER 10, 1862, Lincoln wrote to Carl Schurz, "The administration . . . distributed to its party friends as nearly all the civil patronage as any administration ever did." This was certainly no exaggeration of the break in the diplomatic service which the triumph of the Republican party brought about. Not only were those found in office Democrats, but a very large proportion were from the South; for Buchanan had aimed to give the slave states, not a proportional representation in the higher civil posts, but an equality. The almost complete change in personnel was less important than the change in weight and character. Until 1861 there had never been a time, except for brief periods under Jackson and Taylor, when some member of the administration had not been possessed of direct experience in foreign affairs. From 1861 until John Hay became secretary of state in 1898 the only members of any administration who had such experience were Carl Schurz under Hayes, and Levi P. Morton and J. W. Foster under Harrison. While there continued to be brilliant men and occasionally accomplished diplomats in foreign posts, it is obvious that they were not called upon to share in the outlining of our national foreign policy. It seems also a safe conclusion that the aggregate of ability employed in

Change in diplomatic service

[1] For the history of the Civil war, historians are as much indebted to the late Charles Francis Adams, son of the minister to Great Britain at that time, as they are to Henry Adams, another son, for the diplomacy of the Napoleonic period. His researches and conclusions, which have appeared in many essays, will shortly be combined in his forthcoming life of his father. Rhodes's *History of the United States*, vols. iii.–vii. is also strong on the diplomatic side.

diplomacy, relative to that in other forms of politics, was not so great as previously.

Of the men who took charge in 1861, Lincoln was not only without diplomatic experience, but without such knowledge of American international interests as most public men had previously possessed. Fortunately he **Lincoln** knew it, and seldom intervened; when he did, it seems to have been in all cases beneficially. His profound understanding of human nature reached below diverging national characteristics and touched the common basis of humanity. In a crisis when public opinion so largely controlled the international situation, such an endowment was of inestimable value.[1]

His secretary of state, William F. Seward, was one of the most complex personalities of his perplexing generation. With an absolute conviction of the ultimate triumph of what he believed to be right, he was perfectly **Seward** ready to compromise principle for temporary convenience. Yet he was never content to let Providence work alone, but aided it with all the finesse of which his astute mind was capable. With a practicality thus genially founded in philosophy, he nevertheless at times surrendered himself to an intellectual emotionalism as dangerous to a man of his responsibility as it is useful to the orator. The only such deflection during his diplomatic career occurred at its very opening. Before assuming office he said, in an address to the New England Society of New York, that if we were attacked by a foreign power "all the hills of South Carolina would pour forth their population to the rescue." Becoming secretary, he advised, on April 1, 1861, the development of quarrels with Great Britain and France as a means of restoring unity at home. Lincoln made no comment, but when, on May 21, he looked over the draft of Seward's dis-

---

[1] Abraham Lincoln, *Complete Works*, ed. J. G. Nicolay and John Hay, 2 vols., New York, 1894; *Abraham Lincoln, a History*, by Nicolay and Hay, 10 vols., New York, 1890; Gideon Welles, *Lincoln and Seward*, New York, 1874.

patch to our minister in England incorporating this policy, he took the sting out of it. He cut out a reference to "that hour" when we should "cease to be friends, and become once more, as we have twice before been forced to be, enemies of Great Britain"; in the description of her conduct he changed "wrongful" to "hurtful"; and he added, "This paper is for your own guidance only and not to be read or shown to any one." From this time Seward's handling of affairs was always competent and sometimes masterly, though he continued to evince an even greater penchant for writing diplomatic notes to be read at home than had the secretaries of the fifties.[1]

The dispatch of May 21, thus modified by Lincoln, was further toned down by our minister, who wrote that he "tried
Adams
to act up to [his] instructions at the same time that [he] softened as well as [he] could the sharp edges." The appointment of Charles Francis Adams to the court of St. James was as fortunate, in its lesser way, as the election of Lincoln to the presidency. Of a family, education, and manner to compel the respect of the English, he had, if not the genius of his father John Quincy Adams, at any rate high ability, all the family backbone and sturdy Americanism, and added thereto a somewhat greater tact. Treading a path where any slip was apt to lead to war, and where many of those with whom he associated hoped to see him slip, he maintained himself immune from criticism. His business was to see that nothing happened, and his career was marked by many important things that failed to happen.

Confiding more and more in Adams abroad, Lincoln and Seward relied at home chiefly on Charles Sumner. With a
Sumner
background of foreign travel and a wide English acquaintance, he became in 1861 chairman of the senate committee of foreign affairs, a post which he held till 1871. A scholar, with some knowledge of interna-

[1] Frederick Bancroft, *The Life of William H. Seward* (2 vols., New York, etc., 1900), vol. ii.

tional law, and a cultured gentleman, he was a favorite with the foreign diplomats at Washington, who found him the most congenial of the men high in office. Throughout the war his advice seems to have been sound and useful.[1]   As important in routine matters as Sumner on critical occasions was William Hunter, chief clerk of the state depart- **Hunter** ment. Holding office from 1829 to 1886, he contributed a continuity of knowledge and practice the value of which it is hard to exaggerate.

On April 12 this new administration found itself confronted by a condition of domestic hostility. On April 19, without intending to do so, it recognized that this hostil- **Blockade** ity constituted civil war. It was its purpose to treat the movement as a rebellion, a purely domestic affair. The first essential, however, was to cut off the hostile states from all connection with the outside world. Devoted to the raising of great staple crops, the South purchased many of its necessities instead of producing them; its commerce cut off, therefore, exhaustion would be but a matter of time. Secretary Welles thought that we could accomplish this end by declaring the ports closed; but, as we did not hold the ports, such a regulation would obviously have to be enforced at sea. Accordingly the cabinet decided upon a blockade, which Lincoln proclaimed April 19. In the leading case, that of the *Amy Warwick*, our own supreme court declared that this blockade could rest upon no other basis than that of a change of status in the South making it enemy's country, and hence that the government's act constituted a recognition of belligerency or a state of war. Upon the maintenance of this blockade depended, so far as human judgment can tell, the success of the attempt to restore the Union by arms. Its effectiveness, as against the South, depended on the navy, as against foreign nations, upon diplomacy.[2]

[1] Charles Sumner, *Works* (15 vols., Boston, 1875–83), vi. 153–242, 474–486; "Letters of Richard Cobden to Charles Sumner, 1862–1865," *Amer. Hist. Review*, ii. 306–319.

[2] Gideon Welles, *Diary* (3 vols., Boston, etc., 1911), i. 165, 172 ff.

The United States now found herself in the reverse of the situation that she had occupied during the Napoleonic wars: she was now interested in the rights of belligerents rather than in the rights of neutrals. This change of position did not lead to a change of policy, but to a change of stress. We now admitted, as we had previously contended, that to be legal a blockade must be effectively maintained off the ports blockaded. Questions of course arose as to the definition of effective, but on the whole the navy relieved the diplomatic department of any great anxiety on this point. The blockade, at least after 1861, was reasonably efficient.[1]

Still, it was not proof against the alert blockade-runner willing to take the risk of capture. It became the custom to send goods to and from the Confederacy by way of nearby neutral ports, as Nassau in the British Bahamas, a device that made the actual running of the blockade a short though perilous undertaking. A route still safer was that by way of Matamoros, a Mexican port just opposite Brownville in Texas, but communication from this distant border to the interior of the Confederacy was so poor, that the volume of such trade was small. To meet this situation our courts evolved a doctrine of "continuous voyage," asserting that, if the ultimate destination of the cargo was the Confederacy, the vessel carrying it might be seized even on a voyage between two neutral ports, as Liverpool and Nassau. This doctrine somewhat resembled that applied by Sir William Scott, in the case of the *Essex*, to our trade between the French West Indies and France. Its application during the Civil war, however, was confined to the carrying of contraband. Numerous cases occurred in the Nassau trade, as those of the *Dolphin* and the *Bermuda*, which resulted in the condemnation of vessel and cargo. In the case of the *Springbok* the cargo was condemned, but the ship

Maintenance of blockade

Continuous voyage

---

[1] H. L. Wait, "The Blockade of the Confederacy," *Century*, 1898, xxxiv. 914–928.

was released on the ground that there was no "fraudulent connection on the part of the owners with the ulterior destination of the goods." A leading case was that of the *Peterhof*, seized on its way to Matamoros. The supreme court released the vessel on the plea that the blockade did not apply to the inland trade from Mexico to the Confederacy; but as this decision was not rendered till 1866, it did not affect the conduct of the war. On the whole, the doctrine of "continuous voyage" was acknowledged by European powers and did something to assist in the maintenance of the blockade, though seizures under it were actually few.

Our purpose now being to prevent commerce rather than to prey upon it, we had reason to regret our failure to adhere to the Declaration of Paris, which had abolished privateering among its signers. While we, in this new crisis, made use of our merchant marine by purchasing vessels and incorporating them into the navy, Jefferson Davis, on his part, issued commissions to privateers. Seward, therefore, promptly announced that we would now adhere to all the rules of the Declaration, without amendment. France and England, however, while welcoming our adhesion, properly reminded us that these rules could not be held to apply to the Confederacy, whereupon Seward, failing in his purpose to have the Confederate privateers declared pirates, withdrew his offer to join in the agreement.

Declaration of Paris

On the important question of the belligerent right of search our position was developed with the progress of the war. On the other hand, we firmly insisted from the beginning on a rigid interpretation of the duty of neutral nations to prevent their citizens from aiding our opponents. With regard to this duty, however, there was no such general concurrence of opinion as in the case of continuous voyages, and the issue was left to the course of diplomacy.

Belligerent rights and neutral duties

As the main purpose of the national diplomacy was to prevent interference with the blockade, so that of the Confederate diplomacy was to break it up. The situation had long been regarded as possible, and the South faced it with confidence. In the twenties it had been argued that, in case of secession, the North would blockade the southern coast but that European demand for southern cotton would force the opening of the ports. Since then cotton had grown steadily more important to the industrial life of Europe, till by 1861 few southerners doubted that cotton was "king." Their strength lay in the possession of the monopoly of a necessity of life. Complementary to this club which would compel Europe to intervene was the inducement of free trade, which would win the active friendship of some great maritime power. On December 15, 1860, R. Barnwell Rhett, of whom the *Times* correspondent, William Russell, said, "Rhett is also persuaded that the lord chancellor sits on a cotton bale," sought an interview with the British consul at Charleston. He offered a reciprocal freedom of trade as an inducement for an English alliance, and threatened that if Great Britain made difficulties the South would seek France.[1]

Cotton as "king"

To make proper use of such weapons demanded a high degree of diplomatic skill. This the South did not evince. Jefferson Davis attempted more of an oversight of diplomacy than Lincoln did, and failed to show either Lincoln's patience or his good judgment. His secretaries, R. M. T. Hunter and

[1] J. D. Richardson, *Messages and Papers of the Confederacy*, 2 vols., Nashville, 1905; M. L. Bonham, *The British Consuls in the Confederacy*, Columbia University, *Studies*, xliii. No. 3; J. M. Callahan, *The Diplomatic History of the Southern Confederacy*, Baltimore, 1901, and his *Northern Lake Frontier during the Civil War*, Amer. Hist. Assoc., *Report*, 1896, i. 335–359; J. D. Bulloch, *The Secret Service of the Confederate States in Europe*, 2 vols., New York, 1884, and J. R. Thompson, *Diary* (accounts of Confederate naval agents in England); "Dispatch from the British Consul [Robert Bunch] at Charleston to Lord John Russell, [Dec. 15,] 1860," *Amer. Hist. Review*, 1913, xviii. 783–787; J. R. Soley, *The Blockade and the Cruisers*, N. Y., 1883.

Judah P. Benjamin,[1] were both able men, but by no means of the first rank. James M. Mason made a good impression in England as Confederate commissioner there, but he annoyed her government by undue persistence. John Slidell in France apparently did what was possible, but Paris was not the key to the situation as it had been when Franklin had served there.

Confederate diplomatic service

The accepted method of making diplomatic use of cotton was to prevent exportation in order to bring pressure to bear upon the industrial classes, and through them upon the governments of Great Britain and France. This policy, reminding one of Jefferson's embargo, may be said to have been enforced with rigor: during the four years of war about half a million bales only were exported, as against three million bales in 1861. This disparity, however, was due more to the Federal navy than to the Confederate government, for during most of the war that government despite its policy was exporting all the cotton possible in order to purchase necessities. On the whole, however, one may say that the cotton argument was applied, and that if it did not succeed failure was owing to defect in the theory rather than in the detail of its application.

While the main reliance of the South for relief from the blockade was upon foreign intervention, she hoped to use her cotton actively as well. In fact, Alexander H. Stephens held that all available cotton should be purchased by the government, sent to Europe, held for scarcity prices, and the proceeds employed to build a fleet. Davis also wished a foreign built fleet, as a subsidiary weapon against the North and because of the weight he believed it would have with foreign nations. To circumvent the neutrality laws of the great ship-building nation, Great Britain, by technicality, fraud, or favor, became the second great aim of the diplomatic force. The vessels thus to be secured were to be heavy fighting craft to break the

Commerce destroying

[1] Pierce Butler, *Judah P. Benjamin*, Philadelphia, [1907].

blockade and possibly to bombard northern ports, and fast
steamers to harry United States commerce. The latter
were to supplement the crowd of private ventures which
Davis somewhat too optimistically hoped to call out by his
offer to commission privateers.

Desirous of worrying, yet not hopeful of destroying, United
States commerce, Davis had to adopt a policy with reference
to neutral rights. In so doing he decidedly
overplayed his hand. His great card was in
offering immunity to neutral ships, at the same
time making the hazard of capture to United States vessels
high. This would drive United States trade into the hands
of British vessels. On the strength of this favor he sought to
adhere to the Declaration of Paris, except, however, as to
the abolition of privateering. He would continue to use his
privateers to endanger United States merchantmen, and
yet would bind Europe to insist that our blockade either be
impeccably effective or be raised. The first result that he
aimed at, the transfer of our commerce from our own to
British vessels, was largely attained. American merchantmen were forced to pay high insurance rates and charge
high freights, in many cases their owners transferred them
by actual or fraudulent sale to the British flag.[1] Great
Britain, however, did not show her gratitude. Insisting that
an adhesion to the Declaration of Paris must be to the whole,
she did not consider his offer, and the blockade remained.
In 1863, obviously provoked, Davis threatened to change his
regulations and allow the capture of enemies' goods in neutral vessels. In view of the fact that the commerce destroyers at his disposal were British-built, largely British-
manned, and were subsisting in British ports, his threat to
turn them loose on the British merchant marine overreached
the limits of practical diplomacy. It was ignored, nor did

Davis's policy toward neutrals

---

[1] This question of transfer of ownership in time of war has been regulated
since 1910 by the Declaration of London, at least in the case of nations
signing that declaration, of which the United States is one.

he act upon it. Had he done so, the Confederate warships would have been swept from the ocean.

The field of contest for southern and northern diplomacy was practically confined to Great Britain. Of the European powers, Russia, Germany, Italy, and Denmark were friendly to the North, but the last two were not substantially important. Germany bought northern bonds. Russia was moved not only by her traditional desire to see the United States rival Great Britain as a maritime power, but by the sympathy which her humanitarian czar, Alexander, the liberator of the serfs, felt for the efforts to abolish slavery. Her only active manifestation of friendship, however, lay in the visit of her fleets to this country at what seemed to be a critical moment, September, 1863, —a visit undoubtedly as convenient to her as it was pleasing to us. In fact, the only nations whose policies were really interesting at this time were the maritime powers, France and Great Britain. *Attitude of Europe*

Of these, France was distinctly anxious to secure the break-up of the Union. Louis Napoleon was nursing a new last plan for some kind of French colonial empire in America; division would assist his projects. *French policy* He would have welcomed a chance to take part in the war on the side of the South, to renew that policy of liberating nations which, as pursued in Italy, had conferred a lustre on the Second Empire. He was, however, not in a position to disregard Great Britain with whom he was coöperating; for America was primarily a British problem.[1]

The leading political figure in England at the time was Lord Palmerston, the prime minister, well known, to use a word not then coined, as a jingo. He was *English public opinion* distinctly favorable to the South, and was not loath to interfere. His foreign secretary, Lord John Russell, was less decided in his sympathies and less inclined to action.

[1] John Bigelow, *Retrospections of an Active Life, 1817–79*, 5 vols., New York, 1909–13. Bigelow was consul-general at Paris.

Both recognized the necessity of waiting upon public opinion. This force, more potent in Great Britain than in any other country except the United States, and more complex there than with us, seemed at first overwhelmingly pro-southern.

The *Times*, at the zenith of its prestige, if not of its power, was outspoken, and it represented the opinion of the governing class. The Earl of Malmesbury wrote, May 23, Official class 1862: "There is a rumor that the Confederates have been defeated and Beauregard taken prisoner, which everybody regrets. The feeling for the South is very strong in society."[1] This was due partly to an aristocratic elation at the failure of democracy and partly to sympathy with the apparently kindred culture of the plantation aristocracy of the South. Diplomatically the advantage to Great Britain of dealing with two republics in place of one was keenly appreciated. There was an almost universal feeling in England that the South could not be subdued. Edward A. Freeman, the historian, brought out, in 1863, a *History of Federal Government from the Foundation of the Achaian League to the Disruption of the United States*. It was obviously important to stand well with a new nation that possessed no qualms about using British manufactures, an argument just then pointed by the passage, in the national Congress, of the highly protective Morrill tariff.

To the upholders of the great Whig tradition, which from Burke to Trevelyan has so emphatically championed our own Revolution, the spectacle of the North attempt- Whig element ing to bind to itself a reluctant South seemed a new contest of freedom against oppression. To them Lincoln stood in the place of George III. Many of this faction, to be sure, felt that individual freedom was more important than collective, and would have favored the North had its object been emancipation; but that object was expressly denied by Lincoln.

[1] Earl of Malmesbury, *Memoirs of an Ex-minister* (2d ed., 2 vols., London, 1884), ii. 273, May 23, 1862.

The Dissenters, headed by John Bright, stood almost alone, at the beginning, in favor of the North. Strong forces, however, were working to prevent hasty action. Bad harvests in 1860, 1861, and 1862 caused northern wheat to be more essential than southern cotton.[1] The philosophic, moreover, saw a possible good in the cutting-off of the American supply of the latter commodity, since thereby production in other parts of the world might be stimulated and England thus be relieved of her dependence on whatever power possessed our black belt. The great mercantile class seemed to profit more by the continuance of war than it could hope to do by participation or by the triumph of either side. Inasmuch as British-built ships and British crews were already, under the Confederate flag, destroying the only rival merchant marine in existence, the risks of war were unnecessary. These non-sentimental arguments favored a passive policy. The balance of opinion thus created was dangerous, for, since the subject did not appeal to the average Englishman as one of such importance that it must be thought through to a decision, the result might depend upon the fortuitous stress of apparent accident.

Dissenters and mercantile element

England's first act was to issue May 13, 1861, a neutrality proclamation recognizing that a state of war existed. This step certainly seemed to be called for by Davis's invitation to privateers and Lincoln's proclamation of blockade. It was evident that hostilities would take place at sea and neutrals be involved. Great Britain wished "to bring the management of it within the rules of modern civilized warfare." The proclamation is said to have been issued at the request of W. E. Foster, a member of the cabinet and a friend of the North. Although undoubtedly inevitable, its appearance was perhaps a little hasty, especially in view of the fact that it was

England recognizes belligerency

[1] E. D. Fite, *Social and Industrial Conditions in the North during the Civil War* (New York, 1910), 17–21.

known that Adams was due to arrive within a day or two and would undoubtedly expect to be consulted. The news of England's recognition of belligerency came to the North like a slap in the face. Conscious of its own rectitude, northern opinion had not for a moment contemplated the possibility that Great Britain would not sympathize. The North had counted on the fact that we were fighting to free the slave as heavily as the South had counted on cotton. The leaders of opinion seemed to forget that their government had asserted that we were not fighting to free the slave. Indifference in England they could not understand. By a large portion of the North, Great Britain's assertion of neutrality was as little credited as Washington's similar declaration in 1793 had been by France and England. Her recognition of belligerency, taken in connection with the tone of the British press, was believed to indicate an intention to assist the South.

In this situation, on November 8, 1861, Captain Wilkes, commanding the *San Jacinto*, which he was bringing back into home waters, heard that the Confederate commissioners, Mason and Slidell, were sailing from Havana to Europe on the British steamer *Trent*. Without orders, he "searched" the vessel, took off the commissioners, and brought them to Boston. The North went wild with an unreasoning joy. But the mere capture of the two men could hardly have occasioned the lavish outburst of oratorical exuberance in which men ordinarily so sane as Edward Everett, R. H. Dana, and Governor Andrew indulged, even though southern statesmen were supposed to be possessed of some uncanny power of turning black into white. The rejoicing was rather due to the satisfaction of getting a return stroke against England for her belligerency proclamation.

The British government had already considered the possibility of some such exercise of the right of search. British precedent, coming from her practice during the conflict with Napoleon, was favorable to its broadest extension. Lord

Palmerston had asked what could be done if an American war vessel stationed itself off Southampton to intercept all outgoing shipping, and the law officers of the crown could find no answer. Owing to the develop- British policy ment of ocean transportation and the regularity of steam communication, the situation was very different from what it had been forty years before. It was, of course, palpably absurd to imagine any belligerent regularly stationing vessels to query every channel packet, but legally it seemed possible.[1]

When a specific case arose, however, it was obvious that the interference could not be tolerated. Entering the cabinet meeting, Lord Palmerston threw down his hat British de- and said, "I don't know whether you will mands stand it, but I'll be damned if I do." He hit the popular feeling; all England was ablaze with resentment. Parliament took war measures, troops were ordered to Canada, and Lord Russell wrote a ringing demand for the surrender of the commissioners within seven days. There were those, however, who labored for peace, among them Prince Albert, who, when consulted by the queen, modified Russell's dispatch, as Lincoln had Seward's.

Fortunately, in the absence of a cable these national outbursts were not simultaneous and could not quickly react on each other. By the time Russell's ultima- Release of tum reached the United States, public opinion Mason and there had cooled by its own reflection and by Slidell the advice of men like Sumner. The administration was anxious to get out of the scrape if it could do so without violating the national sense of honor. Appreciating the situation, therefore, Lord Lyons, the British minister, presented Russell's note without reference to its being an ultimatum.[2]

[1] T. L. Harris, *The Trent Affair*, Indianapolis, 1896; R. H. Dana, *Trent Affair*, in Wheaton's *Elements of International Law*, 8th ed., 1866, pp. 644 ff.; C. W. Battine, *The Crisis of the Confederacy*, London, 1905.

[2] Lord [T. W. L.] Newton, *Lord Lyons: a Record of British Diplomacy*, 2 vols., London, 1913 (this work, however, makes little use of Lyons's enor-

On December 26, Seward replied that the capture of the
Trent was justified by the fact that the commissioners were
contraband of war engaged in a continuous voyage from the
Confederate states; that Captain Wilkes, however, had failed
to conform to international law in allowing the *Trent* to
proceed and thus preventing a judicial review of his action;
and consequently that the United States would surrender
Mason and Slidell. In this affair, Seward, or public opinion
coercing Seward, perhaps lost to the United States an opportunity for securing British assent to our nation-old chal-
Result of the lenge of the indiscriminate extension of the
Trent affair belligerent right of search. The prompt surrender of the commissioners on the ground that Captain
Wilkes had exceeded his belligerent powers would while
conciliating British opinion, at the same time have obtained
a national triumph. Yet the actual result was satisfactory
in that it prevented war if it did not restore good feeling.
James Russell Lowell put in the mouth of Jefferson Davis
the words:

> " 'T wuz a beautiful dream, an' all sorrer is idle,—
> But *ef* Lincoln *would* ha' hanged Mason an' Slidell!
> They ain't o' no good in Európean pellices,
> But think wut a help they'd ha' ben on their gallowses!
> They'd ha' felt they wuz truly fulfillin' their mission,
> An', oh, how dog-cheap we'd ha' gut Reecognition!"

This episode over, the British government had an opportunity to deliberate on its policy. Its next step, if it
Significance of were to take one, would be recognition of the
a   recognition independence of the southern Confederacy.
of independ-
ence Such recognition need not involve hostilities
with us. It would give the Confederacy prestige, which
doubtless could be cashed in the form of a loan; but, if Great
Britain accompanied her recognition with an assurance of
neutrality, as she doubtless would, it would give the South

mous correspondence within the United States); Edmund Fitzmaurice,
The Life of . . . Second Earl Granville, 1815–91 (3d ed., 2 vols., London,
1905), vol. i.

no belligerent rights that it did not already possess. When France acknowledged our independence in 1778, Great Britain considered the act cause for war; but when we first, and after us Great Britain, recognized the independence of the Spanish-American states, Spain did not consider it cause for war. The difference lay partly in the fact that Spain had less chance to recover her colonies than Great Britain had, and partly in the relative standing of the nations. In the present case, the United States was not prepared to acknowledge that she had no hope of recovering the South.

Recognition of the Confederacy by Great Britain must almost inevitably have been met by war on our part. Public sentiment, already bitter, was during 1862 constantly exasperated by the disastrous activity of the Confederate cruisers built in Great Britain with what we considered the connivance of that government. The floating of a Confederate loan in the spring of 1863 was regarded as still further evidence of malintent. After the battle of the *Monitor* and *Merrimac* we began to be overconfident of our naval strength; even Secretary Welles considered himself ready for the British navy.[1] No small portion of the press carried a chip on its shoulder. Regardless of the exigencies of the military task already before us, a controlling fraction of the North undoubtedly felt, as the West had felt in 1812, that, if it was obvious that we had to fight Great Britain, we might as well do so openly;—that her recognition of the Confederacy would be the throwing down of the glove. The ingrained hatred of European interference was perhaps still more fundamental. Seward instructed Adams to suspend his diplomatic functions in the event of an announcement of recognition.

With the British government it was a question of time and circumstance. In November, 1861, Adams had told Palmerston that the North would probably not try to coerce a hostile population, that it merely wished to give the latent

[1] Welles, *Diary*, i. 495.

Union sentiment in the South opportunity to develop. The defeat of McClellan before Richmond in July, 1862, Cabinet pro- seemed to show that this attempt had failed. gram September 14, Palmerston wrote to Russell favoring recognition. Russell replied with the suggestion that mediation be offered first, and that a cabinet meeting be held September 23 or September 30 to discuss the matter. Lord Granville, who was absent with the queen, proposed further delay, and a meeting was finally arranged for October. Russell set to work on the preparation of a memoir to present the case for mediation and subsequent recognition.

In the interval W. E. Gladstone, chancellor of the exchequer, the coming man but many years junior to Palmerston Cabinet delay and Russell, touched on the subject at Newcastle. "There can be no doubt," said he, "that Jefferson Davis and other leaders of the South have made an army; they are making, it appears, a navy, and they have made what is more than either, they have made a nation." His position was promptly attacked by a fellow cabinet member, Sir George Cornwallis Lewis. For cabinet members in Great Britain thus to commit themselves on subjects which have not yet been decided by the cabinet as a whole, and thus to differ, is not unknown, but it is always indiscreet. As a result it was decided that recognition could wait awhile, long enough to allow the party chiefs to assert themselves and to discipline Gladstone. The matter was dropped for the time.

The cabinet therefore met Parliament, February 5, 1863, without a declared policy. Interest thereupon centred in Parliamentary an attempt to force its hand through Parliadiscussion ment. A member, Mr. Roebuck, had an interview with Napoleon, who urged him to press the matter. On June 30 he introduced a motion instructing the government "to enter into negotiation with the great powers of Europe for the purpose of obtaining their coöperation in the recognition" of the Confederacy.

This seeming climax, however, is deceptive; the real crisis had passed. The final argument had always been in the hands of the North, and had by this time been made effective. Great Britain could not take *Emancipation proclamation* action perpetuating slavery. Universal emancipation outweighed cotton. With the advantage of its sentimental appeal, this consideration was equally strong from a practical standpoint. Between 1854 and 1860 the northern workingman had been brought over from a passive to an actual opposition to slavery, by insistence on the economic disadvantage to free laborers of competition by labor-owners. The British laboring-man had gone through his education earlier, with such effect that the very population most severely hit by the cotton famine, the operatives of the Lancaster mills, had nevertheless steadily stood by the North. Supported through their distress by the splendid organization of British philanthropy, they found their situation begin to improve with the coming of Indian and Egyptian cotton in 1863; [1] and if they had any doubt as to the purpose of the North it was absolved by Lincoln's preliminary emancipation proclamation of September 22, 1862.

Whether this proclamation had anything to do with the postponement of the critical cabinet meeting it is impossible to say, but it is noticeable that the news of it *Effect of emancipation* reached England between the calling of the meeting and its postponement. Between that time and June, actual emancipation was proclaimed, January 1, 1863. Lincoln did not allow the effect of the proclamation to be lost upon English opinion. Throughout the war he and Seward were continually sending abroad all kinds of informal representatives upon all sorts of missions. The influence of John Bigelow on the French press, and of Thurlow Weed on the English, was probably not great, and many of these roving emissaries caused as much annoyance to Adams as their counterparts had given to Franklin during the Revolu-

[1] R. A. Arnold, *History of the Cotton Famine*, London, 1864.

tion. Henry Ward Beecher, however, was a real ambassador
to the people, and Lincoln himself wrote a public letter to the
working-men of London. On the whole, the development of
a pro-northern sentiment was rather by a raising of interest
in the indifferent or the uninformed than by a converting
of the pro-southern classes, although the Whig element began
to turn. Many moderates moreover, were decidedly influenced by the northern victories of Gettysburg and Vicksburg, July 3 and 4, 1863. It was, however, on July 13, three
days before the news of these victories reached England that
Roebuck, realizing the change in the balance of opinion,
withdrew his motion. It was Lincoln, not Grant and Meade,
who prevented recognition.

Even with the crisis past, there still remained a twofold
danger. With the proceeds of their loan the Confederates
were having built by Laird, the great British
iron-master, war vessels, rams of such formid-

The Laird
"rams"

able fighting capacity that they caused the sensitive quills
of our press to stand erect with horror as they saw them,
omnipresent, destroying our poor blockading fleet, laying
the Atlantic coast under tribute, and ascending our rivers
and creeks for the devastation of the interior. There was
more chance, however, that some episode would arise out of
their building that would tip the still swaying balance of
British opinion, or would impress that of the United States
as an act of war. Adams, with growing confidence, pressed
upon Russell the duty of preventing these vessels, whose
progress was regularly reported in the newspapers, from
being delivered into the hands of the Confederacy. Russell
promised to investigate, but his law officers discovered that
the vessels had been sold to a French firm, and that there
was no "evidence capable of being presented to a Court of
Justice" that they were intended for the Confederacy. Actually they did not know that a contract existed by which
the French firm was to turn them over to Confederate agents
when they were once beyond British jurisdiction. Adams

however, rightly believed that this was the case. On September 5, therefore, hearing that one ship was about to depart, he wrote to Russell: "I can regard it no otherwise than as practically opening to the insurgents full liberty in this Kingdom, to conduct a campaign against the northern seaports. . . . It would be superfluous in me to point out to your Lordship that this is war." Russell had no intention thus to provoke war. Two days before Adams's letter was written he had ordered the rams detained. This closed the episode; the rams never afterwards were within reach of the Confederacy.

With September, 1863, the triumph of northern diplomacy was complete. Davis's next message to the Confederate Congress is a petulant admission of defeat. **Triumph of the North** Nevertheless, the Confederacy did not give up its hope of foreign aid or its attempt to secure it. Alexander H. Stephens even favored abolishing slavery to win it.[1] All subsequent plans, policies, and projects, however, were actually dependent upon military success, which could not come on any grand scale without foreign aid, without the breaking of the blockade. The situation was an *impasse*. Chance might work for the Confederacy, but no diplomatic skill would avail for rescue.

[1] See also M. D. Conway, *Autobiography* (2 vols., Boston, etc., 1904), ch. xxi.

CHAPTER XXIII

THE CIVIL WAR AND THE MONROE DOCTRINE

FROM the date of President Monroe's message of 1823 to the Civil war there had been no new European colony established in America, no transfer of territory from one European nation to another, and no controlling intervention by European powers in American affairs. This inactivity had not been due to any unwillingness to interfere, or even to a lack of desire, but to a recognition of the fact that owing to its position, the United States was actually stronger over most of the continental area than any European power could be, and that her friendship was more valuable than the spoils that might be snatched in a general scramble for plunder.

Practical effect of the Monroe Doctrine

In answering questions as to the national policy asked by the governments of Argentina and Brazil in 1825, Clay had been careful to state that "our declaration must be regarded as having been voluntarily made, and not as conveying any pledge or obligation the performance of which foreign nations have a right to demand." Until the Mexican war our policy was negative, and we avoided entanglements in the ever-changing complications of Spanish-American politics. This left a field open for the exercise of European influence, and by mediation and advice European governments sought to gain a hold without actually coming into collision with us. In 1827, for instance, Austria and Great Britain sought to arrange peace between Brazil and Portugal, and Great Britain did actively intervene. After 1845, our ministers are often found taking a mediating part in South American disputes,

Interpretation of the Monroe Doctrine

but without any strong insistence in our exclusive right to tender such good offices.

The centre of European interest was the mouth of La Plata, the bone of contention between Argentina, Brazil, and Uruguay. In the latter country French influence was strong, and from 1838 to 1849 was constantly on the alert. This foothold French influence in Uruguay was seized upon with vigor by the second French republic in 1848, and Eugène Guillemot was sent to represent her. He reported, December 12, 1848, "Two opposed elements contend at present in all South America, the local element and the European. . . . Around the first group all the tendencies, stationary and retrograde . . .; around the other, colonization, expansion, in all good senses, agricultural, industrial, and commercial. But let the local element prevail, and a new element, influence, and perhaps control, the Anglo-American, will not be long in appearing in the midst of the social torpor, if not anarchy, and will produce a complete and without doubt violent renovation, and more or less our exclusion as well as that of Europe."

March 19, 1849, Guillemot advised that France send six thousand troops to Montevideo: "It is not a conquest that France will make for herself, it will be only a vast rendezvous of emigration for the use of Europe that she will open. . . . South America is occupied nearly entirely by natives of Iberian descent. A fruitful germ of our nation ought to be deposited among them, and if some day the Anglo-Americans pretend to pass over Panamá and descend towards Cape Horn, it is well that they find at least on the route a people of our race, not less hardy than theirs, which may serve to head the column of the others." He was not unmindful of the Monroe Doctrine, just then being insisted upon by Polk; but he put too much stress upon its temporary, humanistic element of opposition to monarchy, and too little on the fundamental opposition to European influence. April 10, 1849, he wrote,

"Let France declare her disinterested views in the matter, and the Americans of the North will find nothing to say, especially as republican France has rights other than those of monarchical France, they know it and they say it." No permanent establishment of French power or population came from this program; but its formulation at a period when the French people, released from administrative control, found opportunity to express their national enthusiasms, shows that the vision of an American empire had not died.[1]

The division of the United States in 1861, and the consequent paralysis of her forces, therefore released European **Seward's adjustable policy** ambitions and projects which her power had repressed. The first country to take advantage of the new situation was Spain. In 1861 either Spain or the Spanish authorities in Cuba managed by some method to receive from the Dominican Republic, the eastern and formerly Spanish portion of the island of Santo Domingo, a request for annexation. This voluntary reincorporation of a former colony raised a delicate question with reference to the interpretation of the Monroe Doctrine; and the difficulty was increased by the fact that, owing to southern opposition to the recognition of a negro republic, we had never been on terms of diplomatic intercourse with the island government which thus determined on suicide, although we had maintained a consul there for most of the period since 1800. Nevertheless, Seward hesitated not a moment as to the applicability of our traditional policy. April 2, 1861, he wrote to the Spanish minister at Washington that, should Spain sustain this action, the President would "be obliged to regard" her "as manifesting an unfriendly spirit towards the United States, and to meet the further prosecution of enterprises of that kind in regard to either the Dominican Republic or any part of the American continent or islands

---

[1] Eugène Guillemot, *La politique et l'avenir de la France dans l'Amériqu du Sud:* also British Public Record Office, *Foreign Office Records, Bueno Ayres,* 1846.

with a prompt, persistent, and, if possible, effective resistance." Spain disregarded the threat, and on July 1, 1861, the Spanish minister announced to Seward the annexation of Dominica. Carl Schurz, our new minister in Spain, asked for instructions, and in August, 1861, Seward wrote to him that circumstances prevented him from giving a definite answer. This change of tone needed no explanation, but it illustrates the influence of the Civil war on the Monroe Doctrine. In refraining from answering Schurz's question, Seward alike saved himself from offending Spain when he had not the power to awe or oppose her, and left open the door for future protest. Meanwhile, by an indirection of statement, he attempted to lead Spain to suppose that this tolerance of a situation which we had so often declared intolerable, was due to her "observance of the blockade and the closing of Spanish ports to the insurgent privateers." The supreme test of our passivity came when, in 1863, war broke out between the Spanish government and the islanders. Seward promptly declared our neutrality.[1]

Although Spain was interested in this undertaking to the extent of sending more than thirty thousand troops to the island, the task of maintaining her local hold, Spain leaves in spite of the neutrality of the United States, Dominica was so exhausting that in 1865 she voluntarily surrendered her claim. Spain's reoccupation of Dominica seems to have been part of a general, though vacillating, purpose on her part to take advantage of our weakness in order to inaugurate an active American policy. In 1864 she went Spain and to war with Peru, and some of her representa- Peru tives claimed that, as she had never recognized Peru's independence, she might without violation of any established sovereignty recover the Chincha islands. Seward, more at ease than in 1861, ordered our minister at Madrid, now G. Koërner, to make known to the Spanish government that

[1] Carl Schurz, *Speeches, Correspondence, and Political Papers* (6 vols. New York, etc., 1913), i. 185–205.

we could not accept such an argument or "regard with indifference" an attempt at re-annexation. The Spanish government disclaimed any idea of encroachment, but occupied the islands, and in 1866 announced that it might take possession of them without any intention of acquiring territory, but merely to reimburse itself for the expense of the war by the sale of guano. It was now too late. Our new minister in Spain, J. P. Hale, was instructed that, in case of even such a temporary occupation, the United States could not be expected "to remain in their present attitude of neutrality." The Civil war was over, and Spain withdrew.

The same successive adjustment of our policy to circumstance that has been observed in the case of Spain is to be found in the more important issue of the activity of France in Mexico. The latter country was the scene of constant revolution and guerrilla warfare. The claims of United States citizens that in Buchanan's administration had seemed to him to warrant our interference were paralleled by those of the citizens of all other foreign nations doing business there, particularly those of Great Britain, France and Spain. These nations were in 1860 moving toward interposition, and Buchanan, in his message of December 3, 1860, regretted that we had not taken action earlier. "We should thus," he said, "have been relieved from the obligation of resisting, even by force should this become necessary, any attempt by these Governments to deprive our neighboring Republic of portions of her territory—a duty from which we could not shrink without abandoning the traditional and established policy of the American people."

In 1861 the Mexican Congress voted to defer the payment of interest on foreign bonds; whereupon Great Britain, France, and Spain decided that action must be taken. They invited the United States to join them, but she refused. In a convention signed at London, October 31, 1861, they decided forcibly to demand "more efficacious protection for the persons and the properties of their subjects, as well as the fulfillment of obligations." The high contracting parties engaged "not to seek for themselves . . . any acquisition of territory . . . or any special advantage, and not to exercise in the internal affairs of Mexico any influence of a nature to prejudice the right of the Mexican nation to choose and to constitute freely the form of its government." Nevertheless, Schurz wrote to Seward, November 16, 1861, of the intriguing rivalries for the throne of Mexico. The importance of the movement of the allies was indicated by the choice of General Prim, the leading man in Spain, to head it. He assured Schurz, before embarking, of his sympathy with the United States.

Once in Mexico, the allies occupied a number of customs-houses and collected the duties, but in April, 1862, Spain and England made an arrangement with the government and withdrew.[1] France was left. This was the opportunity for which Napoleon had been working. His basis for interference was not so much the French claims, which consisted chiefly of bonds with a face value of fifteen million dollars, purchased by the firm of Jecker for seven hundred and fifty thousand from an ephemeral revolutionary government, as the hope that the Second Empire might, by carrying out the French national aspirations, successfully fulfill the colonial vision of the First. Morny, Napoleon's relative and confidential adviser, believed that the United States was a menace to Europe, and wished to create in Mexico an empire that would become the protector of all the Latin republics and with them constitute a power capable of resisting us.

Mexico a French question

With such views in mind, Napoleon, on the withdrawal of the other powers, presented an ultimatum and ordered his army on to the city of Mexico. Finding no stable government with which to treat, the French commander called an

[1] H. Léondaron, "L'Espagne et la question du Mexique, 1861–1862," *Annales des Sciences Politiques*, 1901, xvi. 59–95.

assembly of Mexican notables to deal with the situation.
Amid the confusion of local factions and personal rivalries
that divided the land there ran one main
line of division,—that between the Church
party and the Liberal party. The latter, under
Juarez, was in the field fighting the French; the other Napoleon hoped to use as the local basis for French influence.
His notables were chosen with that end in view, and they
proved docile to his leading. Under his tutelage they decided that an empire on the Napoleonic plan afforded the
best basis for security, and asked the Archduke Maximilian
of Austria, to rule over them. Napoleon calculated on establishing in America an empire that would be strong and yet
dependent upon his support, and on gaining in Europe the
gratitude of the pope and of Austria.[1]

Formation of
the Mexican
empire

The situation thus presented to us was, both technically
and practically, more difficult than that produced by Spain
in Dominica. Technically it was so because
this was not a question of annexation, but
prima facie an exhibition of popular sovereignty. Napoleon's
was plainly the guiding hand, yet to the eye the marionette
notables moved of their own volition. Practically it was
more dangerous because of the greater strength of France.
Spain was simply no longer afraid of us, of France we ourselves were fearful. We could not acquiesce in such a way as
to find our hands tied after the war was over; on the other
hand, if we protested too vigorously we should not only be
making useless threats, but might give Napoleon an excuse
for breaking from England's lead and interfering in our Civil
war. On February 3, 1863, he offered to act as mediator
between the North and South, and, when the North firmly
rejected that offer, it was only England's influence that prevented his recognition of the Confederacy. Napoleon and the
Confederacy mutually cultivated each other; Slidell was con-

Danger of our
situation

[1] *Lettre à M. Duchon Doris*, Bordeaux, 1864; "Mme. Adam's Reminis-
cences," *Nation*, 1905, lxxxi. 521–522.

cerned in the Napoleonic attempt to influence the British Parliament through Roebuck; Benjamin attempted to bribe Napoleon by a million bales of cotton. Almost to the day of Lee's surrender the hope of Napoleon's intervention persisted in the South. Of Seward's first dispatch on the subject, in which he assured France of our neutrality in her war with Mexico, and with reference to the new empire said that it would be neither easily established nor useful, his friend Weed wrote to him: "Your dispatch on Mexican matters breaks no eggs. It makes a record, and there, I hope, you are at rest." Napoleon, on hearing that Seward's dispatch had arrived, eagerly asked if there had been a protest. Rather annoyed than relieved by its mild indefiniteness, he asked that we follow the example of the powers of Europe except Russia, by recognizing Maximilian as emperor. Seward replied that he understood there was still opposition to the Austrian, and that he should prefer to err on the side of neutrality.

Seward and Napoleon

Seward's policy of avoiding offence to France and yet of leaving the future unpledged, was undoubtedly wise, but in pursuing it he was forced to deal not only with Napoleon but with our own newspapers and with Congress. In April, 1864, the House of Representatives unanimously resolved that it could not accord with United States policy to acknowledge a monarchical government established under the auspices of any European power on the ruins of an American Republic. The French foreign minister, Drouyn de l'Huys, learning of the resolution, greeted our minister, Dayton, with the question, "Do you bring us peace or bring us war?" He brought Seward's explanation that the foreign policy of our country was directed by the President.

Seward and Congress

The close of our war left us masters of the situation; but the task of getting rid of Maximilian was a delicate one, for there was the chance that our aroused and militant public sentiment would force Napoleon into war to defend his prestige. General Grant looked on the whole movement as a "direct act of war," and it was proposed that an army **Seward and the army** of our volunteers, Union and Confederate, be reënlisted across the Mexican border to serve under Juarez in driving out the French. General Schofield was detached for twelve months to head this organization.

Seward met this dangerous proposition by finesse. He called Schofield to him and asked him to go to France in- **Seward allows Napoleon a diplomatic victory** stead. "I want you to get your legs under Napoleon's mahogany," said he, "and tell him he must get out of Mexico." Schofield did not happen to dine with Napoleon, but Seward informed France that peace would be put in "imminent jeopardy" by the further retention of French troops in Mexico. Realizing, however, that Napoleon, by reason of the domestic situation in France, could face war more easily than a confessed defeat, Seward gave him a seeming victory by assuring him, February 12, 1866, that after the French evacuation the United States would continue the same neutrality between Juarez and Maximilian that she had previously preserved between Juarez and the French. This recognition constituted a triumph of French diplomacy, though a triumph that every one knew was hollow, for Maximilian could not stand a year unsupported by France. Accepting this way out, so wisely prepared for him, de l'Huys replied. "We receive this assurance with entire confidence and we find therein a sufficient guarantee not any longer to delay the adoption of measures intended to prepare for the return of our army." [1]

Hearing of the probable abandonment of Maximilian by the French, his countrymen of Austria prepared to enlist an army for his defence. Seward promptly directed John

[1] C. A. Duniway, *Reasons for the Withdrawal of the French from Mexico,* Amer. Hist. Assoc., *Report,* 1902, i. 312–328; Latané, *Diplomatic Relations of the United States and Spanish America,* 221–265; Henry Wheaton, *Elements of International Law,* 8th edition by R. H. Dana, London, etc., 1866.

Lothrop Motley, our minister at Vienna, to challenge such an attempt peremptorily. Motley, the least satisfactory of our literary appointments, raised many diffi- **Seward and** culties in carrying out this policy, among others **Austria** that it did not harmonize with the earlier tone which we had adopted. Seward replied, "I refrain from discussing the question you have raised, whether the recent instructions of this department harmonize entirely with the policy which it pursued at an earlier period of the European intervention in Mexico." Europe understood, if Motley did not, that the close of our war had changed the situation. Austria promised to prevent the departure of the volunteers.

The American residuum of European interference soon vanished with the withdrawal of the support which had brought it into being. Maximilian's native **Fate of Maxi-** Mexican forces yielded to those of Juarez, and **milian** he himself was captured. Upon learning that he was condemned to be shot in the back as a traitor, Austria, France, and Great Britain appealed to the United States to save him. We expressed sympathy and recommended clemency to Juarez, but we would not intervene in a matter domestically Mexican. Maximilian was shot. The Monroe Doctrine was once more established, and more firmly established than it was in 1860, for it had practically been recognized by France, Spain, and Austria. The Austrian court, however, has never since been an altogether pleasant residence for an American minister.

That Great Britain does not appear in this crisis of the Monroe Doctrine seems strange to many critics. Bernhardi wrote in 1901: "Since England committed the **Great Britain** unpardonable blunder, from her point of view, **and the Mon-** of not supporting the Southern States in the **roe Doctrine** American war of Secession, a rival to England's world-wide empire has appeared . . . in the form of the United States of North America." In part this apparent neglect of opportunity was due to the fact that, although her prime minister was jingoistic, there was in England at this time a strong sentiment that colonies were unprofitable, and that it was the universal tendency for them to ripen and drop from the parent tree. Still, Canning himself would probably not have acted otherwise. What Great Britain wanted was commercial opportunity, and of that the independence of Spanish America was sufficient guarantee to the cheapest producer in the world. The only portions of America that England might desire were Cuba and the Isthmus; but the first was Spain's, the second was protected by the Clayton-Bulwer treaty. If Great Britain showed a lack of enterprise in not pushing her interests during the Civil war, at least she was spared recognizing the Monroe Doctrine at its close.

It was probably more nearly a deviation from British policy to allow other European powers, like Spain and France, to acquire permanent interests in America. On that point England had been in agreement with us since 1823; the conflicts between us had arisen when we were endeavoring to extend our interests. Her acquiescence in this case was due to her practical alliance with Napoleon, and perhaps to a well-justified cynical belief that nothing would come of it.

Great Britain and European interference

Just after the war, in 1867, the House of Representatives endeavored to hoist Great Britain on our favorite petard by declaring that the organization of the Dominion of Canada, the union of the several British provinces, constituted such a change of status in American affairs as to constitute a violation of the Monroe Doctrine. The failure of the administration to urge this forced interpretation upon Great Britain deprived her of an opportunity of replying to it.

The Monroe Doctrine and Canada

In 1870 Grant gave expression to a corollary of the Doctrine which had for some time been recognized: "Hereafter no territory on this continent shall be regarded as subject to transfer to a European power;" that is even by one European power to another. In fact, from 1823 to the present day the only violation of this principle has been the unimportant cession of the island of Saint Bartholomew by Sweden to France in 1878.[1]

Grant's corollary of the Monroe Doctrine

[1] Coolidge, *The United States as a World Power*, 113.

CHAPTER XXIV

THE AFTERMATH OF THE CIVIL WAR

THE resolution protesting against the formation of the Dominion of Canada was indicative of a feeling of hostility to Great Britain which was the most absorbing factor in our diplomacy from 1865 until 1871. Based primarily upon our disappointment at England's lack of sympathy with the national government during that struggle, nourished by the frank unfriendliness of a large section of the English press and much of her literature, it found many substantial issues which gave occasion for its expression.

The direct loss that we sustained by the depredations of the Confederate commerce-destroyers, which Great Britain's lax interpretation of neutrality allowed to range the ocean to the very end of the war, was less than the indirect loss which they caused by imperilling all vessels bearing the American flag. Eight hundred thousand tons of American shipping were transferred to foreign flags, chiefly that of Great Britain, and what was left to us found itself hampered by almost prohibitory insurance rates. Both these sores were kept open and irritated by the failure of the American merchant marine to rise again. Its decline, which was due to a variety of causes unrelated to the war, had begun about 1857. The most important was the introduction of iron ships, which could be more cheaply constructed in Great Britain. To the natural advantages which that country possessed was added our protective tariff system, which increased the cost of our ship-building without being able to offer any compensatory protection to the ship-owners, engaged as they were in a free international competition. Quite as important, too, was the terrific drain upon our resources of capital, credit, and labor produced by the era of internal expansion which the close of the war ushered in. The rewards coming from the development and exploitation of our own country were incomparably greater than those from any industry competing directly with that of foreign nations. The transfer of his fortune from shipping to railroads, made at this time by Commodore Vanderbilt, was the act of a far-seeing business man. His example was followed by many other Americans concerned in shipping, whether as owners or sailors, and few natives now embarked in the old profession.

These considerations, however, did not at the time sink into the national consciousness, which perceived merely that until the Civil war our merchant marine had been a leading American interest, and that after it our flag had almost disappeared from competitive trade routes. The events of the war afforded a simple explanation, and anger was hot against Great Britain as the instrument of the change.[1]

Great Britain held responsible

Other subjects of dispute naturally arose with a nation with which our connections were so numerous. It became a question, for instance, whether the main channel of the strait of Juan de Fuca ran north or south of the archipelago of San Juan, whether the islands fell to us or to Great Britain. The activities of the American and British representatives on the spot might at any time cause an explosion.[2] Then, too, in 1866 Marcy's reciprocity treaty with Canada ran through its prescribed course, and we notified Great Britain that we did not care to continue it. This reopened the wasp's nest of the fisheries question in an atmosphere provoking irritation.

Boundary and the fisheries

[1] W. L. Marvin, *The American Merchant Marine*, New York, 1902.

[2] This is one of the questions that might have afforded a basis for Seward's foreign-war panacea. See Mrs. G. E. Pickett's "Wartime Story of General Pickett," *Cosmopolitan*, vol. lv, pp. 752–760.

To these problems was added that of the Fenian agitation. An Irish nationalistic and republican movement, its leaders

Fenian movement

planned to make the United States the basis for their effort to invade Canada, spread terror in England, and force the independence of Ireland. Archbishop Hughes had visited Ireland during the Civil war, and had successfully stimulated the emigration of young men to the United States for the purpose of enlisting in the Union armies. As an additional motive he urged that they would secure military training that would prove useful for "ulterior" purposes. He meant the defence of the Papal States; but he was supposed to refer to the freeing of Ireland, and that was the hope that fired thousands of Irish volunteers. In 1866 the Fenians invaded Canada across the Niagara river, but accomplished nothing. In April of the same year an attempt was made to seize the island of Campo Bello, just across the New Brunswick border from Maine, to proclaim a republic, and to secure recognition from the United States; but this expedition also came to nothing.[1] It is not without significance that in July the House of Representatives passed a bill to allow the sale of ships and munitions of war to foreign citizens and governments at peace with the United States though at war with other countries.

The chief danger of the Irish movement arose from the fact that many of the Fenians were naturalized American citizens,

Irish influence

and many were veterans of our Civil war. When they got into difficulties, therefore, they appealed to an American public sentiment already alert to take offence against the British government. The political influence of the Irish leaders, moreover, was so potent that few politicians dared oppose them. In 1868 the House passed by 104 to 4 a bill authorizing the President, in case American citizens were arrested for political reasons by a foreign power, to suspend commercial relations and detain a corresponding

[1] John Rutherford, *The Secret History of the Fenian Conspiracy*, 2 vols. London, 1877.

number of the citizens of the offending government, indiscriminately selected. This bill Sumner succeeded in modifying in the Senate, but still it passed in good round terms. Seward, always on close terms with the Irish leaders, in this case found any temptation that he may have had to play up to them checked by the weightiest of balancing considerations. Just when we were urgently pressing upon Great Britain our claims for damages based on her failure to perform her neutral duties, we could not permit ourselves to be lax. The government, while protecting as far as possible the rights of American citizens, vigorously enforced the laws that prevented the use of our territory as a base of hostile operations.

The crux of the negotiations between the two governments was our demand for damages arising from what we claimed to be Great Britain's violation of neutrality. Her statutory provision for the performance of her neutral duties was found *Great Britain's practice of neutrality* in her foreign enlistment act of 1819. Although this forbade the fitting out of armed vessels, the Confederate commissioners were legally advised that the purchase of vessels and the purchase of arms were both legal, but that the two could not be combined in British waters. Acting on this advice, Captain Bullock, the Confederate naval representative, contracted for several vessels, of which the *Florida*, the *Shenandoah*, and most important, the *Alabama* got to sea in the manner suggested. Although in April, 1863, the British government prevented the *Alexandria* from being similarly handed over, the courts sustained the Confederate agents. In this latter case the lord chief baron instructed the jury: "If you think the object was to build a ship in obedience to an order, and in compliance with a contract, leaving those who bought it to make what use they thought fit of it, then it appears to me the Foreign enlistment act has not been in any degree broken." The American claims for damages rested not only on the construction of these vessels, but also upon the fact that, by a liberal interpretation of the right of belligerent vessels to take on enough provisions to reach a home port, they were allowed to use British ports as bases for their operations.

On October 23, 1863, the detention of the Laird rams having shown that the British government had changed its Futile negotia- practice with regard to the building of hostile tions warships, Adams offered to submit to arbitration our claims for damages caused by those already built. Lord Russell said that the construction of British statutes could never be submitted to arbitration, that the question involved the honor of the country and so was not appropriate for arbitration. It was, of course, obvious that the question was not the construction of British statutes, but the adequacy of those statutes, as interpreted by the British courts, to the maintenance of neutrality; but the negotiation dropped. It was renewed under Russell's successor, Lord Stanley, but agreement was at first prevented by the question as to the limits of the arbitration,—whether it should be confined to claims for damages directly inflicted, or should be extended to include those suffered indirectly, such as insurance, cost of pursuit, and the commercial loss of our merchant marine.

In 1868 Reverdy Johnson, who succeeded Adams, arranged a convention with Lord Stanley dealing with this Johnson- and other subjects. It gave up our claims for Clarendon indirect damages, and so was not entirely satis- convention factory to Seward; nevertheless it was submitted to the Senate. February 10, 1869, Seward wrote to Johnson: "The confused light of the incoming administration is already spreading itself over the country. . . . With your experience in legislative life, you will be able to judge for yourself of the prospects of definite action upon the treaties during the remainder of the present session."

The confused light broke in a lightening flash when, on April 13, 1869, Sumner reported the convention unfavorably from the committee on foreign affairs. In one of his most carefully prepared orations he denounced the agreement and proclaimed his policy. Our direct claims, he contended, were no compensation for our losses; the indirect claims, particularly those based on the **Sumner's policy** substitution of the British merchant marine for our own, were greater and must be made good. Fundamentally, however, our grievance against Great Britain rested on the fact that by her premature and injurious proclamation of belligerency she had prolonged the war for at least two years; and for the cost she should pay. Sumner's total bill amounted to two and a half billion dollars. "Whatever may be the final settlement of these great accounts," he declared, "such must be the judgment in any chancery which consults the simple equity of the case." [1]

The explanation of this preposterous demand is revealed in a memorandum of Sumner's of January 17, 1871: "The greatest trouble, if not peril, being a constant source of anxiety and disturbance, is from the Fenians, which is excited by the proximity of the British flag in Canada. Therefore the withdrawal of the British flag cannot be abandoned as a condition preliminary of such a settlement as is now proposed. To make the settlement complete the withdrawal should be from this hemisphere, including provinces and islands." As Adams had purchased Florida and Polk New Mexico with our claims, as Jackson had proposed to buy Texas, so Sumner would purchase all British America.

Fantastic as was his proposition, it was the result of thought, it rested on facts, and to its execution he devoted his utmost skill; as much may be said of any **Sumner's vision** conscientiously constructed house of cards. He knew that his English friends, many of them highly placed and whom he regarded as the real men of that country, believed colonies to be a burden, that they would in time become free, that Canada would ultimately become part of the United States. Cobden had written to him in

[1] Sumner, *Works*, Boston, 1874–1883, 53–93.

1849: "I agree with you that nature has decided that Canada and the United States must become one for all purposes of intercommunication. Whether they also shall be united in the same Federal Government must depend upon the two parties to the union. I can assure you that there will be no repetition of the policy of 1776, on our part, to prevent our North American colonies from pursuing their interests in their own way. If the people of Canada are tolerably unanimous in wishing to sever the very slight thread which now binds them to this country, I see no reason why, if good faith and ordinary temper be observed, it should not be done amicably." As a matter of fact, Gladstone, who became prime minister in 1869, fifteen years later surrendered British authority in the Transvaal and withdrew from the Soudan. Sumner's plan to remove all causes for dispute with Great Britain, to take another step in our inevitable expansion over the continent without a drop of blood, to assure the dominance in the United States of northern views by thus adding to the northern element, was fitted together from the best thought of his generation.

As Calhoun in his absorption over the Texas question failed to see the fallacy in his syllogistic argument for annexa-

Sumner's madness

tion, so Sumner, rapt in his vision, utterly failed to take cognizance of human nature. To inaugurate an era of brotherly love and lavish exchanges of brotherly favors by presenting a bill for two billion and a half dollars, was not tactful. To suppose that his friends in England would coöperate in fixing everlasting stigma upon the name of Great Britain by acknowledging that she had injured us to that extent, was to lose sight of realities. To imagine that a people strong and dominant as the English would leave those friends in power one minute after they made such a proposition was to display inexcusable ignorance. The only palliation of Sumner's conduct was that he lived in a generation which saw such visions, and that even the more conservative often yielded to them, as Seward had done when he evolved his foreign-war panacea at the opening of the Civil war. One would more readily grant him excuse if he had not regarded with such self-righteous horror others who had been or were endeavoring to carry out such visions, as Jackson, Calhoun, Polk, and Grant.

The importance of Sumner's speech was enhanced by its popular reception and by the fact that it might be presumed to voice the sentiments of the new administra- Closing of ne-tion. The Johnson-Clarendon convention was gotiations rejected by a vote of 54 to 1; Grant, the new President, being a military hero, was expected by many to favor an aggressive policy; and Motley was sent to England as distinctly of Sumner's choice. When the latter, in his first interview, told Lord Clarendon that the belligerency proclamation was "the fountain head" of all the woes caused "to the American people, both individually and collectively, by the hands of Englishmen," the British government concluded that we would insist on Sumner's views, and put an end to the negotiation.

This result was unfortunate, for as a matter of fact the two governments were just approaching an understanding. Not only was the Gladstone ministry friendly Friendly atti-to the United States, but British public senti- tude of the two governments ment was beginning to perceive that it was ad-vantageous for Great Britain to yield. Sir Thomas Baring, inheriting the friendly sentiments of his house, argued that Great Britain, with her immense commerce and her prepared navy, was the last power to admit the extemporizing of commerce-destroyers in neutral ports. In time of war, even with a land-girt power, every neutral harbor, he urged, would be a safe lurking-place for her enemies; the only method of prevention would be universal war.[1] The American administration, also, was inclined to agreement. The new secretary of state, Hamilton Fish, had actually instructed Motley to speak of the belligerency proclamation merely as

[1] John Morley, *Life of Gladstone*, 3 vols., London, etc., 1903.

indicating "the beginning and the animus of that course of conduct which resulted so disastrously to the United States;" and even this clause was inserted only because of the violent insistence of Sumner.

In spite of this approach in the views of the two governments, it was a delicate task to reopen the negotiation as neither government wished to take the first step. Fortunately it happened that Caleb Cushing, for the United States, and John Rose, for Great Britain, two able and accomplished diplomats, were in Washington negotiating in regard to certain claims of the Hudson Bay Company recognized by the treaty of 1846 and by a convention of 1867. Finding by informal conversations that the ground was secure, Rose on January 11, 1871, presented a memorandum suggesting that all questions in dispute be made the subject of a general negotiation and treaty. It was at this time that Sumner, being invited as chairman of the committee on foreign affairs to read Rose's note, revealed his plan for securing Canada. It was obvious that he stood in the way of any settlement. Grant had already been incensed by Motley's disregard of his instructions and by Sumner's opposition to his own favorite project, the annexation of Santo Domingo, an irritation which became mutual when Grant requested Motley to resign, and, on his refusal, removed him. The climax was now reached, and Grant successfully used his influence with the Senate to secure Sumner's removal from his chairmanship. The ground was ready for another of our great clearing-house agreements with Great Britain.[1]

The negotiation was conducted at Washington by a commission of marked distinction. On the American side were Fish, secretary of state, Schenck, minister to Great Britain,

Reopening of negotiations

---

[1] This whole negotiation has been the subject of much controversy. In addition to Moore's *Arbitrations* and the forthcoming life of C. F. Adams, see D. H. Chamberlain, *Charles Sumner and the Treaty of Washington*, Cambridge, Mass., 1902; Caleb Cushing, *The Treaty of Washington*, New York, 1873; and Rhodes, *United States*, vi. 337–368.

Justice Nelson of the supreme court, E. R. Hoar of Massachusetts as interested in the fisheries, and G. H. Williams of Oregon to present the San Juan controversy. The commission Although certainly less able than our delegations at Paris in 1783 or at Ghent in 1815, the body was skilled and representative. The British commission far exceeded in dignity, as probably in ability, any previously sent to us by a foreign power; its makeup was significant of our growth in international importance. The chairman was Earl de Grey, and with him were Viscount Goderich, president of the privy council, Sir Stafford Northcote, Sir Edward Thornton, British minister at Washington, Sir John Alexander Macdonald, minister of justice for Canada, and Montague Bernard, professor of international law at Oxford.

After thirty-seven sittings the treaty was signed, May 8, 1871. It dealt first with claims for damage done by the *Alabama* and other British-built commerce- "Alabama claims" destroyers. This question was to be submitted to a tribunal of five arbitrators, one each to be selected by the president of the United States, the queen of Great Britain, the king of Italy, the president of the Swiss confederation, and the emperor of Brazil. This tribunal was to meet at Geneva, and was to base its decisions on three rules for the conduct of neutral nations: "First, to use due diligence to prevent the fitting out . . . within its jurisdiction, of any vessel which it has reasonable ground to believe is intended to cruise . . . against a Power with which it is at peace . . .; secondly, not to permit . . . either belligerent to make use of its ports or waters as the base of naval operations . . .; thirdly, to exercise due diligence in its own ports and waters . . . to prevent any violation of the foregoing obligations and duties." The insertion of "reasonable ground to believe," taken from our neutrality act of 1838, was a distinct American triumph. Great Britain would not acknowledge that this had been the rule during the Civil war, but was now willing to have the cases decided on that basis, in order to establish it as the rule for the future.

Another but less elaborate tribunal, of one commissioner appointed by each country and one by both together, was **Other Civil war claims** to decide upon all other claims, British and American, that had arisen during the Civil war.

Articles xviii to xxi of the treaty dealt with the fisheries. The principle of reciprocity was again applied, Great Britain granting us the privileges necessary for the con-**The fisheries** duct of our fishing industry, and the United States conceding free entry of fish oil, and sea fish. Upon the contention by the British government that the privileges granted to us were more valuable than those which its subjects received, it was left to a commission, the third and arbitrating member of which was to be appointed by the Austrian minister at London, to investigate the matter and assess the compensatory sum, if any, that we should pay.

Article xxvii gave the United States the free navigation of the St. Lawrence forever, and Great Britain similar use **Border questions** of the Yukon, Porcupine, and Stikine. With England's free use of the Columbia established in 1846, this agreement opened up all the important international rivers with which the two countries were concerned. By the same article the government of Great Britain agreed to urge the Dominion of Canada, and that of the United States promised to use its influence with those of the states concerned, to open up all their respective canals connected with the navigation of the Great Lakes on terms of equality to both nations; and by article xxviii the United States allowed the free navigation of Lake Michigan. Articles xxix and xxx provided for the shipping of goods in bond across the border and back under regulation. By article xxxi Great Britain engaged to urge the Canadian government to impose no export duty on Maine lumber floated down the St. Johns under the provisions of the treaty of 1846.

By article xxiv the question of the San Juan channel was submitted to the decision of the emperor **Boundary** of Germany.

Comprehensive as was this treaty, and unique in calling the direct attention of most of the crowned heads of Europe to our affairs, it was overshadowed in interest **Geneva arbitration** by the Geneva arbitration which it evoked. Never before had such important and irritating international disputes voluntarily been submitted to judicial settlement. The commission was equal to the significance of its task. Grant appointed Charles Francis Adams, who became its president, and Queen Victoria chose Sir Alexander Cockburn, lord chief justice of England; the commissioners from Italy, Switzerland, and Brazil were also men of note. The American case was presented by William Evarts, M. R. Waite, B. R. Curtis, and Caleb Cushing, the first the leader of the bar, the second later to be chief justice, and the third a former member of the supreme court. The case which they were to present was prepared by J. C. Bancroft Davis.

At this time the American public sentiment that had applauded Sumner was still in existence, Sumner himself, a power of unknown strength, was still watch- **Arbitration in danger** ful, the Fenian agitation was again attracting attention, and a presidential campaign was coming on. The administration, therefore, did not venture to admit that it had surrendered all our indirect claims in the treaty of Washington. It instructed our counsel to insist, not indeed on those for the cost of two years of war, but for compensation for the transfer of our commerce to the British merchant marine, as covered by the clause of the treaty that read, "acts committed by the several vessels which have given rise to the claims generally known as the '*Alabama* Claims.'" British public opinion considered this instruction an act of bad faith, and the Gladstone government proposed to withdraw from the arbitration, knowing that, if it consented to submit the consideration of this question to the tribunal, it would itself be instantly overthrown. There was no possibility that these claims would be allowed by the tribunal; yet the United States would not give over presenting them, nor Great Britain allow their presentation.

A point of honor in each case, backed by a public sentiment vociferously led, and in our case at least certainly not Adams's solution representative, seemed likely to wreck the tion work. Such factors, however, seldom have decisive weight in controversies between Anglo-Saxons. The solution in this case was found by Adams. At his suggestion the arbitration tribunal itself announced, June 19, 1872, that it would not consider such claims. Great Britain was satisfied, and the United States acquiesced; we could at least assert that they had been considered. Our direct claims were granted, and by the final decision of September 14, 1872, the sum of fifteen and a half million dollars was awarded us. The commission on other Civil war claims granted British subjects about two million dollars for illegal imprisonment and other such losses incidental to war. The emperor of Germany decided in our favor in the case of the channel through the strait of Juan de Fuca, giving us the islands in dispute.[1]

Thus the difficulties between the United States and Great Britain growing out of the Civil war were settled, the treaty of 1846 was clarified, some standard questions, such as the navigation of the St. Lawrence, were settled "forever," and some, like the fisheries, were settled for a period of years. The terms of the treaty itself reveal a new factor in the relations of the two countries that was liable to be a disturbing element in the future, namely, the deference of the government of Great Britain to the Dominion of Canada. On the other hand, and most important of all, the form of the treaty marked it as the longest step yet taken by any two nations toward the settlement of their disputes by judicial process.

[1] T. W. Balch, *The Alabama Arbitration*, Philadelphia, 1900.

CHAPTER XXV

ROUTINE, 1861–1877

WHILE the problems peculiar to the war received most of the attention that the public had to spare for diplomatic affairs, between 1861 and 1877, they did not relieve the administration from the necessity of handling routine business and continuous policies.

One immediate result of the passing of governmental control to the North was the recognition and establishment of diplomatic intercourse with the negro governments of Hayti, now a republic after a succession of empires, and of Liberia. The latter had been a protégé of the United States ever since it was founded in 1819 to serve as a home for our emancipated slaves; we had protected it from foreign interference, but had not so to speak, recognized it socially. The other American negro nation, Dominica, we recognized as soon as Spanish control was withdrawn, and we have never since refused recognition to any nation because of its race. We made a first treaty with Liberia in 1862, with Hayti in 1864, with the Dominican Republic in 1867; and possibly our first treaty with the kingdom of Madagascar in 1867 should come under this head.

A similar change is to be found in our policy toward the slave trade. Seward's convention of 1862, allowing mutual search in certain specified parts of the ocean, with trial by mixed courts, has been mentioned. The area of ocean subject to this arrangement was extended in 1863, and in 1870 the provision with regard to mixed courts was dropped. In 1890 we joined in a general international act for the suppression of the trade, and in 1904 in a similar act for the suppression of the trade in white women. After our own abolition of slavery we readily co-

349

operated in stamping it out everywhere. It is of course to be noted that the danger of an arbitrary and dangerous use of the mutual right of search in times of peace, of which there were grounds to justify fear in the earlier period, had disappeared by 1870, owing to the change in our relative strength and the development of international law.

The sweep of our treaty relations was already so comprehensive that the only first treaty we made with any nation aside from the negro governments was that with Orange Free State in 1871. The formation of the kingdom of Italy in 1861 and of the German empire in 1871 did not require special attention, for they inherited treaty obligations from their controlling or constituent states; but, as new questions arose, treaties were made, with Italy in 1868 and with Germany in 1871.

First treaties

Even during the Civil war we did not drop our pursuit of claims, and we hotly renewed the chase when the war was over. In 1863 and 1868 Peru and the United States submitted their mutual claims to arbitration, the balance in both cases being in our favor. In 1866 the American claims against Venezuela were arbitrated, and about a million and a quarter dollars were awarded to us. A mutual arbitration with Mexico, begun by a treaty of 1868, gave a balance of about four million to our citizens. In 1871 our claims against Spain based on the revolution in Cuba were started on their long history by the consummation of a treaty. Finally during the Franco-Prussian war we came near becoming liable for a violation of neutrality by our own government in the sale of arms owned by the nation to France,[1] but the episode resulted in no ill consequences.

Claims

The area covered by our extradition treaties was increased by the addition of Belgium, Ecuador, Italy, Nicaragua, the Ottoman empire, Salvador, and Spain. Where treaties did not exist, the surrender of fugitives from justice by virtue

[1] Adolf Hepner, *America's Aid to Germany in 1870–71*, St. Louis, 1905; Schurz, *Speeches, etc.*, v. 33–37.

of international courtesy was a delicate matter for us. We
would not surrender those fleeing from punishment for political offences or from military service, and so we
were loath to ask other nations for the return   **Extradition**
of our own fugitives. The action of the Spanish government
in turning over to us the notorious Boss Tweed, in 1876, before the formation of our treaty with her, was therefore
much appreciated.

A new line of diplomatic activity was represented by treaties for the protection of trademarks, made with Russia
and Belgium in 1868, France in 1869, and   **Trademarks,**
Austria in 1871. A still more remarkable ex-   **weights and**
tension of the scope of diplomacy and of our   **measures, and**
          copyrights
acceptance of the principle of international coöperation was
our participation, in 1875, in an international convention
for the establishment at Paris of a bureau of weights and
measures to be maintained at the joint expense of the contracting nations. Diplomacy, however, was not allowed to
take any steps toward similar protection for authors by
means of international copyrights. As the most conspicuous
example of the use of the same language by two great nations, Great Britain and the United States really occupied
a unique position with reference to this question, and the
latter was the greatest pirate in that form of theft. The
matter had long been urged upon us by Dickens, the greatest
sufferer, and by many of our own authors and public men.
Collectively, however, we showed no more disposition to
surrender our profits than had the pirates of Barbary.
The sums involved were greater than those at stake in
our relations with the North African states, and the moral
delinquency must probably be judged to be about the
same.[1]

Continuing the policy of freeing the navigation of great
international rivers, the United States, acting in agreement
but not in formal coöperation with other powers, made

[1] R. R. Bowker, *Copyright, its History and its Law*, Boston, etc., 1912.

a treaty with Hanover in 1861, opening the Elbe, and one with Belgium in 1863, opening the Scheldt. In each case Freeing river navigation we paid a proportional part of a capital sum which was divided among various nations "pro rata to their navigation."

Although the definite undertaking of the first transcontinental railroad through our territory in 1862 diminished Transcontinental communication the interest in the isthmus routes, and its completion in 1869 lessened their importance, we continued our policy of obtaining the right of free use and the guarantee of their neutrality. In a treaty with Honduras in 1864 we undertook a guarantee of the proposed "Interoceanic railroad" through that country in return for the establishment of free terminal ports for trade and commerce, but we made the agreement conditional upon our right to withdraw on six months' notice if dissatisfied with our treatment by the company. A treaty with Nicaragua in 1867 gave us free use of her isthmus even for troops, in return for a guarantee of neutrality in which we agreed to ask other nations to join. Now, with the change in the conditions of transportation, it was a question whether such treaties might not be more of a burden than an advantage. Fish wrote to Baxter, our representative in Honduras, May 12, 1871, "The guarantee to Honduras of neutrality of interoceanic communication does not imply that the United States is to maintain a police or other force in Honduras for the purpose of keeping petty trespassers from the railway."

Although we made numbers of commercial treaties during this period, we pressed the policy of reciprocity less con- Hawaiian reciprocity spicuously than heretofore. In the treaty of Washington the fisheries were dealt with on that basis, but in much more restricted form than in Marcy's treaty on the same subject. The treaty with the Hawaiian islands in 1875 was a conspicuous exception. This was the most thorough application of the principle into which we had ever entered. It was on the basis of entry customs free, and included practically all articles of exchange, the most important being Hawaiian-grown sugar. It amounted practically to a customs union, and represented not so much a general commercial policy as our growing conception that Hawaii was another of our special interests.

Although in the Pacific, Hawaii is for purposes of our policy to be regarded as connected with the American continents. With the further side of that ocean we continued to develop our diplomatic relations, although **Japan** with the passing of our merchant marine and the substitution of petroleum for whale oil, our material interests declined. With Japan we entered into a convention in 1864, fixing her duties on certain of our exports; but this agreement cannot be considered as an example of reciprocity, for we made no corresponding concessions. The most interesting point in our Japanese relations, however, was our apparently unconscious adoption of a new practice with regard to international relations. In America we refused to admit European interference; in Europe we refrained from interfering; in Asia we began to show a willingness actively to coöperate with European powers. In 1864 we took part with Great Britain, France, and the Netherlands in "chastising" Mori Daizen, feudatory prince of Najato and Suwo, who, in defiance of the Tycoon, closed the straits of Shimonoseki; and we united also in demanding compensation from the Tycoon, receiving our fourth share of the three million dollars that he paid. In 1866 we joined the same powers in exacting from Japan a revision of her tariff, the rates being fixed by the treaty. This regulation proved burdensome to Japan after the revolution and the establishment of the power of the Mikado, and in 1872 a Japanese embassy made a circular tour to secure its reconsideration, as well as that of the earlier treaties which excepted foreigners from the jurisdiction of the native courts and gave the various consuls judicial power over their respective citizens. Secretary Fish wrote, September 14, 1874, "The President is impressed with the importance of continued concert between the treaty powers in Japan, at least until after the revision of the treaties, and until the government of Japan shall have exhibited a degree of power and capacity to adopt and to enforce a system of jurisprudence and of judicial administration, in harmony with that of the Christian powers, equal to their evident desire to be relieved from the enforced duties of extraterritoriality."

With China our relations were particularly pleasant. Anson Burlingame, whom Lincoln sent as minister, was so highly regarded there that in 1868 he returned to the United States accredited Chinese minister to her and other western powers. Representing China, he concluded a treaty with us in 1868. This granted China the right to appoint consuls to reside in the United States, but without such extraterritorial powers as our consuls exercised in China. We agreed, in case China wished aid in internal improvements, to designate suitable engineers and to recommend other nations to do the same. The most important clause was that prohibiting the importation of coolies or forced emigrants. This precaution was called for by the bringing into this country of thousands of laborers who were practically slaves, many of whom were employed in the construction of the Pacific railroads. The prohibition is probably more to be connected with the attempt to stamp out the last remnants of slavery than with the feeling against Chinese labor. The latter sentiment, however, was daily growing stronger on the Pacific coast, and the Burlingame treaty was violently attacked because of its failure to deal with the broader question.[1]

By far the most important routine duty of diplomacy,

---

[1] M. R. Coolidge, *Chinese Immigration*, New York, 1909; G. F. Seward, *Chinese Immigration in its Social and Economical Aspects*, New York, 1881; F. W. Williams, *Anson Burlingame and the first Chinese Mission to Foreign Powers*, New York, 1912.

however, was that of establishing the international status of our naturalized citizens. Seward wrote, August 22, 1867, "The question is one which seems to have been ripening for very serious discussion when the breaking out of the Civil war in this country obliged us to forego every form of debate which was likely to produce hostility or even irritation abroad." The bill of 1868 providing for the defence of American citizens abroad declared that the "right of expatriation" was "a natural and inherent right of all people," and that naturalized citizens of the United States should receive the same protection as native citizens. It was obviously necessary for the administration to press our position upon the attention of foreign countries, and it was fortunate that the handling of this delicate problem fell to the historian George Bancroft, from 1867 to 1874 minister first to the several German states and then to the German empire. Educated in Germany and a scholar of repute, he possessed the kind of ability and distinction that particularly appealed to that nation. His relations with Bismarck were very friendly. Once kept waiting for an audience because the Turkish representative was granted precedence based on ambassadorial rank, he protested that our national importance gave us the right to equality of treatment in matters of business regardless of rank. He was never again kept waiting, although his claim to equality of treatment had no basis in diplomatic custom.[1]

In 1868 he obtained a treaty with the North German Union. The German governments acknowledged the right of their citizens to transfer their allegiance by five years' uninterrupted residence accompanied by naturalization. A subsequent residence of two years in Germany was to be

[1] M. A. D. Howe, *The Life and Letters of George Bancroft*, 2 vols., New York, 1908; J. S. Wise, *A Treatise on American Citizenship*, Northport, N. Y., 1906; F. G. Franklin, *The Legislative History of Naturalization*, Chicago, 1906.

held as a renunciation of United States citizenship, and naturalized citizens remained liable to punishment for acts committed before emigration. This treaty was rapidly followed by similar agreements with other German states, Baden, Bavaria, Hesse, and Württemburg, all in 1868. Treaties were made with Belgium and Mexico in the same year, with Sweden and Norway in 1869, with Austria in 1870, and with Ecuador in 1872.

Treaties with German states

Our agreement with Great Britain was almost as important as the one with Germany. The impressment problem was not likely to come up again, but the Fenians were giving the question of the international status of our British-born citizens every twist of which it seemed capable. The acts for which they were arrested in Great Britain were generally criminal, such as the dynamiting of public buildings, an offence for which our native citizens would have been equally punishable; but cases did arise in which the question of nationality was important. The Gladstone government rightly determined that the doctrine of indefeasible allegiance was inapplicable to existing world conditions, and evinced its willingness to take the question up. Most appropriately the American negotiator was Motley, Bancroft's professional colleague. In this case he successfully carried out the purpose of the government and in 1870 concluded a treaty more satisfactory than those with the German states, in that it contained no reference to punishment for offences previous to naturalization or to an automatic relapse of nationality after two years' residence in one's native land.

Treaty with Great Britain

These treaties provided for most of our naturalized citizens at the time, and the United States has since successfully insisted upon similar principles in the case of nearly all other countries from which she has recruited her population. Bancroft's treaty with Germany really marked the turning-point in the world's attitude towards the question of allegiance. Many details,

Questions unsettled

however, remained unsettled. The status of a foreigner who had declared his intention of becoming a citizen and had not completed his naturalization was anomalous. Many of our states, moreover, admit to the suffrage in less than five years. Questions have arisen as to the liability of a foreigner subject to military conscription who leaves home before reaching the age of service but does not become an American citizen until after passing that age. The question of the validity of naturalization papers has proved annoying, as they have been bought and sold for the protection they afford. One of the most trying problems has arisen from the undoubted right of any nation to exclude foreigners. This right we have not denied, but we have objected to discrimination between our naturalized and our natural citizens. In 1912 we denounced our treaty with Russia because of her discrimination against our citizens of the Jewish race.

Such questions have from 1868 to the present day taken up a large proportion of the time and attention of our state department and diplomatic service. No number of precedents seems able to prevent the development of new situations. In general **Present position of naturalized citizens** the government has insisted upon its sole right to determine the validity of its papers, but it is always willing to investigate cases brought to its attention. It has not conceded the right of foreign governments to punish our citizens for the act of emigration, but it has admitted that evasion of military service is a punishable act. It has not continued to extend its protection to naturalized citizens who are known to have taken up their permanent residence in their native countries. Upon the whole, these questions, though still handled by the diplomatic staff and liable at any time to cause an international rupture, may be said to have become matters of legal detail, their fundamental principles being well understood and generally accepted.

With all these matters of routine upon his mind, in addition to the pressing necessities of the Civil war and its results, and with a weather eye always directed to politics, Seward, most indefatigable of our secretaries of state, did not lose his vision of peaceful expansion.[1] One stroke of luck enabled him to confirm his prophecy of 1861 with regard to Russia's building on the Arctic the outposts of the United States. Our interest in Alaska was not new. Senator Gwin of California had brought up the question of its purchase in 1859, and the matter was talked over with the Russian minister. The latter did not express indignation at the suggestion, but thought that the five millions mentioned as a price was too small. After the war interest reappeared in the Pacific coast states, but was not sufficiently strong to set our machinery in motion. In fact, when in 1867 Russia offered Alaska to us, the general sentiment of the country viewed our acceptance of the proposition as a favor.[2]

Seward and expansion

Alaska

Seward, however, leaped to the opportunity, yet not so far as to lose his diplomatic address. Stoeckl, the Russian minister at Washington, suggested ten millions as a proper price, Seward five millions. Stoeckl proposed to split the difference, and Seward agreed if Stoeckl would knock off the odd half-million. Stoeckl finally said that he would do so if Seward would add two hundred thousand as special compensation to the Russian American Company, making the price seven million two hundred thousand. Elate, Seward roused Sumner from bed at midnight, and the three drew up the agreement between then and four o'clock. The treaty ceded all Russia's territory in America, and ran a boundary through Behring strait and sea, dividing the islands. It provided, as usual

Seward's activity

[1] T. C. Smith, "Expansion after the Civil War, 1865–1871," *Political Science Quarterly*, 1901, xvi. 412–436.

[2] H. H. Bancroft, *Alaska* (San Francisco, 1886), ch. xxviii.; see also O. Straus, *The American Spirit*, New York, 1913, and in *Providence Journal*, June 4, 1905.

that the civilized inhabitants were to become United States citizens, but said nothing of their incorporation into the Union.

To secure the acceptance of the treaty seemed to be more difficult than to make it. To this task Sumner devoted himself. He delivered a speech setting forth with learning and appreciation the possibilities of the territory, but his success was perhaps due less to his material arguments than to the general impression that we owed a favor to Russia, to an undercurrent of belief that this was our part of a secret bargain, as a result of which Russia had lent us her fleet in 1863. From this hazy impression two facts emerge; in the first place, there was no such bargain; in the second place, one fleet did actually come to New York and another to San Francisco with sealed instructions to put themselves at our service in case of intervention by Great Britain and France. While the czar probably was sympathetic with the North and saw with regret the disappearance of our merchant marine, it is doubtful whether his action was chiefly prompted by these considerations. Russia was in 1863 as much alarmed at the prospect of intervention by Great Britain, France, and Austria in her affairs as we were at the possibility that England and France might interfere in ours. The Poles were once more writhing under Russian rule and most of Europe was protesting at Russia's atrocities. When, therefore, in May, 1863, Seward refused an invitation from France to join the protest, his reply, based on the Monroe Doctrine, may well have excited the czar's gratitude. Moreover, the Russian fleets more probably came to our harbors for their own protection than for ours; that of the Pacific had no winter harbor in the East and dared not go home, that of the Atlantic, lying on the Spanish coast, dared not go through the English Channel, a fear analogous to that with which, in the late Japanese war, Russia's fleet passed so nervously through those unfriendly waters.

Russia and the United States

The legend of Russia's aid, however, was apparently the decisive factor in securing the acceptance of the treaty, and **Success of the** has afforded the main basis for a somewhat **treaty** curious friendship between the two nations ever since. When, in 1871, the grand duke Alexis visited this country, Oliver Wendell Holmes greeted him with the lines,

> "Bleak are our coasts with the blasts of December,
> Throbbing and warm are the hearts that remember,
> Who was our friend, when the world was our foe."

Seward also thought of securing the annexation of Hawaii, but his main interest was devoted to the Caribbean. The **Hawaii** National Democratic Convention in 1856 declared, "That the Democratic party will expect of the next administration that every proper effort be made to increase our ascendancy in the Gulf of Mexico and to **Gulf of Mexico** maintain permanent protection to the great outlets through which are emptied into its waters the products raised out of the soil and the commodities created by the industry of the people of our Western valleys and of the Union at large." It was true that, with Florida far flung to the south and untraversable, our Mississippi commerce must in time of war run the gauntlet, by one exit of five hundred miles threatened by Spanish Cuba and the British Bahamas and protected by our solitary and isolated port of Key West, or else must, by the other exit, pass Cuba and the British Jamaica, with no harbor of refuge. This danger was brought so vividly before the minds of those in authority by the exigencies of the Civil war, that at that time we actually leased the harbor of St. Nicholas from Hayti.

In January, 1865, Seward broached the question of purchasing from Denmark the island of St. Thomas, whose splendid harbor, just to the east of Porto Rico, would **Danish islands** secure us a convenient naval station for the protection of the eastern route. After much bargaining, a treaty was at length drawn up ceding both St. Thomas and St. Johns for seven and a half millions, subject to a popular vote by the inhabitants in favor of annexation, a condition upon which Denmark vigorously insisted in opposition to the views of Seward. After some contest a vote was taken which resulted in our favor. To the effort to get the treaty ratified, however, the same popular opposition was demonstrated that encountered the Alaska treaty, but in this case popular sentiment was not caught by Denmark, though she too had proved to be our friend in the war. The House voted that it would not appropriate the money, the Senate laid the treaty on the table, and when Grant came in he dismissed it as a "scheme of Seward's." [1]

Meantime, in 1867 George Bancroft was instructed to stop at Madrid, on his way to Berlin, to attempt the purchase of Culebra and Culebrita, islands in the same Spanish locality belonging to Spain; but as usual, islands that country would not entertain the proposal to sell her colonies.

A more important undertaking, however, was taking shape. In 1866 Admiral Porter was sent to inspect Samana Bay, in the Dominican republic, with reference to its Samana Bay use as a naval station. It was situated near the islands already considered, and proved to be in many ways ideal for the purpose. In February, 1868, a convention was drawn up with the Dominican government providing for a twelve years' lease, in return for a million in gold and a million currency in the form of arms. President Baez, who wanted the arms, was not uninclined to sell out the whole republic while his government still had a going value, and proposed annexation, to be carried into effect without the formality of a popular referendum. Seward, taking a different view of the latter question from that which he had assumed in the case of the Danish islands, demanded a popular vote; but it still seemed possible to bring the negotiation to a head in an acceptable form.

[1] James Parton, *The Danish Islands*, Boston, 1869.

President Johnson, who left Seward a very free hand in diplomacy, referred to the subject in his annual message of 1868: "Comprehensive national policy would seem to sanction the acquisition and incorporation into our Federal Union of the several adjacent continental and insular communities as speedily as it can be done peacefully, lawfully, and without any violation of national justice, faith, or honor. . . . I am satisfied that the time has arrived when even so direct a proceeding as a proposition for an annexation of the two Republics of the island of St. Domingo would not only receive the consent of the people interested, but would also give satisfaction to all other foreign nations." Seward took up the question with General Banks, chairman of the House committee on foreign affairs, and a resolution favoring it was introduced. A test vote, however, was defeated 110 to 63. In the summer of 1868 Seward wrote to our representative in Hawaii, "The public mind refuses to dismiss" domestic questions "even so far as to entertain the higher but more remote questions of national expansion and aggrandizement."

Proposal to annex San Domingo

Although Grant threw aside the Danish treaty, and his secretary, Fish, refused to entertain a proposition from the Swedish minister for the purchase of her West India islands, the San Domingo proposal took on a new lease of life with the new administration. Grant made it his particular policy; perhaps he felt safer with a scheme of Baez's than with one of Seward's. He proceeded like a cavalry officer on a raid. He sent as his secret and personal agent General Babcock, who speedily concluded a treaty. This document provided among other things that the United States should pay a million eight hundred thousand dollars, assume the national debt in return for the public lands, and protect the Dominican republic until a free expression of the public will could be given. This promise was made concrete by the fact that Babcock was accompanied by three men-of-war, instructed

Swedish islands

Grant and San Domingo

to protect the Dominican government, and "if Haytians attack the Dominicans with their ships, destroy or capture them." If one compares this policy of protection during the pendency of annexation with the cautious words of Calhoun in the case of Texas, one is reminded of the remark, "What is the constitution among friends?" But probably Grant himself did not even consider the constitution in this connection.

The agreement continued, the President "promises privately to use all his influence in order that the idea of annexing the Dominican Republic to the United *Defeat of Babcock treaty* States may acquire such a degree of popularity among members of congress as will be necessary for its accomplishment." Grant presented the treaty to the Senate, January 18, 1870, and by message and interviews faithfully carried out his word. Nevertheless, the treaty was rejected, June 30, by a tie vote.

Meanwhile President Baez had busied himself with floating a loan on the London market, which would be assumed by the United States in case of annexation. British *Renewal of the proposal* financial interests strongly favored annexation. In spite of the rejection of the treaty and the outbreak of domestic revolution, he assured his congress, "The measure will, nevertheless, succeed in the end, for it is a necessity in the progress of humanity, whose unseen agent is Providence itself." The seen agent in this case was Grant. He extended his protection for a year, and in his next message to Congress applied the lash of foreign intrigue. Should the treaty be ultimately refused, he said, "a free port will be negotiated for by European nations in the Bay of Samana. A large commercial city will spring up, to which we will be tributary without receiving corresponding benefits, and then will be seen the folly of our rejecting so great a prize." At last he secured from Congress authority to send a *San Domingo commission* commission to report on conditions, and, confident in the value of his proposal, appointed for the mission able and honorable men,—Benjamin F. Wade, Andrew D.

White, and Samuel S. Howe. They were accompanied by A. A. Burton and Frederick Douglass, who served as secretaries. The commission made a well-balanced and not unfavorable report, but the proposition was dead.

Fruitless as it proved in itself, the San Domingo question influenced many other things. Sumner reported it unfavorably from the Senate committee, and thereby earned Grant's enmity, a fact which largely accounted for the latter's willingness to depose him when he stood, next winter, in the way of the treaty of Washington. The debate, too, was the only exhaustive one on expansion between the Mexican and the Spanish wars. In a great speech in the Senate, January 11, 1871, Carl Schurz summed up the reasons that defeated, in this period, the dream of expansion which Seward and others had brought over from the last. He feared that this was but a step in a general campaign of expansion that would stretch us through the West Indies and Mexico to the isthmus. He feared the incorporation into the Union of these tropic territories, where self-government had never flourished, where free labor was never successful. Our true expansion had been westward, migration followed isothermal lines, and we now embraced the habitat suited to the nations from whom we had drawn and should continue to draw our people; San Domingo was not a proper home for them. He believed that the protection of a naval station so far away would raise more problems than it would solve. The irregularities of the President's conduct he condemned, foreign ambitions he scouted, and he made easy fun of "manifest destiny." He did not, however, call attention to a fact which undoubtedly had much to do with the popular sentiment against expansion, namely, that the movement had just before the war become so identified with southern interests that the North was suspicious of every such suggestion.[1]

Meanwhile, from 1868 to 1878 insurrection in Cuba the

[1] Schurz, *Speeches*, etc., ii. 71–122.

desired invited our attention. As Grant made San Domingo his specialty, so his secretary of state assumed direction of the Cuban question. Although Grant first ap-   Grant and pointed Elihu Washburne to this position, it   Fish was merely with the idea of honoring an old friend. After five days' service Washburne resigned and was promptly appointed minister to France, where he played a useful and distinguished part during the Franco-German war and the Commune. He was succeeded as secretary by Hamilton Fish, who outserved Grant three days. A less aggressive man than Seward, serving under a more interfering President than either Lincoln or Johnson, he achieved less and deserved no particular fame for originality. He was, however, trained, skilled, dignified, and wise. He played somewhat the same rôle with Grant that Marcy had with Pierce.[1]

The Cuban situation was particularly complicated by reason of the rapid change of governments in Spain,—the overthrow of Isabella in 1870, the formation   Cuban insur-
of a constitutional monarchy under Amedeo   rection
of Savoy in 1871, the proclamation of a republic in 1873, and the return of the Bourbons under Alfonso in 1874. In Cuba also the population was divided, the native "volunteers" fighting the insurrectionists even more bitterly than did the Spanish troops. Sympathy for the insurgents was keen in the United States, and the presence of native Cubans in our country and of American naturalized Cubans in the island led to constant agitation for us to take a hand in the conflict. To these considerations were added the traditional, though not then dominant, belief that Cuba was eventually destined to become part of the United States.

The three questions which we had to consider were neutrality, mediation, and intervention. On the first one our policy was to some extent dictated by our contemporary dispute with England. Criticizing her issuance of the bellig-

[1] F. E. Chadwick, *Relations of the United States and Spain—Diplomacy* (New York, 1909), chs. xiv–xix.

erency proclamation, Fish desired to restrain us from taking similar action, particularly as the insurgents possessed no

Belligerency

ports or marine. In this object he was successful, although the President and Congress were restive. Grant, it is said, had for a long time a proclamation ready to sign, in his desk. The fact that we did not recognize belligerency did not, however, relieve us of our neutral duties, which we vigorously performed, although we were not able entirely to prevent aid from this country reaching Cuba.

Mediation was offered by Fish in 1869, Marshal Prim having expressed his willingness to consent even to Cuban inde-

Mediation

pendence. The exigencies of Spanish politics, however rendered it impossible for her government to agree to any terms upon which we would act. In 1874, we made another offer, in which, a year later, we asked Great Britain, Germany, Prussia, Italy, and Austria to join. The United States "neither sought nor desired any physical force or pressure, but simply the moral influence of concurrence of opinion as to the protraction of the contest." Italy did act, but again there was no result.

Intervention by force we did not try, though Fish used the possibility of it as a goad to move Spain to activity in

Intervention

meeting our demands. Peaceably, however, we were constantly intervening. In the instructions to Caleb Cushing, who was sent to Spain in 1874,—the situation having at length convinced the government that we needed a minister of ability there,—Fish explained our Cuban policy and our special interest in the island. Commercially as well as geographically, he argued, it was more closely connected with us than with Spain; civil dissension there produced an effect on us second only to that produced in Spain; the local Spanish government was able to injure our citizens, but we could obtain reparation only by the slow and cumbrous method of applying to Spain. The United States had no desire for annexation; but "the desire for independence on the part of the Cubans" "is a natural and legitimate aspiration of theirs, because they are Americans, and while such independence is the manifest exigency of the political interests of the Cubans themselves, it is equally so that of the rest of America, including the United States."

With these special interests as a reason and the possibility of intervention as a motive force, we successfully insisted on maintaining a certain supervision of the con- Influence in test.   Partly at our instance, Spain finally Cuba adopted a system of gradual emancipation of slaves, a step which Buchanan had so feared she would take at the instance of Great Britain. Spain also promised us reform in local government, and modified her methods of conducting the war. In 1871 a convention was signed submitting to arbitration the claims of our citizens growing out of the hostilities in Cuba. Spain, however, would not admit her responsibility for losses by act of the insurgents, though we claimed that, since we had not recognized a state of war, her responsibility was complete.

In 1873 the seizure on the high seas of the *Virginius*, flying an American flag and with American papers, caused an outburst of popular indignation that seemed likely Virginius affair to drive us from our policy of watchful peace. The incident was rendered still more acute by the summary trial and condemnation to death of the crew. The fact that the Spanish government ordered a suspension of the sentences illustrated Fish's point with regard to the diplomatic inconvenience of the situation; for many executions took place before the reprieve was delivered in Cuba. Our attorney-general decided that the *Virginius* was improperly using our flag, and that she was engaged in filibustering contrary to our law, but that Spain had no right to seize her while flying our flag on the high seas, belligerency not being recognized. We demanded indemnity, the return of the *Virginius*, a salute to our flag, and the punishment of the officers guilty of the execution of the crew, an act "inhuman and in viola-

tion of the civilization of the age." Spain called attention
to the fact that in the case of *l'Amistad* our supreme court
had exercised the right of going behind the official papers
and examining the actual status of the vessel. On this point
we yielded, omitting our demand for a salute. Our other
conditions were accepted. In carrying them out, however,
Spain almost drove us into war. The trial of her officers
was not pressed, and the general responsible for the executions was promoted. On being returned, moreover, the
Virginius straightway sank, by the machinations, it was believed, of the Spanish officers in charge. The administra-
End of insur- tion, however, kept its hand on the situation,
rection and Grant in his annual message of December,
1875, announced that our relations with Spain were friendly.
General Martinez de Campos, the new governor-general of
Cuba, proved tactful and efficient, and the insurrection
gradually died out.

The diplomatic problems of the Civil war had practically
been solved by 1872, but the continuity of personnel and of
Significance of domestic conditions serve to give a unity to
the Civil war the whole period from 1861 to 1877. The most
important in our diplomatic history since independence, its
record was marked not so much by progress as by our success in outriding a storm. Our stake was not independence
but unity, and our success in preserving unity was not solely
and perhaps not mainly of domestic importance. Division
meant not only the severing of established ties, but increased
liability to quarrel. Peaceful acceptance of secession in 1861
would have been followed, not by perpetual peace between
North and South, but by perpetual imminence of war, un-
ceasing preparation for war, and ultimately not by one war
but by many. The freedom to expend all our resources upon
our own internal development would have been sacrificed,
and the military system of Europe would have been transferred to America. And not the system only. Our predominance in America once lost, there were abundant in-

dications that the powers of Europe would have extended the scope of their politics to our continents; foreign armies and navies would have been within striking distance. America would no longer have escaped that dualism of European politics, that tricky balance, in which every domestic concern of European royalty, every street broil in a European capital, becomes a makeweight which, if not instantly adjusted, may upset the whole. Our escape was due to a partly unconscious but wholly determined national will which employed our armies, our navies, and our statesmen for the purpose. Diplomacy was not our savior, but it performed its full duty, and those who shaped it deserve eternal gratitude.

Devoted primarily to this great task, the period was not barren of routine progress. The most notable advance lay in the defining of the relationships of our naturalized citizens to the countries of their birth; the most interesting new policy was that of international coöperation in the Pacific. Our various accepted policies were adjusted to meet the needs of the time, and current matters were kept well in hand. The continual agitation for expansion resulted in nothing but the addition of Alaska, and that was one of the most nearly accidental happenings of our history. The people were satisfied with their territory, and by 1877 the idea had developed that expansion was contrary to our national policy and our indisposition to expand had become almost a passion.

Progress, 1861 to 1877

CHAPTER XXVI

BAITING THE LION, 1877-1897

THE period between 1877 and 1897 marks the lowest point in the conduct of our diplomacy. The long and able services

Break in continuity

of Seward and Fish had given dignity and continuity to the period from 1861 to 1877, and their previous experience in public life had reduced to a minimum the deflection from policies previously developed. In the new period, administrations of short duration reversed each other and paid little attention to the past. There was some continuity between the policies of Evarts, secretary under Hayes from 1877 to 1881, and those of Blaine, who served under Garfield in 1881, though Evarts would not have admitted it. Frelinghuysen, coming in under Arthur in December, 1881, changed Blaine's policies, only to have his own reversed by Bayard, whom Cleveland appointed in 1885. Bayard was inclined to conform to the traditions of our history, but he was seriously hampered by Congress. Harrison brought in Blaine again in 1889, and the two united in discarding what their predecessors had done, but otherwise for the most part pulled different ways, until Blaine resigned in 1892, to be succeeded by John W. Foster, who was well equipped but served too short a time to make himself felt. In 1893 Cleveland and his party effectually checked what the Republicans had set in train.

Never before had diplomacy been so much at the mercy of politics. In the fifties the attempt was to arouse national

Politics and diplomacy

interest in general policies; in this period particular questions of diplomacy were thrown into the balance to turn a few votes. Particularly popular was the diversion of twisting the tail of the British lion, which animal proved to be peaceable, though not easily led by this method to any useful end.

During these years we did not put into office any really great diplomat. The secretaries of state were all exceptionally able men, but the position had become **Lack of great** primarily political. James G. Blaine seems to **diplomats** have had some genius for diplomacy, as well as a real purpose, but his superficiality was so much greater than that of Henry Clay, whom he imitated, that comparison is odious. His lack of knowledge of international law was conspicuous even in his own generation, and the influence of his splendid and magnetic personality which might have compensated for this defect was lost by the ineptness of his agents, some of them forced upon him and some for whom he was himself responsible.

The whole mechanics of diplomatic intercourse had been changed by the laying of the Atlantic cable in 1866. This was particularly true of our own service. **Effect of the** Owing to distance and the frequent difficulty **Atlantic cable** of communication, our representatives abroad had always enjoyed a remarkable degree of freedom and responsibility, which they had used to the uttermost, as is illustrated by the careers of John Jay and Soulé. As *Mr. Dooley* says of our ministers, they "led a free an' riochous life, declared war, punched Prime Ministers in th' ey', an' gin'rally misbehaved" themselves, "an' no wan at home cared. . . . Be the time they knew anything about it it was old news an'" they were "up to some other divilment. But now, how is it? Sure an Ambassador is about as vallyable as a tillyphone op'rator. He has to make connections an' if he listens or cuts in he's fired. He's a messenger an' a slow wan fr'm wan Government to another." With the concentration of business at the home department, the position of foreign representative became less attractive to able men with a future. They accepted it as a vacation or an honorable retirement, or because of the social ambition of their wives.

With the flooding of Europe by Americans of wealth, bent upon pleasure or social advancement, a chief occupation Social distrac- of the American ministers became the securing tion of introductions for their countrymen at the courts to which they were accredited. It was in general a thankless task, as the absence of fixed social rank in America left their selections for the honor to the caprices of their own choice; consequently every capital city became the fighting-ground of cliques of Americans for and against the embassy. Involved in society as they were, such offices could be used as stepping-stones to social position at home; hence they came to be sought by men of wealth, whose easiest method of securing them was by contribution to the party campaign funds. Cleveland's appointment to Italy, in 1893 of James J. Van Alen, who had given fifty thousand dollars to the Democratic fund, aroused such a storm of protest throughout the country, that he was barely confirmed by the Senate, and in decency was forced to decline the position. This was not the only case of the kind, however, nor the last.

The competition of the rich for these posts doubtless had something to do with the failure of Congress to raise the sal-
Rich and poor   aries to meet the increased cost of modern living, and it became almost impossible for a man without private resources to accept appointment. On the other hand, the éclat of some embassies did not prevent the exigencies of domestic politics from forcing the appointment of many men whose social training was as lacking and more obvious than their intellectual deficiencies.

There were always exceptions however,[1] and in particular the mission to Great Britain maintained its distinc-
Mission to   tion. With John Adams, Thomas Pinckney, Great Britain   John Jay, Rufus King, James Monroe, William Pinkney, John Quincy Adams, Richard Rush, Albert Gallatin, Martin Van Buren, Edward Everett, George Bancroft, James Buchanan, Charles Francis Adams, Reverdy

[1] A. D. White, *Autobiography*, 2 vols., New York, 1905.

Johnson, and John Lothrop Motley among its previous
holders, the line was continued by James Russell Lowell,
Edward J. Phelps, Robert Lincoln, and Thomas F. Bayard.
The loss of diplomatic responsibility was here more than made
up by the growing sense that the American minister in England was representative of one people to the other; and the
position was regarded as one of eminence.

While the importance of the diplomatic service was de-
clining, that of the consular service was increasing with the
change of trade conditions. Not only was inter- Commercial
national exchange assuming larger relative changes
proportions, but American trade was becoming less special-
ized. With the development of Argentina, our exports of
provisions encountered more active competition. In many
lines of manufacture, moreover, as in leather goods and
agricultural machinery, the supply was coming to exceed
the needs of the home market, and a foreign market was
demanded. The aid of the government was therefore once
more called in, as it had been in the early days of the republic,
to assist our commercial interests. This could be done in
part by national policy, and Blaine and Cleveland proposed,
the one reciprocity, the other free trade. Much of it, however, must be done by the collection and diffusion of information by our consuls, and by their activity in establishing
friendly relations with foreign business men.

Although the consular service had grown to cover almost
every port and shipping point of the world, its selection remained at the mercy of politics. With the Consular
adoption of civil service reform in 1883, efforts service
were made to extend the merit system to this branch; but
they were unsuccessful. On the whole, however, the results
were better than might have been expected. The lack of
special training and experience was not so important here
as in diplomatic positions, and the politicians who were appointed were by profession shrewd and apt at dealing with
men and clever at picking up information. Although they

did not particularly command the respect of the educated classes of other countries or of their own, and though some of them created difficulties that might not otherwise have occurred, they were on the whole efficient in promoting business.[1]

While no advances in the routine of diplomacy are to be looked for, developments already started continued to make progress. For one thing, the range of our ex-
Extradition tradition treaties was extended. The passage of an act by the Canadian Parliament in 1889, authorizing the government to surrender fugitives from justice even where no treaty existed, seemed to close that haven to our embezzlers. Although for certain reasons it failed to be put into operation for some time, it appears to have deterred many recreants from taking refuge there. With the toils of international agreement closing round them, criminal fugitives of all kinds continued to furnish much of the business of diplomacy.

The movement for the protection of trademarks continued, and many treaties were made on the subject. More
Trademarks important was our adhesion, in 1883, to a con-
and copyright vention for the International Protection of
Industrial Property, which covered patents, trademarks, and commercial names. In 1891 Congress at length authorized the President to enter into agreements regarding international copyright, which he could make valid by proclamation. This step was speedily followed up, and copyright has become practically universal in its extent.

We also joined, in 1886, in an international agreement for the protection of submarine cables, and in 1890 in an
International international union for the publication of cus-
coöperation toms tariffs. Our participation in the latter year in an international act for the suppression of the African slave trade has already been noticed. This tendency to enter freely into agreements with foreign countries on general subjects was a natural result of the improvement of communica-

[1] Consular reports have been published monthly since 1880.

tion and the increase of intercourse, conditions which made the necessity for mutual understanding greater and more apparent. It was in no wise in opposition to our fundamental doctrine of avoiding entangling alliances, though a certain sensitiveness developed by our isolation caused many Americans to feel that such communications might corrupt our manners.

First treaties we made only with Servia in 1881, with Corea in 1882, and with Egypt and the new Congo Free State in 1884. Claims we followed up with our ac- First treaties customed zeal. Our bag was not so large as and claims usual, and proved rather troublesome. It included numerous conventions with Hayti beginning in 1884, and with Venezuela beginning in 1885. In the case of Portugal, in 1891, we joined Great Britain in an arbitration fixing the compensation which Portugal should pay to each of us as a result of her taking possession of the Lourenço Marques railroad. The treaty with Ecuador in 1893 concerned only one claimant, an Ecuadorian naturalized in the United States. The convention with Chili in 1892, had almost cost a war before it was concluded. A mutual arbitration convention with France in 1880 recoiled, giving her a balance of over six hundred thousand dollars. Our several treaties with Spain, and one with Mexico in 1897, produced nothing during this period.

The standard question of the fisheries had seemed to be settled by the treaty of Washington, but circumstances worked against the permanency of this agree- Treaty of ment. The mackerel suddenly changed their Washington habits, deserting the Canadian waters for our fisheries own. In 1882 only one of our vessels took advantage of our privileges. The arbitrators under the clause of the treaty providing for special compensation to Great Britain, of whom the umpire was chosen by Austria, made their estimates on previous records and ordered us to pay five and a half million, or $458,333.33 per year, for our supposed advantage. Not unnaturally we did not care to renew this bargain when the fixed period of its duration expired.[1]

Congress ordered that notice of the termination of the agreement be given and in 1885 it came to an end. There-

Failure to renew reciprocity

upon the Canadian authorities began to make themselves disagreeable to our deep-sea fishers, who, although they did not need to fish within the three-mile limit, were obliged to use Canadian harbors. In 1886 the *David J. Adams* was seized for buying bait and ice, and other cases soon followed. The purpose of the Canadians was to force a renewal of reciprocity, which would allow free entry of their fish into the United States. Cleveland was desirous of treating on these terms. In fact, the American government had generally favored even more extensive reciprocity with Canada, and under Grant had endeavored to bring it about. In 1888 the administration submitted a treaty to the Senate on the old basis. American fishermen, however, were unwilling to admit equal competition, particularly as fishing bounties had been discontinued in 1866; and their representatives in the Senate succeeded in defeating the treaty. The fishermen's proposal for the payment of a lump sum by the nation, on the other hand, was opposed by the western interests, which felt that it was enough to pay a higher price for their dried cod without paying additionally in the way of taxes. Consequently no new treaty could be agreed upon, and for many years, the fishing industry rested on a *modus vivendi* agreed to in 1888 pending the acceptance of Cleveland's treaty. This temporary agreement was based on the principle of exacting a payment of a license fee of a dollar and a half per ton for those vessels whose owners wished the freedom of the Canadian harbors. This method of allowing those who used the privileges to pay for them worked satisfactorily, and under it the fishery flourished. With the introduction of steamers to supply the fleet, the industry became more self-sufficing,

[1] J. B. Henderson, *American Diplomatic Questions*, New York, etc., 1901.

till in 1898, out of 1427 New England schooners, only 79 took licenses.

While we were struggling for in-shore and harbor privileges on the east coast of America, we were assuming a very different position in the west. The first fruits of Alaska were seal skins. In 1870, in order The Alaska seals to regulate the industry and prevent the extermination of the seals, the sole right of killing was granted to the Alaska Commercial Company, which was limited to one hundred thousand a year. These were to be killed at the breeding grounds on the Pribilof islands, and were to be bachelor seals. The government royalties seemed destined to pay the purchase price of the islands.

The seals, however, had no appreciation of these provisions for their own safety. Once a year they took a cruise of many months into the Pacific, returning up Destruction of the seal herds the coast of British Columbia. When at home, moreover, they sported recklessly beyond the three-mile limit and the protection of the American flag, thus exposing themselves to the unregulated attack of adventurers from all the Pacific coasts, but particularly of Canadians. With dynamite, undistinguishing between bachelors and mothers of families, indiscriminately tearing up many of the valuable skins, they laid waste the herds.

The herds diminished; whether owing to the annual slaughter of one hundred thousand prospective fathers, or to the uncounted slaughter of whole families, became Assertion United States of claim to marine jurisdiction over Behring sea ultimately a burning issue between British and American scientists. In 1881 the collector of San Francisco, grieved at the prospect of the extermination of another native American race, propounded the theory that all of Behring sea, to the line of the treaty of 1867 dividing Russian territory from American, "is considered as comprized within waters of Alaska territory." In 1886 the United States revenue cutter *Corwin* seized three British vessels, which were later condemned by the United States District Court at Sitka for violating American waters. This action the secretary of state, Bayard, refused to sustain diplomatically, but seizures continued to be made. To meet the actual situation, Bayard wrote to France, Germany, Japan, Russia, and Great Britain, asking them to coöperate "for the better protection of the fur-seal fisheries in Behring Sea." Negotiations went on rapidly and a general agreement seemed probable, when, on May 16, 1888, Lord Salisbury, the British minister of foreign affairs, announced that the Canadian government had asked him to suspend action. As our Senate had rejected the northeastern fishery treaty on May 7, it seems reasonable to suppose that this was a counter stroke.

In March, 1889, Congress, largely through Blaine's influence, asserted that Behring sea was under the territorial jurisdiction of the United States. This asser-
Blaine's policy tion Blaine undertook to defend. It was opposed to the policy of free navigation of rivers and bays, which we had almost consistently pursued from the year of Independence, and ran counter to the general current of the world's opinion, which we had done much to set in motion. Both Great Britain and the United States had protested the czar's *ukase* of 1821, which had asserted territorial control of Behring sea and part of the northern Pacific. Our treaty of 1867 did indeed run a boundary line through the waters of that sea, but this division could not be held binding on other nations unless it could be shown that Russia had owned the sea. Blaine's argument was based on historical misinformation, questionable instances drawn from British practice, and the supposed good of humanity.

After a rather quarrelsome negotiation, a *modus vivendi* was arranged in January, 1891, forbidding all killing of
Arbitration seals, except seven thousand five hundred for the sustenance of the natives. February 29, 1892, an arbitration treaty was signed. The commission created was to take up the whole question, historical, legal,

and economic. If it decided that the United States had no exclusive right to the sea, we were to pay damages for the seizure of British vessels. In this case also the commission was to decide upon measures suitable for the preservation of the seals. The arbitration tribunal was a dignified body of seven members. It met at Paris, and the American case was presented by Edward J. Phelps, Frederic R. Coudert, and Henry Cabot Lodge.

The issue narrowed down to the meaning of "Pacific ocean" in the treaties of the United States and Great Britain with Russia in 1824 and 1825. Our claim that Behring sea was by nature *mare clausum* was given up. Stress was also laid upon the common-law protection for domestic animals when beyond their owner's land; but Lord Salisbury's argument that seals were *feræ naturæ*, and so *res nullius*, seems to have been nearer the fact. The decision was not unnaturally against us, and we finally, though reluctantly and not until 1898, paid about half a million dollars' damages. The protective regulations, providing for a closed season, no killing at sea within sixty miles of the Pribilof islands, no use of steamers or of explosives, and special licenses and flags for the vessels engaged, proved ineffective. Great Britain and the United States disagreed as to the changes necessary to make them so, and other nations were not bound by even the existing regulations. During this period, therefore, diplomacy failed to protect the seal herds. Our attempt to sacrifice a cherished principle to obtain this end had succeeded with regard to neither the end nor the principle. Although agreement had in 1888 halted because of the dispute concerning the fisheries on the opposite coast, it seems probable that the note of bombast introduced by Blaine, and the national antagonisms thus aroused, were the weightiest causes of final failure.

In 1878 Lieutenant Wyse received a concession from the government of Colombia, formerly New Granada, for a French company that desired to build an interoceanic canal across the isthmus of Panama. Ferdinand de Lesseps, director of the Suez canal, was put at the head of the new

French concession at Panama

company, and the scheme was launched with effusion. In 1879 a scientific congress was assembled at Paris to discuss the engineering problems involved, and the United States government was represented by two distinguished naval officers. Our interest in the canal problem, long dormant, suddenly revived, the most effective spur being De Lesseps's suggestion, in 1879, of a joint international guarantee of neutrality.[1]

March 8, 1880, President Hayes announced in a message to Congress: "The policy of this country is a canal under

Hayes's policy

American control. The United States cannot consent to the surrender of this control to any European power or to any combination of European powers. . . . An interoceanic canal across the American Isthmus will essentially change the geographical relations between the Atlantic and Pacific coasts of the United States. . . . It would be the great ocean thoroughfare between our Atlantic and our Pacific shores, and virtually a part of the coast line of the United States. . . . No other power would under similar circumstances fail to assert a rightful control over a work so closely and vitally affecting its interest and welfare." Evarts proposed to Colombia that all cessions be considered as subject to the treaty of 1846, and that we have the right to erect fortifications at the mouths of the canal.

This certainly had not hitherto been the policy of the United States, who has always asserted the general principle

Blaine's policy

of universal freedom of use, analogous to our idea of the freedom of international waters and of a joint international guarantee. It was, however, endorsed in 1880 by Congress, which based it on the Monroe Doctrine,

[1] Freeman Snow, *Treaties and Topics in American Diplomacy* (Boston, 1894), 337–347; T. J. Lawrence, *Essays on some Disputed Questions in Modern International Law* (Cambridge, Eng., 1884), Nos. ii–iii.

and was joyously taken up by Blaine in 1881. He announced to our representatives in Europe that it was "nothing more than the pronounced adherence of the United States to principles long since enunciated." Our guarantee, he maintained, needed no "reinforcement, or accession, or assent from any other power;" a pledge that during a war in which either the United States or Colombia was engaged hostile military forces should be permitted to pass through the canal was "no more admissible than on the railroad lines joining the Atlantic and Pacific shores of the United States"; we should object to any concert of European powers for guaranteeing the canal.

The last two positions at least were in direct contravention to the Clayton-Bulwer treaty, which seems to have escaped Blaine's attention. On November 1, however, he took it up. That treaty, he said, was more than thirty years old; it was for the special purpose of facilitating the construction of a canal which had never materialized; conditions had now changed with the development of our Pacific slope; by forbidding the fortification of the canal, we practically gave it to Great Britain, as she could control it with her fleet; the treaty was not consistent with "our right and long established claim to priority on the American continent;" the entrance of France had changed the situation; finally, we wished to fortify the canal, and, in company with the country in which it was located, to control it. Frelinghuysen, on becoming secretary, added that the English occupation of British Honduras constituted a violation of the treaty, and repeated that "a protectorate by European nations" would be a violation of the Monroe Doctrine, which we had declared "at the suggestion of the official representative of Great Britain."

It must have been a joy to the British foreign office to answer such dispatches as these, of which it received so many during this period. Lord Granville replied in a series of

notes. He pointed out that the Clayton-Bulwer treaty was
not a special contract, that it distinctly stated, indeed,
that its purpose was to declare a general policy.
British case for
the Clayton- The United States, he was able to show,
Bulwer treaty had specifically agreed that British Honduras
should not be considered a part of Central America. He
remarked that the Monroe Doctrine had not prevented the
formation of the treaty; and he might have added that
Canning, so far from urging its declaration, had immediately
upon its announcement set about to defeat it. He called
attention to the development of the Pacific slope in Canada
as well as in the United States, and in one note Lord Salisbury added that the building of the transcontinental railroads had actually decreased our special interest in the canal.
With regard to the age of the treaty, thirty years probably
seemed less in England than in America. Lord Granville
might also have referred to Seward's instructions to Adams
in 1866 when we were seeking a naval station at Tiger
island in Honduras, suggesting that, although the treaty
was really out of date, yet, so long as its binding force
"should remain a question, it would not comport with
good faith for either party to do anything which might
be deemed contrary" even "to its spirit." He might
have shown, too, that Fish in 1872, and Evarts in 1880,
had recognized its existence. The discussion closed without result.

Meanwhile we did not confine ourselves to argument.
We proposed to construct a rival canal on the Nicaraguan
route. In December, 1884, Frelinghuysen
Nicaragua
plan   negotiated a treaty with that country, providing
that such a canal be built under United States auspices and
practically under her control. This treaty was withdrawn
by Cleveland, who reverted to our traditional policy of a
canal internationally guaranteed, Such a highway, he said,
"must be for the world's benefit, a trust for mankind, to be
removed from the chance of domination by any single power,

nor become a point of invitation for hostilities or a prize for warlike ambitions."

Had Cleveland shared the desire of his Republican predecessors to find the Clayton-Bulwer treaty void, he might have attacked it during his second administra- The Mosquition on better grounds than Blaine found. toes
The irritating question of the Mosquitoes seemed to have been settled in 1860 by a treaty between Great Britain and Nicaragua. With the revival of interest in the mouth of the San Juan river, however, adventurers among the tribe began to scent the possibility of profit in emphasizing the semi-independence which that treaty, as interpreted by an arbitrating decision of the emperor of Austria in 1881, gave them. Nicaragua, unwilling to allow interference with the bargain which she seemed to be driving with the United States, asserted her authority, whereupon the Mosquitoes called in Great Britain, who answered the call. In spite of protests from the United States, British marines were landed at Bluefields in 1894. Complicated as were the legal arguments in the case, there seems to be no doubt that this interference on the part of Great Britain was in violation of the spirit of the treaty which she was trying to uphold. In fact the point was apparently appreciated by her government; the marines were withdrawn, and in 1895 the matter was temporarily settled, but not beyond the possibility of revival, by the submission of the Mosquitoes to Nicaragua.

The agitation over the canal question did not, during this period, accomplish any definite result. The canal was not built, the Clayton-Bulwer treaty remained, No progress and the United States had not even definitely changed its mind.

CHAPTER XXVII

BLAINE, OLNEY, AND THE MONROE DOCTRINE [1]

THE development of our policy toward Spanish America during this period was, to 1892, almost entirely the work of Blaine, whose handling of this subject was comprehensive and constructive. The negative influence of the Monroe Doctrine in preserving the territorial integrity and independence of the free nations of our continents had undoubtedly been great, but the hope of Adams and Clay for a sympathetic union with them, accompanied by a leadership on our part, had not been realized. Great Britain had won and held the import trade, her rivals being France, Spain, and to an increasing extent Germany. The United States actually lost ground between 1860 and 1880, although she consumed more and more Brazilian coffee. The immigration of Germans into Brazil and of Italians into Argentina was laying a more substantial basis for influence than any we possessed.

Intervention in America to 1880

The first part of Blaine's policy was developed under Garfield. He planned to have the United States assume the position of sole mediator in the disputes continually arising between the several American powers, and between them and European powers. On this subject we had not previously taken a definite stand. In 1851 we had joined with France and Great Britain in mediating between Hayti and the Dominican Republic; and sometimes our representatives had acted in a mediating capacity, but more often those of France or Great Britain had done so.

Mediation between Europe and America

Blaine's first opportunity appeared in the dispute between

[1] Latané, *Diplomatic Relations of the United States and Spanish America.*

384

France and Venezuela. The former country had claims against the latter, and proposed to seize the customs houses and collect the sum due, a proceeding by no means unusual. To prevent this desecration of American soil by French marines, Blaine vigorously urged Venezuela to acknowledge the French claim, and suggested that the money be paid to our agent at Caracas; if it were not paid within three months, he threatened, the United States herself would seize the customs houses and collect the money. This proposal to act as collecting agent came to nothing at the time, for Frelinghuysen did not continue the policy; as foreshadowing a course of action later much discussed and sometimes followed out, it is, however, important.[1]

With regard to disputes between American powers Blaine did not claim exclusive authority. June 25, 1881, he wrote to Fairchild, minister in Spain, protesting against the proposal to submit to Spain the arbitration of the boundary between Colombia and Costa Rica. He based his protest on the fact that, *Objection to European mediation between American powers* since in the treaty of 1846 we had guaranteed Panama to Colombia, we should have been consulted. In using this special ground, he obviously refrained from denying the right of Spanish-American states to ask European states to serve in such a capacity under ordinary circumstances or that of European states to accept the invitation.

He planned, however, to make such recourse unnecessary by having the United States serve as a permanent and impartial umpire. Already in 1880 Colombia and *United States as elder sister* Chili had agreed to make the president of the United States a permanent arbitrator between them. In 1881 the settlement of a dispute between Chili and Argentina is said to have been "due to the unremitting efforts of the representatives of the United States in both countries." In 1881 Mexico and Guatemala having a boundary dispute, the latter applied to us as the "natural protector of the

[1] Edward Stanwood, *James Gillespie Blaine*, Boston, etc., 1905.

Central American territory." Blaine offered to arbitrate.
He told Mexico that we were satisfied with our own territory
and that she should be content with what was justly hers;
that he should consider any hostile movement by Mexico
against Guatemala as "not in harmony with the friendly
relations existing between us, and injurious to the best interests of all the republics of this continent. This country,"
he declared, "will continue its policy of peace even if it cannot have the great aid which the coöperation of Mexico would
assure; and it will hope at no distant day to see such concord
and coöperation between all the nations of America as will
render war impossible."

His greatest chance came in the war raging between Chili
and Peru and Bolivia for the possession of the nitrate mines
situated near the junction of their national
boundaries. Evarts had already offered mediation and protested against European intervention. Blaine emphasized both points. He informed
France that the American republics were our younger sisters,
removed from the European system. To Chili and Peru he
sent messengers of peace. They were not, however, well
chosen, for each became the partisan of the country to which
he was sent. Blaine, deeply in earnest, at length sent a
competent man, William H. Trescott of South Carolina,
whose diplomatic experience dated back to 1852 and whose
skill and scholarship were everywhere acknowledged. He
was instructed to warn Chili against making excessive demands as a result of her victories, and to suggest that, if
she did, we would secure the coöperation of other American
powers to coerce her into reasonableness.

The Peru-
Bolivia-Chili
war

These instructions are to be taken in connection with
the second great principle upon which Blaine was acting,
that of Pan-Americanism. November 29, 1881,
he invited all the independent nations of
America to meet for a discussion of arbitration. They were
not, to be sure, to take up "exciting" questions, but were to

Pan-American
arbitration

inaugurate an era of peace in America for the future, and the emanation of their good will might serve to assuage present passions based on past lawlessness. This opportunity was lost. Frelinghuysen feared that this meeting of a "partial group of our friends" might offend Europe; accordingly, although many nations accepted the invitation, he indefinitely postponed the conference, and he discourteously recalled Trescott.

Blaine employed the leisure between his two terms of office in preparing the public mind to support his Pan-American plans on a basis even broader than he had suggested in 1881. In 1882 he wrote *The Foreign Policy of the Garfield Administration.* He secured the passage by Congress of an amendment to the consular bill of 1884, providing for a commission of three to obtain information as to the advisability of a Pan-American Congress. Charlatan and genius, he sought to recommend his plan of peace and coöperation in America by a persistent baiting of Europe. He fostered the dispute with Great Britain concerning the fisheries and Behring sea; he became discredited among the intellectual class at home as a jingo; and when he returned to office the Spanish minister of foreign affairs moved an increase in the West Indian fleet.

> Blaine's influence on Congress and public opinion

Nevertheless he made progress. Congress had already, in 1888, passed a bill calling a Pan-American Congress, which Cleveland allowed to become a law without his signature. It was to discuss not arbitration alone, but customs union, weights

> Call for first Pan-American Congress

and measures, copyright, trademarks and patents, communications, common coinage, and indeed anything that seemed suitable. Europe scoffed, and Spanish America was not enthusiastic. The president of Chili told his congress that he had accepted "out of polite regard for a friendly government." Señor Romero, the veteran Mexican minister at Washington, said that there was a general fear that its object was "to secure the political and commercial ascendency of the United States on this continent." [1]

The congress was well attended and ably managed by Blaine, who was elected its president. Nothing could be Meeting of the done on the subject of arbitration; but uniform Congress sanitary regulations were drawn up, the survey of an intercontinental railroad was arranged, the principle of the free navigation of international rivers was endorsed, and agreements, not quite universal, were made concerning trademarks, patents, and extradition. The formation of reciprocity treaties between the several nations was recommended. One thing of real importance was accomplished,—the foundation of the Bureau of the American Republics, located at Washington, supported jointly by the nations concerned, and charged with the collection of information. Actually permanent, its functions grew till it became a lasting, though not a strong, element of union.[2]

The vitality of the whole scheme rested on the development of commercial relations, a process that Blaine sought Reciprocity to stimulate by treaties of reciprocity. Such treaties had been authorized in 1884, and a few were drawn up under Arthur, but they were withdrawn by Cleveland. In 1890 the Republican majority in Congress was working over the McKinley tariff bill. In this document sugar, coffee, hides, and other such commodities, our most important assets for international customs bartering, were put on the free list. If the bill passed in this form, therefore, we should have no favors to offer American countries. Blaine threw himself into opposition. July 11, 1890, he wrote to Senator Frye, "There is not a section or a line in the entire bill that will open a market for another bushel of [American] wheat or another barrel of pork." His position was supported by western sentiment, and Senator Hale of Maine offered an

[1] Romero, M. "The Pan-American Conference," *North American Review,* 1890, cli. 354–367, 407–421.
[2] Bureau of the American Republics, *Bulletins,* 1891, etc.

amendment representing his views. His plan provided for a duty on the commodities in question, but empowered the President "to declare the ports of the United States free and open to all products of any nation of the American hemisphere upon which no export duties are imposed, whenever and so long as such nation shall admit to its ports, free of all" duties of whatsoever nature, certain enumerated products of the United States, or such other products as might be agreed upon. This amendment was not passed, but in substitution for it one proposed by Senator Aldrich was adopted, which left the enumerated articles on the free list, but authorized the President, when in his judgment the duties imposed on the agricultural and other products of the United States by nations producing the enumerated articles were "reciprocally unequal and unjust," to declare in force a prescribed list of duties.[1]

This rule, being applicable to all the world, deprived Blaine of his weapon for specially cementing together the nations of America. Nevertheless he went **Reciprocity in** to work actively to use it to open markets for **operation** American exports, and his efforts were continued by his successor, Foster, with the result that agreements were entered into with Brazil, Spain (for Cuba and Porto Rico), Austria, Nicaragua, Honduras, and with France for herself and her colonies. Colombia, Hayti, Venezuela, and Spain with reference to the Philippines, were informed that unless certain specified duties were removed by March 15, 1892, the President would enforce the duties provided by the act. In 1894, before it was possible to determine what effect this policy was to have on our trade, the Democratic Wilson tariff was enacted, and Cleveland's first secretary of state in his new term, Gresham, informed the countries concerned that the duration of these agreements depended on the duration of the act, and were therefore void.

[1] F. W. Taussig, "Reciprocity," *Quarterly Journal of Economics*, ii. 314–346 (1893), vii. 26–39.

The great tragedy of Blaine's ambition, however, resulted from the civil war in Chili. In that contest we had not taken part, but once more our minister had been ill selected to represent us at so critical a point. His name being Patrick Egan, he sympathized with the anti-English party, and was sufficiently demonstrative to have stirred up decided feeling among its victorious opponents. This feeling had been increased by our over strict interpretation of our neutral duties in seizing the *Itata*, a vessel carrying arms to the successful party. It happened that under these circumstances, on October 16, 1891, some sailors from our cruiser *Baltimore*, who went ashore at Valparaiso, were assaulted, one officer was killed, and seven seamen were wounded. Blaine and Harrison were both being talked of for the next Republican nomination. The latter insisted upon dealing with the matter with a high hand in order to win votes, particularly the Irish ones. Blaine could not be left behind, and a blustering policy was adopted, with primary reference to the effect that the episode would have at home. For a time war seemed imminent; diplomatic relations were suspended and an ultimatum dispatched. Chili grudgingly yielded, but the suspicions with which the Spanish-American states had regarded Blaine were confirmed, and the memory of his pleasing personality and eloquent appeals for kindliness and coöperation vanished.

Although Blaine seemed to make little impression on the solid opinion of his time, some of his policies have proved to be permanently American. The idea of United States control of the canal, which was not original with him but which he made his own, returned later, and apparently to stay. So, too, the conception of the United States as an intermediary between American and European nations is incorporated in our statute books in the case of San Domingo. He was among the first of our public men to observe the changing conditions of our commerce. That with this ability he should have combined the arts of the blatant hawker after votes, thereby uselessly aggravating the powers of Europe; that, with the splendid scope of his plan of international coöperation in America, he should in the eighties have imagined that the two hemispheres could be divided, not in political ideals as Adams in the twenties has said they were, but commercially, were evidences of a power of intuitive perception unaccompanied either by comprehensive knowledge or by a capacity for thinking things through.

Richard Olney, who formulated President Cleveland's conception of the Monroe Doctrine, was Blaine's opposite in every respect. Clear-cut and logical, he **The Venezuela question** thought his problem through to the bitter end, and did not have the imagination to see that the end was bitter. The occasion for the declaration of the Olney doctrine arose out of a dispute between Great Britain and Venezuela. It was a question of boundary, and ran back to the demarcation line of Alexander VI. More particularly, the situation was that the Spaniards had settled on the Orinoco, the Dutch on the Esequibo, without ever determining the line between them. In 1814 the Dutch had ceded western Guiana to the British, and a little later the Spanish settlements had declared their independence as Venezuela.

Both Great Britain and Venezuela had extended their claims to the uttermost, the former to the mouth of the Orinoco, the latter to the mouth of the Ese- **Rise of the controversy** quibo; from 1841 they had been at controversy. Of the two, Venezuela, fearing Great Britain, was the more anxious for a fixed line. In 1876 she appealed to us, as "the most powerful and oldest of the Republics of the new continent," to lend to the others our "powerful moral support in disputes with European nations." Evarts, Frelinghuysen, and Bayard all expressed their interest. Blaine was collecting material on the subject in 1881, and probably would have taken some action had he continued in office. In 1890 he instructed Lincoln to proffer our good offices and to suggest an informal conference of the three countries.

Meantime the question had become acute, owing to the discovery of gold in the region in dispute and the probabil- **Cleveland and Venezuela** ity of actual occupation. Cleveland therefore proposed to handle it with vigor. He referred to it in his message of 1894, expressing his hope for arbitration, and Congress recommended such action to both parties. England refused, as she had in the case of Lincoln's suggestion, to submit the whole question, but she would arbitrate within fixed limits. It was at this point that Secretary Gresham died and Olney took office. It was not, however, as a result of Gresham's death that the United States policy showed that sudden acceleration which became a nine days' wonder for the whole world; the change had already been determined upon by Cleveland. He believed that, in accordance with the non-colonization pronouncement of Monroe, the boundaries of foreign colonies in America had become fixed, that they were determinable by judicial process, and must be so determined lest in a contest between a strong European nation and a weak American one the line might be pushed back and the area of freedom curtailed. To insist upon such a judicial settlement was, he urged, our duty and privilege.

June 20, 1895, Olney sent his dispatch setting forth these views. To the more usual phrases of the Monroe Doctrine **The Olney doctrine** he added, "That distance and three thousand miles of intervening ocean make any permanent political union between a European and an American state unnatural and inexpedient will hardly be denied." Not content with thus proclaiming the ultimate extinction of European colonial possessions, he announced with reference to the present, "Today the United States is practically sovereign on this continent, and its fiat is law upon the subjects to which it confines its interposition." Great Britain, he declared, could not be considered as a South American power;

if she advanced her frontier, she would be acting contrary to the Monroe Doctrine. In order that we might know that no such extension was taking place, full arbitration was necessary. The President, he said, must be informed of her policy before the next meeting of Congress; "if he is disappointed in that hope" the result will be "calculated to greatly embarrass the future relations between this country and Great Britain."

Lord Salisbury in a long dispatch controverted these statements, and refused to admit the intervention of the United States between Great Britain and Vene-   Cleveland and zuela. In a special message of December 17,   Great Britain 1895, Cleveland dealt with the matter in a manner similar to that which Polk had made use of in connection with Oregon, but more vigorously. He recommended that we appoint a commission of our own to investigate the facts. If its report should show that Great Britain was extending her territory, nothing would remain but to accept the situation, to recognize its plain requirements, and to deal with it accordingly.

War spirit ran high, but it is only fair to President Cleveland to say that he was throughout probably conscious of the irresistible weight of the forces making for   The settle-peace between Great Britain and the United   ment States. He was not bluffing, for he was prepared to meet the call; but he did not expect to be called. Like Polk, he was "looking England in the eye." Venezuela prepared her case for the benefit of our commission, and Great Britain brought out a timely parliamentary Blue Book, which answered the same purpose. February 27, 1896, Sir Julian Pauncefote, who long and ably represented Great Britain at Washington, was empowered to discuss the question. In order to avoid yielding, Lord Salisbury suggested a general arbitration tribunal to adjust all questions between us; but this was refused. After a year of negotiation, February 2, 1897, an arbitration between Great Britain and Venezuela was arranged. Although to a degree Great Britain's action in treating of the matter with us constituted an acknowledgment of our special position on the continent, she did not formally recognize it, and she did not conclude without having forced a compromise,—namely, that the arbitrators were to act on the rule that adverse possession for fifty years should make good title, a limitation upon which she had long insisted. The tribunal met at Paris in 1899, and was distinguished by the presence of Ex-President Harrison as counsel for Venezuela. The result was largely favorable to Great Britain, but it gave Venezuela control of the mouth of the Orinoco. A dispute between Great Britain and Brazil concerning the southern boundary of Guiana was in 1901 submitted to arbitration without controversy.[1]

As an exposition of the Monroe Doctrine, Olney's dispatch pushed interpretation to an extreme. It was as much an extension of the original intention as was Blaine's. If Blaine could see nothing but America, Olney could see nothing but the United States. If his statement that colonies in America were but transitory was provocative to Europe, his assertion that the fiat of the United States was law upon this continent was equally provocative to other American powers. They could not grasp its consistency with Cleveland's statement that the Monroe Doctrine found "its recognition in those principles of international law which are based upon the theory that every nation shall have its rights protected and its just claims enforced." They considered our assertion of authority in connection with what they believed to be our designs. The really harmless statement of President Hayes, that an isthmian canal would be part of the coast line of the United States, they regarded as a threat to all countries

Blaine and Olney compared

[1] Henderson, *American Diplomatic Questions*, 411–443; Grover Cleveland, *Presidential Problems*, New York, 1904; Richard Olney, "International Isolation of the United States," *Atlantic Monthly*, 1898, lxxxi. 577–588; Hiram Bingham, *The Monroe Doctrine an Obsolete Shibboleth*, New Haven, 1913.

between us and it.   Our protection of Venezuela, therefore, failed to increase our popularity in America.   In this respect Olney seems to have been guilty of an ignorance which Blaine avoided.   His remark that "the states of America, South as well as North, by geographical proximity, by natural sympathy, by similarity of governmental constitutions, are friends and allies, commercially and politically, of the United States," could scarcely have compressed more errors into fewer words.   It contrasts with Blaine's effort to make precisely those hopes, facts.

CHAPTER XXVIII

GROWTH OF AMERICAN INFLUENCE IN THE PACIFIC

WHILE both political parties were doing their best to deepen the Atlantic, and the careless words of so many of our statesmen were preventing any diplomatic understanding with Spanish America, our influence in the Pacific, unbacked by policy and largely unnoticed, was rapidly extending. Foremost among the pioneers were the missionaries, who were carrying their ministrations to every coral isle and penetrating the vast bulk of China, to whose awakening they were ultimately to contribute so much. In China their ministry was distinctly recognized by the treaties of 1858 and 1868, and everywhere, as American citizens, they carried the protection of our name and extended the duties of our diplomacy. The whaler had become a less customary visitant in the Pacific, but the trade was not entirely dead. Regular commerce with the East was not relatively so important as in the first part of the century, but absolutely it was growing and demanded the constant attention of our state department and our representatives abroad.[1]

In Japan we took a benevolent interest. In returning to her in 1883 our portion of the Shimonoseki indemnity, we

American influence in the Pacific

[1] J. M. Callahan, *American Relations in the Pacific and the Far East, 1784–1900*, Johns Hopkins University, *Studies in Historical and Political Science*, 1901, xix. Nos. 1–3; J. W. Foster, *American Diplomacy in the Orient*, Boston, etc., 1903; W. E. Griffis, *America in the East, a Glance at our History, Prospects, Problems, and Duties in the Pacific Ocean*, New York, 1899; A. T. Mahan, *The Problem of Asia and its Effect upon International Policies*, Boston, 1900; A. R. Colquhoun, *The Mastery of the Pacific*, New York, etc., 1902; E. E. Sparks, *National Development, 1877–1885 (American Nation*, vol. xxiii.), chs. xiii–xiv. All these were written after the Spanish war.

performed an unusual act of international courtesy. With
Japan's desire for commercial autonomy we exhibited sympathy, which was checked, however, by our international convention of 1866, and by our suspicion as to her readiness for the judicial autonomy for which she was equally desirous. In 1878 we concluded a commercial treaty with her, surrendering our tariff rights; but, as it was not to go into effect until the other treaty powers had similarly surrendered theirs, it served merely as an expression of our good will. We finally left it for Great Britain to be the first absolutely to recognize the accomplished modernity of the empire in 1804, but we followed with a treaty of the same year. Our general relations continued to be of special friendliness.[1]

With China there was much the same spirit, but just as our territorial acquisitiveness, actual or suspected, has always prevented that sympathy for which we have hoped in America, so the vase of our friendship with the Far East began to show a flaw. As subjects for missionary effort, and as honest merchants with whom to deal, we respected the Chinese while we condescended to them. As competitive laborers in our country we both disliked and feared them. Concentrated as it was on the Pacific coast, this sentiment had the advantage of being the dominant political issue there. The electoral vote of California began to veer with the attitude of parties on this question, and by 1880 the Californian position became the embodied national will.

In 1879 Congress passed a bill excluding the Chinese, but, as this action was in contradiction to the Burlingame treaty, President Hayes vetoed it. To accomplish the same end by diplomacy he sent a special commission. Following the precedent of calling upon the best talent in the country to deal with such emergencies, instead of relying on our regular diplomatic staff, he selected

[1] W. E. Griffis, *Townsend Harris, First American Envoy in Japan*, Boston, etc., 1895.

President James B. Angell of the University of Michigan, and Trescott, with John F. Smith to represent California. They succeeded in obtaining a treaty permitting us to limit or suspend, though not absolutely to prohibit, the immigration of laborers. In accordance with this treaty we passed an exclusion act in 1882.

Successfully evading the law, however, the Chinese continued to come. More vigorous measures being necessary to carry out our purpose, we again nego-

Treaty of 1894 with China

tiated in 1888, and in spite of the failure of the treaty passed a new and more effective act in that year. Other laws followed, the most important being the Geary act of 1892, requiring the registration of all Chinese in this country. The question as to the return, after leaving the country, of those once resident here added to the diplomatic difficulty of the situation. At length in 1894 a new treaty was signed prohibiting by its own terms the immigration of Chinese laborers for ten years. "Officials, teachers, students, merchants, or travellers for curiosity or pleasure" were exempted, but they must carry certificates. This took the question through the period, but our success was not without the loss of some regard.

Our interest in the Pacific, however, was not confined to our relations with other nations resident upon it: we were becoming one of the most important resident nations ourselves. The definite acquisition of Oregon with Puget Sound in 1846, and of California with the bay of San Francisco in 1848, gave us the best commercial coast line on its western shores, and the annexation of Alaska in 1867 stretched a finger round toward Asia.[1]

Territorial expansion on the Pacific coast

From time to time the American flag was raised over a number of the Pacific islands. In 1812 Commodore Porter, cruising in the Pacific, named and annexed Madison island;

[1] F. H. Skrine, *The Expansion of Russia, 1815-1900*, Cambridge, Eng., 1903.

but name and flag alike soon vanished from it. Ephemeral national occupation was taken from time to time of guano islands. By a succession of United States laws The Pacific the President was authorized, after proper for- islands malities, to maintain these as national possessions while the guano was being extracted, but without incurring any obligation of perpetual possession. Although some of them were situated in the Caribbean and elsewhere, the majority were in the Pacific; in the eighties over fifty were reported as claimed by Americans in that ocean. The hold of the United States in such cases was not only temporary but slight; still conflicting claims of persons and nations, and complaints as to conditions on them, demanded constant attention by the department of state. The occupation of the appropriately named Midway island by the navy in 1867 has been held to have brought it permanently within our sovereignty.

More important was our connection with the inhabited islands, the first general interest being excited by the island kingdom of Samoa. This earthly paradise, Samoa which Stevenson has made the home of romance and faery, was the scene of diverting wars between the natives and of Gilbertian intrigues between the American, German, and English consuls. Like the "three kings of Chickeraboo," they smoked at Apia, the capital, and dreamed of circumventing their rivals. Three hundred foreigners, mostly of the beach-combing variety, divided the trade of the islands. That of the United States and Great Britain had ceased to grow, but the Deutsche Handels-und Plantagengesell-schaft für Südseeinseln zu Hamburg was extending its sales and taking in payment therefor land titles of the significance of which the natives had as little idea as the American Indians had had of theirs. The tendency, therefore, was for the American and English consuls to cooperate against the German.[1]

[1] R. L. Stevenson, *A Footnote to History: Eight Years of Trouble in Samoa,* New York, 1892.

In 1872 one of our naval officers secured an agreement with a local chieftain giving us harbor privileges. In 1875 a German agent named Steinberger obtained a commission of inquiry from the United States government, and with this as authority attempted to set up a government under our protection; but our consul secured his deportation. In 1878 we made a treaty with the kingdom. This gave us the right to use the harbor of Pagopago, in the island of Tutuila, as a naval station. We on our part agreed, "If, unhappily, any differences should have arisen, or shall hereafter arise, between the Samoan government and any other government in amity with the United States, the government of the latter will employ its good offices for the purpose of adjusting those differences upon a satisfactory and solid foundation." Although this pledge did not constitute a protectorate, it was from time to time so interpreted by our consuls. At any rate, it seems to have been somewhat of a departure from our tradition of avoiding entangling obligations.

Our first diplomatic relations with Samoa

In 1884 the German consul, on pretext of an agreement with King Malietoa, hoisted the German flag over the royal hut. In 1886 the American consul once more proclaimed our protectorate. Our government, being appealed to under the treaty of 1878, sent a commission to investigate, and in accordance with their report Bayard sought to come to an agreement with the German and British ministers at Washington. A conference was arranged, but failed to agree. Meantime a quarrel between King Malietoa and the German consul culminating opportunely at the time of the arrival of a German warship, the consul deposed and deported the king, and substituted for him another, Tamasese. Uprose at this point Mataafa, a native champion of island rights, and refused to recognize Tamasese. The German warship *Adler* bombarded Mataafa's villages, while the American consul, Sewall, steamed his launch between the *Adler* and the shore. Finally, De-

Approach of the crisis

cember 18, 1888, Mataafa surrounded a German landing party, and killed fifty of its members.

German public opinion demanded satisfaction and the vindication of German arms; American public sentiment, touched by the heroism of the Samoans, demanded that our government protect them; Great Britain, jealous of Germany as a new rival in the colonial field, stood with the United States. All three sent warships, and it was a possibility that any day might bring news that their animosities, stimulated by the tropic heat, had resulted in hostilities. On March 16, 1880, a hurricane descended on Apia, blowing bad feeling away before it. Every one, the sailors of the three nations as well as the natives, showed helpfulness and good feeling, and the air in Samoa cleared. *The crisis and the hurricane*

Meantime, in the real world Bayard and Bismarck were trying to reach a permanent solution of these troubles. Bayard, in accordance with American traditions, insisted that the basis of such a solution must be the authority of the natives; Bismarck could see no permanence for trade except in European control. At length, and after rather heated controversy, the Washington conference was revived in Berlin. The United States sent a commission headed by John A. Kasson, another veteran in diplomacy, who, like Trescott, was often called in for critical service. In 1889 there was concluded the General Act of Berlin, which recognized the independence of Samoa, but gave preponderance of authority to a chief justice and a president of the municipal council of Apia, to be chosen by the three powers, the United States, Great Britain, and Germany. *General Act of Berlin*

Trivial as was this affair, its significance as illustrating the interplay of old and new forces in American diplomacy is great. Some importance attaches to the appearance of a new bogy, the German empire. In 1871 that power was supposed to want Samana Bay; the first actual evidence of rivalry with us appeared in the Samoan affair, and other instances were to *Implications of the Samoan episode* arise. In this case, the real obstacle to agreement was the traditional American belief in the right of local self-government. Had we believed in the extension of the colonial system, division of the islands and compromise would have been easy. In the end, however, the United States, though she saved the form of independence for Samoa, was forced to consent to its violation in substance, thereby becoming herself involved in a very spider's web of entangling alliance. It was the third such international agreement into which we had entered. The first, the treaty of 1866 between Great Britain, France, Holland, Japan, and ourselves, was perhaps only an agreement by concert. It was, however, already proving troublesome, and would doubtless have entangled us seriously in the future had not rising Japan shaken it off. The second was an agreement concerning Morocco, entered into in 1880, including most European powers, and having to do with the protection of foreigners and their native protégés in that country. Apparently harmless in itself, it involved us, though not materially, in the great Algeciras conference that bid fair to plunge Europe into war in 1906. It is important to note that none of these agreements had to do with Europe or the Americas, and that two were concerned with the Pacific.[1]

Richest and most strategically important of the island groups of the Pacific was Hawaii, where we had possessed from the beginning the really predominant interest. As early as 1820 we had appointed an "agent . . . for commerce and seamen," and in the same year the first of our missionaries arrived there. The latter was particularly well received by the King Kamamaha, the Napoleon of the Pacific, who had consolidated the whole group of islands into a strong kingdom. The missionaries aided him in establishing a civilized government, reduced the language to writing, and codified the laws; their children became land-owners and sugar-planters, an

American interests in Hawaii

[1] Schurz, *Speeches*, etc., v. 1–10.

opulent and fascinating aristocracy, preserving their American ism of race and education. Our interests there were still further advanced by the establishment of reciprocity in 1875, and our commerce offered a substantial basis for a claim to priority.[1]

This we had put forth as early as 1842, when Webster said that the government of Hawaii should not be the object of interference by foreign powers. In 1843 *Diplomatic protection of Hawaii* a British naval officer made one of those unauthorized seizures of the islands which so often result in the permanent extension of British territory. Legaré instructed Everett to protest, and declared that, if Great Britain persisted, we might be justified even in using force, a warning which practically included Hawaii within the American continents and under the protection of the Monroe Doctrine. The British withdrew. An appearance of interest by France in 1851 led Fillmore to reiterate our views. Although Blaine, or some subordinate, forgot to invite her to the Pan-American Congress in 1889, it may be said to have been the American contention from the time of Webster that Hawaii was constructively and in the general sense American. Because of the priority of our interests, Bayard in 1888 refused to join with England and France in a joint guarantee of the government.

Our protection was several times asked, and while any such formal arrangement was refused, it was practically extended. Marcy and Seward were anxious for annexa- *Discussion of annexation* tion. Fish summed up the situation well in 1873: "There seems to be a strong desire on the part of many persons in the islands, representing large interests and great wealth, to become annexed to the United States. And while there are, as I have already said, many and influential

[1] W. F. Blackman, *The Making of Hawaii*, New York, etc., 1899; L. A. Thurston, *A Hand-book on the Annexation of Hawaii*, [St. Joseph, Mich., 1897]; M. H. Krout, *Hawaii and a Revolution*, New York, 1898; Liliuokalani, *Hawaii's Story by Hawaii's Queen*, Boston, 1898; Chalfant Robinson, *History of two Reciprocity Treaties*.

persons in this country who question the policy of any insular
acquisitions, perhaps even any extension of territorial limits,
there are also those of influence and of wise foresight who see
a future that must extend the jurisdiction and the limits of
this nation, and that will require a resting spot in the mid-
ocean, between the Pacific coast and the vast domains of
Asia, which are now opening to commerce and Christian
civilization." The feeling against expansion was too strong
to be overcome, however, especially since the advantage of
reciprocity made it seem unnecessary. Without annexation,
even the navy was provided for: by a Senate amendment to a
renewal of the reciprocity treaty in 1884, which was accepted
by the Hawaiian government, we were to have the exclusive,
right to use Pearl harbor as a coaling and repair station.

Nevertheless, Blaine in 1881 seriously considered annexation, for the bogy of foreign influence was appearing. In a
Blaine and confidential dispatch to our minister, Comly, he
Hawaii said that we must take the islands if the native
population continued to decline. "Throughout the continent, north and south," he wrote, "wherever a foothold
is found for American enterprize, it is quickly occupied, and
this spirit of adventure, which seeks its outlet in the mines of
South America and the railroads of Mexico, would not be
slow to avail itself of openings of assured and profitable enterprize even in mid-ocean."

Before Blaine came in again foreign influence had taken
on a definite form. The king had died, and had been suc-
British influ- ceeded by Queen Liliuokalani, who had married
ence in Hawaii a Scotchman, and whose successor, the crown
princess Kaiulani, was the daughter of an Englishman and
had been educated in England. Blaine appointed a personal
friend, J. L. Stevens, as minister. On February 8, 1892,
Stevens wrote: "At a future time, after the proposed treaty
shall be ratified, I shall give you a more elaborate statement
of facts and reasons why a 'new departure' by the United
States as to Hawaii is rapidly becoming a necessity, that a

protectorate is impracticable, and that *annexation must be the future remedy or else Great Britain will be furnished with circumstances and opportunity to get a hold on these islands which will cause* future serious embarrassment to the United States. At this time there seems to be no immediate prospect of its being safe to have the harbor of Honolulu left without an American vessel of war. Last week a British gunboat arrived here, and it is said will remain here for an indefinite period." Foster, succeeding Blaine, June 29, 1892, asked Stevens for two series of reports, one public and one confidential. On November 20, 1892, Stevens in one of the latter discussed the terms of annexation. Scenting a revolution, he asked how to use the United States naval force which had been sent to the harbor.

On January 14, 1893, the queen abolished the constitution drawn up and administered largely by the American element, and proclaimed a new one based on absolutism and native home rule. At 2 P. M., January 16, the American element organized a committee

Revolution and annexation

of safety; at 4:30 P. M. the United States forces landed at the request of Stevens. The next day a provisional government was organized and was at once recognized by Stevens; the queen surrendered under protest. Envoys of the new government were sent to the United States by the next steamer, and passage was refused to the envoy of the queen. February 14 a treaty of annexation was drawn up at Washington.

On March 9 President Cleveland withdrew this treaty from the consideration of the Senate and soon after sent a commissioner to investigate the facts of the revolt. The latter could not obtain evidence that Stevens was in collusion with the men who

Cleveland rejects annexation

held the very quiet meeting at 2 P. M., January 16, although the landing of our troops at 4:30 P. M., seemed to indicate his complicity. It was clear, however, that the only solid force behind the revolt was the presence of United States marines, and that the leaders had counted upon them. Moreover, although the only proper pretext for the landing of the seamen was the protection of American citizens and property, yet they were stationed in a portion of the city where there was nothing American to protect. Cleveland recalled Stevens, and December 19 requested the new government to restore the queen. This it refused to do; and even if the majority of the population preferred the native dynasty, their preference was not strong enough, at any rate, to drive them to serious revolt, nor did Cleveland venture to use force. The provisional government became permanent, waiting for a return of Republican control in the United States and a renewed opportunity for annexation.[1]

Even if Hawaii was theoretically part of the American continent, practically it was far out in the Pacific, and even Our position in 1897 if it was still independent, its government was as American as that of Texas between 1836 and 1845. With Alaska and Midway island in our possession, with Hawaii American, and Samoa under our joint control, we were by 1897 halfway across to Asia.

The period from 1877 to 1898 was one of flux. No strong current of popular interest or purpose was apparent, and 1877–1898 a period of flux the surface of diplomacy was choppy with the wind of circumstance, but some eddies in the stream indicated new conditions not fully understood. The most important development was that of our interests in the Pacific, a process which had gone on for the most part independently of diplomacy, but which must before many years involve diplomatic action. Similarly, the impending changes in our commercial position arising from the growth of an export trade in manufactures was sure to concern the diplomat sooner or later. Of more immediate moment was the oscillation of our opinions as to the status of the isthmian canal which had become an imminent possibility. Our interest in Spanish America was increasing; there were some signs of a more special interest in the Caribbean, but no one

[1] *Senate Reports*, 53 Cong. 2 sess., ii. No. 227.

felt certain what our policy there would be. In a general way, also, it was evident that international associations were becoming closer; but whether we should be a dog in the manger or a gracious participant, and whether participation would mean the abandonment of our policy of self-contained abstinence from European politics, no one could tell.

CHAPTER XXIX

THE SPANISH WAR

WHEN William McKinley became President in 1897, he shared with an overwhelming majority of Americans the

The war spirit

view that our destiny was peace and our inheritance complete. The fact that we had, without becoming involved in war, passed through a period when diplomatic leadership was vacillating when it was not weak, and when the virile manhood of the country had been trained to battle, seemed to assure the future. It is possible, however, that the spiritual impulse to war is strongest when the horrors of past struggles have had time to become blurred, when the veteran, respected and reminiscent, embroiders its glories and its satisfactions. Neither the war of 1812 nor the Spanish war was necessary. Those responsible for both justified themselves by referring to causes which had long been in existence. The development of the crisis in each case was in large measure due to the rise of a new spirit.

The pugnacity and nationalism of Blaine and Olney were due in part to an apprehension, in part to a reflection, of a

Demonstrations of patriotism

general militancy and a demonstrative patriotism. During the later eighties and nineties public schools began to teach respect for the flag, assemblies began to rise at the playing of the national anthem or to be chidden for not rising, the comic opera began to exhibit the national emblems and to be condemned for so doing. American history and military drill came to be commonly taught in schools and colleges. A new generation of historians dedicated themselves to the study of our past; patriotic societies awakened the popular interest in the deeds of their ancestors. In a material way this sentiment found expression in the regeneration of our navy, which, from its Civil war bulk and efficiency, had sunk to such a point that in 1891 the prospect of war with Chili caused not entirely unjustifiable panic on the Pacific coast.

The occasion that gave point to this national assertiveness was the outbreak of a new revolt against Spanish rule in Cuba. This began in 1895, and in character *Cuban insurrection* resembled the ten years' insurrection of 1868 to 1878. Cubans themselves were divided, hence the struggle took on the nature of a civil war. The Spanish troops and volunteers were able to drive the insurrectionists to the mountains; but these, running in a long ridge from one end of the island to the other, offered countless fastnesses for refuge and for use as posts from which to attack the plantations in the plains at their foot.[1]

Innumerable causes of friction between the United States and Spain were inherent in the situation. The Cubans planned to conduct the war from the United *American assistance* States as a base. Many Cubans of wealth resided in the United States, and that sympathy for revolution which has never failed among us promised assistance. A Cuban committee headed by the inspiring name of Ethan Allen raised the Cuban flag over its headquarters in New York. Cuban bonds were sold, and the press generally expressed its hope for the success of the movement. Irritating as all this was to Spain, she had no cause to complain unless words were transmuted into action. This Cleveland tried to prevent, by ordering our neutrality laws to be enforced. In spite, however, of an administration that seemed to be conscientiously rigid, aid did reach Cuba. The Spanish govern-

[1] Chadwick, *Relations of the United States and Spain, Diplomacy;* Louis Le Fur, *Etude sur la guerre hispano-américaine de 1898,* Paris, 1899; J. H. Latané, *America as a World Power 1897–1907.* (*American Nation,* vol. xxv.), chs. i.–iv; E. J. Benton, *International Law and Diplomacy of the Spanish-American War,* Baltimore, 1908; Achille Viallate, *Les préliminaires de la guerre hispano-américaine et l'annexation des Philippines par les Etats-Unis, Revue Historique,* 1903, lxxxii. 242–291.

ment asserted that its delay in quelling the insurrection was due to this assistance.

The causes for irritation on the part of the United States were numerous. American capital was invested in the American interests island, particularly in the tobacco industry, and was therefore subject to loss. Many of our citizens, particularly natives of Cuba naturalized in the United States, were residents and were doing business there, and these were continually in trouble. Official complaints and inquiries by our government include such subjects as the maltreatment of naturalized Americans, their irregular trial and condemnation for participation in the revolt, the destruction of American property, the expropriation of property of United States citizens for military use, the methods of dealing with American vessels thought to be running the blockade, the Spanish prohibition of the export of leaf tobacco to the injury of American interests, the withdrawal of Spanish protection from American plantations and other property, to say nothing of the harsh treatment of the correspondents of the American press recklessly seeking news in the dungeon's mouth.

The fact that Spain had not yet settled our claims arising out of the last war did not diminish our insistence. These Disputes between Spain and United States claims were actually paid in 1898, but we were at odds not only over Spanish delay but also over theory. Since we had recognized no state of war, we still held her responsible for the acts of the insurgents, such as the destruction of some property and the levy of assessments to secure the exemption of still more, a responsibility which Spain continued to deny, as she had done in 1871. This conflict of opinion was, however, less provocative of bad feeling than the annoyance to which we were constantly subjected in the delay caused by the necessity of dealing with every petty case through Madrid. Complaints came to our consul-general at Havana, from him went to Washington, and thence to Madrid; Madrid sought the facts from Havana, and on receiving them, if there were no controversy, sent its orders to Havana.

While such calls by the hundreds almost clogged our state department, the people did not confine their attention to the sufferings of our own citizens. The conduct of the war itself was the leading topic of their comment. *American sympathy* After Martinez de Campos had driven the insurgents from the fields but failed to dislodge them from the mountains, he was succeeded by General Weyler, the "Butcher," as he came to be known in America. He adopted two methods of subduing the rebels. One was that of the corral, a system of wire fences and blockhouses stretched across the island, and gradually pushed forward with the hope of penning the insurgents up in one end. The other method was that of starving them out by destroying everything eatable within their reach. To accomplish this object, Weyler caused the population of infected areas to be brought together in reconcentrado camps, and crops and granaries to be burned. This policy involved the virtual imprisonment of many American citizens and the giving over of their property to destruction. Executed with all the Spanish indifference to suffering, the prevailing lack of sanitary knowledge, and the inadequacy of Spain's financial resources, the reconcentrado camps became pest-holes filled with starving unfortunates.

The horror of the American public at these atrocities so near their own territory was inflamed, as the pressure of their opinion upon the government was constantly increased, by the attention which the *Influence of the press* press devoted to Cuban affairs. The boast of an important American journalist that it cost him three millions to bring on the war need not be taken seriously. In spite of the brilliancy of his sensational strokes, it was upon other papers than his that the solid elements which pushed Congress to action based their opinion. It was by no particular design that the press as a whole exploited the Cuban question; it was the question of the day upon which Americans wanted news. It was on the reports of such men as Consul-General Lee and Senator Proctor, and of reliable and known correspondents, that the effective majority formed its views. If, however, the American people had not possessed such an instrument as their press to circulate the opinions of Lee and Proctor, to ascertain the facts that they wished to know, their interest might have remained dormant and the war might not have occurred.

Cleveland, intent on peace, enforced neutrality, refused to recognize belligerency, but offered mediation and threatened **Development** intervention. Sherman, McKinley's secretary **of policy** of state, followed the example of Fish by asserting our right to oversee the conduct of the war. June 26, 1897, he wrote: "The inclusion of a thousand or more of our own citizens among the victims of this [the reconcentrado] policy, the wanton destruction of the legitimate investments of Americans to the amount of millions of dollars, and the stoppage of avenues of normal trade—all these give the President the right of specific remonstrance, but in the just fulfillment of his duty he cannot limit himself to these formal grounds of complaint. He is bound by the higher obligations of his representative office to protest against the uncivilized and inhuman conduct of the campaign in the Island of Cuba. He conceives that he has a right to demand that a war, conducted almost within sight of our shores and grievously affecting American citizens and their interests throughout the length and breadth of the land, shall at least be conducted according to the military codes of civilization." In a later dispatch he called attention to the fact that conditions in the camps imperilled our own health. On July 16 he wrote to Woodford, our minister in Spain, that public opinion strongly demanded recognition, and that beyond recognition lay intervention. He asked whether Spain could offer a solution.

The death of the Spanish prime minister, the conservative

Canovas, in the following fall, and the appointment of the
liberal Sagasta, seemed to promise alleviation. In November,
Spain promised to break up the reconcentrado   Change of
camps; the queen regent issued decrees for the   Spanish policy
establishment of legislative autonomy in Cuba and substituting Blanco for Weyler; and on December 6, McKinley
told Congress that we must allow time enough to determine
the success of the new system. Our government, however,
more and more earnestly urged upon Spain that the struggle
in Cuba could not be indefinitely prolonged without necessity
for action on our part; and in March it began to grow restive.

During this watchful pause in the development of our
policy two episodes inflamed the public mind. Dupuy de
Lôme, the Spanish minister at Washington, in   De Lôme epi-
a private letter to a Madrid editor visiting   sode
Havana, characterized McKinley as a vacillating and time-
serving politician. This letter fell into the hands of the
American press. On the same day on which it was published,
February 9, 1898, Woodford was instructed to demand his
recall. De Lôme, upon seeing the facsimile of his letter in a
newspaper, cabled his resignation. It was accepted, and
he thus escaped the punishment he should have received.
Although our state department expressed satisfaction, it
would have been more conducive to peace had he been recalled.

On January 24, 1898, we expressed our intention of sending a warship on a friendly visit to Havana, the *Maine* was
sent, and on February 15, in Havana harbor,   The blowing
an explosion utterly wrecked the ship and   up of the
killed 266 of the crew, besides wounding 60.   Maine
A large portion of the American public at once attributed
this catastrophe to the action of Spain, the more conservative laid it to the individual action of Spanish officers. T. B.
Reed, speaker of the House of Representatives and an opponent of war, suggested, but not openly, that the insurgents
blew up the vessel in order to bring on war. Spain naturally

urged internal combustion as the cause. Among these conflicting theories, that of Spanish responsibility was the most general in the United States, and "Remember the Maine" became a popular call to action. Responding to the new impulse, Congress could no longer be held in check. March 9 J. G. Cannon introduced a bill granting fifty million to the President for war preparations; and still more definite action was inevitable unless it were prevented by some decided change in the situation.

The administration exerted itself to change the situation. In the age and infirmity of Secretary Sherman, the manage-
Last effort for ment of the negotiation at Washington was
peace undertaken by the assistant secretary of state, President McKinley's close friend, William R. Day. The cable was kept hot with messages between him and Woodford, who was in constant touch with the Spanish administration. The latter did not want war any more than we did, but feared humiliation. It regarded Cuba as already lost, but it must save its face with the Spanish public.

March 27, 1895, Day enumerated our demands to Woodford: anmesty until October 1, during which negotiations
United States should be conducted through the President of
demands the United States; immediate abolition of the reconcentrado policy, and admission, which had heretofore been refused, of relief from the United States for the suffering; should the negotiations prove unsuccessful, the President was to act as arbiter. The demand for facilities to examine the *Maine* in order to ascertain the cause of the explosion had already been made. Under these terms the Spanish government writhed, fearing to yield completely, and yet realizing the necessity of yielding in substance. March 31 it abrogated the reconcentrado system in the western provinces and offered to refer the question of the *Maine* to arbitration. April 3, Woodford cabled that, should the President ask the Pope to intervene, the latter's suggestion for an immediate amnesty would be accepted. Spain would also, he

intimated, feel less humiliated in yielding, if we withdrew our fleet now in Cuban waters. "I can get the peace that you have worked so hard for," he protested. Day replied, "Would the peace you are so confident of securing mean the independence of Cuba? The President cannot hold his message longer than Tuesday."

On April 5 Day was informed that the reconcentrado policy was abolished over the entire island, and Woodford cabled asking if an amnesty by the queen regent, dated April 6, and prefaced, "at the request of the Holy Father, and in sincere hope and belief that during this suspension permanent and honorable peace may be obtained," would be sufficient. "Please read this," he added, "in the light of all my previous telegrams and letters. I believe that this means peace, which the sober judgment of our people will approve long before next November, and which must be approved at the bar of final history." Day said that the President would lay the whole matter before Congress. On April 6 a joint note of the powers was presented, appealing "to the feelings of humanity and moderation of the President and of the American people." A similar note was presented to Spain, and at length, on April 9, an amnesty based on this appeal was granted and negotiation with the insurgents authorized. On April 10 Woodford cabled that the negotiation would result in autonomy, independence, or cession to us, according to our wishes.

Spain's hesitating acceptance

By this time, so far as our government knew, there remained no American citizen in a Cuban prison, the reconcentrado policy had been stopped, American relief had been admitted, most questions arising in Cuba could be settled directly through our consul at Havana, Fitzhugh Lee, arbitration on the *Maine* controversy had been offered, and amnesty had been granted. In two respects our terms had not been exactly met, that the negotiation during the amnesty be conducted officially through the President, and that the President be arbi-

The diplomatic status, April 10, 1898

ter if the negotiation failed. Our minister, however, assured the government that its decision would govern the result. This solution McKinley seems to have been content to accept; yet it may be well questioned how valuable was the assurance of a government that dared not announce its decision to its own people. Spanish public opinion was as excited as our own. The less educated believed that war would be successful; and many of those who realized that it would not, preferred war to the revolution which they feared if the crown should yield to the United States. However sincere the government of Sagasta, there was no guarantee that Sagasta could remain in office. Under these circumstances the President would not have been justified in resisting the sentiment of Congress that war was necessary.

On April 11 he sent in his message, already delayed a few days in order to allow Americans to leave Cuba and to permit **McKinley and** the completion of war preparations. He **Congress** recommended forcible intervention, but recognition of neither belligerency nor independence; whereupon Congress, entirely out of hand, adopted joint resolutions, on April 17, calling upon Spain to withdraw from Cuba and authorizing the President to use our forces to compel her to do so. It was further resolved that the United States did not desire Cuba, and "that the people of the island of Cuba are and of right ought to be free and independent." In this last resolution vanished, apparently forever, the cherished hope and frequently expressed conviction of our statesmen from Jefferson to the Civil war, that Cuba must inevitably become part of the United States.

Since neither Spain nor the United States had adhered to the Declaration of Paris, they were free to practice privateering. On April 26, 1898, however, the **Rules of war** President of his own initiative proclaimed the principles of that declaration, and on May 7 a proclamation of the queen regent announced that practically the same rules would be observed by Spain.

The administration had already determined, in the event of war, to attack the Spanish empire not only in Cuba but also at its other extremity, the Philippines. Those far-away islands had appeared in our diplomacy The Philippines as early as 1786, when Rufus King suggested that trade concessions there might be obtained from Spain in part payment for Jay's proposed surrender of the navigation of the Mississippi for a term of years.[1] Historically they might have been supposed to fall under the wing of the Monroe Doctrine, for the Spaniards regarded them as part of the western hemisphere; in fact it was the supposition that they fell within the continuance of Alexander VI's demarcation line that gave Spain her first title to them. Actually, moreover, their connection with Europe had been westward until the independence of Spanish America barred the way. But it is not probable that such considerations as these influenced young Captain Dewey when, at the time of the *Virginius* affair, he proposed, in case war should break out, to take the vessel which he was commanding on the west coast of Mexico across the Pacific and attack Manila.[2] To him it was merely that Manila was a vulnerable point; and it was probably the same reason that moved the administration in 1898 to order Commodore Dewey and his fleet to attack that port. It is also to be observed that for a belligerent American fleet in Asia there were but three alternatives,—to return home, to be interned in a neutral port, or to occupy an enemy's harbor. Moreover, it was doubtless felt that a natural result of peace might be the concession to us of a harbor of our own in the East, which would prevent the recurrence of a similar situation. On May 1, by the battle of Manila Bay, Dewey made good his position in the best harbor of the archipelago.

The war having gone against her, Spain, on July 22, 1898, through the French ambassador Cambon, made the first

---

[1] King to Gerry, June 4, 1786, Mass. Hist. Soc., *Proceedings*, 1866, pp. 9–12.
[2] George Dewey, *Autobiography*, New York, 1913.

approach for peace. On July 30 Day replied, stating our general terms; Spain was to relinquish all her claim to Cuba and immediately to withdraw; she was to grant us as indemnity all her remaining West India islands and a selected island in the Ladrone group, in the mid-Pacific; "the United States," he declared, "will occupy and hold the city, bay, and harbor of Manila, pending the conclusion of a treaty of peace which shall determine the control, disposition, and government of the Philippines." These terms Spain accepted, August 7, with the statement that she did not *ipso facto* relinquish the Philippines; and on August 12 a protocol of agreement was signed.

Opening of peace negotiations

The treaty of peace was to be drawn at Paris. The President appointed as president of the commission Day, who had succeeded Sherman as secretary of state on April 26, and who on September 16 resigned that post to undertake this new service. With him were senators Davis, Frye, and Gray, and Whitelaw Reid. The commission was conspicuously fortunate in having as its secretary the publicist John Bassett Moore, who had been connected with the state department from 1885 to 1891, thus overlapping the long tenure of Hunter, and who had just now been serving as assistant secretary of state. The Spanish commissioner least unknown to America was Don Eugenio Montero Ríos.

The peace commission

The negotiations from our point of view were the simplest in which we had ever been engaged, for we stood in a position to demand what we wanted. The trouble was, we were not entirely certain what we did want. The Spanish delegates were particularly disturbed over the debt secured by Cuban revenues. The other Spanish-American States had, on receiving recognition from Spain, assumed their debts; but, as this one had been incurred in the effort to subdue Cuba rather than in an attempt to improve her condition, our commissioners would not consent that the new island government should be saddled with it. The United States, never

avaricious of money from a defeated enemy, released Spain
from all claims resulting from the insurrection, and agreed to
adjudge and pay them herself. It is interesting to note that
the domestic commission appointed for their settlement
adopted the Spanish contention that Spain was not responsible for the acts of the insurgents and that "concentration and
devastation are legitimate war measures." On one point we
yielded to the desires of Spain. She was unwilling, on
abandoning Cuba, to deliver it to the insurgents, a sense of
honor and prudence combining to urge her to this position.
We therefore agreed to receive the island in trust. The island
which we selected in the Ladrone group, Guam, was ceded
to us.

By far the chief feature of the negotiation, however, was
the disposition of the Philippines. McKinley stated in
August: "I do not want any ambiguity to be   Status of the
allowed to remain on this point. The negotia-   Philippines
tors of both countries are the ones who shall resolve upon the
permanent advantages which we shall ask in the archipelago,
and decide upon the intervention, disposition, and government of the Philippines." On October 31 the American
commissioners formally suggested the cession of the whole
group to the United States. Apparently the chief evidence
before the commission to lead to this decision was the report
of General Merritt, who brought directly from Manila the
views of Admiral Dewey. He pointed out that we wanted
one of the islands as a coaling station, and that what we left
some other nation, stronger than Spain, would take. He
felt that the actual situation in the islands was bad, and that
in some way we were responsible for its cure.

The foreign bogy in this case was Germany. It is quite
possible that Germany, on the lookout for colonies, had
before our war considered the acquisition of the   Minor points
islands. The action of her Pacific fleet during
our occupation of Manila harbor was calculated to excite such
suspicion, and, her prompt purchase, in 1899, of everything

that we left to Spain in that ocean is further evidence of her desires. As the Philippines were not in America, our non-transfer corollary of the Monroe Doctrine did not apply to them; but it was obvious that the value of a naval station there would be much diminished if surrounded by the possessions of a strong naval power like Germany.

That the question of the disposition of the islands was not more complicated was due to Admiral Dewey's knowledge of Conditions in the islands international law and his tact. He found an insurrection going on there similar to that which we had found in Cuba; but, while maintaining friendly relations with the insurrectionists and coöperating with them, he refrained from recognition. It was evident that, should the forces of Spain be withdrawn, widespread murder and destruction of property would take place; on the other hand, should we leave the islands in the hands of Spain, we would leave civil war, and would abandon the islanders, who under their leader Aguinaldo had been coöperating with us. The suggestion of Carl Schurz, that we turn the islands over to Belgium or Holland, was hardly within the cognizance of practical international politics, if indeed it was consistent with international morality. It was this situation which seemed to Admiral Dewey to involve us in some responsibility.

It can hardly be that a question of this magnitude was left to the commissioners, particularly under a President so American public opinion notably characterized by keeping his ear to the ground as was McKinley. It is impossible to believe that the decision was not made at Washington, and in accordance with the pressure of what the administration believed to be public opinion. When Dewey won the battle of Manila Bay, the idea of expansion so far afield was novel to the great majority of Americans. As the sentiment for "all Mexico" developed during our war with that country, so an expansionist feeling developed in the United States during the summer and fall of 1898. Engendered by the reasons already given, it received direction from two forces particularly powerful at the White House—the influence of capital seeking new fields for exploitation, and the enthusiasm of the missionary element filled with the idea of the good that we might do there. With many to whom the diffusion of Christianity by the organized work of religious bodies was not a leading purpose, a general belief in the civilizing function of our race, just then set forth in Kipling's *White Man's Burden*, was a deciding consideration.[1]

The Spanish commissioners were forced to accept the American proposition, sugared as it was by the payment of twenty millions. The annexation of territory not a part of the American continents, thickly populated by a foreign race, and not likely ever to become predominantly American constituted in each particular a departure from our previous policy. The last two differences the Philippines shared with Porto Rico, included in the same treaty.[2] An additional divergence was made in the provision that the civil rights and political status of the inhabitants "of the territories hereby ceded to the United States shall be determined by the Congress." Their religious freedom only was secured by the treaty. In all previous annexations provision had been made for incorporation into the United States, except in case of Alaska, and there all except the native Indians were to have the rights of citizens of the United States.[3] For the first time we were acquiring colonies. What

Terms of the treaty

[1] Herbert Croly, *M. A. Hanna* (New York, 1912), 279–280, attributes much influence to Senator Orville Platt.

[2] Whitelaw Reid, *Problems of Expansion*, New York, 1912; H. von Holst, *The Annexation of our Spanish Conquests*, Chicago, 1898.

[3] The Russian treaty provided: "The inhabitants of the ceded territory . . . with the exception of uncivilized native tribes, shall be admitted to the enjoyment of all the rights . . . of citizens of the United States." The Spanish treaty declared of native Spaniards that, if they did not assert their Spanish citizenship, they should be considered "to have adopted the nationality" of the territory in which they might reside; and it added,

the Federalists had contended for in the Louisiana debate was now the national policy. The treaty was signed on December 10, 1898.

"The civil rights and political status of the native inhabitants of the territories hereby ceded to the United States shall be determined by the Congress."

CHAPTER XXX

IMPERIALISM AND GREAT BRITAIN

THE Spanish war brought to light, and accelerated in progress, a spirit which may properly be called imperialism. That democratic regard for simplicity which had prevented the appointment of foreign representatives of the highest official rank yielded, in 1893, to the appointment of ambassadors, though not so far as to provide for their maintenance on an equality with those of other nations. The attempt to give a similar titular precedence to our naval officers, who often perform semi-diplomatic functions, made slower progress; Dewey, as a special reward, was made admiral (1899), and the grade of vice-admiral has just (1915) been created. After the war, moreover, the regular army was increased to double its previous size. Although this enlargement had special reference to the occupation of the Philippines, the steady and very much greater increase of the navy has been based on more general grounds.

This spirit was voiced by Rear-admiral Alfred Thayer Mahan, and by Theodore Roosevelt. Both trained historians, and with a wide knowledge of other peoples and of world politics, they were able to avoid many of the errors and inconsistencies which had marred the programs of Blaine and Olney. Mahan in a series of studies of naval history published between 1883 and 1913, pointed out the importance of sea power in the world's history, its relations to the future of the United States, and the necessity of our maintaining a large navy and securing strategic bases for naval operations. He tried to bring public sentiment to a realization of the fact that the United

423

States could not safely remain forever aloof, and that it should not confide too trustingly in the hope for universal peace. His books received even more attention abroad than at home, and belong as much to the international literature of the discussion of peace and war, which now began to divide the world of thought, as to the literature of American history. These views were shared by Roosevelt, who from his return from Cuba at the close of the Spanish war for a dozen years rode a wave of popularity whose crest seemed ever to mount higher. As President from 1901 to 1909, he was able to give them effect. The navy, whose record against Spain had made a profound impression on international opinion, was increased until it eventually ranked just after those of Great Britain and Germany; its efficiency was tested and at the same time thrust upon the attention of the world by its circumnavigation of the globe by order of the President in 1907. The impression which this latter event made whether at home or abroad, was scarcely so great as that created by the brilliant and dashing personality of President Roosevelt himself. It seemed evident that a nation so equipped and so led, and that of its own choice, would play a larger part in world movements than the United States had done in the past.

The war probably had no effect on the fact or the form of Hawaiian annexation. McKinley, to be sure, shortly after his inauguration, conveyed to Carl Schurz the impression that the subject would not be pressed;[1] but those best informed realized that the return of the Republican party meant annexation. The war, nevertheless, hastened the process. July 7, 1898, a treaty negotiation was cut short by the passage of a joint resolution providing for annexation on the old terms of incorporation into the United States. A new note was struck, however, by the protest of the Japanese government, based on the disturbance of the balance of power in the Pacific, and on the possible effect

Hawaii

[1] Schurz, *Speeches*, etc., vi. 270, 271.

upon the large number of its citizens who were laborers and merchants in the islands.[1]

Of the influence of the Spanish treaty on the final settlement of the Samoan question, on the other hand, there can be no doubt. Constant difficulties having arisen under the General Act of Berlin, and our scruples at the extinction of native rule having become deadened, we agreed, on December 4, 1899, to a treaty of division. This gave us the island of Tutuila, whose fine harbor of Pagopago we had had the right to use since 1878. Germany took the other islands, and Great Britain received compensation elsewhere. This treaty contained no provision for incorporation or civil rights. While this negotiation, with the reassertion of our claim to Midway island, or rather islands, and the occupation of the neighboring Wake island in 1900, completed the tale of our acquisitions, it does not indicate the extent to which the colonial policy was applied. A treaty was once more negotiated for the purchase of the Danish islands, but it was rejected by the Danish parliament. As there was some doubt whether the Isle of Pines, to the southwest of Cuba, belonged to that government, the matter was left open in our treaty with the new nation in 1903. Negotiation, however, resulted in giving it to her.

More important than all the rest was the action of Congress. That body made use of the discretion left it by the treaty with Spain to establish the Spanish cessions upon a basis definitely colonial, without reference to their future incorporation into the United States. In the case of Cuba we conscientiously carried out our obligations both to Spain and to the islanders, by handing its government over to the latter as soon as they were organized to receive it and competent to protect persons and property. In so doing, however, we insisted on certain permanent conditions prescribed by Congress and known as the "Platt

Samoa

Tutuila

Midway and Wake islands

Colonial governments

[1] Moore, *Digest,* i. 504.

amendment." These conditions provided that Cuba should never allow any foreign power or powers to impair its inde-

Platt amendment pendence in any way; that the government should contract no debt which could not be paid by a sinking fund from the ordinary revenues; that the United States should have the right to intervene in Cuba "for the preservation of Cuban independence, the maintenance of a government adequate for the protection of life, property, and individual liberty, and for discharging the obligations" with respect to the rights and property of Spanish subjects under the treaty of Paris; that Cuba should provide for the sanitation of her cities, and should grant the United States "lands necessary for coaling or naval stations" and for cognate purposes. By the treaty embodying these provisions we practically added a protectorate to our colonies.

The change involved in the sudden extension of our territory almost to the Asiatic coast, and still more in our new

Attitude of Europe spirit, did not escape the attention of Europe. The general sentiment was at first one of disapproval. In France, Spanish bondholders were at first

France alarmed by the war, and then were indignant at our refusal to impose the Cuban debt on the island government. German opinion was influenced by the

Germany fact that we apparently had forestalled its government in taking over the Philippines, and it was kept excited by the exchange of discourtesies between the officers of the two fleets. Austria, never friendly, remember-

Austria ing the fate of Maximilian, was distressed at the losses of the queen regent of Spain, a member of the Hapsburg house. The feeling of Italy had been con-

Italy tinually aggravated by repeated lynchings of Italian subjects in the United States. In affairs of that kind the United States government was unable to afford the protection of its courts, as the punishment for such offences fell within the jurisdiction of the states, whose courts often failed to do their duty. The most important case was that at New Orleans in 1891, but others occurred in Colorado in 1896, at Hahnville, Louisiana, in 1896, and at Tallulah in the same state in 1899. In each of these instances, Congress voted indemnity, but this wergeld did not entirely assuage the national ill-feeling.

To these special sources of discontent was added a general resentment at the sudden apparition of a new world power which might upset the nicely adjusted balance of international politics. More immediately alarming was the fact that the balance of trade seemed already upset. In 1895 we had exported less than fifty millions more than we imported, in 1900 over five hundred million more; and much of the surplus consisted of manufactured goods. Credits accumulated at New York, which seemed likely to become the financial centre of the world.[1] Our bankers began to talk of the financing of the loans of foreign governments, an industry which had previously been monopolized by London, Paris, and Berlin, and which carried with it a vast influence in world politics. This condition was in part temporary, due to the "dumping" by our trusts, at under-cost prices, of the accumulated supplies of overproduction, a practice very unpopular at home where prices were kept up behind the protection of our tariff wall, but equally unpopular abroad, where it was feared that these low prices would undermine established industries. Joined with the fear of German competition, it formed the basis of Joseph Chamberlain's somewhat later campaign for protection in England. The United States loomed so gigantic on the horizon of industrial and diplomatic competition, which are always closely connected, that during the years immediately following the Spanish war, talk of European combination to oppose her advance was in the air.

Great Britain was the one great power who, in spite of her industrial fears, welcomed the rise of the United States. Her population had more appreciation of the humanitarian

Balance of power and balance of trade

[1] Coman, *Industrial History*, 327–331.

impulse that lay behind our intervention in Cuba. Her statesmen hoped much from our moral assistance. She was at that
time diplomatically in a position which Lord

Great Britain
Salisbury described as one of "spendid isola-
tion," but which was not without its dangers, particularly in
view of the impending Boer war. Somewhat exaggerating the
Anglo-Saxon character of our population, her orators called
attention to the ties of blood and the world destiny of our
common race. For the first time in our national history there
was a real cordiality between the two peoples, though it was
most demonstrative on the part of the English. An alliance,
formal or informal, with the United States they would have
greeted with enthusiasm.

The task of adapting American foreign policy to these new
conditions raised our diplomacy to an importance equal to

Diplomatic
that which it had possessed in the early days of

task
the republic and during the Civil war. To
adjust the nation to its new position without sacrificing the
principles developed in the past was an operation of a delicacy hardly exceeded by that of preserving our neutrality
during the French revolutionary wars, or of keeping Europe
neutral while we ourselves were fighting. It was the more
difficult because of the divided tones in which the voice of
the past came down through the confusion of the eighties and
nineties. That its importance was appreciated is evident
from the struggle for control which was almost continuously
waged between the administration and the Senate. In the

Executive
latter the leadership was generally with Sen-

versus Senate
ator Lodge, long a member of the committee
on foreign affairs; but his leadership did not mean control.
Except in one case, in which it acted alone and in one other
in which it joined with the House, namely, in ordering the abrogation of the Russian treaty, the power of the Senate has
been confined to checking or modifying the policy of the administration. The direction of policy has been with the
executive.

Fortunately, at this time the main burden fell upon John Hay, secretary of state from September, 1898, to June, 1905. Beginning public life as private secretary to President Lincoln, he had passed the years since *John Hay* that time in minor diplomatic posts, in journalistic and literary work, and in an advantageously placed social position at home and abroad, until his appointment by President McKinley as ambassador to Great Britain in 1897. Somewhat predisposed by his European associations to think in the terms of the great powers, he was least successful in his dealings with the Spanish-American nations. His knowledge of international law, of historic tendencies, and of men was, however, in its combination unsurpassed in his day. He possessed such an Americanism as can exist only when based on a complete knowledge of American development. Most of all, during his tenure he divorced the office of secretary of state from politics. Under McKinley he was left with a free hand in his own department, and he himself did not interfere in others; under Roosevelt the latter's vigorous personality asserted itself on particular questions, but the general policy remained Hay's. In diplomatic ability and accomplishment he is to be ranked with Franklin and John Quincy Adams. His successor, Elihu Root, who served *Elihu Root* till January, 1909, brought to the office an unrivalled legal knowledge and a compelling geniality of approach.

From 1897 to 1913 there was an unusual degree of continuity in the diplomatic service, accompanied by some regularity of promotion. Thus Henry White, *Diplomatic service* employed in minor but responsible posts from 1879 until Cleveland's second term, was again called into service and appointed successively as secretary of the London embassy, as ambassador to Italy and later to France, and to many special missions and international conferences. David Jayne Hill, an eminent student of diplomatic history, served in Switzerland, the Netherlands, and Germany. John

Barrett was minister to Spain in 1894, and later to Argentina, to Panama, and to Colombia; he took part in many international conferences, and became director-general of the Pan-American Union in 1905. C. P. Bryan was minister successively in China, Brazil, Switzerland, Portugal, Belgium, and was ambassador to Japan; Charlemagne Tower was ambassador to Austria, Russia, and Germany; J. G. A. Leishman was minister to Switzerland and Turkey, and ambassador to Italy and Germany. The triple embassy of Oscar Straus to Turkey, 1887–1889, 1898–1901, and 1909–1910, and the long service of Whitelaw Reid in England, 1905 to 1913, are noticeable. All these were men of ability, and they had an opportunity to acquire diplomatic experience of which most of them took advantage. If some of them indulged in an ostentation of extravagance a bit offensive to good taste, at least they were representative of an important element among their countrymen, and they spent their money on the whole with grace.

The action of President Wilson, in 1913, in removing nearly all the heads of missions shows that the elements of continuity and promotion found between 1897 and 1913 were due to the maintenance in power of one political party, and that it is still our policy, as it always has been, to have the ministers represent the administration rather than constitute the culminating rank of a permanent staff. Wilson's attempt to appoint men of training and experience to certain significant posts however, indicates a desire to recognize merit.

Wilson and the diplomatic service

The consular service has still more markedly improved. In 1864 the proposition of 1856 for the appointment of a permanent staff was revived in a very modified form. Thirteen consular clerks or pupils, removable only with the consent of the Senate, were thereafter to be appointed. The substitution of salaries for fees also made gradual progress, until it was made complete in 1906, with the unimportant exception of consular agents.

Consular service

Meantime the development of civil-service reform led to a continuous attempt to include the consular service under its provisions. Although this attempt has failed, it has not been without its results. President Cleveland announced a system of appointment by examination and promotion. Although McKinley was hardly rigid in adhering to this, President Roosevelt returned to it with emphasis, and the decision of President Wilson to treat the service as out of politics promises permanence.[1]

This administrative systematization has fortunately been accompanied by an effective backing of popular support. The industrial interests of the country have urged improvement, and have coöperated in bringing it about. Educational institutions *Interest in consular service* have also responded to the national need, especially in the attention devoted to the study of modern languages, Spanish in particular, and in the offering of courses designed to equip students for consular positions. With the promise of a continuous career, it has become possible to advise many young men to take up the service as a life work, and at the same time the position by becoming businesslike has become less attractive as a vacation for the exhausted politician.

Working under these conditions, Secretary Hay undertook to achieve a new settlement of outstanding disputes with Great Britain, such as had been accomplished in 1794, 1815 to 1818, 1842, and 1871. *Relations with Great Britain* The friendship of Great Britain for the United States, still represented at Washington by the veteran Sir Julian Pauncefote, was an advantage, though it required some caution to prevent that friendship from becoming entangling. This situation became particularly delicate during the Boer war, but our experience in the art of neutrality prevented any real difficulties. The main obstacles were the now definite decision of the American people to have an American canal, and the fact that, since many of our disputes were between

[1] Civil Service Commission, *Reports*, annual.

the United States and Canada, Great Britain was obliged to defer in large measure to that powerful colony.

A commission appointed in 1898 to agree upon questions at issue between the United States and Canada found twelve topics for discussion: seals, fishing, the Alaskan boundary, transit of goods through each other's territory back to the original country, or to a third country, transit of criminals, wreckage and salvage, alien labor,— particularly the importation of Chinese into the United States across the Canadian boundary,—reciprocity, mining rights, the navigation of the Great Lakes, and the marking of the boundary line. These matters the commission failed to settle outright, but negotiation was continuous. In 1908 the transit of criminals, the question of wreckage and salvage, and the marking of the frontier were provided for.

Canadian disputes

The more exciting question of the Alaskan boundary had already been settled. This had first assumed importance with the discovery of gold on the Yukon in 1898. The dispute grew out of the treaty of 1825 between Russia and Great Britain, and chiefly out of the provision that the boundary was to follow the crest of the mountains parallel to the coast from the parallel of latitude of 56° to the intersection of that line with the parallel of longitude of 141°, but was never to be more than ten marine leagues from the coast following its sinuosities. This arrangement was sufficiently complicated, but it was rendered more so by the deep and irregular indentations of the Alaskan coast line. Great Britain claimed that the line ran along the crests nearest the ocean, from peak to peak, crossing the bays, giving her the heads of several of them and thus access to the sea. The United States held that the line must be everywhere ten leagues from sea water, thus entirely cutting off a great part of Canada from the ocean. A *modus vivendi* was agreed upon in 1899, and in 1903 the question was submitted to arbitration, but by a commission composed of three members from each nation, without an umpire. The

Alaskan boundary

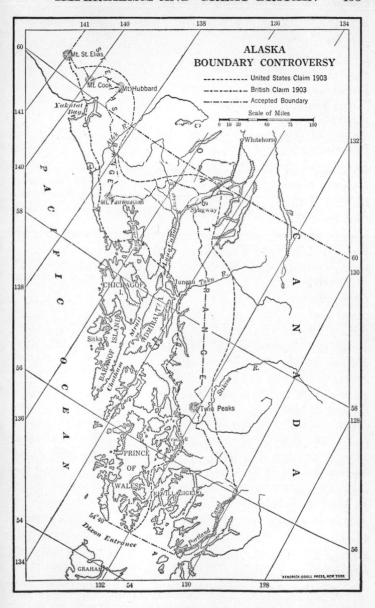

ALASKA
BOUNDARY CONTROVERSY

--------- United States Claim 1903
-·-·-·-·- British Claim 1903
-··-··-··- Accepted Boundary

Scale of Miles
0 10 20   50   75   100

KENDRICK-ODELL PRESS, NEW YORK

American commissioners were Senator Lodge, Elihu Root, and Senator Turner to represent the Northwest. Maintaining the American position in all except a few minor points, they were supported by Chief Justice Alverstone of England; and so the boundary was fixed according to our views.[1]

The question of fishing was threefold, involving the protection of the Alaskan seals, the securing of privileges from **Fur seals** the Dominion of Canada, and the securing of privileges from the separate jurisdiction of Newfoundland. In case of the seals, the British legislation resulting from the Behring sea arbitration lapsed in 1899, at the end of the prescribed five-year period, and the sea was thus open to Canadians to within three miles of the Pribilof islands, with no limitation as to methods. In 1897 we had prohibited our own citizens from engaging in open-sea killing, but Canadian opinion would not permit Great Britain to reciprocate in any way. In the United States the feeling among those interested was so strong that at one time it was proposed that we kill off all the herds. It was not until the administration of President Taft, in 1911, that the matter was settled by a joint treaty with Japan, Russia, and Great Britain, whereby pelagic killing was for the time being altogether prohibited and these countries were to have pro rata shares of the kill on land. An act of Congress of 1912 prohibited all killing whatsoever on land for a term of years.

Our fishing difficulties with Canada were settled by a treaty of 1908, which provided a permanent international **Canada and** fisheries commission. It was with Newfound-**Newfoundland** land that the most trying situation existed, rendering negotiation and fresh causes of irritation constant. In 1902, in accordance with a new diplomatic method accepted by Great Britain, Hay negotiated a treaty with Premier Bond of Newfoundland on the familiar basis of admitting fish from the Banks to our markets free of duty in return for the privileges that we desired. Again, however, as

[1] George Davidson, *The Alaska Boundary*, San Francisco, 1903.

in 1888, the fishing interests in the Senate were strong enough to defeat the treaty, by insisting that it was the national duty both to afford economic protection to the industry and to obtain such international advantages as might be necessary. The final defeat of this treaty in 1904 led to retaliatory legislation by Newfoundland in 1905 and 1906, in which every possible port regulation that could distress our fishermen was resorted to. While the governments of Great Britain and the United States temporarily quieted matters by an annual *modus vivendi*, they sought agreement. Great Britain maintained the right of Newfoundland to make any port regulations which ostensibly applied to both nations equally, and which were in its judgment, necessary to the preservation of the fishing or to the maintenance of order and morals. The United States admitted that there must be such port regulations as were necessary for the preservation of the fishing, but claimed that, as these determined the conditions under which she was to enjoy the privileges accorded to her by the treaties of 1783 and 1818, her assent to them was necessary. In 1909 the matter was submitted to a tribunal composed of members of the Hague Permanent Court of Arbitration, which was, in addition, to recommend rules for the conduct of the fishing. The decision was mainly in favor of Newfoundland, but in accordance with the recommendations an agreement between Great Britain and the United States was reached. It seems probable that this century-old dispute is happily ended. The Americans are to enjoy such privileges as the right to buy bait and take on necessary water, without suffering undue annoyance from local laws.[1]

The all-important subject of trade relations with Canada reached no special crisis until, in 1911, a reciprocity treaty was concluded under Taft's administration and largely by his personal influence. The rejection of this treaty as the

[1] P. T. McGrath, "The Atlantic Fisheries Dispute," *Review of Reviews,* 1910, xli. 718–724.

result of a nationalistic uprising in Canada and the defeat
of the Laurier government, seemed to presage a period of still
greater strain than in the past. Some of the
things aimed at by reciprocity, however, the
new United States tariff bill of 1913 accomplished without the
exaction of specific compensation, and it may lead to a better
understanding. Only five of the twelve questions of 1898
remain to be settled, but in regard to all of them except
alien labor and mining rights the existing agreements are not
unsatisfactory. The new questions that have arisen, such as
the use of international rivers for irrigation, seem not to be
serious.

Reciprocity

The other-important British interest in America has been
the interoceanic canal. It had finally become obvious
that such a canal would be constructed, and
either by, or under the auspices of, the United
States government. Yet the Clayton-Bulwer treaty still
held. In 1900, therefore, Hay and Pauncefote arranged a
compact to meet these conditions. This new treaty, like
that of Clayton and Bulwer, was based on the principle of international neutralization, and it asked other
nations to join in the guarantee. As this arrangement was
unsatisfactory to public opinion in the United States, the
Senate amended it by specifically abrogating the Clayton-
Bulwer treaty, by allowing the United States to fortify the
canal, and by leaving out the general invitation to adhere
to the agreement. In consequence of these amendments,
Hay and Pauncefote drew up, in 1901, a new treaty providing
for the abrogation of the Clayton-Bulwer treaty. In return
for this concession by Great Britain, which allowed the United
States to acquire territory in Central America, the last-
named power adopted certain prescribed rules. The second
of these forbade the blockade of the canal, but allowed the
United States to "maintain such military police along the
canal as may be necessary to protect it against lawlessness
and disorder." Under a rather liberal interpretation of this

Clayton-
Bulwer treaty

permission, the United States plans to fortify the canal in the hope of rendering it impregnable to attack. Rules three to six regulated the use of the canal in time of war. Rule one ran: "The canal shall be free and open to the vessels of commerce and of war of all nations observing these Rules, on terms of entire equality, so that there shall be no discrimination against any such nation, or its citizens or subjects, in respect of the conditions or charges of traffic, or otherwise. Such conditions and charges of traffic shall be just and equitable."

This last rule became the subject of much controversy after 1912, when Congress, in fixing the rates of traffic, exempted from all charge vessels engaging under certain conditions in the coastwise, or **Canal tolls** rather coast-to-coast, trade of the United States. Primarily intended to decrease the cost of transcontinental freight, and to have its effect on the rates of the transcontinental railroads, the law plainly violated the provisions of the treaty. Great Britain promptly protested, and President Wilson in 1914 recommended that Congress repeal the discriminating exemption. The acceptance of the recommendation by Congress was a notable manifestation of our intention of recognizing treaty rights.

It is not only in thus preventing our carrying out of a domestic policy that the Hay-Pauncefote treaty has proved a stumbling-block in our way. The purpose of our change of canal policy was not so much **Military use of the canal** commercial as military. A canal internationally guaranteed would need no fortification, but would be equally available to all nations. The policy of making the canal American involved the expense of fortifying it and of maintaining a garrison there, the compensation being that our fleet could do double duty, could be available for use in either ocean. By the terms of the treaty, however, it is probable that the value of any other fleet with which we may be contending will equally be doubled, as the canal is open to the war vessels of other nations even when at war with us, if those nations observe the rules laid down in the treaty. This being the case, it might seem that, since we are not allowed to exclude their war vessels, we need not be at the expense of fortification. In the absence of the international guarantee arranged for in the Clayton-Bulwer treaty and in the first Hay-Pauncefote treaty, however, it is obvious that the only means we have of seeing that the rules are observed is the ability to enforce them on the spot. By the terms of agreement all we have secured by our canal diplomacy is the obligation to maintain by our own power, and without any compensating exclusive use, a neutrality which the nations of the world would have been glad to guarantee. The canal has become a vulnerable spot, at the mercy of any power able to seize it, except Great Britain which is bound by the treaty. Authority and power are of course not synonymous. Having made use of our right to acquire territory and to fortify the canal, we have acquired the power to exclude other nations, if we care to disregard our treaty obligations. Such disregard, however, is always provocative of trouble, and may be dangerous. The experience of the United States with the Clayton-Bulwer treaty should emphasize the advice of Washington and Jefferson, to avoid entangling alliances, if we wish to maintain our freedom to change our mind.

It is apparent that the questions at issue between Great Britain and the United States have since the Spanish war been much less critical than those of earlier periods, that most of them have been settled, and that the difficulties of the future are likely to be of diminishing significance.

CHAPTER XXXI

SPANISH AMERICA

IN clarifying her relations with Great Britain, the United States removed only one diplomatic obstacle from the path of the canal. It remained for her to decide Nicaragua versus Panama whether she wished a canal by way of Nicaragua or of Panama, and then to make arrangements with the nation that owned the chosen isthmus. In Congress there was a strong sentiment in favor of the former way, and Nicaragua was willing to grant us such conditions as we considered necessary. By the Spooner act of 1902, however, the President was authorized to proceed with the Panama route, which he preferred, if he could make satisfactory arrangements within a reasonable time. President Roosevelt determined to build the canal by Panama, and he at once made the enterprise his particular policy. The first step was to obtain the concession which was still legally held by the successor of de Lesseps's company. This was bought for forty million dollars, and title to the Panama railroad was subsequently purchased.

More difficult was the negotiation with the republic of Colombia, of which Panama was one of the constituent states. We regarded as essential to the construction Position of and operation of the canal full possession of a Colombia strip of territory on each side, with ample rights of fortification and police, and for this we were willing to pay. Hay accordingly arranged a satisfactory treaty with Herran, the Colombian minister, giving us, not sovereignty, but control for ninety-nine years, with privileges of renewal, of a six-mile strip. After four months' debate, however, this treaty was rejected by the Colombian senate in July, 1903. Although

Colombia had a perfect right to do this, and though her motives were not properly open to question, President Roosevelt prepared to act without her assent. He ordered our minister to leave Bogota, and prepared a message proposing to Congress that we begin to dig the canal. He argued, or at least asserted, that Colombia, in rejecting a reasonable and generous offer, had violated the treaty of 1846. He believed that her motive was to obtain more money, and declared that the world could wait no longer on her sloth and avarice. An agreement, he believed, might be made with the state of Panama.[1]

To those who are ready for the fray weapons are sent. Like Polk, Roosevelt was able, when Congress met, to present a simpler course, for which, however, unlike Polk, he did not have to incur the direct responsibility. Not unnaturally, the citizens of Panama were deeply incensed that their only prospect for future greatness was likely to be blocked, perhaps forever if the Nicaraguan route should be chosen. The situation was attractive to adventurers, and offered all the possibilities of intrigue familiar to the readers of Richard Harding Davis. When in August, 1903, it was announced that Panama would revolt, the attitude of the United States government was not such as to discourage action.

The state of Panama

October 10, 1903, President Roosevelt wrote to Dr. Albert Shaw, editor of the *Review of Reviews:* "I enclose you, purely for your own information, a copy of a letter of September 5th, from our minister to Colombia. I think it might interest you to see that there was absolutely not the slightest chance of securing by treaty any more than we endeavored to secure. The alternatives were to go to Nicaragua against the advice of the great majority of competent engineers—some of the most competent saying that

Roosevelt's policy

[1] W. L. Scruggs, *The Colombian and Venezuelan Republics,* Boston, 1900; Achille Viallate, *Les Etats-Unis et le canal interocéanique,* in his *Essais d'histoire diplomatique américaine* (Paris, 1905), 57–206.

we had better have no canal at this time than go there—or else to take the territory by force without any attempt at getting a treaty. I cast aside the proposition made at this time to foment the secession of Panama. Whatever other governments can do, the United States cannot go into the securing by such underhand means the cession. Privately, I freely say to you that I should be delighted if Panama were an independent state; or if it made itself so at this moment; but for me to say so publicly would amount to an instigation of a revolt, and therefore I cannot say it." [1]

Fully alert to the possibilities, the administration watched the Isthmus. November 2 the naval officer commanding our observation squadron was ordered: "Maintain free and uninterrupted transit. . . . Prevent landing of any armed force with hostile intent, either government or insurgent, either at Colon, Porto Bello, or other point." At 3.40 P. M., November 3, the acting secretary of state telegraphed to the Isthmus that an uprising was reported to be taking place there. A reply of 8.15 P. M. stated that there had been none yet, but that it was rumored that there would be one during the night. On November 4 independence was proclaimed. The only active hostility was in the city of Panama, on the Pacific, beyond our reach, where the Colombian gunboat *Bogota* dropped a few shells on the morning of the 4th and killed a Chinaman. At noon we warned the commander to shell no more. At 11.55 A. M. on November 6, the state department was informed: "The situation is peaceful. Isthmian movement has obtained so far success. Colon and interior provinces have enthusiastically joined independence. Not any Colombian soldiers known on isthmian soil at present. *Padillo* equipped to pursue *Bogota*. Bunau Varilla has been appointed officially confidential agent of the Republic of Panama at Washington." At 12.51 P. M. Hay acknowledged the receipt of this note.[2]

The administration and the revolution

---

[1] *Nation*, 1904, lxxix. 328.
[2] *Senate Docs.*, 58 Cong. 2 sess., No. 51.

On the same day Hay instructed our acting consul on the spot to negotiate with the new government. November 13 Bunau Varilla was received at Washington; December 7 a treaty, drawn up by Hay, was signed; December 12 a minister was appointed. This quick recognition of the new republic was contrary to our consistent practice of waiting till independence was soundly established, as illustrated by our conduct in relation to the Spanish-American revolutions from Spain, the Texan revolution, and the government of Maximilian, and as emphasized by our attitude toward the contemplated recognition of the Confederacy. To be sure, the Isthmus was quiet; but it was because we had prevented the Colombian forces, amply able to restore order, from intervening. Such interposition on our part was not, as President Roosevelt subsequently claimed it was, in accordance with local precedents.[1] We had a number of times, under the treaty of 1846, landed troops to protect the railroad, but we had successfully protected it without occupying the whole Isthmus. Senator Hoar seems to have been justified in his statement of December 17, 1903, that no revolution had up to that date interfered with the isthmian traffic.[2] Such previous interventions, moreover, had been to carry out the treaty; in this case the purpose was to overthrow it. In compensation for the right of free transit we had guaranteed the Isthmus to Colombia, we now intervened to prevent Colombia from enforcing her sovereignty. These points were cleverly met by Roosevelt in his message to Congress, and by Hay in his correspondence relating to the episode. They urged among other things that the validity of the union of the several states of the Colombian republic, and particularly of Panama, was extremely complicated from a constitutional point of view. The relation of Panama to Colombia had actually varied from independence to incorporation as a department. To suggest that

Recognition of Panama

---

[1] *House Docs.*, 58 Cong. 2 sess., No. 1.
[2] *Congressional Record*, 58 Cong. 2 sess., pp. 316–318; 2191–2000.

an outside power might take cognizance of such internal conditions was of course obviously inconsistent with our policy, and before the Civil War cemented our own union would have been dangerous. It was not, however, the real defense upon which the administration relied. Its real excuse was, rather, the plea by which Jefferson justified to himself the Louisiana purchase, a transaction so contrary to his constitutional scruples,—the plea that the situation was one which never could happen again, and was of such unparalleled importance as to exempt it from the ordinary laws of morality and of nations.

The new republic met our needs more completely than Señor Herran had done. The United States received full rights, as "if it were the sovereign," of "a zone five miles on each side" of the canal; she also secured the right to fortify the canal, and to obtain additional naval stations within the republic. In return she paid ten million dollars down, and agreed to pay a quarter of a million a year, beginning nine years from date. The United States guaranteed the independence of Panama. The constitution of Panama contains the following clause: "The Government of the United States of America may intervene anywhere in the Republic of Panama for the re-establishment of constitutional peace and order if this should be disturbed, provided that by virtue of public treaty said nation should assume or have assumed to guarantee the independence and sovereignty of this Republic." Though our guarantee was made in the light of this clause, intervention is merely a right that has been granted to us, not a duty that we have assumed. Yet it can hardly be denied that by the events of 1903 we acquired in the canal zone a colony, and in Panama a protectorate. It is worth noting that between 1846 and 1903 there were fifty-three riots and revolutions on the isthmus, and since then, peace.[1]

[1] Aragon, *Republica de Panamá y la diplomacia contemporanea, Revista Positivista* (Mexico), 1904; Schurz, *Speeches*, etc., vi. 389–403, 434–436; Rafael Reyes, *The Two Americas*, New York, 1914.

Until the Spanish war it had been one of our unrealized ambitions to dominate the Gulf of Mexico, and thus secure Control of the the outlet of the Mississippi. Although we Caribbean Sea failed to win Cuba in that war, we obtained enough hold on that island to give us the control we wished, a control which has recently been strengthened by the completion of the railroad to Key West. With the undertaking of the canal as a national enterprise, the control of the Caribbean became equally necessary. By 1903 we had already, with our naval station at Guantanamo in Cuba, in addition to Porto Rico and Panama, a strategic preponderance in that sea which it has been the apparent intention of the government to maintain and strengthen. The only danger lies in the possibility of European influence over some of the republics situated about it, a peril that has involved a careful consideration of the exact bearing of the Monroe Doctrine upon the situation.

European interference with the political affairs of those states it obviously remains our intention to prevent, and European this policy doubtless extends to the exclusion mediation of European mediation in the case of a revolutionary contest in any one of them, a policy underlying our present (1915) attitude with respect to Mexico. Other possible avenues of European approach would be mediation between two warring republics, and the collection of claims. With regard to the first, no case has yet arisen clearly indicating whether the administration would follow the earlier practice of allowing mediation, or whether it would adopt Blaine's policy of discouraging it, or whether we would absolutely prevent it. There can be no doubt, however, that in any such case our own good offices would be promptly offered, and that we should resent their rejection in favor of any other country. The existence of the Permanent Court at The Hague, established in 1899, has simplified this problem by providing a recourse equally acceptable to Europe and America.

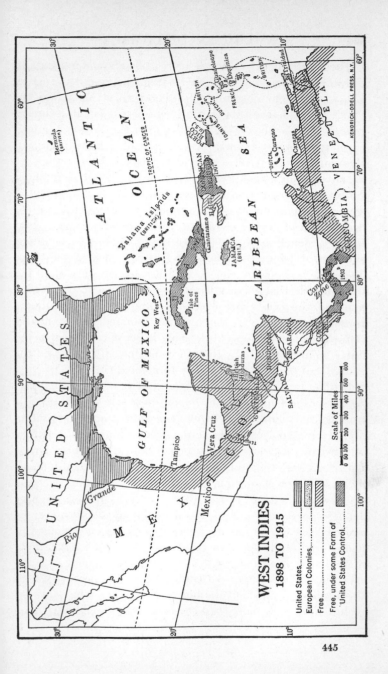

WEST INDIES
1898 TO 1915

United States..........
European Colonies..........
Free..........
Free, under some Form of
United States Control..........

Scale of Miles
0 50 100 200 300 400 500 600

KENDRICK-ODELL PRESS. N.Y.

The question of claims is more difficult and important. These are of two kinds. One rests upon the duty of every European claims government to protect with all its power the lives of its citizens legally resident in a foreign country. The recent (1914) attitude of the Wilson administration in connection with the killing of a British subject, Benton, by the Mexican revolutionists indicates that we do not assume responsibility in such cases, but that under certain circumstances we do undertake to act as intermediary. The question of property is a different one; or at least, if the destruction of personal and tangible property is analogous to the destruction of life, that of public debts may be differentiated. Such debts give rise to many perplexing questions. They are sometimes contracted by governments that fail to establish themselves; through non-payment of interest many of them, as those of Santo Domingo and Honduras, mount to proportions beyond any immediate possibility of payment; and, worse still, being in most cases contracted for temporary purposes, they have not usually increased the capacity of the debtor countries to meet them.

In 1902 Luis M. Drago, foreign minister of Argentina, presented to the United States government the view that "the Drago Doctrine public debt cannot occasion armed intervention nor even the actual occupation of the territory of American nations by a European power." [1] This "Drago Doctrine" was a slight modification of the principle advanced by his fellow country-man, Carlos Calvo, that "the collection of pecuniary claims made by the citizens of one country against the government of another country should never be made by force." It has excited much discussion among diplomats and students of international law. It is true, however, that capitalists have in the past loaned money with the expectation that their own country would if necessary help them collect it, and that the borrowing countries have in consequence received more than they otherwise would have done

[1] *House Docs.*, 58 Cong. 2 sess., No. 1, p. 4.

and at lower interest rates. Hay refused to accept Drago's views, and in the case of Venezuela, which called forth the suggestion, failed also to take the position assumed by Blaine in 1881 with reference to the same country. He did not protest, as in many previous similar cases we had **Forcible collection of debts** not protested, at the blockade of the Venezuelan coast by a joint German, British, and Italian squadron. It is important to observe, however, that the United States was fully and officially informed that this blockade was for the sole purpose of collecting the claims in question, which included both government loans and destruction of private property; and that the matter was submitted to arbitration at our suggestion and by our active assistance. In 1907 the United States submitted the Drago Doctrine to the Hague Conference, in the modified form, that force should not be used in such cases unless the creditor nation had first proposed arbitration and this had been refused or ignored by the nation against which the claim was made. In this form it was endorsed by the Conference.

The possibilities of such interference, particularly when the debts were obviously beyond the unassisted resources of the debtor country, excited much anxiety **Roosevelt's doctrine of police power** in the United States. So long as we recognized the principle of the forcible collection of debts, the only method of preventing the occasional, and perhaps at times long-continued, presence of foreign fleets in American waters was to assume the duty of collection ourselves. Even the Drago Doctrine would not prevent the enforcement of claims for the destruction of private property. In messages of 1903 and 1904 President Roosevelt said: "That our rights and interests are deeply concerned in the maintenance of the [Monroe] Doctrine is so clear as hardly to need argument. This is especially true in view of the construction of the Panama Canal. As a mere matter of self-defence we must exercise a close watch over the approaches to this canal, and this means we must be thoroughly alive to our interests in the Caribbean Sea." "When we announce a policy, such as the Monroe Doctrine, we thereby commit ourselves to the consequences of the policy." . . . "Chronic wrongdoing, or an impotence which results in a general loosening of the ties of civilized society, may in America, as elsewhere, ultimately require intervention by some civilized nation, and in the Western Hemisphere the adherence of the United States to the Monroe Doctrine may force the United States, however reluctantly, in flagrant cases of such wrongdoing or impotence, to the exercise of an international police power."

This policy of intervention to prevent wrongdoing, whether to our own citizens or to those of other countries, resembled The "Big the policy advocated by Blaine. The absence Stick" of any sugar-coating in its pronouncement, however, justifies the popular differentiation in terms, Blaine's being known as the "Elder Sister" policy and Roosevelt's as the "Big Stick."

The conspicuous example of this new extension of the Monroe Doctrine—our assumption of responsibility for the Santo Do- good behavior of Latin America—occurred in mingo the case of the negro republic of Santo Domingo. In 1905 President Roosevelt made a treaty with its government whereby we were to undertake the adjustment of its obligations and the administration of its customs houses. This agreement was not ratified at once, or in its first form, by the Senate, but in 1907 a convention which preserved the main features of the plan was accepted.

This action added, at any rate for the time being, a new protectorate to our list, and thereby increased our territorial New protec- hold on the Caribbean. In 1911 somewhat torates similar arrangements were made by Secretary Knox with Nicaragua and Honduras. Although circumstances have thus far prevented their execution, the drawing up of a new treaty with Nicaragua, on practically the same basis, by Secretary Bryan in 1913 indicates that such trusteeship may be regarded as an accepted national policy. While we do not absolutely prohibit European intervention for the collection of debts, we aim to make such intervention unnecessary by acting as intermediary.

The "Big Stick" has also been evident in the frequent and penetrating applications of our police power for the defence of our own interests. In Cuba, by United States intervening in 1908 and by threatening in-intervention tervention in 1912, we have, in accordance with the Platt amendment, insisted on peace and order. In Venezuela we threatened to use force to establish our claims, which were subsequently submitted to the Hague conference. We forcibly intervened in Honduras, and have continually used force in Nicaragua in the hope of establishing peace. In the case of the latter country, at least, we have ourselves exercised a latitude of interference which we would not permit to European powers without vigorous protest. It remains the theory of the United States that such intervention shall not control the right of the people to constitute their own government, but we approach the position of insisting that they shall have a stable government. So far as European powers are concerned, we do not prohibit their intervention to protect the lives and property of their subjects; but we insist, as against them, that their intervention shall be strictly confined to that purpose, and as against the American nation involved, that it shall be in a condition to render such intervention unnecessary.

It is not, however, European nations alone that we wish to keep from interference in American affairs. With the rise to power of Japan and the immense po-Japan and tentialities of immigration from that country Magdalena and from China, the attitude of these countries Bay toward America has become a matter of concern. There is no doubt that we shall apply to them all the prohibitions that we maintain against Europe, although in their case we have not the justification of non-interference in Asia. It was, moreover, with special reference to Japan that a new corollary of the Monroe Doctrine was proposed in 1912. This was in the form of a resolution presented by Senator Lodge, declaring that, "When any harbor or other place in the American continents is so situated that the occupation thereof for naval or military purposes might threaten the communication or the safety of the United States, the government of the United States could not see, without grave concern, the possession of such harbor or other place by any corporation or association which has such relations to another government not American as to give that government practical power of control for naval or military purposes." Though passed by a vote of 51 to 4, it was not, however, accepted by President Taft. In 1913 President Wilson attempted to put it upon less nationalistic grounds by enlarging its scope so as to make it extend to an opposition to all special "concessions" to foreign syndicates, for it is his belief that capital should find ample protection in the general laws of a country, and that, if it cannot, its investment will inevitably lead to political complications such as we wish to avoid. His attitude seems already to have prevented the execution of the plan of the English Pearson syndicate in Colombia. A still further method of meeting this situation has been developed by the attempt to secure for the United States a preëmption of all possible interoceanic canal routes in America. Those of Nicaragua and Colombia are now covered by treaties with those countries, which are as yet (1915) unratified.

The intensification of the Monroe Doctrine since the Spanish war has been confined, as to fact, to the Caribbean. Dr. Shaw, of the *Review of Reviews*, and very close to President Roosevelt, wrote editorially, "Control of the canal and dominance in the Caribbean Sea would suffice to assure the Monroe Doctrine." It is not to be supposed that the administration intended to withdraw the Monroe Doctrine from connection with the more southern

Scope of new policies

countries; but it certainly did not actually apply to them its additions to that doctrine, which was in part due to the fact that their governments were more firmly established than those about the Caribbean. President Roosevelt said in 1904, "Any country whose people conduct themselves well can count upon our hearty friendship." We helped mediate between Chili and Argentine, but we did not protest when in 1902 they made Edward VII. arbiter in their disputes, and we accepted in 1909 the same monarch, and later George V, as arbiter between Chili and the United States.

All Spanish America, however, has been included in our attempts to establish continental coöperation. In 1907, at our initiative joined with that of Mexico, the Central-American states agreed to a series of treaties and conventions establishing a court of arbitration, and looking toward a renewal of that union which existed for a few years after their separation from Spain. Andrew Carnegie presented them with a palace at San José, in Costa Rica, for the use of their court. *Relations with Spanish America in general*

In 1899 President McKinley proposed a second Pan-American congress, and we endeavored to popularize the idea by the holding of a Pan-American exposition at Buffalo in 1901. It was there that President McKinley met his death, but as a result of his initiative a congress was held in 1901 at the City of Mexico. This congress put on record a number of far-reaching resolutions and adopted a few useful regulations, its most important undertaking being an effort to make the meeting of such congresses regular. The result is that they have since then been held every five years, the third—the second of the new series —at Rio Janeiro in 1906 and the next at Santiago of Chili in 1911. Although these congresses have steadily improved the conditions of international intercourse, they cannot be said to have led to any marked advance toward our goals of trade supremacy and sympathetic understanding. Our trade has grown, to be sure, and with it our regular steam- *Pan-American congresses* ship connection. It still, however, consists chiefly of importations, many of them brought to us by tramp steamers, which, arriving in New York, take on an American cargo for Europe, where they load with manufactured goods for South America. Our exports, except those that go to countries near by, like Mexico, have not generally equalled those of Great Britain nor has their growth kept pace with those of Germany and Belgium.[1]

Sympathy cannot exist without interest, and interest is languid in the United States, where news from every part of the world is presented more voluminously and read more eagerly than that from any part of Spanish America, except, again, Mexico. Among the Spanish Americans there is plenty of interest in us, but not understanding, or at least kindly understanding. The aggressions of the United States against Spain and Colombia, her decided firmness in dealing with the countries of the Caribbean, the threatening and condescending language of President Roosevelt, far from changing the opinion that a majority of their public men have always held in regard to us, have only confirmed it. They still fear our continued aggression, a fear from which the repeated assertions of Roosevelt and of Wilson fail to free them. In addition, the powerful and firmly established governments of Argentina, Brazil, and Chili resent the arrogance of our tone.

They feel no necessity for the defence of the Monroe Doctrine; they deny the assertion that our fiat is law upon the American continents, while they realize that in fact that is the basis of our action. It was with the idea of quieting this apprehension and sensitiveness that Root in 1906, while still secretary of state, visited South America, and that Secretary Knox in 1912 visited the Caribbean states, omitting Colombia by request. It is said to have been with the intention of counteracting the effect of the "Big Stick" on the minds of the people of the

Lack of interest on the part of the United States

Suspicion in Spanish America

[1] Bureau of the American Republics, *Annual Reports*, 1891, etc.

great South-American powers that Ex-President Roosevelt undertook his journey to South America in 1913–14. Nevertheless, our not unnatural refusal to submit our differences growing out of the treaty of 1846 and the revolution in Panama to arbitration by the Hague court, remains a stumbling-block. Secretary Knox endeavored to appease Colombia by a treaty granting her financial compensation and gaining for us control of a possible canal route though her territory. Secretary Bryan succeeded in making such a treaty, which added an expression of our regret that misunderstandings had arisen. This treaty, however, has not yet been approved by the Senate.[1]

[1] For a recent and clear-headed discussion of the whole subject see John Bigelow, *American Policy: The Western Hemisphere in Its Relation to the Eastern*, New York, 1915; cf. R. G. Usher, *Pan-Americanism*, New York, 1915.

CHAPTER XXXII

THE PACIFIC

INTO the diplomacy of the Pacific the new régime plunged joyously, stripped of past policies and entangling alliances. New start in By our treaty of 1894 with Japan and the the Pacific return of the Simonoseki indemnity we had freed ourselves from the consequences of joint action under Seward and Fish, and by the division of Samoa from the complications of the General Act of Berlin. From the consequences of our situation, however, we were not so free. No other country possessed so much Pacific coast-line as we did: the North Pacific was strategically ours. Our possessions were widely scattered, however, and, in spite of the attempts of Congress, by customs duties and by education, to knit them together, they could not be held apart from the current of Asian development. We were forced to become participants in the affairs of the Far East.[1]

We found there England, France, Germany, and Russia, all strongly entrenched in commerce and territory. Japan, International modern and ambitious, was already by the situation help of her geographical position a great power. China, inert but containing no one knew what possibilities of greatness, was prey about which the others hovered expectantly but somewhat gingerly. With Japan it was a question of dealing as with an equal. With China the question was less of dealing with her than about her, and it was quickly evident that our only choice was between be-

[1] Latané, *America as a World Power;* J. W. Foster, *American Diplomacy in the Orient,* Boston, etc., 1903; Coolidge, *The United States as a World Power,* 313–374; A. T. Mahan, *The Interest of America in International Conditions,* Boston, 1910; T. J. Lawrence, *War and Neutrality in the Far East,* 2d edition, London, etc., 1904.

coming one of the concert of powers or leaving them to apportion the empire according to their desires.

In 1898 Germany secured by lease from China the port of Kiauchau, Russia got in the same way Port Arthur and Talien-wan, France, Kwangchau Bay, Great "Spheres" of Britain, Wei-hai-wei and Mirs Bay, and Italy influence obtained the right to develop the port of Sanmun, Japan, as a result of her recent war with China, had already obtained the separation of Corea from Chinese jurisdiction. In these transactions, the United States took no part, though she temporarily profited by the opening of these places to trade. It was believed, however, that these leased ports might become the centres of spheres of influence, the commercial advantages of which the respective powers would seek to monopolize. On the possibility, therefore, that we might be deprived of our natural share of Chinese commerce, Hay, on September 6, 1899, instructed our ambassadors at London, Berlin, and St. Petersburg to ask for declarations in favor of open trade.

Meantime there began in China a religious and conservative movement against the "foreign devils," and particularly against the missionaries. Sweeping all before "Boxer" them, and winning the support of the empress troubles dowager, the "Boxers" got possession of Peking and besieged the foreign embassies. Under such circumstances the only possible policy for the United States was to join with the other powers in a military expedition for the relief of the legations. That relief once effected, however, there were untold possibilities of further interference. The lives and property of individuals, particularly of missionaries, must be atoned for in some manner that would render a recurrence of a similar movement unlikely. France, as protector of Catholics in the Orient, might demand indemnity for the native Christians slain; and such demands might easily assume a bulk that would render payment impossible except by cession of territory, or they might take the form of putting the empire in a straight-jacket. With these possibilities in mind, Hay determined to assume the advantage of leadership, and on July 3, 1900, announced the policy of the United States. "If wrong be done to our citizens," he declared, "we propose to hold the responsible authors to the uttermost accountability." Peking being in anarchy, the power and responsibility "are practically devolved upon the local provincial authorities. So long as they are not in overt collusion with rebellion and use their power to protect foreign life and property, we regard them as representing the Chinese people, with whom we seek to remain in peace and friendship." The President will coöperate with the powers in protecting American interests, and "in aiding to prevent a spread of the disorders to the other provinces of the Empire and a recurrence of such disasters. It is of course too early to forecast the means of attaining this last result; but the policy of the Government of the United States is to seek a solution which may bring about permanent safety and peace to China, preserve Chinese territorial and administrative entity, protect all rights guaranteed to friendly powers by treaty and international law, and safeguard for the world the principle of equal and impartial trade with all parts of the Chinese Empire." To this policy he invited the powers to adhere by similar declarations.

The two fundamental ideas of this circular note, which was sent to Berlin, Brussels, The Hague, Lisbon, London, Madrid, Paris, Rome, St. Petersburg, Tokio, and Vienna, were the preservation of the territorial and administrative entity of China, and the "open door" to the world's trade. These ideas have become almost as firmly established in the American mind with regard to China, as the Monroe Doctrine is with regard to America. Furthermore, by his prompt action and especially by the manner of it, Secretary Hay established a leadership in the concert of powers which, although entirely temporary and personal, gave dignity and power to our appearance in this new relationship. He succeeded in establishing a reputation for being a man of his word similar and equal to that which Franklin had enjoyed, and he knew how to seize upon that exact moment when international opinion rendered the carrying out of an idea practical but needed a strong and respected leader to make itself effective. He had learned from Lincoln to step ahead of the crowd without ceasing to step with it. His thorough acquaintance with diplomacy as it existed, did not blind him to new currents of thought as yet little recognized by diplomatic staffs, but destined to shape their activities. The powers promptly concurred in disclaiming any desire to partition China, and some of them admitted the principle of the "open door." On this basis the expedition for the relief of the legation in Peking was undertaken.

The matter of negotiation, involving first an agreement between the powers and then a joint negotiation with China, was difficult, but it was ably handled, the United States being represented by E. H. Conger and W. W. Rockhill, and China by Prince Ching and Li Hung Chang. The Chinese agreed, September 7, 1901, to make expiatory punishments and memorials, to pay an indemnity, and to improve the facilities of communication; both the physical route to Peking and the organization of the foreign office. Rockhill, the special commissioner, reported to Hay, November 30, 1901: "While we maintained complete independence, we were able to act harmoniously in the concert of powers . . . we retained the friendship of all the negotiating powers, exerted a salutary influence in the cause of moderation, humanity, and justice, secured adequate reparation for wrongs done our citizens, guaranties for their future protection, and labored successfully in the interests of the whole world in the cause of equal and impartial trade with all parts of the Chinese Empire."

Preservation of China's integrity

Our coöperation in the expedition against the Boxers not only assisted in preserving the territorial integrity of China, but helped establish the principle of the "open door." Hay had asked the assent of the powers that had spheres of influence in China to three propositions,—that treaty ports within leased territory be not interfered with; that the tariff charged be that of China and be under Chinese administration, unless the leased ports were made "free " of all duties; and that no discriminating harbor dues or transportation charges be levied in such "spheres." To these propositions he had, by December, 1899, secured the adhesion of France, Germany, Great Britain, Italy, Japan, and Russia, although the latter country was somewhat guarded in its commitment. By thus establishing these important items he confirmed his leadership in the development of the policy of the powers toward China.

Establishment of the " Open Door "

On February 8, 1904, Hay again assumed leadership by inviting Germany, Great Britain, and France to unite with the United States in urging Japan and Russia to recognize the neutrality of China in the war which they were beginning, and to localize hostilities within fixed limits. This effort was successful. In January, 1905, Russia announced to us that China was not neutral and could not preserve neutrality; hence that she should be forced to consider Chinese neutrality "from the standpoint of her own interests." Mr. Hay was able to convince Russia of the inexpediency of such action. His circular note of January 10, 1905, setting forth our hope that the war would not result in any "concession of Chinese territory to neutral powers," brought equivalent disclaimers from Germany, Austria-Hungary, France, Great Britain, and Italy. The culmination of this leadership was reached in President Roosevelt's offer, in 1905, of our good offices to bring the war to a close. In the treaty of Portsmouth, which concluded it, both the territorial and the administra-

The United States and the Russo-Japanese war

tive entity of China, as well as the policy of the "open door," were formally respected, although a way was left for their subsequent violation in spirit.

Philander C. Knox, who became secretary of state in 1909, carried out this policy by a circular note of 1912 proposing non-intervention in the Chinese revolu- **Non-intervention in China** tion, then in progress. Although such was the actual conduct of most of the powers, the action of Russia in recognizing the independence of Mongolia before acknowledging the new government of China was an ominous exception; while the attitude of Great Britain with reference to Tibet and that of Japan in Manchuria have long constituted false notes in the concert for the preservation of China's territorial and administrative integrity. Japan's action has also threatened the openness of trade.

Secretary Knox, however, devoted most of his attention to securing opportunities for American capital to share in the development of Chinese resources, This **"Dollar" diplomacy** movement, popularly known as "dollar" diplomacy, though not confined to China, was most important there. His treaty of 1911 with Honduras was based on the assumption of the foreign debt of that country by an American syndicate, headed by J. P. Morgan, in return for concessions. In 1910 he attempted to have the Manchurian railroads turned over to a syndicate, and urged China to grant to an Anglo-American body concessions in the same province. These attempts were unsuccessful, but an Anglo-American, French, and German company received a concession to build a railroad in the Yangtse valley. His most important effort, however, was to secure a right for the United States to participate in the loan required by the new government in 1912.

As finally arranged, this loan was to be shared equally by the bankers of Great Britain, France, Germany, Japan, Russia, and the United States. If its political character was not rendered sufficiently obvious by the inclusion of Japan and Russia, which had no money to lend, it was written plainly enough in the terms upon which the credit was "Six power" to be given to China. That government, loan though anxious for the money, was unwilling to be bound by the engagements proposed, a hesitation which probably caused recognition of the Chinese republic to be withheld in order that pressure might be brought to United States bear upon it. On March 18, 1913, President withdraws from "six Wilson reversed this policy. He led the way power" loan in the recognition of the new republic, and withdrew the government support from the "six power" loan. "The conditions of the loan," he said, "seem to us to touch very nearly the administrative independence of China itself, and this administration does not feel that it ought, even by implication, to be a party to those conditions." As a result, the American bankers withdrew from the syndicate. Although this action is in line with his attitude toward concessions to syndicates in Spanish America, the administration did not go so far in China as to oppose the activities of others; and the five remaining powers continued their negotiations.

Our relations with China herself have been simple and good-natured, particularly during the agreeable mission of United States Wu Ting Fang to this country. The question and China of Chinese immigration has been left on the basis of the treaty of 1894, which was continued in 1903.[1] In the treaty that perpetuated it, new ports, inland navigation, and mining rights were opened up, and trademarks, patents, and copyrights were provided for. Missions were placed upon an exceptionally strong basis, which allowed societies to rent and lease lands and buildings in any part of the empire, and exempted Chinese Christians from taxation for the support of "religious customs and practices contrary to their faith." An elaborate tariff was made a part of the

[1] A. P. C. Griffin, *Select list of References on Chinese Immigration*, Library of Congress, 1904.

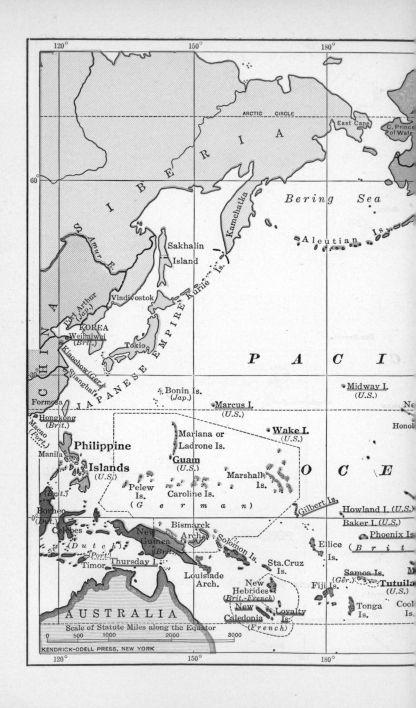

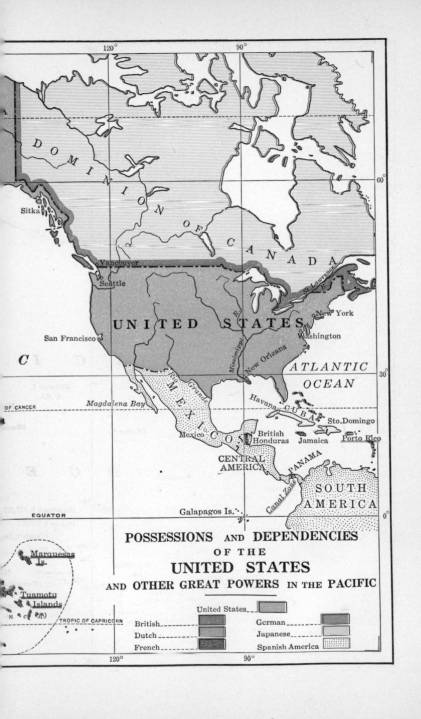

POSSESSIONS AND DEPENDENCIES
OF THE
UNITED STATES
AND OTHER GREAT POWERS IN THE PACIFIC

treaty. Finally, the use of a portion of the Boxer indemnity fund to aid Chinese students to study in this country bids fair to increase the friendliness between the two peoples.

With Japan the situation has been very different. With that country we now have more points of contact than with any other nation except Great Britain. United States The fact is, though it is not yet recognized and Japan politically, that this embassy has taken the position held by that of Spain until 1898, as the second in importance. In addition to the direct questions involved by a large trade and an unpopular immigration, we have to deal with Japan as occupying Chinese territory in Manchuria, as well as in her relations to Spanish America, which are founded on a large and increasing immigration to nearly all of those republics. The situation is further complicated in the United States by the belief that Japan desires Hawaii and the Philippines, and in Japan by a disappointment, to say the least, that we secured the latter islands, as well as by resentment at our attitude toward Japanese emigrants.

The first difficulty lay in the objection on the part of a large element of American public opinion, particularly on the Pacific coast, to Japanese immigration. Japanese This objection was partly racial and partly immigration due to the fear of competition in the labor market with the overflowing populations of the Orient. The position and the self-conscious pride of Japan made impossible any such treaty arrangement as was made with China. In fact the treaties of 1894 and 1911 both granted a mutual right of immigration. Under these trying circumstances Secretary Root succeeded in putting the question at rest, by an agreement, expressed in a series of notes exchanged in 1907 and 1908, whereby the Japanese government itself undertook to prohibit the emigration of laborers to the United States. A similar understanding between Japan and Canada prevents the danger of the smuggling of coolies across the border, and a United States law prevents Japanese labor already resident in Hawaii from migrating to the states. In this way Japanese pride was saved, and the desire of American opinion was for the time being met.

The problem of the position of Japanese now resident in the United States has proved more perplexing. By treaty they
Japanese in the United States
are secured the rights of citizens of the most favored nation, but they are ineligible to citizenship. In the case of the Italians, who were unpopular in the nineties, the securing of the franchise has, politically at any rate, secured them full acceptance. The Japanese, being politically negligible, are at the mercy of legislation in so far as they are not protected by treaty rights. Their privileges have been interfered with by legislation in several states, in such a way, the Japanese government claims, as to violate our treaty obligation. The chief complaint has been of California. In 1913 the legislature of that state, after many years of agitation with regard to their use of schools and other privileges, adopted a small measure of discrimination by prohibiting leases of agricultural land for more than three years to persons "ineligible to citizenship." In the actual situation this restriction applies almost entirely to the Japanese. The qualifications for citizenship are of course a purely domestic affair; but the making of the standard of eligibility a rule for granting further favors, when that standard applies almost wholly to one nation, certainly raises a delicate question under the most favored nation clause.

This dispute still persists, but otherwise our relations have been exceptionally friendly. The floating of a Japanese
Japanese-American understanding
loan in the United States at the time of the war with Russia established a tie, and our coöperation in China was generally conducive to good feeling. In 1908 Secretary Root and the Japanese ambassador exchanged notes to the effect that their wish was for the peaceful development of their commerce on the Pacific; that "the policy of both governments, uninfluenced

by any aggressive tendencies, is directed to the maintenance of the existing status quo in the region above mentioned, and to the defense of the principle of equal opportunity for commerce and industry in China;" that they both stood for the independence and integrity of China; and that, should any event threaten the existing conditions, "it remains for the two governments to communicate with each other in order to arrive at an understanding as to what measures they may consider it useful to take."

In thus defending our interests in the Pacific, and at the same time exerting a decided influence on international policy, even to the point of having possibly prevented the dismemberment of China, with so little resulting international bad feeling and that of a character practically inevitable and without becoming involved in any entangling alliance, American diplomacy has shown itself at its best and worthy of the early traditions of the republic.[1]

Avoidance of entangling alliances

[1] W. R. Thayer, "John Hay," *Harper's Magazine*, 1915, especially 836–842, throws much light on Hay's personality and on diplomatic problems, particularly the Alaska boundary and the canal problem. His life of Hay will appear in 1915.

CHAPTER XXXIII

ROUTINE AND ARBITRATION [1]

WITH our policy of dominance in the Caribbean, of exclusion of foreign influence throughout Spanish America, of
Africa equal compromise with Great Britain in British North America, of participation in Eastern Asia, of non-interference in Europe, Africa remains open. Our joining in an international receivership for Liberia in 1912, must, of course, be attributed to a special parental interest in that little republic; but our participation in the Algeciras conference in 1906 was merely an accidental result of our signing the act of 1880 concerning Morocco, and led to no entangling consequences. The Senate ratified the "General Act" of the conference with the distinct assertion that it was not to be deemed a departure on our part from our traditional policy of having nothing to do with "the settlement of questions which are entirely European in their scope." We have no African policy.

With Turkey, a power partly European and partly Asiatic, the United States has also assumed no special attitude. It
Turkey has followed the example of European nations in reserving to its own consuls the jurisdiction over its own citizens. This matter has been the subject of perennial dispute, as differing texts have been found of our treaty of 1830, upon which our claim to the privileges of extraterritoriality have been chiefly based. Our insistence upon the practice, however, was placed by Hay in 1900 on the most favored nation clause, and we have maintained it. What action will be taken now that Turkey has (1914) abrogated

[1] *American Year Book*, 1910. This annual and the *International Year Book* give good accounts of the diplomacy of each year.

the privilege in the case of all nations, is uncertain; the most favored nation clause ceases to have any significance in the connection, and our treaty is abrogated with the rest. We have taken no part in the concert of powers which has so often intervened and remonstrated as a result of conditions within the Turkish empire. In 1894 the Senate passed resolutions looking to expostulation because of reported "atrocities;" but President Cleveland stated that, since the European powers were bound together in the matter by the treaty of Berlin, we could not take action without inconvenience, and that he had already declined an invitation of the Turkish government to investigate conditions.

The protection of our citizens there has, however, been a perpetual source of annoyance and dispute. These controversies have been chiefly of two classes, those relating to missionaries, and those having to do **Missions** with naturalized citizens of Turkish origin. Our missions, particularly numerous in Syria and including the important Roberts College at Constantinople, have been permitted, and have enjoyed protection. By an agreement of 1874, definitely interpreted in 1910, they have even been allowed to hold property. Our whole position has been simplified by the fact that united Europe demands the fullest freedom in such matters, and that we have since 1903 claimed and have not been denied, equal treatment. Our position has been that whatever concessions of this character have been granted European nations, become automatically ours by right. In the case of injury to missions or to other American property during the disorders so frequent in Turkey, we have never succeeded in making the Sublime Porte acknowledge our claims by formal treaty. In one instance, however, indemnity was virtually granted by an agreed overpayment for the construction of a Turkish war vessel by an American firm.

The situation of our naturalized natives of Turkey is

extremely disagreeable, and, owing to the increased immigration of Armenians and Syrians to this country, the matter has been of growing importance. Turkey allows expatriation only by permission and on condition of renewing Turkish citizenship immediately upon return to the empire. European nations, having no large interchange of population with Turkey, have acquiesced in this position; and the United States has been obliged to follow their example. Natives of Turkey who have become naturalized in the United States, therefore, whether with or without the permission of the Turkish government, cannot expect from the United States that full protection afforded to native American citizens or naturalized citizens born elsewhere than Turkey. This does not, however, mean that they are neglected. The United States embassy and consular officials are always on the alert, and have actually afforded a protection sufficiently efficacious to make it worth while to forge American passports. It is this lack of definite agreement and the possibility of accomplishing so much by personal effort, that makes the embassy at Constantinople so important. It is generally given to a man of personality, and it was here that Oscar S. Straus did so much to ameliorate conditions. Legally the conditions with regard to naturalization are similar in Russia, but there the subject has been handled on the basis of general understandings, which for a long time worked fairly satisfactorily. The dangers inherent in the situation however, are illustrated by the dispute over Russia's decision to exclude entirely Russian Jews naturalized in America, which led in 1912 to the denunciation of our treaty of commerce with that country by Congress.

In Europe itself the shadow of the profound and united animosity, which succeeded the Spanish War, quickly vanished with the realization that our new policy was not aggressive in fields particularly interesting to that continent,—that we did not threaten the equipoise of European power, that our gigantic trade balances were not eternal, that New York did not take the place of European capitals as the center for foreign loans. Perhaps, too, there was a feeling that, if we were strong, it would be good policy to cultivate us.

Change in attitude of Europe

Quick to perceive these facts, the Kaiser became demonstrative in his friendliness, sending his brother Prince Henry to visit us, presenting the nation with a statute of Frederick the Great and Harvard University with the material to fill a Germanic museum, leading the way in the cultivation of international good will by the establishment of exchange professorships, and asking President Roosevelt's daughter to christen his new racing yacht, the building of which in America was a compliment to a national industry of which we are justly proud. France, less successful in engaging the popular attention, followed in his wake with a statue of Rochambeau, which recalled to our people when reading one morning newspaper, the aid that she had given us under his leadership during our Revolution. She too provided exchange professorships. This effusive friendship was harmless, and, if it did not much affect the stand taken by Germany on American pork, it at least provided a pleasanter atmosphere for negotiation.

With Europe, the question of immigration to the United States has far-reaching possibilities. The floods of immigrants that have lately come to our shores from that continent have excited the apprehension of widely differing classes of our population.

European immigration

Senator Lodge has made himself spokesman of the movement toward exclusion, and the labor element has complained of being exposed to the competition of newcomers satisfied with a low standard of living. This agitation has taken form in the exclusion of persons with disease, with criminal records, or those likely to become dependent upon the public for support. As a further precaution, Congress in 1912 and twice

in 1914 passed acts establishing a literary test. The first
of these was vetoed by President Taft, and the other two met
a like fate from President Wilson. Nevertheless some
further legislation is probable in the near future.

While such action would not necessarily lead to foreign
complications, yet the laws that we already have give rise
Roumanian to many minor diplomatic problems, and in
note 1902 Secretary Hay took a new stand with
many potentialities. On July 17 of that year he wrote to
our minister accredited to Roumania concerning a proposed
convention in regard to naturalization. After discussing our
general policy, he added: "It behooves the State to scrutinize
most jealously the character of the immigration from a foreign
land, and, if it be obnoxious to objection, to examine the
causes which render it so. Should those causes originate
in the act of another sovereign State, to the detriment of
its neighbors, it is the prerogative of an injured State, to
point out the evil and to make remonstrance; for with nations, as with individuals, the social law holds good that the
right of each is bounded by the right of the neighbor." He
found that the action of Roumania made life intolerable to
the Jews. "Removal under such conditions is not and cannot be the healthy, intelligent emigration of a free and self-
reliant being. It must be, in most cases, the mere trans-
plantation of an artifically produced diseased growth to a
new place." Our opposition was not to Jews, but to out-
casts and paupers. We would make no treaty by which,
under existing conditions, we were forced to take them, or
by which they were to be prevented from returning to
Roumania.[1]

Our action in this matter was limited to our remonstrance
and our refusal to make a treaty. The suggestion of Secretary Bryan, in 1913, to the Bucharest conference of the Balkan states, that it permit full religious liberty, seems to have

[1] Cyrus Adler, *Jews in the Diplomatic Correspondence of the United States*
Amer. Jewish Hist. Soc., *Publications*, No. 15 (1906).

been in accordance with this policy. Our national annoyance at the forced immigration due to the artificial stimulation caused by the advertisements and solicitations of steamship lines, has not reached the point of definite diplomatic action; but we have called the attention of the nations concerned to the subject, and have met with sympathetic response from Italy. The prospective opening of the Panama canal, with the possibility of water transit to the Pacific Coast, caused the subject to receive special attention in 1914.

Undue stimulation of immigration

The routine problems of diplomacy did not require quite so much attention during this period as in that from the Civil to the Spanish war, although the number of actual cases was far greater. We made first treaties only with Ethiopia, more commonly known as Abyssinia, and with San Marino. The area of extradition practically covered the globe, and the protection of our trademarks, patents, and copyrights became almost world-wide. Claims we arranged with Brazil, Chili, Great Britain, Guatemala, Hayti, Peru, Russia, Salvador, and Venezuela. These were all submitted to some form of arbitration.

First treaties, extradition, and trade-marks

Although our ocean merchant marine remained relatively small, we took no steps to improve it that involved our relations with other countries. The era of maritime discrimination, except in regard to coasting trade, had passed. For the maintenance of their commercial flags at sea, nations had come to rely on subsidies and on the creation of conditions favorable to ship-building and employment. Congress was continually and earnestly urged to adopt a subsidy policy, but refused to do so. Such legislation as was adopted from time to time rather repressed than encouraged the development of a marine under our flag. The laws concerning the registration of vessels, granting the right to carry the American flag, made it difficult to register foreign built vessels, the intention being to encourage

Merchant marine

domestic ship-building. The various tariffs, however, by protecting the materials for ship-building, increased its cost. While thus making American built ships more costly, the government was not able to afford them compensating protection, for the competition of the ocean marine is international, and equality is the most that can be obtained by international agreement. It was hoped that the tariff law of 1913 would remove some of the disadvantages under which we labored, but conditions since its passage have been so unusual as to render it impossible to estimate its effect. The outbreak of the great war of 1914, therefore, found us in the position that Jefferson described in his report of 1793; chiefly dependent for our foreign intercourse upon the marines of warring foreign nations. The situation thus created led to a widespread interest in the problem, from which some consistent and effective national policy may result. Already (March, 1915) the opening of American registry to foreign built vessels has brought us half a million tons of shipping. President Wilson's proposal for a nation-owned marine suggests interesting possibilities.

The attempt to create openings for our commerce was constant and more successful. In 1903 a special reciprocity treaty was made with Cuba. The Dingley tariff act of 1897, authorized the President to negotiate, within two years, reciprocity treaties providing for a twenty per cent reduction of duties, such agreement to be subject in every case to the ratification of the Senate and the approval of Congress. J. A. Kasson was appointed special commissioner to secure such treaties, and obtained them with Great Britain in behalf of Barbadoes, Bermuda, British Guiana, Turk island and Caicos, and Jamaica, also with the Argentine Republic, France, the Dominican Republic, Ecuador, and Denmark. Although Senator Cullom, chairman of the senate committee on foreign affairs, strongly urged that the treaties should go into effect immediately upon their ratification by the Senate, that view was not

Reciprocity

pressed, and at the suggestion of Senator Spooner each of
them was amended by the addition of the clause "not to
take effect until the same shall have been approved by the
Congress." This admission of the power of Congress as a
whole in these particular cases left open the general question of the rights of the President and Senate to make such
treaties. Under these circumstances, only the treaty with
France was accepted, in 1898, with an amendment in 1902.[1]

In addition, the Dingley act gave the President power to
apply by proclamation varying fixed minimum and maximum tariffs to different countries according
to their treatment of us. This measure proved **Maximum and minimum rates**
to be a powerful weapon in preventing retalia-
tory and discriminating tariffs. It became the constant
business of our diplomats to watch the commercial policies
of foreign governments, and with the threat of high or the
offer of low rates to secure favorable treatment for our
merchants. Such agreements were made in 1900 with Italy,
Germany, and Portugal, and in 1902 an additional one was
arranged with Portugal; in 1906 one was made with Spain
and a substitute one with Germany; and in 1908 the treaty
with France was supplemented by such an agreement. In
1906 the President, without formal compact, but in consideration of tariff changes in Switzerland, proclaimed a
low rate on our imports of her products. With the passage
of the Payne-Aldrich tariff act in 1910, all these agreements
fell. A similar minimum and maximum provision in the latter
act, however, afforded opportunity for similar agreements,
and a tariff mission was able promptly to make arrangements
with most of the countries with which we trade heavily.
These again ceased to be of force with the passage of the
Underwood tariff of 1913, which nevertheless authorized
the President "to negotiate trade agreements with foreign
nations," providing for mutual concessions "looking toward
free trade relations and further reciprocal expansion of trade

[1] S. M. Cullom, *Fifty Years of Public Service*, Chicago, 1911.

and commerce." These are to be ratified in each case by both houses of Congress.

It was only natural that, with our new and wider international relationships and the constant progress of international agreement, the scope of our international acts should expand also. In 1898 we adopted as a *modus vivendi* during our war with Spain, articles relating to the conduct of hostilities drawn up at a Geneva convention of 1864. In 1899 we adhered to a Convention regulating the Importation of Spirituous Liquors into Africa, and in 1906 to a new agreement on the same subject. In 1900 we were parties to an additional Act for the Protection of Industrial Property, in 1902 to a Convention on Literary and Artistic Copyrights, in 1903 to an International Sanitary Convention. In 1902 we united with most of the American powers in a Convention for the Arbitration of Pecuniary Claims, and in 1905 in an International Sanitary Convention of which the other signatories were Central and South American states. In 1904 we joined in an international exemption of hospital ships from the payment of dues. In 1905 we shared in the establishment of an International Institute of Agriculture at Rome, of which the first director was an American. In 1906 we were signatory to an International Red Cross Convention for the amelioration of the condition of the wounded of the armies in the field, in the same year to an agreement for the unification of the Pharmacopœial Formulas for Potent Drugs, and in 1907 to the establishment of an International Office of Public Health.

During the whole of this period one of the most absorbing subjects of our diplomacy, as well as of popular interest in diplomacy, was the movement for the improvement of the conditions of war and for the customary settlement of international disputes by judicial process. Arbitration in special cases has been a historic policy of the United States. Blaine's attempt to establish it as a

International agreements

Peace movement

general practice for all America showed, as did so many of his policies, a premonition of the coming movement. In the period following the Spanish war many of our leaders welcomed it with enthusiasm. President Roosevelt endorsed it, and Secretaries Hay, Root, and Bryan, as well as President Taft, made it a leading purpose. The education of public sentiment in the direction of universal peace was organized on a colossal scale as a result of the munificence of Andrew Carnegie and Edwin Ginn, and of the activity of A. K. Smiley, who since 1882 has called the believers in peace to annual conferences at Lake Mohonk. The pressure of always-impending war in Spanish America, however, excited those countries to a somewhat earlier application of arbitration as a general practice, and the tremendous cost of war armaments in Europe, combined with the militant patriotism of its great powers, have given the question a greater popular vitality there than with us.

The first important step in the direction of peace was the calling by the Czar of the first Hague conference, which met in 1899. This body adopted certain principles to govern the conduct of war on land and sea, Hague conferences and established a permanent court of arbitration to sit at the Hague. The second conference, held in 1907, adopted additional rules with regard to the conduct of war, reorganized the court, and declared the principle that the contract debts of one government to another should not be collected by force. Andrew Carnegie gave funds for the building of a palace for the work of the court, to the furnishing of which various nations presented evidences of their regard for peace.[1]

The formation of a permanent court stimulated the resort to arbitration. The United States joined in sending many

[1] W. I. Hull, *The Two Hague Conferences*, Boston, 1908; Moore, *American Diplomacy*, ch. viii.; J. W. Foster, *Arbitration and the Hague Court*, Boston, 1904; Lake Mohonk Conference on International Arbitration, *Reports*, 1895, etc., Assoc. for International Conciliation, *International Conciliation*, 1907, etc. (issued monthly).

cases to it, particularly its long-standing claim against Mexico for the "Pious fund," and suggested the court as a recourse General arbitration agreeable to us for the settlement of Spanish-American disputes with European powers. More important was the impetus which it gave to the adoption of general arbitration treaties providing for future cases. In 1902, for instance, Spain and Mexico came to a ten years' agreement for the compulsory reference to the Hague court of all their troubles that could not be settled by diplomacy.

A model treaty known as the mondel, or world treaty, was devised by the Conference. This provided that all differences The model treaties of a legal nature as well as all those relating to the interpretation of treaties, which could not be settled by diplomacy, and which did not affect vital interests, independence, or honor, should be referred to the Hague Court. This reference was not to be automatic, but every dispute which arose between the contracting nations was to be made the subject of a special protocol or agreement. The point gained for judicial settlement, was that the contracting nations bound themselves to make such arrangements. The treaty itself was to be of five years' duration. It was a very tentative step, but it was hoped that if generally accepted, it would land mankind somewhat nearer the goal of universal peace. Secretary Hay concluded treaties in general accord with this model with a number of nations, and President Roosevelt referred them to the Senate.

In that body there was general approval, tempered by fear that they might lead to cases involving the bonds which Attitude of Senate have been repudiated by a number of our states. The Senate was also alarmed because no provision was made that the special protocols in each case should be submitted to it for approval. If all such international disputes were simply to be sent by the President to the Hague, the prestige of the Senate would be decidedly diminished. President Roosevelt wrote Senator Cullom, chairman of the committee on foreign affairs, that it was "absurd and probably mischievous to treat" the question of state debts " as possible to be raised." On the subject of reference, however, both he and Hay were emphatic that it was intended to be kept in the hands of the President, and that it should be kept there; whereupon the Senate straightway amended the treaties by substituting the word "treaty" for "special agreement," thus removing the doubt and keeping the matter in its own hands.[1]

President Roosevelt was so deeply incensed at this action that he refused to go on with the treaties. Secretary Root, with the approval of President Taft, however, renewed the project and secured a large number in the amended form. In 1908 and 1909 we made them with Austria-Hungary, China, Costa Rica, Denmark, France, Great Britain, Hayti, Italy, Japan, Mexico, the Netherlands, Norway, Paraguay, Peru, Portugal, Salvador, Spain, Sweden, and Switzerland. *Acceptance of the treaties*

In 1913 Secretary Bryan sought to extend the scope of arbitration still farther by carrying out one of the recommendations of the second Hague conference looking to the postponement of hostilities, from whatever cause, pending an investigation of the facts. This suggestion, reminding one of the "pause twenty minutes before you spank" principle, which has done so much to reduce the corporal punishment of children, would help offset the exciting effect of the telegraph and the cable, which have enabled the popular excitement in two countries to react so quickly and so constantly. Secretary Bryan's proposal met with so prompt a response from most of the countries with which we have habitual dealings, that in the summer of 1914 twenty such treaties were submitted to the Senate. *Bryan's policy*

The years from 1898 to 1913 may be regarded as a period by themselves, partly because of the continuity of personnel in the diplomatic staff, and partly from the fact that prac-

[1] Cullom, *Fifty Years of Public Service.*

tically all terminable difficulties had been settled by the latter year. It was a period replete with new policies and with Period 1898 the development of old ones to suit new con-to 1913 ditions, and over the whole period hung the uncertainty as to whether, should the opposing party come to power, these new departures would be confirmed, or dropped or changed. The administration of President Wilson does indeed bid fair to mark a turning point in international relationships, and to usher in a new period. Mainly, however, this diplomatic change has been the result of new factors introduced from the outside, of the great calamity of the present (1915) world war. The situation has altered, but American policy has remained comparatively unchanged. The traditional American policies have been maintained and the most of the new ideas introduced under McKinley, Roosevelt, and Taft, having been endorsed by the opposing party, are in fair way to become traditions. Those few which were reversed, as Secretary Knox's "dollar diplomacy" may be considered as still subjects of domestic controversy.

In many respects the outstanding feature of this period was, as for that from 1815 to 1829, the clearing of the board of minor Routine and questions of all kinds,—boundaries, fisheries, cit-commerce izenship, claims, and treaty interpretations,— some of them old problems, some new, but all interfering with cordial international relationships. Never before had we been quite so free from such food for quarrelling as we were by 1913. In this period, as in all others, diplomacy sought to aid commerce, its attempts were perhaps somewhat more positive than before, but were of such a character that it is difficult to estimate their effect.

Much more spectacular was the expansion of territory. The new acquisitions were more remarkable for the novelty Expansion of of their characteristics than for their extent. territory For the first time we violated Jefferson's injunction to make no annexations that would require a navy for their defense. In the case of the Philippines there was the further novelty that we professed an intention of holding them only until they should be ready for independence. In reality far more important than the exten- Expansion of sion of our dominions was our entrance into influence the diplomacy of eastern Asia. Although still avoiding entangling alliances, we nevertheless engaged in the problems of the Far East as an equal participant with the great powers of Europe. Our purposes were limited to the preservation of the integrity of China and the open door for trade, ideas that appealed to the ideals of our own people, and were calculated to command the acquiescence if not the heartfelt approval of foreign nations. At the same time we cordially coöperated with other nations in general measures for the protection of commerce, for the peaceful settlement of international disputes, and for the humane conduct of war, if war must be.

Our most striking single achievement was the settlement on a new basis, in accordance with our changed opinion, of the status of isthmian transit. Although Isthmian this determination of the question has proved policy its worth by allowing the actual construction of the long-planned canal, it can hardly be regarded as diplomatically satisfactory, or as likely to withstand the strain of a war to which we ourselves should be a party. In connection with the canal we have developed a distinct Caribbean policy, which has not been thoroughly differentiated from what we call the Monroe Doctrine, but which is actually different.

The Monroe Doctrine itself has continued its growth by accretion; even more than the Constitution has it been adjusted to meet new wants, while preserving Persistence of the sanctity of an established and revered the Monroe name. Although monarchy and republicanism Doctrine cease to stand in such striking opposition as they did in 1823, the European system of alliances and balance of power is still a real something which we wish to avoid, and have thus far successfully avoided. Though our relations have grown, and will continue to grow, increasingly intimate, we have not become a part of the European system. It is, however, still a possibility, as it was in 1823, that we may by our own action or by the force of circumstances, become a member of it. It is still the wish of some European statesmen that this may become the case, and some Americans are not adverse to the idea. The fact that for ninety years, ever since our declaration against further colonization, there has been no establishment of new European colonies in America decidedly strengthens our continued insistence on that point. On the other hand, the fact that in the same ninety years the only colonies in America from which European authority has been removed are Alaska, Cuba, and Porto Rico somewhat deadens the force of Secretary Olney's declaration that all the colonies are destined to break off their dependence. Fortunately he set no date. If any new case should occur, we should probably still maintain the position announced by Polk in the case of Yucatan, that we could not with equanimity see even the voluntary passing of any American territory under European jurisdiction; and probably, we should also hold the position taken by Grant, that we should object to the transfer of any colony from one European power to another, at least where such transfer was likely to change the status of American affairs. The development of an American unity to confront the duality of Europe, which Adams and Clay planned, which Blaine did so much to promote, was pressed in this period with vigor and with some success, but must be held to be a long way from accomplishment. Our American policy is still the policy of the United States.

The most important new features or corollaries of our policy were our announcements that, with a view to reducing the opportunity for European interference, we were willing, by mediation, advice, guardianship, and practical protectorates, to insure the carrying out by American governments of their general obligations to Europeans. To what extent we are ready to

New corollaries of the Monroe Doctrine

push this supervision is a matter to be determined in each case, but there can be no doubt that we would go farther within the region of our special interest, the Caribbean, than elsewhere. It is significant that the new corollary of the Wilson administration, to the effect that we will recognize only governments founded on justice and law, was not applied in the case of Peru, where a military government was promptly recognized at the very time when we were protesting against the government of Huerta in Mexico.

CHAPTER XXXIV

MEXICO

WHEN Woodrow Wilson became President, March 4, 1913, he found himself in a position somewhat similar to that of

Wilson administration

Jefferson in 1801, of Jackson in 1829, and of Lincoln in 1861. Most of the diplomatic problems of the time had been set at rest, and policies for dealing with routine affairs had been adopted and were running smoothly. He called to the position of secretary of state William Jennings Bryan, who, being without experience in matters of state, would naturally be expected to be chiefly interested in the general politics of the administration. In selecting John Bassett Moore as counsellor of the state department, however, he secured the promise of sound judgment and continuity of action.[1]

Wilson at once reversed one policy of the previous administration by withdrawing the assistance of diplomacy to

Change of policy

Americans seeking concessions in China, and announced a new extension of the Monroe Doctrine by opposing concessions to foreign corporations by American nations. The second of these new departures promised to make up to the state department the loss of labor which the first might cause. Of the three unsettled and exciting questions left to him, two were the dispute with Great Britain concerning the canal toll, and that relating to the position of Japanese residents in this country. Both these matters he endeavored to settle by domestic action. In the interest of the second one, Secretary Bryan visited California and attempted to forestall action by her legislature, but this attempt failed, and the controversy con-

[1] Resigned March 4, 1914.

tinues. In the matter of tolls, the President recommended Congress to revoke its action. This it did, and that question has vanished.

The third and most important problem was that of Mexico. Contiguous, within the range of our Caribbean policy, and powerful, Mexico had always demanded Relations with a large share of our diplomatic attention. To Mexico these causes of interest have usually been added those arising from her internal disorder; but that factor had come to be excluded from our consideration during the long presidency of Porfirio Diaz, which had given a peace that seemed established. The intimacy of our relationship is indicated by forty agreements, treaties, and conventions made in the forty years between 1868 and 1908. These included, besides the usual subjects of international negotiation, arrangements with regard to boundary, the pursuit of Indians, provision for the navigation of the Rio Grande, and the equitable distribution of the waters of that river. The agreements finally culminated in a general treaty of arbitration and the meeting of Taft and Diaz in 1910.

While the governments were thus intimate, and in general friendly, the citizens of the United States were infiltrating Mexico. This infiltration, however, was dif- Foreign interests in ferent from that which Alaman saw and feared terests in in Texas, it was most largely an infiltration of Mexico capital. Peace had opened up enormous possibilities of development, for which Mexico could furnish the opportunity and the labor, but not the accumulated capital necessary to combine the two. The rewards promised to capital were correspondingly great and it was furnished in large amounts. Mining companies and railroad corporations invested enormous sums, and ranching companies, rubber plantation companies, and municipal utility companies scattered their shares broadcast. Private individuals engaged in great undertakings, and to hasten development the Mexican government itself borrowed heavily. This capital came from all the investing countries of the world, but chiefly from the United States. In 1912, President Taft estimated that a billion dollars had been invested by Americans. This capital did not go unaccompanied. It sent its representatives to Mexico, and in addition, organizing ability

Foreign population in Mexico

and expert service were needed. Thousands of Americans, with many English, French, and Germans, found employment there. Spaniards continued, as always, to be numerous. Although the foreign colony at the City of Mexico was large, the majority of these foreigners were not to be found in compact settlements, but scattered about the country, managing mines, ranches, and plantations, and living in the midst of a population overwhelmingly native. The one important exception was an agricultural colony of American Mormons in the north.

When, therefore, in November, 1910, Francisco Madero inaugurated a revolution, the event became at once a matter

Revolution of Madero

of high concern for the United States and for other foreign powers. While France, Spain, Germany, Great Britain, and the United States were all interested in the protection of the lives and property of their citizens, the United States was additionally disturbed over the relation of the revolt to the Monroe Doctrine, as well as over the possibility of frontier disturbances. The latter question was the more immediately alarming, as the revolution was to some extent sectional in character and in the beginning was localized in the north, the strategic points being those at which the railroads ran out of Mexico into United States territory. Juarez, Porfirio Diaz, and Larado ultimately became the scene of fighting, and stray bullets sometimes crossed the frontier and killed Americans upon American soil. In March, 1911, therefore, President Taft ordered the mobilization of twenty thousand United States troops on the frontier, with a fleet at Galveston. The rumors that these forces were intended to take part in a forcible intervention, however, Secretary Knox dismissed as "foolish stories." We did, in point of fact preserve our neutrality according to our customary principles.

The speedy collapse of the Diaz government was a surprise to most Americans, who were unaware of the general unrest and dissatisfaction which his failure to **Madero's** broaden the limits of popular government and **success** relieve the distress of the agricultural laborers had excited. While those with financial interests in Mexico regretted the passing of a government apparently strong and sympathetic with their aims, the general public in America came to sympathize with Madero, as the press spread the complaints of the revolutionists. There was, therefore, general satisfaction in the United States when, in May, 1911, Diaz resigned and left the country and, in October, Madero was elected president.

The government of the latter was at once recognized, but was never able to establish peace. Even in 1911 the United States warned him that fighting was not to **United States** take place where American lives and property **and Madero** would be endangered; and our army was kept ready for action. Nevertheless, while favoring the new government, we preserved strict neutrality, and in 1912 Congress took an additional step in the development of our neutral system by the passage of an act authorizing the President, whenever he should "find that in any American country conditions of domestic violence exist which are promoted by the use of arms and munitions of war procured from the United States," to prohibit trade in such articles. Taft acted at once upon this authority, but he exempted purchases by the government of Madero.

In February, 1913, however, Madero was overthrown by Felix Diaz and General Huerta. Madero and his vice-president, Suarez, were killed under circum- **Revolution of** stances which strongly indicated official assas- **Huerta** sination, and on February 27 Huerta was proclaimed president. His authority was at once rejected by Governor

Carranza of the state of Coahuila, who denied its constitutionality and insisted upon a return to the governmental methods prescribed by the constitution.

It was under these circumstances that Wilson became President and undertook the management of the problem. **Wilson and Huerta** Before his policy was developed, Great Britain, on May 3, and France, Germany, and other countries in quick succession, recognized Huerta. This Wilson refused to do, and in explaining his action he formulated a new policy which remains the latest extension of the Monroe Doctrine. His purpose was to use non-recognition as a means of discouraging the establishment of governments in Spanish America that were based on violence, and on violation of the constitution of the country involved and of the laws of morality. "We dare not," he declared, "turn from the principle that morality and not expediency is the thing that is to guide us and that we will never condone iniquity because it is most convenient to do so." This is a departure from our traditional policy of recognizing *de facto* governments, although there exists one precedent in the threat of the Roosevelt administration not to acknowledge a revolutionary leader in the Dominican Republic even if he succeeded. Our practical protectorate over that country however, together with its size, constituted important differences.

President Wilson's attitude of non-recognition is by all odds the most aggressive turn that has ever been given to **The policy of "non-recognition"** our Spanish-American policy, as it involves practical intervention in the domestic affairs of those republics. To ascertain the facts obviously means investigation. In actual operation the force created by such a policy of non-recognition consists in the lack of stability which it gives to the government under our disapprobation, and the consequent inability of the latter to borrow money. It is plainly President Wilson's belief that a government not founded on the popular will constitutionally expressed, and without our recognition, is a house built upon the sands. Should such a government establish itself, however, the situation might be inconvenient.

In accordance with this policy, Wilson in August, 1913, sent a special but informal agent, John Lind, to convey his terms to Huerta. These were immediate **"Watchful** amnesty, security for an early and a free elec- **waiting"** tion, and the assurance that Huerta would not be candidate for the presidency and that all parties would agree to abide by the results. These terms were rejected; when, therefore, on October 9, 1913, Huerta "purged" the Mexican Congress by imprisoning over a hundred of its members, Wilson informed him that the United States would not accept the result of the election which was soon to be held. Already in August the United States had warned Americans to leave Mexico, the administration had sent war-vessels to assist their departure, and Congress had appropriated money for the same purpose. On December 2, the President informed Congress that his policy was one of "watchful waiting." Hoping for the success of the insurrectionists, he soon afterward withdrew the embargo on arms.

Meantime the administration vigorously, and with some degree of success, held both the Huerta government and the insurrectionists to a respect for the lives and **Protection of** property of Americans. It could not, however, **life and** insist on restitution and indemnity, since **property** there was no recognized government to approach on these subjects. The powers of Europe, having recognized Huerta, were in a different position, and it was feared that they might pursue a different policy. This fear was in part removed by a speech of Prime Minister Asquith, on November 10, 1913, in which he announced that, so far as Great Britain was concerned, there was "not a vestige of foundation for such a rumor;" and other nations assured the administration of their intention to respect American policy.

Nevertheless, the presence of British, German, and French war-vessels on the Mexican coast created alarm lest they should feel called upon to land troops to protect their citizens. Senator Bacon, chairman of the Senate committee on foreign affairs, admitted that we could not deny their right to do so, but said he considered "it far better that a request be made to the United States to land marines" when protection was necessary, "so as to avoid the possibility of the slightest conflict between the United States and the European Powers." The killing of Benton, an Englishman, by the revolutionary forces of General Villa in March, 1914, brought this question of protection to a head. Secretary Bryan asserted that, since Great Britain, having recognized Huerta and not recognized belligerency, could in no way treat with the Constitutionalists, and yet could not be expected to let the matter pass unnoticed, we should be allowed to serve as intermediary, with the understanding, however, that we thereby assumed no responsibility. This policy was acquiesced in by both Great Britain and, after some hesitation, by Villa's superior officer, General Carranza. Should another case occur, therefore, the United States will undoubtedly handle it as next friend of both parties.

The question arose whether the condition in Mexico constituted another of the traditional opportunities for American expansion. The infiltration of American capital and citizens, and the subsequent development of occasions for interference, were already there; the governor of Texas encouraged Texan citizens to cross the frontier in self-defence, the governor of Oregon prepared his militia for war with Mexico, and a bill for the annexation of northern Mexico was introduced into Congress. Even the final symptom, the fear of the intrusion of foreign influence in case we did not intervene, appeared. Japan had for some time been supposed to be seeking an entrance into Mexico. In 1912 the proposed purchase of

Magdalena bay for a Japanese colony excited the Senate to its adoption of Senator Lodge's resolution on the subject of concessions to a syndicate that might lead to the establishment of a foreign power on American territory. The sending of Felix Diaz by Huerta on a special mission to Japan in 1913 seemed to confirm the suspicion of undue intimacy, but the refusal of that government to receive him somewhat quieted our apprehension. In March, 1914, Senator Fall of New Mexico called for immediate intervention to prevent Germany from taking action in Mexico.

On the other hand, the process of expansion by the growth of American interests in foreign countries and the subsequent adhesion of these countries to the United States seems, except in case of Hawaii, to have been completed in 1845. The acquisition of the Philippines, although it gave evidence of our desire to anticipate other countries, was exceptional. It has been the theory, moreover, that our occupation of those islands is to last only until they shall obtain the capacity for self-government, an idea which the Wilson administration has endeavored to make the basis of its Philippine policy. Alaska was an instance of happy and largely accidental anticipation; annexation promoted expansion rather than the reverse. Our other acquisitions belong to the category of naval stations, and are to be attributed rather to our imperialistic tendencies than to our traditional expansive habits.

In spite of the dreams of a continental republic that Seward reflected, and in spite of our confident expectations of Cuba, the only settled portion of Spanish America that we have secured is Porto Rico. That island we took possession of because it was obviously foolish to have fought the Spanish war without putting an end to our century and a quarter of difficulties with Spain by excluding her, as Sumner said of Great Britain, from the "hemisphere"; and, having taken it from Spain, we could do nothing but annex it. In no settled portion of

Character of expansion into Spanish America

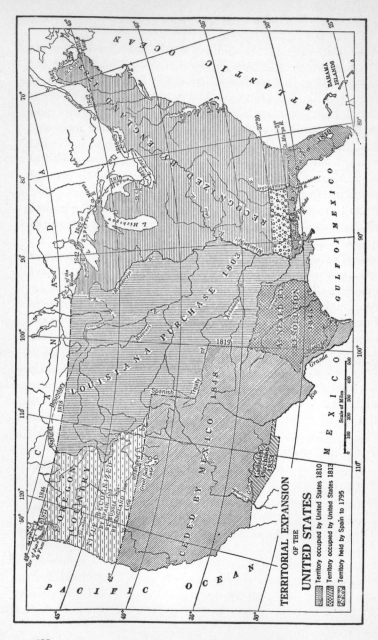

TERRITORIAL EXPANSION
OF THE
UNITED STATES

Territory occupied by United States 1810
Territory occupied by United States 1813
Territory held by Spain to 1795

488

Spanish America have we ever established a concentrated population, or acquired a preponderance of numbers or of influence, or established a likelihood of such a preponderance; nor has any Spanish-American population shown an inclination to become incorporated into the United States. There has always been lacking, therefore, that local germ which has been the moving cause of annexation in each natural case. Financial interests and the temporary residence of our citizens in a foreign country have never yet led us to acquire that country. Had Buchanan taken northern Mexico in pledge for our claims in 1858, it is possible that such a germ might have developed there; but the possibility of it now seems remote.

It is evident that we will not allow Mexico to become the seat of a power threatening our control of the Caribbean; but there is no probability that we shall ever receive from Mexico, or even from a part of The Vera Cruz episode Mexico, any authentic request for annexation, or that we shall in this case depart from President Wilson's pronouncement that "the United States will never again seek one foot of territory by conquest." In fact the very act which seemed to Spanish-American opinion most indicative of an intention on our part to conquer Mexico, was turned by President Wilson into the most convincing demonstration it has received of the sincerity of our constant protestation to the contrary. While our government refused to recognize either Huerta or Carranza as officially representative of Mexico, it was in constant relationship with both. In April, 1914 its relations with Huerta became so strained that it was decided to undertake a military occupation of Vera Cruz. This was accomplished not without bloodshed. Although the administration announced that hostilities would not be carried farther, the opinion was widespread that war and at least temporary conquest would result. The people of the United States were strongly divided as to the probability and wisdom of such action, Europe was deeply interested.

Spanish America was still more intensely aroused, and its press and public men were very generally convinced of the ambitions of the United States. In this crisis Argentina, Brazil, and Chili, known as the A B C powers, offered their mediation. This the Wilson administration promptly accepted, subject to certain restrictions, and a conference was The A B C   arranged at Niagara. The Mexican factions mediation   showed themselves less amenable to suggestion than the United States, and practically nothing was done towards solving the internal problems of Mexico. The attitude of the United States, however, was made clear to Spanish America, and the subsequent withdrawal of the American troops from Vera Cruz confirmed the impression, that it was guided by no motives of territorial aggrandizement.

CHAPTER XXXV

THE GREAT WAR

THE shadow which impending war had for some years cast over Europe, had not reached America, and the events of August, 1914, took almost everyone in the United States by complete surprise. They cannot be said, however, to have found the country unprepared. The teachings of Washington, the reverence for the Monroe Doctrine, the consistent practice of a century and a quarter, had furnished a policy and a general understanding of the requirements of that policy. The almost universal desire was for neutrality, and both government and people realized that neutrality was not merely a passive state but involved active duties. It was realized also that neutrality could not save the nation from all the consequences of war, and that the utmost vigilance would be required to protect the national interests.

Neutrality

History seemed to be repeating itself, and as nation after nation joined in the conflict, the conditions obtaining between 1793 and 1815 seemed to reappear. But actually history never repeats, and differences as important as the resemblances were soon evident. The first worry to which the country was subjected was the flight of the tens of thousands of American travellers who found themselves for a time, stranded, moneyless and without means of transportation, in the belligerent countries. The world had grown so much smaller in the hundred years, so many new strands of connection united the nations of the world, that war was bound to touch neutral individuals more intimately than ever before. On the other hand, the settlement of the naturalization question

Contrast between 1793 and 1915

rendered a revival of the impressment problem impossible. The sympathies of the American people were divided as they had been before, but now the basis for this division was not political theory but racial kinship. Still more important was the change in the relative weight of the United States among the nations of the world. While national interests were involved by the conflict and apt to be affected by its results, no sane opinion could suppose that the integrity of the national territory or what could properly be called vital interests were endangered.

The greatest disturbance was in commerce. In 1793, war had found the nation with a merchant marine ready not only to do its own carrying, but also to undertake much of that of the nations at war; in 1914, the country was largely dependent upon the marines of the belligerents, and the immediate tying up of the German marine left it for a time ill supplied. It followed that the United States was more interested than before in the rules and practices of war as they affected the treatment of belligerent vessels by belligerents. This interest, however, did not carry with it very extensive rights, and the main activity of the government was, as it previously had been, with the protection of American vessels.

Dislocation of commerce

The policy of the Allies, that is of the powers allied against Germany, Austria, and Turkey, was similar to that which Great Britain had pursued in the conflict with Napoleon, but somewhat simpler. On the one hand they wished to keep the oceans open for their commerce, on the other, to cut off Germany and Austria from all connection with the outside world. By the early months of 1915 the first object had been practically accomplished in all seas except those within the radius of action of submarines having their bases on the German or Belgian coasts. The accomplishment of the second was rendered difficult by the fact that several neutral countries, Italy, Switzerland, Holland, and Denmark. abutted on Ger-

Contraband and continuous voyage

man or Austrian territory, and that the Baltic remained in the control of the German fleet, thus protecting intercourse with the outside world through Norway and Sweden. To close these channels, the Allies resorted to the doctrines of contraband and of continuous voyage. The attitude which the United States had assumed in the Civil War, rendered it difficult for her to protest against a rather rigorous interpretation of the latter doctrine. With regard to contraband, the most serious question arose in connection with cotton. The decreased demand for this article constituted the most serious economic effect of the war on the United States. When it was proposed in addition to class it as contraband, thus checking its export to Germany, a vigorous and effective protest was made and it was left as a legitimate article of neutral trade.

That the Allies were slow in resorting to blockade was due to the changed conditions of naval warfare, which made it more dangerous than before to patrol a hostile **Blockade** coast line. Their inability to control the Baltic, moreover, rendered the effect of a regular blockade doubtful. In February, 1915, however, Germany, on the ground that the Allies were exceeding their rights as belligerents by declaring all foodstuffs contraband regardless of whether they were intended for combatants or non-combatants, announced a quasi-blockade of the British Isles by submarines. The Allies responded by declaring, first a virtual blockade of Germany and Austria, and then, on our complaint at its unusual nature, a real blockade. They argued that they were in a position to carry out the spirit of the law of blockade, though not its letter. This clash of decrees called to mind that between Napoleon and Great Britain, each power defending its position, not in law, but on the ground of retaliation. The effort of both to conciliate American opinion, however, marked a decided change. The German policy was directed only against belligerent ships, though neutrals were warned that they might incur danger;

the Allies promised compensation for all financial losses under the operation of their system. Analogous to these questions were those with regard to the use of mines. Although the Hague Conference had drawn up rules regulating their employment, whether of the floating or anchored variety, actual warfare produced situations which were unprovided for, and which involved the security of neutral commerce.

The desire of the United States to improvise as rapidly as possible a merchant marine, led to a revival of the question
Transfer of vessels of the transfer of merchant vessels from belligerent to neutral powers, which had so much angered the American public during the Civil War. The Declaration of London of 1910 had prohibited such transfer, and to this the United States had adhered, but doubtful cases remained. In 1915 the *Dacia*, sailing from the United States to Germany, was seized by France on the ground of illegal change of ownership, and became the occasion for a test case.

A matter which attracted even more attention was the sale of contraband to belligerents. There was no question
Trade in contraband that international law sanctioned such trade; it was merely subject to the risk of interference by the opposing belligerent. The supplying of the demands for such articles, moreover, did much to offset the industrial distress caused by the dislocation of customary occupations. On the other hand, in the actual conditions of the war, such trade was confined to the Allies and was of substantial assistance to them. The act of Congress, moreover, authorizing the President to suspend such trade in the case of conflicts in America, had created a disposition to regard such prohibition as a step in international progress. Consequently a strong demand arose in the United States, backed by the elements favorable to Germany and by many of those opposed to all war, that the government put a stop to the traffic. The administration, however, refrained in this case

as in others from deviating in any way from the established practices of neutrality.

The United States government, indeed, followed a policy strictly conservative. It refused to act on the protests received from the various countries based on alleged acts of their opponents in violation of the laws of war. It followed established practice in all cases where precedent existed, and where it did not, based its policy on reasoned implications from previous cases of a similar nature. When the practices of the belligerents seemed to it to constitute violations of the laws of nations and at the same time to infringe the rights of Americans, it did not have recourse to bombastic complaint, but expressed its views in carefully drawn protests which might serve as bases for reclamations at the return of peace. The predicament of Americans caught abroad at the beginning of the war was handled with energy. Congress voted money to assist them, the government undertook the forwarding of private funds during the time that private exchange was suspended, and naval vessels were sent to bring home those who could not secure other accommodation. To encourage the development of the merchant marine the administration proposed a national corporation in which the government should be a stockholder, but Congress failed to approve this suggestion.

Congress equally failed to change its policy with regard to national defense. The support of the navy was continued upon the scale previously fixed, but neither it nor the army were further increased. Public opinion took up this question, but divided upon it. On the one hand it was urged that the United States was ill prepared to face contingencies which the continuance of war or the conclusion of peace might very possibly produce. Many believed that the new conditions resulting from the war would inevitably detach the United States from so much of its policy of isolation as still remained, and that it must be prepared to play its part as a world power. On the other hand, the movement for disarmament, supported by those who believed that judicial settlement might be substituted for war, received new impulse from the horrors of modern warfare. Many of the leaders of this movement were as dissatisfied with the government as were those favoring greater armaments. They wished the President to take the lead in bringing about peace by offering mediation. The great majority of the people, however, accepted the lead of the administration. Although extreme utterances on every side of every question attested the existence of free speech, the press and conversation alike reflected a very general following of President Wilson's advice that the spirit as well as the letter of neutrality be kept, and as yet (April, 1915) the war has not become in any way a party question.

CHAPTER XXXVI

SUCCESS AND ITS CAUSES

Our diplomacy has, on the whole, served the national needs and purposes exceptionally well. No other nation has been confronted so continually by the problem of neutrality, and for none has it assumed such protean shapes; yet it is impossible to see how we could, with foreknowledge, have improved our handling of it in any large way. For no other nation has the problem of protecting its citizens abroad been so difficult, owing to the great numbers of our naturalized citizens and the variety of their origin; but at the present day, and for a long time past, an American passport is nowhere inferior to any other certificate of nationality. Although our merchant flag was ill-treated during the wars of the French Revolution and the Napoleonic period, we won for it later, in the teeth of Great Britain, a freedom almost unique.

The policies for the building up of our merchant marine and the furtherance of our commerce have been chiefly determined by internal considerations, but diplomacy has in all cases eventually, though with difficulty, laid open the path for the execution of those policies internationally. The government has been able to offer our people as great opportunities for the exercise of their activities beyond the national boundaries as any other nation has enjoyed; our Newfoundland fisheries, for example, have been even more caressingly watched over than have those of France. It has also successfully protected them in the enjoyment of their national resources, the only important exception being the practical destruction of the seal herd of Behring sea. The territory desired by our people for their expansion has been obtained, excepting to the north. There, meeting the equal force of Great Britain, we are left with a straight line as the result of the impact. The study of the measuring of each stretch of that line, however, reveals the fact that we obtained all that we had the power to demand.

Erratic and experimental divergencies in our diplomacy have been few. Of these, Jefferson's embargo must be considered the greatest, and it was diplomatically unsuccessful and disastrous. To err with Napoleon, however, does not indicate lightness of mind; and the embargo in the United States, like the continental system in Europe, hastened an internal development that was sure to come. Our many and varied attempts at an unnatural expansion failed because they were unnatural, and left no serious effects. Our foreign wars have all been turned to account—even that of 1812, which was saved from being a national calamity only by the skill of our diplomats at Ghent.

This success has rested upon a continuity, both of detail and of general policy, which is remarkable in a nation that in a hundred and fifty years has gone through all the stages of evolution from a second-rate colony to a great power. This continuity must in a considerable degree be attributed to that juristic tone which until very recently has been a predominating factor in our public life. Well advised in the beginning, particularly by Franklin, we accepted a system of international law which appealed to our ethical sense and fitted our position and interests. To this we clung with an unequaled persistence and exactitude, and it is in large part through our efforts that this system has become the basis of the accepted international law of to-day.

That in handling innumerable petty cases and frequent pressing crises we were able to preserve an impressive consistency of practice, was not primarily due to the efforts of our diplomatic staff in foreign countries. Efficient as it was at some periods, and brilliant as have been some of the men composing it at every stage, it had after 1829 no element of cohesion, unless between 1897 and 1913, and it has at all times been marred by the presence of incompetent or unsuitable individuals. The home administration of diplomacy, however, has exhibited a continuity of service and a conspicuous ability which give it rank with our supreme court. John Jay, John Quincy Adams, William Hunter, and John Bassett Moore cover the whole period of our diplomacy, and represent an almost constant service within the state department or easy availability for advice to it. Other series equally striking may be named. Jefferson and Buchanan were always powerful, and for much of the time in control, from the beginning of independence to Civil war; Seward and Hay, from 1849 to 1905. William Hunter and A. A. Adee together served in the state department from 1829 to the present day (1915); counting the years when they overlapped, their combined service falls just six years short of a century. Such personal oversight has meant a growth from precedent to precedent which has gradually resulted in a self-carrying tradition for those minor matters that do not reach the public ear.[1]

The consistency with which general policies have been applied in the greater episodes, as such have arisen, is due to the force of a governing public opinion. It is probably true that the growth of democracy has made diplomacy more difficult in most countries than it previously had been. That the reverse has been true in the United States has been due, in the first place, to the juristic habit of mind already mentioned. The Monroe Doctrine has been popularly regarded as a law; its successive extensions have been looked upon in the same light as the new powers which the courts have successively found by implication in the constitution.

More important has been the simplicity of our leading and essential policy. The harmonizing of conflicting ideas, when they have presented themselves, has proved beyond our grasp. The one deliberate purpose which our diplomacy has

[1] Gaillard Hunt, *Department of State of the United States*, N. H., 1914.

completely failed to bring about has been that of winning the sympathy and acquiring the leadership of Spanish America. The reason is obvious; not the sentiment of Pan-Americanism, but the deep-seated nationalistic conception of United States dominance, has primarily moved us. From the day in 1794 when Wayne rode round the British fort at the rapids of the Maumee and dared its commander to fire, we have, with the exception of brief periods after the first abdication of Napoleon and during the Civil war, been the dominant American power. In 1823 we announced the fact to the world, and at the same time first became generally conscious of it ourselves. Every corollary added to the Monroe Doctrine has been a renewed assertion of the fact, and has presented an added means of maintaining it.

Dominance is not a policy but a talent: the responsibility is for its use. Our employment of our position has rested upon a feeling that long antedated it, that even antedated our ancestors' migration to America. They wanted to be let alone, the colonies in 1776 wanted to be let alone, to seek their future in their own way. In return they were willing, not exactly to let every one else alone, but at least to confine their activities to the limits within which they were actually in control. Franklin rejected the idea of colonial representation in the English Parliament; he wished not legislative participation in the empire, but legislative independence within the colonial area. This was the reverse side of the Monroe Doctrine. In America we were dominant; by confining our activities to America we could be dominant wherever we were active. It is this simple and fundamental idea that has impressed itself on the American mind, and has become the touchstone by which public opinion judges all diplomatic questions. With such a task as keeping adjusted a balance of power, democracy is probably incompetent to deal, with its accustomed practicality the democracy of America has determined that it will have no balance of power in America, and will not meddle with it where it exists.

INDEX

INDEX

A

Aberdeen, Lord, Mexican policy, 253, 262, 270; Oregon, 267.

Abyssinia, treaty with United States, 469.

Acadia, French, boundary dispute, 230.

Adams, Charles F., minister to England, 8, 306, 316, 321, 372; instructions, 319; protests delivery of Confederate rams, 322, 340; successor, 340; in Geneva board, 347; characterized, 306; cited, 322, 382.

Adams, David J., fishing-vessel, seized, 376.

Adams, John, diplomat, 1, 115, 188; commissioner to France, 38; Holland, 38; peace commissioner, 41, 46, 48; minister to England, 52, 59, 60, 83, 372; commercial treaties, 54; treats with Barbary States, 56; arranges Dutch loan, 78; vice-president, 81; president, 130; appointments, 131, 138; French policy, 133, 134, 137–139; views on neutrality, 92; on isolation, 211; characterized, 38, 39; cited, 34, 39, 59, 60, 92, 133.

Adams, John Q., diplomat, 2, 8, 241, 306, 429, 499; mission to Prussia and Sweden, 129; at Berlin, 143; minister to Russia, 163, 170, 179, 188; on commission to England, 179; on Ghent commission, 180, 183, 185; secretary of state, 188; president, 188, 214; fisheries policy, 192; trade, 199; Florida, 199–202, 208, 341; Spanish-American, 207–218, 297; slavetrade, 237; objects to British cooperation, 210–214, 293; Pan-American policy, 214, 215, 284, 478; slave-trade, 237; Texas policy, 246, 247, 250–252; member of Congress, 227, 256; supports Jackson, 228; argues l'Amisted case, 239; minister to England, 372; characterized, 188, 222; opinions cited, 81, 104, 120, 126, 140, 189.

Adams, Samuel, gains foreign sympathy, 24; predicts separation of East and South, 41.

Adams, William, peace commissioner, 180.

Adee, A. A., service in state department, 499.

Adet, P. A., minister to United States, 127; recall, 128, 130; Canadian intrigues, 131; western, 131.

Adler, German warship, 400.

Admiralty Courts, organized by Genêt, 99; British, 111, 112, 114, 122, 156, 157, 236, 339.

Africa, trade with United States, 55, 85; Napoleon's dealings with, 131; slaves returned to, 239; pirates of, 351; international relations, 464.

Aguinaldo, Emilio, Philippine leader, 420.

Aix-la-Chapelle, treaty of, 16.

Alabama, Confederate cruiser, 339; claims against, 345; commission on, 347.

Alaman, Louis, Mexican secretary, cited, 243; warnings heeded, 247; Texan views, 252; views on American expansion, 481.

Alamo, story of, 248.

Alaska, Russian fur-trade, 209; purchase of, 358, 398, 406, 478, 487; seal industry, 377, 434; boundary dispute, 432; settled, 434; status of inhabitants, 421.

Alaska Commercial Company, sealing monopoly, 377.

Albert, Prince, labors for peace, 317.

503

Aldrich, Sen. Nelson, on reciprocity, 388, 471.

Alexander I, of Russia, fosters Holy Alliance, 204; foreign policy, 179.

Alexander II, of Russia, emancipator, 312.

Alexander VI, Pope, confirms Spanish claims, 10; demarcation line, 11, 12, 391, 417.

Alexis, Grand Duke, visits America, 360.

Alfonso XII, king of Spain, 365.

Algeciras, conference at, 402; United States takes part, 464.

Algiers, official piracy, 55, 56; holds Americans as slaves, 56; treaty with, 85; raids Atlantic, 114; American expedition against, 141; French capture, 223; Dey of, cited, 141.

Aliens, control of, 80.

Allegheny River, 17.

Allen, Ethan, head of Cuban committee, 409.

Alverstone, Lord Chief Justice, on Alaskan boundary commission, 434.

Amazon River, navigation of, 287.

Ambrister, R. C., hanged, 200.

l'Ambuscade, captures *Little Sarah*, 103.

Amelia Island, privateers use, 200.

American Fur Co., rivals, 173.

American Revolution, diplomacy during, 1, 23; causes, 35; European interest in, 24, 25; piracy, 56; after effects on commerce, 62; frontier loyalty, 67, 69; trade during, 70, 81, 108.

Americans, relations with Indians, 64–66, 72, 74, 116; sympathies in French Revolution, 95, 96; man French privateers, 98, 102.

Ames, Fisher, supports Jay treaty, 122; cited, 86, 144, 121.

Amiens, treaty of, 143.

l'Amisted, slave carrier, case tried, 239; as precedent, 368.

Amoy, port opened, 223.

Amsterdam, printing centre, 24; financial, 34; market, 35; burgomaster, 36.

Amy Warwick, admiralty case, 307.

Andrew, Gov. J. M., *Trent* affair pleases, 316.

Angell, J. B., on Chinese commission, 398.

Anglican Church, position in United States, 52.

Antelope, admiralty case, 237.

Apia (Samoa), consular intrigues in, 399, 401.

Appalachian Mountains, as boundary, 98.

Appalachicola River, as boundary, 19.

d'Aranda, Count, Spanish minister, 33; treats with Jay, 44, 142.

Arbitration, familiar to English colonists, 22; of boundaries, 186; of slave indemnity, 191; Indian annuities, 194; northeast boundary, 228, 234; *Creole* case, 239; northwest boundary, 270; seizure of fishing vessels, 287; idea of permanent, 279; fisheries, 285; Civil war claims, 344–347; Geneva court, 347, 348; of Spanish-American claims, 350; Cuban claims, 367; Portuguese, 375; French, 375; fisheries, 375; sealing rights, 378; between American powers, 385, 386; proposed in Venezuelan dispute, 392, 393; in *Maine* affair, 414; of Alaska boundary, 432, 434; of fisheries, 435; Pan-American court of, 451; Venezuelan claims, 447; other claims, 469; "Pious fund" claims, 474; scope, 340, 474, 475; American advocates of, 472, 473; treaties, 474, 475, 481; Spanish-American practice of, 473, 474.

Arbuthnot, Alexander, hanged, 200.

Archangel, port open, 163.

Argentine Republic, commercial treaty with, 285, 287; later relations, 324; European relations, 325; competition with, 373; Italian immigration, 384; diplomatic service to, 430; foreign minister, 446; dispute with Chile, mediated, 451; attitude toward United States, 452; reciprocity treaty with, 470; offers mediation, 490.

Arizona, New Mexico includes, 279.

Arkansas, early history, 253; emigrants, 257.

Armed Neutrality. See Neutrality.

Armenians, status in United States, 466.

Armstrong, Gen. John, letter cited, 150; minister to France, 170.

Arnold, Benedict, at siege of Quebec, 75.

Aroostook River, trouble in valley, 230, 235.

Arthur, C. A., president, 370; appointments, 370; reciprocity policy, 388

Ashburton, Lord, treats with Webster, 233, 234, 237; views cited, 233; letter to, 239.

Asia, trade with United States, 54, 196, 223; diplomatic activity in, 353, 477; American interests, 464.

Asquith, H. H., premier, Mexican policy, 485.

Astor, J. J., plans for Northwest, 173.

Astoria (Ore.), founded, 173, 254; American flag over, 185; property title, 185; Americans lose, 265.

Atlantic cable, effect on diplomatic intercourse, 300, 316, 371.

Austin, Stephen, rouses sympathy for Texas, 248.

Austria, offers mediation, 41; war with France, 95; signs Holy Alliance, 204; quells Italian revolt, 204; England seeks alliance, 240; extradition treaty, 284; returns Kotzka to United States, 289; mediator, 324, 375, 383; policy toward Maximilian, 333; irritation against United States, 333, 426; trade-mark treaty, 351; naturalization, 356; Russian relations, 359; Cuban, 366; reciprocity with, 389; diplomatic service to, 430; policy in Far East, 458; war policies (1915), 492.

Azores, Islands, as boundary, 10.

B

Babcock, Gen. O. E., San Domingo mission, 362, 363.

Bacon, Sen. A. C., Mexican policy, 486.

Baden, naturalization treaty with, 356.

Baez, Pres. Buenaventura, annexation policy, 361–363.

Bagot, Sir Charles, minister to United States, 191.

Bahamas, British, trade, 308; position threatens Gulf trade, 360.

Bainbridge, Capt. William, brings "tribute" to Algiers, 141.

Balkan states, conference of, 468.

Baltic Sea, control of, 493.

Baltimore (Md.), trade centre, 161.

Baltimore, marines from, killed, 390.

Bancroft, George, minister to Germany, 355; ability, 255; makes treaty, 356; mission to Spain, 361; England, 372; cited, 278.

Banks, Gen. N. P., member of Congress, 362.

"The Banks." See Newfoundland.

Barbados, reciprocity with, 470.

Barbary States, pirates, 13, 55; consular service to, 81; United States pays "tribute," 84, 132; treaties with, 85, 141, 222; piracy stopped, 196, 204, 223; profits of pirates, 351.

Barclay, Thomas, concludes Morocco treaty, 56.

Baring, Sir Thomas, American policy, 343.

Baring Brothers, firm of, 233.

Barlow, Joel, French sympathy, 96; minister to France, 171.

Barrett, John, diplomatic service, 430.

Barron, Commodore James, commands *Chesapeake*, 159.

Basle, treaty of, terms, 123, 130.

Bassano, Duc de, French foreign minister, 170.

Bastile, fall of, 94.

Bathurst, Lord, treaty interpretation, 192; letters to, cited, 82, 181.

Bavaria, desires commercial treaty, 53; naturalization treaty with, 356.

Baxter, Henry, agent in Honduras, 352.

Bayard, J. A., peace commissioner, 179, 180, 183.

Bayard, T. F., secretary of state, 370, 378, 391, 400, 403; minister to England, 373; Samoan policy, 400.

Bayonne, trade decree, 166.

Beaumarchais, Pierre de, agent of Vergennes, 26; cited, 27.

Beauregard, Gen. P. G. T., English sympathy for, 314.

Beckwith, Maj. George, British agent, 90; cited, 90.

Beecher, H. W., English influence, 322.

Behring Sea, fisheries, 5, 434, 497; jurisdiction disputed, 377, 378, 387.

Behring Straits, boundary through, 358.

Belgium, commercial treaty with, 285; extradition, 350; trade-mark, 351; navigation, 352; naturalization, 356; diplomatic service to, 430; export trade, 452.

Belize, British settlement, 292, 293; boundaries, 295, 381, 382.

Benjamin, J. P., Confederate secretary, 311; French policy, 331.

Benton, W. S., British subject, killed in Mexico, 446, 486.

Benton, Sen. T. H., Oregon views, 256.

Berlin, American commissioner to, 31; Samoan conference at, 401; General Act of, 401, 425, 454; financial centre, 427; diplomatic service to, 455; treaty of, 465.

Berlin Decree, terms, 158; revoked, 168.

Bermuda Islands, ownership, 29; American acquisition suggested, 40; reciprocity with, 470.

Bermuda, admiralty case, 308.

Bernard, Montague, on claims commission, 345.

Bernhardi, Gen. von, on British policy, cited, 333.

Berthier, Alexandre, cited, 149.

Biddle, Nicholas, author, 148.

Bigelow, John, in France, 321.

Bismarck, Prince Otto von, relations with Bancroft, 355; Samoan policy, 401.

Black Warrior, seized by Spain, 300, 301.

Blaine, J. G., diplomat, 8; secretary of state, 370, 403; reciprocity advocate, 373, 388, 389; arbitration, 472; Behring Sea contention, 378, 379; Panama policy, 381, 383; Spanish-American, 384–386, 391, 394, 444; Pan-Americanism, 386, 478; trouble with Chili, 390; presidential ambition, 390; Hawaiian policy, 404; "Elder Sister," 448; characterized, 371, 387, 390, 391; cited, 381, 385, 388, 404; The Foreign Policy of the Garfield Administration, cited, 387.

Blanca, Florida, Spanish minister, 26.

Blockade. See International Law.

Blount, William, conspirator, 134.

Bluefields (Nicaragua), British marines land at, 383.

Boer War, impending, 428; diplomatic difficulties, 431.

Bogota, American minister recalled, 440.

Bogota, Colombian gunboat, 441.

Bolivar, Gen. Simon, revolutionary leader, 89, 203, 206.

Bolivia, commercial treaty with, 223, 285, 287; Peru-Chili war, 386.

Bonaparte, Joseph, King of Spain, 150, 203.

Bonaparte, Louis, King of Holland, 167.

Bonaparte, Napoleon, dealings with United States, 8, 101, 138, 139, 142–146, 148–150, 154, 155, 164–170, 175, 178, 201, 209; Africa, 131; navy defeated, 152; on Louisiana, cited, 145, 146; orders to Dantzig, 166; English policy, 155, 158; at Elba, 155; Russian policy, 169, 170, 179; fall of, 177, 179; continental system, 165, 167, 190, 493, 498.

Bond, Sir Robert, Newfoundland premier, 434.

Bond, Phineas, British consul, 87; letter cited, 122, 154.

Borneo, commercial treaty with, 286.

Boston, port of, 177, 316.

Boundaries, Northeast, 15, 16, 117, 186, 228–232, 234; Hudson Bay region, 16; Florida, 19, 20, 124; Continental Congress discusses, 40, 46; peace commissioners discuss (1782), 46, 48; (1814), 182;

Cherokee, 72; Northwestern, 194; Western, 201, 202; Louisiana, 148–151; Canadian-American, 186; 498; commissions appointed, 186, defined, 218; Texas, 266, 271; between islands, 337, 347.

Bounties, to American fishermen, 193, 194.

Bowles, W. A., adventurer, 89; letter cited, 89.

"Boxer" troubles, 455, 461.

Brandy, trade in French, 61.

Brant, Joseph, Iroquois leader, 65.

Brazil, settled by Portuguese, 11, 12; Portugal loses, 203; empire of, 204; slavery in, 236; commercial treaties, 216, navigation question, 287; relations with United States, 324, 452; Europe, 325; German immigration, 384; war with Portugal, 324; represented on Geneva board, 347; reciprocity with, 389; British dispute, arbitrated, 394; diplomatic service to, 430; offers mediation, 490.

Breda, Treaty of, 14.

Bremen, commercial treaty with, 197.

Bright, John, favors North, 315.

British America, fisheries, 192; trade with, 197; Sumner's policy, 341.

British Guiana, reciprocity treaty with, 470.

Brittany, fishermen of, 108, 110.

Brougham, Lord, questions British policy, 254.

Brown, John, colonizing schemes, 75.

Bruni, treaty with, 286.

Bryan, C. P., diplomatic service, 430.

Bryan, W. J., secretary of state, 448, 480; draws up Colombian treaty, 453; note to Balkan States, 468; arbitration advocate, 473, 475; Japanese policy, 480; Mexican, 486.

Buchanan, James, secretary of state, 268, 282; minister to England, 282, 294, 300, 372; mission to Spain, 301; president, 282; expansionist, 281, 282, 297, 300; diplomatic policy, 304; Californian, 275; Mexican, 277, 278, 297, 328,

489; Central American, 295, 296; Cuban, 299, 367; opinion of Clayton-Bulwer treaty, 293; diplomatic service, 2, 499; characterized, 282; cited, 278, 297, 328.

Bucharest, conference of Balkan states at, 468.

Buenos Ayres, revolt in, 203; United States envoy to, 206; English investments, 215; commercial treaties, 216.

Buffalo (N. Y.), Pan-American Exposition at, 451.

Buffer State, of Indians, proposed, 181, 183, 184, 246.

Bullock, Capt. J. D., makes ship contracts, 339.

Dulwer, Sir H. L, makes treaty, 282, 293.

Bunau Varilla, Panama agent, 441, 442.

Bureau of American Republics established, 388.

Burgoyne, Gen. John, surrender, 29.

Burke, Edmund, friend of America, 314.

Burlingame, Anson, mission from China, 354.

Burr, Aaron, at siege of Quebec, 75; French sympathies, 104; vice-president, 147; conspiracy, 147, 148.

Burton, A. A., commission secretary, 364.

Bustamante, Anastasio, Mexican president, 247.

Butler, Anthony, minister to Mexico, 221.

Butter, trade in, 76, 110.

C

Cabot, John, explorer, 10, 13.

Cadore, Duc de, French foreign minister, letter, cited, 168.

Caicos, reciprocity with, 470.

Calhoun, J. C., a "War Hawk," 171; secretary of state, 221, 225, 261, 268; on maritime law question, 238; Texas policy, 261–266, 272, 298, 342, 363; Oregon, 267–269; diplomatic ability, 221, 261; letter to, cited, 259; opinions, 261.

California, Spain holds, 205, 209,

257; Russian fort in, 209; Russia gives up claim to, 213; American interests, 245, 253, 257–259, 274; British, 257–259; Mexico, 274, 278; gained from Mexico, 279; gold discovered, 286, 291; Alaskan interest, 358; coast line important, 398; Chinese problem, 397, 398; Japanese, 462, 480.

California, Lower, ownership, 275.

Calvo, Carlos, collection of claims theory, 446.

Cambon, J. M., French ambassador, 417.

Campo Bello Island, Fenians attack, 338.

Campos, Gen. Martinez de, Cuban governor, 368; campaign, 411.

Canada, French colony, 13, 17; English conquer, 17; ceded, 18; trade encouraged, 60; governor-generals, 63, 67, 114, 230; French sympathies in, 97, 102, 131, 232; British loyalty, 153, 178; American trade, 176; desires northern New York, 181; annexation proposed, 174, 182, 232, 299; Sumner's view, 342, 344; Cobden's, 342; fishing regulations, 194, 285, 376, 434, 435; revolts in, 232; reciprocity treaty, 285; expires, 376; (1911), rejected, 435, 436; Dominion organized, 334; Americans protest, 336; Fenians invade, 338; minister of justice, 345; relations with England, 346, 434, 435; extradition act, 374; Alaska seal interests, 377, 378, 434.

Canadian Gazette, policy, 181.

Canals, Hudson-Lake Champlain, 197; Erie Canal, 197; Isthmian, 290, 291, 380, 382, 436–444, 469, 480, 481.

Canning, George, dealings with J. Q. Adams, 8, 293; minister of foreign affairs, 164, 188, 206, 237, 293, 334, 382; rejects Erskine's agreement, 165, 166; Spanish-American policy, 210–217; ability, 189, 215; cited, 214.

Cannon, J. G., introduces war preparation bill, 413.

Canovas, del Castillo, Antonio, Spanish prime minister, death, 413.

Canso, Gut of, waters closed, 193.

Canton, trade with, 55, 286.

Cape Cod, blockade south of, 176; north of, 177.

Cape Horn, route via, 286.

Cape Verde Islands, as boundary, 10.

Caracas (Venezuela), intrigues in, 89; American agent at, 385.

Caribbean Sea, privateers, 207; commerce, 286, 360; American interests, 444, 448, 450–452, 464, 477, 479, 481, 489.

Carmichael, William, American minister to Spain, 123.

Carnegie, Andrew, presents arbitration palace, 451; peace palace, 473; pacifist, 473.

Carnegie Institution, historical study, 244.

Caroline, Canadians seize, 232, 233; case settled, 234.

Carranza, Gen. Vincenzio, denies authority of Huerta, 484; constitutionalist leader, 486; not recognized, 489.

Carroll, John, appointed bishop, 52.

Cartier, Jacques, American discoveries, 13.

Cass, Lewis, minister to France, 240; secretary of state, 241, 282.

Castlereagh, Lord, in peace negotiations, 179; instructs commissioners, 182; slave-trade policy, 236.

Catherine II of Russia, doctrine of armed neutrality, 37, 179.

Cattrell, Stephen, Canadian official, cited, 67.

Central America, commercial treaty with, 216, 285; route via, 290; neutrality guaranteed, 293; American immigration, 296; *status* of British Honduras, 382; United States acquires territory in, 436; arbitration court, 451.

Civil service reform, development, 431.

Civil war, diplomacy during, 3; neutral rights, 6; encourages humanitarianism, 241; diplomatic effects, 331, 368; Irish enlistments, 338; commercial straits, 360; claims against England, 339–348.

Chaleurs, Bay of, boundary, 20, 230.

Chamberlain, Joseph, protection advocate, 427.

Champlain, Lake, as boundary, 20; settlements along, 67; battle on, 178; outlet, 231.

Charles III, of Spain, vacillation, 26, 31, 42.

Charles V, of Germany, colonial policy, 12; foresight, 290.

Charleston (S. C.) British agents at, 90, 310; Genêt reaches, 98; schemes in, 99; French privateers at, 103; British Consul at, 310.

Chatham, Earl of. See William Pitt.

Cheese, trade in, 58.

Chesapeake, affair with Leopard, 159, 165, 174.

Chile, commercial treaty with, 223; relations strained, 375, 390, 409; accepts mediation, 385, 451; Bolivia-Peru war, 386; president, cited, 387; civil war, 390; resents United States arrogance, 452; offers mediation, 490.

China, trade with United States, 55; commercial treaty with, 223, 286; five ports opened, 223; open to missions, 286; Burlingame treaty, 354; missionary interests, 396, 455, 460; Boxer troubles, 455–457; emigration question, 397, 398, 449, 460; diplomatic service to, 430; international interests in, 454, 455; relations with Japan, 455, 461; United States, 432; integrity of, 456–458, 459, 463, 477; neutrality recognized, 458; "six power" loan, 460; revolution, 459; arbitration, 475.

Chinese, employed in Pacific coast, 286; exclusion of, 397, 398.

Canadian problem, 432.

Chincha Island, Spain's claims, 327.

Ching, Prince, represents China, 457.

Choate, Rufus, Senator, report cited, 225.

Chocolate, trade in, 108.

Choiseul, Duc de, predicts American Revolution, 25.

Christopher Island, ownership, 35.

Church of England. See Anglican Church.

Claiborne, W. C. C., governor of Orleans territory, 151.

Claims, Spanish-American, 226, 284, 350, 375, 469; French spoliation, 226–228, 375; Mexican, 251, 274, 328, 350, 375, 474; Civil war, 339–348; British, 344, 469; Russian, 469; Portuguese, 375; against Tycoon, 353; Spanish, 410; problems under Monroe Doctrine, 446; Treaties, 226, 345, 375.

Clarendon, Lord, British minister, 295; convention with Johnson, rejected, 343.

Clark, G. R., takes western forts, 33, 69; colonizing schemes, 75; French sympathy, 97; French commission, 102, forces separated, 105.

Clark, William, explorer, 148.

Clarkson, Thomas, opposes slave-trade, 236.

Clay, Henry, a "War Hawk," 174, 178; peace commissioner, 179, 180, 185, 189; attacks administration, 189, 206; secretary of state, 189, 214, 291; Pan-American policy, 214, 284, 478; conciliates France, 228; influence of, 371; characterized, 189; cited, 291.

Clayton, J. M., secretary of state, 282; English treaty, 282, 292, 293.

Cleveland, Grover, appointments, 370, 372, 389; free trade advocate, 373; fisheries policy, 376; canal, 382; Pan-American, 387; Venezuela, 391; opposes reciprocity, 388; conception of Monroe Doctrine, 392, 394; Hawaiian policy, 405, 406; Cuban, 409, 412; Turkish, 465; civil service under, 431; cited, 382, 394.

Coahuila, Texas joined to, 247, 248; governor, 484.

Coasting trade, embargo not applicable, 160, 177; cut off by war, 177; canal tolls exemption, 437.

Cobden, Richard, American views, cited, 341, 342.

Cochrane, Admiral Thomas, aids Spanish-America, 206.

Cockburn, Sir Alexander, on Geneva board, 347.

Cocoa, trade in, 119, 153.

Coffee, trade in, 108, 109, 119, 153, 284; in McKinley tariff, 388.

Collot-d'Herbois, Jean M., French agent, 134; instructions, cited, 131.

Colombia, commercial treaty with, 216; United States influence, 217, 385; extradition, 285; Panama neutrality treaty (1846), 291, 295, 379, 380, 385, 439, 440; grants de Lesseps canal concession, 379; boundary dispute, 385; affected by reciprocity, 389; diplomatic service to, 430, 440; rejects Herran-Hay treaty, 439; Pearson syndicate, 450; treaty (1915), 450; resentment against United States, 452.

Colon (Panama), revolt in, 441.

Colonial wars, causes, 15, 16.

Colorado, Italians lynched in, 427.

Colorado River, free navigation, 279.

Columbia River, first white man enters, 93; Lewis and Clark, 148; Americans settle on, 173; claim, 253, 267; navigation free, 346.

Columbus, Christopher, effect of discoveries, 10.

Comet, carries slaves, 238.

Comly, J. M., minister to Hawaii, 404.

Commerce, relations with diplomacy, 5, 54–57, 77, 85–87, 222, 497; pirates menace, 55; defence measures, 156, 281; non-importation agreements, 156, 157; non-intercourse, 163, 164, 166, 167; embargoes, 115, 160, 161; prospers, 163, 283; declines, 190; war of 1812 affects, 187, 196; encouragement of, 241, 283; consular aid, 373, 476; balance of trade, 58, 284, 427, 467; special licenses, 153, 164, 167, 177; open door policy, 455; in war of 1915, 492; via Scheldt, 5; Danish Straits, 5; Spanish colonial 15, 57; American, 53, 62, 109; Dutch, 109; with British North America, 5, 67, 68, 118, 197; British Empire, 57–62, 119, 152; Latin-America, 5, 161, 286, 287, 452; Asia, 5, 54, 55, 199, 223, 455; Africa, 54, 55; Europe, 61, 62, 152–154, 156, 159, 163, 164, 224, 225; West Indies, 5, 6, 77, 118, 119, 156, 161, 198, 222, 298; Pacific, 92, 93, 118, 197, 285, 396, 398, 403, 461, 462; Mediterranean, 55, 56, 62, 77, 85, 125, 141, 196. See also Reciprocity and Merchant Marine.

Confederacy, blockade runners, 308, 309; commerce destroyers, 319, 336; rams, 322; diplomacy of, 310, 311, 321, 330; British relations, 316–319, 321–323, 339; recognition of, 442.

Confederation, diplomacy of, 1; British distrust, 60; failures of, 62, 68, 71, 72, 77, 79, 124; diplomatic problems, 64, 67, 190; growth of population, 69; Western problems, 73.

Conger, E. H., commissioner to China, 457.

Congo Free State, treaty with, 375.

Congress, creates departments, 80; discusses merchant marine, 85–87; resentment against England, 87; considers Jay treaty, 122; increases army and navy, 133; reports to, 156; non-importation agreement, 157; special session, 160; passes embargo, 160; non-intercourse act, 169; war sentiment, 171; declares war, 174; Spanish-American resolutions, 206; neutrality acts, 207, 232; calls out militia, 230; abolishes slave-trade, 237; recognizes Texan republic, 251; debates annexation, 265; annexes, 274; Oregon question, 269; receives Polk's war message, 276; military policy, 281; Mexican policy, 297; Cuban, 302; passes Morrill Tariff, 314; opposes Maximilian's empire, 331; refuses Denmark treaty, 361; relations to diplomacy, 370; authorizes international copyright, 374; Panama canal action, 380, 439; Pan-American, 387; Chinese exclusion acts, 397, 398; Cuban action, 416, 425; Philippine, 425; seal fisheries, 434; votes lynching indemnities, 427; canal tolls, 437; abrogates Russian treaty, 466; immigration policy, 467, 468; refuses ship subsidies, 469; powers over treaties, 471; acts on sale of munitions, 483; Mexican policy, 485, 486; aids Americans in Europe, 495.

Connecticut River, source, 231, 235.

Connolly, John, British agent, 68.

Constantinople, American college at, 465.

Constitution, strengthens central authority, 79; executive under, 80, 105; Congress, powers, 80, 225; ambiguities, 80, 471.

Constitution, wins fight, 190.

Consular service, early organization, 81, 82; growth, 221; "pupils," 283, 430; commercial importance increases, 373; politics dominates, 373; bill of *1884,* amended, 387; improvement in, 430, 431; popular interest, 431.

Continental Congress, first meeting, 23; measures adopted, 23; message from Beaumarchais, 27; parties in, 31, 46; appoints commissioners, 32, 33, 41; members, 39, 81; considers peace terms, 40, 41, 44; instructs peace commissioners, 46; treatment of Loyalists, 48, 64; relations with Papacy, 51; relations with Anglican Church, 52.

Contraband. See International Law.

Convention of *1802,* renewed, 202.

Convention of *1818,* terms, 192–195; ambiguities, 193.

Convention of *1828,* terms, 269.

Convention of *1831,* terms, 223.

Convention for the Arbitration of Pecuniary Claims, parties to, 472.

Convention on Artistic and Literary Copyrights, parties to, 472.

Convention regulating the Importation of Spirituous Liquors into Africa, United States adheres to, 472.

Convention of London, terms, 328, 329; United States does not sign, 328.

Coolies, importation of Chinese, 354; smuggling of, 461.

Cooper, J. F., diplomatic service, 221.

Copyrights, international, 351, 374, 469.

Corea, treaty with, 375; separated from China, 455.

Cornwallis, Lord, surrenders, 42.

Corwin, seizes British vessels, 377.

Costa Rica, commercial treaty, 285; boundary dispute, 385; arbitration, 475.

Cotton, trade in, 119, 164, 196, 224, 225, 253, 262, 284; as "King," 310, 311, 315, 316, 321; contraband (*1915*), 493.

Coudert, F. R., on seal-fisheries commission, 379.

Crampton, Sir J. F. T., British minister, dismissed, 288.

Creole, slave mutiny on, 238; case settled, 239.

Crimean war, neutral problems, 288.

Crockett, David, frontier hero, 248.

Cuba, United States reversionary interest, 6, 78, 208–210, 245; ownership, 203, 205, 206; England's relations, 217; seeks independence, 217; European interest, 282; slavery in, 236, 297, 301, 302; revolution in, 350; position threatens Gulf commerce, 360; Santo Domingo relations, 326; reciprocity with, 389, 470; insurrection of *1895,* 409, 420; methods of war, 409, 411, 412; American sympathy, 409; interests, 410; policy, 297–302, 365, 368, 413–419, 425, 426, 427, 444, 449, 478, 487; Spain promises autonomy, 413; Roosevelt's service in, 424; owns Isle of Pines, 425.

Culebra Island, sale refused, 361,

Culebrita Island, sale refused, 1, 361.

Cullom, Sen. Shelby, in foreign affairs committee, 474; views in reciprocity treaties, 470.

Cumberland River, settlements in, 69, 102; intrigues of settlers, 77, 89; junction, 105.

Curtis, B. R., on Geneva board, 347.

Cushing, Caleb, diplomat, 344; on Geneva board, 347; minister to Spain, 366; instructions, cited, 366, 367.

D

Dacia, seizure of, 494.

Dallas, G. M., minister to England, 295.

Dana, Francis, commissioner to Russia, 31, 170; policy, 264.

Dana, R. H., *Trent* capture pleases, 316.

Danelson, A. J., United States agent in Texas, 273.

Danish Islands, sale refused, 360, 361, 425.

Danish sound, right of free passage, 5, 287.

Danton, G. J., French leader, 103.

Dantzig, Napoleon's orders to, 166.

Darien, colonists, 205.

Dauphin, pirates capture, 56.

Davie, Gov. W. R., on French commission, 137.

Davis, Sen. C. K., Spanish treaty commissioner, 418.

Davis, J. C. B., prepares American claims case, 347.

Davis, Jefferson, commissions privateers, 309, 312, 315; as diplomatist, 310, 312; appointments, 310, 311; message to his Congress, 323; British policy, 311; neutral policy, 312; Lowell satirizes, 318.

Davis, R. H., author, 440.

Day, W. R., conducts Spanish negotiations, 414, 415, 418; terms cited, 418; secretary of state, 418.

Dayton, W. L., minister to France, 331.

Deane, Silas, agent to France, 23, 24; reaches Paris, 27; recall, 31.

Debt, foreign, source of danger, 78.

Debts, collection of British, 48, 60, 64, 118.

Declaration of Independence, effect on American policy, 23, 27.

Declaration of London (*1910*), terms, 494.

Declaration of Paris, terms, 288, 309; not signed by United States, 288, 416; Seward and, 309; attitude of Confederacy, 312.

Delaware River, Swedes settle on, 14.

Democracy, American experience in, 8, 499, 500.

Democrats, platform of *1856*, cited, 360.

Denmark, armed neutrality, 37; commercial treaty, 197; claims, 226; forbids slave-trade, 236; Danish sound question, 287; Civil war policy, 313; proposed cession of St. Thomas, 360, 361; reciprocity, 470, 475; neutrality problems (*1915*), 492.

Detroit (Mich.), British fort, 63; garrison, 90; militia, 84.

Deutsche Handels-und-Plantagen-gesell-schaft für Südseeinseln zu Hamburg, intersets in Samoa, 399.

Dewey, George, Mexican coast service, 417; capture of Manila, 417, 420; Philippine views, 419, 420; made admiral, 423.

Diaz, Felix, aids Huerta, 483; Japan mission, 487.

Diaz, Pres. Porfirio, length of service, 481; meets Taft, 481; overthrow, 483.

Dickens, Charles, urges international copyright, 351.

Diplomacy, American, birth of, 1; golden age, 2; aids expansion, 2; politics dominates, 2, 220, 259, 264, 281, 283, 304, 370; Civil war problems, 3; nadir of, 3; study of, 4; protects fisheries, 5; international routes, 5; popular control of, 8; first event in, 11, 12; basic documents, 18, 19; early problems, 20; colonial experience, 21, 22; direct methods, 21; relations to Congress, 80, 370; to parties, 304; service not attractive, 81, 371, 372; special missions, 81; consular service, 81, 82, 373; organization during Revolution, 23, 24; successes, 50, 139, 185, 213, 222; failures, 77, 79, 87, 188; gains French support, 31; seeks that of Spain, 33; religious problems, 52; Western, 73, 77; brilliant period, 188; daring, 213; bluff, 271, 295; in Nootka Sound affair, 88, 93; in French claims case, 226–228; based on neutrality, 6, 100, 101, 152, 428; recognition of new governments, 101, 208, 484; secures extradition, 117;

favors international commissions, 117, 397; Hamilton's influence, 138; problems change, 190, 196, 242, 245, 286, 288, 289, 336, 398, 401; "shirt-sleeve," 220, 241, 271, 304, 370, 457; permanent arbitration policy, 279; service systematized, 283; relation to commerce, 196, 284, 286, 406, 471, 476; international waterways, 287, 351; marine jurisdiction, 287; transportation policy, 290–295; Cuban, 298–302, 365–368; triumph of Northern, 323; anti-British feeling a factor, 336, 338; service to negro states, 349; extension of field, 351, 353, 357, 396, 406; significance of Civil war problems, 368, 369; affected by Atlantic cable, 371; social side emphasized, 81, 372, 430; appointment of ambassadors, 423; represents administrations, 430; affected by Spanish war, 428, 438, 454, 477; high standards, 463; "Open Door" policy, 458, 477; "Dollar" diplomacy, 459, 476; peace movement, 472; continuity, 4, 188, 429, 475, 498, 499; broken, 370; personal, 8, 22, 137, 180, 188, 189, 220, 221, 242, 261, 283, 304, 498, 499.

Dissenters, favor North, 315.

Divine right, doctrine of, 204, 205, 207, 209, 211.

Dolphin, admiralty case, 308.

Dominican Republic, Cuban relations, 326; Spanish, 327, 329; American, 344, 384; first treaty 349; annexation proposed, 361–364; mediation accepted, 390; reciprocity treaty with; public debt, 446; United States protectorate, 448, 484; revolution in, 484.

Dooley, Mr., on diplomatic service, cited, 371.

Dorchester, Lord, Canadian Governor-general, 67; injudicious speech, 83, 114, 116.

Dorset, Duke of, cited, 60.

Douglass, Frederick, commission secretary, 364.

Drago, L. M., public debt doctrine, 446, 447.

Droit d'aubaine, abolished, 54, 224.

Droit detraction, abolished, 224.

Dumas, C. W. F., friend of Franklin, 26.

Dumauriez, Gen. C. F., letter cited, 96.

Durham, Lord, Canadian report, 232.

Dutch, plunder Spanish colonies, 13; settle in Hudson, 13; cede American claims, 14; England gives neutral rights, 14, 36; theory of international law, 29, 54; smugglers, 35; neutrality aids American Revolution, 22, 35; consider armed neutrality, 38; England declares war on, 38; relations with Indians, 65; loan to United States, 78; cede western Guiana, 391.

E

East, sectional interests, 71, 98.

East India Company, monopoly, 54.

East Indies, trade with, 197.

Eastport (Me.), British demand, 182.

Ecuador, commercial treaty with, 223; extradition, 350; naturalization, 356; claims, 375; reciprocity, 470.

Edward VII, of England, arbiter, 451.

Egan, Patrick, minister to Chili, 390.

Egypt, French expedition to, 136; treaty with United States, 375.

Elba, Island of, Napoleon at, 155.

Elbe River, navigation opened, 352.

Elliot, Capt. Charles, British agent in Texas, 265, 266.

Ellsworth, Oliver, chief justice, 137; on French commission, 137.

Emanuel, admiralty case, 156.

Embargo, of *1794*, provisions, 115; of *1807*, 160; effects, 160–162, 177; Washington Irving's ridicule of, cited, 161; repeal of, 162; and Napoleon, 165, 166; failure, 498.

Encomium, carries slaves, 238.

English Channel, Russians fear to pass, 359.

Enterprise, carries slaves, 238.

Erie, Lake, as boundary, 46; battle on, 178.

Erskine, D. M., minister to United States, 159; instructions, 164; recall, 165, 166.

Esequibo River, Dutch on, 391.

Essex, admiralty case, 156, 308.

Ethiopia. See Abyssinia.

Europe, interest in American Revolution, 24, 25; opinion of United States (*1789*), 78; of Jay treaty, 122; Spanish-American attitude, 203, 204, 324, 325, 328, 385; collection of debts 447, 449; intervention in America, 204, 210–213, 282, 324, 451; respects Monroe doctrine, 218, 324; revolutions in, 204, 208, 280; expatriation problems, 289; recognizes Texas republic, 259; needs cotton, 310; balance of power, 3, 184, 205, 369, 427, 467, 477; interest in Civil war claims, 347; protests Russian outrages, 359; military system, 368, 473; opinion of Pan-American Congress, 387; of acquisition of Philippines, 426, 466; international agreements, 402; relations with Turkey, 465, 466; with Far East, 477; emigration problems, 467–469; Mexican interests, 485; War of *1915*, 491.

Evarts, W. H., in Geneva board, 347; secretary of state, 370, 380, 382, 386, 391.

Everett, Alexander, letter of Adams to, 207.

Everett, Edward, minister to England, 262, 372, 403; dispatch on Cuba, 282, 299; secretary of state, 282, 294; on *Trent* affair, 316.

Executive, relations with Senate, 428, 471.

Expansion, American, Mexican view, 243, 244; historical, 244, 245; Sumner's, 342; theory of, 280, 300, 301, 486, 487–489; leaders, 282, 297, 300; Central American problems, 296; Cuban, 300, 302; Alaskan, 358, 369; San Domingo, 362; Hawaiian, 404; Philippine, 420; Mexican, 486, 489; debated in Congress, 364; era of internal, 337; territorial, 476.

Expatriation. See International Law.

Extradition. See International Law.

F

Fairchild, Lucius, minister to Spain, instructions, 385.

Fall, Sen. A. B., Mexican policy, 487.

Fallen Timbers, battle at, 84.

"Family Alliance," provisions, 18, 32, 88.

Far East, international interests in, 454.

Fauchet, J. A. J., minister to United States, 106; dispatches captured, 120; relations with Randolph, 120, 121; successor, 127; cited, 106, 130, 158, 254.

Federalists, commercial policy, 85; British sympathies, 120, 129; use of special missions, 144; lose control, 139; theories, 146, 147, 422.

Fenian movement, American phases, 338, 341, 347, 356.

Ferdinand, King of Aragon, 10.

Ferdinand VIII, restored, 203; colonial system, 205.

Filibustering, Cuban, 298.

Fillmore, Millard, president, 239; appointments, 239; Hawaiian policy, 403.

Finances, Revolutionary War debt, 78; French loan, 97, 101; under Hamilton, 82, 97.

Fish, Hamilton, secretary of state, 343, 362, 365, 366, 382, 412, 454; in British claims commission, 344; Isthmian policy, cited, 352; Japanese, 353, 354; Hawaiian, 403, 404; characterized, 365; length of service, 370.

Fish, trade in, 55, 57, 58, 61, 108, 163, 196; free entry conceded, 346.

Fisheries, Congress discusses, 40, 41; in peace terms (*1782*), 43, 45, 48; (*1812*), 182, 185; protection of, 5, 497; whale, 285; convention of *1818*, 192, 193; bounties, 284; treaty of *1854*, 285; expiration of, 337; treaty of *1871*, 346, 348, 352, 375; expiration of, 376; arbitration of claims, 375; Blaine's policy, 387; disputes, 432, 434, 435.

Fitzherbert, Alleyne, succeeds Grenville, 45.

Florida, as boundary, 12; ceded to England, 19; divided, 19; boundaries, 20, 46, 70; Spain desires, 26, 32, 33; seizes forts, 33; regains, 50; England desires, 91, 200; France, 143; Indians in, 200; boundaries of West, 46, 48, 70, 71, 124, 149, 150; Pitt's policy, 135; United States desires, 144, 181; Spanish claims, 199–201; Jackson invades, 200, 234; ceded to United States, 202, 208, 218, 245, 341; United States reversionary interest, 208, 245; Seminole rising, 250; position affects Gulf trade, 360.

Florida, Confederate cruiser, 339.

Flour, trade in, 76, 111.

Floyd, John, interest in Oregon, 255.

Forbes, J. M., provisions Sebastopol, 288.

Forsyth, John, Secretary of State, 220.

Foster, A. J., minister to United States, 174.

Foster, J. W., diplomatic experience, 304; Secretary of State, 370, 389, 405.

Foster, W. E., in British Cabinet, 315.

Fouché, Joseph, in Napoleon's cabinet, 167.

Fox, C. J., opinion on peace terms, 42; retires, 45; returns to office, 59; foreign minister, 158; appointments, 165; death, 158.

Foxes, Falmouth family, aid American prisoners, 30.

France, claims in America, 13; English rival, 15; Indians aid, 15; privateers, 15; treaties with England, 16; claims Ohio valley, 16, 17; alliance with Spain, 18; cedes colonies, 18, 19; aids American Revolution, 22, 25–27, 30; American agents to, 23, 31; secret agents of, 25; urges Spain to aid, 26; treaties with U. S., 29; war with England, 30, 32; relations with Holland, 36; Russia, 37, 38; recognizes American Independence, 319; reason for aiding Americans, 91; attitude toward neutrals, 38, 108, 109, 126, 138; in American peace negotiations, 42–46, 48–50; protects Cath-

olics in Orient, 51, 455; payments to Barbary pirates, 56; seeks American trade, 61; relations with Indians, 64, 65; loan to United States, 78; in Family Alliance, 88; National Assembly, powers, 92; Convention, 98; Revolution begins, 94; republic proclaimed, 96; United States recognizes, 101; war with "tyrants," 95, 96, 99; hopes for United States aid, 96; instructs Genêt, 97, 98; recalls, 104; Spanish-American policy, 97, 106, 130, 213, 214, 299, 325, 326–333, 384, 385; difficulties of Republic, 106; successes, 116; triumph of Revolution, 132; trade decrees, 127, 128, 166 170; in election of 1796, 130; seeks Louisiana, 130; friction with United States, 128, 133, 136; convention of 1800, 138; obtains Louisiana, 142, 147; English treaty, 143; war with England, 152; non-intercourse act affects, 163–165; colonial trade, 153, 161, 308; diplomatic service to, 189, 226, 240, 301, 331, 365, 429; restores Spanish monarchy, 204; friction over American claims, 226–228, 375; forbids slave-trade, 236; helps suppress, 240; recognizes Texas, 253; desires California, 274; Revolution of 1848, 280; extradition treaty, 284; in Crimean war, 288; relations with Confederacy, 309, 311; with Mexico, 312, 331, 359; with Russia, 359; Hawaii, 403; gains St. Bartholomew Island, 335; trade-mark treaty, 351; interests in Asia, 353, 402, 454, 455; de Lesseps canal, 381; Spanish bondholders anxious, 426; policy in Far East, 458; friendly attitude to United States, 467; reciprocity, 223, 224; with, 389, 470, 471, 473; interests in Mexico, 482, 484, 486; seizes Dacia, 494; fisheries interests, 497.

Francis I, of France, sends colonies, 10.

Franco-Prussian war, American neutrality questioned, 350.

Frankfort, conference at, 36.

Franklin, Benjamin, diplomat, 1, 8,

18, 188; general agent, 21, 26, 27, 30; popularity in Paris, 28, 99; French sympathies, 95; tact, 30; minister to France, 31, 311, 321; peace commissioner, 41, 44, 45, 49; dealings with papal nuncio, 51, 52; with Barbary States, 56; makes commercial treaties, 54; Adams disapproves, 39; outvoted, 46; ability, 429; characterized, 27, 28; influence endures, 498; cited, 39, 43, 49, 53, 56; letter to,

Fraser River, claim to valley, 267.

Frederick the Great, attitude toward neutrals, 38; statue presented, 467.

"Fredonian Republic," proclaimed, 247.

Freeman, E. A., *History of Federal Government from Foundation of Achaian League to Disruption of United States*, cited, 314.

Frelinghuysen, F. T., secretary of state, 370, 385, 387, 391; Panama policy, 381; Nicaragua, 382.

Frémont, J. C., explores California, 258, 274.

French colonists, negotiate with English, 21.

French Institute, papers before, 131.

French Revolution, affects America, 1; dawn of, 94; Terror, 94, 95; effect on trade, 108; diplomacy during, 132.

French Spoliation Claims, 138, 139.

Freneau, Philip, editor, 103.

Frontier, transportation on, 63; character of population, 63; Indian peril, 65, 66, 82–84, 172, 249, 250; loyalty develops, 82, 147, 245; friction with British, 116, 172–174, 230; favors war, 174; Canadian friction, 232, 233; ambitions, 245.

Frye, Sen. W. P., letter to cited, 388; Spanish treaty commissioner, 418.

Fuchow, port opened, 223.

Fundy, Bay of, tributaries, 228.

Fur trade, in Ohio valley, 16; importance, 55, 93; effect of Treaty of Paris, 64; nationality of traders, 172, 182; rivalries, 172, 173; American policy, 192; in Oregon, 255.

G

Gadsden, James, concludes treaty, 290.

Gaines, Gen. E. P., Indian campaign, 250.

Gallatin, Albert, secretary of treasury, 141; estimates, 154; peace commissioner, 179, 180, 183, 185; European respect for, 180, 189; arranges arbitration, 230, 267; letters to, cited, 208, 237; missions to England, 372.

Gallican party, in Continental Congress, 31.

Galveston (Tex.), United States occupies, 200; fleet at, 482.

Gambier, Lord, peace commissioners, 180.

Gardoqui, Don Diego de, Spanish representative, 33, 57, 70, 71, 75, 77.

Garfield, J. A., president, 370; appointments, 370; foreign policy, 384.

Gayoso de Lenns, Manuel, Spanish commandant, 76; cited, 123.

Geary Act, passage of, 398.

Genêt, Edmund C., minister to United States, 96; instructions, 96–98, 131; cited, 98; correspondence, 129; reaches Charleston, 98; Philadelphia, 99; cabinet discusses, 99, 125; recognized, 101; intrigues, 101–103; recall demanded, 103; appeals to people, 103; recalled, 104; cited, 103; successor, 106; disturbing factor, 107.

Geneva, Alabama claims commission at, 345; international interest, 347.

Geneva Convention, rules of war, 472.

George III, of England, 23; asks Russian support, 37; letter of Louis XVI, 30; library, 59; conversation with John Adams, cited, 59, 60; Indian regard for, 66; loses colonies, 89.

George V, arbiter, 451.

Georgia, boundary disputes, 19, 20; retaliatory laws, 61.

Georgia, Strait of, as boundary, 270.

Gerard, C. A., French minister, 41.

Germany, diplomatic service to, 221, 224, 355, 429, 430; commercial treaties with, 224, 225, 471; extradition, 284; Civil War policy, 313; arbitrates channel boundary, 347, 348; forms Empire, 350; naturalization treaties, 355, 356; Cuban relations, 366; Spanish-American trade, 384, 452; Samoan relations, 399–401, 425; colonial ambition, 401, 419, 420, 426, 454, 455; rank of navy, 424; policy in Far East, 458; friendly feeling for United States, 467; interests in Mexico, 482, 484, 486, 487; war policies (1915), 492.

Gerry, Elbridge, commissioner to France, 131, 132.

Gettysburg, moral effects of battle, 322.

Ghent, peace negotiations at, 2, 180, 188, 345, 498; checked, 183; continued, 184; concluded, 186.

Gibraltar, Spain wants to regain, 26, 43, 44, 49.

Gibraltar, Straits of, Portuguese fleet guards, 114.

Gillespie, Lieut. A. H., sent to Monterey, 274.

Ginn, Edwin, pacifist, 473.

Ginseng, commercial importance, 55, 93.

Girondists, fall of, 103.

Gladstone, W. E., colonial policy, 342; American, 343, 347, 356; cited, 320.

Goderich, Viscount, in claims commission, 345.

Godoy, Don Manuel, Spanish statesman, 143.

Goliad, story of, 248.

Goulburn, Henry, peace commissioners, 180, 183; British minister, 246.

Grain, trade in, 55, 58, 61, 67, 108, 110, 315, competition in, 373, tariff, 388.

Grant, Ulysses S., victories, 322; opinion of French policy in Mexico, 332, 343; president, 335; Monroe Doctrine corollary, cited, 335, 478; foreign policy, 343, 344, 361, 365; appointments, 347; message cited, 368.

Granville, Lord, in British Cabinet, 320; on Clayton-Bulwer treaty, 381, 382.

Gray, Capt. Robert, enters Columbia River, 93, 148.

Gray, Sen. George, Spanish treaty commissioner, 418.

Great Britain, defeats Armada, 13; Florida ceded to, 19; Spain makes war on, 32; negotiates with, 33; treaties with (1763), 70, (1783), 70; French colonial rival, 15; treaties with France, 16; Canada ceded to, 18; claims in America, 13, 14; desires Ohio valley, 17; European hatred of, 24; Franco-American alliance against, 29, 30; friction with Holland, 35, 36; war, 38; payment to Barbary pirates, 56; discusses American peace terms, 42–50; distrusts Confederation, 60, 61; first American minister, 87; in Nootka Sound affair, 88–93; resists French Revolution, 94, 95, 203, 205; war with France, 99, 152; Napoleon's policy toward, 155, 158, 169; pride in victory over France, 180; United States, trade, 57–63, 86, 87, 198, 222, 285; embargo affects, 161; nonintercourse act, 163, 165; relations with neutrals, 14, 36–38, 102, 105, 108, 110, 118, 163; international law position, 54, 110–116, 124, 129, 159, 168, 169, 179, 183, 191, 193, 197, 236, 241–309, 316, 339, 349, 350; need of impressment, 113; naval supremacy, 14, 108, 152, 189, 237; trade policy, 59, 60, 153, 154, 156–160, 164, 198, 199, 205, 206, 270; orders in council, 111, 112, 120, 156, 159, 161, 164, 168, 169, 177, 183; holds frontier forts, 63, 64, 84, 116, 178; agrees to evacuate, 117; frontier policy, 68, 116, 147; Louisiana, 134, 135; relations with Indians, 64–66, 68, 82, 83, 116, 172, 182, 185, 292, 294, 295, 383; friction with United States, 114, 174; pays indemnity, 118; in War of 1812, 174–178; peace negotiations, 178–185; convention of 1818, 192–195; dislike of America, 181;

upholds balance of power, 205; Spanish-American policy, 206, 209–217, 324, 334, 384; anti-slavery, 216, 236, 246, 253, 254, 262, 263–265, 298, 301, 321, 333, 367; Oregon, 254–257, 265, 267–271; Texas, 253, 254, 260–266, 269–271; California, 257–259, 269, 274, 275; spoliation claims against, 226, Northeastern boundary dispute, 228–232, 234; Canadian policy; 232, 294, 348, 378, 432, 434, 435, 464; diplomatic service to, 188, 189, 222, 278, 282, 294, 295, 300, 306, 340, 343, 344, 372, 373, 429, 430; high grade of, 372; in Crimean war, 288; Russian relations, 359; central American policy, 292–296; Clayton-Bulwer treaty, 293, 381, 382; Cuban policy, 299, 366, civil war policy, 310–323, 359; aftermath, 336, 339–344; claims commission, 344–348; in relation to Monroe Doctrine, 333, 343; interests in Asia, 353; expatriation problems, 356; in seal-fisheries dispute, 378, 379; Venezuela affair, 391–394; Japanese relations, 353, 397, 402; Samoan, 399–401, 425; Hawaiian, 403, 405; rank of navy, 424; cordial toward United States, 427, 428; exports, 452; policy in Far East, 454, 455, 458; authorizes reciprocity with colonies, 470; Russian treaty (1825), 432; Alaska boundary dispute, 432, 434; fisheries, 435; seal fisheries treaty, 434; Isthmian policy, 436–438; canal tolls dispute, 480; interests in Mexico, 482, 484, 486; war policies (1915), 492.

Great Lakes, navigation rights, 432.

Greece, insurrection in, 204, 212; Americans aid, 207; commercial treaty with, 223.

Green, B. E., views in California, 259.

Green, Duff, confidant of Calhoun, 264; in Texas, 265.

Greenville, treaty at, 84, 122.

Grenville, Lord, foreign minister, 87, 89, 90, 116, 117, 122.

Grenville, Thomas, British minister

to France, 42; additional powers, 44; recalled, 45;

Grenville, W. W., letter to, cited, 67.

Gresham, W. Q., secretary of state, 389; death, 392.

Grey Earl de, on claims commission, 345.

Greytown (Nic.), English seize, 292.

Guadaloupe Island, rich in sugar, 18; exhange proposed, 49; trade, 108, 134.

Guam Island, ceded to United States, 419.

Guantanamo (Cuba), naval station, 444.

Guatemala, commercial treaty with, 285; boundary dispute, 385, 386.

Guiana, boundary disputed, 391, 394.

Guillemot, Eugène, agent to Uruguay, cited, 325, 326.

Guizot, F. P. G., French premier, 240.

Gunn, James, Georgia Senator, 135.

Gwin, Sen. W. McK., Alaskan policy, 358.

H

Hague, The, American minister to, 136.

Hague Conference (1899), called by Czar, 473; acts of, 473, 494; (1907), endorses modified Drago Doctrine, 447; recommendations, 475.

Hague Permanent Court of Arbitration, 8, 453; functions, 444; settles fisheries dispute, 435; Venezuelan claims submitted to, 449; established, 473; palace presented, 473; Spain and Mexico resort to, 474; scope of jurisdiction, 474.

Hahnville (La.), Italian lynched at, 427.

Haldiman, Gen. Frederick, refuses to surrender frontier ports, 63.

Hale, J. P., minister to Spain, instructions, 328.

Hale, Sen. W. G., tariff views, 388.

Halifax, American trade, 177; route via, 182, 230; admiralty court, 157.

Hamburg, commercial treaty with, 197; interests in Samoa, 399.

Hamilton, Alexander, financial policy, 82, 97, 106; meets English agent, 90; English sympathies, 91, 92, 95; French policy, 99–101, 136–138; differs with Jefferson, 99, 104, 125; Republicans distrust, 115; intimacy with British minister, 120; stoned, 120; commands army, 135; cited, 135.

Hammond, George, British minister, 64, 87, 181; frontier policy, 116; successor, 122.

Hammond, J. H., letter to, cited, 264.

Hannegan, E. A., Indiana senator, vote, 279.

Hanover, commercial treaty with, 224; navigation, 352.

Harmer, Gen. Josiah, Indians defeat, 83.

Harris, Sir James, British diplomat, 37.

Harrison, Benjamin, presidential ambition, 390; counsel for Venezuela, 394; appointments, 304, 370.

Harrison, W. H., Indian dealings, 172.

Hartford Convention, proposed, 184.

Hartly, David, commission, 58.

Harvard University, Germanic Museum, 467.

Hats, Leghorn, trade in, 55.

Havana, route via, 316, 410, 411; Maine destroyed in harbor, 413.

Hawaii, American relations, 223, 245, 286, 297, 352, 353, 360, 362, 402–406, 424, 487; missionaries in, 402; British, 403, 405; Japanese, 461, 462.

Hawkins, Sir John, colonial dreams of, 205.

Hay, John, diplomat, 8, 188, 499; secretary of state, 304, 429; ambassador to England, 429; dealings with England, 431, 434, 436; Canada, 434; Panama, 441; China, 455–458; views on Drago Doctrine, 447; Turkey, 464; Roumania, 468; arbitration attitude, 473–475; characterized, 429, 457; cited, 368.

Hayes, R. B., president, 304; appointments, 304, 370; on Monroe Doctrine, 394; Chinese exclusion, 397; Panama canal policy, message cited, 380.

Hayti, negro republic, 217, 264; diplomatic relations with, 349, 375; affected by reciprocity, 389; arbitration treaty with, 475.

Heber, Bishop Reginald, missionary zeal, 255; "From Greenland's Icy Mountains," 255.

Hemp, trade in, 110.

Henfield, Gideon, arrested, 102.

Henry VII, of England, sends Cabot's expedition, 10.

Henry, Prince, visits United States, 467.

Henry, John, British agent, 174, 176.

Henry, Patrick, gains foreign sympathy, 24; refuses mission to France, 137.

Hermosa, carries slaves, 238.

Herran, P. A., Colombian minister, arranges treaty, 439, 443.

Herrera, J. J., Mexican president, 275.

Hervey, Lionel, British agent in Mexico, 215; recall, 215, 216.

Hesse, naturalization treaty with, 356.

Hides, in McKinley tariff, 388.

Hill, D. J., diplomatic service, 429.

History Teachers' Magazine, cited, 243.

Hoar, E. R., on British claims commission, 345.

Hoar, Sen. George, cited, 442.

Holland, claims in America, 13; decline, 14, 110; trade during Revolution, 22, 34–36; war with England, 38, 43; treaty with United States, 39; in American peace negotiations, 44–46; peace with England, 50; diplomatic service to, 81, 140, 188; American trade, 164, 167.

Holland, war with France, 95; France annexes, 167; neutrality problems, 492; Japanese relations, 353, 402.

Holmes, O. W., greeting to Alexis, cited, 360.

Holy Alliance, terms, 204; failures, 208; relations with England, 237.

Honduras, Bay of, English in, 292, 294, 295; Honduras, Isthmus of, route via, 295; treaty concerning, 352; English occupation, 381, 382; Honduras, Republic of, reciprocity with, 389; public debt, 446, 459; American protectorate, 448; forcible intervention, 449; treaty with, 459.

Honolulu, gunboats in harbor of, 405.

Hopewell, treaty of, 83.

Horses, trade in, 58.

Horseshoe Bend, battle at, 178.

Hortalie, Rodriguez, and Company, aids American Revolution, 26.

House of Representatives, relation to diplomacy, 80, 121; to Senate, 225, 428; impeachments, 134; resolutions, 331, 334; speakers, 171, 413; members, 86, 227, 300; Fenian sympathy, 338.

Houston, Samuel, Tennessee governor, 248; Texas leader, 248–250, 260.

Howe, John, British agent, 176.

Howe, S. S., on San Domingo commission, 364; aids Greece, 207.

Howick, Lord, issues order in council, 159; dispatch, cited, 159.

Hudson, Hendrik, American discoveries, 13.

Hudson Bay, rival claims, 16; British control trade, 118.

Hudson Bay Company, American rival, 173; absorbs Northwestern Co., 186; in Oregon, 255; protect priests, 256; claims negotiated, 344.

Hudson River, Dutch colony on, 13, 14.

Huerta, Gen. Victoriano, government not recognized, 479, 483, 489; defeats Madero, 483; president, 483; European recognition, 483, 486; Japan policy, 487.

Hughes, Archbishop John, visits Ireland, 338.

Huguenots, massacre of French, 12.

Hülseman, Baron, Austrian minister, 282.

Humphreys, David, minister to Spain, 140.

Hungary, revolution in, 281.

Hunter, R. M. T., Confederate secretary, 310.

Hunter, William, service in state department, 307, 418, 499.

"Hunters' Lodges," organized, 233.

Huron, Lake, as boundary, 46, 186, 235.

Huskisson, William, British trade policy, 198.

l'Huys, Drouyn de, French foreign minister, 331; cited, 332.

I

Iberville River, as boundary, 19, 149–151.

Ile d'Orleans, ceded to England, 19.

Illinois, emigrants, 257.

Immigration, Chinese, 397, 398, 449, 460; Japanese, 461; European, 467–469; Roumanian, 468; undue stimulation of, 469.

Imperialism, United States disclaims, 280, 281; tendency toward, 423–426.

Impressment. See International Law.

Independence (Mo.), emigrant centre, 257.

Indiana, Indian tribes, 65, 84; territorial governor, 172.

Indians, in colonial wars, 15; in War of 1812, 178; Continental Congress, seeks support, 23; sell lands, 172; "buffer state" proposed, 181, 183, 184, 246; fur trade, 192; annuities, 194; among frontier population, 63; relations with English, 65, 66, 114, 116, 118, 172, 182, 185; Americans, 65, 66, 69, 72, 172; Cherokee, treaty, 72, 83; intrigues, 89; Chickamauga, 72; Chickasaw, 72; Choctaw, 72; Creeks, 72; chief, 73, 83, 89; treaty, 83; intrigues, 89; Delaware, 65; Florida, 200, 201, 250; Iroquois, relations with English, 17; colonial negotiations with, 21; power of confederacy, 64, 65; Miami, 65; Mosquito, British relations, 292, 294, 295,

383; Northwestern tribes, 65; Oregon, missions to, 255, 256; Texas, 248-250; Shawnee, 65; Southwestern, 72; Spanish trade with, 73, 74, 123; raid against, 76; Wyandot, 65; Yucatan, 296; wars with, 83, 84, 117; treaty, 122, 182.

Industrial Property, Act for Protection of parties to, 472.

Industrial Property, Convention for International Protection of, 374.

Inness, Harry, colonizing schemes, 75.

International co-operation, 374, 378.

International Institute of Agriculture, 472.

International law, tendencies, 7; affecting colonial claims, 17; informal system, 21; continental views, 54, 111; rights of foreigners, 53; strain of Napoleonic wars, 187; armed neutrality, 37, 110, 179; blockade, 111, 119, 159, 168, 169, 174, 175, 177, 288, 307-312, 315, 493; building enemies' ships, 340, 342; collection of debts, 446, 447; continuous voyage, 308, 309, 318, 492, 493; contraband, 36, 54, 100, 111, 119, 124, 128, 129, 138, 154, 288, 318, 442, 493, 494; embezzlement, 235; expatriation, see naturalization; extradition, 117, 235, 284, 350, 351, 374, 388, 469; flag, use of, 240, 312, 367; free ships, free goods, 29, 36, 54, 110, 119, 124, 129, 138, 207, 288; hospital ships, 472; impressment, 113, 157-159, 164, 175, 182, 289, 356, 492; indemnity, 182, 191, 238, 239; marine territorial jurisdiction, 287; mines, 494; most favored nation, 224, 464, 465; naturalization, 7, 114, 289, 355-357, 466, 468, 491; navigation, right of, 70, 71, 119, 197, 285, 287, 378, 380, 388; neutral goods in enemies' ships, 288; privateering, 54, 102, 103, 105, 106, 119, 288, 309, 416; prizes, 102, 105, 118, 119, 124; recognition of governments, 442, 484; "Rule of 1756," terms, 112;

validity of treaties, 90-101, 191; violation of territory, 234; visit and search, 54, 113, 157, 159, 164, 236, 237, 239, 241, 282, 309, 316, 318, 349, 350; waterways, 5, 70, 197, 287, 291; wounded, treatment of, 288, 472.

International office of Public Health, parties to, 472.

International Red Cross Convention, signatories, 472.

International Sanitary Convention, parties to, 472.

Ireland, colonies appeal to, 23; Fenians plan to free, 338.

Irish, political power in United States, 338, 390.

Isabella, Queen, of Castile, 10.

Isabella, Queen of Spain, overthrown, 365.

Isle of Pines, given to Cuba, 425.

Italy, United States trade, 166; commercial treaty, 471; revolt in, 204; Civil War policy, 313; represented in Geneva board, 347; Kingdom of, 350; extradition treaty, 350; offers mediation in Cuba, 300; emigration to Argentina, 384; United States, 469; irritation over lynchings, 426, 427; American ambassador to, 429, 430; interests in Far East, 455, 458; arbitration treaty, 475; neutrality problems 1915, 492.

Itata, seized, 390.

Izard, Ralph, commissioner to Tuscany, 31; dislikes French, 34.

J

Jackson, Andrew, deals with Florida Indians, 200; seizes Spanish forts, 200, 201; diplomatic service under, 220, 304; methods, 241; problems of policy, 480; appointments, 221, 248, 250; British policy, 222; French, 226-228; Texas, 250, 252, 265, 341; messages cited, 227, 228, 251.

Jackson, F. J., minister to United States, 165, 176.

Jacobins, American club, 99, 103.

Jamaica, position threatens Gulf trade, 360; reciprocity with, 470.

Jameson, J. F., views on American expansion, 243, 244.

Japan, commerce with, 286; Perry's expedition, 286, 303; American relations, 353, 396, 461–463, 480; European, 353, 402; commercial treaty with, 397, 454; arbitration, 475; seal fisheries, 434; protests Hawaiian annexation, 424; diplomatic service to, 430; affected by Monroe Doctrine, 449, 450; world-power, 454, 459; relations with China, 455, 458; war with Russia, 458; Manchurian policy, 459, 461; Canadian, 461; Mexican, 486, 487.

Jay, John, diplomat, 1; commissioner to Spain, 32, 33; distrusts Spain, 34; France, 34, 44–46, 91, 137; in peace negotiations, 44–46, 58, 74, 142; secretary of foreign affairs, 57, 70, 71; mission to England, 115, 126, 128, 372; instructions, 115; welcome, 116; concludes treaty, 84, 117–119; error in, 119; burned in effigy, 120; views on French treaty, 99; chief justice, 81, 115; Mississippi proposal, 417; independent action 371; length of service, 499; characterized, 32; cited, 32, 34.

Jecker and Company, firm of, buys bonds, 329.

Jefferson, Thomas, peace commissioner, 41; makes commercial treaty, 54; treats with Barbary states, 56; minister to France, 54, 81; secretary of state, 81; resigns, 104; views on merchant marine, 85, 86, 196; on validity of treaties, 99, 100; on expansion, 476; on neutrality, 102, 103, 106; on isolation, 211, 438; French sympathies, 95, 136; fears English, 91; differs with Hamilton, 99, 125; presidential candidate, 129, 130; president, 140; appointments, 141, 157, 158; problems of policy, 480; Barbary states policy, 141, 222; Cuban, 208, 209; Louisiana, 144, 145, 148; trade, 155–157, 190, 498; closes American harbors, 160; Madison consults, 163; length of public service, 499;

theories, 140, 154, 160, 165, 181; justifies Louisiana purchase, 442; cited, 28, 85, 86, 91, 95, 106, 208, 209, 470.

Jews, protest against persecution of, 357; treatment by Roumania, 468.

Johnson, Andrew, president, 362, 365; message, cited, 362.

Johnson, Reverdy, treats with England, 340, 373; convention rejected, 343.

Jones, Anson, president of Texas, 266, 272.

Jones, J. P., American commodore, 30; enters Texel, 36; French sympathies, 96.

Juan de Fuca, Straits of, channel, 337, 348.

Juarez, Gen. B. P., resists French in Mexico, 332; captures Maximilian, 333.

Juarez (Mex.), fighting at, 482.

K

Kaiulani, Hawaiian princess, 404.

Kamamaha, King of Hawaii, 402.

Kanakas, employed on Pacific coast, 286.

Kaskaskia (Ill.), Clark captures, 33, 69.

Kasson, J. A., on Samoan commission, 401; reciprocity treaty commissioner, 470.

Kentucky, relations with England, 67, 68; pioneers, 69; governor, 102; intrigues with Spain, 76, 123; France, 102, 105; constitutional convention, 76; admitted to Union, 82; militia praised, 174.

Key West, position isolated, 360; importance of railroad to, 444.

Kiauchau, port leased, 455.

King, Rufus, minister to England, 129, 135, 189, 372; successor, 158; suggests Philippine trade concessions, 417; fears loss of West, 71; cited, 135; letter to, cited, 137.

King's Mountain, battle of, 69.

Kipling, Rudyard, White Man's Burden, cited, 421.

Knox, Gen. Henry, secretary of war, cited, 83; letter to, cited, 84.

Knox, P. C., secretary of state, 448, 459, 483; visits Caribbean states, 452; proposes Colombian treaty, 453; Chinese policy, 459; "dollar diplomacy," 476.

Koerner, G., minister to Spain, instructions, 327.

Kossuth, Louis, visits America, 280, 281.

Kossta, Martin, case of, 282, 289.

Kwangchau Bay, port opened, 223; port leased, 455.

Kwang-Chow. See Kwangchau.

L

Labrador, fisheries, 192.

Ladrone Islands, American interests, 418, 419.

Lafayette, Marquis de, American sympathy, 27, 94; proscribed, 99.

Laird, William, British ship-builder, 322, 340.

Lakes, Great, trade route, 68; navigation rights on, 182, 191, 346.

La Plata River, navigation of, 287; dispute over mouth of, 325.

Lard, trade in, 225.

Laredo (Mex.), fighting at, 482.

Larkin, T. O., consul at Monterey, 274.

La Salle, Robert Cavalier, Sieur de, explorer, 201.

Laurens, Henry, commissioner to Netherlands, 31, 38; captured on ocean, 38; peace commissioner, 41; imprisoned, 42.

Laurier, Sir Wilfred, government defeated, 436.

Lazzari, Mgr., diary of American Revolution, 24.

Leather goods, trade in, 373.

Lebrun, C. F., letters to, cited, 96, 102.

Leclerc, Gen. V. E., San Domingo expedition, 143; death, 145.

Lee, Arthur, deals with Beaumarchais, 27; commissioner to France, 31; irritates Spain, 31; dislikes French, 34.

Lee, Fitzhugh, consul-general at Havana, 412, 415.

Lee, R. E., surrender, 331.

Lee, William, commissioner to Berlin, 31; meets de Neufville, 37; drafts treaty, 37, 38.

Legaré, H. S., secretary of state, 221; Hawaiian policy, 403; death, 260.

Leishman, J. G. A., diplomatic service, 430.

Le Louis, admiralty case, 236.

Leo XIII, proposed as Cuban mediator, 414, 415.

Leopard, affair with Chesapeake, 159, 174.

Leslie. See Panton, Leslie and Co.

Lesseps, Ferdinand de, head of canal company, 380, 439.

Lew Chew Islands, commercial treaty with, 286.

Lewis, Sir G. C., American views, 320.

Lewis, Meriwether, explorer, 148.

Lexington, Battle of, rouses America, 159.

Liberia, American relations, 349; international receivership, 464.

Li Hung Chang, represents China, 457.

Liliuokalani, Queen of Hawaii, 404; abolishes constitution, 405.

Lincoln, Abraham, compared with Franklin, 28; diplomatic influence, 305, 306, 310, 317, 322; appointments, 304–306, 354; proclaims blockade, 307, 315; English opinion of, 314; Emancipation proclamation, 321; effects, 321; letter to London working-men, 322; private secretary, 429; political wisdom, 457; problems of policy, 480; cited, 304.

Lincoln, Robert, minister to England, 373, 392.

Lind, John, mission to Mexico, 485.

Linn, L. F., Missouri senator, 255; Oregon bill, 256.

Liston, Robert, British minister, 122, 134.

Little Belt, fights President, 174.

Little Democrat, French privateer, 103.

Little Sarah, captured, 103.

Livingston, Edward, House leader, 121; diplomatic ability, 220; death, 220.

Livingston, Robert, secretary of

foreign affairs, 23, 57; minister to France, 140, 146, 149, 150, 226, 227; letters to, cited, 34, 53, 92.

Lodge, H. C., Senate leader, 428; on Alaskan boundary commission, 434; seal fisheries, 379; Magdalena Bay resolution, 450, 487; immigration views, 467.

Logan, Dr. George, peace mission, 136.

Lôme, Dupuy de, Spanish minister, indiscretion, 413.

London, 73, 81, 123, 129, 165, 180, 210, 262, 429, 455; interest in American Revolution, 24; loses American trade, 35; distributing centre, 61; financial, 362, 427; fur-market, 64.

Lopez, Gen. Narciso, Cuban leader, 298; death, 299.

Louis XVI, interest in America, 25; adopts middle course, 260; recognizes American Independence, 30, 42; powers, 92; beheaded, 99; American treaty, 100.

Louis Napoleon, Civil War policy, 313, 330, 331; colonial plans, 313; Mexican, 329–333; offers mediation, 330; British relations, 334.

Louis Philippe, American policy, 227.

Louisburg, English capture, 15, 16; give back, 16.

Louisiana, French possession, 17; ceded to England and Spain, 19; England desires, 91, 134; France, 97, 98, 102, 130; Spanish policy, 73, 74, 123, 124; governor, 75; cedes to France, 142, 143; France to United States, 145, 146, 165, 188, 199, 224; problems, 147; boundaries, 148–151, 185, 194, 202; loyalty doubtful, 181; effect of purchase, 187; justification of, 443.

Lourenço Marques Railroad, seized by Portugal, 375.

L'Ouverture, Toussaint, rules San Domingo, 134, 136; captured, 143.

Lowell, J. R., diplomatic service, 221, 373; "Bigelow Papers," cited, 318.

Loyalists, interests safeguarded, 48; leniency recommended, 60; treatment of, 64; settle in Ontario, 66; in Natchez, 71; bitter feeling, 66; in War of 1812, 178; compensation refused, 118.

Lübeck, commercial treaty with, 197.

Lumber, trade in, 58, 67, 346.

Luzerne, Anne Cesar de la, French minister to United States, 33; instructions, 50.

Lyons, Lord, British minister, 317.

M

Macdonald, Sir J. A., on claims commission, 345.

McGillivray, Alexander, Creek chief, 73; visits New York, 83; rival, 89; cited, 77.

Machinery, farm, trade in, 373.

McClellan, Gen. G. B., fails before Richmond, 320.

McKean, Thomas, Pennsylvania judge, 136.

McKenzie, Alexander, explorer, 254.

MacKenzie, A. S., confers with Santa Anna, 276.

Mackerel, trade in, 58, 108; desert Canadian waters, 375.

McKinley, William, elected president, 408; appointments, 412, 429; Cuban policy, 413; Hawaiian, 424; Philippine, 419, 420; de Lôme's opinion of, 413; forbids privateering, 416; civil service under, 431; proposes Pan-American Congress, 451; foreign policy, 476; cited, 419.

McLane, Louis, secretary of state, 220; minister to England, instructions, 222.

McLaughlin, Dr. John, Hudson Bay Co., factor, 255.

McLeod, Alexander, case of, 233, 234.

Macon Bill, No. 2, provisions, 167.

Madagascar, treaty with, 349.

Madawaska, French fief, 230.

Madero, Francisco, leads revolution, 482; elected president, 483; overthrown, 483.

Madison, James, diplomat, 8; member of Congress, 86; declines office, 104; secretary of state, 141; Florida policy, 149–151; minister to

England, 158; president, 163; re-election, 175; foreign policy, 163, 211; British, 165, 168–170, 174, 179, 184; English resentment, 181; views, cited, 100, 158; letter to, 209.

Madison Island, annexation, 398.

Madrid, 33, 73, 130, 150, 327, 361, 410.

Madrid, Treaty of, 14.

Magdalena Bay, Japanese interest in, 449, 487.

Magellan, Ferdinand, circumnavigates world, 11.

Mahan, Rear Adm. A. T., naval authority, 423.

Maine, boundary dispute, 230, 234, 235, 272; lumber trade, 346.

Maine, destruction of, 413; cause disputed, 413, 414; arbitration offered, 415.

Malietoa, King of Samoa, 400.

Malmesbury, Earl of, Southern sympathy, 314.

Malta, desires United States trade, 55.

Manchester, Duke of, commission, 58.

Manchuria, relations with Japan, 459, 461.

Mangouret, M. A., French consul, 99.

"Manifest Destiny," theory of, 199, 200, 296, 301; scouted by Carl Schurz, 364.

Manila, captured by Dewey, 417, 419; held by United States, 418; German attitude, 419.

Manila Bay, battle of, 417, 420.

Manufactures, growth of, 284.

Marbois, Barbé, French agent, 145, 146; *Mémoire*, captured, 45.

Marcy, W. L., dispatch on Koszta case, 282, 289; secretary of state, 282, 283, 285, 288, 297, 300, 302; reciprocity treaty, 337; fisheries, 352; relations with Pierce, 365; Hawaiian policy, 403.

Maria, pirates capture, 56.

Marshall, John, constitutional authority, 2; commissioner to France, 131, 132; secretary of state, 138; court decisions, 237.

Martinique, trade, 108, 134.

Mason, G. T., Virginia senator, 120.

Mason, J. M., Confederate commissioner, 311; captured, 316; released, 318.

Mason, J. Y., minister to France, 301; special Spanish mission, 301.

Massachusetts, limits curtailed, 46; interest in fisheries, 48; merchant marine, 163; whigs control, 227; boundary dispute, 230, 235.

Mataafa, Samoan leader, 400, 401.

Matamoras (Mex.), port, 308, 309.

Maumee River, British fort on, 83, 84, 116, 500.

Maurepas, Comte de, French prime minister, 25.

Maximilian, Archduke, Mexican emperor, 330, 331, United States policy toward, 332, 442; death, 333, 427.

Meade, Gen. George, in Civil War, 322.

Mecklenburg-Schwerin, commercial treaty with, 285.

Mediation, offered, in American Revolution, 41; in War of *1812*, 178; Spanish-American, 208, 324; French claims dispute, 228; Civil War, 330; Cuban insurrections, 366, 412; Hayti-Dominican dispute, 384, 390; European, in American disputes, 384–386, 444; offered by A. B. C. powers, 490.

Mediterranean Sea, piracy on, 55, 56; abolished, 196; commerce, 85, 141, 159.

Merchant marine, development, 85–87, 109, 110, 152–154, 157, 163, 169, 190, 284; risks, 154, 156, 161, 164, 177; reciprocity aids, 196, 197; subsidies, 284, 469; registration rules, 470, 494; in Civil War, 309, 312; decline after war, 336, 337, 353, 359, 469, 492.

Merrimac, Monitor defeats, 319.

Merritt, Gen. Wesley, advises peace commission (*1898*), 419.

Merry, Anthony, British minister, 147.

Mexico, as boundary, 12; mines, 74, 75, 89, 123; revolts from Spain, 203; independence, 213; France desires, 205; Napoleon's views on, 209; Russian relations, 213; seeks alliances, 214; English relations, 90, 215, 216, 253, 270, 271, 275, 276, 278, 328, 329; plans of Congress, 216, 276; land policy, 246; commercial treaties, 216, 223, 224, 279; slavery in, 246, 247; diplomatic service to, 221, 258, 273; claims treaty, 226, 375; report to Congress of, cited, 243; American interests in, 245, 248, 297, 452, 481; defers payment, 328; Texas question, 248–254, 260, 263, 265, 271–276; California, 257–259, 274, 275, 279; war with United States, 277, 278; terms of peace, 279; Gadsden treaty, 290; Yucatan revolt, 296; revolution chronic, 297, 328, 481; trade with Confederacy, 309; relations with Second Empire, 328–333; discourages American settlers, 247; Spanish relations, 328, 329; allies collect duties in, 329; Empire founded, 320; arbitration of claims, 350, 474; naturalization treaty, 356; arbitration, 475, 481; boundary dispute, 385, 386; minister, cited, 387; favors arbitration court, 451; relations with United States 1915, 444, 479, 481; foreign interests in, 481, 486; American, 482, 485–487; Madero government, 482; Huerta, 483, 484, 486.

Mexico, City of, Americans take, 277; French, 329; Second Pan-American Congress, 451; foreign colony in, 482.

Mexico, Gulf of, tributaries, 32, 187; commerce on, 33; control of, 253, 360, 444.

Michaux, André, French agent, 102.

Michilimackinac (Mich.), British fort, 63; trade-centre, 173.

Michigan, Lake, right of navigation, 285, 346.

Middle West, demands open Mississippi, 5.

Midway Islands, annexation, 399, 406, 425.

Milan decree, terms, 158; revoked, 168.

Military service, liability of naturalized citizens, 357.

Milk River, source, 195.

Mines, Mexican, 74, 75, 89, 90, 123; foreign interests in, 481, 482; nitrate, 386.

Mirabeau, Comte de, defeat in Assembly, 92.

Miranda, Francisco de, adventurer, 89; revolutionary plans, 90, 96, 134, 135, 139, 203, 290; death, 203.

Miro, Estevern, Louisiana governor, 75; intrigues, 76, 77; cited, 76.

Mirs Bay, port leased, 455.

Missionaries, American, in Oregon, 255, 256; in Pacific, 396; China, 286, 455, 460; Hawaii, 402; Turkey, 465; desire Philippines as field, 421.

Mississippi River, as boundary, 19, 40, 41, 46, 74, 135, 151, 201; source, 116, 118; Spain holds, 5, 32, 33, 63, 70, 75, 87, 90; French hold mouth, 16; Americans, 181; free navigation demanded, 41, 43, 48, 57, 70, 72, 97, 197, 245; opposed by East, 71; granted, 124, 125, 147; English demand, 182, 185, 195; French designs in valley, 142; America secures, 194; fur-trade on upper, 173; outlet for commerce of, 360, 444.

Missouri, Spanish intrigues in, 75; slavery struggle in, 252; emigrants, 257; senator, 255.

Missouri River, as boundary, 148; source, 195; fur-trade on, 173.

Mobile (Ala.), French colony, 19, 149; Americans occupy, 151; British threaten, 181.

Mohammedans, plunder Spanish colonies, 13.

Mohonk, Lake, conferences at, 473.

Molasses, trade in, 119.

Mongolia, independence recognized, 459.

Monitor, defeats *Merrimac*, 319.

Monongahela River, joins Allegheny, 17.

Monroe, James, minister to France, 104; welcome, 107, 115, 126; mission, 127; recall, 128; indiscretion, 128, 129, 131, 132; poor diplomat, 141, 188; Louisiana purchase, 144–146, 149, 150; minister to England, 158, 372; special mission, 158;

secretary of state, 170, 188; instructs peace commissioners, 182; president, 188; Spanish-American policy, 201, 210, 211, 251; Oregon, 255; states "doctrine," 211, 212, 324.

Monroe Doctrine, development, 1, 2; basis, 211; stated, 212, 213; Canning's opinion of, 214, 215, 382; influence on national policy, 217, 218, 353, 359; extensions of, 218, 296, 334, 403, 417, 420, 448, 450, 477–479, 484, 499, 500; real author, 218; Polk revives, 268, 281, 325; Polk's corollary, 296; effect of Clayton-Bulwer treaty, 293, 382; practiced effects, 324, 326; during Civil War, 324–334; in Maximilian affairs, 333; Grant's corollary, 334; base of Panama policy (1880), 380; Blaine and Olney's conception of, 384–395; affects Caribbean situation, 444, 450, 477; question of claims, 446, 448; Roosevelt's corollary, 448; Lodge's corollary, 450; Wilson's corollaries, 450, 478, 484; Spanish-America resents, 452; Mexican problems, 482.

Monterey (Cal.), American consul, instructions, 274; British consul, 257; Americans seize, 258.

Montevideo, French relations, 325.

Montreal, trade centre, 67, 118, 122, 125, 173, 197; Americans desire, 174.

Moore, J. B., Spanish treaty commission secretary, 418; state department counsellor, 480, 499.

Moose Island, British demand, 182, 186.

Morgan, Col. George, Western schemes, 75.

Morgan, J. P., interests in Honduras, 459.

Mori Daizen, chastised by Europe, 353.

Mormons, American, in Mexico, 482.

Morny, Duc de, Mexican policy, 329.

Morocco, official piracy, 55; treaty with, 56, 85; international agreement with, 402; Algeciras conference, 402, 464.

Morris, Gouverneur, mission to England, 87; minister to France, 104; recall, 104.

Morton, L. P., diplomatic experience, 304.

Mosquitoes (Indian tribe), 292, 295, 383. See Nicaragua.

Motley, J. L., minister to England, 343, 373; instructions, 344; removal, 344; to Austria, 333; concludes treaty with England, 356.

Moultrie, Gov. William, receives Genêt, 98.

Mount Vernon, Washington at, 120.

Munster, treaty of, 14.

Murray, W. V., minister to Holland, 136; on French commission, 137.

Muscat, commercial treaty with, 223.

N

Nacodoches, Spanish fort, 202; Americans occupy, 250.

Najato, prince of, 353.

Naples, interest in American Revolution, 24; American trade, 55, 164, 167; insurrection in, 204; commercial treaty, 223; claims treaty, 226; extradition, 285.

Nashville (Tenn.), pioneers, 69.

Nassau, port of, 238, 308.

Natchez (Miss.), possession disputed, 33, 71; American interests, 245; trade centre, 70; commandant, 76.

Natchitoches, French fort, 202.

National Era, Mexican policy, 278.

National Gazette, policy, 103.

Naturalization. See International Law.

Navarro, Martin, Spanish intendant, cited, 73, 74.

Navigation. See International Law.

Navy, in War of 1812, 178; in Civil War, 409; rebuilding, 409.

Navy, steady increase in, 423; efficiency tested, 424; rank, 424; increase refused, 495.

Navy Island, militia rendezvous, 232.

Necker, Jacques, French statesman, 43.

Nelson, Hugh, minister to Spain, 209, 210; instructions, cited, 297.

Nelson, Justice Samuel, on British Claims commission, 345.

Nesselrode, Count Karl Robert, English sympathy, 169.

Netherlands, King of, arbitrates, 230, 235; interests in Asia, 353; diplomatic service to, 429; arbitration treaty, 475. See Holland.

Neutrality, position of Holland (1688), 14, 22, (1776), 35, 36, (1779), 38; lax enforcement, 22; doctrine of armed, 37, 38; John Adams's views, 92; Jefferson's, 102, 104; Washington's, 125; cabinet discusses, 99; proclamation issued, 100, 105; law of 1794, 105; problems (1789–1812), 6, 90–92, 95, 100, 107, 127–129, 136, 152, 169, 170; obligations (1789–1812), 106, 118, 169; rights (1789–1812), 14, 108, 110–114, 118, 124, 126, 127, 156, 159, 167, 170, 175; indemnity for violations, 118, 124; England proclaims, 206; United States, 207; problems (1812–1829), 196, 207, 208; Great Britain's interpretation lax, 336, 338; American act of 1838, 345; problems (1829–1872), 232, 249–251, 288, 299, 327, 330, 332, 339; obligations (1829–1872), 288, 309, 339, 345; rights (1829–1872), 288, 308, 309, 312, 342, 345, 390, 493; in Franco-Prussian war, 350; of Isthmian routes, 352, 380; in Cuban insurrection, 365, 409, 412; in Boer war, 431; of China, in Russian-Japanese war, 458; in Mexican revolutions, 483; in European war, 491, 493–496.

Neufville, Jean de, drafts treaty, 36.

Neuville, Baron Hyde de, minister to United States, 200, 201.

New Brunswick, boundary dispute, 230, 235.

New England, settlement of, 13; captures Canadian ports, 15; fishing interests, 40, 41, 192, 377;

commercial, 71; embargo hurts, 161; carrying trade, 55, 177.

New England Society, of New York, address to, cited, 305.

New Granada. See Colombia.

New Hampshire, claims Vermont lands, 67.

New Madrid (Mo.), proposed colony, 75.

New Mexico, United States claims, 274; obtains, 279, 341.

New Orleans (La.), French settle, 16; ceded to England, 19; trade centre, 70, 98; Americans desire, 73; English designs against, 90; French, 102; place of deposit, 124, 144, 145; Pitt's plan for, 135; Spanish intendant, 144; ceded to United States, 146; Pakenham's expedition against, 181, 184; filibustering expeditions from, 298; Italian lynched at, 427.

New York, Indian tribes, 64; claims Vermont lands, 67; Canada desires northern, 181; Canadian trade, 197; militia equip in, 232.

New York City, Indian chiefs visit, 83; British agent at, 90; trade centre, 161, 173, 199, 285, 427, 452, 467; filibustering expeditions, 298; Russian fleet visits, 359; Cuban head-quarters, 409.

Newfoundland, ceded to England, 16; fisheries, 40, 41, 45, 48, 108, 192, 285, 434, 435, 497; embargo hurts, 161; War of 1812, 177; not a part of Canada, 434.

Niagara (N. Y.), fort, 63, 182; mediation conference at, 490.

Niagara River, Iroquois on, 65; international waterway, 181; Fenians cross, 338.

Nicaragua, international route, 135, 290; rival of Panama, 291, 292, 295, 440; Indians, 292; British relations, 292, 383; American, 296, 297; extradition treaty with, 350; right of way through, 352; proposed canal treaty, 382, 383; reciprocity with, 389; canal policy, 439; protectorate over, 448; forcible intervention, 449; treaty (1915), 450.

Nicholas II of Russia, calls first Hague Conference, 473.

Ningpo, port opened, 223.

Nipissing, Lake, as boundary, 20, 40, 46.

Nitrate mines, South American, 386.

Non-importation, colonial agreements, 156; law of *1806*, 157.

Non-intercourse act, terms, 163; effects, 164, 166, 167; renewed, 169.

Nootka Sound, English settlement, 88; Spanish ships raid, 88; controversy over, 89 92, neutrality difficult, 100; Treaty of, 92.

North, Lord, resigns, 42; return to office, 59.

North Carolina, settles Tennessee, 69; Indian relations, 72; governor, 137.

Northcote, Sir Stafford, in claims commission, 345.

North German Union, naturalization treaty, 355.

Northwest, British policy in, 68, 116, 172; Indian tribes, 172; northwest coast, Russian advance, 205, 206, 209, 212.

Northwest Territory, governor, 83.

Northwestern Fur Co., rival, 173; title to Astoria, 185; absorbed, 185.

Norway, commercial treaty with, 197; extradition, 285; naturalization, 356; arbitration, 475; neutrality (*1915*), 492.

Nova Scotia, desired by United States, 40.

Nueces River, as boundary, 271.

O

Ohio, Indian tribes, 65, 84.

Ohio River, claims to valley, 16, 17; ceded to England, 19; as boundary, 20, 40, 116; branches, 68; junction, 105; pioneers in valley, 245.

Oil, trade in, 164, 285; free entry conceded, 346.

Oldenburg, commercial treaty with, 285.

Olliwochica, Indian leader, 172.

Olney, Richard, secretary of state,

8, 391, 392; Venezuela policy, 391; conception of Monroe Doctrine, 392–395, 478; characterized, 391, 395; cited, 392, 395.

Onis, Don Luis de, negotiates with Adams, 200, 201, 246.

Ontario, loyalists settle in, 66; relations with England, 178.

Ontario, Lake, as boundary, 46; naval fights in, 178, 190.

Orange Free State, treaty with, 350.

Oregon, American claims, 93, 148, 186, 195, 202, 214, 245, 265, 267, 200, 270, joint occupation, 105, 254–257, 269, 271; treaty signed, 270; fur-trade in, 255; missionaries, 255, 256; rush of settlers, 257, 291; importance of coast line, 398; attitude toward Mexico (*1915*), 486.

Orinoco River, Spanish on, 391; Venezuelan control of, 394.

Ostend Manifesto, terms cited, 301.

Oswald, Richard, British minister to France, 42, 43; new commission, 45.

Oswego (N. Y.), British fort, 63.

Ottoman Empire, commercial treaty with, 223; in Crimean war, 288; diplomatic service to, 430; extradition treaty, 350; relations with United States, 464–466; war policies (*1915*), 492.

P

Pacific Ocean, commerce, 92, 93; international co-operation on, 353, 354, 369; interpretation of term, 379; growth of American influence, 396, 402, 463; territorial expansion on, 398, 454; islands acquired, 398, 399, 404, 418, 425.

Padillo, Panama gunboat, 441.

Pagopago, naval station, 400, 425.

Paine, Thomas, French sympathy, 96.

Pakenham, Sir Richard, British minister, 262; correspondence with, 263, 267.

Pakenham, Gen. Sir Edward M., New Orleans expedition, 181.

Palmerston, Lord, Central American policy, 294; Civil War, 313, 317, 319; cited, 317.

Panama, international route, 135, 286, 290; Spanish-American congress, 214, 291; United States delegates, 216; American interests in, 245; neutrality guaranteed (treaty of *1846*), 291, 385, 442; Nicaragua a rival, 291, 439, 440; railroad built, 295; de Lesseps canal, 380; title bought by United States, 439; relations with Colombia, 439–442, 453; United States recognizes, 442; guarantees independence, 443; constitution, cited, 443; relations with United States, 443.

Panama Canal, fortifications, 436–438; tolls, 437, 480, 481; strategic importance, 444; opening, 469.

Panama City, revolt in, 441.

Pan-American Congress, success of first, 388; Hawaii not included, 403; sessions, 451.

Pan-American Exposition, at Buffalo, 451.

Pan-American Union, director-general, 430.

Pan-Americanism, policy of Adams and Clay, 214; of Blaine, 386; action of Congress, 387; later, 451.

Panton, Leslie & Co., Indian trade, 73.

Papacy, relations with United States, 51, 55.

Papal bulls, confirm Spanish claims, 10; importance, 10, 11.

Papal States, diplomatic service to, 280; plan to defend, 338.

Paraguay, commercial treaty with, 285, 287; arbitration, 475.

Parana River, navigation of, opened, 287.

Paredes y A., Gen. M., Mexican president, policy, 275, 276.

Paris, 73, 81, 138, 150, 204, 311, 418; interest in American Revolution, 24; American representatives in, 27, 28, 33, 96, 99, 104, 132, 145, 188, 345; international bureau, weights and measures, 351; seal fisheries arbitration court, 379; Venezuelan, 394; engineering congress, 380; financial centre, 427.

Paris, treaty of (*1781–3*), 18; discussion of terms, 40–50, 66; Indians angry at, 65; interpretation, 67, 70, 115, 117, 139, 186, 192, 194, 195; (*1898*), 418–422.

Parker, Josiah, Virginia Member of Congress, 121.

Parliament, toleration of Lord Shelburne, 59; passes navigation act; (*1788*), 60.

Parrott, W. S., United States agent in Mexico, 273.

Passamaquoddy Bay, islands, 186.

Patriotism, demonstrations of, cultivated, 408.

Pauncefote, Sir Julian, discusses Venezuelan dispute, 393; friendly to America, 431; Hay treaty, 436.

Peace movement, growth of, 472, 473, 496.

Pearl Harbor, coaling station, 404.

Pearl River, as boundary, 151.

Pearson syndicate, Colombian plans, 450.

Peel, Sir Robert, American policy, 233, 269, 270.

Peking, foreign embassies besieged, 455, 456; relieved, 457.

Pensacola (Fla.), Spanish colony, 19; trading-post, 73; Jackson seizes, 200, 201.

Perceval, Spencer, issues order in council, 159.

Perdido River, as boundary, 19, 149–159.

Perignon, Gen. Marquis de, minister to Spain, 130.

Perry, Commodore Matthew, Japan treaty, 286.

Persia, commercial treaty with, 285.

Peru, mines, 75; revolution in, 203; commercial treaty with, 223, 285; claims, 226; war with Spain, 327; arbitration of claims, 350; Bolivia-Chili war, 386; arbitration treaty, 475; new government recognized, 479.

Peterhof, admiralty case, 309.

Petroleum, supersedes whale-oil, 353.

Pharmacopœal Formulas for Potent Drugs, agreement to unify, 472.

Phelps, E. J., on seal-fisheries commission, 379.

Philadelphia, seat of Continental Congress, 23, 24, 33, 45, 70, 75; frivolity of, 39; port, 70, 76, 87, 103; trade centre, 161; Genêt at, 99, 101.

Philip II, of Spain, succeeds to throne, 12.

Philippines, ownership, 12; relations with United States, 245; reciprocity with, 389; early history, 417; negotiations for, 418; American sentiment concerning, 420, 421, 476, 487; army of occupation, 420; Japanese relations, 461.

Pickering, Timothy, secretary of state, 121, 135, 288; maritime law policy, 129; English sympathies, 121, 137; successor, 138; cited, 129, 176.

Pierce, Franklin, president, 281; first message, 281; expansionist, 282; appointments, 282, 292, 300, 365; Cuban policy, 300; cited, 300.

Pike, Capt. Zebulon, explorer, 148.

Pinchon, L. A., French minister, 144.

Pinckney, Charles, minister to Spain, 140.

Pinckney, C. C., minister to France, 128; not received, 129–131; one of commission, 131, 137; reply to Talleyrand, 132; cited, 137.

Pinckney, Thomas, minister to England, 87, 123; envoy to Spain, 123; concludes treaty, 124; replaced, 129.

Pinkney, William, mission to England, 158, 372; tact, 165; recall, 169.

Piracy, menace to colonies, 13; of Barbary States, 55, 114, 132; slave-trade question, 237.

Pitt, William, Earl of Chatham, friend of colonies, 17, 25; trade policy, 110.

Pitt, William, premier, 60, 88, 89; fears frontier clash, 116; French policy, 132; Louisiana, 134.

Pius IX, assumes pontificate, 280.

Platt Amendment, terms, 425, 426; enforced, 449.

Plattsburg, battle of, 181.

Poinsett, Joel, mission to Buenos Ayres, 206.

Poles, treatment by Russia, 359.

Polk, James K., elected president, 265; appointments, 273, 282; Texas policy, 266, 267, 278, 440; Oregon, 267–271, 393; Mexican, 271–279, 341; California, 267, 274, 277; extends Monroe Doctrine, 296, 325, 478; characterized, 267, 279; cited, 276, 277.

Polly, admiralty case, 156.

Pompey the Great, destroys pirates, 56.

Pontiac, conspiracy of, 65.

Poor Richard's Almanac, author, 27.

Porcupine River, navigation free, 346.

Porfirio Diaz (Mex.), fighting at, 482.

Pork, trade in, 58, 76, 110, 467; in McKinley tariff, 388.

Port Arthur, leased to Russia, 455.

Port Royal. See Louisburg.

Porter, Admiral David, annexes Madison island, 398.

Porter, Admiral David D., inspection cruise, 361.

Porto Bello, Panama town, 441.

Porto Rico, ownership, 35, 135, 203; effort to free, 217; slavery in, 236; reciprocity with, 389; United States acquires, 421; strategic importance, 444; change of owners, 478, 487.

Portugal, colonial relations with Spain, 11, 12; United States trade with, 56, 57, 163; diplomatic service to, 81, 140, 430; guards Gibraltar, 114; loses Brazil, 203; commercial treaty, 223, 471; claims, 226; forbids slave-trade, 236; war with Brazil, 324; pays American claims, 375; arbitration treaty, 475.

President, fights Little Belt, 174.

Press, influence in causing Spanish war, 411.

Pribilof Islands, sealing industry, 377, 379, 434.

Prim, Juan, Count de Reus, Mexican expedition, 329; Cuban policy, 366.

Privateering. See International Law.

Privateers, French, 15, 98, 102, 103; American, 29; in war with France,

133; of *1812*, 177; Spanish-American, 200, 207; Confederacy, 309, 312, 315.

Prizes. See International Law.

Proctor, Sen. Redfield, report on Cuba, 412.

Provisions, contraband, 111, 119–121, 124, 128, 154, 164, 493; competition in trade, 373.

Prussia, American commissioner to, 31; commercial treaties with, 53, 54, 129, 197; privateering prohibited, 54; diplomatic service to, 81, 140, 188; war with France, 95; war debt, 167; signs Holy Alliance, 204; head of *Zollverein*, 224; England seeks alliance with, 240; Cuban relations, 366.

Puget Sound, ownership, 267, 270; coast importance, 398.

Q

Quebec, province created, 20; boundaries, 33, 40, 46, 228.

Quebec Act, provisions, 20.

Quebec, City of, French stronghold, 13, 16; Americans besiege, 75; trade centre, 118, 125, 197; route via, 182, 230.

Quitman, Gen. J. A., Cuban filibustering, 298; Member of Congress, 300.

R

Railroads. See Transportation.

Rambouillet, decree of, 167, 168.

Randolph, Edmund, secretary of state, 104; indiscretion, 120, 121; *Vindication*, 120.

Randolph, John, opinion of non-importation, cited, 157; minister to Russia, 221.

Rayneval, Gerard, secretary to Vergennes, 33; mission to England, 44.

Reciprocity, (*1815–1829*), 196–199; (*1830–1860*), treaties, 223–225, 285, 337, 346, 352, 376, 389, 403, 404; "most favored nation" dispute, 224; policy of Blaine, 373, 388; endorsed by Pan-American Congress, 388; with Canada, 432,

435, 436; under Dingley tariff, 470; Payne-Aldrich, 471; Underwood, 471.

Reed, T. B., opposes Spanish war, 413.

Reid, Whitelaw, Spanish treaty commissioner, 418; ambassador to England, 430.

"Restook," 230.

Review of Reviews, editor, 440, 450.

Rhett, R. B., Southern leader, 310.

Rhode Island, France said to desire, 78.

Rice, trade in, 55, 57, 225.

Richelieu River, trade route, 67.

Richmond (Va.), Confederate capital, 320.

Riga, port open, 163.

Right of search. See International Law.

Rio Grande, boundary, 148, 201, 246, 277, 279; source, 272, 274; as American troops on, 273, 276; navigation of, 481.

Rio Janeiro, Pan-American Congress, 451.

Rios, Don E. M., Spanish treaty commissioner, 418.

Roberts College, protected by Turkey, 465.

Robertson, James, intrigues with Spain, 77.

Robespierre, M. M. I., French leader, 103.

Rochambeau, Comte de, statue of, presented, 467.

Rockhill, W. W., commissioner to China, report cited, 457.

Rockingham, Marquis of, favors peace, 42; death, 45.

Rocky Mountains, as boundary, 194, 271.

Rodney, Adm. G. B., seizes St. Eustatius, 38.

Roebuck, J. A., member of Parliament, 320, 322, 331.

Roman Catholic Church, aids Spain, 15; first American bishop, 51, 52; political sympathies, 207; missions in Oregon, 256; Far East, 455.

Romanzoff, Count, French sympathy, 169.

Rome, diplomatic centre, 10.

Romero, Señor Matias, Mexican minister, cited, 387.

Roosevelt, Alice, christens German yacht, 467.

Roosevelt, Theodore, voices imperialist spirit, 423; navy policy, 424; relations with Hay, 429; civil service under, 431; Panama policy, 439–443; doctrine of police power, 447–450, 452; Santo Domingo intervention, 448; Spanish-American fears, 452; South American trip, 453; mediator, 458; arbitration attitude, 473–475; foreign policy, 476, 484; cited, 440, 441, 451.

Root, Elihu, secretary of state, on Alaska boundary commission, 434; visits South America, 452; Japanese policy, 461, 462; arbitration advocate, 473, 475; ability, 429.

Rose, John, English diplomat, 344.

Roumania, relations with United States, 468.

Rouse's Point, in dispute, 231.

Rousseau, J. J., influence in America, 24.

"Rule of 1756." See International Law.

Rush, Richard, minister to England, 189, 191, 210, 237, 372; instructions cited, 210.

Russell, Lord John, foreign secretary, 8, 313, 322, 323, 340; Civil War papers, 317, 320.

Russell, Jonathan, legation secretary, 170; peace commissioner, 180, 185.

Russell, William, *Times* correspondent, cited, 310.

Russia, international relations, 37, 178, 179, 209, 213, 240, 313, 331, 357, 359, 379, 432; offers mediation, 41, 178, 179; American trade, 53, 163, 169; diplomatic service to, 81, 163, 221, 430; dealings with Miranda, 89; British treaty, 111; French invasion, 155, 170, 178; arbitrator, 191, signs Holy Alliance, 204; policy in northwest, 205, 206, 209, 211–214, 218, 254, 281; Crimean war, 288; neutrality treaty, 288; Civil War policy, 313, 359, 360; frees serfs, 313; Alaska treaty, 358, 359; treat-

ment of Jews, 357, 466; Poles, 359; treaty with England, 432; seal fisheries treaty, 434; policy in Far East, 454, 455, 458, 459; Congress abrogates treaty with, 428, 466; war with Japan, 458, 462.

Russian American Company, compensation, 358.

Ryswick, Treaty of, 16.

S

Sabine River, as boundary, 201, 202, 240.

Sackett's harbor, British demand, 182.

Sagasta, P. M., Spanish prime minister, 413, 416.

St. Augustine (Fla.), French designs on, 99.

St. Bartholomew Island, ownership, 35; ceded to France, 335.

St. Clair, Gov. Arthur, Indians defeat, 83, 116.

St. Croix Island, ownership, 35.

St. Croix River, as boundary, 46,117, 186; source, 228; command of, 182.

St. Eustatius Island, entrepôt, 35; governor, 36; British seize, 38.

St. Germain, treaty of, 13.

St. John Island, cession proposed, 360.

St. John River (Florida), Huguenot massacre on, 13.

St. John river (New Brunswick), as boundary, 40, 46; valley in dispute, 228; international waterway, 235, 346.

St. Joseph (Mich.), British fort burned, 33.

St. Lawrence river, as boundary, 20, 40, 46, 186, 228; British hold, 63, 68, 87, 197; settlements in basin, 66, 67; opened to United States, 125; international waterway, 181; right of navigation, 197, 285; granted, 346, 348; tributaries, 228.

St. Louis (Mo.), trade-centre, 173.

St. Marks (Fla.), Spanish fort, 200, 201.

St. Nicholas, port leased, 360.

St Petersburg (Petrograd), American minister at, 170, 188, 455.

St. Thomas Island, cession proposed, 360.

Saligny, Alphonso de, French agent in Texas, 265.

Salisbury, Lord, dealings with America, 8; in seal-fisheries dispute, 378, 379; in Clayton-Bulwer treaty dispute, 382; Venezuelan, 393; cited, 428.

Samana Bay, desirable naval station, 361, 363, 401.

Samoa, international interests in, 399–401, 406, 425; American relations, 245, 399–401, 406, 425; independence recognized, 401, 402; division of islands, 425, 454.

San Francisco, Russian fleet visits, 359; collector of port, 377; San Francisco, bay as boundary, 92; importance, 275, 398.

San José (Costa Rica), arbitration court palace, 451.

San Ildefonso, treaty of, 143.

San Jacinto, battle of, 250.

San Jacinto, stops *Trent*, 316.

San Juan archipelago, ownership, 337, 345, 347, 348.

San Juan river, mouth of, 292, 383.

San Marino, treaty with United States, 469.

Sanmun, port leased, 455.

San Salvador, commercial treaty with, 285; extradition, 350; arbitration, 475.

Santa Anna, Gen. Antonio Lopez de, revolutionary leader, 247–249, 251; exiled, 276; Polk's negotiations with, 276; intrigues, 277.

Santa Fé, Texan expedition against, 252; Mexican post, 272.

Santiago of Chili, Pan-American Congress at, 451.

Santo Domingo, divisions of, 326; trade, 108, 109, 134, 165, 166; leader, 134, 136; Le Clerc's expedition to, 143, 145; freedom, 153.

Sardinia, commercial treaty with, 223; insurrection in, 204; in Crimean war, 288.

Savoy, Amadeo de, king of Spain, 365.

Saxony, desires commercial treaty, 53.

Scheldt River, commerce *via*, 5; navigation opened, 352.

Schenck, R. C., minister to England, 344.

Schenectady, burned, 15.

Schofield, Gen. J. M., on Mexican duty, 332; mission to Napoleon, 332.

Schurz, Carl, diplomatic experience, 304; minister to Spain, 327, 329; speech on expansion, 364; Philippine views, 420; cited, 424.

Scotch-Irish, in Kentucky, 69.

Scott, Sir Walter, cited, 239.

Scott, Sir William, admiralty decisions, 156, 236, 308.

Scott, Gen. Winfield, on Northeastern frontier, 230.

Seabury, Samuel, consecration as bishop, 52.

Seals, fisheries problem, 377, 432, 434, 497.

Sectionalism, influences diplomacy, 71, 282.

Senate, relation to diplomacy, 80; acts on Jay treaty, 119; members, 174, 222, 225, 364, 428; relation to House, 225, 428; to executive, 428; acts on Zollverein treaty, 225; Oregon, 270; San Domingo, 363; Canadian reciprocity, 376, 378, 435; Algeciras "General Act," 464; Turkish atrocities, 465; arbitration, 474, 475; treaty making power, 471.

Servia, treaty with, 375.

Sevastopol, in Crimean War, 288.

Seven Years' War, trade during, 109.

Servier, John, Tennessee leader, 69, 77.

Sewall, H. M., consul at Samoa, 400.

Seward, W. H., dealings with England, 241, 318, 319, 321, 339, 340, 382; France, 331–333; Mexico, 329; Spain, 326, 327; privateering policy, 309; slave-trade, 349; naturalization, 355; views on expansion, 281, 305, 306, 326, 333, 358–362, 403, 487; length of public service, 370, 499; indiscretion, 305, 317, 342; characterized, 305, 306; cited, 340, 355, 362, 382.

Shanghai, port opened, 223.

Shaw, Albert, letter to, cited, 440; editorial, cited, 450.

Sheffield, Lord, "Observations on the Commerce of the United States," influence, 59.

Shelburne, Lord, liberal opinions, 42, 60; controls ministry, 45; resigns, 58; cited, 45.

Shelby, Isaac, Kentucky governor, 102; cited, 105.

Shenandoah, Confederate cruiser, 339.

Sherman, John, secretary of state, 414; Cuban policy, 412; successor, 418; cited, 412.

Shimonoseki, indemnity returned, 397, 454.

Shimonoseki Straits, closed, 353.

Ship-building, American industry, 58; government policy toward, 85, 469, 470; growth, 109; decline, 336.

Short, William, American minister to Spain, 123, 140.

Siam, commercial treaty with, 223, 286.

Silks, trade in, 55, 284.

Singleterry, John, arrested, 102.

Sitka (Alaska), United States court at, 378.

Slavery, Missouri question, 252; Texas, 253, 254, 262; in Cuba, 298, 301, 302, 367; growth of opposition, 321, 354; Alex. H. Stephens views, 323.

Slave trade, African, 55, 58; prohibited, 79; English opposition to, 191, 216, 236; European, 236; American, 236, 237; Mexican, 246; suppression difficult, 236, 238, 239, 241; declared piracy, 237; legislation after *1862*, 349, 374.

Slidell, John, minister to Mexico, 273–275; Confederate commissioner, 311; captured, 316; released, 318; agent in France, 331.

Smiley, A. K., pacifist, 473.

Smith, Adam, influences Lord Shelburne, 58.

Smith, Ashabel, Texas representative, 264.

Smith, J. F., on Chinese commission, 398.

Smith, Robert, secretary of state, 163; successor, 170.

Smuggling, by Dutch, 35, 36; between England and France, 164.

Society of Holy Trinity for Redemption of Captives, activity, 55, 56.

Sorrel River, trade route, 67.

Soudan, British withdrawal, 342.

Soulé, Pierre, minister to Spain, 283, 300; independence in office, 371.

South, in diplomatic service, 304.

South America, commerce, 5.

South Sea Bubble, speculation, 205.

Southwest, character of settlers, 69; trade, 69; relations with Indians, 83, 89.

Spain, holds Mississippi River, 5; trouble with colonies, 6; papal aid, 10, 15; colonial relations with Portugal, 11, 12; extends empire, 12; pirates molest colonies, 13; Armada defeated, 13; recognizes rival colonies, 14, 21; colonial commerce, 15; aids France, 18; cedes Florida, 19; acquires Louisiana, 19; neutrality lax, 22; aids American Revolution, 26, 27, 108; offers mediation, 32; war with England, 32, 37; American commissioner to, 31, 32, 34; American policy, 33, 91; seizes British forts in Florida, 33; Michigan, 34; neutral trade, 38; in American peace negotiations, 43–45, 49, 50; gains Floridas, 50; payments to Barbary, 56; United States trade, 57, 63, 77, 163, 166, 167, 177; controls Mississippi, 69, 70, 71, 87, 147, 197; treaties with England, 70; Western intrigues, 73–77, 123; Indian policy, 73, 74, 83, 123; diplomatic service to, 81, 123, 209, 283, 300, 301, 327, 366, 385, 412, 430; in Nootka Sound affair, 88–93; Family alliance, 88; effect of Jay treaty, 122; vacillation, 123; war with France, 95, 97, 99; treaty with United States, 124, 134; international law position, 124, 237; evacuates disputed ports, 139, 142; cedes Louisiana, 143, 147, 150; Bonaparte regime, 150, 203; disputed boundary, 199–202; cedes Floridas, 202, 207; insurrection in, 204; monarchy restored, 204; relations with Spanish-America, 203, 210–213, 251, 296, 326–329, 361, 384, 387, 391; claims treaty, 226, 350, 375; forbids slave trade, 236; gives up Oregon claim, 254; Cuban relations, 298, 326, 330, 365–368; domestic situation, 365; emancipation policy, 367; in Virginius affair, 366, 367; reciprocity with, 389; commercial treaty, 471; war with America, 409–417; peace terms, 418–421, 487; Cuban debt problem, 418, 426; arbitration with Mexico, 474; United States, 475; interests in Mexico, 482.

Spanish-America, mines, 75; revolutionary leaders, 89, 96, 97, 203; discontent in, 135; European relations, 385; Burr's designs on, 147; trade valuable, 155; revolutions, 203, 205, 226; United States trade with, 206; interest in, 7, 208, 209; relations with, 210–219, 226, 284, 319, 384, 390, 406, 442, 464, 484, 489, 490, 500; England's relations with, 206, 209–217, 319, 334; calls a congress, 214; Pan-American attitude, 387, 390, 451; foreign concessions in, 450, 460; relations with Japan, 461; joins in Sanitary Conventions, 472.

Spooner, Sen. J. C., amends reciprocity treaties, 471.

Spooner Act, provisions, 439.

Springbok, admiralty case, 308.

Stanley, Lord, foreign policy, 340.

Staples, loan to Mexico, 215.

Steinberger, A. B., German agent, 400.

Stephens, A. H., favors fleet, 311.

Steuben, Baron Friedrich von, demands surrender of frontier posts, 63.

Stevens, Edward, American consul 136.

Stevens, J. L., minister to Hawaii,

cited, 404; favors annexation, 405; recalled, 406.

Stevenson, R. L., interest in Samoa, 399.

Stickine River, navigation free, 346.

Stockton, Admiral R. F., sent to Monterey, 274.

Stoeckl, Baron, Russian minister, sale of Alaska, 358.

Straus, Oscar, minister to Turkey, 430, 466; betters conditions, 466.

Suarez, Pino, Mexican vice-president, killed, 483.

Suez Canal, director of, 380.

Sugar, trade in, 108, 109, 119, 153; Hawaiian, 353; in McKinley tariff, 388.

Sullivan, Gen. John, expedition against Iroquois, 64.

Sumner, Charles, senator, 306, 339, 340, 364; views in foreign policy, 317, 340–344, 347; removed from chairmanship, 344, 364; works for Alaska treaty, 358, 359; characterized, 306, 307, 342; cited, 341.

Superior, Lake, as boundary, 46.

Supreme Court, powers over treaties, 80.

Suwo, prince of, 353.

Sweden, American colonists, 14; armed neutrality, 37; treaties with, 54, 129, 197, 285, 356, 475; American minister to, 188; forbids slave-trade, 236; cedes St. Bartholomew to France, 335; American cession refused, 362; neutrality (*1915*), 492.

Switzerland, commercial treaty with, 285; represented in Geneva board, 347; diplomatic service to, 429, 430; trade agreement with United States, 471; arbitration, 475; neutrality problems (*1915*), 492.

Syria, missions in, 465.

Syrians, status in United States, 466.

T

Tackle, T., British agent, cited, 82, 181.

Taft, W. H., president, 435; seal fisheries treaty, 434; reciprocity,

435; immigration policy, 468; Japan, 450; arbitration, 475; Mexican, 481, 482.

Talien-wan, port leased, 455.

Talleyrand, C. M. de, American policy, 131–133, 136–138, 142, 143; cited, 142, 143, 149, 150.

Tallulah (La.), Italian lynched at, 427.

Tamasese, King of Samoa, 400.

Tar, trade in, 57.

Tariff, customs, 85; protects fisheries, 193, 194; affects ship-building, 336, 470; Morrill, 314; McKinley, 388; Wilson, 389; Dingley, 470, 471; Payne-Aldrich, 471; Underwood, 471.

Taylor, Zachary, Mexican campaigns, 273, 276; diplomatic service under, 304; instructions to, cited, 273; president, 304.

Tea, commercial importance of, 54, 55, 196, 199, 284.

Tecumseh, forms confederacy, 172.

Tehuantepec, Isthmus of, canal proposed, 216, 290, 295.

Temple, Sir John, British consul-general, 87.

Tennessee, offshoot of North Carolina, 69; Spanish intrigues, 77; admitted to Union, 82; French intrigues, 102, 105; English, 134; governors, 134, 248.

Tepic (Cal.), British consul, 257.

Texas, Spanish boundaries, 201, 202; United States reversionary interest, 208, 209, 245, 246; claims treaty, 226; rush of settlers, 245, 481; land titles, 245; "Fredonian republic," 247; joined to Coahuila, 247; Mexican forts in, 247; American leaders, 248; Indian negotiations, 248; declares independence, 248; gained American aid, 249; annexation question, 250, 251–254, 259–266, 272, 274, 341; slavery, 253, 262–266, 298, 301; boundary, 271, 279; truce with Mexico, 273; United States gains, 279; attitude toward Mexico (1915), 486.

Texel, John Paul Jones at, 36.

Thames, battle of, 178.

Thiers, M. J. L. A., cited, 166.

Thompson, Waddy, minister to Mexico, cited, 258, 274.

Thornton, Sir Edward, British agent, 144; on claims commission, 345.

Tibet, relations to Great Britain, 459.

Tiger Island, naval station sought, 382.

Tippecanoe, battle of, 172.

Tobacco, trade, 57, 76, 164, 225; Cuban plantations, 410.

Tobago, France acquires, 50.

Tordesillas, treaty of, 11, 13.

Tower, Charlemagne, diplomatic service, 430.

Trade-mark treaties, 351, 469.

Trafalgar, battle at, 152.

Transportation, ocean, 63, 70, 289, 817; trans continental railroads, 289, 290, 352, 382, 437; canals, 290–293, 295, 346, 380 383; Isthmian railroad, 295, 303, 352.

Transvaal, British withdrawal, 342.

Treaties, arbitration, 474, 475, 481; claims, 226, 345, 375; commercial, 14, 29, 39, 53, 54, 118, 119, 124, 129, 197, 216, 223, 279, 285–287, 352, 397; extradition, 350, 374; model, 474; naturalization, 355, 356; reciprocity, 223–225, 285, 337, 346, 352, 376, 389, 403, 404, 470; seal fisheries, 434; trademarks, 351, 374; of Aix-la-Chapelle, 16; Alaska Purchase, 358–361; Amiens, 143; Basle, 123, 130; Berlin, 465; Breda, 14; Clayton-Bulwer, terms, 293, 295, 334, 438; interpretation, 282, 293, 381–383; abrogated, 436; Family Alliance, 18, 26, 32; Florida Purchase, 202; Gadsden Purchase, 290, 295; of Ghent, 2, 70; negotiated, 178–185, 235; terms, 185, 186, 190, 237; interpretation, 191; error in survey, 231; Greenville, 84, 122; Guadaloupe Hidalgo, 277–279; Hay-Pauncefote, 436–438; Holy Alliance, 88, 123, 204; failures, 208; manifesto, 209; Hopewell, 83; Jay's, provisions, 117, 119, 173, 192, 197, 235; adventures, 119–122; effects, 122, 123, 126, 127, 130; neutral clause expires, 157; Louisiana Purchase, 146, 147;

Madrid, 14; Munster, 14; Nootka Sound, 92, 267; Oregon, 270; Paris (1763), 18, 19, 40–50, 77, 115; Paris (1898), 426; Portsmouth, 458; Quadruple Alliance, stops Barbary piracy, 196, 204; Spanish-American attitude, 212; Ryswick, 16; St. Germain, 13; San Ildefonso, 143, 149, 150; San Lorenzo, 124; Tordesillas, 11, 13; Utrecht, 16; Victoria, 12; Washington, 345, 352, 364, 375; Wayne's, 122, 182; Webster-Ashburton, 234, 235, 269; Westminster, 14; Zaragoza, 12. See names of countries.

Trent, affair of, 316–318.

Trescott, W. H., South American mission, 386, 387; on Chinese commission, 398; ability, 401.

Trevelyan, Sir G. O., upholds American Revolution, 314.

Tripoli, official piracy, 55.

Trist, N. P., peace commissioner, 277, 278.

Troppau, meeting of allies, 204.

Tuhl, Baron de, Russian minister, 209.

Tunis, official piracy, 55; treaty, 85.

Turgot, A. R. J., attitude toward America, 25, 26; reputation, 43.

Turk Island, reciprocity with, 470.

Turner, Sen. George, in Alaskan boundary commission, 434.

Turpentine, trade in, 58.

Turreau, L. M., minister to United States, 166.

Tuscany, American commissioner to, 31.

Tutuila Island, naval station, 400; ceded to United States, 425.

Tyler, John, president, 225; foreign policy, 225, 233, 239, 256; Texas, 260, 264, 266; unpopularity, 225, 264.

Tweed, Boss, surrendered by Spain, 351.

Two Sicilies, commercial treaty with, 223; extradition, 285; neutrality, 288.

U

United States, isolation policy, 1, 2, 125, 134, 137, 139, 171, 187, 190, 211, 212, 220, 324, 375, 407, 438, 463, 477, 495; world-power, 3, 4; problems of neutrality, 6, 90–92, 100, 152, 154, 156, 169, 170, 175, 207, 208, 232, 249–251, 288, 330, 332, 339, 350, 352, 409, 483; treaty with France, 29; seeks recognition by Spain, 32; England, 44; in peace negotiations, 43–46; English trade, 57; foreign debt, 77; treaties with England, 70, 77; direction of foreign policy, 81; financial strength, 82; Indian policy, 82–84, 172, 194, 245; relations with Barbary States, 84, 85; in Nootka Sound affair, 90–93; French diplomacy in, 96; recognizes French republic, 101; recalls Morris, 104; neutral claims, 109, 110, 113, 158, 288; England injures trade, 112; naturalization policy, 114, 289, 355–357; treaty with Spain, 124; resents British aggressions, 114, 158, 160, 166; passes embargo, 115; sends embassy, 115; compromises treaty difficulties, 117–119; friction with France, 128, 133, 136, 226–228; foreign intrigues in, 131; Convention of 1800, 138, 143; buys Louisiana, 146; carrying trade, 156, 157, 161, 167, 169, 196, 198, 222; in War of 1812–14, 174–178; peace negotiations, 178–185; effect on neutral trade, 185; position in 1815, 186; European prestige, 189; growth of navy, 189, 190, 424; in Florida dispute, 199–202; recognizes de facto governments, 212, 280; Spanish-American sympathy, 206, 207; problems, 210–219; trade, 223; slavery sentiment, 217, 237; claims treaties, 226–228; Northeastern boundary dispute, 228–235; abolishes slave-trade, 236; enforcement lax, 238, 247; public land policy, 246; Texas sympathy, 248; recognition, 251; annexation question, 253–254, 260–266, 271–276; Missouri question, 252; Oregon, 255–257, 267, 270, 271; California, 257–259, 274; Mexican War sentiment, 277, 278; increase of territory, 279; expansion process, Mexican view, 243, 244; historical, 244, 245; theory of, 280, 281; sympathy with European revolutions, 280, 281; Isthmian policy, 290–295, 390, 406, 436–438, 450, 477, 481; Cuban, 299–302, 365–368; Southern blockade, 307–312, 315; irritation at England, 316, 322, 336, 337; Spanish-American policy, 324, 327, 350, 385, 489; dealings with Second Empire, in Mexico, 329–333; Irish immigration, 338; enlistments, 338; war claims against England, 339–348; seal-fisheries dispute, 378, 379; interest in de Lesseps canal, 380; interpretation of Clayton-Bulwer treaty, 381, 382; proposed Nicaragua canal treaty, 382; Venezuela dispute, 391–394; relations with China, 397, 398; Samoa, 399–401; Hawaii, 402–406, 424; isolation policy violated, 402; in Spanish war, 409–417; peace terms, 418–422; changes in policy, 421, 422, 425; imperialist spirit in, 424; colonial policy, 425, 443; Chinese immigration question, 397, 398, 432; Alaska boundary, 432, 434; fisheries, 435; Panama treaty, 443; Santo Domingo protectorate,. 448; intervention doctrine, 449; continental cooperation, 451; Spanish-American distrust of, 452, 489, 490, 500; interest in Far East, 455; Chinese policy, 456–462; relations with Japan, 461–463, 481; Africa, 464; Turkey, 464–466; Mexico, 481–490; international agreements, 472; neutrality problems (1915), 491, 493–496.

United States, wins fight, 190.

Upshur, A. P., secretary of state, 220, 260, 262; killed, 260.

Uruguay, European relations, 325.

Uruguay River, navigation of, opened, 287.

Utrecht, treaty of, 16.

V

Valparaiso (Chili), killing of marines at, 390.

Van Alen, J. J., appointment to Italy, criticized, 372.

Van Berkel, E. T., Amsterdam burgomaster, 36.

Van Bibber, Abraham, American agent, cited, 36.

Van Buren, Martin, secretary of state, 2, 220, 222; president, 252; minister to England, 372; Texas policy, 252.

Vancouver Island, English settlement, 88, 270; American claim, 267, 271.

Vanderbilt, Commodore Cornelius, promoter, 292, 337.

Vaughan, Benjamin, secret mission, 45; returns to France, 45; letter, cited, 59.

Venezuela, revolution, 203; commercial treaty, 223; arbitration of claims, 350; convention with, 375; French claims, 385; reciprocity affects, 389; British controversy, 391, 393, 394; American interests, 391, 393–395; intervention threatened, 449; international blockade, 447.

Venice, desires United States trade, 55.

Vera Cruz (Mex.), United States occupies, 489; leaves, 490.

Vergennes, Count de, urges aid to America, 25; directs French policy, 26, 28, 31, 33, 36, 39; subordinates, 96; in peace negotiations, 43, 44, 46, 49, 61, 137; difficult position, 43; characterized, 43; cited, 25.

Vermont, in Revolution, 67, 69; sends commissioners to Canada, 67; British control possible, 68; not recognized by Congress, 67; admitted to Union, 82; trade agreements with England, 87, 118, 122, 197.

Verona, Congress of, 204; principles, cited, 204.

Verrazano, Giovanni de, explorer, 13.

Vicksburg, moral effects of capture, 322.

Victor, Gen. C. P., on Louisiana expedition, 143; instructions, 148, 149, 201.

Victoria, Queen, appointments, 347.
Victoria, treaty of, 12.
Vienna, American commissioner to, 31.
Vienna, Congress of, 180; wrangles, 184.
Vienna, Decree of, 166, 167.
Villa, Gen., revolutionary leader, 486.
Vincennes (Ind.), French settle, 16; Clark captures, 33, 69.
Virginia, English colony, 13; in French and Indian war, 17; re-taliatory laws, 61; emigrants, 69; Kentucky part of, 76; convention of, *1788*, 72; hurt by embargo, 162.
Virginius, affair of, 367, 368.
"Visit and Search." See International Law.
Voltaire, F. M. A. de, cited, 17.

W

Wade, B. F., on San Domingo commission, 363.
Wagram, battle of, effects, 166.
Waite, M. R., on Geneva board, 347.
Wake Island, United States occupies, 425.
Walker, William, Nicaragua intrigues, 296, 297.
Walpole, Lord, on maritime law, cited, 179.
War of *1812*, causes, 6, 175; effects, 2.
War Hawks, beliefs, 171, 175.
Ward, H. G., British minister, 247.
Warville, Brissot de, American voyage, 96.
Washburne, Elihu, secretary of state, 365; minister to France, 365.
Washington, George, president, 1; in French and Indian war, 17; supporters, 31; appointments, 80, 81, 87, 104; foreign, 63, 91, 99–101, 104, 123, 129, 188, 211; success of, 124; Indian policy, 82, 83, 125, 173; task unfinished, 93, 125; accepts Bastile Key, 94; neutrality proclamation, 100; supplementary, 105; receives Genêt, 101; press attacks, 103; disapproves Jay treaty, 120; signs, 120; contest with House, 121; farewell address,

125, 438; commander-in-chief, 135; formality of, 140; strength of character, 95, 125; cited 63, 123.
Washington (D. C.), 179, 191, 200, 210, 227, 250, 256, 262, 294, 307, 326, 344, 345, 358, 387, 400, 401, 413, 441, 442; burned, 184; seat of government, 276; Bureau of American Republics at, 388.
Wasp, wins fight, 190.
Waterways, international, 5, 70, 197, 287, 291, 346, 351.
Wayne, Gen. Anthony, moves against Indians, 83, 116; defeats them, 84, 117; treaty, 122; Cumberland manoeuvers, 105; on Maumee, 500.
Webster, Daniel, oration for Greece, 207; secretary of state, 222, 233; Ashburton treaty, 234, 237; British policy, 234, 239–241, 294, 403; Oregon, 269; California, 274; Mexico, 258, 260, 278; presidential ambitions, 235; characterized, 221; letters cited, 233, 252, 271, 282.
Weed, Thurlow, in England, 321; letter cited, 331.
Weights and measures, joint bureau of, 351.
Wei-hai-wei, port leased, 455.
Welles, Gideon, blockade policy, 307; confidence in navy, 319.
Wellesley, Marquis of, minister of foreign affairs, 168.
Wellington, Duke of, victory over French, 178; desires American peace, 180; American campaign proposed, 184; aids Spain, 205.
West, development, 71; sectionalism, 71, 72; discontent, 72, 77, 82, 144, 172–175; foreign intrigues, 72–77, 98, 102, 116, 131; loyalty, 148, 152; in War of *1812*, 178.
West Indies, Spanish, 12; ownership, 25; diplomatic importance, 20; England sends troops to, 49; Spanish claims relinquished, 418; British, 29; trade important to America, 58, 77, 161, 176, 193, 198, 199; forbidden, 59–61, 87, 153, 198, 199, 218; temporarily open, 122, 124; direct trade open, 222; admiralty courts, 112, 114,

122; slave-trade forbidden, 238; slaves freed, 238; French, trade with America, 61, 134, 156, 158, 165, 176, 308; with France, 108; with England, 156; guarantee, 99, 101; ready for war, 102; need neutral trade, 106; England blockades, 112.

Westminster, Treaty of, 14.

Weyler y Nicolau, Gen. Valeriano, Cuban campaign, 411.

Whale oil, trade in, 61, 396; petroleum supersedes, 353.

Wharton, Francis, letter to, cited, 261.

Wheat. See Grain.

Wheaton, Henry, diplomatic ability, 221; German negotiations, 224, 225; *An Inquiry into the Validity of the British Claim to a Right of Visitation and Search*, cited, 240.

Whiskey Rebellion, "confessions" of Randolph, 120.

White, A. D., on San Domingo commission, 364.

White, Henry, diplomatic promotion, 429.

Wilkes, Capt. Charles, visits Oregon coast, 256; stops *Trent*, 316; exceeds powers, 318.

Wilkinson, James, colonizing scheme, 75; at siege of Quebec, 75; intrigues with Spain, 76, 123, 136; Burr, 147; occupies Mobile, 151; Texas speculations, 245.

Willamette River, American settlers on, 267.

William III, of England, 14, 36.

Williams, G. H., on British claims commission, 345.

Wilson, Woodrow, president, 430; diplomatic policy, 430; civil service, 431; canal tolls, 437, 481;

European claims, 446; opposes foreign "concessions," 450, 460, 480; Spanish-American attitude, 452; Chinese policy, 460; vetoes literacy test, 468; merchant marine policy, 470; foreign, 476, 479, 480, 489, 496; Japanese, 480; Mexican, 484, 489; Philippine, 487.

Wine, trade in, 223.

Wisconsin, fur-trade, 173.

Woodford, S. L., minister to Spain, 412–415.

Woods, Lake of, as boundary, 46, 116, 186, 194, 235.

Wordsworth, William, cited, 94.

Württemburg, naturalization treaty with, 356.

Wu Ting Fang, Chinese minister, 460.

Wyse, Capt, concession from Colombia, 379.

X

X. Y. Z. correspondence, 133.

Y

Yangtse River valley, railroad, 459.

Yazoo River, as boundary, 20, 48, 70, 71, 139; settlements, 75; settlements planned, 75.

York, Sir Joseph, British minister, 38.

Yorktown, British surrender, 22, 42.

Yrujo, C. M., Spanish minister, 144.

Yucatan, international relations, 296, 478.

Yukon River, navigation free, 346; gold discovered, 432.

Z

Zaragoza, treaty of, 12.